AutoCAD® 14
Bible

AutoCAD® 14 Bible

Ellen Finkelstein

IDG
BOOKS
WORLDWIDE

IDG Books Worldwide, Inc.
An International Data Group Company

Foster City, CA ✦ Chicago, IL ✦ Indianapolis, IN ✦ New York, NY

AutoCAD® 14 Bible

Published by
IDG Books Worldwide, Inc.
An International Data Group Company
919 E. Hillsdale Blvd., Suite 400
Foster City, CA 94404
www.idgbooks.com (IDG Books World Wide Web site)

Library of Congress Catalog Card No.: 97-73636

ISBN: 0-7645-3092-5

Printed in the United States of America

10 9 8 7 6 5

1O/QT/QT/ZZ/IN

Distributed in the United States by IDG Books Worldwide, Inc.

Distributed by Macmillan Canada for Canada; by Transworld Publishers Limited in the United Kingdom; by IDG Norge Books for Norway; by IDG Sweden Books for Sweden; by Woodslane Pty. Ltd. for Australia; by Woodslane (NZ) Ltd. for New Zealand; by Addison Wesley Longman Singapore Pte Ltd. for Singapore, Malaysia, Thailand, and Indonesia; by Norma Comunicaciones S.A. for Colombia; by Intersoft for South Africa; by International Thomson Publishing for Germany, Austria and Switzerland; by Distribuidora Cuspide for Argentina; by Livraria Cultura for Brazil; by Ediciencia S.A. for Ecuador; by Ediciones ZETA S.C.R. Ltda. for Peru; by WS Computer Publishing Corporation, Inc., for the Philippines; by Contemporanea de Ediciones for Venezuela; by Express Computer Distributors for the Caribbean and West Indies; by Micronesia Media Distributor, Inc. for Micronesia; by Grupo Editorial Norma S.A. for Guatemala; by Chips Computadoras S.A. de C.V. for Mexico; by Editorial Norma de Panama S.A. for Panama; by Wouters Import for Belgium; by American Bookshops for Finland. Authorized Sales Agent: Anthony Rudkin Associates for the Middle East and North Africa.

For general information on IDG Books Worldwideís books in the U.S., please call our Consumer Customer Service department at 800-762-2974. For reseller information, including discounts and premium sales, please call our Reseller Customer Service department at 800-434-3422.

For information on where to purchase IDG Books Worldwideís books outside the U.S., please contact our International Sales department at 317-596-5530 or fax 317-596-5692.

For information on foreign language translations, please contact our Foreign & Subsidiary Rights department at 650-655-3021 or fax 650-655-3281.

For sales inquiries and special prices for bulk quantities, please contact our Sales department at 650-655-3200 or write to the address above.

For information on using IDG Books Worldwideís books in the classroom or for ordering examination copies, please contact our Educational Sales department at 800-434-2086 or fax 317-596-5499.

For press review copies, author interviews, or other publicity information, please contact our Public Relations department at 650-655-3000 or fax 650-655-3299.

For authorization to photocopy items for corporate, personal, or educational use, please contact Copyright Clearance Center, 222 Rosewood Drive, Danvers, MA 01923, or fax 978-750-4470.

 is a trademark under exclusive license to IDG Books Worldwide, Inc., from International Data Group, Inc.

ABOUT IDG BOOKS WORLDWIDE

Welcome to the world of IDG Books Worldwide.

IDG Books Worldwide, Inc., is a subsidiary of International Data Group, the world's largest publisher of computer-related information and the leading global provider of information services on information technology. IDG was founded more than 25 years ago and now employs more than 8,500 people worldwide. IDG publishes more than 275 computer publications in over 75 countries (see listing below). More than 90 million people read one or more IDG publications each month.

Launched in 1990, IDG Books Worldwide is today the #1 publisher of best-selling computer books in the United States. We are proud to have received eight awards from the Computer Press Association in recognition of editorial excellence and three from *Computer Currents'* First Annual Readers' Choice Awards. Our best-selling *...For Dummies®* series has more than 50 million copies in print with translations in 38 languages. IDG Books Worldwide, through a joint venture with IDG's Hi-Tech Beijing, became the first U.S. publisher to publish a computer book in the People's Republic of China. In record time, IDG Books Worldwide has become the first choice for millions of readers around the world who want to learn how to better manage their businesses.

Our mission is simple: Every one of our books is designed to bring extra value and skill-building instructions to the reader. Our books are written by experts who understand and care about our readers. The knowledge base of our editorial staff comes from years of experience in publishing, education, and journalism — experience we use to produce books for the '90s. In short, we care about books, so we attract the best people. We devote special attention to details such as audience, interior design, use of icons, and illustrations. And because we use an efficient process of authoring, editing, and desktop publishing our books electronically, we can spend more time ensuring superior content and spend less time on the technicalities of making books.

You can count on our commitment to deliver high-quality books at competitive prices on topics you want to read about. At IDG Books Worldwide, we continue in the IDG tradition of delivering quality for more than 25 years. You'll find no better book on a subject than one from IDG Books Worldwide.

John Kilcullen
CEO
IDG Books Worldwide, Inc.

Steven Berkowitz
President and Publisher
IDG Books Worldwide, Inc.

Eighth Annual
Computer Press
Awards ≥1992

Ninth Annual
Computer Press
Awards ≥1993

Tenth Annual
Computer Press
Awards ≥1994

Eleventh Annual
Computer Press
Awards ≥1995

Credits

Acquisitions Editor
Andy Cummings

Development Editors
Jenna Wallace
Susan Pines

Technical Editor
Christal Elliott

Copy Editors
Deb Kaufmann
Carolyn Welch

Project Coordinator
Katy German

Book Design
Drew R. Moore

Graphics and Production Specialists
Jude Levinson
Laura Carpenter
Ed Penslien
Mary Penn
Elyse Kaplan-Steinberger
Deirdre Smith

Quality Control
Mick Arellano

Proofreader
David Wise

Indexer
Rebecca Plunkett

About the Author

Ellen Finkelstein learned AutoCAD in Israel, where she always got to pour through the manual because she was the only one who could read it in English. After returning to the United States, she started consulting and teaching AutoCAD as well as other computer programs, including Microsoft Word, Excel, and PowerPoint. Ellen has written tutorial textbooks on Word and PowerPoint in Peter Norton's *Introduction to Computers* series. Her first book was *AutoCAD For Dummies Quick Reference* and she was a contributing author to *AutoCAD 13 Secrets,* both published by IDG Books Worldwide.

For MMY for teaching me that there's more to life than meets the eye.

Preface

Welcome to the *AutoCAD 14 Bible*. AutoCAD 14 is the most powerful CAD software product available for PCs today. It can perform nearly any drawing task you can give it. This book is designed to be your comprehensive guide to the entire AutoCAD program.

AutoCAD Release 14 is the fastest, smoothest AutoCAD yet. Many features have been added that are not even mentioned in this book because you never see them — you just notice that there are fewer regenerations, drawings load faster, and file sizes are smaller. In addition to these refinements, of course, are the many new features covered in this book that will make your drawing easier and faster.

This book covers every major AutoCAD feature. It will start you out if you are a beginner and bring you through an advanced level if you are already using AutoCAD regularly. It provides a solid reference base to come back to again and again as well as short tutorials to get you drawing. I've also added a number of sidebar profiles to show how companies out in the real world use AutoCAD. Finally, the CD-ROM is chock full of drawings, AutoLISP programs, and third-party reference material. This book should be all you need to make full use of that expensive program called AutoCAD.

Is This Book for You?

AutoCAD 14 Bible covers all the essential features of AutoCAD and includes clear, real-life examples and tutorials that you can adapt to your needs.

Although I fully cover AutoCAD basics, I have included material on the many advanced features such as the AutoCAD SQL Environment for accessing external databases, AutoLISP, 3D modeling, rendering, and ways to customize AutoCAD. The following should help you decide if this book is for you.

If you are a new AutoCAD user

If you are new to AutoCAD, the *AutoCAD 14 Bible* will guide you through all you need to know to start drawing effectively, whatever your field.

If you are upgrading to Release 14

This book highlights all the new features of Release 14 and will help you to make the transition as seamlessly as possible.

If you are upgrading from AutoCAD for DOS

For users who are new to the world of AutoCAD for Windows 95, this book will help you learn how to use the new interface for familiar commands. All instructions are given using Windows 95 menus and toolbars so you will quickly learn how to take fullest advantage of the graphical user interface for faster, easier drawing.

If you are switching from another CAD program

You already know what CAD is all about. This book will clearly explain the AutoCAD way of drawing the models you have already been drawing. In addition, there is a great deal of essential information about transferring information from other formats.

Other Information

If you are an advanced AutoCAD user but need tips and secrets for getting the most out of AutoCAD, this book will probably not add too much to your already great store of knowledge. I refer you to *AutoCAD Secrets* also published by IDG Books Worldwide — a great book for advanced AutoCAD users.

If you want to learn about Windows 95, look for a book that focuses on it. This book assumes you know the basics of Windows 95, although the instructions in this book are usually detailed enough to get you through any task. For more information about Windows 95, try *Windows 95 For Dummies* by Andy Rathbone (IDG Books Worldwide) or *Windows 95 Bible* by Alan Simpson (IDG Books Worldwide).

If you want just the basics; You probably didn't buy AutoCAD if you want just the basics. AutoCAD LT might serve your needs better. However, if you do have AutoCAD and want a more basic book, I recommend *AutoCAD For Dummies,* 2nd Edition, by Bud Smith (IDG Books Worldwide) and my *AutoCAD For Dummies Quick Reference*, also published by IDG Books Worldwide.

AutoCAD and Windows Versions

The *AutoCAD 14 Bible* covers AutoCAD Release 14 for Windows 95. However, most of the information also applies to Release 13c4, which was Autodesk's first release for Windows 95. Almost everything also applies to Windows NT versions of AutoCAD as well, although some of the screens will look slightly different.

Conventions Used in This Book

Given all the ways in which you can execute a command in AutoCAD, you'll find it useful to read through this section, which describes the typographical conventions used in this book.

AutoCAD commands

It is time to accept that AutoCAD is running on Windows 95 and to use standard Windows 95 conventions for menus and toolbars. To indicate choosing a command from the menu, for example, I say choose View⇨Paper Space, which means that you should click the View menu with your mouse or puck/stylus and then click the Paper Space menu item.

Some of AutoCAD's toolbar buttons have flyouts, which are equivalent to submenus. They are called flyouts because they fly out when you click the button on the main toolbar, displaying even more buttons. Therefore, to indicate which button to choose, I may need to tell you to choose (or click) Zoom Extents from the Zoom flyout of the Standard toolbar. Although I haven't yet found a good alternative, this is not completely satisfactory for two reasons. First, it's a mouthful! Second, the flyout names do not appear, making it hard to know which is the Line flyout. However, you can look in Appendix B where each toolbar and flyout is shown along with its name. Also, in most cases it will be obvious which flyout I'm talking about.

AutoCAD is unique in that every command also has a *command name* that can be typed on the command line that appears at the bottom of your screen. Command names are shown in capital letters, as in CIRCLE.

AutoCAD prompts, your input, and instructions

In the Step-by-Step exercises, most instructions are written in the same font and style you are reading now. However, when I reproduce the AutoCAD command line, I show AutoCAD's prompts in a nonproportional font and the input you should provide in bold. Other instructions (such as Type in the first coordinate) are shown in italic. Comments that I use to explain what is happening are in regular text. Here's a sample Step-by-Step section:

1. With your left mouse button (also called the pick button), choose Line from the Draw toolbar.

```
_line From point: 0,0 ↵ (This arrow means to press Enter)
To point: 10,0 ↵
To point: 10,7 ↵
To point: 0,7 ↵
To point: 0,0 ↵
To point: ↵
```

In this exercise, you simply click the proper toolbar button, type in the X,Y coordinates shown in bold, and press Enter when indicated.

Mouse and keyboard terms

You can draw in AutoCAD using a mouse or a puck. The mouse is familiar to all users. A puck is used with a digitizing tablet. Because most AutoCAD users do not have a digitizing tablet, I will not directly refer to it in this book. If you have one, follow the instructions for using the mouse in the same way, using your puck.

A mouse can have two or more buttons. Many AutoCAD users like using a mouse with at least three buttons, because you can customize the buttons to suit your needs. However, since many users have only two buttons, I assume only two. The left mouse button is used to choose commands and toolbar buttons and to pick points in your drawing. For this reason, it is sometimes called the *pick button*. The right button is equivalent to pressing Enter (also called Return). For this reason, it is sometimes called the *return button*. In Windows 95, the right button is used to display shortcut menus.

If I say,

- ✦ choose Tools⇨Toolbars
- ✦ click Line on the Draw toolbar
- ✦ select the circle in your drawing

it means to use the left button of your mouse.

When I say, press Enter, it means to press the key that is marked Enter, Return, or ↵. Usually I use the bent arrow picture (↵) to indicate that you should press Enter.

Tip

In most cases when I say press Enter, you can also use the return (right) button of the mouse.

I also use the mouse terms shown in Table I-1.

Table I-1 AutoCAD Mouse Terms	
Term	**Description**
Cursor	The shape on your screen that shows you where the mouse is pointed. It can take a number of shapes, such as crosshairs, pickbox, or arrow. Also known as the mouse pointer.
Pickbox	A type of cursor consisting of a small box, used to select drawing objects.
Crosshairs	A type of cursor consisting of intersecting lines.
Pick	Point to a drawing object and click the left mouse button.
Click	Press the left mouse button once and release it.
Double-click	Press the left mouse button twice in rapid succession.
Drag	Move the mouse cursor, causing drawing objects to move with it.
Click and drag	Click the left mouse button and hold it down while you move the mouse, dragging an object on your screen with it.
Choose	Click a menu item, toolbar button, or dialog box item. You can sometimes choose an item using the keyboard as well.
Right-click	Press the right mouse button once and release it.
Shift and click	While holding down the Shift key, press the left mouse button once and release it.
Select	Highlight an object in a drawing by picking it or using another object selection method, or highlight text in a dialog box or text document.

What the Icons Mean

AutoCAD 14 Bible is liberally sprinkled with icons — small symbols in the left margin that call your attention to noteworthy points.

The Release 14 icon means that a feature is new to Release 14, or includes features that existed in Release 13 but have been significantly changed.

A Note icon alerts you to some important information that requires special attention.

A Tip shows you a way to accomplish a task more efficiently or quickly.

The Cross-reference icon refers you to a related topic elsewhere in the book.

The CD-ROM icon highlights references to related material on the CD-ROM. I use this icon whenever an exercise uses a drawing on the CD-ROM, or to reference other material on the CD-ROM.

The Caution icon means you should pay special attention to the instructions because there is a possibility you could cause a problem otherwise.

How This Book Is Organized

This book is divided into seven parts plus appendixes.

Part I: "AutoCAD Basics" — This part contains five chapters that provide the background information you need to start drawing. It starts with a "quick tour" that gets you drawing right away, and then covers how to start a drawing, use commands, specify coordinates, and set up a drawing.

Part II: "Drawing in Two Dimensions" — Part II covers all the commands and procedures for drawing and editing in two dimensions. In addition I discuss how to control the drawing process with layers, zooming, and panning. Also included in this part are dimensioning, plotting, and printing.

Part III: "Working with Data" — This part covers the many ways to organize and share data, including blocks, attributes, external references, and external databases.

Part IV: "Drawing in Three Dimensions" — Here I explain everything you need to know to draw in three dimensions. I also discuss how to present 3D drawings using hiding, shading, and rendering techniques.

Part V: "Organizing and Managing Drawings" — This part helps to relate AutoCAD to the rest of the work world by discussing how to set standards, manage drawings, and work with other applications. It concludes with a chapter on AutoCAD and the World Wide Web.

Part VI: "Customizing AutoCAD" — In this part, you are introduced to the tools you need to customize commands, toolbars, linetypes, hatch patterns, shapes, fonts, menus, and help files. There is a chapter on script files, which are AutoCAD's method of creating macros.

Part VII: "AutoLISP" — This part is a two-chapter discussion of AutoLISP to help you get the most out of AutoCAD.

Appendix A gives instructions for installing AutoCAD. Appendix B displays all the menus and submenus as well as the toolbars and their flyouts. Appendix C lists new, changed, and discontinued commands and system variables. Appendix D covers all the ways to get help on AutoCAD, and Appendix E explains what is on the CD-ROM.

How to Use This Book

You can use this book in two ways: as a reference or as a learning tool.

AutoCAD 14 Bible is organized as a reference that you can refer to whenever you get stuck or when you try to do something for the first time. Each chapter covers a topic completely, making it easy to find what you're looking for. Each Step-by-Step exercise can be done on its own without doing the other exercises in the chapter. You can easily look up a topic and do an exercise on it without having to go through the entire chapter. There is also a complete index where you can look up the feature you need.

However, the overall organization of the book is from simple to complex, and each chapter has several step-by-step sections. This allows you to use the book as a tutorial — from beginning to end. You can then go back and redo any exercise when you need to refresh your memory on a particular feature.

For newcomers to AutoCAD, Parts I and II are essential. After that you can refer to chapters that interest you. Parts III and V are also useful for beginners. Intermediate users will probably be familiar with most of the material in Part I and will be more likely to skip around looking for the specific topics they need.

However, don't forget that many of the new features for Release 14 are introduced in Part I. There is enough material in this book to bring intermediate users up to a fairly advanced level.

I have designed this book to be comprehensive and to include every significant feature of AutoCAD. Therefore, do not be concerned if some of the material seems too advanced. It will be there when you are ready for it.

Doing the Exercises

AutoCAD is a very customizable program. This book assumes that you are working with the default setup. However, a number of changes may have been made to your system that could result in menus, toolbars, and drawings appearing differently from those shown in this book. If you installed AutoCAD yourself and made some adjustments, you know what changes you made. However, if you are using a computer that was set up by someone else, it may help to talk to that person first, to see what changes were made.

In addition, during the course of the exercises in this book you will make certain changes in AutoCAD's setup. Most of these are minor changes that any user would make while drawing. All changes that could have serious consequences, such as customizing the menu, are accompanied by Cautions and Tips for safety. For example, when customizing the menu, you will be instructed to copy the menu template file to a new name, and you will then work with the new menu file, not the original one. Nevertheless, if you are working on a network or sharing AutoCAD with someone else, it is proper computer etiquette to consult with others who may be affected by the changes you make.

If you do the exercises, I recommend that you do them from the beginning. Important instructions are given during earlier exercises that may affect your system later. For example, one of the first exercises is to create a new folder to hold your drawings from the exercises. This folder keeps your exercise drawings separate from other drawings created in your office. However, each exercise stands on its own so that you can go back and do only the exercise you need.

Cross-Reference
You can create your own AutoCAD configuration that ensures that changes you make will not affect others. Instructions for doing this are in Appendix A under the heading "Creating Your Own Configuration."

The exercises in *AutoCAD 14 Bible* have been carefully checked by a technical reviewer to ensure accuracy. However, there are always situations that we cannot anticipate, either due to varying hardware/software configurations or customization within AutoCAD. If you have a problem with an exercise, contact me at the e-mail address listed at the end of the Preface so I can correct the problem in the next edition of the book.

About the CD-ROM

The CD-ROM contains all the drawings you need to do the exercises and tutorials in this book. These drawings save you time in learning AutoCAD's features. In addition, the CD-ROM includes the drawings that result once you have finished an exercise or tutorial. In this way, you can check what you have done if you wish.

The CD-ROM is also chock-full of resource material that I hope you will find useful for many years to come. The contents of the CD-ROM are listed in Appendix E.

Contacting the Author

I would be happy to hear from you. The best way to contact me is by e-mail at ellenfinkl@compuserve.com. You can also use the U.S. Postal Service (aka snail mail) and write to me care of the publisher.

Acknowledgments

I would like to offer special thanks to Ellen Camm, who has supported me throughout the past two years and kept me busy working for IDG Books. I'd also like to thank Andy Cummings, Anne Friedman, Deb Kaufmann, Katy German, and all the people at IDG Books who helped with the production of this book.

Special thanks to Jenna Wallace, whose superb organizational skills and good nature helped immensely. Also thanks to Christal Elliott for her knowledgeable technical editing of this book.

Thanks to David Walsh for contributing the material for Chapter 20 on ASE and to Jerry Coley, Head QA Engineer at Autodesk, for contributing the two chapters on AutoLISP. Thanks to Brian Souder at Autodesk for providing material for the CD-ROM.

Many people contributed drawings for this book. I'd like to thank all of them. They have helped make this book the most comprehensive book on AutoCAD available.

Finally, I would like to thank my family, who helped out while I was writing, writing, and writing. Without their support, I could not have completed this book.

Contents at a Glance

Contents

Part VII: AutoLISP   913

Part VIII: Appendixes   953

AutoCAD Basics

The five chapters in Part I provide all the basics you need to start drawing in AutoCAD. These chapters are essential for the beginner, but even current users will find some new tips and points, especially related to features that are new for Release 14. If you feel you know enough to skip to Part II, skim this part first for Release 14 icons to bring yourself up to date. Some of the best new features of Release 14 are introduced here.

Starting to Draw

Learning AutoCAD is a bit like trying to decide what came first — the chicken or the egg. On one hand, there are many basics you need to know before you can start drawing. On the other hand, it is very difficult to understand those basics if you haven't had the experience of drawing something. In this chapter you resolve this problem by drawing a simple rectangle. The next few chapters then fill you in on the basics you need to move on to more complex drawings. By experiencing the drawing process first, the initial learning curve will be easier and smoother.

Getting Acquainted

AutoCAD, created by Autodesk, is the most widely used technical drawing program anywhere, with over 1.25 million registered users. Autodesk is the fourth-largest PC software company in the world. According to Autodesk, CAD stands for computer aided design, but can also stand for computer aided drafting or drawing.

The first version of AutoCAD came out in 1982 running under DOS. AutoCAD was the first significant CAD program to run on a desktop computer. At the time most other technical drawing programs ran on high-end workstations or even mainframes. AutoCAD's success has been attributed to its famous *open architecture,* which means that many of the files that AutoCAD uses are plain text (ASCII) files that you can easily customize to your needs. The support of AutoLISP, a programming language designed especially for AutoCAD, has also been a major factor in making AutoCAD the standard for serious technical drawing.

As a result, AutoCAD is the most flexible drafting program available, applicable to all fields. AutoCAD's support for foreign languages, including those using other alphabets, is unparalleled, making AutoCAD virtually without serious competition abroad. As a result, AutoCAD is used in all fields and in well over 125 countries.

Through a high level of technical innovation and expertise, Autodesk has created a program with unequaled features and capabilities, including 3D modeling and visualization, access to external databases, intelligent dimensioning, importing and exporting of other file formats, and many more.

Autodesk has developed what it calls a virtual corporation which includes programmers who create software designed to work with AutoCAD (called third-party software), dealers who provide technical support and training specific to a user's field, and an education network providing training and courses to over one million users each year. This setup provides a strong network of support to users throughout the world.

The major disciplines that use AutoCAD are:

✦ Architectural (often called AEC for architectural, engineering, and construction)

✦ Mechanical

✦ GIS (Geographic Information Systems)

✦ Facilities management

✦ Electrical/electronic

✦ Multimedia

However, there are many other lesser-known uses for AutoCAD, such as pattern making in the garment industry, sign making, and so on.

In this book, I try to provide examples from many fields. The world of AutoCAD is very broad, and it is worthwhile to see the many approaches that AutoCAD makes possible.

Now, let's start!

Starting AutoCAD

This section starts the quick tour of AutoCAD, designed to make AutoCAD seem easy and simple. The first step is to start AutoCAD.

This book covers AutoCAD Release 14 running on Windows 95. When you turn on your computer, Windows 95 starts automatically and you see your desktop. Every computer is set up somewhat differently, so you may need to adjust the following steps slightly. If you didn't install AutoCAD yourself and are unfamiliar with the folders (also called directories) on your computer, you should first talk to someone who is familiar with your computer system.

Cross-Reference If you need help installing AutoCAD, turn to Appendix A.

Windows 95 offers several ways to launch a program, but the simplest is to follow these steps:

Step-by-Step: Starting AutoCAD Release 14 in Windows 95

1. Click Start on the Taskbar at the bottom of your screen.

2. Choose Programs.

3. Choose AutoCAD. (On your system, it may appear as AutoCAD R14 or something similar.)

4. If a submenu opens up, choose AutoCAD again. (On your system, it may appear as AutoCAD R14 or something similar.)

5. AutoCAD opens, loads the menu, and displays the Startup dialog box, shown in Figure 1-1. You can choose from one of five options. For now, choose Start from Scratch.

6. Choose English as the default setting and click OK. AutoCAD creates a blank drawing ready for you to start drawing.

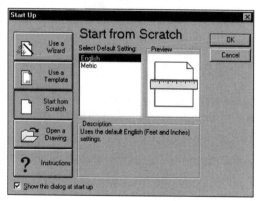

Figure 1-1: The Startup dialog box.

The Startup dialog box is new for Release 14. The heading in the Startup dialog box varies according to which button you choose.

✦ Choose Use a Wizard to let AutoCAD guide you through the process of setting up a drawing.

✦ Choose Use a Template to use a template (formerly called a prototype drawing) as the basis for your drawing.

✦ Choose Start from Scratch to start a drawing with default settings.

✦ Choose Open a Drawing to open an existing drawing.

Notice that you can uncheck Show this dialog at startup. If you do so, AutoCAD opens a blank drawing based on default settings each time. This is equivalent to choosing Start from Scratch.

You can also turn the display of the Startup dialog box on and off by choosing Tools⇨Preferences and clicking the Compatibility tab.

If you use AutoCAD a lot, you will probably prefer to have a shortcut to AutoCAD on your desktop. Follow these steps to create one.

Step-by-Step: Creating a Shortcut for AutoCAD on the Desktop

1. On the desktop, double-click My Computer.

2. If the window lists more than one drive, double-click the drive that contains AutoCAD.

3. Double-click the folder containing the *acad.exe* file. (This is the file that launches AutoCAD.) By default, it is called ACADR14.

4. With the right mouse button, click *acad.exe.*

5. Choose Create Shortcut from the menu.

6. Find the new shortcut in the folder window (it is probably called *Shortcut to acad.exe*) and drag it to the desktop.

7. Click the name of the shortcut to highlight it.

8. Type a shorter name for your shortcut, such as **AutoCAD**, and press Enter. Your shortcut should look like Figure 1-2.

You can now double-click your new shortcut to open AutoCAD.

Shortcut icon

Figure 1-2: An AutoCAD shortcut on the desktop is the fastest way to open AutoCAD.

Using the AutoCAD Interface

You are probably impatient to start drawing but first you need to get the lay of the land.

Figure 1-3 shows the screen when you first open AutoCAD. Your screen may look somewhat different — remember that AutoCAD can be customized in many ways — but the general features will be the same.

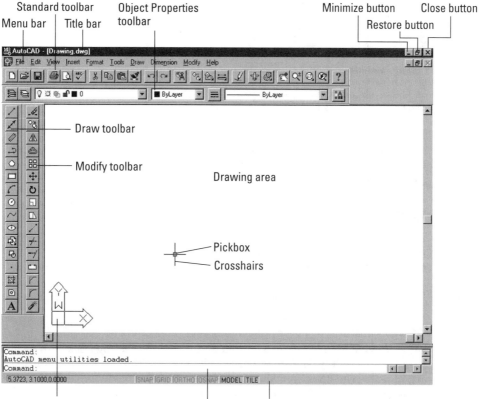

Figure 1-3: The AutoCAD screen.

There are four important areas on the AutoCAD screen. These are discussed in the next sections.

The drawing area

The main blank area in the middle of the screen is where you draw. You can compare this to a sheet of drafting paper except that this piece of paper can be any size — even the size of a huge factory!

To specify a point, it is the universally accepted convention to put the X coordinate first, then a comma, and then the Y coordinate. Figure 1-4 shows some coordinates on X and Y axes.

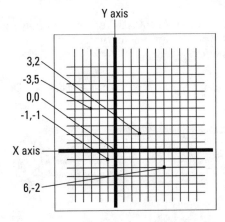

Figure 1-4: Some X,Y coordinates.

Cross-Reference

Chapter 4 is devoted to explaining how to specify coordinates. If you want to create three-dimensional models, you would add a Z coordinate when specifying a point. Three-dimensional coordinates are discussed in Chapter 21.

The UCS icon

Notice the symbol with two arrows at the bottom left corner of the drawing area in Figure 1-3. This symbol is called the UCS (User Coordinate System) icon. The arrows point to the positive directions of the X and Y axes.

Note

For now, ignore the W on the UCS icon.

The crosshairs

In the drawing area of Figure 1-3, notice the two intersecting lines with a small box at their intersection. The small box is called the pickbox because it helps you to pick objects. The lines are called crosshairs. They help you judge the location of the mouse cursor in relation to other objects in your drawing.

Move your mouse around. The pickbox and crosshairs move with your mouse. At the bottom of your screen, on the left end of the status bar (described later in this chapter), you can see the X,Y coordinates changing as you move the mouse.

The menus and toolbars

At the top of your screen is the title bar, and directly beneath the title bar is a menu bar. Below that are two rows of toolbars. In addition, there are two more toolbars, the Draw and Modify toolbars, which may be floating somewhere on your screen or docked at any side of the screen. Figure 1-3 shows them docked at the left side of the screen. The menus and toolbars together allow you to give AutoCAD commands to draw, edit, get information, and so on.

When you install AutoCAD out of the box, the menus and toolbars appear as shown in Figure 1-3. However, you can customize both the menus and toolbars to suit your needs so your screen may appear somewhat differently. There are also many more toolbars provided by AutoCAD that you can display when you need them. Some examples of the toolbars are Dimensioning, Solids, Render, and External Database. You will learn about all these and more in this book.

Release 14 provides Draw and Modify menus that are very similar to the Draw and Modify toolbars.

The Bonus menu item appears only if you choose a full installation when you install AutoCAD. It does not appear if you choose a typical installation. The Bonus menu items are explained in Appendix A.

The command line

At the bottom of the screen you see a separate window showing approximately three lines of text. (It can be changed to show as many lines as you like.) Notice the word Command:. This is the command line. All commands can be executed by typing them on the command line.

Even if you use a menu item or toolbar button to execute a command, you need to look at the command line to see how AutoCAD responds. Often, AutoCAD provides you with options that must be typed in from the keyboard. Also, anything you type appears on the command line. For example, when you type in coordinates specifying points, they appear on the command line. To see more of the command line, press F2 to open the AutoCAD Text window. You can then scroll back through previous commands. Press F2 again to close the window.

The status bar

At the very bottom of the screen is the status bar, as shown in Figure 1-3. At the left are the X,Y coordinates. As you move your mouse around, these change. There are also several buttons that you will learn about later.

Getting Started

Now you are almost ready to draw your first lines. It is worthwhile to first take a minute to get accustomed to using the toolbars to give AutoCAD a command.

Toolbars and flyouts

On the Draw toolbar, move the mouse cursor over the first button. You see a ToolTip that says Line, as shown in Figure 1-5. Also notice the status bar, which tells you that this button creates straight line segments.

Tip

If a ToolTip is not self-explanatory, look on the status bar. It provides some additional information.

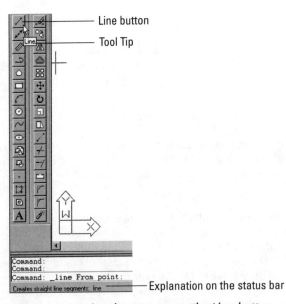

Figure 1-5: Moving the cursor over the Line button.

Tip

If you inadvertently execute a command that you don't want, press Esc. The command line prompt (Command:) returns.

Your first drawing

For this exercise, simply follow the instructions exactly. When you type the X and Y coordinates (shown in bold), type the first number, a comma, then the second number, with no spaces between them. If you haven't read the Introduction, now is a good time to go back and read the part that explains how to follow the Step-by-Step exercises.

Don't worry if you do not understand everything you are doing. It will all become clear as you progress through this book.

Step-by-Step: Drawing a Rectangle

Follow the prompts below. As explained in the Introduction, what you type appears in bold. Instructions to you in command sections appear in italic.

1. Start AutoCAD. When the Startup dialog box appears, choose Start from Scratch. Choose English from the Select Default Setting box. Click OK.

2. With your left mouse button (also called the pick button), choose Line from the Draw toolbar. Notice that the command name is repeated on the command line.

```
Command: _line From point: 0,0 ↵ (This arrow means to press
Enter)
To point: 10,0 ↵
To point: 10,7 ↵
To point: 0,7 ↵
To point: 0,0 ↵
To point: ↵
```

3. The command line prompt appears again, ready for a new command. To make the rectangle fill up the screen, type the following shown in bold:

```
Command: zoom ↵
All/Center/Dynamic/Extents/_Previous/
Scale(X/XP)/Window/<Realtime>: e↵
```

The rectangle is centered and fills most of the screen, leaving a small space at the edges of the drawing area. The ZOOM command with the Extents (e) option brings the outer extents of the drawing to the edges of your screen. You will learn more about the ZOOM command in Chapter 8.

4. Keep your drawing open. You will save it later in this chapter. It should look like Figure 1-6.

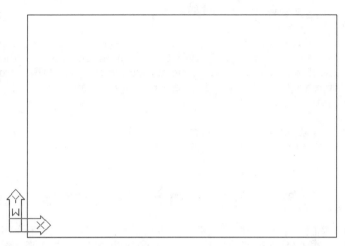

Figure 1-6: Your first drawing.

Help! My drawing doesn't look like the figure

If your drawing doesn't look like the figure, there could be several reasons. Try one of the following.

✦ You may have made a mistake. If you think that's the case, choose File⇨New and choose No when AutoCAD asks if you want to save your changes. Choose Start from Scratch in the Startup dialog box and click OK. Then follow the prompts again.

✦ You may have started AutoCAD based on a template instead of choosing Start from Scratch. Choose File⇨New and choose No when AutoCAD asks if you want to save your changes. Choose Start from Scratch in the Startup dialog box and click OK. Then follow the prompts again.

✦ If your drawing still seems wrong, put the CD-ROM in your CD-ROM drive. Choose File⇨Open and use the Open dialog box to find *ab-acad.dwg* on the CD-ROM. Choose *ab-acad.dwg* and click OK. Then follow the prompts again.

One of the above should solve your problem.

You may be wondering what units the coordinates you typed refer to. For now, you can think of them as inches, although they can actually be whatever you want. Therefore, you could print out the drawing as a rectangle of 10 inches by 7 inches.

You have learned several things — how to start a command using the toolbar (the LINE command), how to type in X,Y coordinates on the command line, and how to end the LINE command (by pressing Enter without typing in any coordinates). You also used the ZOOM command by typing it on the command line. Most of AutoCAD builds on these basic skills.

Saving a Drawing

Saving a drawing is similar to saving any other file in Windows 95. You should get in the habit of saving your work every 10 to 15 minutes to avoid losing your work in case your computer system crashes.

For your work with this book, you should create a new folder so your exercise drawings don't get mixed up with other drawings. Although this is a standard Windows 95 function, I am including the steps here because they are so important. You will use Windows Explorer.

The following directions leave up to you where to create this new folder. Each computer system is organized differently. If you are unsure what to do, choose the drive (not the folder) where AutoCAD is installed and create a new folder there. (Most computers have only one drive.) I do not recommend creating a subfolder in the AutoCAD folder (which is usually called *acadr14*) because it is too easy to make a mistake and delete necessary AutoCAD files!

Step-by-Step: Creating a New Folder

1. Move the mouse cursor down to the Taskbar at the bottom of your screen and click Start.

2. Choose Programs.

3. Choose Windows Explorer. Windows Explorer opens.

4. On the left pane, click the drive where you want to create the new folder. If you don't know where to create the folder, choose the drive where AutoCAD is installed. If you are on a network, choose the drive that represents your computer.

5. If you want to make a subfolder (a folder within a folder), choose the folder where you want to create the subfolder.

6. From the Explorer menu, choose File⇨New⇨Folder.

7. A new, highlighted folder appears in the right pane, called *New Folder*. (You may have to scroll down to see it.)

8. Type **AutoCAD Bible** for the folder name and press Enter.

Now you are ready to save your drawing. Saving a drawing for the first time is different from saving it subsequently, because you have to name the drawing the first time you save it. The important point is to save the drawing in the right drive and folder. You should save this drawing (and all drawings you create using this book) in the special folder you created in the Step-by-Step session just completed.

Caution

It is essential to create a folder for your drawings as described in the previous steps before you go on to exercises in the rest of the book.

Step-by-Step: Saving a Drawing for the First Time

1. The rectangle you created earlier in this chapter should still be on your screen. Click Save on the Standard toolbar. The Save Drawing As dialog box opens.

2. Click the Save In drop-down list box. If necessary, choose the drive where you created your *AutoCAD Bible* folder.

3. Double-click the *AutoCAD Bible* folder you created for this book. You may need to scroll down to display the folder name.

4. In the File Name box, choose a filename. Type **ab1-1** and press Enter (or click Save).

AutoCAD saves your drawing under the name *ab1-1.dwg*. You can use a different name if you like, but this will help you organize your drawings from this book. It just means that this is the first drawing from Chapter 1 of the *AutoCAD 14 Bible*.

On the
CD-ROM

The CD-ROM includes a small program, *savea.lsp,* that automatically backs up your drawing to the floppy drive after you have saved it on your hard drive. If you like to back up to a diskette regularly for safety, this can be useful. Look in *\Software\Chap01*.

Exiting AutoCAD

As with any Windows program, there is more than one way to exit. The simplest is to use the Close box at the top right corner of your screen. Click it and AutoCAD closes.

If you're very observant, you will notice the word *Quit* on the command line as you exit. You can also exit AutoCAD by typing **quit** on the command line and pressing Enter.

Another method is to choose File⇨Exit.

If you have made any changes to your drawing since last saving it, AutoCAD asks you if you want to save your changes. Choose Yes or No as your situation requires. Choosing Cancel returns you to your drawing.

Summary

In this chapter you explored the AutoCAD screen and started to draw. You created a folder for your drawings for this book, saved your drawing in that folder, and exited AutoCAD.

You may have several questions at this point, but "well begun is half done." The next chapter explains all the ways to start a new drawing as well as to open an existing drawing.

♦　　♦　　♦

Opening a Drawing

Opening a Drawing Using the Default Template

AutoCAD offers a number of options for opening a drawing. These options create a great deal of flexibility and save you time as well. You can create complex templates to avoid doing the same basic setup and drawing over and over.

Release 14 introduces a new drawing type called a *template*. It is just like the templates in your word processor. Previously, the term *prototype* was used, but the prototype was a regular drawing.

To open a drawing based on the default template, choose Use a Template from the Start Up dialog box. AutoCAD displays the Use a Template dialog box, which lists all the available templates, as shown in Figure 2-1. The first one is *Acad.dwt. Acad* is an abbreviation for AutoCAD and *Acad.dwt* is the default template. This template then becomes the basis of your subsequent work. However, the new drawing is named *Drawing.dwg*. When you save and name your drawing, the original *Acad.dwt* template file is unaffected.

♦   ♦   ♦   ♦

In This Chapter

Opening a new drawing using the default template

Working with templates

Starting from scratch

Opening a new drawing from within AutoCAD

Opening an existing drawing

Using an existing drawing as a prototype

Exiting a drawing and AutoCAD

♦   ♦   ♦   ♦

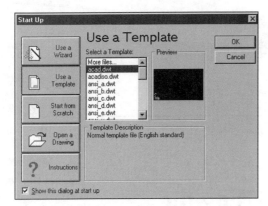

Figure 2-1: Using the Use a Template dialog box to open a drawing based on *Acad.dwt.*

If you are already in AutoCAD, you can start a new drawing based on *Acad.dwt* by choosing File➪New. The Startup dialog box opens. Choose Use a Template and *Acad.dwt* appears along with all the other templates AutoCAD provides. Click OK and a new drawing opens, using *Acad.dwt* as its template.

Step-by-Step: Opening a Drawing Based on Acad.dwt

1. Start AutoCAD.

2. In the Start Up dialog box, choose Use a Template.

3. Choose *Acad.dwt* from the Select a Template list. (In most cases, it is selected by default.)

4. Choose OK. You now have a blank drawing called *Drawing.dwg*, as shown in Figure 2-2.

Working with Templates

A template contains ready-made settings to get you started drawing quickly. These settings include the size of the drawing (called limits), the unit type (such as decimal or architectural), and others. An important part of setting standards in an office where people work together on drawings is the creation of a template so that all users work with an identical setup.

A template may contain more than just settings — it often contains a complete title block, for example, and may include boilerplate (standardized) text as well.

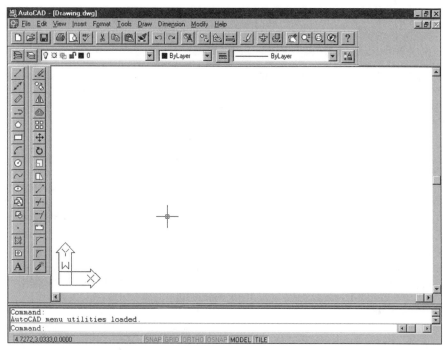

Figure 2-2: When you start a drawing based on a template, AutoCAD opens a drawing called Drawing.dwg.

Customizing Acad.dwt

To customize *Acad.dwt,* open a drawing based on it as described in the previous section. Make any changes you wish. Click Save on the Standard toolbar. In the Save Drawing As dialog box, click the Save as type drop-down list box. Choose Drawing Template File (*.dwt). Click Save.

Without templates, you would have to set up your drawing each time you start a drawing — a time-consuming project. Over time, the use of templates saves hours and hours of work.

Caution

Don't change *Acad.dwt* if you are using someone else's computer and copy of AutoCAD without first checking with that person. It can be a frustrating experience to open a drawing based on *Acad.dwt* and find that all the settings are different.

Spotlight on AutoCAD Users
Creative Edge in Fairfield, Iowa

Creative Edge has literally carved out its own niche in CAD/CAM. This company uses AutoCAD to create drawings that are then used to cut out shapes of almost any material imaginable. Creative Edge provides services to architects, interior designers, and even individual homeowners.

Here's how the process works. Creative Edge accepts anything from a completed drawing to a sketch on a napkin as the front-end input. An example is the Radisson Hotel in Rapid City, South Dakota, shown below. In this case, Creative Edge's in-house artist and vice president Harri Aalto created the design. Once the design is finalized, an AutoCAD drawing is created from the design. Often, the design is digitized by putting the artwork on a large digitizer and picking points with the puck. Here you see a close-up of the central part of the drawing, showing Mount Rushmore.

Then the company's programmers use NC Polaris by NC Microproducts, Inc. (phone number 214-234-6655) to convert the drawing into numerical code. This program determines a cutting path for every section of the drawing. Here you see the first few lines of the code created from the Radisson Hotel AutoCAD drawing.

```
%
;INW12.OUT
F20.000;PRE-OFFSET
G92XY
G91
G41
H1
N1177A
G0X2.0787Y4.2481;_RAPID_TO_PIERCE
/P200;_CUTTER_ON
G91
G3X.1764Y.0121I.0821J.0942
G3X.3383Y.3909I-56.3796J49.1335
```

This code is input into one of Creative Edge's 16 high-pressure water-jet cutters, which cuts out the pieces in the chosen material. In this case, the pieces were cut out of marble, granite, limestone, and brass. Other common materials are vinyl, linoleum, ceramic tile, titanium, stainless steel, and composites such as bullet-proof materials. Finally, the pieces of cut stone were set into the floor of the hotel's lobby. As you can see, the results are stunning.

Credit: Thanks to Harri Aalto of Creative Edge, Fairfield, IA, for the drawing and the photo below.

Creating your own templates

You may want several templates to choose from on a regular basis. For example, you may create drawings of several sizes. AutoCAD lets you easily create as many templates as you wish. To create your own templates, either start a drawing based on *Acad.dwt* and make the changes you want or open an existing drawing that already has some of the settings you want and make any further changes you need.

✦ If you start a drawing based on *Acad.dwt,* choose Save from the Standard toolbar. In the Save Drawing As dialog box, click the Save as type drop-down list box. Choose Drawing Template File (**.dwt*). In the File Name text edit box, type a name for your template. Click Save.

✦ If you open an existing drawing, choose File➪Save As. In the Save Drawing As dialog box, click the Save as type drop-down list box. Choose Drawing Template File (**.dwt*). In the File Name text edit box, type a name for your template. Click Save.

Name your templates in a way that clearly differentiates them from regular drawings. You may want drawings set up for each of the standard paper sizes (A through E), with a title block in each. An example would be *tb-a.dwt, tb-b.dwt (tb* meaning title block), and so on.

Most AutoCAD users take advantage of these techniques as a standard practice. You can usually make profitable use of a template or previous drawing as a basis for a new drawing.

Opening a Drawing with Default Settings

Occasionally you want to open a drawing without any settings. It is actually impossible for a drawing to have no settings at all, but you can open a drawing with the minimum possible presets. You might want to do this if you are working on someone else's computer and don't want to take the time to get rid of a large number of complex settings that are not helpful for your work.

To open a drawing with the fewest possible settings, choose Start from Scratch from the Start Up dialog box. Choose either English or Metric as the default setting and click OK.

Opening a New Drawing from Within AutoCAD

If you are already working on a drawing in AutoCAD and want to start a new drawing, choose New on the Standard toolbar. If you have not saved your changes to the current drawing, AutoCAD displays a message asking you if you want to do so. Choose Yes to save your changes and No to discard them. AutoCAD opens the Create New Drawing dialog box, as shown in Figure 2-3.

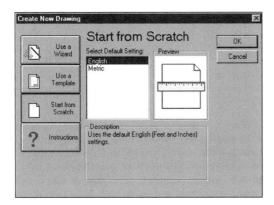

Figure 2-3: The Create New Drawing dialog box.

Choose one of the options and press Enter. The Use a Wizard option is discussed in Chapter 5.

Opening an Existing Drawing

To open an existing drawing when starting AutoCAD, choose Open a Drawing from the Start Up dialog box when you start AutoCAD. AutoCAD displays the last few drawings you opened in the Select a File box. To open one of these files, choose it and click OK.

If your drawing is not listed, choose More files from the Select a File box and click OK. AutoCAD opens the Select File dialog box, as shown in Figure 2-4. In the Look in drop-down list box, choose the drive where your drawing resides. In the main box, double-click the folder you need. Then choose your drawing. The Preview box lets you quickly look at the drawing to see if it's the one you want. Click Open. AutoCAD opens the drawing.

Note

Drawings created and saved in Release 12 do not show previews. Drawings created in Releases 13 and 14 have previews unless this feature has been disabled.

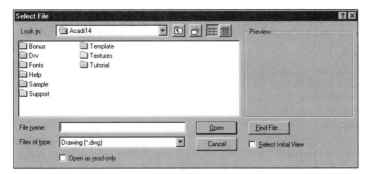

Figure 2-4: The Select File dialog box is equivalent to the Open dialog box in most Windows programs.

To open an existing drawing once you have already started working in AutoCAD, choose Open from the Standard toolbar. The Select File dialog box appears. Choose a drawing as explained earlier and click Open.

Tip   As with other Windows programs, you can double-click the drawing file to open it immediately without clicking Open.

All dialog boxes that open or save files, like the Select File dialog box, now support many new Windows 95 features. You can display the files in a list with or without details. Click the List icon to see a simple list. Click the Details icon to see file size and the last date and time the file was saved. Right-click inside the dialog box to open a shortcut menu with even more options. You can click the name of a drawing to highlight it and then click it once more to rename it (but don't double-click it — that will open the drawing). If you are familiar with Windows 95 dialog boxes already, you will enjoy the new capabilities of AutoCAD's open and save dialog boxes.

Step-by-Step: Opening a Drawing

1. If AutoCAD is not open, start AutoCAD. In the Start Up dialog box, choose Open a Drawing. In the Open a Drawing screen, choose More files.

 2. If AutoCAD is already open, click Open on the Standard toolbar.

On the CD-ROM

3. In the Select File dialog box, choose the drive for your CD-ROM drive in the Look in drop-down list box.

4. In the main box, double-click the *Results* folder.

5. In the main box, click *ab1-1.dwg*.

6. Click Open. AutoCAD opens the drawing. Keep this drawing open for the next exercise.

Using an Existing Drawing as a Prototype

Another option is to use an existing completed drawing as a prototype. Commonly, you need to draw a series of related drawings, perhaps several related electrical schematics or a group of similar apartments in an apartment complex. When a significant part of the first drawing is applicable to subsequent drawings, don't start over — open a new drawing based on the first drawing and simply make the necessary changes.

To use an existing drawing as a prototype, first open the drawing. Then choose File➪Save As and save the drawing under a new name.

Exiting a Drawing

Unfortunately, you can open only one drawing at a time. As a result, you never actually exit a drawing while remaining in AutoCAD. Instead, you have two choices:

✦ Exit AutoCAD entirely.

✦ Open a new or existing drawing without exiting AutoCAD.

Tip   If your computer has enough memory, you can open AutoCAD more than once and use the Windows 95 Taskbar to switch between drawings.

In the next exercise, you exit a drawing by exiting AutoCAD.

Step-by-Step: Exiting a Drawing and AutoCAD

On the CD-ROM   If you did the last Step-by-Step exercise, you have drawing *ab1-1.dwg* on your screen. If you didn't do that exercise, open *ab1-1.dwg* from the *Results* folder of the CD-ROM.

1. Choose File⇨Save As. The Save Drawing As dialog box opens, as shown in Figure 2-5.

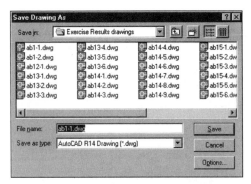

Figure 2-5: The Save Drawing As dialog box.

2. In the File name text box, change the file name to *ab2-1.dwg*. Select your *AutoCAD Bible* folder and choose Save.

3. Choose Line from the Draw toolbar. Follow the prompts:

```
From point: 10,.5 ↵
To point: 6,.5 ↵
To point: 6,0 ↵
To point: ↵
```

Your drawing should look like Figure 2-6.

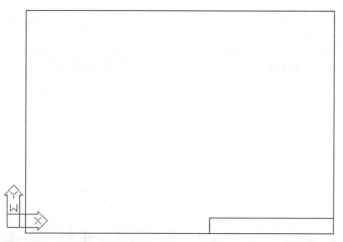

Figure 2-6: A simple title block.

4. Choose File⇨Exit.

5. Because you haven't saved the changes to the drawing, AutoCAD asks if you want to save them, as shown in Figure 2-7.

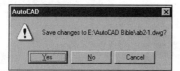

Figure 2-7: If you try to exit AutoCAD without saving the changes you made to a drawing, AutoCAD gives you a chance to save the changes.

6. Choose Yes. AutoCAD saves the drawing and exits AutoCAD.

Summary

In this chapter you explored the various ways of opening a drawing. While you can open a drawing from scratch, usually you use a template as the basis for a new drawing. Templates may have only settings or may contain drawing objects such as various size title blocks.

The default template is *Acad.dwt*. You may customize *Acad.dwt* or create your own templates. You can use any existing drawing as a prototype for a new drawing by opening the file and resaving it with a new name — choose File⇨Save As. You exit a drawing by exiting AutoCAD or opening a new drawing.

In the next chapter you learn all about using commands.

✦   ✦   ✦

Using Commands

The Windows Interface

Due to AutoCAD's long history and recent conversion to
Windows, the way you give AutoCAD commands, called the
user interface, is somewhat unique. You can give the same
command in several ways. In this chapter you learn about
these ways and start to feel comfortable with all of them.

Commands are important because you can't do anything in
AutoCAD without executing a command. In a word processing
program, you can simply start typing; in a spreadsheet program, you can begin by entering data; but nothing much happens in AutoCAD without giving it commands.

Using AutoCAD's menus

Many new commands have been added to AutoCAD over the
years. Often, older commands that were no longer necessary
were kept to maintain compatibility. In most Windows programs, all commands are included in the menus, but in
AutoCAD a number of these older commands, as well as certain rarely used commands, are not found in the menus.
Other than this idiosyncrasy, AutoCAD's menus are similar to
those of other Windows programs.

The screen menu

In early releases, AutoCAD provided a menu on the right side of the screen, called the screen menu. If you are just moving from the DOS version to the Windows version of AutoCAD, you may be used to the screen menu — however, I strongly suggest you adjust to the new interface. You will find its consistency with other Windows programs to be an advantage.

If you must have the screen menu, you can easily display it. Choose Tools⇨Preferences. If the Display tab is not on top, click it. Choose Display AutoCAD screen menu in the drawing window. Click OK.

AutoCAD's current default is to *not* show the screen menu, so I do not use it in this book. Therefore, the word *menu* always means the pull-down menu at the top of the AutoCAD screen.

A menu item can do three things. As in all Windows programs, the menu provides cues to let you know what is going to occur when you click on a menu item. Table 3-1 explains how this works.

Table 3-1 Menu Symbols and What They Mean	
Symbol	*Menu Action*
No symbol appears after the menu item	Executes a command
. . .	Opens a dialog box
▶	Displays a submenu

The View menu, shown in Figure 3-1, includes all three types of menu items.

Figure 3-1: The View menu.

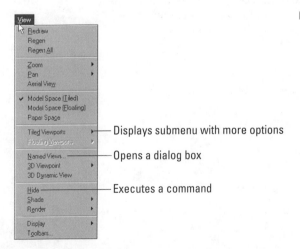

— Displays submenu with more options

— Opens a dialog box

— Executes a command

To see how a menu with a submenu works, try this Step-by-Step exercise.

Step-by-Step: Using a Submenu

On the CD-ROM

1. Open *ab2-1.dwg* from the *Results* folder of the CD-ROM.

2. Choose the View menu and point to the Zoom menu item. You may click it, but it is not necessary. The submenu opens.

3. Move the mouse pointer over to the submenu. You now have a choice of a list of ZOOM command options.

4. Choose Out from the submenu. The title block gets smaller, as if you have zoomed out using a movie camera lens.

5. Do not save this drawing.

It's worthwhile to look at the command line whenever you click a menu option. The ZOOM command is repeated on the command line and a list of options appears. Notice that they are mostly the same as those on the submenu, with some minor differences. For example, the Out option that you just used is not available on the command line. This is actually equivalent to using the Scale option that appears on the command line with a value of .5. AutoCAD's menu often offers pre-set options of commands to make your work simpler.

Using dialog boxes

Dialog boxes offer the user a simple way to control AutoCAD without memorizing a lot of technical command and option names. They guide you through a task by clearly laying out all the choices.

If you're familiar with any other Windows program, you're familiar with dialog boxes. AutoCAD, because of its complexity, has some very complicated dialog boxes. Nevertheless, you will find navigating them a familiar experience.

As a brief example, look at the Units Control dialog box, which allows you to define the type of units AutoCAD uses in your drawing. It has most of the features you see in AutoCAD's dialog boxes and is shown in Figure 3-2.

Figure 3-2: The Units Control dialog box is typical of many dialog boxes.

Step-by-Step: Using a Dialog Box

This Step-by-Step exercise can be done with any drawing on screen.

1. Choose Format⇨Units. The Units Control dialog box opens. Notice the two sections headed Units and Angles.

2. The default unit is Decimal. Choose Architectural. Notice how the display of units in the Precision box changes.

3. Choose each type of unit and watch how the units change.

4. Choose Decimal again.

5. Click the Precision drop-down list box. The default precision is four decimal places. Choose two decimal places.

6. Now choose various angle options on the right side of the dialog box. The angle options determine how angle measurements are shown.

7. Choose the default again, Decimal Degrees.

8. In the Precision drop-down list box, choose two decimal places.

9. The Direction button at the bottom of the dialog box has an ellipsis (...). This has the same meaning for dialog boxes as it does for menus — it opens another dialog box. Click Direction. The Direction Control dialog box opens. This dialog box allows you to change the standard convention that East is 0 degrees, North is 90 degrees, and so on. You can also change the standard that degrees increase in a counter-clockwise direction.

10. Click Cancel because you don't want to change these conventions. You return to the Units Control dialog box.

11. In the Precision drop-down list box for Angles, choose 0 to return this specification to its original setting. (If your setting was different from the default, you may want to return it to the way it was when you opened the dialog box.)

12. In the Precision drop-down list box for Units, choose 0.0000 to return this specification to its original setting. (If your setting was different from the default, you may want to return it to the way it was when you opened the dialog box.)

13. Click OK.

Tip

If a dialog box has a question mark (?) icon in the top right corner, click it to change the cursor to a question mark. Then click on any item in the dialog box to display a brief explanation of that item.

Toolbars

Toolbars provide a quick way to execute a command with one click of the mouse button. On the other hand, the little picture on the toolbar button is not always self-explanatory. Until you get used to the location of the buttons, you may find yourself wandering (with the mouse cursor) from button to button, reading ToolTips. However, once you are familiar with the location of most of the toolbar buttons, toolbars may become a favorite way to execute commands.

Cross-Reference

Toolbars can be customized to suit your needs. You can also create your own toolbars from scratch, perhaps containing your favorite command combinations. Toolbar customization is covered in Chapter 29.

According to my count, AutoCAD provides 12 toolbars. If you include all their flyouts, there are 50! Normally, you have only the Standard, Object Properties, Draw, and Modify toolbars showing. You can open other toolbars as you need them.

Release 14

Release 14 introduces a new Toolbars dialog box that lets you show and hide toolbars, as well as create, customize, and delete them. You use this dialog box in the next Step-by-Step exercise to make toolbars bend to your will.

Step-by-Step: Manipulating Toolbars

This Step-by-Step exercise can be done with any drawing on screen.

1. Point to the top edge of the Draw toolbar with the mouse pointer, click, hold down the mouse button, and drag the toolbar until it is under the left side of the Object Properties toolbar (which is the second toolbar under the menu bar) and changes to a straight horizontal line. When you release the mouse button, the toolbar docks under the Object Properties toolbar.

2. Point to the Modify toolbar and drag it in the same way you did for the Draw toolbar until it is docked under the right side of the Object Properties toolbar. Your screen should look something like Figure 3-3.

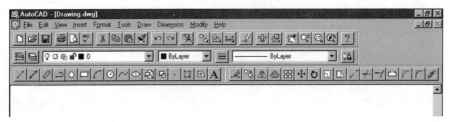

Figure 3-3: Docking the Draw and Modify toolbars at the top of the screen.

3. To try another configuration, point to the edge of the Draw toolbar. Drag the toolbar to the left side of the screen until the dotted shape shows a one-column vertical toolbar.

4. In the same way, drag the Modify toolbar to the right side of the screen. Your screen should look like Figure 3-4.

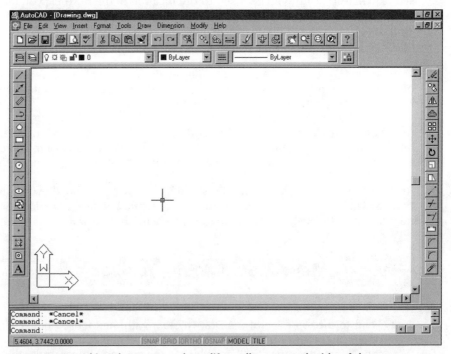

Figure 3-4: Docking the Draw and Modify toolbars at each side of the screen.

5. Choose View⇨Toolbars. Choose Dimension in the Toolbars dialog box and click Close to display the Dimensioning toolbar, which provides tools to allow you to show measurements in your drawing.

6. Point to the fourth button. The ToolTip says Radius Dimension. This button lets you create a dimension showing the measurement of the radius of a circle.

7. With the mouse, point to the bottom edge of the toolbar until the mouse cursor takes the shape of a double-headed arrow.

8. Click and drag downward. The toolbar changes shape.

9. Drag the Dimensioning toolbar by its title bar down to the bottom edge of the drawing area (onto the horizontal scrollbar) until the dotted shape becomes a horizontal bar. The Dimensioning toolbar docks at the lower edge of the screen, as shown in Figure 3-5. There's not as much screen space as before, but the toolbars are off the drawing area.

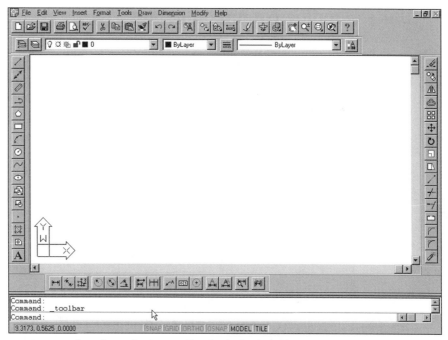

Figure 3-5: The Dimensioning toolbar is docked at the bottom of the screen.

10. To close the Dimensioning toolbar (which you would do when you are finished placing dimensions in your drawing), drag it by its narrow gray border onto the drawing area and click the Close button at the right of its title bar.

11. You may leave the Draw and Modify toolbars where they are or return them to their original positions — it's up to you.

As you can see, it's worth the time to learn how to move, place, show, and hide toolbars. This small effort can greatly increase your comfort with drawing in AutoCAD.

The Command Line

You have already seen how every command you give AutoCAD is echoed on the command line, although sometimes using slightly different words, syntax, and options. You have also given a command by typing it directly on the command line (the ZOOM command in Chapter 1).

Understanding command names

All commands have a special one-word command name. This may or may not be the same as the command that appears on the toolbar's ToolTip or on the menu. But you can be sure of one thing — every command can be executed by typing its name on the command line. Some users prefer to use the command line because they find it faster than searching for a command on a menu or toolbar. Most users use a combination of command line, menu, and toolbar commands.

Some of the commands are easy to type, such as LINE or ARC. Some are long and difficult to remember, as with DDLMODES or DDEMODES. Such command names can quickly drive you to use a menu or toolbar.

Release 14 has significantly improved the ease of command line entry. You can now edit what you have typed on the command line (previously, you had to start over if you made a mistake). If you type a long command and make a mistake, you can backspace up to the mistake and retype the last part correctly. Table 3-2 shows how to use the keyboard edit keys to edit the command line.

Table 3-2 Command Line Editing Keys	
Key	**Function**
Backspace	Backspaces through the text on the command line, erasing each letter as it backspaces
Left arrow	Moves backward through the text of the command, without erasing anything
Right arrow	Moves forward through the text of the command, without erasing
Home	Moves the command line cursor to the beginning of the text
End	Moves the command line cursor to the end of the text

Key	Function
Insert	Toggles between Insert/Overwrite mode. Insert mode inserts text. Overwrite mode types over existing text. Note that there is no status line confirmation of which mode you are in.
Delete	Deletes the character to the right of the command line cursor
Ctrl+V	Pastes text from the Clipboard

In Release 14 you can now scroll through and reuse previous command line entries. To repeat the last line you entered, press the up arrow. Press Enter to execute it. To see more of the command line entries, press F2 on your keyboard to open the text screen. Scroll (or use the up and down arrows) until you find the entry you want, highlight it, then right-click and choose Paste To CmdLine from the shortcut menu. AutoCAD pastes the highlighted text into the current command line. You can also copy selected text from the command line history or the entire history to the Clipboard.

Switching from the mouse to the keyboard and back is time-consuming. In general, if you are picking points using the mouse (which is covered in Chapter 4), it's fastest to use menus and toolbars to give commands. If you are typing coordinates as you did in Chapter 1, your hands are already at the keyboard, so in that case it's easiest to type commands at the keyboard.

If you like typing in commands, you can create short versions of the command names. These are called *aliases*. Several are already included with AutoCAD. Aliases are covered in Chapter 29.

Responding to command options

Many commands have a number of options from which you need to choose. Choosing an option on the command line is easy:

✦ To choose an option on the command line, type the letter that is capitalized in the option name — usually (but not always) the first letter of the option. You can type the letter in lowercase. Press Enter.

✦ To choose a default option on the command line, which appears in angled brackets like `<Realtime>`, simply press Enter or provide the point or value required.

At this point, additional options may appear or you may be prompted to select a point or an object.

You can click the right mouse button in place of pressing Enter.

The ARC command offers many ways of defining an arc. The following exercise shows how to use options in the ARC command starting with the toolbar and continuing on the command line. In Chapter 1 you typed in coordinates to specify points. Here you pick points on the screen directly with the mouse.

Cross-Reference

Arcs are fully covered in Chapter 7.

Step-by-Step: Using Command Options

1. Open a new drawing using the *acad.dwt* template.

2. Click Arc on the Draw toolbar.

3. Look at the command line. You see the following prompt:

   `Center/<Start point>:`

   The start point is the default option. Move the mouse cursor anywhere in the middle of the screen and click to specify the start point. This is called *picking* a point.

4. Now you see the `Center/End/<Second point>:` prompt. Let's say you want to specify the end of the arc. Because Second point is the default, type **e** ↵. AutoCAD responds with the `End point:` prompt.

5. Pick any other point on the screen.

6. At the `Angle/Direction/Radius/<Center point>:` prompt, pick any point for the center point (the default). As you move the mouse, AutoCAD displays the resulting arc even before you pick the point, as shown in Figure 3-6. The arc is created and the command ends. Don't worry at this point if the arc is partly off the screen or doesn't appear as you expect.

7. Do not save this drawing.

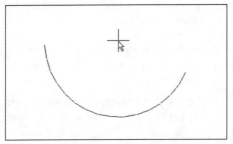

Figure 3-6: Creating an arc using the Start point, End, and Center options.

Note

You may have noticed that AutoCAD places an underscore (_) before each command. This allows translation to foreign languages and can be ignored.

Sometimes a command has so many options that AutoCAD opens a dialog box. This offers a more structured and informative way of letting you choose command options.

Command Techniques

To make working with commands easier, AutoCAD offers shortcuts for repeating and canceling commands as well as sophisticated undo and redo options. You can also use certain commands once you have started another command.

Repeating commands

The most common way to repeat the command you have just used is to press Enter at the Command: prompt. The last command appears again. You can also click the right mouse button for this.

If you know in advance that you will be using a command several times, you can use another technique — type **multiple**, a space, and the command name on the command line. The command automatically reappears on the command line until you press the Esc key. For example, you could type **multiple arc** if you knew you were going to draw several arcs in a row. When you were finished drawing the arcs, you would press Esc.

Canceling commands

As with any Windows program, press Esc to cancel a command that you have already started. The Command: prompt reappears.

Prior to Release 13 of AutoCAD, Ctrl+C was used to cancel a command. However, this key combination is the Windows shortcut for copying data to the Windows Clipboard. Therefore, if you have been using Ctrl+C to cancel a command, you should get used to using the Esc key instead.

The following exercise covers the techniques for repeating and canceling commands.

Step-by-Step: Repeating and Canceling a Command

1. Start a new drawing using the *acad.dwt* template.

2. Choose Circle on the Draw toolbar.

3. At the `3P/2P/TTR/<Center point>:` prompt, pick a center point anywhere near the center of the screen.

4. At the `Diameter/<Radius>:` prompt, move the mouse cursor and click the pick button when you see a medium-sized circle. AutoCAD draws a circle.

5. Click the right (return) mouse button. The CIRCLE command appears again.

6. Follow the prompts below:

```
3P/2P/TTR/<Center point>: 2p ↵
First point on diameter: Pick any point on the screen.
Second point on diameter: Press Esc.
```

AutoCAD responds with `*Cancel*` and returns you to the `Command:` prompt without finishing the command that was in progress.

7. Do not save this drawing.

Undoing a command

Most Windows applications offer Undo and Redo commands on the Standard toolbar. AutoCAD is no different. Some applications remember a list of your last several actions so that you can undo them one by one. AutoCAD remembers every command you execute starting from the time you open a drawing. You can therefore undo every action and return your drawing to its condition when you opened it.

Actually, AutoCAD has a few obvious exceptions. For example, if you print a drawing, you can't unprint it, and you can't unsave a drawing, either. Similarly, commands that provide you with information, such as the coordinates of a point, cannot be undone.

Note

Some commands have their own undo options.

The U command

Each time you click Undo on the Standard toolbar AutoCAD undoes one command. If you undo all the commands, you get the message:

```
Everything has been undone
```

On the command line, you may notice that AutoCAD echoes only u. Actually, AutoCAD has two related command names, U and UNDO. When you choose Undo from the Standard toolbar, AutoCAD actually executes the U command, which undoes one command at a time.

The UNDO command

The UNDO command is more complex and offers several options. It can only be typed at the command line, since it has no menu item or toolbar button. When you start UNDO you see the following options on the command line:

```
Auto/Control/BEgin/End/Mark/Back/<Number>:
```

As you can see by the angled brackets, `Number` is the default option. If you type in a number, for example **3**, AutoCAD undoes your last three commands. Typing **1** is equivalent to using the U command. Table 3-3 explains the other options:

Table 3-3
Options of the UNDO Command

Option	How to Use It
Auto	Can be On or Off. Applies to a menu item that executes more than one command at a time. When Auto is On (the default), the entire menu item is undone in one step. When Auto is Off, UNDO undoes each step one at a time.
Control	Offers three suboptions. All, the default, gives you the full UNDO capability. None disables the UNDO command. One allows you to undo only one step at a time, effectively turning the UNDO command into the U command.
Begin	Works with the End option. This starts a group at the current point of the list of commands. Then, when you use the End option, UNDO undoes all the commands in the group. The U command also undoes everything within a group.
End	Undoes all commands in the group created by using the Begin option.
Mark	This option works with the Back option. It is somewhat similar to the Begin option, but you can place several marks as you work.
Back	When you use this option, AutoCAD undoes only to the most recent Mark point. The next Back option you use undoes to the Mark point before that.

Note

AutoCAD lists the commands it is undoing to help you figure things out. The word *Group* means that a group of commands is being undone. However, sometimes the word *Group* is used even for a single command. This is not significant and the word *Group* can be ignored.

Tip

The Begin/End and Mark/Back options are useful when you are trying something new and want to be able to undo a whole series of commands in one undo command in case things don't work out as planned.

Caution   Using the Back option when no Mark has been created undoes everything you have done in a drawing session! Luckily, AutoCAD warns you with a message:

```
This will undo everything. OK? <Y>
```

Type **n** if you do not want to undo everything.

Redoing a command

The REDO command redoes the effect of the last U or UNDO command. It only works on one command, so you can only use it once, unlike the U and UNDO commands. It must be used immediately after a previous U or UNDO command.

The following exercise lets you practice the U, UNDO, and REDO commands.

Step-by-Step: Undoing and Redoing Commands

1. Start a new drawing using *acad.dwt* as the template.

2. Choose Line on the Draw toolbar.

3. Draw one line and press Enter to exit the command.

4. Choose Arc on the Draw toolbar.

5. Using the default options, pick any three points to draw an arc.

6. Choose Circle on the Draw toolbar.

7. Pick one point to be the center of the circle and another nearby point to specify the radius. Your drawing now contains a line, an arc, and a circle, and looks something like Figure 3-7. Of course your objects will look different because you picked different points.

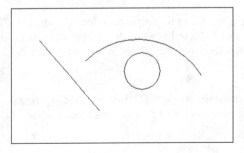

Figure 3-7: Your drawing should contain a line, an arc, and a circle.

8. Click Undo on the Standard toolbar to execute the U command. The circle disappears.

9. Type **undo** on the command line. Then type **2** ↲. The arc and the line disappear.

10. Click Redo on the Standard toolbar. The line and arc reappear because they were erased by the last undo command.

11. Do not save this drawing. If you are continuing on, keep the drawing on the screen for the next Step-by-Step exercise.

Using the OOPS command

Cross-Reference

The OOPS command undoes the most recent command that erased an object, even if you have used other commands in the meantime. It brings that object back to the screen. It is discussed further in Chapter 18.

Using one command within another command

Certain commands can be used within another command. These are called *transparent* commands. Once the transparent command is completed, the original command continues its regular operation. Many transparent commands help you display the drawing differently so you can complete the original command easily.

Step-by-Step: Using a Transparent Command

1. From the last exercise you have a line and an arc on the screen. If not, start AutoCAD using *acad.dwt* as the template and draw a line and an arc anywhere on the screen.

2. Choose View⇨Zoom⇨Out. The drawing zooms out, appearing smaller.

3. Choose Circle from the Draw toolbar. The following prompt appears:

```
Command: _circle 3P/2P/TTR/<Center point>: Pick any point on your
screen.
Diameter/<Radius> <2.4075>:
```

Note

The default number at the end of the prompt is left over from the last circle drawn. The number on your command line may be different.

4. At this point, you want to see the drawing closer up to properly decide where to place the radius of the circle. Choose View⇨Zoom⇨In. The following appears on the command line (You may need to press F2 to see the entire prompt.):

```
_zoom
>>All/Center/Dynamic/Extents/Previous/Scale(X/XP)/Window/
<Realtime>: 2x
Resuming CIRCLE command.
Diameter/<Radius> <2.4075>:
```

5. Pick any point to define the radius of your circle.

6. Do not save this drawing.

Looking at the prompts carefully, note three features.

✦ The ZOOM command is preceded by an apostrophe. This is the sign of a transparent command. If you want to type a transparent command on the command line, you need to type the apostrophe before the command name.

✦ The prompt for the transparent command is preceded by >>. This helps you distinguish between the prompts of the original command and the transparent command that is embedded in it.

✦ When the transparent command is complete, AutoCAD tells you. In this case you see Resuming CIRCLE command.

Commands that create or edit objects cannot generally be used transparently. Transparent commands are usually those which change settings, such as zooming the visual display, changing running object snap modes, or changing layer visibility settings. Experiment using transparent commands, and you will soon find them indispensable.

Of Mice and Pucks

For the sake of simplicity, this book assumes that you are using a mouse, but many people use a digitizing tablet and a puck (or a stylus). A typical digitizing tablet and puck are shown in Figure 3-8. It has buttons like a mouse but also has crosshairs on a transparent area that you can use for accurately picking points from a paper drawing.

Figure 3-8: A .digitizer and puck.

Credit: Thanks to CalComp for this photograph.

The digitizing tablet includes an area that represents the screen you draw on as well as a customizable command area that you use for AutoCAD commands. This command area of the tablet functions as another menu. Figure 3-9 shows the default tablet provided with AutoCAD. This is generally customized to suit individual needs. Each square is equivalent to a toolbar button and executes a command when you click it. The top area is left blank for you to include your own commands. This area is often used to insert parts from a library of standardized parts. Examples would be gaskets and valves in a mechanical drawing environment, or doors and windows in an architectural environment.

The square area in the right center represents the drawing area. In this area, the puck functions like a mouse to access menus and dialog box options. The tablet can also be used for a process called *digitizing*, which means transferring data on paper to AutoCAD. This is often done by putting a paper document directly on the tablet and using the entire tablet as a drawing area. Because the puck has crosshairs on a transparent surface, you can pick points on the drawing, which then become endpoints of lines, for example.

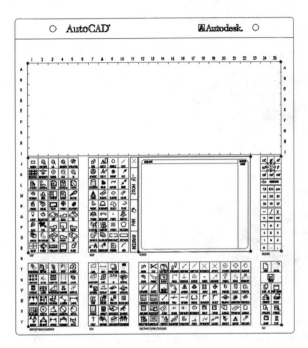

Figure 3-9: The standard tablet menu.

In-Program Help

AutoCAD has so many commands with so many options that every user needs help at some time. AutoCAD comes with a very complete help system. I call it an In-Program help system. This type of help used to be called online help, but that term has come to mean help available on the Internet.

See Appendix D for that kind of help, among others.

Getting help on a command

The easiest way to get help on a command is to start the command and press F1. The help screen for that command opens up. Figure 3-10 shows the screen that opens when you type **zoom** ↵, and then press F1.

If you're observant and look on the command line, you see that AutoCAD treats the request for help as a transparent command.

To get information on a menu item, click the menu and press F1. A screen opens showing the entire menu. Click the menu item for which you want help.

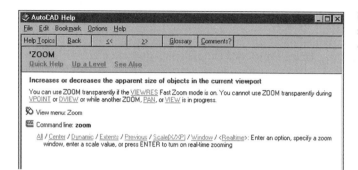

Figure 3-10: The help screen for the ZOOM command.

Choosing Help⇨Contents gives you the help table of contents. Figure 3-11 shows the help table of contents. Double-clicking Command Reference leads you to help on AutoCAD's commands and system variables. The User's Guide is the electronic equivalent of AutoCAD's manual. The How To selection provides step-by-step procedures for many common actions in AutoCAD.

Cross-Reference

System variables are discussed in Chapter 5; Appendix C lists many system variables.

Figure 3-11: The help table of contents.

Release 14

AutoCAD's help feature has been updated to have the look and organization of other Windows help programs.

Using the help index

If you have an idea in your head but don't know the command name, you may want to use the index. Choose Help⇨AutoCAD Help Topics and click the Index tab. The index is an alphabetical listing of topics. In the first box, type the first few letters of the word or words for which you want help. As you type, the list in the second box jumps to the closest match. When you have found the topic you want, highlight it and click Display. Sometimes subtopics appear from which you can choose.

Using the Find tab

The last tab in AutoCAD's Help Topics window lets you find keywords from all the words in the in-program help screens. The first time you use this feature, it creates a database of all the words in the help screens, and then you can search for a word.

Working with help screens

Once you have arrived at the help screen you want, look for two useful features.

✦ You see phrases underlined in green. Click on any of these to jump to further information relating to that phrase.

✦ At the top of most screens are several buttons. The selection of buttons depends on which aspect of help you are accessing. These buttons assist you to navigate the help system quickly and easily. Table 3-4 explains these buttons and their use.

| | Table 3-4 |
| | Help Screen Buttons |

Button	Action
Help Topics	Displays the main Contents screen, with the last-used tab on top
Back	Returns you to the last help screen you viewed
<<	Switches to the previous page
>>	Switches to the next page
Print	Prints the help topic
Glossary	Opens AutoCAD's extensive alphabetical glossary of terms
Options	Lets you copy or print the topic, or keep the help topic on top while you work

The help window also has its own menu bar that you can explore. From the menus you can copy to the Clipboard, print help topics, and create bookmarks.

Using the tutorials

When you choose Help from the menu bar, you can also choose four other helpful items.

✦ Quick Tour — this is a great way to get a quick review of AutoCAD.

✦ What's New — this lists all the new, changed, and deleted commands, as well as other changes in Release 14.

✦ Learning Assistance — this is a whiz-bang, multimedia tutorial on CD-ROM.

✦ AutoCAD Help Topics⇨Contents⇨Tutorial — this is a thorough 10-lesson tutorial, complete with sample drawings.

The tutorials are a great way to get accustomed to AutoCAD. Even if you know AutoCAD and are upgrading from an earlier version, the What's New list is very helpful.

Step-by-Step: Using In-Program Help

1. If AutoCAD is not open, start AutoCAD with the *acad.dwt* template. If AutoCAD is already open, this exercise can be done with any drawing on the screen.

2. Choose Circle from the Draw toolbar. At the prompt, press F1 on the keyboard. The Circle help screen opens.

3. Click 2P, which appears in green and underlined. The 2P — 2 Points (CIRCLE) screen opens. Read the description of how to use the 2P option.

4. Click the Close button at the top right of the help screen. Press Esc to exit the CIRCLE command.

5. Choose File⇨AutoCAD Help Topics.

6. Click the Contents tab if it is not on top. Double-click User's Guide. From the list, double-click Getting Started, then double-click Accessing Commands. Click Using the Command Line. Read the text.

7. At the bottom of the screen, click Copying Text to the Command Line. Read the text.

8. Click on Help Topics.

9. Click the Index tab.

10. In the text box at the top, type **transparent commands** and click Display.

11. Read the text. When you are done, click the Close button.

Summary

In this chapter you have learned all you need to know about how to use AutoCAD's commands. AutoCAD has menus, dialog boxes, and toolbars that are fairly typical of any Windows program. In addition, every command has a command name that can be typed at the Command: prompt. You can repeat any command by pressing Enter or clicking the right mouse button at the Command: prompt.

AutoCAD has a sophisticated capability for undoing commands. You can also redo the last command undone. Many commands can be used transparently, that is, within another command.

AutoCAD's in-program help is an excellent resource when you have a question.

In the next chapter I explain how to specify coordinates, an essential skill to learn before you start to draw.

✦   ✦   ✦

Specifying Coordinates

Understanding the X,Y Coordinate System

Specifying points on the screen is one of the most fundamental tasks in AutoCAD. Unless you know how to specify a point, you can't draw anything real, whether a house or a gasket. Most objects you draw have a specific size, and you need to give AutoCAD that information. Drawing lines, arcs, and circles is accomplished by specifying the coordinates of points on the screen. As with most tasks, AutoCAD offers many ways to accomplish this.

Remember when you studied geometry and trigonometry in high school? You created graphs by drawing X and Y axes. Then you plotted coordinates on graph paper. AutoCAD works the same way.

Look at the UCS (User Coordinate System) icon on your screen, shown in Figure 4-1.

Figure 4-1: The UCS icon shows the direction of the X and Y axes.

The arrow marked *X* points along the X axis in the positive direction. That means that as you go in the direction of the arrow, the X coordinates increase. The arrow marked *Y* points along the Y axis in the positive direction.

In this way, every point on the screen can be specified using X and Y coordinates. This is called a Cartesian coordinate system.

Cross-
Reference

As explained in Chapter 1, the universal convention is to place the X coordinate first, then a comma (but no space), and then the Y coordinate. Refer to Figure 1-4 in Chapter 1 for some sample coordinates.

By default, the intersection of the X,Y axes is 0,0. Use negative numbers for points to the left of the X axis or below the Y axis.

Drawing units

What do the coordinates measure? When you draw in AutoCAD you draw in undefined units. That means, a line from point 3,0 to point 6,0 is three units long. While you are drawing, these units can be anything — a millimeter, a centimeter, a meter, an inch, a foot, or a mile, to list some common examples.

In reality, you should know exactly what the units represent. After all, you don't want your 33-foot-wide house to end up 33 inches wide!

When you set up a drawing, you specify how units are displayed, for example, whether partial units show as decimal points or fractions. I cover units in the next chapter, Chapter 5. However, you don't actually specify what the units represent until you print or plot your drawing — covered in Chapter17.

In AutoCAD, you customarily draw full size. That means, if you are drawing a plan for a factory that will be 120 feet long, you create lines with those measurements. On the screen, you can zoom in to see small details or zoom out to see the whole factory, so the actual line lengths can be whatever you want. It is only when you need to print those 120-foot-long lines on a real sheet of paper that you have to tell AutoCAD to plot out your drawing at a reduced scale.

Types of measurement notation

Users are typically familiar only with the type of notation used in their own field, whether scientific, architectural, engineering, or whatever. However, you should be at least somewhat familiar with all the major forms of measurement notation.

Note

If you are using engineering or architectural units, AutoCAD displays parts of inches differently than the format you must use to type them in. You must type in coordinates without any spaces, because AutoCAD interprets a space as equivalent to pressing Enter and ends your input. Use a hyphen between whole and partial inches, for example, 3'2^1/$_2$". (You can omit the " after the inches because AutoCAD assumes inches in engineering and architectural units if no symbol follows a number.) However, this appears on the status bar as 3'-2^1/$_2$". This can be confusing because AutoCAD places the hyphen in a different place and uses a space between the whole and partial inches.

Typing Coordinates

You have already practiced typing coordinates in previous chapters. There are actually several forms of coordinates that you can enter from the keyboard. These are covered in the next few sections.

Absolute Cartesian coordinates

When you type a line and enter the actual coordinates, such as a line from point 3,2 to 6,9, you are using absolute Cartesian coordinates. Absolute coordinates are measured from 0,0. These coordinates are probably familiar to you from high school geometry class.

Step-by-Step: Entering Absolute Cartesian Coordinates

1. Start a new drawing in AutoCAD using the Start from Scratch option and English measurement.

2. Choose Line from the Draw toolbar. Follow the prompts below:

```
From point: -10,-5 ↵
To point: 21,-5 ↵
To point: 21,49 ↵
To point: -10,49 ↵
To point: -10,-5 ↵
To point: ↵ to end the command.
```

 3. Most of the lines are off the screen. By default, a new drawing starts with 0,0 at the lower left corner of your screen, so negative coordinates do not show. Choose Zoom Out from the Zoom flyout on the Standard toolbar.

4. If you still cannot see the entire rectangle, click Zoom Out again, until you can see it. Your picture should look like Figure 4-2.

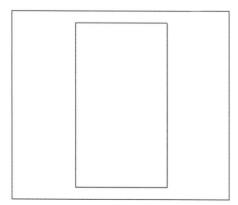

Figure 4-2: A rectangle drawn using absolute coordinates.

Note

If AutoCAD responds `Point or option keyword required,` you have entered a coordinate incorrectly. Try again. Also, don't forget that you can UNDO a command if you make a mistake.

5. Start the LINE command again and follow the prompts:

```
From point: -8,-2 ↵
To point: 19,-2 ↵
To point: 19,21.5 ↵
To point: -8,21.5 ↵
To point: -8,-2 ↵
To point: ↵ to end the command.
```

6. Once more start the LINE command and follow the prompts:

```
From point: -8,22.5 ↵
To point: 19, 22.5 ↵
To point: 19,46 ↵
To point: -8,46 ↵
To point: -8,22.5 ↵
To point: ↵ to end the command.
```

7. Save this drawing in your *AutoCAD Bible* folder as *ab4-1.dwg*.

You can now see that you have drawn a simple window, as shown in Figure 4-3.

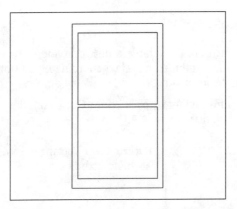

Figure 4-3: A window drawn with absolute coordinates.

Two questions might have occurred to you during this exercise. First, isn't there a better way of entering absolute coordinates? Typing them in is slow and prone to error. Second, how do you know the absolute coordinates for what you are drawing? Read on for the answers.

Relative Cartesian coordinates

In practice, you usually do not know the absolute coordinates of the points you need to specify in order to draw an object. Whether you are drawing an architectural layout, a physical object (as in mechanical drawing), a three-dimensional model, or an electrical schematic, you don't have X,Y coordinates to work from. However, you often do have the measurements of what you are drawing. Usually, you start from any suitable point and work from there. In this situation, you know only the length of the lines you are drawing (if you are drawing lines). There is no 0,0 point in real life. Relative coordinates were developed for these situations.

Relative coordinates specify the X and Y distance from a previous point. They are called relative coordinates because they only have meaning relative to a point previously specified. Suppose you need to draw a window. You can start the window from any point. From there, you have the measurements you need. (The measurements may be shown on a piece of paper you're working from or you may have the actual window sitting next to you so you can measure it.)

You tell AutoCAD that the coordinates are relative by using the @ symbol. (It's over the 2 on the keyboard, and you have to hold down the Shift key to type it.) For example, if you start a line by picking any point with the mouse, and you know it should be two units long, you can specify the next point as @2,0. AutoCAD creates a line starting with the first point you picked and ending 2 units to the right, as shown in Figure 4-4. The line is horizontal because the Y coordinate is 0. In a relative coordinate, this means that the Y distance does not change.

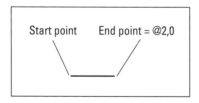

Figure 4-4: A line whose start point could be anywhere and whose endpoint was specified with the relative point @2,0 is a horizontal line two units long.

Relative Cartesian coordinates are often used for lines drawn at 90-degree angles, that are either horizontal or vertical. These are called *orthogonal* lines. When you create a diagonal line from point 3,3 to point @2,5 you don't know how long the line is.

When you specify a positive number such as the 2 in @2,0, AutoCAD assumes the positive direction. However, if you want to draw a line in the negative direction of an axis, type a minus sign before the number. Figure 4-5 shows how to draw lines in four directions using relative coordinates.

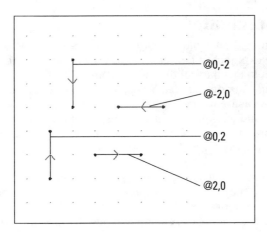

Figure 4-5: Drawing lines in the four orthogonal directions using relative coordinates. The arrow on each line shows the direction of the line.

Polar coordinates

Another common situation is to know the distance and angle of a point from either 0,0 or a previous point. In this case, you can use polar coordinates, which can be either absolute or relative. Most commonly you use relative polar coordinates.

Polar coordinates take the form *distance<angle*. (To type the angle symbol, use the Shift key to access the sign above the comma on your keyboard.) Relative polar coordinates must have the @ sign before the coordinate.

Angles are almost universally measured according to the diagram in Figure 4-6, although AutoCAD allows you to change this system. The positive and negative angles shown next to each other are interchangeable. Use whichever is more meaningful to you.

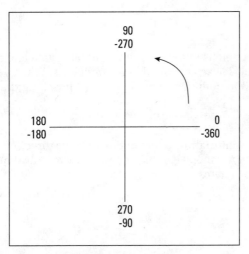

Figure 4-6: The standard angle measurement system.

In this series of steps you draw part of a portico, the decorative molding above a door. Because it is an architectural design, you use architectural units. In this case, only inches are used, which don't need to be specified. You can specify feet by using the apostrophe (also called a *prime*) after any number.

When typing architectural units, partial inches are indicated by fractions in the form 3/4. You need to separate the fraction from the whole inches by a hyphen. This can be a little confusing since the hyphen is also used for negative numbers. For example, to draw a horizontal line of 5-1/4 inches to the left, you would type @-5-1/4,0. (The 0 indicates no change in the Y axis because it is a horizontal line.)

In this drawing you see *blips* that mark points that you specify. Choose Redraw on the Standard toolbar to make them go away.

Step-by-Step: Using Relative and Polar Coordinates

1. Open *ab4-a.dwg* from the CD-ROM. As you move your mouse around, notice that the coordinates displayed on the status bar are in architectural units, that is, in feet and inches.

2. Choose File➪Save As and save the drawing in your *AutoCAD Bible* folder as *ab4-2.dwg*.

The next steps involve some complex typing. If you get an error message from AutoCAD, try typing the coordinate again. If you realize you made a mistake after pressing Enter, click Undo on the Standard toolbar.

3. Start the LINE command. Follow the prompts below:

```
Command: _line From point: Pick any point at the lower left
corner of your screen.
To point: @0,-3/4 ↵
To point: @75-1/4,0 ↵
To point: @0,3/4 ↵
To point: @-75-1/4,0 ↵
To point: ↵ to end the command.
```

4. Start the LINE command again. Follow the prompts:

```
To point: ↵. This starts the line at the last endpoint you
specified.
To point: @4-3/4,0 ↵
To point: @43<40 ↵
To point: @43<320 ↵
To point: @-2-1/4,0 ↵
To point: @39-7/8<140 ↵
To point: @39-7/8<220 ↵
To point: ↵ to end the command.
```

5. Save your drawing. You have created a portion of a portico, which goes over a window of a house, shown in Figure 4-7.

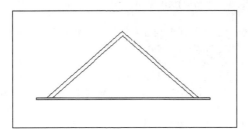

Figure 4-7: Part of a portico over a window, drawn using relative Cartesian and polar coordinates in architectural notation.

Tip

You can type @ at the first prompt of any drawing command to pick the last coordinate specified.

Notice that using relative coordinates, both Cartesian and polar, is much more realistic than using absolute coordinates. However, typing in all those coordinates is still awkward. Typing in coordinates is often the only way to get exactly what you want. Nevertheless, several other techniques for specifying coordinates are easier in many circumstances.

Orthogonal mode

As mentioned earlier in this chapter, lines drawn at 0, 90, 180, and 270 degrees are called orthogonal lines. When in orthogonal mode — *Ortho* mode as it's called for short — you can only draw orthogonal lines. Ortho mode also affects editing. For example, with Ortho mode on you can only move objects vertically or horizontally. Combined with snap and grid, Ortho makes drawing easier and more efficient. Ortho is also great for Direct Distance Entry, discussed in the next section.

Double-click ORTHO on the status bar to toggle Ortho mode on and off.

Tip

Orthogonal mode only affects points picked directly on the screen. Any relative or absolute coordinates typed on the command line override orthogonal mode.

Direct distance entry

One shortcut for entering coordinates is direct distance entry. Once you specify the start point of a line, at any To point: prompt, simply move the mouse cursor in the direction you want the line to go and type in the line's length. It works best in orthogonal mode.

Tip

You can use direct distance entry for any command that requires you to specify a coordinate and a direction.

Step-by-Step: Using Direct Distance Entry

1. Open drawing *ab4-b.dwg* from the CD-ROM.

2. Choose File⇨Save As to save the drawing in your *AutoCAD Bible* folder as *ab-4-3.dwg*. Notice in the status bar that ORTHO is on.

3. Start the LINE command and at the `From point:` prompt, type **2,2** ↵.

4. Move the mouse horizontally to the right, type **.5** ↵.

5. Move the mouse up vertically (in the 90-degree direction), type **.5** ↵.

6. Move the mouse horizontally to the right, type **2** ↵. Your drawing should look like Figure 4-8.

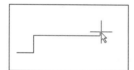

Figure 4-8: Drawing with direct distance entry allows you to specify coordinates by typing in a length after you move the pointer in the desired direction.

7. Move the mouse up in the 90-degree direction, type **.5** ↵.

8. Move the mouse to the left in the 180-degree direction, type **2** ↵.

9. Move the mouse up in the 90-degree direction, type **.5** ↵.

10. Move the mouse to the left in the 180-degree direction, type **.5** ↵.

11. Move the mouse down in the 270-degree direction, type **1.5** ↵.

12. Your drawing should look like Figure 4-9.

13. Save your drawing.

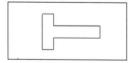

Figure 4-9: The completed drawing of a bolt.

Displaying Coordinates

In Chapter 1, I introduced you to the coordinate display on the status bar, and you may have noticed the coordinates moving as you moved the mouse. AutoCAD gives you three coordinate display modes to use:

✦ **Dynamic absolute coordinates:** Absolute coordinates that change as you move the mouse, shown in Figure 4-10.

`1.9209, 6.6721 ,0.0000`   **Figure 4-10:** Dynamic absolute coordinates.

✦ **Static absolute coordinates:** Absolute coordinates that change only when you specify a point, shown in Figure 4-11. The coordinate display is dimmed.

`1.9850, 6.7362 ,0.0000`   **Figure 4-11:** Static absolute coordinates.

✦ **Dynamic polar coordinates:** Polar coordinates that change continuously as you move the mouse, shown in Figure 4-12. They appear once you have already specified a point and are ready to specify a new point, as when you are in the process of drawing a line.

`2.8451<57,0.0000`   **Figure 4-12:** Dynamic polar coordinates.

You can change the coordinate display in three ways:

✦ Press Ctrl+D.

✦ Press the F6 key.

✦ Double-click the coordinates area on the status bar.

For purposes of this chapter, I ignore the Z coordinate that follows the X and Y coordinates. In two-dimensional drawings, the Z coordinate is always zero.

The following steps acquaint you with the coordinate display options.

Step-by-Step: Using Coordinate Display Options

This exercise can be done with any new or existing drawing open on the screen.

1. Look at the coordinate display on the status bar. It should be shown in black. If the coordinates are shown in gray, press F6 on your keyboard.

2. Move the mouse around in a few directions. Notice how the coordinates constantly change with the mouse movement.

3. Press F6. The coordinate display is grayed out. The command line shows `<Coords off>`.

4. Move the mouse around again. The coordinate display does not change with the movement of the mouse.

5. Start the LINE command.

6. Watch the coordinate display as you pick any point at the `To point:` prompt.

7. Pick several other points and watch as the coordinate display changes only when you pick a point. This is the static coordinate display.

8. Press F6 again without ending the LINE command.

9. Move the mouse to another point you would like to pick but watch the coordinate display before you pick the point. This time the length and angle of the new line segment is shown. These are dynamic polar coordinates.

10. Pick a few more points, watching the polar coordinates.

11. Press F6 again to return to dynamic absolute coordinates.

12. Press Enter to end the LINE command. Do not save your drawing.

The next sections introduce three new ways to specify coordinates.

Picking Coordinates on the Screen

The easiest and quickest way to specify coordinates is to pick them directly on the screen with the mouse. AutoCAD offers several techniques to help you do so accurately.

Release 14 lets you adjust the size of the crosshairs that cross the cursor. By default, they are now 5 percent of screen size. In previous releases, the crosshairs covered the entire screen. To change the crosshair size, choose Tools⇨Preferences and click the Pointer tab. In the Percentage of screen size text box, you can type a new percentage or use the arrows to incrementally increase or decrease the percentage. Choose Apply, then OK.

Snap settings

The SNAP command is often an alternative to tedious entry of coordinates. This command creates an invisible grid (which you can make visible using the GRID command, discussed in the next section). Once you turn on snap, the mouse cursor can only move to the grid points.

You can set the snap size to anything you want. For example, if all your measurements are rounded off to the nearest .25 unit, you can set your snap to .25.

The snap technique is not very useful when you need to draw to three or more decimal places of accuracy. And when you are zoomed out in a large drawing, the snap points may be so close together that you cannot easily find the one you want. But in the right situation, snap is one of the quickest, most accurate drawing techniques available.

To set the snap size, choose Tools⇨Drawing Aids to open the Drawing Aids dialog box, shown in Figure 4-13. In the X Spacing text box of the Snap section, type the spacing you want between snap points. Click OK.

Tip

Usually you want the X spacing (going across) to be the same as the Y spacing (going up and down). You need to specify only the X spacing, and AutoCAD automatically changes the Y spacing to equal the X spacing. They will only be different if you type a different number in the Y Spacing box.

You can also turn snap on in this dialog box by clicking the On check box. However, the most common way to turn snap on, once you have set the spacing, is to double-click SNAP on the status bar.

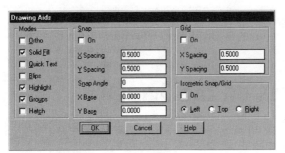

Figure 4-13: The Drawing Aids dialog box.

The grid

Sometimes you may find it helpful to see a grid of points to help get your bearings while you draw, as shown in Figure 4-14. Notice how you can quickly judge the approximate width of a window pane, knowing that the grid points are $1/2$ foot apart. If you turn on snap, the grid helps you visualize the snap points. However, the grid does not have to be set to the same size as snap.

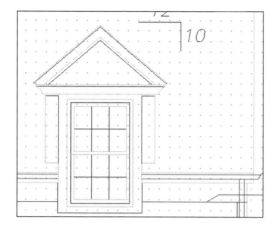

Figure 4-14: A portion of a drawing with the grid turned on and set to 6 inches.

Credit: Thanks to Henry Dearborn, AIA, Fairfield, Iowa, for this drawing.

The smaller the grid size and the further out you zoom, the denser the grid. At a certain point, AutoCAD issues a message, Grid too dense to display, and refuses to display the grid.

Some users find the grid annoying, but when you first start to use AutoCAD you may find it helpful. Even accomplished users can take advantage of the grid, especially when starting a new drawing.

Tip If you are working with a small snap size and the grid is too dense, set the grid to twice the size of the snap.

To set the grid size, choose Tools⇨Drawing Aids to open the Drawing Aids dialog box, shown in Figure 4-13. In the X Spacing text box of the Grid section, type the spacing you want between grid points. Click OK.

Tip As with the snap feature, you usually want the X spacing (going across) to be the same as the Y spacing (going up and down). You need to specify only the X spacing, and AutoCAD automatically changes the Y spacing to be the same. They will only be different if you type a different number in the Y Spacing box.

You can turn Grid on in this dialog box by clicking the On check box, but the most common way to turn the grid on, once you have set the spacing, is to double-click GRID on the status bar.

Step-by-Step: Using Snap and Grid

1. Open *ab4-b.dwg* from the CD-ROM.

2. Choose File⇨Save As to save the drawing in your *AutoCAD Bible* folder as *ab4-4.dwg*.

3. Choose Tools⇨Drawing Aids. The Drawing Aids dialog box opens. In the Snap section, change the X Spacing to **.5**.

4. Click in the Grid section. Notice the Y Spacing of Snap automatically changes to .5 also. Change the Grid X spacing to **.5** and click OK.

5. On the status bar, double-click SNAP, GRID, and ORTHO. The grid appears.

6. If the grid doesn't take up most of the screen, type **zoom** ↵, then type **a** (for All) ↵.

7. Move the mouse around and watch the coordinates on the status bar. They only show halves of units because you have set the snap to .5.

8. Start the LINE command and at the `From point:` prompt, pick coordinate 2.000,2.000 by looking at the coordinates on the status bar. (For now, ignore the third Z coordinate, which is always 0.0000.)

9. Move the mouse around and watch the coordinates. If you don't see polar coordinates (for example 3.0000<0), press F6 twice until you see polar coordinates.

10. Move the mouse to the right until the coordinates read 1.5000<0, as shown in Figure 4-15, and click the pick (left) button. You have drawn a horizontal line with a length of 1.5 units.

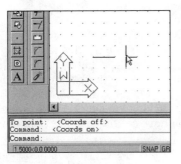

Figure 4-15: Drawing a 1.5 unit horizontal line to the right with snap on. The crosshair covers part of the line, making it invisible.

11. Click the right mouse button to end the LINE command.

12. Move the mouse cursor away from the end of the new line and back to it again, and the absolute coordinates appear. They should be 3.5000,2.0000.

13. To start the next line .5 units to the right of the last line, click the right mouse button to start the LINE command again. Then move the cursor until the coordinates say 4.0000,2.0000 and click to start the line.

14. Move the cursor to the right of the screen until the coordinates say 8.5000<0 (if the status bar displays absolute coordinates, press F6 twice) and click. End the LINE command.

15. Right-click to start the LINE command, move the cursor until the absolute coordinates show 13.0000,2.0000 and click.

16. Draw a horizontal line to the right with a length of 1.5 units with polar coordinates visible on the status bar (1.5000<0) and end the LINE command.

17. Start the LINE command and use the coordinate display to draw the following line segments starting from 3.5000,1.5000:

```
.5<0
3.0<90
.5<180
3.0<270
```

18. End the LINE command.

19. Start the LINE command and draw the following line segments starting from 12.5,1.5 and end the LINE command.

```
.5<0
3.0<90
.5<180
3.0<270
```

20. Starting from 2,4 draw a 1.5 unit line at 0 degrees.

21. Starting from 4,4 draw an 8.5 unit line at 0 degrees.

22. Starting from 13,4 draw a 1.5 unit line at 0 degrees.

23. Save your drawing. Your drawing should look like Figure 4-16.

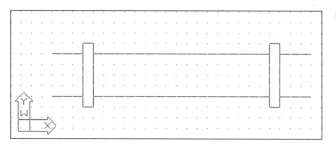

Figure 4-16: The completed pipe section.

As you no doubt experienced, this is a much easier way to draw compared to typing in coordinates. Note that drawing with snap on works better when you are drawing small objects. However, even when drawing an office building, you spend a great deal of time working on small details that may be easier to draw with snap on.

Object snaps

Often you need to draw an object relative to a previously drawn object. For example, you may need to start a line from the endpoint or midpoint of an existing line. AutoCAD offers a feature called object snaps (OSNAPS for short) that allows you to specify a point by snapping to a geometrically defined point on an existing object. This is a very precise and efficient way to draw.

Start an object snap in one of these three ways:

✦ Click the Object Snap flyout on the Standard toolbar and choose the object snap you want.

✦ Access the cursor menu by holding down Shift and clicking the right mouse button. Choose the object snap you want with the left mouse button.

✦ Type the object snap's abbreviation on the command line.

On three-button mice, you can customize the middle button to show the object snaps. Customizing the mouse is discussed in Chapter 33.

Table 4-1 lists the object snaps. The abbreviation is used to type the object snap from the keyboard.

Table 4-1: AutoCAD's Object Snaps		
Object Snap	**Abbreviation**	**Uses**
Endpoint	end	Lines, arcs
Midpoint	mid	Lines, arcs
Intersection	int	Intersection of lines, circles, arcs
Apparent Intersection*	app	The intersection that would be created if two objects were extended until they met
Center	cen	Circles, arcs, ellipses
Quadrant	qua	Nearest quadrant (0, 90, 180, or 270 degree point) of a circle, arc, ellipse

* Apparent Intersection also applies to 3D objects that appear to intersect due to the angle of view.

Object Snap	Abbreviation	Uses
Perpendicular	per	Starts or continues a line, circle, ellipse, arc perpendicular to another object
Tangent	tan	Finds point on arcs, circles, ellipses that are tangent to another object. See Figure 4-17.
Node	nod	Points (discussed in Chapter 7)
Insertion	ins	Insertion point of text or a block (inserting text is covered in Chapter 13; blocks are discussed in Chapter 18.)
Nearest	nea	Nearest point on any object
Quick	qui	Used with another object snap (as in qui,int) to find the most recently created object in the aperture box that satisfies the object snap. Used when there are many objects in a drawing causing AutoCAD's calculation process to slow down.

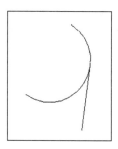

Figure 4-17: A line drawn tangent to an arc.

On the CD-ROM

I have included an AutoLISP program on the CD-ROM that replaces the Quadrant object snap, letting you specify any angle you want for the object snap. For example, you can choose to snap to point at the 10-degree angle on a circle. You can find it in *\Software\Chap04\Apt*.

Note

When drawing a line, we think of it as having a starting point and an ending point. Once the line is drawn, however, both of these points are considered endpoints in terms of object snaps. When picking a point, pick a point on the line closer to the endpoint you want. The same applies to arcs. Although the arc prompts read Start point and End, both are considered endpoints for purposes of object snaps.

Release 14

One of the most exciting new features of Release 14 is AutoSnap™, which makes it much easier than before to work with object snaps. When you move the cursor near the geometric point you have specified, such as an endpoint, AutoCAD lets you know in three ways:

✦ Marker — an object snap shape appears. Each object snap has a differently shaped marker.

✦ SnapTip — a label that displays the name of the object snap. SnapTips are like the ToolTips you see when you point to a toolbar button.

✦ Magnet — a pull that gently moves the cursor toward the geometric point.

Figure 4-18 shows an endpoint marker and SnapTip.

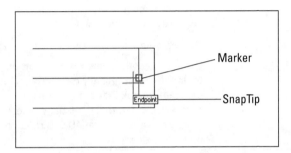

Figure 4-18: Release 14's new AutoSnap™ feature shows you the endpoint of the line.

You can customize the AutoSnap™ feature to suit your needs, or make it go away completely if you wish. Choose Tools⇨Object Snap Settings to open the Osnap Settings dialog box. Click the AutoSnap™ tab, shown in Figure 4-19.

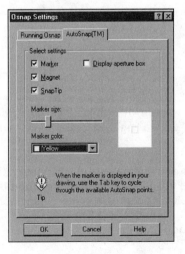

Figure 4-19: The AutoSnap™ tab of the Osnap Settings dialog box.

You can individually turn on and off the marker, SnapTip, and the magnet. You can also change the marker size and color. If you wish, you can display the aperture box, which previous releases of AutoCAD used to let you pick an object snap point. (You probably don't want to display both the marker and the aperture — it can be somewhat confusing.)

Most drawing tasks use one or two object snaps; in the following steps you practice most of them by using some simple, though meaningless, objects.

Step-by-Step: Using Object Snaps

1. Start a new drawing using the Start from Scratch option and English units.

2. Save the drawing in your *AutoCAD Bible* folder as *ab4-5.dwg*.

3. Start the LINE command. Follow the prompts below:

```
From point: 4,3 ↵
To point: @3.5<0 ↵
To point: ↵ to end the command.
Start the LINE command again.
LINE From point: 4,2 ↵
To point: @3.5<0 ↵
To point: ↵ to end the command.
```

4. Your drawing should look something like Figure 4-20. The circled numbers are reference points for this exercise.

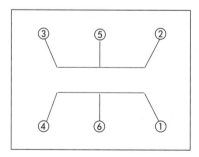

Figure 4-20: Two parallel lines.

5. Start the LINE command again. At the `From point:` prompt, click the Object Snap flyout on the Standard toolbar and choose Snap to Endpoint, as shown in Figure 4-21.

Figure 4-21: Choosing the Endpoint object snap from the Object Snap flyout of the Standard toolbar.

6. Move the mouse cursor near ① of Figure 4-20 until you see the endpoint marker and SnapTip, and pick.

7. At the `To point:` prompt, choose Snap to Endpoint from the Object Snap flyout of the Standard toolbar.

8. Pick point ② when you see the endpoint marker and SnapTip, and end the LINE command.

9. To draw another line between the other endpoints, start the LINE command again and move your cursor into the drawing area. At the `From Point:` prompt, hold down Shift and right-click once. The object snap menu appears. Use the left mouse button to choose Endpoint from the shortcut menu.

Note   When you right-click to get the object snap menu, the mouse pointer must be in the drawing area. If it is on a toolbar, you get the Toolbars dialog box. If that happens, click Close and try again.

10. Pick point ③, as shown in Figure 4-20.

11. At the `To point:` prompt Shift+right-click again and choose Endpoint.

12. Pick point ④, as shown in Figure 4-20. End the LINE command.

13. Start the CIRCLE command. Specify the 2P option. At the `First point on diameter:` prompt, type **mid** ↵.

14. Pick a point near ⑤ when you see the midpoint marker and SnapTip.

15. At the `Second point on diameter:` prompt, type **mid** ↵.

16. Pick a point near ⑥ when you see the midpoint marker and SnapTip.

17. Start the ARC command. At the `Center/<Start point>:` prompt use the Object Snap flyout to choose the Center object snap.

18. Point to any point on the circumference of the circle. When you see the center marker and SnapTip, pick the marker. This puts the start point of the arc at the center of the circle.

19. At the `Center/End/<Second point>:` prompt, use the cursor menu to choose the Quadrant object snap.

20. Choose a point on the circumference of the circle near the right (0 degrees) quadrant of the circle.

21. At the `Endpoint:` prompt, use any method to choose the Endpoint object snap.

22. Pick the endpoint at ① in Figure 4-20.

23. Start the LINE command. At the `From point:` prompt, use the Object Snap flyout to choose the Snap to Intersection object snap.

24. Pick the intersection of the arc and the circle.

25. At the `To point:` prompt, type **per** ↵.

26. Pick a point near ⑤ when you see the perpendicular marker and SnapTip.

27. Save your drawing. Your drawing should look like Figure 4-22.

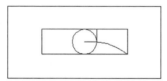

Figure 4-22: The finished drawing, created using the Endpoint, Midpoint, Center, Quadrant, Perpendicular, and Intersection object snaps.

Running object snaps and OSNAP mode

The Endpoint object snap is probably the most commonly used of all the object snaps. You might have a drawing project in which you need to use the Endpoint object snap often. You can set a *running object snap,* which keeps one or more object snaps on until you turn them off.

Tip

Some users like to work with three or four running object snaps on at once, such as Endpoint, Midpoint, Center, and Intersection.

To set running object snaps, choose Tools⇨Object Snap Settings to open the Osnap Settings dialog box, as shown in Figure 4-23. Click the Running Osnap tab, if necessary, choose the object snaps you want, and click OK. Click any checked object snap to clear it. Choose Clear All to clear all running snaps.

A great new feature of Release 14 is the OSNAP button on the status bar. When the button is on, your running object snaps are active. If you want to turn them off temporarily, just double-click the OSNAP button. This ability to toggle running object snaps on and off make them much more useful. It is now feasible to work with running object snaps on almost all the time, knowing that you can turn them off at the double-click of a button. The result is that accurate drawing is faster and easier.

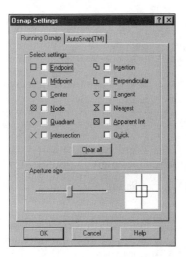

Figure 4-23: Use the Osnap Settings dialog box to set running object snaps.

The following exercise gives you a chance to make full use of the new OSNAP features.

Step-by-Step: Using Running Object Snaps with OSNAP mode

1. Start a new drawing using the Start from Scratch option with English units. Save it in your *AutoCAD Bible* folder as *ab4-6.dwg*.

2. Choose Tools⇨Object Snap Settings to open the Osnap Settings dialog box. Verify that the Running Osnap tab is displayed. Choose Endpoint. Make sure all other object snaps are not checked and click OK.

3. Start the LINE command and start the line at 2,2.

4. Turn on Ortho mode by double-clicking ORTHO on the status bar.

5. Move the mouse in the $0°$ direction and type **6** ↵.

6. Move the mouse up in the $90°$ direction, type **3** ↵, and end the LINE command.

7. Start the ARC command. At the `Center/<Start point>:` prompt, pick the endpoint at ①, shown in Figure 4-24. (Look for the marker and SnapTip.)

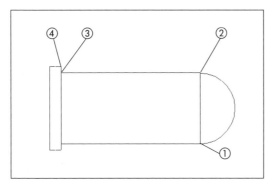

Figure 4-24: Drawing a steam boiler with an Endpoint running snap.

8. At the `Center/End/<Second point>:` prompt, type **e** ↵ to specify the end of the arc. Pick the endpoint at ②, shown in Figure 4-24.

9. At the `Angle/Direction/Radius/<Center point>:` prompt, type **a** ↵ to specify the angle, and type **180** ↵.

10. Start the LINE command and at the `From point:` prompt, pick the endpoint at ② in Figure 4-24.

11. Move the mouse to the left in the 180° direction, type **6** ↵, and end the LINE command.

12. Choose Tools⇨Drawing Aids. Set the Snap X Spacing to 0.25. Click OK.

13. Start the LINE command. At the `From point:` prompt, place the cursor .25 units above ③ in Figure 4-24 (at 2,5.25). However, you see the Endpoint marker and SnapTip indicating that AutoCAD finds the endpoint of the last line you drew. Since you want a point just above the endpoint, double-click OSNAP on the status bar. Now pick point 2,5.25.

14. At the `To point:` prompt, pick point 2,1.75.

15. Press F6 twice to get polar coordinates. Follow the prompts:

```
To point: Pick .5<180
To point: Pick 3.5<90
Double-click OSNAP again to turn it on.
To point: Pick the endpoint at ④ in Figure 4-24.
To point: ↵
```

16. Save your drawing. If you are going on to the next exercise, leave it open.

Even if you have running object snaps, if you specify an object snap during a command, it overrides the running object snap. For example, having a running Endpoint object snap does not mean you cannot use a Midpoint object snap for any specific drawing command.

By default, if you type absolute or relative coordinates, they take precedence over any running object snaps. This lets you leave running object snaps on but override them with typed coordinates whenever you wish. In general, the default gives you the most control and flexibility. However, Release 14 lets you change this default to give running object snaps precedence. To change the default, choose Tools⇨Preferences and choose the Compatibility tab.

From

Object snaps help you draw an object based on a geometrical point of an existing object. However, sometimes you want to draw an object starting near an existing object or geometrical point. Before Release 13, you had to draw a temporary line from the existing object to your intended start point. Then you used object snap to create the new object. Finally, you erased that extra line you created.

From lets you create a new object starting at a known distance and direction from an existing object. It's like creating one or more invisible lines between the existing object and the new object, helping you start the new object in the proper place.

Here's how to use the From feature:

1. Start a command to draw an object, such as LINE.

 2. Choose Snap From on the Object Snap flyout of the Standard toolbar (or From on the cursor menu). You can also type **from** on the command line.

3. AutoCAD prompts you for a base point, which you usually provide using an object snap, such as Endpoint.

4. Choose an object to tell AutoCAD which object you want the object snap to refer to.

5. AutoCAD prompts you for an Offset, which you provide using relative coordinates.

6. Continue your command.

The following exercise shows how to use the From feature.

Step-by-Step: Using From

1. Open *ab4-6.dwg*, which you created in the last Step-by-Step, or continue using it if it is still on the screen. If you did not do the last exercise, open it from the *Results* folder of the CD-ROM. Make sure Ortho mode is still on. Double-click SNAP on the status bar to turn snap off. OSNAP mode should be on.

2. Save the drawing as *ab4-7.dwg* in your *AutoCAD Bible* folder.

3. Start the LINE command.

4. Choose the Object Snap flyout on the Standard toolbar and drag down to the second button, Snap From.

5. AutoCAD prompts you for a base point. Pick the endpoint near ① in Figure 4-25.

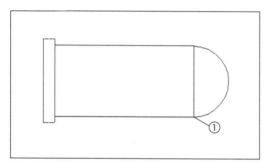

Figure 4-25: Using the From feature to complete the steam boiler.

6. At the `<Offset>:` prompt, type **@-1,.5** ↵.

7. You are now ready to continue the line at the `To point:` prompt. Move the cursor in the 90° direction and type **2** ↵.

8. Move the mouse in the 180° direction and type **1** ↵.

9. Move the mouse in the 270° direction and type **2** ↵.

10. Move the mouse in the 0° direction, find the Endpoint marker of the start point of the first segment of the line, and pick the point. End the LINE command.

11. Save your drawing. It should look like Figure 4-26.

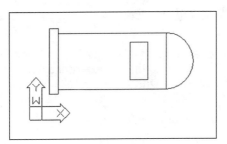

Figure 4-26: The completed steam boiler.

Locating points with tracking

Tracking is a new feature for Release 14. The purpose of tracking is to let you specify a point based on the coordinates of two other points. Imaginary orthogonal lines are drawn from the two points you specify, and tracking locates their intersection. Tracking performs a function similar to point filters, discussed in the next section, but is easier to use. In some cases, tracking can be used in the place of the From object snap, often with Direct Distance Entry. Tracking locates coordinates that are not yet explicit in the drawing and is usually used with object snaps.

Tracking is intended for use in two dimensions only. For 3D point location, use X, Y, and Z point filters.

To use tracking, follow these steps:

1. Start a command.

2. At any prompt where you need to specify a point, choose Tracking from the Object Snap flyout of the Standard toolbar or from the cursor menu. You can also type **tk** ↵.

3. At the First tracking point: prompt, specify the first point you want to use to create the final point. If possible, use an object snap to do so.

4. At the Next point (Press ENTER to end tracking): prompt, specify the second point. You can use an object snap or Direct Distance Entry (from the first point) to specify the second point. Notice that the cursor is constrained to orthogonal movement from the first point you chose.

5. Press Enter to end tracking. AutoCAD specifies the imaginary intersection of the two points you picked.

Figure 4-27 shows how you can use tracking to specify the center of a circle at the center of a rectangle. At the prompt for the center, start tracking and use object snaps to pick the midpoints of two of the sides of the rectangle. When you end tracking, AutoCAD uses the intersection of two imaginary lines drawn from the midpoints of the two sides of the rectangle as the center of the circle. Thus the circle is centered in the rectangle. In Figure 4-27, the midpoint object snap was also used to specify the radius.

Both the center of the rectangle and its top-right corner can be located by the same two tracking points. Move the cursor toward the desired point before specifying the second tracking point to ensure that you get the point you want.

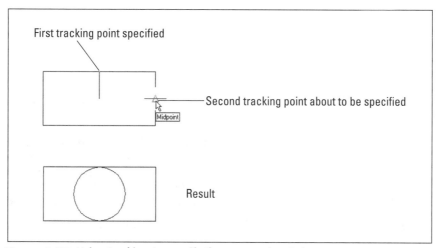

First tracking point specified

Second tracking point about to be specified

Midpoint

Result

Figure 4-27: Using tracking to specify the center of a circle.

When you use tracking to draw, the object you are drawing disappears! Tracking does this because it is waiting to determine the point that tracking will specify. This can be disconcerting. If you are drawing a series of lines, only the current segment disappears. However, if you are drawing the first segment of a line, the entire line disappears. When you end tracking, everything reappears.

Step-by-Step: Locating Points with Tracking

On the CD-ROM

1. Open *ab4-c.dwg* from the CD-ROM.

2. Save the drawing as *ab4-8.dwg* in your *AutoCAD Bible* folder. This is a section of a simple plan layout of an apartment. OSNAP is on with a running object snap set to Endpoint. ORTHO is on.

3. Start the LINE command. At the `From point:` prompt, pick the endpoint at ① in Figure 4-28.

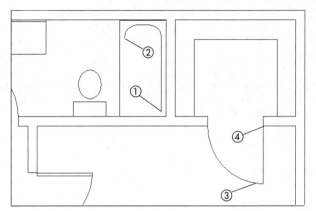

Figure 4-28: The plan layout needs the tub and door to be completed.

4. Choose Tracking from the Object Snap flyout of the Standard toolbar. At the `First tracking point:` prompt, choose the endpoint at ①. At the `Next point (Press ENTER to end tracking):` prompt, move the cursor to the left, and then pick the endpoint at ②. Press Enter to end tracking. AutoCAD picks the intersection of imaginary lines running orthogonally from ① and ②.

5. At the `To point:` prompt, pick the endpoint at ② in Figure 4-28. End the LINE command.

6. Start the LINE command again. At the `From point:` prompt, pick the endpoint at ③ in Figure 4-28. If you have trouble finding the right endpoint, press Tab until the arc is highlighted, letting you know that AutoCAD has found the end-point of the arc.

7. At the `To point:` prompt, start Tracking. At the `First tracking point:` prompt, choose the endpoint at ③. At the `Next point (Press ENTER to end tracking):` prompt, pick the endpoint at ④. Press Enter to end tracking.

8. At the `To point:` prompt, pick the endpoint at ④ and end the LINE command.

9. Save your drawing. It should look like Figure 4-29.

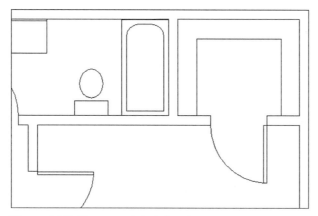

Figure 4-29: The completed drawing.

Point filters

Point filters allow you to specify a coordinate using the X coordinate of one existing object snap and the Y coordinate of another. You construct an X,Y coordinate based on coordinates of existing objects.

Here's how to use point filters:

1. Start a command to draw an object.

2. To specify a coordinate, type **.x** or **.y** on the command line. You can also find point filters on the cursor menu (Shift+right-click).

3. AutoCAD prompts you for a point. Generally, you specify the point by using an object snap.

4. AutoCAD prompts you for the other coordinate value, which you generally provide using an object snap. (If you are working in 2D, ignore the request for a Z coordinate.)

5. Continue your command.

Tip

You do not need to use existing coordinates for both the X and Y portions of the coordinate. For example, you can construct an X,Y coordinate by using the Y coordinate of an existing line and picking the X coordinate anywhere on the screen.

Point filters are often used in 3D drawing. See Chapter 21.

The following Step-by-Step exercise lets you practice using 2D point filters on the same drawing you used in the previous exercise.

Step-by-Step: Using 2D Point Filters

1. Open *ab4-c.dwg* from the CD-ROM.

2. Save it as *ab4-9.dwg* in your *AutoCAD Bible* folder. ORTHO and OSNAP are on. A running object snap is set for endpoint.

3. Start the LINE command.

4. At the From point: prompt, pick the endpoint at ① in Figure 4-30.

5. At the To point: prompt, type **.x** ↵. At the .x of prompt, pick the endpoint at ② in Figure 4-30.

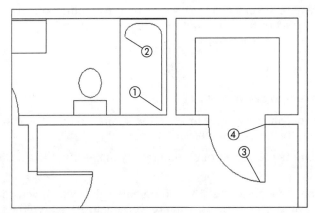

Figure 4-30: Using point filters to specify the start of a line.

6. AutoCAD responds with the (need YZ): prompt. (Since you are drawing in 2D, you can ignore the Z.) Choose the endpoint at ① in Figure 4-30. AutoCAD draws the line segment to the point defined by the X coordinate of ② and the Y coordinate of ①.

7. At the To point: prompt, pick the endpoint at ②. End the LINE command.

8. Start the LINE command again. At the From point: prompt, pick the endpoint at ③. If necessary, press Tab until you see the arc highlighted so you know you have the endpoint of the arc.

9. At the `To point:` prompt, type **.y** ↵. Pick the endpoint at ④ in Figure 4-30.

10. At the `(need XZ):` prompt, pick the endpoint at ③.

11. At the `To point:` prompt, pick the endpoint at ④. End the LINE command.

12. Save your drawing.

Summary

You have learned a great deal about specifying coordinates in this chapter. These skills are the basis for all your future work with AutoCAD.

In AutoCAD, you can specify absolute and relative Cartesian and polar coordinates by typing them on the command line. You can display coordinates in three modes — dynamic absolute, static absolute, and dynamic polar.

Orthogonal mode restricts drawing and editing to the horizontal and vertical directions. Direct Distance Entry lets you move the cursor in the direction you want to draw and type in only a distance.

Snap restricts cursor movement to an invisible grid. You can set the spacing to whatever you wish. Turn on snap by double-clicking SNAP on the status bar.

Turn on Grid mode to display a visible grid. You can set the spacing of the grid to whatever you wish. Turn on Grid by double-clicking GRID on the status bar.

Object snaps let you reference geometric points of existing objects. The new AutoSnap feature visually confirms the geometric points. The From feature creates an offset from an existing object. You can set running object snaps that continue until you turn them off. The new OSNAP button on the status bar lets you easily turn running object snaps on and off.

Tracking lets you find the intersection of two points and use that intersection whenever you need to specify a coordinate. Point filters offer a similar capability, letting you build a coordinate from existing objects.

The next chapter introduces you to the basics of setting up a drawing.

✦　　✦　　✦

Setting Up a Drawing

✦ ✦ ✦ ✦

In This Chapter

Setting the unit type

Setting drawing limits

Presetting the drawing scale

Inserting a title block

Laying out a drawing

Understanding system variables

Using the MVSETUP command

✦ ✦ ✦ ✦

The Setup Process

Often the first step after you start a new drawing is to set its size and unit type. These and other setup options are discussed in this chapter. Many of these settings can be saved in a template so that they are available to you whenever you start a new drawing.

To create a customized template, open any drawing. Make changes as described in this chapter and save the drawing as a template by choosing Drawing Template File (*.dwt) from the Save as type drop-down list box in the Save As dialog box.

Release 14 offers two wizards that help you set up a drawing. From the Start Up dialog box, choose Use a Wizard. You can then choose Quick Setup or Advanced Setup. Because Advanced Setup includes the Quick Setup settings, I cover the Advanced Setup in this chapter. I also explain how to set up your drawing the old-fashioned way.

Unit Types

When you choose Use a Wizard from the Start Up dialog, and then Advanced Setup, AutoCAD displays the dialog box shown in Figure 5-1. Step 1 determines the unit type. The unit type can be saved in a template.

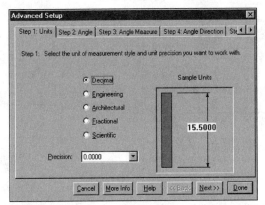

Figure 5-1: Step 1 of Advanced Setup determines the type of units you want to use in your drawing.

As mentioned earlier, the coordinates you use in AutoCAD are measured in units that can represent any real-world measurement, such as inches or millimeters. A surveyor might even use miles as the base unit. However, different disciplines customarily express units differently, and you should use the unit type appropriate for the type of drawing you are creating. AutoCAD offers five types of units, as shown in Table 5-1.

The sample measurement column shows how a line 32.5 inches long would be displayed in the various unit types.

Table 5-1		
Unit Types		
Unit Type Name	**Sample Measurement**	**Description**
Decimal	32.50	Number of units, partial units in decimals
Engineering	2'-8.50"	Feet and inches, partial inches in decimals
Architectural	2'-8 1/2"	Feet and inches, partial inches in fractions
Fractional	32 1/2	Number of units, partial units in fractions
Scientific	3.25E+.01	Base number + exponent

Notice how the engineering and architectural units translate a line of 32.5 units into 2'8-1/2". Engineering and architectural units assume a unit of one inch unlike the other unit types, which can represent any measurement.

The unit type affects how coordinates are shown on the status bar and how AutoCAD lists information about objects. Coordinates are also generally input using the type of units you have chosen, although AutoCAD accepts coordinates in any of the unit types.

Note

As mentioned in Chapter 4, if you are using engineering or architectural units, AutoCAD displays parts of inches differently than the format you must use to type them in. You must type coordinates without any spaces, because AutoCAD interprets a space as equivalent to pressing Enter and ends your input. Use a hyphen between whole and partial inches, for example, 3'2-1/2". (You can omit the " after the inches because AutoCAD assumes inches in engineering and architectural units if no symbol follows a number.) However, this appears on the status line as 3'-2 1/2". This can be confusing because the hyphen is in a different place, and AutoCAD inserts a space between the whole and partial inches.

Setting the drawing units

To set the units, choose the type of units you want on the Units tab of the Advanced Setup dialog box. Choose a precision in the Precision drop-down list box, and then click Next.

**Cross-
Reference**

To set drawing units without the wizard, choose Format➪Units to open the Units Control dialog box, shown in Figure 5-2. Look in Chapter 3 for a brief overview of this dialog box in the Step-by-Step exercise, *Using a Dialog Box.*

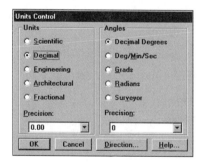

Figure 5-2: The Units Control dialog box.

The left side of the Units Control dialog box lets you choose which unit type you want to use. In the precision box in the Units section, click the arrow and a list of precision options drops down. Click the one you want.

Caution

AutoCAD rounds off measurements to the nearest precision value you choose. Let's say you choose a precision of two decimal places, using Decimal units. You want to draw a line 3.25 units long, but when you type in the coordinate, by accident you hit the 4 key at the end, resulting in a line 3.254 units long. AutoCAD shows this line as 3.25 units long, making it difficult for you to spot the error. Therefore, it is a good idea to set a higher precision than you need to show.

Setting the angle type

Step 2 of the Advanced Setup Wizard, shown in Figure 5-3, lets you set the angle type.

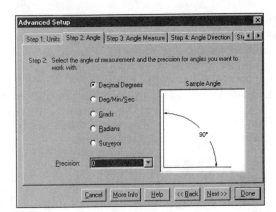

Figure 5-3: Setting the angle type.

As with units, your choice of angle type depends on your profession and work environment. Decimal degrees is the default. Table 5-2 lists the types of angles.

Table 5-2		
Angle Types		
Angle Type Name	**Sample Measurement**	**Description**
Decimal Degrees	32.5	Degrees, partial degrees in decimals
Deg/Min/Sec	32°30'0"	Degrees, minutes, and seconds
Grads	36.1111g	Grads
Radians	0.5672r	Radians
Surveyor	N 57d30' E	Surveyor (directional) units

Note

A minute is $\frac{1}{60}$ of a degree and a second is $\frac{1}{60}$ of a minute. Grads and radians are simply alternate ways of measuring angles. A grad is a metric measurement equal to $\frac{1}{100}$ of a right angle. Radians measure an angle by placing a length, equal to the radius, along the circle's circumference. Radians range from 0 to 2 * PI instead of from 0 to 360 as degrees do. A radian is equivalent to 57.32 degrees. Surveyor units measure angles in directions, starting with north or south and adding an angle in degrees, minutes, seconds format that shows how far the angle is from north or south and in which direction (east or west).

Choose the type of angle measurement you want. In the precision box, click the arrow and a list of precision options drops down. Click the one you want.

Cross-Reference

Changing these settings does not automatically change the way your dimensions appear. These are changed using the Dimension Styles dialog box, which is discussed in Chapter 15.

Once you have chosen the angle type and the precision, click Next. As with the unit type, you can set the angle type without the wizard by choosing Format➪Units to open the Units Control dialog box (shown in Figure 5-2).

Setting the angle measure and direction

Step 3 of the Advanced Setup Wizard, shown in Figure 5-4, is where you set the angle measure.

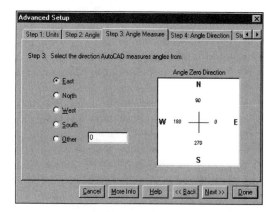

Figure 5-4: Selecting the angle measure.

According to standard convention, you measure angles so that 0 degrees starts to the right, in the East direction. To change this convention, choose the direction for 0 degrees, and then click Next.

AutoCAD displays Step 4, shown in Figure 5-5.

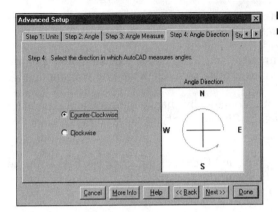

Figure 5-5: Setting the direction of angle measure.

The standard also increases degrees in a counter-clockwise direction. However, if you need another arrangement, you can customize how angles are calculated. Choose Counter-Clockwise (the default) or Clockwise and click Next.

To set the angle direction without the wizard, choose Direction in the Units Control dialog box. The Direction Control dialog box opens, as shown in Figure 5-6.

Figure 5-6: The Direction Control dialog box.

Here you can choose to have 0 degrees start in a direction other than East. You can also choose to increase degrees in the clockwise direction. Choose OK twice to return to your drawing.

Note

Changing the angle direction affects what happens when you input angles and what you see in the coordinate display. It does not change the absolute coordinates, which are set according to the UCS (User Coordinate System) icon. Using and customizing the UCS icon is covered in Chapter 8.

In this exercise, you practice setting the drawing units with the Units Control dialog box.

Step-by-Step: Setting the Drawing Units

1. Open a new drawing using the *acad.dwt* template.

2. Save the drawing as *ab5-1.dwg* in your *AutoCAD Bible* folder.

3. Choose Format⇨Units to open the Units Control dialog box.

4. In the Units section, choose Architectural.

5. Click the arrow to the right of the Precision drop-down list box. Choose 0'-0 1/8".

6. In the Angles section, choose Deg/Min/Sec.

7. In the Precision box, choose 0d00'.

8. Click OK.

9. Start the LINE command. Follow the prompts:

```
From point: 2,2 ↵
To point: @1 <0 ↵
To point: @6-3/4<153 ↵
To point: 2,2 ↵
```

10. End the LINE command.

11. Type **zoom** ↵. Type **a** ↵ to zoom to the entire drawing. Save your drawing. If you are continuing through the chapter, keep it open.

Note You would not actually use Deg/Min/Sec for angles in an architectural drawing, but the exercise gives you the opportunity to set the angular units.

Drawing Limits

Step 5 of the Advanced Setup Wizard, shown in Figure 5-7, lets you specify the area of your drawing, also called the *limits*. The drawing limits are the outer edges of the drawing, specified in X,Y units. You need to set only the lower-left and upper-right corners of the drawing. Together, these two points create an invisible bounding rectangle for your drawing.

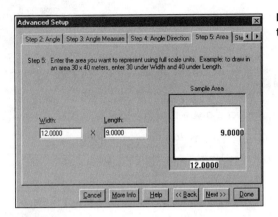

Figure 5-7: The Area tab lets you set the drawing limits.

Almost universally, the lower-left limit is 0,0, which is the default. This also lets you use 0,0 as a reference for entering absolute coordinates. Therefore, the upper-right corner really defines the drawing size. Remember that you typically draw at life size in AutoCAD. Therefore, the size of your drawing should be equal to the size of the outer extents of what you are drawing plus a margin for a title block and perhaps for annotation and dimensioning. If you want to show more than one view of an object, as is common in both architectural and mechanical drawing, you need to take this into account.

To decide on drawing limits, you need to consider what the drawing units mean for you. Generally, the smallest commonly used unit is used, often inches or millimeters. Therefore, if you are drawing a plan view of a house which is approximately 40 feet across (in the X direction) by 30 feet deep (in the Y direction), this translates to a top-right corner of 480,360. Adding room for a title block brings you to about 500,380.

Tip

You can draw outside the drawing limits. However, the drawing limits setting affects the size of the grid if you turn it on. This can help you visualize the size of your drawing if you don't have a title block. The ZOOM command with the All option also uses the drawing limits to resize the display, although it displays the entire drawing if the drawing is outside the limits. Setting the limits properly makes a ZOOM All more useful.

Setting drawing limits

To set the drawing limits, type in a width and a length on the Step 5: Area tab. AutoCAD shows the result in the Sample Area as shown in Figure 5-7. Then click Next.

To set drawing limits without the wizard, choose Format⇨Drawing Limits. Press Enter to accept the lower-left corner default of 0,0 that appears on the command line. Then type in the upper-right corner coordinate that you want and press Enter. In the next Step-by-Step exercise, you set limits without the wizard.

Step-by-Step: Setting the Drawing Limits

On the
CD-ROM

1. If you did the previous exercise, continue to use *ab5-1.dwg.* Otherwise, open *ab5-1.dwg* from the *Results* folder of the CD-ROM.

2. Save the drawing as *ab5-2.dwg* in your *AutoCAD Bible* folder.

3. Choose Format⇨Drawing Limits.

4. Press Enter to accept the lower-left default.

5. Type **16,10** ↵.

6. Start the LINE command. Follow the prompts:

```
From point: 0,0 ↵
To point: 16,0 ↵
To point: 16,10 ↵
To point, 0,10 ↵
To point: 0,0 ↵
```

7. End the LINE command.

8. Save your drawing. If you are continuing through the chapter, keep it open.

Understanding scales

You need to consider the fact that your drawing will most likely be plotted onto a standard paper (sheet) size. The standard orientation for drafting (and the default for most plotters) is landscape orientation, meaning that as you look at the drawing the paper is wider than it is tall. Figure 5-8 shows an example. These conventions have carried over from the days of hand drafting. (In a computer program, this is not really necessary, as you can rotate the drawing when you plot it.) To scale a drawing onto a piece of paper in a pleasing manner requires a rectangular shape that somewhat resembles the proportions of standard paper sizes.

In addition, although you specify the scale at plotting time, it helps to be aware of the scale you will use when plotting your drawing at the outset. The scales used for GIS (Geographical Information Systems), where you might be drawing an entire county, will be different from those used when drawing a house. The scales used in mechanical drafting are again totally different. In fact, in mechanical drafting, if you are drawing a very small object, such as a 2" screw-plate, you may scale up, that is, enlarge the drawing when plotting.

One important reason for establishing the scale at the beginning is to ensure that text, whether annotations or dimensions, is readable in its final plotted form. Applying a scale makes it possible to ensure that text remains a reasonable size even as the rest of the drawing is scaled up or down. Scale also affects dotted and dashed lines as well as line widths.

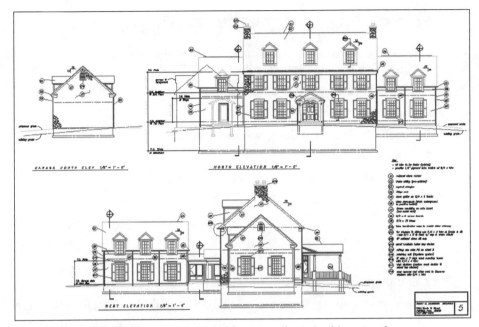

Figure 5-8: Drawings are usually oriented horizontally, as in this example.

Credit: Thanks to Henry Dearborn, AIA, Fairfield, Iowa, for this drawing, which I have somewhat altered.

Some drawings are not scaled. Examples are electrical or electronic schematics. These drawings are representations of electrical or electronic connections but do not resemble the actual physical object that will eventually be created from the drawing. These drawings can be any size as long as they are clear and organized.

Cross-Reference

You can place various views of your drawing on an imaginary piece of paper, called paper space, to prepare it for plotting. See Chapter 17 for more on paper space and plotting.

When determining your scale to try to fit a drawing on a sheet of paper, be aware that a plotter cannot print on the entire sheet. There is a margin around the edge that is not available for drawing. Plotters differ in this respect. The plotter's manual can provide this information for you. On average, you can assume a ½-inch margin on each side, so that you should subtract one inch from both the length and width sheet measurements to determine the actual drawing space. Table 5-3 shows standard U.S. sheet sizes.

			Table 5-3			
Standard Paper Sheet Sizes in the United States (in inches)						
Size	*Width*	*Height*	*Size*	*Width*	*Height*	
A	11	$8^{1}/2$	D	34	22	
B	17	11	E	44	34	
C	22	17				

Table 5-4 lists standard metric sheet sizes.

			Table 5-4			
Standard Metric Paper Sheet Sizes (in millimeters)						
Size	*Width*	*Height*	*Size*	*Width*	*Height*	
A4	297	210	A1	841	594	
A3	420	297	A0	1189	841	
A2	594	420				

Scale formats

A scale is generally indicated in the format *plotted size:actual size*. Because you draw at actual size in AutoCAD, the actual size is also the drawing size. For example, a scale of $^{1}/4"=1'$ means that $^{1}/4"$ on the drawing, when plotted out on a sheet of paper, represents one foot in actual life — and in the AutoCAD drawing. This is a typical architectural scale. A windowpane one foot wide would appear $^{1}/4"$ wide on paper.

From the scale, you can calculate a scale factor. To do this, the left side of the scale equation must equal 1, and the two numbers must be in the same measurement (for example, both in inches). This requires some simple math. For $^{1}/4"=1'$, you would calculate as follows:

$^{1}/4"=1'$

1"= 4'   Multiply both sides of the equation by 4

1"= 48"   Change 4' to 48"

Therefore, the scale factor is 48. This means that the paper plot is $1/48$ of real size.

In mechanical drawing, you might draw a metal joint that is actually 4 inches long. To fit it on an $8^1/2 \times 11$ sheet of paper, you could use a 2"=1" scale, which means that 2" on the paper drawing equals 1" in actual life and the AutoCAD drawing. Calculate the scale factor:

2" = 1"

1" = $1/2$"

The scale factor is $1/2$. This means that the paper plot is twice the real size.

You will use the scale factor when you set the size for text in Chapter 13 and for dimensions in Chapter 15.

Most professions use certain standard scales. Therefore, you do not usually have a choice to pick any scale you wish, such as 1":27'. Instead, the conventions of your profession, client, or office dictate a choice of only a few scales. Table 5-5 lists some standard architectural scales.

Table 5-5		
Typical Architectural Scales		
Scale Factor	*Plotted Size*	*Drawing/Actual Size*
(480)	$1/40$"	1'
(240)	$1/20$"	1'
(192)	$1/16$"	1'
(96)	$1/8$"	1'
(48)	$1/4$"	1'
(24)	$1/2$"	1'
(16)	$3/4$"	1'
(12)	1"	1'
(4)	3"	1'
(2)	6"	1'
(1)	1'	1'

Civil Engineering scales are somewhat different and range to larger sizes — a bridge is bigger than a house — as shown in Table 5-6.

Table 5-6
Typical Civil Engineering Scales

Scale Factor	Plotted Size	Drawing/Actual Size
120	1"	10'
240	1"	20'
360	1"	30'
480	1"	40'
600	1"	50'
720	1"	60'
960	1"	80'
1200	1"	100'

Table 5-7 shows some typical metric scales that could be used for any purpose. You would most typically work in millimeters, but these could represent any metric measurement.

Table 5-7
Typical Metric Scales

Scale Factor	Plotted Size	Drawing/Actual Size
5000	1	5000
2000	1	2000
1000	1	1000
500	1	500
200	1	200
100	1	100
75	1	75
50	1	50
20	1	20
10	1	10
5	1	5
1	1	1

Deciding on a scale and sheet size

Once you know the size of your drawing and the scales appropriate for your situation, you need to consider the sheet size of the paper that you will plot on. Again, you often find that certain factors limit your choices. Your plotter or printer may be limited to certain sheet sizes. The conventions used in your discipline or working environment also affect your decision. You may be working on a series of drawings that are all to be plotted on the same size sheet of paper.

As an example, the architectural drawing in Figure 5-8 is 175' wide by 120' high. The two most typical scales for a drawing of a house are $1/4"=1'$ and $1/8"=1'$. You might have a choice of sheet sizes A, B, or C. The following steps show the calculations you need to do in order to decide on a scale, obtain the scale factor, and determine the appropriate sheet size.

For this exercise, you need only a sheet of paper and a pencil. Use Figure 5-8 as a guide.

Step-by-Step: Determining the Scale and Sheet Size

1. To calculate the plotted size of the drawing at $1/4"=1'$, you can start with the width, which is 175'. Take $1/4$ of 175 to get the width of the drawing in inches, which is $43^3/4"$.

2. Take $1/4$ of the height, 120', to get the height of the drawing in inches, which is 30".

3. A size C sheet (see Table 5-3) is 22" × 17", which is too small for a $43^3/4"$ × 30" drawing.

4. Recalculate the drawing at $1/8"=1'$. Take $1/8$ of 175 to get $21^7/8"$. Take $1/8$ of 120 to get 15".

5. The actual drawing space (minus the margins the printer requires) on a size C sheet is about 21" × 16". The height of the drawing at this scale is adequate, but the width is $7/8"$ too long. Therefore, the best bet is to simply make the drawing $7/8"$ narrower, since the drawing has some extra room. This lets you fit the drawing on a size C sheet.

6. To calculate the scale factor of a $1/8"=1'$ scale, multiply 1' × 8 to get 8' and convert it to inches, which is 96 (8 × 12).

Resizing a drawing slightly to fit a standard scale factor and sheet size is a typical task. There is no actual setup step for setting the drawing scale, but you use it when you insert text or dimensions and when you plot the drawing.

Inserting a Title Block

Step 6 of the Advanced Setup Wizard, shown in Figure 5-9, lets you insert a title block.

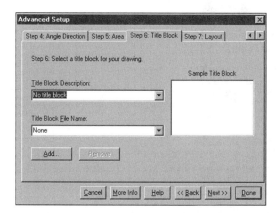

Figure 5-9: Use Step 6 of the Advanced Setup Wizard to insert a title block.

A title block is a rectangle that bounds your drawing and includes spaces for the drawing title, company name, drafter name, and so on. You can choose the title block from either its description or its filename. AutoCAD displays the title block in the Sample Title Block area. You can create your own title blocks, save them as drawing files, and add them to this list by clicking Add. Remove title block drawings that you know you never use by clicking Remove.

Cross-Reference

As explained in Chapter 2, you can create your own title block, make a template from it, then open a drawing based on that template.

When you have chosen a title block, or decided to choose the default No title block option, click Next.

Laying Out a Drawing

Step 7 of the Advanced Setup Wizard, shown in Figure 5-10, lets you use paper space to lay out a drawing for plotting.

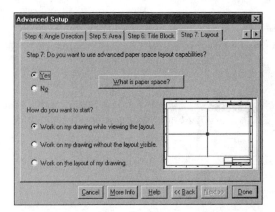

Figure 5-10: In Step 7 of the Advance Setup Wizard, you specify whether to use paper space to lay out a drawing.

Cross-
Reference

Unless you understand paper space, you should choose No and click Done. I cover paper space in Chapter 17. If you understand paper space, click one of the options under the section How do you want to start?

✦ Choose Work on my drawing while viewing the layout if you want to see the paper space layout but work on your drawing.

✦ Choose Work on my drawing without the layout visible to work in model space — the type of space where you usually draw — instead of paper space.

✦ Choose Work on the layout of my drawing to enter paper space and set up the layout of the drawing.

You have now completed the Advanced Setup Wizard.

Common Setup Options

Cross-
Reference

As explained in Chapter 2, most of the process discussed in this chapter can be streamlined by creating templates. You may wish to create templates for the most common scales and sheet sizes you use.

There are a few other items that are generally set up in advance and are included in a template. The following are covered in other chapters of this book:

Cross-
Reference

✦ *Layers* (covered in Chapter 11) allow you to organize your drawing into meaningful groups. In an architectural drawing, for example, you might create a layer for walls, another for doors, one for electrical fixtures, and so on.

✦ *Text styles* (covered in Chapter 13) let you format the font and other text characteristics.

✦ *Dimension styles* (covered in Chapter 15) format the dimensions that measure your objects.

Setting blips

Certain aspects of the interface can be customized and saved in a template. For example, you can turn on blips so that AutoCAD creates a mark when you pick a point. If you turn them on and save the drawing as a template, they will appear in any drawing based on that template. Blips can be helpful as reference points in certain cases, but they are off by default.

Step-by-Step: Changing the Blips Setting

1. If you did the previous exercise, continue to use *ab5-2.dwg*. Otherwise, open *ab5-2.dwg* from the *Results* folder of the CD-ROM.

2. Save the drawing as *ab5-3.dwg* in your *AutoCAD Bible* folder.

3. Type **blipmode ↵ on ↵**.

4. Turn on Ortho mode.

5. Start the LINE command. Follow the prompts:

   ```
   From point: 2,2 ↵
   To point: Move the cursor down. .5 ↵
   To point: Move the cursor to the right. 1  ↵
   To point: Move the cursor up. .5 ↵
   ```

6. End the LINE command. Notice the blip marks.

7. Choose Redraw from the Standard toolbar. The blip marks disappear.

8. Save your drawing.

Setting snap, grid, and ortho

If you know you will be using snap, grid, and ortho a lot in certain drawings and you know the suitable settings for snap and grid, you can set these and save them in a template. In other cases, you might want to leave them off and turn them on only when you need them.

System variables

When you change settings in AutoCAD such as the unit type, angle type, drawing limits, or blip marks, you are actually changing AutoCAD's *system variables.* These are simply settings that AutoCAD stores in each drawing or in the AutoCAD configuration file (which stores settings that apply to all drawings). Usually you don't need to pay any direct attention to them, but they are the nuts and bolts behind the dialog boxes you use to change the settings. When you start customizing AutoCAD, you need to learn about them. Programming code cannot access dialog boxes. Also, a few system variables are accessible only by typing them directly on the command line. Appendix C provides more information on system variables. Throughout this book, I occasionally mention system variables when it is useful to use them directly. For example, blipmode is both a command and a system variable. When you changed the blips setting in the Step-by-Step exercise, you used a command to directly set the system variable.

Some system variables store information about a drawing or the drawing environment, such as the drawing name and path. These are *read-only*, meaning that you cannot change them. They exist to provide information and are often used in AutoLISP programs.

As of AutoCAD Release 13, you can type system variables on the command line, just like AutoCAD's regular commands.

Step-by-Step: Setting the Drawing Aids and Creating a Template

Cross-Reference

1. Continue from previous exercise or open *ab5-3.dwg* from the *Results* folder of the CD-ROM.

2. Save the drawing as *ab5-4.dwg* in your *AutoCAD Bible* folder.

3. Choose Tools⇨Drawing Aids.

4. The Snap section is set to 0'0-1/2". In the Grid section, change the X spacing to 0'1". Click OK.

5. Double-click SNAP and GRID on the status bar to turn them on.

6. Using the coordinate display as your guide, draw line segments from $2^1/2$, $1^1/2$ to @$^1/2$<270 to @11"<0 to @$^1/2$<90. End the LINE command.

7. Save your drawing. It should look like Figure 5-11. Notice how the grid and snap settings facilitate the drawing process. The architectural units create a different drawing experience than decimal units would. Setting up a drawing creates a drawing environment suited to your work needs.

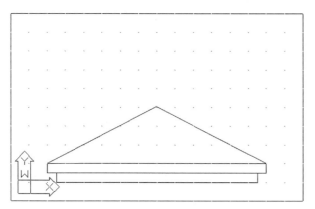

Figure 5-11: The final architectural drawing.

 8. Choose File➪Save As. In the Save Drawing As dialog box, click the Save as type drop-down list box and choose Drawing Template File (*.dwt).

 9. In the File name text box, change the name to *archroof.dwt*. Click Save.

 10. In the Template Description dialog box, type the following and click OK:

```
Arch units, 16,10 limits, blips, snap & grid
```

 11. Choose File➪New. Choose the Use a Template option. In the scroll box, choose the archroof template and choose OK. AutoCAD opens a new drawing using the template.

 Do not save this new drawing.

The MVSETUP Command

The MVSETUP command is used in two different ways — to set up a drawing and to create viewports in paper space.

Cross-
Reference

Paper space is discussed in Chapter 17.

When used to set up a drawing, MVSETUP simply provides a routine to walk you through some of the basic setup functions discussed in this chapter. It is similar to the Quick Setup Wizard, but you type your responses on the command line. To use MVSETUP, type **mvsetup** on the command line. AutoCAD responds with the following prompt:

```
Units type (Scientific / Decimal / Engineering /
Architectural / Metric):
```

Choose the option you want. Then AutoCAD displays a list of scale factors appropriate to the units option you chose. At the `Enter the scale factor:` prompt, type in a scale factor.

Finally, AutoCAD prompts you to set the drawing limits with the following two prompts:

```
Enter the paper width:
Enter the paper height:
```

After each prompt, enter a number based on the size of the paper you plan to plot on. AutoCAD draws a rectangle of the size you indicated for the drawing limits.

Summary

In this chapter you learned all about setting up a drawing so that it behaves the way you want it to. You can use Release 14's new Quick or Advanced Setup Wizards to walk you through the process. Setting the unit type is an important setup task. You should also set the limits of a drawing before starting to draw. When starting to draw, you need to consider the scale you will use to plot the drawing. AutoCAD uses system variables to change and store most settings. You can also use MVSETUP to set up a drawing.

This chapter ends Part I on AutoCAD Basics. Now that you know the basics, you can go on to Part II, Drawing in Two Dimensions. The next chapter covers drawing simple lines, polygons, rectangles, and special infinite construction lines.

✦   ✦   ✦

Drawing in Two Dimensions

Now that you have the basics under your belt, it's time to draw. In Part II you learn the techniques for basic drawing and editing in AutoCAD. After chapters on drawing simple lines and curves, I explain the details of how to control the display of your drawings. There are also chapters on text and dimensioning. Separate chapters cover getting information from your drawing and drawing complex objects. Part II winds up with a chapter on plotting and printing.

Drawing Simple Lines

The LINE Command

If you have been reading through this book from the beginning, you have already drawn a lot of lines while learning the
basics of AutoCAD. However, you can still learn a few tricks of
the trade by focusing on the LINE command itself.

To draw a line, choose Line from the Draw toolbar. At the
`From point:` prompt, specify any point. Continue to specify
points until you are finished. Press Enter (or use the right
mouse button) to end the command.

The LINE command is one of those commands that assumes
you will continue to use it over and over. For this reason,
AutoCAD repeats the `From point:` prompt until you press
Enter.

Most commands show all their options on the command line
or in a dialog box. The LINE command, however, has three
hidden but essential options, described in Table 6-1.

Table 6-1	
LINE Command Options	
Option	*Description*
Undo	After creating any line segment, type **u** ↵ (for undo) to undo only the last line segment you created — without exiting the LINE command.
Close	After creating at least three line segments, type **c** ↵ (for close) to automatically draw a line from the endpoint of the last segment to the original start point, thereby creating a closed figure.
↵	If you previously drew a line, press Enter at the From point: prompt to start the line at the endpoint of the last line. If you most recently drew an arc, press Enter to start the line at the endpoint of the arc and draw it tangent to the arc.

Step-by-Step: Using the LINE Command

1. Start a new drawing using the Start from Scratch option.

2. Save the drawing in your *AutoCAD Bible* folder as *ab6-1.dwg*.

3. Start the LINE command. At the From point: prompt, choose any point in the center of your drawing.

4. Double-click ORTHO on the status bar.

5. Move the cursor to the right in the 0° direction and type **.4667** ↵.

6. Type **@.7341<129** ↵.

7. Move the cursor to the right in the 0° direction and type **.4668** ↵.

8. That was a mistake. Type **u** ↵.

9. The To point: prompt reappears. With the cursor still in the 0° direction, type **.4667** ↵.

10. Type **c** ↵ to close the figure. This ends the LINE command.

11. Start the LINE command again.

12. At the From point: prompt, press Enter. The line starts at the previous endpoint.

13. Type **@.8071<270** ↵ and press Enter or the right mouse button to end the LINE command.

14. Save your drawing. It should look similar to Figure 6-1.

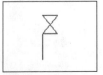

Figure 6-1: The completed gate valve schematic.

Spotlight on AutoCAD Users:
Military mapping with AutoCAD

The Transportation Engineering Agency (TEA) is a small federal agency in eastern Virginia. TEA assists other military agencies with preliminary planning to deploy Army vehicles and equipment overseas. TEA publishes the Ports for National Defense Publications, reports that provide overview information and maps to help military agencies select seaports. The reports also suggest what equipment and personnel military port operators should bring to the port, and what type of equipment the seaport can easily handle. The maps do not need to be as precise as most maps since their purpose is to show the general features of each port.

To begin the reports, TEA project engineers visit the seaports to gather maps, photographs, videotape, and brochures. They next mark up the maps in the brochures or from reference books and pass these copies to illustrators. TEA computer illustrators scan the maps and trace roads, cranes, railroad tracks, parking areas, and buildings onto the scanned drawing. TEA typically uses AutoCAD's main competitor, MicroStation, to make maps for these reports.

Recently, project engineer Paul Burgener realized that time was lost marking and proof-reading hard copies passed back and forth between project engineers and illustrators. Paul's idea was to digitize and annotate the maps with AutoCAD. He places an original map on a digitizing tablet and uses the puck to draw over the lines of the map. With the help of Mountain Software's Vector™ AutoCAD add-on program, Paul develops ready-to-publish maps, complete with solid-fill coloring. The map shown here is an example. Paul also creates the text with bold TrueType™ fonts. (Mountain Software can be reached by e-mail at jerry@mtnsoft.com, by phone at 304-746-0246, or at its Web site at http://www.mtnsoft.com.)

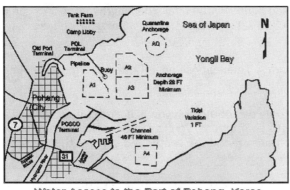

Water Access to the Port of Pohang, Korea

After Paul exports the maps as Windows Metafiles (.WMF format), TEA's layout artists easily import them into Microsoft Word for Windows™ and FrameMaker™ for desktop publishing.

Credit: Thanks to Paul Burgener for this account. He can be reached by e-mail at burgener@bigfoot.com.

Chapter 11 explains how to draw dashed and dotted lines. Chapter 16 explains how to create polylines, which combine lines segments and curves into one object. Chapter 16 also covers multilines — sets of parallel lines that you draw all at once.

Rectangles

 Use the RECTANG command to create a rectangle by specifying the two diagonal corners. Choose Rectangle from the Draw toolbar.

AutoCAD prompts you for the two corners and creates the rectangle. You can specify the two corners using any method of specifying coordinates. For example, if you know the rectangle should be 6" wide and 3" high, you can specify the second point as @6,3.

 In Release 14, the RECTANG command has several new options. You can chamfer and fillet the corners as you create the rectangle. Chamfering and Filleting are covered in Chapter 10. You can also create a 3D box using the Elevation, Thickness, and Width options (see Chapters 21 and 23). In most cases, you simply specify two corners and create a two-dimensional rectangle.

 The RECTANG command creates a polyline, meaning that all four sides of the rectangle are one object, instead of four separate line objects. Polylines are covered in Chapter 16.

Polygons

 Polygons are multisided closed figures with equal side lengths. AutoCAD can draw polygons with anything from 3 to 1,024 sides. To draw a polygon, choose Polygon from the Draw toolbar.

First choose the number of sides. Then choose one of three methods of defining the polygon, as described in Table 6-2.

If you type a radius, the bottom edge of the polygon is horizontal. However, if you pick a point for the radius with your mouse, you can choose the orientation of the polygon. Rotate the mouse cursor around the center and you see the polygon rotate. Pick when you like what you see.

 Actually, when you type a radius, the bottom edge aligns with the snap rotation angle, which is usually 0. Chapter 8 explains how to change this angle.

The POLYGON command creates a polyline, meaning that the entire polygon is one object, rather than a series of line segments.

Table 6-2
POLYGON Command Options

Option	Description
Edge	Type e ↵ to choose the Edge option and specify the two endpoints of any edge of the polygon. AutoCAD completes the polygon.
Inscribed in circle	After specifying the center, type **i** ↵, and specify the radius from the center to a vertex (point). This defines the polygon with reference to an imaginary circle whose circumference touches all the vertices of the polygon.
Circumscribed about circle	After specifying the center, type **c** ↵, and specify the radius from the center to the midpoint of a side. This defines the polygon with reference to an imaginary circle whose circumference touches all the midpoints of the polygon's sides.

Tip

In the exercise that follows, I indicate inches with a double-prime (") and feet with a prime ('). It is not necessary to type the double-prime for inches, but you may find it clearer when a measurement has both feet and inches. When you have a measurement that is only in inches, it saves time to leave out the double-prime.

Step-by-Step: Drawing Rectangles and Polygons

On the CD-ROM

1. Open *ab6-a.dwg* from the CD-ROM.

2. Save the drawing in your *AutoCAD Bible* folder as *ab6-2.dwg.* Verify that snap and grid are on, set at 1″.

3. Choose Rectangle from the Draw toolbar.

4. At the `Chamfer/Elevation/Fillet/Thickness/Width/<First corner>:` prompt, move the cursor to 1'0″,1'0″ and click. At the `Other corner:` prompt, type **@2'1″,1'9″** ↵.

5. Start the RECTANG command again. At the `Chamfer/Elevation/Fillet/Thickness/Width/<First corner>:` prompt, press Shift + the right mouse button and choose the From object snap. Shift + right-click again and choose the Endpoint object snap. Pick the bottom left corner of the rectangle. At the `Offset:` prompt, type **@2,2** ↵ to start the second rectangle 2″ up and 2″ to the right of the first rectangle.

6. At the `Other corner:` prompt, type **@1'9″,1'3″** ↵.

7. Click the right mouse button to start the RECTANG command again. At the prompt, find 1'7",2'6" (on a snap point) and click. At the `Other corner:` prompt, type **@11",2"** ↵.

8. Again start the RECTANG command. At the prompt, find 2"0",2'7" and click. At the `Other corner:` prompt, type **@1,-5** ↵. (You don't need to type the double-prime for inches.)

9. Start the POLYGON command. At the `Number of sides:<4>:` prompt, type **5** ↵. At the `Edge/<Center of polygon>:` prompt, type **1'9",2'7"** ↵ to indicate the center.

10. At the `Inscribed in circle/Circumscribed about circle (I/C) <I>:` prompt, press Enter to accept the default. This means you indicate the radius from the center to the vertices. (If your prompt shows <C> as the default, type **i** ↵.)

11. At the `Radius of circle:` prompt, type **.5** ↵. AutoCAD draws the pentagon.

12. Repeat steps 9–11, using a center of 2'4",2'7".

13. Start the POLYGON command again. At the `Number of sides <5>:` prompt, type **3** ↵.

14. At the `Edge/<Center of polygon>:` prompt, type **e** ↵ to choose the Edge option.

15. At the `First endpoint of edge:` prompt, choose the top-left corner of the faucet rectangle (2'0",2'7"), which is on a snap point.

16. At the `Second endpoint of edge:` prompt, choose the top-right corner of the faucet rectangle. AutoCAD completes the triangle.

17. Turn off the grid to get a better look at the drawing. You have completed the sink, which should look like Figure 6-2.

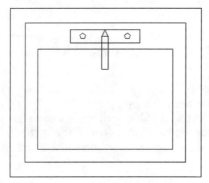

Figure 6-2: The completed sink, drawn using rectangles and polygons.

Credit: Thanks to Bill Wynn of New Windsor, Md., for this drawing, which he created in his AutoCAD class as part of a plan drawing of an entire house.

Construction Lines

Sometimes you want to create a line that is used solely for the purpose of reference. For example, you might want to

◆ Draw two lines from the midpoint of two perpendicular lines so that you can use their intersection as the center for a circle;

◆ Draw a line from one object to another to indicate visually the relationship between the two objects;

◆ Draw lines to find the center of a polygon so you can draw a line from that center;

◆ Draw a line through the center of an object shown in cross-section so you can show dimensions from the center line to the edge of an object.

You could use regular lines for these purposes. However, construction lines (also known as *xlines*) are unique in that they extend infinitely in both directions. This makes them especially useful in seeing the relationships among various objects in your drawing.

Of course, construction lines are not actually infinite. However, they extend to the edge of the drawing area on your screen, and if you zoom out to see more of your drawing, they expand so that they always extend to the edge of the screen.

Note

If you zoom to show the extent of your drawing, AutoCAD ignores the xlines and shows you just the extents of the regular objects in your drawing. The ZOOM command is covered in Chapter 8.

Cross-Reference

Construction lines are especially helpful when working in 3D. See Part IV of this book.

The XLINE command offers several ways to create construction lines. Start the command by choosing Construction Line from the Draw toolbar. You see the following prompt:

```
Hor/Ver/Ang/Bisect/Offset/<From point>:
```

Table 6-3 lists the possible options. AutoCAD continues to prompt you for more points so that you can continue to draw construction lines. This is similar to the LINE command.

Table 6-3 XLINE Command Options	
Option	**Description**
From point	This option lets you define the xline with two points. At the `From point:` prompt, choose a point. At the Through point: prompt, specify another point.
Hor	To draw a construction line parallel to the X axis, type **h** ↵ to choose the Horizontal option. AutoCAD responds with the `Through point:` prompt. Specify one point.
Ver	To draw a construction line parallel to the Y axis, type **v** ↵ to choose the Vertical option. AutoCAD responds with the `Through point:` prompt. Specify one point.
Ang	Type **a** ↵ (for Angle). AutoCAD responds with the `Reference/<Enter angle (0)>:` prompt. If you enter an angle, AutoCAD asks for a through point. Or you can type **r** ↵ and choose a line as a reference, then provide an angle and a through point. AutoCAD calculates the angle of the construction line from the angle of the reference line.
Bisect	To draw a construction line that bisects (lies in the middle of) an angle, type **b** ↵. AutoCAD responds with the `Angle vertex point:` prompt. Choose any point that you want the construction line to pass through. Then at the `Angle start point:` prompt, choose a point that defines the base of the angle. At the `Angle end point:` prompt, choose a point that defines the end of the angle.
Offset	To draw a construction line parallel to a line, type **o** ↵. You can specify the offset distance by typing in a number or use the Through option to pick a point through which the construction line should pass. Either way, the next step is to select a line. If you specified an offset distance, AutoCAD asks `Side to offset?`. Respond by picking a point on the side of the base line on which you want the construction line to appear.

Rays

Rays are similar to construction lines, except they start at a specific point and extend to infinity in one direction only. If you need a line to extend only in one direction, using a ray may be less confusing.

To draw a ray, choose Draw⇨Ray. At the `From point:` prompt, specify the start point for the ray. At the `Through point:` prompt, specify another point. AutoCAD continues to ask for through points. Press Enter to end the command.

You can use object snaps with construction lines and rays. Construction lines and rays can be edited like any other objects.

Step-by-Step: Drawing Construction Lines and Rays

On the CD-ROM

1. Open *ab6-b.dwg* from the CD-ROM. This drawing is similar to the pipe you drew in Chapter 4. A simple cross-section view has been added.

2. Save the drawing as *ab6-3.dwg* in your *AutoCAD Bible* folder.

3. Choose Construction Line from the Draw toolbar.

4. At the `From point:` prompt, choose point ①, shown in Figure 6-3.

5. At the `Through point:` prompt, choose point ②, shown in Figure 6-3.

6. Press Enter to end the command. Notice that the construction line is drawn in green and with a noncontinuous linetype. This is to distinguish it from the main drawing.

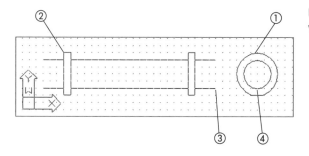

Figure 6-3: The pipe with cross-section.

7. Choose Draw⇨Ray.

8. At the `From point:` prompt, choose point ③, shown in Figure 6-3.

9. At the `Through point:` prompt, choose point ④, shown in Figure 6-3.

10. Save your drawing.

Summary

This chapter covered all the ins and outs of lines — including how to draw lines, rectangles, polygons, construction lines (xlines), and rays.

The next chapter explains how to draw curves and point objects. Curves include circles, arcs, ellipses, and donuts (sometimes called doughnuts).

✦   ✦   ✦

Drawing Curves and Point Objects

Curved Objects

AutoCAD offers a number of ways to create curved objects. You can draw circles, arcs, ellipses, and donuts (also called doughnuts). In this chapter I also cover point objects which are neither curves nor lines, but don't deserve their own chapter.

Cross-Reference Several complex objects involve curves, such as polylines, splines, regions, and boundaries. These are covered in Chapter 16.

Circles

Circles are common objects in drawings. In mechanical drawings, they often represent holes or wheels. In architectural drawings, they may be used for doorknobs, trash baskets, or trees. In electrical drawings they are used for various kinds of symbols.

Understanding the circle options

 AutoCAD provides five ways to draw a circle. To draw a circle, choose Circle from the Draw toolbar. AutoCAD responds with the 3P/2P/TTR/<Center point>: prompt. Table 7-1 describes how to use these options.

Table 7-1
Five Ways to Draw a Circle

Option	Description
Center Radius	This is the default. Specify the center and then the radius. You can type the radius as a distance or pick a point on the circumference.
Center Diameter	Specify the center. Type **d** ↵ and type the length of the diameter.
2P	2P stands for 2 point. Type **2p** ↵. Specify one point on the circumference, then an opposite point on the circumference. These two points define the diameter of the circle.
3P	3P stands for 3 point. Type **3p** ↵. Specify three points on the circumference.
Tangent, Tangent, Radius	Type **t** or **ttr** ↵. AutoCAD prompts Enter Tangent spec: and provides an aperture to let you pick a point. Then AutoCAD prompts Enter second Tangent spec: and you pick a second point. These points can be any points on the object(s) you want your circle to be tangent to. Finally, type in a radius.

Tip   You can also create a circle tangent to other objects by using the 2-point (2P) or 3-point (3P) method and picking those points with the Tangent object snap.

Drawing circles

Drawing circles is fairly straightforward. Often you can use object snaps to define part of the circle. The following exercise uses the most common methods of creating a circle.

Step-by-Step: Drawing Circles

On the CD-ROM

1. Open *ab7-a.dwg* from the CD-ROM.

2. Save the file as *ab7-1.dwg* in your *AutoCAD Bible* folder. This is a drawing of an air compressor from which all the circles have been removed. OSNAP is on and a running object snap is set for endpoints.

3. Choose Circle from the Draw toolbar. Type **2p** ↵. At the First point on diameter: prompt, pick the endpoint at ① in Figure 7-1. At the Second point on diameter: prompt, pick the endpoint at ②.

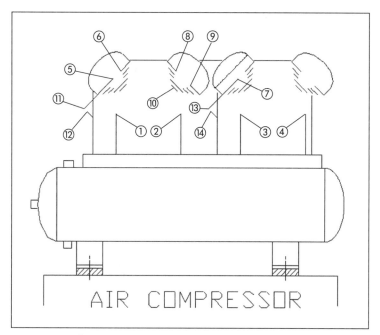

Figure 7-1: The air compressor without its circles.

4. Repeat the CIRCLE command by pressing the right mouse button. Type **2p** ↵. Pick the endpoints at ③ and ④ in Figure 7-1.

5. Repeat the CIRCLE command by pressing the right mouse button. At the 3P/2P/TTR/<Center point>: prompt, pick the endpoint at ⑤. At the Diameter/<Radius>: prompt, pick the endpoint at ⑥.

6. Repeat the CIRCLE command by pressing the right mouse button. At the 3P/2P/TTR/<Center point>: prompt, pick the endpoint at ⑦. At the Diameter/<Radius>: prompt, type **d** ↵, then type **.25** ↵.

7. Repeat the CIRCLE command by pressing the right mouse button. At the 3P/2P/TTR/<Center point>: prompt, type **3p** ↵. At the First point: prompt, pick the endpoint at ⑧ in Figure 7-1. At the Second point: prompt, pick the endpoint at ⑨. At the Third point: prompt, choose the Midpoint object snap and pick the midpoint ⑩.

8. For the last circle on the right, choose any method you wish to draw a circle. The circle should be the same size and placement as the second circle from the left.

9. Repeat the CIRCLE command. At the 3P/2P/TTR/<Center point>: prompt, choose the Center object snap and pick anywhere on the circumference of the circle whose center is ⑦. At the Diameter/<Radius>: prompt, type **.05** ↵.

10. Repeat step 9 to create a circle inside the circle whose center is ⑤ and whose radius is .05.

11. Repeat the CIRCLE command. At the `3P/2P/TTR/<Center point>:` prompt, pick the endpoint at ⑪. At the `Diameter/<Radius>:` prompt, pick the endpoint at ⑫.

12. Repeat step 11, choosing the endpoint at ⑬ for the center of the circle and the endpoint at ⑭ for its radius, as shown in Figure 7-1.

13. Save your drawing. It should look like Figure 7-2.

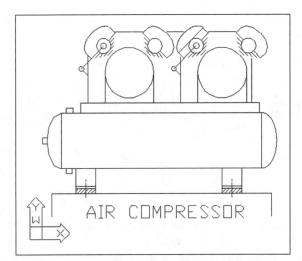

Figure 7-2: The completed air compressor.

Credit: Thanks to the U.S. Army Corps of Engineers at Vicksburg, Mississippi, for this drawing. They maintain a Web site of drawings at `http://cadlib.wes.army.mil`.

Cross-Reference

It may have occurred to you that this task would have been easier if you could simply have copied one circle to another location instead of creating it from scratch each time. I cover copying in Chapter 9.

Arcs

An arc is a portion of a circle. Therefore, to define an arc, you not only have to define a circle — for example, by specifying a center and a radius — but you must define the start and end points of the arc as well. This can be done in many ways. AutoCAD offers several methods of defining an arc. The method you pick depends on the information you have about the arc you want to draw.

Understanding arc options

There are many arc options. Making sense of them may seem overwhelming, but once you understand the parts of an arc and AutoCAD's terminology, you can choose the options that suit your needs. Only three pieces of information define an arc. The parts of an arc are shown in Figure 7-3. Refer to these parts as you read through the arc options.

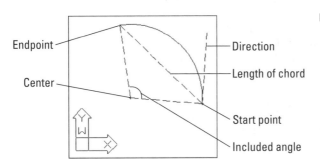

Figure 7-3: The parts of an arc.

Figure 7-4 shows the flow of the arc options. When you start the ARC command, you have two options, Start point and Center. Depending on which you choose, more options become available.

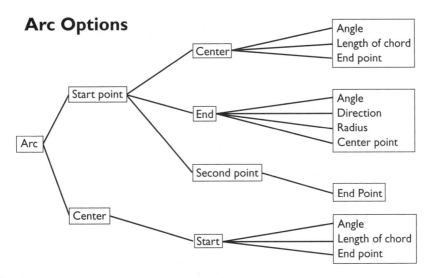

Figure 7-4: The ARC command options.

You can also press Enter at the first arc prompt to draw a second arc starting from the endpoint of a previous arc. The new arc continues in the same direction as the end of the first arc. The only other prompt is the endpoint.

Drawing arcs

To draw an arc, choose Arc from the Draw toolbar and follow the prompts. As with circles, object snaps are often helpful when drawing arcs.

When drawing an arc using the Start, End, and Radius options, the three specifications actually define two possible arcs, one minor and one major. AutoCAD draws the minor arc by default. (A minor arc is less than half a circle.) If you enter a negative number for the radius, AutoCAD draws the major arc.

The options requiring an angle also define two possible arcs, one drawn counter-clockwise and one drawn clockwise. AutoCAD draws the counter-clockwise arc by default. If you enter a negative number for the angle, AutoCAD draws the arc clockwise.

Step-by-Step: Drawing Arcs

1. Open *ab7-b.dwg* from the CD-ROM.

2. Save it as *ab7-2.dwg* in your *AutoCAD Bible* folder. ORTHO is on and units are set to Fractional. OSNAP is on and running object snaps are set for intersection, center, and endpoint. In this exercise you draw part of the sealing plate shown in Figure 7-5.

3. Start the LINE command. Start at 2,3 and use Direct Distance Entry to create a 7-unit horizontal line to the right. End the LINE command.

Cross-
Reference

4. Draw another line starting at 5-1/2,1-5/8 and draw it 2-3/4 units long in the 90-degree direction. These two lines are construction lines and would ordinarily appear in a different color and linetype than the object you are drawing. (You learn about colors and linetypes in Chapter 11.)

5. Draw a circle with its center at the intersection of the two lines (use the Intersection object snap) and a radius of 11/16.

6. Use the Center object snap to draw another circle with the same center as the first circle and a radius of 1.

7. Draw a third circle. Choose the From object snap from the shortcut menu. Use the Center object snap and pick either of the first two circles you drew. The offset is @-1-15/16,0. (That means 1-15/16 units to the left of the center of the first two circles.) Its radius is 3/8.

8. Draw a fourth circle. Choose the From object snap from the shortcut menu. Use the Center object snap and pick either of the first two circles. The offset is @1-15/16,0. The radius is 3/8.

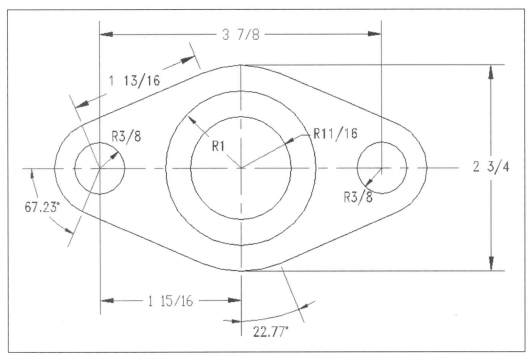

Figure 7-5: The dimensioned sealing plate for a valve.

Credit: Thanks to Jerry Bottenfield of Clow Valve Company in Oskaloosa, Iowa, for this drawing.

9. Choose Arc from the Draw toolbar. Follow the prompts:

```
Center/<Start point>: Choose the From object snap.
Base point: Use the Center object snap to pick the center of the left-
most circle.
<Offset>: @-5/8,0 ↵
Center/End/<Second point>: c ↵    Use the Center object snap to pick
the center of the leftmost circle.
Angle/Length of chord/<End point>: a ↵
Included angle: 67.23 ↵
```

10. Start the LINE command. At the `From point:` prompt, press Enter to continue the line in the same direction as the end of the arc. At the `Length of line:` prompt, type **1-13/16** ↵.

11. Choose Arc from the Draw toolbar. Follow the prompts:

```
Center/<Start point>: Use the Endpoint object snap to pick the end of
the line you just drew.
Center/End/<Second point>: c ↵ Use the Center object snap and pick
any point on one of the large central circles.
Angle/Length of chord/<End point>: Use Endpoint object snap to pick
the lower end of the vertical construction line.
```

12. Repeat the ARC command. Follow the prompts:

```
Center/<Start point>: c ↵ Use the Center object snap and pick any
point on one of the large central circles.
Start point: Use the Endpoint object snap to pick the endpoint of the arc
you just completed.
Angle/Length of chord/<End point>: a ↵
Included angle: 22.77 ↵
```

13. Start the LINE command. At the `From point:` prompt, press Enter to continue the line in the same direction as the end of the arc. At the `Length of line:` prompt, type **1-13/16** ↵.

14. Start the ARC command. Follow the prompts:

```
Center/<Start point>: Use the Endpoint object snap to pick the end-
point of the line you just drew.
Center/End/<Second point>: e ↵
End point: Choose the From object snap.
_from Base point: Use the Center object snap to pick the center of the
rightmost circle.
<Offset>: @5/8,0 ↵
Angle/Direction/Radius/<Center point>: r ↵
Radius: 5/8 ↵
```

15. Save your drawing. You will complete this drawing in Chapter 10 by creating a mirror image. Your drawing should look like Figure 7-6.

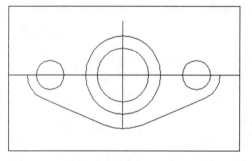

Figure 7-6: The partially completed sealing plate, created using lines, circles, and arcs.

Ellipses and Elliptical Arcs

AutoCAD provides three options for creating ellipses. You can also create elliptical arcs, which are simply partial ellipses.

Like a circle, an ellipse has a center. The difference, of course, is that an ellipse has a longer radius along its major axis and a shorter radius along its minor axis, as shown in Figure 7-7.

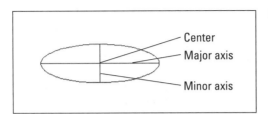

Figure 7-7: The parts of an ellipse.

Understanding ellipse options

You can draw ellipses by defining a center first. Another option is to define the axis endpoints first. If you want to draw an elliptical arc, you must specify the start and end angle.

Ellipses

The default option is to specify endpoints 1 and 2 of the first axis. Then you specify the second axis distance, which is the radius from the first axis line to the circumference along the second axis. Instead of specifying a second axis distance, you can choose the Rotation option. The rotation option defines the minor axis by defining an angle from 0 degrees to 90 degrees, which is the ratio of the major axis to the minor axis. (Actually, AutoCAD only accepts up to 89.4 degrees.) When the angle is 0, you get a circle. As the angle increases, the ellipse gets flatter and flatter until you reach 89.4 degrees. A 45-degree angle results in a minor axis whose length is the square root of the major axis length.

Instead of specifying endpoints, you can type **c** to specify the center of the ellipse. Then specify the endpoint of the first axis, which can be either the major or the minor axis. Finally, specify the other axis distance, which is the radius from the center to the circumference along the second axis. Again, instead of specifying the second axis distance, you can define the ellipse using the rotation option.

Elliptical arcs

To draw an elliptical arc, choose the Arc option. The first prompts are the same as for an ellipse, because you must first define the ellipse. Then AutoCAD continues with the Parameter/<start angle>: prompt, offering the following options:

Start angle	This is the default. Specify the start angle, which AutoCAD redefines along the major axis. AutoCAD responds with the Parameter/Included/<end angle>: prompt.
End angle	Specify the end angle to complete the ellipse arc.
Included angle	After specifying the start angle, you can complete the arc by specifying the included angle.

Parameter   Choose this option to define the arc portion by the ellipse's area rather than its included angle (which defines the arc portion by its circumference). AutoCAD responds with the `start parameter:` and `end parameter:` prompts. By typing in angles, you define the percent of the full ellipse's area that you want to include. (For example, starting at 15 degrees and ending at 105 degrees includes 90 degrees. AutoCAD then draws 1/4 of an ellipse.) AutoCAD also offers options to return to regular angle specification.

Drawing ellipses

To draw an ellipse, choose Ellipse from the Draw toolbar.

Besides the information AutoCAD explicitly requests in the prompts, you need to know the angle of the first axis you define. Not all ellipses are horizontal or vertical. You specify this when you specify the second point of the first axis. The second axis is automatically perpendicular to the first axis.

When you draw an elliptical arc, AutoCAD introduces a helpful but sometimes confusing feature. While you are defining the arc angles, AutoCAD redefines 0 degrees along the major axis. This helps you define the included angle in an orientation that relates to the ellipse, rather than the usual orientation where 0 degrees is to the right.

Step-by-Step: Drawing Ellipses and Elliptical Arcs

On the CD-ROM

1. Open *ab7-c.dwg* from the CD-ROM.

2. Save it as *ab7-3.dwg* in your *AutoCAD Bible* folder. The drawing shows an empty conference room. Snap is on, set to 6". OSNAP is on with a running object snap set for endpoints.

3. Choose Ellipse from the Draw toolbar. At the `Arc/Center/<Axis endpoint 1>:` prompt, type **c** ↵. At the `Center of ellipse:` prompt, choose 8',10', which is a snap point. At the `Axis endpoint:` prompt, move the cursor to the right until the coordinates read 3'<0 and pick. (If necessary, press F6 until you see polar coordinates.) At the `<Other axis distance>/Rotation:` prompt, move the cursor up until the coordinates read 6'6"<90 and pick. This completes the conference table.

4. Repeat the ELLIPSE command. Follow the prompts:

```
Arc/Center/<Axis endpoint 1>: a ↵
<Axis endpoint 1>/Center: c ↵
Center of ellipse: Pick 8',3', a snap point.
Axis endpoint: Move the cursor to the right until the coordi-
nates read 1'<0 and pick.
<Other axis distance>/Rotation: Move the cursor up until the
coordinates read 6"<90 and pick.
Parameter/<start angle>: 162 ↵
Parameter/Included/<end angle>: 18 ↵
```

5. Turn off ORTHO. Start the LINE command. At the `From point:` prompt, use the Endpoint object snap and pick the right side of the elliptical arc. At the `To point:` prompt, press F6 to change to absolute coordinates (if necessary) and pick the snap point 8'6",3'. End the LINE command.

6. Start the LINE command. At the `From point:` prompt, choose the Endpoint object snap and pick the left side of the ellipse arc. At the `To point:` prompt, pick the snap point 7'6",3'. End the LINE command.

7. Start the ELLIPSE command again. Follow the prompts:

```
Arc/Center/<Axis endpoint 1>: a ↵
<Axis endpoint 1>/Center: Use the Endpoint object snap to
pick the endpoint of the line on the right.
Axis endpoint 2: Use the Endpoint object snap to pick the
endpoint of the line on the left.
<Other axis distance>/Rotation: @3<90 ↵
Parameter/<start angle>: Use the Endpoint object snap to pick
the endpoint of the line on the right.
Parameter/Included/<end angle>: Use Endpoint object snap to
pick the endpoint of the line on the left.
```

8. Choose Ellipse from the Draw toolbar. At the `Arc/Center/<Axis endpoint 1>:` prompt, pick point 2',18', a snap point. At the `Axis endpoint 2:` prompt, pick point 2',16', also a snap point. At the `<Other axis distance> /Rotation:` prompt, move the cursor to the right until the coordinates read 6"<0 (also a snap point) and pick. This completes the small side table.

9. Your drawing should look like Figure 7-8. Save your drawing.

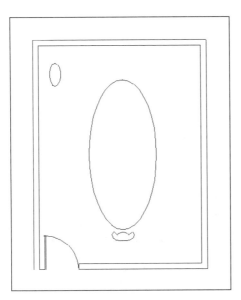

Figure 7-8: The conference room with a conference table, a chair, and a side table.

Donuts

A donut consists of a pair of concentric circles. The circles have the same center, but you define a diameter for each. AutoCAD accepts both DONUT and DOUGH-NUT if you type in the command. Donuts are often used in electrical drawings and to create symbols. They can also represent holes in an object. If the inner circle's radius is zero, you create a circle.

The setting of the FILL command determines whether AutoCAD fills in the donut. Type **fill** ↵ and type **on** ↵ or **off** ↵. Fill is on by default. Turning FILL off creates a radial pattern of lines, as shown in Figure 7-9.

Tip

If you have many filled objects in your drawing, AutoCAD may need to take some time to display the drawing. You can save time by turning FILL off while you draw. Then turn FILL on just before you need to print or plot the drawing.

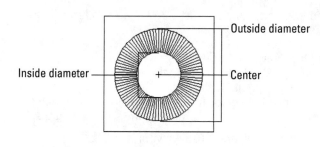

Figure 7-9: The parts of a donut, shown with FILL off.

Understanding DONUT options

The DONUT command has the following prompts:

`Inside diameter <0.5000>:`	Type the diameter of the inside circle. The number in brackets is the diameter of the last inside circle you defined.
`Outside diameter <1.0000>:`	Type the diameter of the outside circle. The number in brackets is the diameter of the last outside circle you defined.
`Second point:`	If you define the inside or outside diameter by picking a point, AutoCAD asks for a second point. Use this technique if you are using object snaps to define the diameters.
`Center of doughnut:`	Specify the center of the donut.

AutoCAD calls the command *Donut* on the menu but uses the spelling *doughnut* in the `Center of doughnut` command option.

Drawing donuts

Drawing donuts is quite easy in AutoCAD. Choose Draw⇨Donut. Then specify the inner and outer diameters and the center. AutoCAD continues to prompt for centers so you can place additional donuts. Press Enter to end the command.

In Release 14, you can use the hatch feature to fill in any object with a solid fill. (Hatching is discussed in Chapter 16.) As a result, the DONUT command is not as essential as it once was. However, it is still an easy way to create filled circles and donut shapes.

You draw some donuts in the next Step-by-Step exercise.

Points

Points are used for reference. For example, you may want to indicate the center of a circle, arc, or ellipse in your drawing. Sometimes, it is helpful to mark a point that you use later as a guide to place another object. Then you may erase the point. This is a typical construction method. In some cases, the From object snap or Tracking can be used instead of a point. However, often it is simpler to create a point first and use it in the next command.

The DIVIDE and MEASURE commands place point objects along an object. These commands are covered in Chapter 12.

Changing the point style

Different disciplines have different conventions for drawing point objects. As a result, AutoCAD provides 20 types of point styles that you can use in your drawing. Before you draw a point, you should set the point style. This setting can be saved in your template.

Choose Format⇨Point Style to open the Point Style dialog box, shown in Figure 7-10.

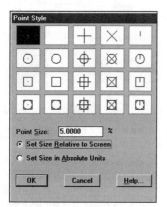

Figure 7-10: Choosing a point style.

To set the point style, click the box showing the style you want. Then set the point size, which has the following options:

✦ **Set Size Relative to Screen:** Use this option if you want the point to always appear the same size, no matter how much you zoom in and out — for example when you are using the point as a reference. The size is set as a percentage of the screen. This option is the default, with the size set to 5% of the screen.

✦ **Set Size in Absolute Units:** Use this option if you want the point to have a real size, just like any other object. The size is set in units. Use this option when you want the point to stay the same size relative to other objects in your drawing.

Click OK to close the dialog box.

Creating points

Once you have determined the point style, you are ready to create points. Choose Point from the Draw toolbar.

You see the following on the command line:

```
_point Point:
```

This just means that AutoCAD executes the POINT command whose prompt is Point:. Specify the point you want, either by picking a point on the screen or typing coordinates. You can use object snaps to specify the point.

AutoCAD automatically repeats the Point: prompt so you can continue to specify points. Press Esc to end the command. (Pressing Enter doesn't work.)

Once you have created a point, use the Node object snap to snap to the point.

Note

If BLIPMODE is on, and you are using the first point style — a small dot — you cannot see the point until you use the REDRAW command to remove the blips. Choose Redraw on the Standard toolbar.

Tip

If you are using the points for temporary reference, instead of erasing them you can set the point style to the second style — no dot — before plotting. The points do not appear on your plot.

When you change the point style, previously drawn points do not automatically change to the new style. However, the REGEN command, covered in Chapter 8, changes all previously drawn points to the new style.

Step-by-Step: Drawing Donuts and Points

On the CD-ROM

1. Open *ab7-d.dwg* from the CD-ROM.

2. Save it as *ab7-4.dwg* in your *AutoCAD Bible* folder. The drawing contains a rectangle and connecting wires for an electrical switch. OSNAP is on. Running object snaps are set for Endpoint, Quadrant, Center, and Node.

3. Choose Format⇨Point Style. The Point Style dialog box opens. Choose the third point type, the cross. The radio button Set Size Relative to Screen should be marked. The Point Size should be 5.0000%. Choose OK.

4. Choose Point from the Draw toolbar. Follow the prompts:

```
Point: Choose the From object snap from the shortcut menu.
Base point: Use the Endpoint object snap to pick the top left corner of
the rectangle.
<Offset>: @.08,-.09 ↵
```

   AutoCAD places the point. Press Esc to end the command.

5. Choose Draw⇨Donut. Follow these prompts:

```
Inside diameter <0.0000>: .04 ↵
Outside diameter <0.5000>: .06 ↵
Center of doughnut: Use the Node object snap to pick the point you
drew.
Center of doughnut: @.19,0 ↵
Center of doughnut: ↵
```

6. Start the POINT command again. Follow the prompts:

```
Point: .x ↵
of  Use the Center object snap to pick the center of the righthand donut.
(need YZ):  Pick a point about halfway between the right donut and the
bottom of the rectangle, as shown in Figure
7-11.
```

7. Start the LINE command. Follow the prompts:

```
From point: Use the Quadrant object snap to pick the right (0 degrees)
quadrant of the left donut. If you don't see the Quadrant SnapTip, press
Tab until it appears.
To point: Use the Node object snap to pick the point you
just drew.
```

8. Press Enter to end the command.

9. Save your drawing. It should look like Figure 7-11.

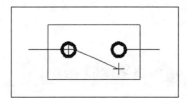

Figure 7-11: The completed electrical switch. The points show as crosses.

Summary

In this chapter you learned how to draw curved objects in AutoCAD.

Circles are probably the most common curved object. You can define circles in five ways. An arc is a part of a circle. Defining an arc is more complex than defining a circle because you must specify where the arc begins and ends.

You define an ellipse by specifying a major axis and a minor axis or, alternately, a center, a major axis radius, and a minor axis radius. AutoCAD can also draw an elliptical arc. First you define the ellipse, then the angle of the ellipse that you want to draw.

Donuts (or doughnuts) are two concentric circles. The space between the circles is filled by default. You define the inner and outer diameters and then the center point.

Points are often used as a construction technique or to mark objects for reference. First choose the point style and size. Then specify the coordinates for the point by picking on the screen or typing.

In the next chapter you learn how to display your drawing for the greatest ease and comfort.

✦   ✦   ✦

Viewing Your Drawing

AutoCAD's Display

By now, if you have been following along, you may have wished you could zoom in to see a particular part of a drawing more closely. You have already used the ZOOM command a few times. In this chapter you learn how to control the display of your drawing to meet all your drawing needs and increase productivity.

Understanding how AutoCAD displays drawings

In order to understand the display options, it helps to know something about how AutoCAD creates the display on your screen.

AutoCAD is a vector program, which means that it stores information about objects in your drawing in terms of coordinates and equations. This information is stored in your drawing's database. However, your screen displays information in terms of tiny dots called pixels. To display your drawing, AutoCAD converts the vector information in the drawing's database to pixels. When you change the drawing display significantly, AutoCAD has to reconvert the object data to pixels, recalculating the coordinates of every object in the drawing. This is called *regenerating*. Perhaps you have seen the message on AutoCAD's command line — Regenerating drawing.

Regenerating an entire drawing can be time-consuming. To avoid having to regenerate the drawing every time you change the display, AutoCAD keeps a *virtual screen* in your computer's memory. The virtual screen covers an area beyond the current display of your drawing and can be accessed very quickly. When you change the display within the virtual display, AutoCAD doesn't have to regenerate the entire drawing — it only redraws it. Redrawing uses the data stored in the virtual screen to refresh the display. A redraw is much quicker than regeneration.

The REGEN and REDRAW commands

You use the REDRAW command to remove blips or to quickly refresh the screen. Use the REGEN command whenever you want AutoCAD to recalculate the entire drawing. In the last chapter, I showed an example when REGEN was necessary — when you change the point style, you need to regen to see the points in the new style. (AutoCAD users use the word "regen" both to refer to the REGEN command and also as shorthand for regenerate or regeneration.)

 However, in most cases, you want to redraw rather than regen because it is quicker. To redraw the screen, choose Redraw from the Standard toolbar.

To regenerate the entire drawing, type **REGEN** at the command line. Certain zooms and pans require a regeneration, which AutoCAD does automatically.

Panning

To *pan* means to move the display without changing the magnification. The word refers to the expression of panning a camera across a scene or view. You pan to view a different part of your drawing. You can pan any amount and in any direction using the PAN command. You can pan vertically and horizontally using the scroll bars.

Using the PAN command

The PAN command moves the display in the direction and distance you indicate without changing the magnification in any way.

 Release 14 introduces *real-time* panning. Real-time panning moves the drawing as you move the cursor. Real-time panning makes panning quick, intuitive, and easy.

 To pan the drawing, choose Pan Realtime from the Standard toolbar. The cursor changes to a hand. Place the cursor anywhere in your drawing, click, and drag in the direction you want the objects to go. If you reach the end of the screen, release the mouse button, move the cursor away from the edge, and drag again. When you reach the edge of the drawing, PAN places a line on the side of the hand where the edge is.

To leave pan mode, press Esc or Enter or start any command via menu or toolbar. You can also right-click to open the cursor menu shown in Figure 8-1. Pan can be used transparently, while you are in the middle of another command.

Figure 8-1: The pan cursor menu.

Use the cursor menu to exit pan mode, switch to real-time zoom, or to choose one of the zoom options listed.

Note

You can use displacement panning (the kind used by Releases 13 and earlier) by choosing View⇨Pan⇨Point. At the Displacement: prompt, choose any point in your drawing. At the Second point: prompt, choose another point where you want the first point to appear. The display then moves in the direction and the distance indicated by the difference between the first and second points.

Using the scroll bars

You can use the scroll bars to pan vertically and horizontally as you would with any Windows program. However, you can't easily predict just how much the drawing view will move. Therefore, the scroll bars are less useful than the PAN command.

You can use the scroll bars in three ways.

◆ Drag the scroll box in the desired direction and the desired amount.

◆ Click on the scroll bar between the scroll box and the up or down arrow.

◆ Click the up or down arrow to move the drawing view slightly.

Step-by-Step: Panning and Scrolling

On the
CD-ROM

1. Open *ab8-a.dwg* from the CD-ROM. This is the air compressor you drew in Chapter 7, but this display is magnified so you cannot see the entire drawing. The air compressor is shown in Figure 8-2.

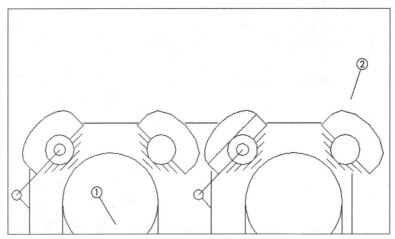

Figure 8-2: The air compressor is zoomed in so that you can only see part of the drawing.

 2. Choose Pan Realtime from the Standard toolbar. Move the cursor to ① in Figure 8-2, click, and drag to ②. The air compressor moves up and to the right. (Note that by the time you get to ②, the display of the air compressor has moved — but you should drag to where ② is on the screen.) Press Esc.

3. The scroll box of the horizontal scroll bar is all the way to the left. Click anywhere in the scroll bar to the right of the scroll box. The air compressor moves to the left.

4. Click anywhere in the vertical scroll bar between the scroll box and the down arrow at the bottom of the scroll bar. The air compressor moves up as you scroll down.

5. Start the PAN command again. Pick a point at the top left corner of the screen and drag to the bottom right corner of the screen. The drawing moves in the direction that you dragged the cursor. Press Esc.

6. Click the right arrow on the horizontal scroll bar three times. The drawing moves to the left slightly each time. Your drawing should look something like Figure 8-3. You may have a different view if you chose slightly different pan points.

7. Do not save this drawing.

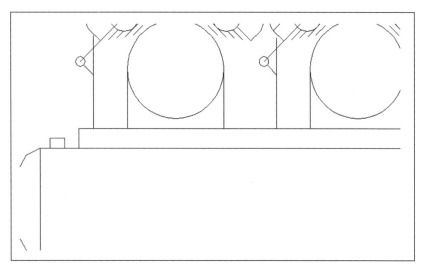

Figure 8-3: The final view. Your view may be somewhat different.

The ZOOM Command

The ZOOM command allows you to zoom in and out of your drawing — like the zoom lens of a camera. When you zoom in, everything is magnified so you can see it more easily, but you see less of the entire drawing. When you zoom out, objects look smaller, but you can see more of the drawing. The ZOOM command has several options that make it easy to see just what you need at an appropriate size.

Zooming does not affect the actual size of objects, just as zooming with a camera lens does not affect the size of the scene you are viewing. Changing the actual size of objects is covered in Chapter 9.

Release 14 introduces *real-time* zoom. The drawing zooms in and out as you move the cursor.

To use real-time zoom, choose Zoom Realtime from the Standard toolbar. The cursor changes to a magnifying glass with a plus sign on one side and a minus sign on the other side. You determine whether AutoCAD zooms in or out depending on the movement of the cursor. To zoom in, click and drag up in the direction of the plus sign. To zoom out, click and drag down in the direction of the minus sign. To continue zooming in or out when you get to the end of the screen, release the mouse button, move the cursor back to its original position, and drag again. A movement from the middle of the screen to the top edge zooms in 100%. A movement from the middle of the screen to the bottom edge zooms out 100%.

Right-click to open the cursor menu to exit zoom mode, switch to real-time pan, or to choose one of the zoom options listed. To end real-time zoom, press Esc or Enter or start any command via menu or toolbar.

Understanding ZOOM options

The Zoom flyout has eight options. There is also a Zoom Previous button on the Standard toolbar. These Zoom options are shown in Table 8-1.

	Table 8-1	
	Zoom Options	
Button	*Option*	*Description*
🔍	Window	This button lets you define a rectangular window as the boundaries of the new display. AutoCAD prompts you for the two corners of the window. Use Window to zoom in on any area already displayed in your drawing.
		Note: When you use Zoom Window, AutoCAD displays everything in the window you specify but reshapes the display to fit your screen. As a result, you may see objects that were outside the specified window.
🔍	Dynamic	Allows you to zoom and pan in one operation. This option is covered in its own section in this chapter.
🔍	Scale	Enter a number to scale the display relative to the drawing limits (a kind of absolute scaling). Enter a number followed by **x** to scale the display relative to the current view (a relative scaling). Enter a number followed by **xp** to scale the display relative to paper space units (discussed in Chapter 17). A number less than one (such as .5) reduces the size of the objects on the screen (such as by half). A number greater than one (such as 2) increases the size of the objects on the screen (such as by two).
🔍	Center	Lets you specify a new center for the display, then a new magnification/height. The current magnification/height is shown in brackets for your reference. Type a smaller number to increase the magnification, making the objects larger. Type a larger value to decrease the magnification, making the objects smaller.
🔍	In	This button is a shortcut for using the Scale option with a value of 2x. See the Scale option.

Button	Option	Description
Out	Out	This button is a shortcut for using the Scale option with a value of .5x. See the Scale option.
All	All	Zooms the display to the greater of the drawing extents or the drawing limits.
Extents	Extents	Zooms to the outer extents of the drawing.
Previous	Previous	Redisplays the last display of your drawing. This option has its own button on the Standard toolbar because it is used so often.

In Release 14, the Extents option does not usually cause a regen. Also, the display is centered rather than shown at the bottom left corner of your screen.

ZOOM Dynamic

The Dynamic option of ZOOM allows you to pan and zoom in one operation. The Aerial View (discussed in the next section) offers more sophisticated options, but the simplicity of ZOOM Dynamic is sometimes just what you need.

When you start ZOOM Dynamic, you see the virtual screen area of the drawing in a blue dashed rectangle. This is also called the *generated* area — the area that was displayed in the last regen operation. Your current view is bounded in a green, dashed rectangle. Your mouse cursor changes to a black rectangle with a large X inside — the Pan view box. When you click the left mouse button, the X changes to a large arrow — the Zoom view box. These are the two modes of ZOOM Dynamic. Each time you click the left mouse button, you switch modes. You can switch back and forth as often as you want. Here's how the two modes work.

✦ **Pan mode:** The box contains an X and can move freely around the drawing. You can therefore pan to any location in the drawing.

✦ **Zoom mode:** The box has an arrow. The left side of the box is fixed at the point where you changed to Zoom mode. As you move the cursor the box expands or shrinks, letting you zoom to any magnification.

When the view box shows the view you want, click the right mouse button or press Enter. AutoCAD pans and zooms to show that view. Figure 8-4 shows the screen during a ZOOM Dynamic operation. Clicking the right mouse button displays the portion of the drawing inside the View box.

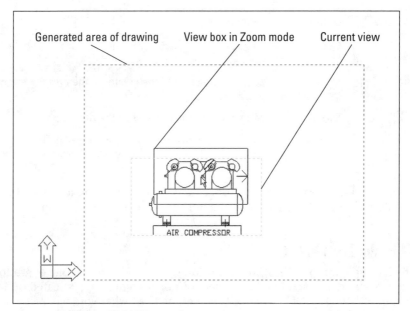

Figure 8-4: Using ZOOM Dynamic.

Step-by-Step: Using the ZOOM Options

On the CD-ROM

1. Open *ab8-b.dwg* from the CD-ROM. This is a drawing of a warehouse, as shown in Figure 8-5.

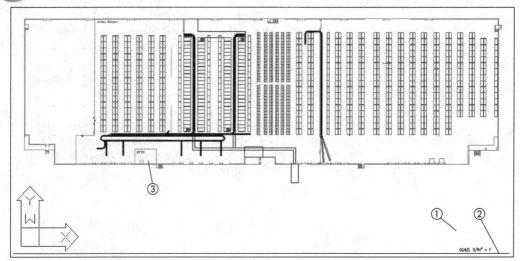

Figure 8-5: A drawing of a large warehouse, with shelving and conveyor belts.

Credit: Thanks to Bryan Kelly of ATI Corporation, Fairfield, Iowa, for this drawing.

2. To read the text in the lower right corner, choose Zoom Window from the Zoom flyout of the Standard toolbar.

3. At the `First corner:` prompt, pick ① as shown in Figure 8-5. At the `Other corner:` prompt, pick ②. AutoCAD zooms in to display the window you specified, as shown in Figure 8-6.

Figure 8-6: Your display should look approximately like this figure after using ZOOM Window.

4. Choose Zoom All from the Zoom flyout of the Standard toolbar.

5. Choose Zoom Previous from the Standard toolbar. AutoCAD quickly returns you to the previous display.

6. Choose Zoom Extents from the Zoom flyout of the Standard toolbar. The drawing fills the screen. In this drawing, the drawing extents are similar to the drawing limits, so you see little difference between using Zoom All and Zoom Extents.

7. Choose Zoom Center from the Zoom flyout. At the `Center point:` prompt, pick ③ in Figure 8-5. At the `Magnification or Height <5177.399>:` prompt, type **500** ↵. AutoCAD zooms in on the office.

8. Choose Zoom Realtime from the Standard toolbar. Place the cursor at the top of the drawing, click, and drag to the bottom of the screen. AutoCAD zooms out the display about 200%.

9. Choose Zoom Scale from the Zoom flyout of the Standard toolbar. Type **2x** ↵. AutoCAD zooms in, doubling the scale of the view and returning you approximately to the previous view of the office.

10. Choose Zoom Dynamic from the Zoom flyout. AutoCAD now displays the entire drawing. The current view is shown with a green dashed line. The mouse cursor is a large box with an X in it. You are now in Pan mode. To zoom in on the right side of the warehouse, move the Pan box to the right of the drawing and click with the pick (left) button.

11. AutoCAD switches to Zoom mode. The Zoom box contains an arrow. Move the mouse to the left to shrink the Zoom box. Notice that the Zoom box is fixed at its left side. When the Zoom box is about half its original size, left-click again.

12. AutoCAD switches to Pan mode again. Move the Pan box to the bottom right corner of the warehouse. This time click with the return (right) mouse button. AutoCAD zooms in on this new view. Your display should look approximately like Figure 8-7.

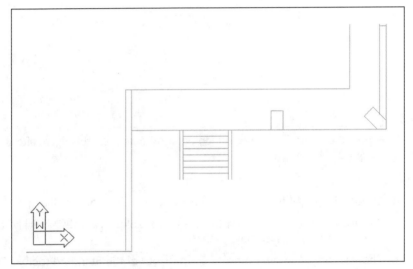

Figure 8-7: The new view of the drawing after using Zoom Dynamic.

 13. Choose Zoom All from the Zoom flyout. Do not save your drawing. If you are continuing on to the next Step-by-Step exercise, leave the drawing open.

 If you have upgraded from an earlier release and wonder where the Zoom options Left and Vmax went, they are no longer listed at the Zoom command prompt, but you can still use either option by typing it in the command line. These options will probably be dropped in the next major release.

Aerial View

Aerial View is a souped-up version of ZOOM Dynamic. You can use Aerial View to pan and zoom. If you need to pan and zoom often, you can leave the Aerial View window open and use it whenever you need to.

 To open Aerial View, click Aerial View on the Standard toolbar or choose View⇨Aerial View. The Aerial View window opens, as shown in Figure 8-8. Like other windows, the Aerial View window can be active or inactive. When active, its title bar is shown in color (usually blue). When inactive, the title bar is gray. Inside the window you see your entire drawing. To close Aerial View, click Aerial View on the Standard toolbar again or click the Aerial View window's own Close button.

Aerial View has its own toolbar and menu. These are explained in the next few sections.

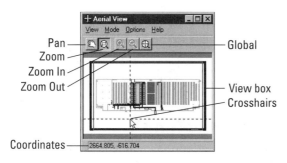

Figure 8-8: The Aerial View window.

You also see a thick black border around your current display, called the View box.

Zooming with Aerial View

While you work in your drawing, the drawing window is active and the Aerial View window is inactive. To zoom using Aerial View:

1. Click anywhere in the Aerial View window to activate it.

 2. If the Zoom button is not chosen (depressed), click it.

3. In the Aerial View window, move the crosshairs until they meet at one corner of the desired view and click and drag.

4. As you move the mouse, the crosshairs change to a rectangle. When the rectangle shows the desired view, click again. In the main drawing window, you immediately see the new zoomed view. In the Aerial View window, the View box adjusts to bound the new view.

After a few zooms, the Aerial View window may no longer show your entire drawing. To quickly zoom out in the Aerial View window, click Zoom Out on the Aerial View toolbar. To quickly zoom in, click Zoom In on the toolbar. To see your entire drawing, click Global on the toolbar. You can then easily zoom in to any location.

Note

The Aerial View Zoom and Pan buttons change the view in the main drawing window. The Zoom In, Zoom Out, and Global buttons change only the view in the Aerial View window. Use these buttons when the Aerial View window does not show the part of the drawing you need to zoom or pan to. Then use the Zoom or Pan buttons.

Panning with Aerial View

Panning is easy with Aerial View.

1. Click anywhere in the Aerial View window to activate it.

 2. If the Pan button is not chosen (depressed), click it.

3. You see a dashed rectangle the same size as the View box. The rectangle moves as you move the cursor.

4. When the rectangle shows the desired view, click. In the main drawing window, you immediately see the new view. In the Aerial View window, the View box adjusts to bound the new view.

If necessary, click Global to see the entire drawing.

Understanding Aerial View options

The Aerial View Options menu contains two options that affect how Aerial View works. Auto Viewport applies only when you have more than one viewport. Viewports are discussed later in this chapter. If this option is checked, the view in the Aerial View window changes as you change the active viewport in the main drawing area.

Dynamic Update determines whether the view in the Aerial View window is continually (dynamically) updated as you edit your drawing. As you can imagine, it takes up additional computer resources (mainly memory) to maintain two views of your drawing at once. If you find that Aerial View slows down your computer (but you don't want to close it entirely), choose this option to turn Dynamic Update off. Choose the option again to turn it on.

Using Aerial View

Aerial View is most useful in a large drawing with lots of detail. You can use it transparently. In the following exercise, you practice using Aerial View.

Don't forget that before you use Aerial Window you need to click in the Aerial View window to activate it. When you return to the AutoCAD window, you need to activate that window as well.

To close Aerial View, click its Close button in the upper right corner of the window.

It can be annoying if you forget to activate the Aerial View window before using it. When you start to define a zoom window, Aerial View uses the first point to activate the window. Your second zoom window point becomes the first zoom window point and . . . confusion ensues. I find it helpful to get in the habit of activating the Aerial View window in its title bar. This purposeful way of activating the window creates a habit that avoids this type of confusion.

Step-by-Step: Using Aerial View

1. Open *ab8-b.dwg* from the CD-ROM if it is not already open from the previous Step-by-Step exercise.

2. Choose Aerial View from the Standard toolbar. The Aerial View window opens. The Aerial View window is not currently active. By default, the Zoom button is depressed.

3. Click the Aerial View window to activate it. At the bottom of the warehouse, somewhat to the left, is a rectangle (it's an office) with some text in it. (If you did the previous exercise, you zoomed into this office using Zoom Center.)

4. To zoom in to the office, use the crosshairs in the Aerial View window to guide you and click once at the top left corner of the office and once at the bottom right corner of the office. AutoCAD zooms in on the office. In the Aerial View window, you still see the entire drawing and the current view is bounded by a thick black box, the View box. Your screen should look like Figure 8-9.

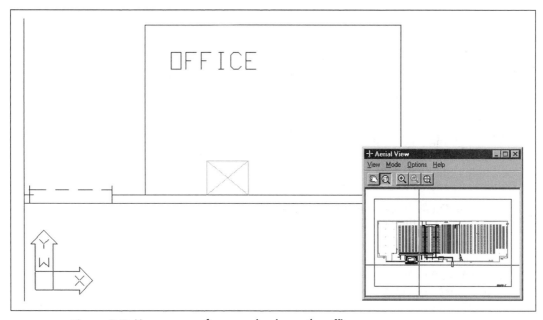

Figure 8-9: Your screen after zooming in on the office.

5. Click Pan in the Aerial View window. Now the cursor is a box the same size as the View box. Move the box just to the left of the View box and click. AutoCAD pans to show some windows to the left of the office.

6. Click Zoom in the Aerial View window. Using the same technique as you used in step 4 above, zoom in on the entire top left quadrant of the warehouse. Zoom in again until you can read the text at the top left corner of the shelving area. (The red columns represent shelving in the warehouse.) Your screen should look approximately like Figure 8-10.

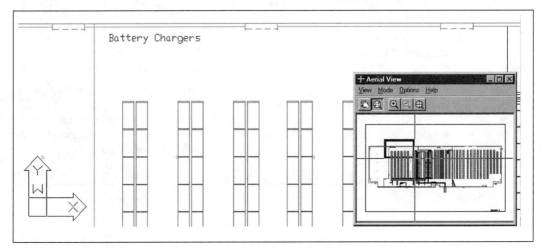

Figure 8-10: Zooming in on the top left corner of the warehouse. You can now see the text, which reads "Battery Chargers."

7. The Zoom button should still be depressed. Use the crosshairs in the Aerial View window to pick a point at the top left corner of the warehouse and another point at the bottom right corner of the warehouse. AutoCAD quickly zooms to display the entire warehouse.

8. Do not save your drawing. Close the Aerial View window. If you are continuing on to the next Step-by-Step exercise, keep the drawing open.

Note   While you are using Aerial View, no commands are executed on the command line. For this reason, you cannot undo individual zooms and pans created using Aerial View.

Named Views

After you have done a lot of panning and zooming in a drawing, you may find that you return to the same part of your drawing again and again, especially if the drawing undergoes a lot of changes. In a large drawing, it can take some time to display the part of the drawing you want, especially if AutoCAD needs to regenerate the drawing. You can speed up the process by saving views.

A view is simply a display of a drawing on your screen. It can show any part of your drawing at any magnification. Once you have the display, you give the view a name and save it. AutoCAD then lets you retrieve that view at any time, without zooming or panning.

Tip In a very large drawing, you can create four or more views as soon as you create the title block — for example, one for each quadrant of the drawing. This helps you move quickly from one section of the drawing to another. As you determine the need for more specific views, you can add them.

Saving a view

First display the view you want to save on the screen. For this purpose, use the ZOOM and PAN commands or Aerial View. Then choose Named Views from the View flyout of the Standard toolbar — or choose View⇨Named Views. This starts the DDVIEW command. The View Control dialog box opens, as shown in Figure 8-11.

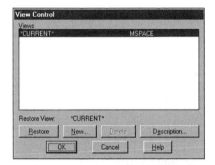

Figure 8-11: The View Control dialog box.

When you first open this dialog box, it shows only one view, called *CURRENT*, which is the current display. Choose New to open the Define New View dialog box, shown in Figure 8-12.

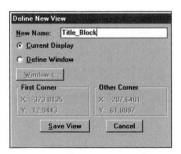

Figure 8-12: The Define New View dialog box.

Type a name for your view in the New Name text box. View names are limited to 31 characters and may not have any spaces, which is why it is common to use the underscore character between words, as you see in Figure 8-12. You can also use a hyphen between words.

Choose Save View to return to the View Control dialog box, where you see your new view listed. Click OK to return to your drawing.

Tip

You can use the Define New View dialog box to define several views at once. To do this:

1. Choose Named Views from the View flyout of the Standard toolbar.

2. Choose New.

3. Type the name of the first view in the New Name text box.

4. Choose the Define Window radio button.

5. Click the Window button. AutoCAD returns you to your drawing.

6. At the `First Corner:` prompt, pick one corner of a rectangular window.

7. At the `Other Corner:` prompt, pick the diagonally opposite corner of the window. AutoCAD returns you to the Define New View dialog box.

8. Choose Save View. AutoCAD returns you to the View Control dialog box.

9. Repeat steps 2–8 for all additional views.

Restoring a view

To restore a view means to display it. The View Control dialog box lets you easily restore any view you have saved.

1. Choose Named Views from the View flyout of the Standard toolbar.

2. Click the view you want to restore.

3. Choose Restore.

4. Click OK.

Using other view control functions

To delete a view, open the View Control dialog box as described above, choose the view you want to delete, click Delete, and click OK.

To get a description of a view, open the View Control dialog box as described above, choose the view you want to see a description of, and click Description. The View Description dialog box opens, which simply provides some statistics about the view. In general, these statistics are more useful for 3D drawings than 2D ones.

Step-by-Step: Working with Views

1. Open *ab8-b.dwg* from the CD-ROM if it is not already open from the previous Step-by-Step exercise.

2. Save it as *ab8-1.dwg* in your *AutoCAD Bible* folder.

 3. Choose View⇨Named Views to open the View Control dialog box.

4. Click New to open the Define New View dialog box.

5. In the text box, type **topleft**.

6. Click the Define Window radio button and then click Window. AutoCAD returns you to your drawing temporarily.

 7. Choose Zoom Window from the Zoom flyout of the Standard toolbar and pick a window that covers the entire top left quadrant of the warehouse.

8. At the `First corner:` prompt, pick the bottom left corner of your screen. At the `Other Corner:` prompt, pick the top right corner of your screen. AutoCAD returns you to the Define New View dialog box.

9. Click Save View. Click OK.

10. Repeat the DDVIEW command. Click New. Type **bottomleft** in the edit box of the Define New View dialog box.

11. Click Define Window, then Click Window. Choose Zoom Dynamic to zoom into a view that displays the bottom left corner of the warehouse. At the `First corner:` prompt, pick the bottom left corner of your screen. At the `Other Corner:` prompt, pick the top right corner of your screen. Back in the Define New View dialog box, click Save View. The View Control dialog box should list both your views, as shown in Figure 8-13. Click OK to close the View Control dialog box.

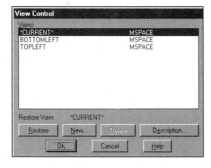

Figure 8-13: The View Control box now lists the views you have saved.

 12. Do a ZOOM Extents. Choose Named Views from the Views flyout of the Standard toolbar. Choose BOTTOMLEFT from the View Control dialog box. Click Restore, then click OK. AutoCAD restores the view.

13. Save your drawing. The views you created are now a part of the drawing database.

Tiled Viewports

Tiled viewports let you divide up the screen into rectangular bounding boxes. You can then show a different view of your drawing in each viewport. The purpose of tiled viewports is to make it easier to draw. For example:

✦ You can see the whole drawing in one viewport and a zoomed in portion of that drawing in another viewport.

✦ You can see widely separated views of a large drawing at one time.

AutoCAD offers two types of viewports — tiled and floating. For more information on floating viewports, see the sidebar of that title in this chapter, and Chapter 17.

Actually, you are already using a tiled viewport since the regular single view of your drawing that you have been working with represents the default of a one-tile viewport.

You may have noticed the TILE button on the status bar at the bottom of your screen. By default the TILE button is on, allowing tiled viewports.

When you turn the TILE button on and off, you are changing the TILEMODE system variable. This variable has two settings, 1 (on) and 0 (off). On allows tiled viewports. Off allows floating viewports.

Tiled viewports have the following characteristics:

✦ No matter how many viewports you have, they always collectively take up the entire screen. They are not separate entities, but a way of dividing up the screen.

✦ Only one viewport can be active at a time. The active viewport has a bold border.

✦ The crosshairs only appear in the active viewport.

✦ The UCS (User Coordinate System) icon (if set to On) appears in each viewport.

✦ Any change you make to your drawing in one viewport automatically appears in every other viewport (or in each viewport that shows the part of the drawing where you made the change).

✦ AutoCAD lets you create up to 96 viewports — but you'll never want to create that many!

✦ You can begin a command in one viewport and finish it in another. For example, you can start a line in one viewport, switch to a second viewport, and end the line there.

✦ You can save and restore viewport configurations.

Figure 8-14 shows a drawing divided into three viewports. Each viewport shows a different view of the drawing.

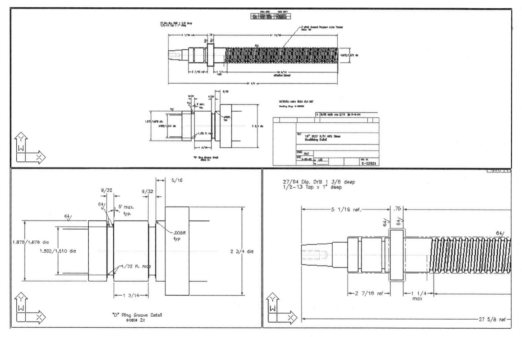

Figure 8-14: A drawing showing three viewports with a different view in each viewport.

Credit: Thanks to Jerry Bottenfield of Clow Valve Company, Oskaloosa, Iowa, for this drawing.

Configuring tiled viewports

Creating tiled viewports involves deciding how you want to divide up the screen. A set of tiled viewports is called a configuration. AutoCAD offers a few simple configurations, but you can create your own by further dividing up any of the viewports. You can also join two viewports. Finally, you can always return to the default of one viewport.

Creating tiled viewports

To create additional viewports (that is, more than the one viewport you always see), choose View⇨Tiled Viewports. This opens a submenu letting you choose from AutoCAD's preset configurations, as shown in Figure 8-15.

Figure 8-15: The Tiled Viewports submenu.

You can choose to create up to four viewports from the submenu, at which point you respond to the options that appear on the command line. For example, if you choose 2 Viewports, AutoCAD responds with the `Horizontal/<Vertical>:` prompt. Type **h** ↵ or **v** ↵ to create two horizontal or vertical viewports. If you choose 4 Viewports, AutoCAD makes four equal viewports, one in each corner. However, if you choose 3 Viewports, AutoCAD offers several options to let you choose the configuration of the three viewports. These options can be confusing.

An easier way to configure viewports is to choose Layout from the submenu. The Tiled Viewport Layout dialog box opens, as shown in Figure 8-16. Here you simply click the image that matches the configuration you want. Click OK to return to your drawing.

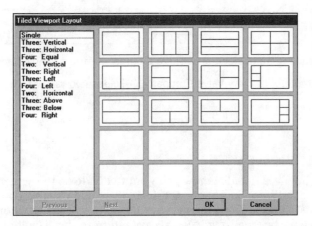

Figure 8-16: The Tiled Viewport Layout dialog box makes it easy to choose a configuration.

The Tiled Viewport Layout dialog box is usually the best place to start creating viewports. However, if the standard configurations do not meet your needs, you can use one of them as a starting point and then use the other options.

The tiled viewport options always work on the *active* viewport. As explained earlier, the active viewport has a bold border and crosshairs. To make a viewport
active, click anywhere inside that viewport. Then Choose View⇨Tiled Viewports
and choose the option you want for that viewport.

Let's say you have four equal viewports, and the top left viewport is active. If you
choose 4 Viewports from the Tiled Viewports submenu while the top left viewport
is active, AutoCAD divides the top left viewport into four viewports. Now you have
seven viewports of the drawing.

Removing tiled viewports

One way to remove a tiled viewport is to join it to another viewport. To join one
viewport to another, choose View⇨Tiled Viewports⇨Join. At the `Select dominant
viewport <current>:` prompt, click the viewport you want to keep or press Enter
if you want to keep the current viewport. At the `Select viewport to join:`
prompt, click the viewport that you want to join into the dominant viewport. You
lose the display in this second viewport as AutoCAD joins the two viewports.

The only other way to remove tiled viewports is to return to the single viewport
configuration — choose View⇨Tiled Viewports⇨1 Viewport. AutoCAD keeps the
display in the current viewport and discards the others.

Using tiled viewports

Once you have created the viewport configuration you want, you are ready to use
it. The first step is to create the views you need in each viewport.

Creating viewport views

Creating views in each viewport involves two steps:

1. Make a viewport current by clicking anywhere inside it.

2. Zoom and pan until you have the view you want.

Tip
Although you can create any collection of views in your viewports, many users
commonly use one viewport to display the entire drawing and the others to display zoomed in views of smaller sections.

Drawing from viewport to viewport

Once you have the viewport configuration and views you need, you can start to
draw. One of the great advantages of viewports is that you can draw from one
viewport to another. In a large drawing, you may need to draw a line from one end
of the drawing to another, but when you display the entire drawing you cannot see
the detail well enough to specify where to start and end the line. The basic steps
to draw from one viewport to another are:

1. Click the viewport where you want to start. This might be a small detail of one corner of your drawing.

2. Start the command and specify any options you need. Specify any necessary coordinates as you usually would.

3. To continue the command in a second viewport, click to activate that viewport. Continue the command, specifying coordinates as necessary.

4. You can continue the command in a third viewport by clicking it. Do this until you have completed the command. If you have a viewport displaying the entire drawing, you immediately see the results in that viewport as well.

Cross-
Reference

You can also use viewports to make changes in your drawing. The commands used to edit your drawing are covered in Chapters 9 and 10.

All commands except those that change the display — such as zooming, panning, and creating views — can be started in one viewport and continued in another.

Saving and restoring viewport configurations

You can save a tiled viewport configuration. If you find yourself creating a particular configuration over and over, you should save it. You can then restore it when needed.

Saving a viewport configuration

Once you have created a viewport configuration that you like, follow these steps to save it:

1. Choose View⇨Tiled Viewports⇨Save.

2. At the `?/ Name for new viewport configuration:` prompt, type a name and press Enter.

Names can be up to 31 characters with no spaces. They can include the dollar sign ($), hyphen (-), and underscore (_).

Unfortunately, AutoCAD has no dialog box for viewport configurations equivalent to the one for views. As explained in the next section, to restore a viewport configuration you must type its name. This makes it wise to choose short names.

Restoring a viewport configuration

After returning to one viewport or using a different configuration, you can restore a saved configuration.

1. Choose View⇨Tiled Viewports⇨Restore.

2. At the `?/Name of viewport configuration to restore:` prompt, type the name of the viewport you want to restore and press Enter.

3. If you don't remember the name of the viewport configuration, type ? ↵. AutoCAD lists the current configuration as well as all saved configurations. AutoCAD then repeats the prompt so you can type the name of the configuration to restore.

Figure 8-17 shows a configuration listing two saved viewport configurations, 3-O-RING and 4-O-RING.

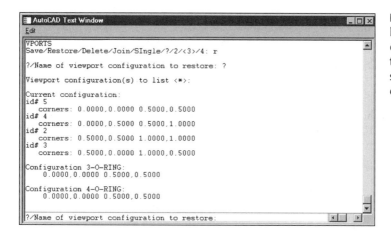

Figure 8-17: A listing of the current configuration and two saved viewport configurations.

Floating viewports

AutoCAD has two types of viewports, tiled viewports, which are discussed here, and floating viewports, which I cover in Chapter 17. These two types of viewports have many similarities, but they have different purposes. Whereas the purpose of tiled viewports is to help you draw and edit your drawing, floating viewports are used to lay out your drawing for plotting.

Floating viewports are created in *paper space*, which lets you treat your screen like a sheet of paper. You create floating viewports and perhaps a title block on this electronic sheet of paper. Each floating viewport can show a different view of your drawing — just like tiled viewports. But floating viewports then let you plot all those views on one sheet of paper. You can't do that with tiled viewports, which are just devices to let you temporarily display your drawing in a way that helps you draw and edit.

Tiled viewports are covered here because they are appropriate for learning how to draw and edit your drawing. Floating viewports are covered in Chapter 17, "Plotting and Printing," because you use them to lay out your drawing for plotting.

Step-by-Step: Creating, Saving, and Restoring Tiled Viewports

1. Open *ab8-c.dwg* from the CD-ROM.

2. Save it as *ab8-2.dwg* in your *AutoCAD Bible* folder.

3. Choose View⇨Tiled Viewports⇨Layout to open the Tiled Viewport Layout dialog box.

4. In the listing at the left of the dialog box, choose the third from last item, `Three:Above`. Click OK. AutoCAD creates three tiled viewports.

5. Click the bottom left viewport. Click Zoom Window on the Zoom flyout of the Standard toolbar and choose a window around the left portion of the threaded model (the upper part of the drawing).

6. Click the bottom right viewport. Click Zoom Window on the Zoom flyout of the Standard toolbar and choose a window around the bottom left portion of the drawing (not including the title block). The results are shown in Figure 8-18.

7. Choose View⇨Tiled Viewports⇨Save. At the `?/Name for new viewport configuration:` prompt, type **3-o-ring** ↵.

8. Click the top viewport. Choose View⇨Tiled Viewports⇨1 Viewport. AutoCAD displays the view shown in the last active viewport.

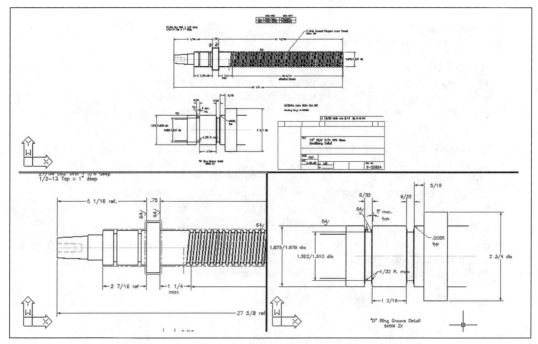

Figure 8-18: The three viewports now display three different views.

9. Choose View⇨Tiled Viewports⇨Restore. At the `?/Name of viewport con-figuration to restore:` prompt, type **?** ↵.

10. At the `Viewport configuration(s) to list <*>:` prompt, press Enter to list the viewport configurations. AutoCAD displays the configuration specifications.

11. At the `?/Name of viewport configuration to restore:` prompt, type **3-o-ring** ↵. AutoCAD restores the viewport configuration, including the views in each viewport.

12. Save your drawing.

Snap Rotation

Not all drawings are vertical and horizontal. In some drawings a significant portion of your objects are drawn at non-orthogonal angles. It can sometimes help to rotate the crosshairs to match the major angles of the drawing.

Consider Figure 8-19. A great deal of this drawing is at an angle. You could handle this in four ways.

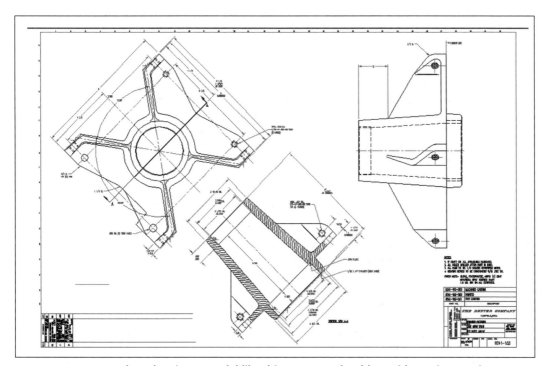

Figure 8-19: When drawing a model like this one, you should consider various options, such as rotating the snap or creating a new UCS.

Credit: Thanks to Robert Mack of The Dexter Company, Fairfield, Iowa, for this drawing.

✦ Draw as normal, specifying the necessary angles.

✦ Rotate the snap, which also rotates the grid and crosshairs.

✦ Create a new UCS (User Coordinate System).

✦ Draw the entire model vertically and rotate it afterward.

Creating a new UCS is covered later in this chapter.

If you need to draw several objects at a certain angle, such as 45 degrees, you can rotate the snap to that angle. AutoCAD rotates the grid and crosshairs to follow suit. This technique works best when the decimal point accuracy required allows you to draw using snap points. It can also be used to guide the cursor at an appropriate angle for direct distance entry.

In Chapter 4 you learned how to use direct distance entry and used it for orthogonal drawing. Rotating the snap makes it easy to use direct distance entry for other angles.

As explained in Chapter 6, when you create a polygon, AutoCAD automatically makes the bottom edge of the polygon horizontal unless you choose the radius by picking a point with the mouse. If you need to create a polygon on an angle and want to type in the radius, a quick solution is to rotate the snap angle. AutoCAD then aligns the bottom edge of the polygon with the snap rotation.

To change the snap rotation angle, choose Tools⇨Drawing Aids to open the Drawing Aids dialog box. In the Snap section, type an angle in the Snap Angle text edit box.

Note that you can also set an X base and a Y base. This simply ensures that the grid goes through a point of your choice, which is very important if you are using snap mode to draw. If you are just starting to draw an object, use the 0,0 base and draw to the existing snap points. However, if you have an existing object and need to add to it, changing the base may be helpful.

You can use the ID command to get the coordinates of a point. Then use these coordinates as the X and Y bases. The ID command is covered in Chapter 12.

Setting X and Y bases does not change the coordinates, which are tied to the UCS. The UCS is discussed in the next section.

Click OK to return to your drawing. Make sure the grid is on. The crosshairs and grid now reflect the new snap angle. Figure 8-20 shows the same drawing with a snap angle of 45 degrees. Notice how the crosshairs now match the angle of the drawing. The crosshairs have been set to 100% of screen size, which is useful when rotating the snap angle.

The grid does not have to be on, but it helps you get your bearings when working with an unusual snap angle.

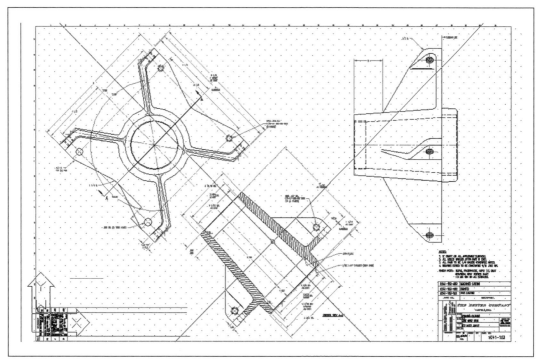

Figure 8-20: The snap angle in this drawing has been changed to 45 degrees. Note that the grid follows the snap.

You can create a new UCS (User Coordinate System) rather than rotate the snap angle. The results are similar, except that when you create a UCS, you also affect the X,Y coordinates. The UCS is much more flexible when you start drawing in three dimensions.

User Coordinate Systems

By default, a drawing is set up using a *World Coordinate System*. This sets the origin of the X,Y points at 0,0 and the angles using the familiar East equals 90 degrees system. When a drawing uses the World Coordinate System, a *W* shows in the UCS icon, as shown in Figure 8-21.

Figure 8-21: The UCS icon with the W symbol, indicating that the drawing uses the World Coordinate System.

You can easily create your own UCS and even save it for future use in the drawing. Creating a UCS is essential for 3D drawing but often useful for 2D drawing as well.

To define a UCS in a 2D drawing, you indicate the angle of the X and Y axes and an origin point. The origin point then becomes the new 0,0 coordinate. AutoCAD offers several options for specifying the UCS.

Understanding UCS options

To create a UCS, choose Tools⇨UCS. (You can also choose a button on the UCS fly-out of the Standard toolbar.) A submenu opens offering the following options, shown in Table 8-2.

Table 8-2
UCS Options

Option	Meaning
Preset	Opens the UCS Orientation dialog box where you can choose one of several preset UCS choices.
Named	Opens the UCS Control dialog box where you can make a named UCS current. You name a UCS when you save it. This dialog box combines the functions of the Previous, Restore, Delete, and List options.
Previous	Displays the previous UCS. AutoCAD remembers up to 10 previous UCSs.
Restore	Restores a UCS that you have previously saved.
Save	Allows you to name and save a UCS.
Delete	Deletes a UCS.
List	Lists saved UCSs.
World	Specifies the default UCS, with the X axis horizontal, the Y axis vertical, and the origin at the initial 0,0 location.
Object	Allows you to align the UCS with an object. In general, AutoCAD uses the most obvious object snap as the origin and aligns the X axis with the object. For example, when you choose a line, the endpoint nearest your pick point becomes the origin and the X axis aligns with the angle of the line.
View	Aligns the X and Y axes with the current view. Used in 3D drawing. AutoCAD arbitrarily sets the origin.
Origin	Specifies a new 0,0 point relative to the current origin.
Z Axis Vector	Specifies which way the Z axis points. This option is not used in 2D drawing.

Option	Meaning
3 Point	Allows you to specify three points. The first point is the origin, the second point indicates the positive direction of the X axis, and the third point indicates the positive direction of the Y axis.
X Axis Rotate	Keeps the current origin and rotates the Y and Z axes around the current X axis. You specify the angle. This is used in 3D drawing.
Y Axis Rotate	Keeps the current origin and rotates the X and Z axes around the current Y axis. You specify the angle. This is used in 3D drawing.
Z Axis Rotate	Keeps the current origin and rotates the X and Y axes around the current Z axis. You specify the angle. Can be used in 2D drawing.

Controlling the UCS icon

By default, the UCS icon is at the bottom left of your drawing. The icon is not necessarily at the 0,0 point, especially if you have panned around your drawing. The value of this is obvious — it keeps the icon out of the way so it does not obstruct your drawing.

You can turn off the UCS icon completely. If you are not working with customized UCSs, you often have no reason to see the UCS in a 2D drawing.

If you create a UCS, you can place the UCS icon at the 0,0 point (the origin). This helps you get your bearings. AutoCAD places a plus sign in the icon to indicate the origin. However, if the origin is out of the current display or so close to the edge that the icon won't fit, AutoCAD places the UCS icon at the lower left corner of your drawing anyway.

To control the UCS icon, choose View⊅Display⊅UCS Icon. (Don't confuse this with Tools⊅UCS, which creates a custom UCS.) A submenu opens with the following items:

✦ **Icon:** Toggles the display of the UCS icon on and off.

✦ **Icon Origin:** Toggles on and off the placement of the UCS icon at the origin.

Using a custom UCS

Although it seems confusing at first, once you try creating your own UCS it becomes easier to understand how the process works. In this Step-by-Step exercise, you create the basic framework for the drawing shown in Figures 8-19 and 8-20, a bearing housing for a commercial dryer.

Step-by-Step: Drawing with a Custom UCS

1. Open *ab8-d.dwg* from the CD-ROM.

2. Save it as *ab8-3.dwg* in your *AutoCAD Bible* folder. ORTHO is on. OSNAP is on and a running object snap is set for endpoints.

3. Choose Tools⇨UCS⇨Z Axis Rotate. Because there are no objects in the drawing, you cannot use the 3 Point or Object options which might otherwise be useful.

4. At the `Rotation angle about Z axis <0>:` prompt, type **45** ↵. The UCS icon and crosshairs are displayed at a 45-degree angle.

5. Choose Rectangle from the Draw toolbar. At the prompt, pick a point at the bottom center of your screen. At the `Other corner:` prompt, type **@3-15/16,31/32** ↵. AutoCAD creates the rectangle at the proper angle.

6. Start the LINE command. At the `From point:` prompt, choose the From object snap. At the `Base point:` prompt, use the Endpoint object snap to pick point ① in Figure 8-22. At the `<Offset>:` prompt, type **@-1/8,0** ↵. At the `To point:` prompt, type **@5-3/16<93.3** ↵. End the LINE command.

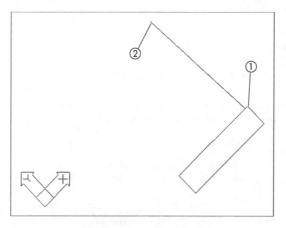

Figure 8-22: Starting to draw the framework for the bearing housing drawn using a customized UCS.

7. Start the LINE command again. Follow the prompts:

```
From point: Choose the From object snap.
Base point: Use the Endpoint object snap to pick point ②.
<Offset>: @1/16,0 ↵
To point: Move the cursor in the 90° direction relative to the UCS.
35/64 ↵
Note: Remember that the UCS has been rotated 45 degrees so 90
degrees looks like 135 degrees. Press F6 twice for polar
coordinates to confirm the 90° direction as you move the cur-
sor.
To point: Move cursor in the 180° direction. 3-9/64 ↵
To point: Move cursor in the 270° direction. 35/64 ↵
To point: c ↵ (to close the figure)
```

8. Start the LINE command. At the `From point:` prompt, choose the From object snap. At the `Base point:` prompt, use the endpoint object snap to pick ① in Figure 8-23. At the `<Offset>:` prompt, type **@1/16,0** ↵.

9. At the `To point:` prompt, again choose From. At the `Base point:` prompt, use the endpoint object snap to pick ②. At the `<Offset>:` prompt, type **@1/8,0** ↵ to complete the model as shown in Figure 8-23. End the LINE command.

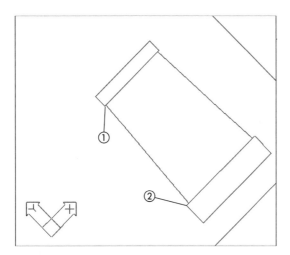

Figure 8-23: The completed framework for the bearing housing.

10. Since you would normally continue working on this drawing, you should save the UCS. Choose Tools⇨UCS⇨Save. At the `Desired UCS name:` prompt, type **45** ↵.

11. To return to the World Coordinate System, choose Tools⇨UCS⇨World. The UCS icon and crosshairs return to their familiar angle.

12. To return to the 45 UCS, choose Tools⇨UCS⇨Named to open the UCS Control dialog box. Choose **45** and click Current. Click OK. AutoCAD restores the 45 UCS.

13. Save your drawing.

Isometric Drawing

An isometric drawing is a 2D drawing drawn to look like a 3D drawing. Every child learns how to draw a box that looks three dimensional. By drawing parallelograms instead of squares, the drawing gives the impression of being in three dimensions. AutoCAD allows you to do the same thing.

Understanding isometric planes

AutoCAD uses the ISOPLANE (short for isometric plane) command to rotate the crosshairs to the special angles required for isometric drawing. You then toggle from left to right to top to draw the three "dimensions" or planes. As you do so, AutoCAD changes the angles of the crosshairs, snap, and grid to the appropriate angles. These angles are 30 degrees for the X axis, 90 degrees for the Z axis, and 150 degrees for the Y axis. As you toggle among the planes, you see the crosshairs take on various configurations of these angles. Figure 8-24 shows the standard isometric cube. You can see three sides — left, right, and top. In the figure, the crosshairs are set to the right isometric plane.

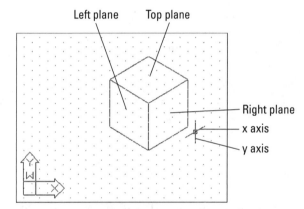

Left plane   Top plane

Right plane

x axis

y axis

Figure 8-24: The isometric cube.

Isometric drawing is not often used for precise drawing because it can be difficult to specify the exact points you need. Also, true 3D drawing has mostly supplanted isometric drawing. It can, however, be used successfully for illustration when exact precision is not necessary.

Tip

Use snap points and object snaps as much as possible in an isometric drawing. Also, set the cursor to 100% of the screen to better visualize the isometric planes.

Drawing in isometric mode

To start isometric mode, choose Tools⇨Drawing Aids to open the Drawing Aids dialog box. In the Isometric Snap/Grid section, choose On. Then choose the plane you want to start working with. Click OK.

Once you are in isometric mode, you can open the dialog box again to change the plane. However, it is easier to press F5 to toggle from plane to plane.

Drawing lines in isometric mode is fairly straightforward if the lines are parallel to one of the isometric plane angles. Circles and arcs in isometric mode must be drawn as ellipses and elliptical arcs. When you are in isometric mode the ELLIPSE command has an Isocircle option.

If you do isometric drawings, check out Isomak13 on the CD-ROM. This shareware program converts 2D objects into isometric models, greatly reducing the time it takes to create isometric drawings. Look in */Software/Chap08/Isomak*.

Step-by-Step: Drawing in Isometric Mode

1. Start a new drawing using the Start from Scratch option.

2. Save the drawing in your *AutoCAD Bible* folder as *ab8-4.dwg*.

3. Choose Tools⇨Drawing Aids. In the Isometric Snap/Grid section, choose On. Choose Left to start with the left plane.

4. In the Snap section, change the Y spacing to .5 and click On. In the Grid section, set the Y spacing to .5 and click On. Click OK to return to your drawing.

5. Start the LINE command. At the `From point:` prompt, use the coordinate display to choose 3.4641,2, which is a snap point. (It may take you a while to find the point — that's okay.) At the `To point:` prompt, choose 6.4952,0.25. At the next `To point:` prompt, choose 6.4952,1.25. At the next `To point:` prompt, choose 3.4641,3. At the next `To point:` prompt, type **c** ↵ to close the left side of the model. All these points are snap points. The results are shown in Figure 8-25.

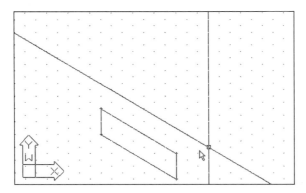

Figure 8-25: The left side of the iron plate. The cursor has been changed to extend to 100% of the screen.

6. Press F5 twice until you see `<Isoplane Right>` on the command line.

7. Start the LINE command again. At the `From point:` prompt, pick 6,4952,1.25. Press F6 twice to get dynamic polar coordinates. At the `To point:` prompt, pick when the coordinates show 2<30. At the `To point:` prompt, use the polar coordinate display to draw a line of 1<270. At the `To point:` prompt, draw a line of 2<210. End the LINE command.

8. Press F5 twice until you see `<Isoplane Top>` on the command line. Start the LINE command. Start the line at 8.2272,2.25, which is a snap point. Press F6 twice to use polar coordinates. Draw a line of 3.5<150 and continue another line of 2<210. End the LINE command. This completes the box.

9. Choose Ellipse from the Draw toolbar. Type **i** ↵ to choose the Isocircle option. At the `Center of circle:` prompt, choose 5.1962,3. At the `<Circle radius>/Diameter:` prompt, type **.5** ↵. AutoCAD draws the ellipse. Your drawing should look like Figure 8-26.

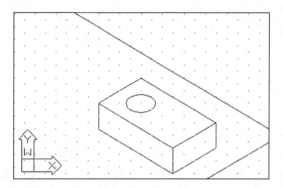

Figure 8-26: The completed iron plate with a hole in it, drawn isometrically.

10. Save your drawing.

Tip

Polar coordinate display is very helpful while drawing isometrically. The coordinates are easier to understand than the unusual absolute snap point coordinates created by ISOPLANE.

Summary

In this chapter you learned how to control the display of your drawing.

You learned about the PAN and ZOOM commands, including Release 14's new real-time pan and zoom and the many ZOOM options. Aerial View can also be used to pan and zoom.

In a large drawing it saves time to save several views of your drawing. You can then retrieve them quickly. Another way to view your drawing is to create tiled viewports. Each viewport can then show a different view of your drawing. You can also draw from viewport to viewport. You can save and retrieve useful viewport configurations.

When working with non-orthogonal angles, you can rotate the snap and grid or create an entirely new User Coordinate System. By viewing your drawing at a different angle, you can make certain drawing tasks much easier.

Use the ISOPLANE command to create isometric drawings, which are 2D drawings that give the appearance of three dimensions.

✦   ✦   ✦

Editing Your Drawing: Basic Tools

Editing a Drawing

No drawing project is ever completed without changes. You make changes in a drawing for many reasons. Some editing processes are simply part of the drawing process, such as copying an object instead of drawing it a second time from scratch. Other types of editing involve making changes to many objects at once, such as moving an entire section of a drawing to make room for newer added objects. You often need to erase, move, rotate, and resize objects.

If you have been following through the exercises in this book, you have not yet made any changes to existing objects. However, you probably felt that some of the drawing you did was repetitive. To avoid drawing the same object over and over, you can draw an object once and then copy it to a new location.

Making changes to a drawing is called *editing*. In order to edit an object, you need to select it. AutoCAD offers numerous techniques for selecting objects. In this chapter I cover the basic editing commands as well as most of the ways to select objects. The rest of the 2D editing commands, as well as three additional selection methods — grips, selection filters, and groups — are covered in the next chapter.

Most of the editing commands are on the Modify toolbar. In most cases, you can either:

✦ Choose the command first and then select the objects the command applies to, or

✦ Select the objects first and then choose the command.

The topic of which comes first, the command or the object, is fully covered later in this chapter.

Understanding object selection basics

When you start editing drawings, the main new skill to learn is how to select objects. The selection options are covered later in this chapter.

The simplest selection technique is to place the pickbox—the box at the intersection of the crosshairs—over the object and click with the pick button. This is known as *picking* an object.

If you choose an editing command before selecting an object, AutoCAD responds with the Select objects: prompt. When you pick an object, AutoCAD highlights it, usually by making it dashed, as shown in Figure 9-1.

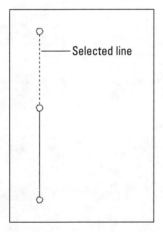

Figure 9-1: The selected line is dashed.

Selected line

AutoCAD continues to provide Select objects: prompts so you can select other objects. Continue to select objects until you have selected all the objects you want to edit. Then press Enter to end the Select objects: prompt.

When you choose the object first, the selected object becomes dashed and you also see one or more small boxes, called grips, as shown in Figure 9-2. Grips are covered in the next chapter.

In the next few Step-by-Step exercises, you use this picking technique to select objects.

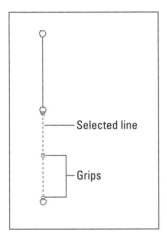

Figure 9-2: The selected line is dashed and also displays grips.

Erasing objects

 Somehow, no drawing is ever completed without erasing an object. The ERASE command is very simple—it has no options. To erase an object, select the object and click Erase on the Modify toolbar. Alternately, click Erase and then select the object.

Step-by-Step: Erasing Objects

On the
CD-ROM

1. Open *ab9-a.dwg* from the CD-ROM.

2. Save it as *ab9-1.dwg* in your *AutoCAD Bible* folder. This drawing is a schematic of a gas extraction well, shown in Figure 9-3.

3. To erase the line at point ① of Figure 9-3, move the mouse until the pickbox at the intersection of the crosshairs is anywhere over the line and click. Notice that the line is dashed and displays grips.

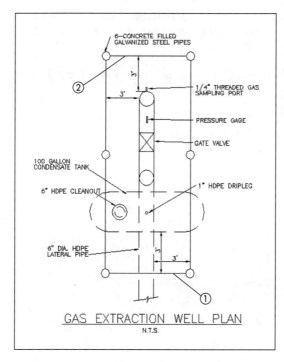

Figure 9-3: The gas extraction well schematic.

Credit: Thanks to the Army Corps of Engineers for this drawing. The COE maintains a Web site of drawings at http://cadlib.wes.army.mil.

  4. Choose Erase from the Modify toolbar. AutoCAD erases the line.

5. Press Enter to repeat the ERASE command.

6. At the Select objects: prompt, pick the line at point ② in Figure 9-3.

7. AutoCAD responds 1 found and repeats the Select objects: prompt. Press Enter to end the Select objects: prompt. AutoCAD erases the line.

8. Save your drawing.

Cross-Reference

The OOPS command restores the most recently erased object and is covered in Chapter 18.

Moving objects

Use the MOVE command to move objects in your drawing. Moving an object is more complex than erasing one, because you need to tell AutoCAD the distance and direction you want the object to move.

To move an object, select it and click Move on the Modify toolbar. Alternately, click Move and then select the object.

When you choose the MOVE command, AutoCAD responds with the following prompt:

```
Base point or displacement:
```

You now have two ways of telling AutoCAD how to move the object or objects:

✦ **Displacement method:** At the `Base point or displacement:` prompt, state the entire displacement as an X,Y coordinate such as 2,3 or a polar coordinate such as 2<60, relative to the point you used to select the object. Because the word *displacement* already implies the relative distance from the object, you do *not* use @. AutoCAD responds with the `Second point of displacement:` prompt. Since you have already given AutoCAD all the information it needs, press Enter. AutoCAD moves the object.

✦ **Base point/Second point method:** At the `Base point or displacement:` prompt, pick a base point. This can be anywhere in your drawing. At the `Second point of displacement:` prompt, specify the distance and angle of movement either by picking a second point on the screen or typing a relative coordinate, using @.

The displacement method requires less input and is simpler when you select the object at a key location, and know the exact displacement so that you can type it in. The only disadvantage is that once you type in the displacement, AutoCAD sometimes displays a confusing drag line and copy of your object or objects. AutoCAD is anticipating that you might specify a second point. Ignore this display, press Enter, and your object or objects move as you specified.

The Base point/Second point method works best when you want to move an object relative to another object on the screen.

Tip   When you move an object, choose an object snap on the object or a nearby related object as the base point for exact results.

Step-by-Step: Moving Objects

On the CD-ROM

1. Open *ab9-b.dwg* from the CD-ROM.

2. Save it as *ab9-2.dwg* in your *AutoCAD Bible* folder. This drawing shows the plan of a bathroom. Each object is a *block,* a set of objects that you can select as one object. (Blocks are covered in Chapter 18.)

3. Pick anywhere on the tub to select it. Notice the grip and dashed lines. Choose Move on the Modify toolbar. Follow the prompts:

```
Base point or displacement: Move the cursor to the Intersection at
① in Figure 9-4 and click.
Second point of displacement: Move the cursor to the Intersection at
② in Figure 9-4 and click.
```

AutoCAD moves the tub to the bottom right corner of the bathroom.

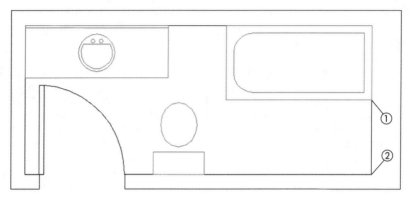

Figure 9-4: The bathroom plan.

Credit: Thanks to Bill Wynn of New Windsor, Md., for this drawing.

4. Choose Move on the Modify toolbar. Follow the prompts:

```
Select objects: Pick the sink.
Select objects: ↵
Base point or displacement: 4 <0 ↵
Second point of displacement: ↵
```

AutoCAD moves the sink 4 feet to the right.

5. Save your drawing.

Copying objects

Copying is very similar to moving. In fact, the only difference is that AutoCAD does not remove the object from its original spot, so that you end up with two objects instead of one.

 To copy an object, select it and click Copy Object on the Modify toolbar. Alternatively, click Copy Object and then select the object.

The COPY command has a Multiple option that lets you make any number of copies from the original object or objects.

 The section "Repeating Commands" in Chapter 3 explains how to repeat any command by typing multiple before any command on the command line.

When you choose the COPY command, AutoCAD responds with the following prompt:

```
Base point or displacement:
```

You now have two ways of telling AutoCAD how to copy the object or objects.

✦ **Displacement method:** At the Base point or displacement: prompt, state the entire displacement as an X,Y coordinate such as 2,3 or a polar coordinate such as 2<60 relative to the point you used to select the object. Because the word *displacement* already implies the relative distance from the object, you do *not* use @. AutoCAD responds with the Second point of displacement: prompt. Since you have already given AutoCAD all the information it needs, press Enter. AutoCAD copies the object.

✦ **Base point/Second point method:** At the Base point or displacement: prompt, pick a base point. This can be anywhere in your drawing. At the Second point of displacement: prompt, specify the distance and angle of movement either by picking a second point on the screen or typing in a relative coordinate, using @.

Step-by-Step: Copying Objects

1. Open *ab9-c.dwg* from the CD-ROM.

2. Save it as *ab9-3.dwg* in your *AutoCAD Bible* folder. This drawing shows part of an electrical schematic. OSNAP should be on.

3. Use ZOOM Window to zoom into the area of the drawing marked ① in Figure 9-5. This shows a 24-volt transformer.

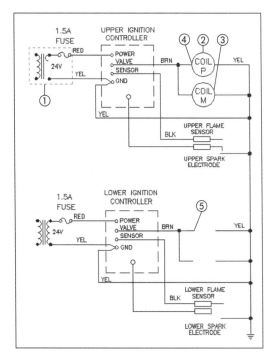

Figure 9-5: The electrical schematic.

Credit: Thanks to Robert Mack of The Dexter Company, Fairfield, Iowa, for this drawing.

4. Note that three of the arcs that make up the right side of the transformer are missing. Pick the arc at ① in Figure 9-6. Choose Copy Object from the Modify toolbar. Follow the prompts.

```
<Base point or displacement>/Multiple: m ↵
Base point: Pick the Endpoint object snap at the top of the arc at ②.
(See Figure 9-6.)
Second point of displacement: Pick the Endpoint object snap at the
bottom of the first arc at ③. (See Figure 9-6.)
Second point of displacement: Pick the Endpoint object snap at the
bottom of the second arc at ④. (See Figure 9-6.)
Second point of displacement: Pick the Endpoint object snap at the
bottom of the third arc at ⑤. (See Figure 9-6.)
Second point of displacement: ↵
```

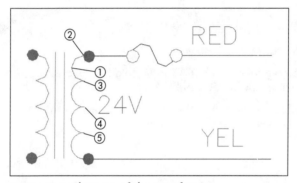

Figure 9-6: Close-up of the transformer.

5. Use ZOOM Previous to return to your previous view.

6. Select the circle at ② in Figure 9-5 (which shows the entire schematic section). Note the grips. You also want to select the text inside the circles, but it's hard to see because of the grips. Press Esc twice to remove the grips.

7. Choose Copy Object from the Modify toolbar. Now select the circle at ② in Figure 9-5 again. This time no grips obscure the text. Separately pick both lines of text inside the circle.

8. Continuing to select objects to copy, select the circle at ③ in Figure 9-5. Also select the two lines of text inside the circle. Press Enter to end the `Select objects:` prompt.

9. At the `<Base point or displacement>/Multiple:` prompt, use the Endpoint object snap to pick point ④ in Figure 9-5. At the `Second point of displacement:` prompt, use the Endpoint object snap to pick point ⑤ in Figure 9-5. AutoCAD copies the two circles with the text.

10. Save your drawing.

Rotating objects

AutoCAD lets you easily rotate an object or objects around a base point that you specify. The base point is usually a point on the object. An object snap is often used. To indicate the rotation, specify an angle of rotation. As explained in Chapter 5, zero degrees is generally to the right, and degrees increase counterclockwise, although you can change this convention. By specifying a negative angle, you can turn objects clockwise.

The simplest way to indicate the rotation is simply to type an angle at the command line. However, the Reference option lets you specify the angle with reference to another angle or an object. At the Reference angle: prompt, you type in an angle or (more likely) specify an angle by picking two points. These are often object snap points on the object. At the New angle: prompt, you type or pick a new angle. This new angle can also be indicated by picking an object snap on another object in the drawing. The Reference option can be used to align the object with another object in your drawing.

To rotate an object, choose Rotate from the Modify toolbar and select an object. Alternately, select an object and then choose Rotate from the Modify toolbar.

On the CD-ROM
I have included an AutoLISP routine, *Mrotate,* on the CD-ROM. This program lets you simultaneously rotate multiple objects. Look in *\Software\Chap09\Mrotate.*

Using CUTCLIP and COPYCLIP to move and copy

If you use other Windows programs, you usually use the Cut command to move and the Copy command to copy. Then you use the Paste command to specify a new location. In AutoCAD these commands are called CUTCLIP, COPYCLIP, and PASTECLIP. (The CLIP refers to the Windows Clipboard.) As in all Windows programs, you can use these commands to move and copy both within the program as well as from program to program.

However, AutoCAD has chosen to give these commands additional options, allowing you to not only specify the new location but a rotation angle and scale as well. These options are identical to those used by the INSERT command, which inserts blocks—sets of objects that you work with as one object. For this reason, I cover these commands in Chapter 18, which discusses blocks.

Step-by-Step: Rotating Objects

1. Open *ab7-3.dwg* from the *Results* folder of the CD-ROM. If you did the Step-by-Step exercise on ellipses in Chapter 7, you can open this drawing from your *AutoCAD Bible* folder.

2. Save it as *ab9-4.dwg* in your *AutoCAD Bible* folder. This drawing shows a conference room, as shown in Figure 9-7.

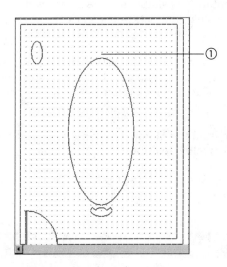

Figure 9-7: The conference room.

3. Double-click GRID on the status bar to remove the grid.

4. Choose Tools⇨Object Snap Settings. Choose Center, Quadrant, and Perpendicular. Click OK.

5. Pick the small elliptical table at the top left corner of the conference room. Choose Rotate from the Modify toolbar.

6. At the `Base point:` prompt, pick the top quadrant of the ellipse, which has a snap point. At the `<Rotation angle>/Reference:` prompt, type **90** ↵. AutoCAD rotates the small table 90 degrees around the base point.

7. Turn off Snap by double-clicking SNAP on the status bar.

8. Start the COPY command. At the `Select objects:` prompt, pick the arc that makes the back of the chair. AutoCAD responds `1 found`. Continue to pick the two lines that make the armrests and the arc that makes the front of the chair, making sure that each time AutoCAD responds `1 found`. Press Enter to end the `Select objects:` prompt.

9. At the `<Base point or displacement>/Multiple:` prompt, locate the Center object snap to pick the center of the arc that makes up the back of the chair. At the `Second point of displacement:` prompt, pick point ① in Figure 9-7. This point doesn't have to be exact.

10. Start the ROTATE command. Follow the prompts:

```
Select objects: Pick all four objects that make up the new chair you
just created and press Enter to end object selection.
Base point: Use the Center object snap to select the center of the arc
that makes up the back of the chair.
<Rotation angle>/Reference: 180 ↵.
```

11. Start the COPY command and select the four objects in the new chair. Press Enter to end object selection. Follow the prompts:

```
<Base point or displacement>/Multiple: m ↵
Base point: Use the Center object snap to select the center of the arc
that makes up the back of the chair.
Second point of displacement: Pick a point about a third of the way
around the right side of the conference table.
Second point of displacement: Pick a point about halfway around the
right side of the conference table.
Second point of displacement: Pick a point about two-thirds of the
way around the right side of the conference table.
Second point of displacement: ↵
```

12. Start the ROTATE command and select the four objects in the first of the three chairs (the top one) you just created. Press Enter to end object selection. At the `Base point:` prompt, choose the Center object snap and pick either arc of the chair. At the `<Rotation angle>/Reference:` prompt, move the cursor around, watch the image of the chair rotate, and click when the chair faces the angle of the table.

13. Repeat Step 10 for the second chair.

14. Start the ROTATE command and select the four objects in the last chair you created using the COPY command. Follow the prompts:

```
Base point: Choose the Center object snap
_center of: Pick either of the chair arcs.
<Rotation angle>/Reference: r ↵
Reference angle <0>: Use the Quadrant object snap to pick the back arc
of the chair.
Second point: Use the Quadrant object snap to pick the front arc of the
chair.
New angle: Use the Perpendicular object snap to choose the conference
table next to the chair.
```

15. Save your drawing.

Scaling objects

Scaling, or resizing, objects is another common editing task in AutoCAD. As with rotating objects, you specify a base point, usually an object snap on the object. The base point is the one point on the object that does not move or change as you scale the object. The most common way to resize an object is to specify a scale factor. The current object has a scale factor of 1. Therefore, to increase the size of the object, type in a number greater than one. For example, a scale factor of 2 doubles the size of the object. To decrease the size of the object, type in a number less than one. A scale factor of .25 creates an object 1/4 of its previous size.

As with the ROTATE command, you can scale using the Reference option. You specify the reference length, usually the current length of the object, by typing it in or using object snaps on the object. At the `New length:` prompt, you can type a new length or pick a point. AutoCAD measures this point from the base point you specified to determine the new length.

To scale an object, choose Scale from the Modify toolbar and select the object. Alternately, select the object and choose Scale from the Modify toolbar.

Step-by-Step: Scaling Objects

1. Open *ab9-d.dwg* from the CD-ROM.

2. Save it as *ab9-5.dwg* in your *AutoCAD Bible* folder. This drawing, shown in Figure 9-8, is part of a valve that is manufactured in several sizes. In this exercise you scale both views to represent a different-size valve piece.

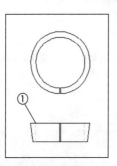

Figure 9-8: The valve piece in two views.

Credit: Thanks to Jerry Bottenfield of Clow Valve Company, Oskaloosa, Iowa, for this drawing.

3. Choose Scale from the Modify toolbar. At the `Select objects:` prompt, pick both circles in the top view (they are actually arcs since they are broken at the bottom) and the two short lines at the bottom of the circles. Press Enter to end object selection. Follow the prompts:

```
Base point: Use the Quadrant object snap to pick the left quadrant of
the inner circle.
<Scale factor>/Reference: r ↵
```

```
Reference length <1>: Use the Quadrant object snap to pick the left
quadrant of the inner circle again.
Second point: Use the Quadrant object snap to pick the right quadrant of
the inner circle.
New length: 1 ↵
```

4. Press Enter to start the SCALE command again. Select all eight lines in the bottom view including the green dashed lines. Be sure that AutoCAD says `1 found` each time. If necessary, use ZOOM Window to zoom in. Press Enter to end object selection when you have finished selecting the lines. Follow the prompts:

```
Base point: Use the Endpoint object snap at point ① in
Figure 9-8.
<Scale factor>/Reference: .4 ↵
```

5. Save your drawing. It should look like Figure 9-9.

Figure 9-9: The valve piece has now been scaled down.

Changing lines and circles

The CHANGE command changes the endpoint of a line and the radius of a circle. This command can also be used to change text and the location of blocks (covered in Chapter 18), but other newer commands do the job better, so CHANGE is now used mostly for lines and circles.

Cross-Reference

CHANGE also lets you change an object's properties—layer, linetype, linetype scale, color, elevation (Z axis coordinate), and thickness. Layer, linetype, linetype scale, and color are covered in Chapter 11. Elevation and thickness are basic 3D concepts that are covered in Chapter 22.

Changing the radius of a circle has the same result as scaling it. However, if the information you have is the new radius rather than the change in scale, the CHANGE command is easier.

To change an object, select it and type **change** ↵ on the command line. Alternately, type **change** ↵ on the command line and select the object.

Caution The CHANGE command works differently depending on whether you select lines or circles. For this reason, it can give unexpected results if you choose lines and circles at the same time. Use the command for either lines or for circles but not for both at once.

Changing lines

If you select one line, the CHANGE command changes the endpoint closest to where you picked the line. AutoCAD prompts you for a change point. When you pick it, AutoCAD brings the endpoint of the line to that change point, as shown in Figure 9-10. You can use an object snap to specify the change point.

If ORTHO is on, AutoCAD makes the line orthogonal, bringing the endpoint of the line as close as possible to the change point you specify, as shown in Figure 9-10.

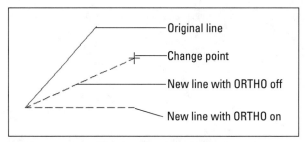

Figure 9-10: Using the CHANGE command on one line.

If you select more than one line, CHANGE works differently—it moves the nearest endpoints of all the lines to the change point so that all the lines meet at one point, as shown in Figure 9-11.

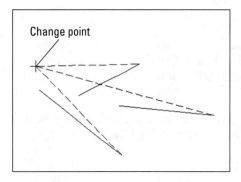

Figure 9-11: Using the CHANGE command on several lines. The original lines are shown as continuous. The new lines, after using the CHANGE command, are dashed.

Changing circles

When you select a circle, AutoCAD prompts you for a change point. If you pick one, AutoCAD resizes the circle so that it passes through the new point. You can also press Enter. Then AutoCAD prompts you to enter a new radius.

If you select more than one circle, AutoCAD moves from circle to circle, letting you specify a new radius for each, one at a time. You can tell which circle is current because of its drag image, which lets you drag the size of the circle.

Note

When you select more than one circle and try to pick a change point, AutoCAD responds `Change point ignored`. At that point, one circle becomes active and you can then pick a change point.

Tip

Another way to change the radius of a circle is to choose Properties on the Object Properties toolbar and select one circle. In the Modify Circle dialog box, you can enter any radius you want. You can use this technique to change other single objects.

Step-by-Step: Changing Circles and Lines

On the CD-ROM

1. Open *ab9-e.dwg* from the CD-ROM.

2. Save it as *ab9-6.dwg* in your *AutoCAD Bible* folder. OSNAP is on, and running object snaps have been set to Endpoint and Perpendicular.

3. Use ZOOM Window to zoom in on the concentric circles at the bottom of the drawing.

4. Type **change** ↵. At the `Select objects:` prompt, pick the innermost circle. Press Enter to end object selection.

5. At the `Properties/<Change point>:` prompt, press Enter so you can type in a radius. At the `Enter circle radius:` prompt, type **3/16** ↵.

6. Use ZOOM Dynamic to zoom in to the top of the release valve. Your view should look like Figure 9-12.

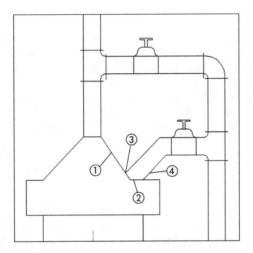

Figure 9-12: The zoomed-in view of the air and vacuum release valve.

Credit: Thanks to the Army Corps of Engineers in Vicksburg, Mississippi, for this drawing.

7. Type **change** ↵. At the Select objects: prompt, pick points ① and ② in Figure 9-12. End object selection. At the Properties/<Change point>: prompt, choose the Endpoint object snap. At the end of prompt, pick point ③ in Figure 9-12. AutoCAD redraws the lines.

8. Pick the line at ④. Press Enter to repeat the CHANGE command. At the Properties/<Change point>: prompt, use the Intersection object snap to pick point ④ in Figure 9-12. AutoCAD trims the line.

Cross-Reference

The TRIM command, discussed in Chapter 11, can make the same change that you just performed with the CHANGE command.

9. Do a ZOOM Extents and save your drawing.

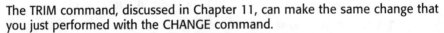

Selecting Objects

If you have been following through the exercises in this chapter, you have probably thought it tedious to individually pick several objects one at a time. Imagine trying to individually pick every object in a drawing just to move all the objects one-half unit to the left! Of course, there is a better way. In fact, AutoCAD offers many ways of selecting objects.

Selected objects are also called the *selection set* of objects.

Selecting objects after choosing a command

When you choose an editing command, AutoCAD responds with the Select objects: prompt. This prompt has 16 options—all you could ever want for selecting objects. To choose an option, type the option abbreviation. Since the Select objects: prompt repeats until you press Enter, you can combine options to select objects for any command.

In the list of options below, the capitalized letters of the option are the abbreviation you type (uppercase or lowercase letters work) at the `Select objects:` prompt.

Window

The Window option lets you pick two diagonal corners that define a window. All objects entirely within the window are selected. Figure 9-13 shows the process of picking the window. Figure 9-14 shows the result—the selected objects are highlighted by appearing with dashed instead of continuous lines.

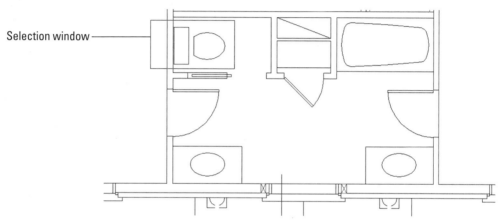

Figure 9-13: Choosing objects with a window. AutoCAD selects only objects that lie entirely within the window.

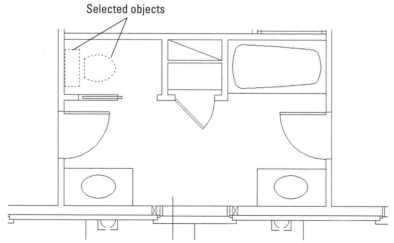

Figure 9-14: The selected objects are highlighted.

Spotlight on AutoCAD Users
R. G. Greer Design Inc., Fergus, Ontario, Canada

R. G. Greer Design Inc. uses AutoCAD and APDesign, third-party software that works directly with AutoCAD (1-888-CADSOFT or http://www.cadsoft.com), to create 3D models for its residential designs. These drawing models are initially used as presentation tools so clients can quickly visualize projects. "Two-dimensional drawings have always been difficult for clients to understand and fully visualize. Three-dimensional models allow perspective views and animation of both the exterior and interior spaces and present a clearer, more tangible design concept for our clients," says Rod Greer, President of R. G. Greer Design. The 2D AutoCAD drawing of a house shown here was designed by R. G. Greer Design Inc. You can see that the complexity of the drawing makes it difficult to visualize the final result.

In the next stage, the drawing models are put to work in construction documents and building estimates. APDesign adds to AutoCAD a parametric database of construction materials, specifications, and cost. The process of drawing objects in AutoCAD is a little different using APDesign's drawing tools. Walls, doors, windows, roofs, and so on are inserted from the APDesign database and linked so that the lines drawn in plan view (looking from the top) represent, for example, a 2×4 Spruce stud at 16" spacing with all the framing information required by local building codes. Also, a value for the cost per lineal foot is attached to the database and can be updated at any time. The 3D models are intelligent and can quickly provide building material quantity estimates through the use of APDesign's Quantity module.

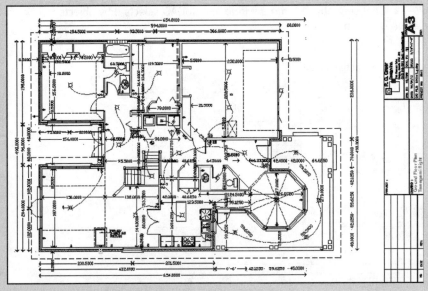

The 2D plan view of the house.

Finally, the drawing model is used for clients who require or desire a rendering—a photo-realistic visualization. The 3D model is used to create a perspective view that can be rendered by computer or by traditional artists. Here you see the computer rendering. What client wouldn't get excited about this house? R. G. Greer Design uses both rendering media, depending on the client's taste. "Computer rendering is still very rigid and exact, which leaves a very contemporary and polished finish. The artist, on the other hand, can reproduce that quality or provide a looser impression of the composition."

The computerized 3D rendering of the house.

Last

The Last option selects the last object you created.

Crossing

Crossing lets you pick two diagonal corners that define a window. All objects entirely *or partly* within the window are selected. Figure 9-15 shows the process of picking the window. Figure 9-16 shows the result—the selected objects are highlighted.

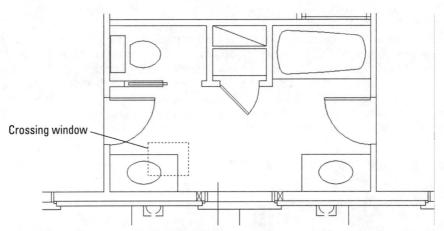

Crossing window

Figure 9-15: Choosing objects with a crossing window. AutoCAD selects any objects that lie within or partly within the window.

BOX

BOX is a combination of Window and Crossing. If you pick the two window corners from left to right, AutoCAD treats it as the Window option. If you pick the two points from right to left, AutoCAD treats it as the Crossing option. By default, you can select objects this way without specifying the BOX option. See the description of implied windowing later in this chapter.

ALL

The ALL option selects all objects in the drawing.

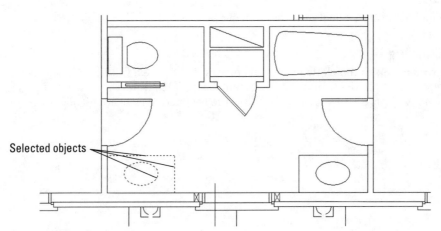

Selected objects

Figure 9-16: The selected objects are highlighted.

Fence

The Fence option lets you specify a series of temporary lines. AutoCAD selects any object crossing the lines. Figure 9-17 shows the process of defining a selection fence. Figure 9-18 shows the result—the selected objects are highlighted.

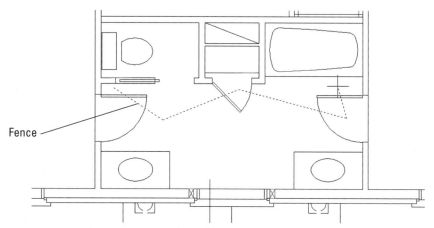

Figure 9-17: Using a fence to select objects.

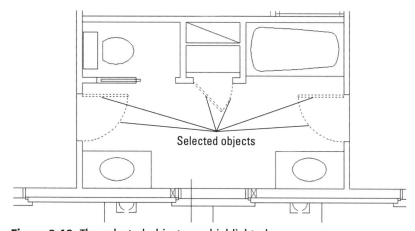

Figure 9-18: The selected objects are highlighted.

WPolygon

The Window Polygon option (Wpolygon) is like Window except that you create a polygon instead of a rectangular window. AutoCAD selects all objects that lie entirely within the polygon.

CPolygon

The Crossing Polygon option (Cpolygon) is like Crossing except that you create a polygon instead of a rectangular window. AutoCAD selects all objects that lie entirely *or partly* within the window.

Group

The Group option selects a named group of objects. (Groups are covered in Chapter 11.)

Add

Use Add after using Remove to start selecting objects again.

Remove

The Remove option lets you deselect objects. Once you use this option, all objects you choose are deselected. Use the Add option to once again select objects.

An alternative to using Remove to deselect objects is to press Shift and deselect objects by picking or implied windowing. Implied windowing is discussed later in this chapter.

Multiple

The Multiple option turns off highlighting as you select objects. This can speed up the selection of large numbers of objects. However, you cannot visually determine which objects are in the selection set.

Previous

Previous automatically selects all objects you selected for the previous command. Objects selected and edited using grips are not remembered for this option. (Grips are covered in the next chapter.)

Undo

Undo deselects the object(s) selected at the last `Select objects:` prompt. (If you removed objects at the last `Select objects:` prompt, Undo reselects them.)

Auto

Auto combines picking with the BOX option. By default, you can select objects this way without specifying this option. See the description of Implied windowing later in this chapter.

Single

When you choose this option, AutoCAD responds with another `Select objects:` prompt. You select objects using any option and then AutoCAD immediately ends the selection process. You don't have to press Enter.

Cycling through objects

It may happen that you have many objects close together in a drawing, making it hard to select the object or point you want. You could always zoom in, but in a complex drawing this can take quite a bit of time. Another trick is to use *object cycling*. At the `Select objects:` prompt, hold down Ctrl and pick at the area where more than one object overlaps. AutoCAD displays the `<Cycle on>` message. One object is highlighted. If it is not the one you want, continue to hold down Ctrl and pick. AutoCAD cycles through the objects. When you have the one you want, release Ctrl. Press Enter to turn object cycling off. You can continue to select other objects or end object selection by pressing Enter.

Selecting objects before choosing a command

When you select objects before choosing a command, your options are more limited than when you choose a command first. Nevertheless, you have enough flexibility for most situations. The reason for the limitation is that the `Command:` prompt is active and anything you might type at the keyboard to indicate a selection option could be confused with a command. You can pick the object to highlight it, use implied windowing, or use the Select command to select objects in advance.

Picking

As you practiced earlier in this chapter, you can directly pick objects at any time, before choosing a command or at the `Select options:` prompt.

Implied windowing

Implied windowing is equivalent to the Auto selection option listed earlier in this chapter. By default, implied windowing is always active. By carefully choosing which way you create a selection window, you determine how AutoCAD selects objects.

✦ **From right to left:** If the first window corner is to the right of the second one, AutoCAD creates a crossing window. AutoCAD selects all objects completely or partially within the window.

✦ **From left to right:** If the first window corner is to the left of the second one, AutoCAD creates a regular selection window. AutoCAD selects all objects completely within the window.

SELECT command

The SELECT command offers another way to select objects before choosing a command. The purpose of this command is simply to select objects. AutoCAD then saves these objects for use with the Previous selection option. Choose an editing command and type **p** ↵ at the `Select objects:` prompt. AutoCAD selects the objects you selected with the SELECT command.

Step-by-Step: Selecting Objects

1. Open *ab9-f.dwg* from the CD-ROM, as shown in Figure 9-19.

2. Draw a line from ① to ② in Figure 9-19. You will use this later to illustrate the Last selection option.

3. Type **select** ↵.

4. To select the six-burner stovetop, pick a point near ③ , being careful that the pickbox at the intersection of the crosshairs doesn't touch any object. Then move the mouse to ④ and pick again. The objects chosen appear dashed to indicate that they have been selected.

5. To select the last object created, the line drawn in step 1, type **l** ↵. It now appears dashed.

6. To select the two walls at the upper right corner, pick a point near ⑤, then a point near ⑥. The walls also become dashed.

7. To select the interior lines on the kitchen's island using a fence, type **f** ↵. Then pick points ⑦, ⑧, and ⑨. Press Enter to end the fence.

8. Type **r** ↵ at the `Select objects:` prompt, and pick the line at ⑩ to remove the external island line picked in step 7. At this point all the selected items should be dashed as shown in Figure 9-20.

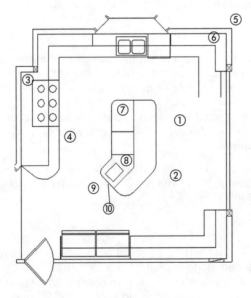

Figure 9-19: A kitchen floor plan.

9. Press Enter to complete the command.

10. Do not save this drawing.

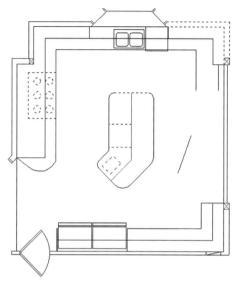

Figure 9-20: Kitchen floor plan with all selected items shown dashed.

Customizing the selection process

AutoCAD uses the Object Selection Settings dialog box to let you customize the way you select objects. To open this dialog box, choose Tools➪Selection. The dialog box is shown in Figure 9-21.

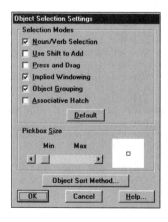

Figure 9-21: The Object Selection Settings dialog box.

This dialog box gives you control over a number of selection features.

Commands and object selection

Certain commands require you to choose objects in a certain order or require objects that have a certain relationship to each other. For example, the TRIM command (covered in the next chapter) requires that you first choose an object to trim to, then the object to trim. If you chose the objects in advance, AutoCAD wouldn't know which object to trim. Only after you choose the TRIM command does AutoCAD know to prompt you exactly for the objects it needs to complete the command. Other commands require that you select objects that are related in some way. The FILLET command (also covered in the next chapter) joins objects that meet—or would meet if extended—by drawing an arc to create a rounded corner. Here again, the command would be meaningless if, say, you chose three or more objects, so AutoCAD requires that you use the command first and then specifically prompts you to select the first object, then the second object.

You can choose objects first with the following commands:

ARRAY	DVIEW	MIRROR
BLOCK	ERASE	MOVE
CHANGE	EXPLODE	ROTATE
CHPROP	HATCH	STRETCH
COPY	LIST	WBLOCK

These commands let you choose any number of objects without restriction, so choosing the objects first and the command second works well.

Noun/Verb Selection

As you already know, the editing process consists of two parts—using a command, such as COPY or MOVE, and selecting objects. In AutoCAD lingo, *noun* means an object in your drawing. *Verb* refers to a command, because a command acts on an object. This option lets you choose whether you want to be able to select objects before choosing a command.

AutoCAD originally required you to choose the command first and then select the objects. However, in Windows programs, you typically select objects before choosing a command. For example, if you are using Microsoft Word and want to erase a sentence, you select the sentence first, then press Del.

By default, AutoCAD enables Noun/Verb Selection, the first option on the Object Selection Settings dialog box.With this option enabled, you can choose objects first —without giving up the ability to choose commands first. This gives you maximum flexibility.

The advantage of choosing objects first is that when you switch between Windows programs, you don't have to change habitual ways of selecting objects. The disadvantage of choosing objects first is that a few AutoCAD commands don't allow you to choose objects first, which can be confusing. Also, when you select objects first, grips appear—sometimes obscuring the objects you need to select.

Use Shift to Add

Use Shift to Add is the second option in the Object Selection Settings dialog box. By default, this option is not selected. In AutoCAD, you often choose more than one object at a time for editing. Therefore, AutoCAD simply lets you choose object after object—when you choose a second object, the first object stays selected— so that you can easily choose any number of objects you want.

However, Windows programs typically let you choose only one object at a time. For example, let's say you select a few sentences in a Windows word processing program. If you then decide to select another group of sentences elsewhere in the document, the first set of sentences are deselected and only the second group is selected. You can add to the first selection using the Shift key as you select. To use a more graphical example, you can choose Drawing from the Standard toolbar in Microsoft Word and draw a few shapes. If you select one shape and then a second shape, choosing the second shape deselects the first shape. However, if you hold down Shift, you can choose any number of shapes at a time.

AutoCAD lets you use this type of selecting if you wish, although it is not the default, probably because selecting more than one object at a time is so common. If you choose this option, after selecting one object, you must hold down Shift to select any additional object.

Press and Drag

One of the ways to select objects is to create a window that includes a number of objects. You are already familiar with creating a similar window from using ZOOM with the Window option. If the Press and Drag option is chosen, you need to click at one corner of the window and, without releasing the pick button, drag the cursor to the diagonally opposite corner. This type of action is typical of Windows programs.

By default, this option is not selected, which means that to create a window you click at one corner of the window, release the pick button, and pick again at the diagonally opposite corner.

Note

This setting does not affect ZOOM Window, which always requires two separate picks.

Implied Windowing

By default, this option is on. Implied windowing means that if you pick any point not on an object, AutoCAD assumes you want to create a selection window. You can then pick the opposite corner to select objects. If you pick the corners from right to left, you get a crossing window. If you pick the corners from left to right, you get a standard selection window. If implied windowing is not on, when you pick a point not on an object, AutoCAD assumes you missed some object and gives you this message on the command line:

```
0 found
```

This option applies when you have chosen a command and see the Select objects: prompt. If you turn this option off, you can still enter the Crossing or Window selection options manually (by typing **c** or **w**). When selecting objects before choosing the command, implied windowing is always on.

Object Grouping

Creating groups of objects is discussed in the next chapter. Groups are sets of objects that you name. If object grouping is on (the default) when you select one object in a group, all the objects in a group are automatically selected. Object grouping is a global setting, but you can also set object grouping on or off for individual groups.

Associative Hatch

A hatch is a pattern or solid that fills in a closed area. Hatching is covered in Chapter 16. Associative hatches are associated with the objects they fill. When this option is off (the default), the hatch pattern is considered separately from the object it fills. Therefore, if you select the hatch pattern, you do not automatically select the object. When this option is on, selecting the hatch pattern automatically selects the object it fills. This allows you to, say, move two objects together by selecting just the hatch pattern associated with them.

Default

This button returns you to the default settings, which set Noun/Verb Selection, Implied Windowing, and Object Grouping on and the other options off. This button makes it easy to change one or two settings temporarily for a specific need and then return to your familiar ways of selecting objects.

Pickbox Size

In Chapter 4, you learned about the aperture, which is the little box at the crosshairs that you use to pick object snaps such as Endpoint or Intersection. The pickbox is the box that you see at the intersection of the crosshairs when selecting (or picking) objects. The Pickbox Size area lets you set the size of the pickbox.

Note

If Noun/Verb Selection is off and grips are disabled, no pickbox appears at the intersection of the crosshairs until you choose an editing command and AutoCAD gives you the `Select objects:` prompt. However, if either Noun/Verb Selection or grips are on, the pickbox is always at the crosshairs, letting you select objects at any time.

Object Sort Method

Click the Object Sort Method button to open the Object Sort Method dialog box, as shown in Figure 9-22.

Figure 9-22: The Object Sort Method dialog box.

You use the Object Sort Method dialog box to specify when AutoCAD processes objects in your drawing in the order in which they were created. Object sorting is used mostly for programming applications that operate on objects and need them to be in the same order they were created—the order in which they exist in the drawing database. By default, object sorting is on for plotting and PostScript output.

Summary

All drawings need to be edited, either as part of the drawing process or to make corrections. When you edit existing objects, you must select them. One of the simplest editing commands is the ERASE command. Two other often-used commands are COPY and MOVE. To rotate an object, specify a base point and rotation angle. To scale an object, specify a base point and scale factor.

The CHANGE command lets you easily change the endpoint of a line (or lines) and the radius of a circle.

The many object selection options make it easy to select just the objects you need to work on. If you select objects before choosing a command, you can pick them one by one or use implied windowing. You can customize many of the object selection features in the Object Selection Settings dialog box.

The next chapter covers the more advanced editing commands.

✦   ✦   ✦

Editing Your Drawing: Advanced Tools

Advanced Editing Commands

This chapter completes the discussion of geometric editing commands — covering the more complex commands used to refine the details of your drawing. Then I discuss grips, which make it easy to move, mirror, rotate, scale, and stretch objects. I end the chapter with a discussion of two ways to control the selection of objects — groups and filters.

Copying and Moving Commands

Three commands allow you to copy objects in very specific ways. MIRROR creates a mirror image. ARRAY creates a rectangular or circular pattern of an object. OFFSET creates parallel objects. Although these commands make copies of objects, they accomplish a result that would be difficult or impossible simply by using the COPY command. The ALIGN command moves objects by aligning them with other objects in the drawing.

Using the MIRROR command

Many drawings have symmetrical elements. Often, especially in mechanical drawing, you can create one-half or one-quarter of a model and complete it simply by mirroring what you have drawn.

To mirror, select an object or objects and then choose Mirror from the Modify toolbar. Alternately, choose Mirror from the Modify toolbar and then select an object or objects.

AutoCAD prompts for the first and second points of the mirror line. This is an imaginary line across which AutoCAD creates the mirrored object. The length of the line is irrelevant — only the direction is important.

Tip   Most mirror lines are orthogonal. Therefore, once you specify the first mirror point, turn on ORTHO and move the mouse in the direction of the second point. You can then quickly pick the second point anywhere on the screen.

AutoCAD then asks if you want to delete the old objects. The old objects refer to the objects you have selected to mirror. If you want to keep them, type **n** ↵. You would keep the old objects when you are building a symmetrical model and want the mirror image to be added to the original object(s). Type **y** ↵ when you want to edit an object — change its orientation — so that only the mirror image is retained in the drawing.

Step-by-Step: Mirroring Objects

On the CD-ROM

1. Open *ab7-2.dwg* from the *Results* folder of your CD-ROM. If you completed the exercise on arcs in Chapter 7, you can open this drawing from your *AutoCAD Bible* folder.

2. Save it as *ab10-1.dwg* in your *AutoCAD Bible* folder.

3. Choose Erase on the Modify toolbar. At the Select objects: prompt, pick the line and two arcs to the bottom-right of the two centerlines, then press Enter. The resulting model should look like Figure 10-1.

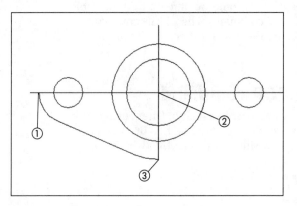

Figure 10-1: A partially completed mounting plate.

4. Choose Mirror from the Modify toolbar. At the `Select objects:` prompt, pick the remaining exterior line and two arcs and press Enter.

5. At the `First point of mirror line:` prompt, pick the intersection ① in Figure 10-1. At the `Second point:` prompt, pick the intersection ②.

6. AutoCAD prompts: `Delete old objects? <N>`. Press Enter to accept the default, No.

7. Choose Mirror from the Modify toolbar. At the `Select objects:` prompt, type **p** ↵ to pick the original lines. Then pick the new exterior line and two arcs and then press Enter.

8. At the `First point of mirror line:` prompt, pick the intersection ②. At the `Second point:` prompt, pick the intersection ③. Press Enter again at the `Delete old objects? <N>` prompt.

9. AutoCAD completes the mounting plate. Save your drawing. It should look like Figure 10-2.

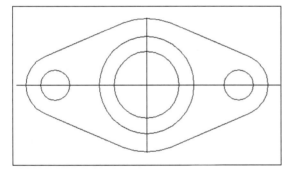

Figure 10-2: The completed mounting plate.

Using the ARRAY command

The ARRAY command creates a rectangular or circular (polar) pattern by copying the object(s) you select as many times as you specify. The ARRAY command is a powerful drawing tool. It can quickly create large numbers of objects — saving a huge amount of time and effort.

AutoCAD Release 14's new lightweight polyline object improves display speed and reduces drawing file size — making it easier to use with the ARRAY command.

To create an array, select the object or objects and choose Array from the Modify toolbar. Alternately, choose Array from the Modify toolbar and select the object or objects.

Rectangular arrays

To create a rectangular array, follow these steps. Figure 10-3 shows an example of a rectangular array.

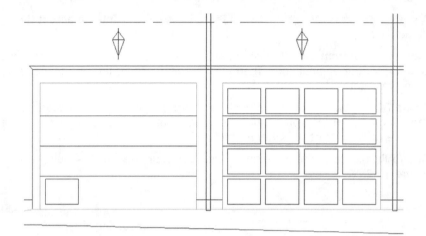

Figure 10-3: The garage door was drawn with one panel as shown on the left side. A rectangular array created the rest of the door panels as shown on the right.

Credit: Thanks to Henry Dearborn, AIA, Fairfield, Iowa, for this drawing.

1. Type **r** ↵ at the `Rectangular or Polar array (R/P):` prompt or press Enter if <R> is shown as the default. (The default is whichever type of array you performed last.)

2. AutoCAD responds with the `Number of rows (---) <1>:` prompt, showing you the direction of rows in parentheses. Type in the total number of rows you want to create.

3. AutoCAD displays the `Number of columns (|||) <1>:` prompt, again indicating in parentheses what columns look like. Type in the total number of columns.

4. AutoCAD responds with the `Unit cell or distance between rows (---):` prompt. Type in the distance between rows. A positive number builds the array upward. A negative number builds the array downward. Alternately, you can pick two points — the start point of the array and the start point of the next row and column. These two points define a *cell,* which specifies in one step the distance between the rows and the columns.

5. If you typed in a distance between rows, AutoCAD displays the `Distance between columns (|||):` prompt. Type in the distance between columns. A positive number builds the array to the right. A negative number builds the array to the left.

AutoCAD creates the rectangular array.

Tip If you need to create a number of copies of an object along a straight path, use a one-column or one-row array instead of the COPY command. It's faster and easier.

Note If you change the Snap angle or the UCS, AutoCAD creates the rectangular array at the angle of the snap or UCS. Chapter 8 explains how to do this.

Polar (circular) arrays

To create a polar array, follow these steps. An example is shown in Figure 10-4.

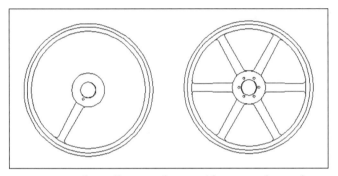

Figure 10-4: The pulley was drawn with one spoke as shown at left. A polar array created the additional spokes.

Credit: Thanks to Robert Mack of the Dexter Company, Fairfield, Iowa, for this drawing.

1. Type **p** at the `Rectangular or Polar array (R/P):` prompt or press Enter if `<P>` is shown as the default. (The default shown is whichever type of array you performed last.)

2. AutoCAD responds with the `Base/<Specify center point of array>:` prompt. A polar array has a center point, like a circle, around which the objects are arrayed. Specify the center point. You can also use the new Base option to specify the base point of the objects to use when arraying.

3. AutoCAD asks for the number of items. If you know how many of the object you want the polar array to have, type in the number (the total number, not the number of copies). If you don't know, press Enter and respond to the next two prompts. AutoCAD figures it out for you.

4. AutoCAD displays the `Angle to fill (+=ccw, -=cw) <360>:` prompt. A 360-degree angle means that the polar array covers an entire circle. Typing **90** would create a quarter-circular array. In parentheses, the prompt explains that a positive angle arrays in a counterclockwise direction; a negative angle arrays in a clockwise direction. If you responded to the `Number of items:`

prompt and can respond to the next prompt, you don't need to respond to this prompt. In that case, press Enter.

5. AutoCAD offers the Angle between items: prompt. If you responded to the last two prompts, AutoCAD omits this prompt. Otherwise, type in the angle (along the circle) between items (from the start of one item to the start of the next).

6. AutoCAD responds with the Rotate objects as they are copied? <Y> prompt. If you respond **y** for yes, AutoCAD rotates the objects around the center point, as well as arrays them. If you respond **n**, AutoCAD keeps the objects at their original angle.

AutoCAD creates the array.

Step-by-Step: Arraying Objects

1. Open *ab10-a.dwg* from the CD-ROM.

2. Save it as *ab10-2.dwg* in your *AutoCAD Bible* folder. It looks like Figure 10-5.

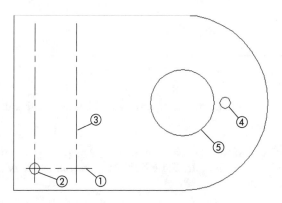

Figure 10-5: A partially completed mounting bracket.

3. Choose Array on the Modify toolbar. At the Select objects: prompt, pick the horizontal centerline ① in Figure 10-5, then press Enter.

4. At the Rectangular or Polar array (<R>/P): prompt, type **r** ↵ or press Enter if <R> is the default.

5. Type **4** ↵ at the Number of rows (---) <1>: prompt. At the Number of columns (|||) <1>: prompt, press Enter to accept the default of 1.

6. At the Unit cell or distance between rows (---): prompt, type **1**↵. AutoCAD places three more centerlines above the original.

7. To add the holes to the pattern again, choose Array from the Modify toolbar.

8. At the Select objects: prompt, pick the circle ② in Figure 10-5, then press Enter.

9. Follow the prompts:

```
Rectangular or Polar array (<R>/P): ↵
Number of rows ( - ) <1>: 4 ↵
Number of columns (|||) <1>: 2 ↵
Unit cell or distance between rows ( - ): Pick the center of circle
②.
Other corner: Pick the intersection of centerlines near ③ in Figure 10-
5.
```

AutoCAD arrays the holes to fit the centerlines.

10. To create a 6-hole bolt circle, pick the hole ④ in Figure 10-5.

11. Choose Array from the Modify toolbar. Follow the prompts:

```
Rectangular or Polar array (R/P) <R>: p ↵
Base/<Center point of array>: Pick the center of the large circle at
⑤ in Figure 10-5.
Number of items: 6 ↵
Angle to fill (+=ccw, -=cw) <360>: ↵
Rotate objects as they are copied? <Y> ↵
```

AutoCAD completes the mounting bracket.

12. Save your drawing. It should look like Figure 10-6.

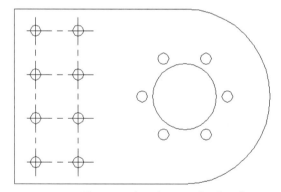

Figure 10-6: The completed mounting bracket.

Offsetting objects

The OFFSET command creates lines or curves parallel to one existing object. The beauty of this command is apparent when you start to create complex objects, such as polylines, which are covered in Chapter 16. You may remember that polygons and rectangles are polylines, meaning that they are treated as one object. Using OFFSET, you can create concentric polygons, for example, in one step. Figure 10-7 shows two concentric polygons. The outside polygon was created with the POLYGON command, and the inside polygon was created using OFFSET.

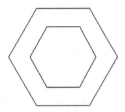

Figure 10-7: Using OFFSET to create concentric polygons.

 To offset an object, choose Offset from the Modify toolbar. You cannot select objects before choosing the command.

AutoCAD responds with the `Offset distance or Through <Through>:` prompt. AutoCAD offers two slightly different ways to specify the offset:

✦ If you type an offset distance, AutoCAD responds with the `Select object to offset:` prompt. You can select one object. Then AutoCAD displays the `Side to offset?` prompt. Pick a point to indicate on which side of the object AutoCAD should create the offset copy. AutoCAD creates the offset and continues to show the `Select object to offset:` prompt so you can offset other objects using the same offset distance. Press Enter to end the command.

✦ If you want to indicate a through point, such as an object snap on another object, type **t** ↵. Then AutoCAD displays the `Select object to offset:` prompt. Pick one object. At the `Through point:` prompt, pick a point through which you want the offset to go. AutoCAD creates the offset.

Step-by-Step: Using the OFFSET Command

1. Open *ab10-b.dwg* from the CD-ROM.

2. Save it as *ab10-3.dwg* in your *AutoCAD Bible* folder. It looks like Figure 10-8.

3. Choose Offset on the Modify toolbar. Follow the prompts:

```
Offset distance or Through <Through>: t ↵
Select object to offset: Pick ① in Figure 10-8.
Select object to offset: ↵
Through point: Pick the center of ②.
Select object to offset: ↵
```

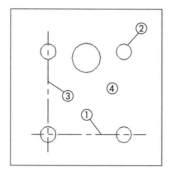

Figure 10-8: A partially completed clamp plate.

AutoCAD copies the centerline through the upper circles.

4. Choose Offset from the Modify toolbar again. At the `Offset distance or Through <Through>:` prompt, type **2** ↵. Pick the centerline ③ at the `Select object to offset:` prompt, and near ④ at the `Side to offset?` prompt. Press Enter to end the command. AutoCAD copies the vertical centerline 2 units to the right of the original.

5. Save your drawing. It should look like Figure 10-9.

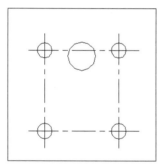

Figure 10-9: The completed clamp plate.

Aligning objects

The ALIGN command lets you move and rotate an object or objects in one procedure. It is especially useful in 3D work. By specifying which points on an object move where, you can align the object with other objects in your drawing, as shown in Figure 10-10.

See Chapter 24 for the use of this command in 3D editing.

Aligning requires several steps. Even so, it can save time when you need to both move and rotate at the same time, especially if you don't know the rotation angle you need. To align an object, choose Modify⇨3D Operations⇨Align and select an object or objects. Alternately, select the object or objects first and then choose Modify⇨3D Operations⇨Align. Then follow these steps:

1. AutoCAD asks for the first source point. Specify a point, usually an object snap on the object you want to move.

2. AutoCAD asks for the first destination point. Specify the point where you want the first source point to end up.

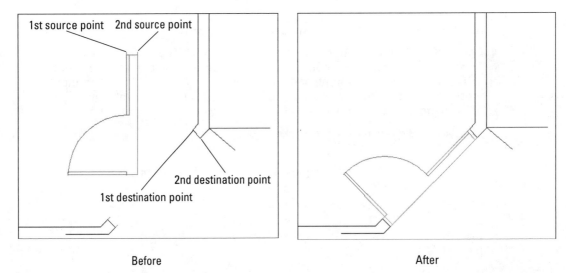

Figure 10-10: Aligning a door with a wall.

3. AutoCAD asks for the second source point. If you press Enter, AutoCAD simply moves the selected objects. To continue to align, specify another point, usually an object snap on the object you want to move.

4. AutoCAD asks for the second destination point. Specify the point where you want the second source point to end up.

5. AutoCAD asks for the third source point. This is used for 3D alignment, to specify how you want to rotate the object in the third dimension. For 2D alignment, press Enter.

6. AutoCAD displays the <2d> or 3d transformation: prompt. This is used for 3D work, letting you confine the rotation of a 3D model to two dimensions. For 2D work, press Enter again to accept the 2d default.

AutoCAD aligns the object(s).

If you align objects using two pairs of points, AutoCAD prompts you to scale the object(s). AutoCAD compares the distance between the two source points and the two destination points to scale the object. You can press Enter to accept the default of not scaling, or type **y** ↵ to choose the Yes option and scale the object(s).

Step-by-Step: Aligning Objects in Two Dimensions

1. Open *ab10-c.dwg* from the CD-ROM.

2. Save it as *ab10-4.dwg* in your *AutoCAD Bible* folder. It looks like Figure 10-11.

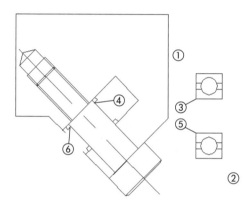

Figure 10-11: A partially completed bearing block.

3. Select the bearing cross-sections on the right using a window, picking near ① then ②.

4. Choose Modify⇨3D Operations⇨Align and follow the prompts:

```
1st source point: Pick the endpoint at ③ in Figure 10-11.
1st destination point: Pick the endpoint at ④.
2nd source point: Pick the endpoint at ⑤.
2nd destination point: Pick the endpoint at ⑥.
3rd source point or <continue>: ↵
Scale objects to alignment points? [Yes/No] <No>: ↵
```

AutoCAD aligns the bearing in its proper position on the shaft.

5. Save your drawing. It should look like Figure 10-12.

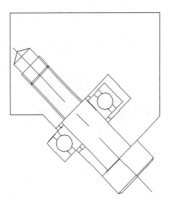

Figure 10-12: The completed bearing block.

Resizing Commands

There are four additional commands that resize objects. The TRIM and EXTEND commands bring the endpoint of an object to another object. LENGTHEN lets you lengthen or shorten a line or arc. STRETCH is used to stretch (larger or shorter) a group of objects, letting you change their direction at the same time.

Trimming objects

As you edit a drawing, you may find that lines or arcs that once perfectly met other objects now hang over. To trim an object, you must first specify the *cutting edge*, which defines the point at which AutoCAD cuts the object you want to trim. You define the cutting edge by selecting an object. You can select several cutting edges and several objects to trim at one time, as shown in Figure 10-13. When you select an object to trim, you must pick the object on the side that you want trimmed (not on the side that you want left remaining). A common use for the TRIM command is to create intersections of walls and doors in architectural floor plans.

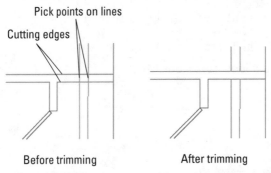

Figure 10-13: Trimming two objects using two cutting edges.

The object you want to trim does not have to actually intersect the cutting edge. AutoCAD can trim an object to a cutting edge that would intersect the object if extended. This is called trimming to an implied intersection, shown in Figure 10-14.

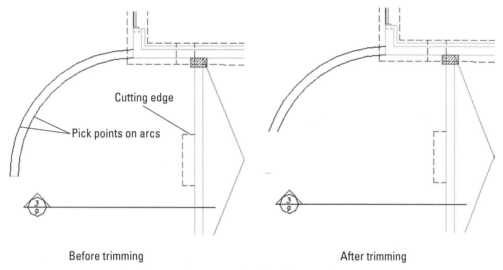

Before trimming   After trimming

Figure 10-14: Trimming two arcs to an implied intersection.

You can trim arcs, circles, elliptical arcs, lines, open polylines, rays, and splines. You can use polylines, arcs, circles, ellipses, lines, rays, regions, splines, text, or xlines as cutting edges.

 To trim an object, choose Trim from the Modify toolbar. You cannot select objects before the command with Trim. AutoCAD displays the `Select cutting edges:` `(Projmode = UCS, Edgemode = Extend) Select objects:` prompt. In parentheses, AutoCAD lets you know the values of the two system variables that affect trimming. Projmode is used only for 3D models. Edgemode is used for implied intersections. When Edgemode is set to 1 (Extend), AutoCAD trims to the implied intersection of the cutting edge and the object to be trimmed. At this prompt, pick the object(s) you want to use as a cutting edge. Press Enter to end object selection.

✦ If you want to trim to an actual intersection, at the `<Select object to trim>/Project/Edge/Undo:` prompt, select objects to trim. Be sure to pick each object at or near the end you want to trim. Press Enter to end object selection. AutoCAD trims the object(s).

✦ If you want to trim to an implied intersection, at the `<Select object to trim>/Project/Edge/Undo:` prompt, type **e** ↵. AutoCAD responds with the `Extend/No extend <No extend>:` prompt. Type **e** ↵. Then select the objects you want to trim at the `<Select object to trim>/Project/Edge/Undo:` prompt. Be sure to pick each object at or near the end you want to trim. Press Enter to end object selection. AutoCAD trims the object(s).

Use the Undo option if the results of the trim are not what you want. You can then continue to select objects to trim.

Tip

Generally, you pick the objects to be trimmed individually. You cannot use windows to select them. However, you can use the Fence object selection method. AutoCAD trims the side of the object that the fence line crosses.

Note

An object can be used as both a cutting edge and an object to be trimmed in the same trimming process.

Step-by-Step: Trimming Objects

**On the
CD-ROM**

1. Open *ab10-d.dwg* from the CD-ROM.

2. Save it as *ab10-5.dwg* in your *AutoCAD Bible* folder. It looks like Figure 10-15.

3. Choose Trim on the Modify toolbar. At the `Select objects:` prompt, pick lines at ① and ② in Figure 10-15, then press Enter.

4. At the `<Select object to trim>/Project/Edge/Undo:` prompt, pick lines at ① and ② in Figure 10-15 again. Be sure to pick them above the intersection as shown. AutoCAD trims the lines. Each line is used as the cutting edge for the other line.

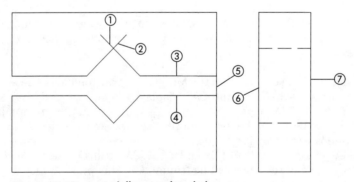

Figure 10-15: A partially completed clamp.

5. Choose Trim on the Modify toolbar again. At the `Select objects:` prompt, pick lines at ③ and ④ in Figure 10-15, then press Enter.

6. At the `<Select object to trim>/Project/Edge/Undo:` prompt, type **e** ↵ to select Edge. Type **e** ↵ again at the `Extend/No extend <No extend>:` prompt to choose Extend.

7. Pick lines at ⑤, ⑥, and ⑦ in Figure 10-15. AutoCAD trims the lines. If you wish, you can add horizontal lines to connect the new endpoints to complete the right view.

8. Save your drawing. It should look like Figure 10-16.

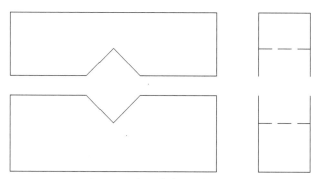

Figure 10-16: The completed clamp in two views.

Extending objects

The EXTEND command has the same prompts as the TRIM command, but instead of extending objects to a cutting edge, it extends them to a *boundary edge* (see Figure 10-17). As with TRIM, when you select an object to extend, you must pick the object on the side that you want extended (not on the side that you want left as is).

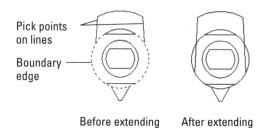

Pick points
on lines

Boundary
edge

Before extending   After extending

Figure 10-17: Extending two lines using an arc as the boundary edge.

The object you want to extend does not have to actually intersect the boundary edge after its extension. AutoCAD can extend an object to a boundary edge that would intersect the extended object if it were longer. This is called extending to an implied intersection, shown in Figure 10-18.

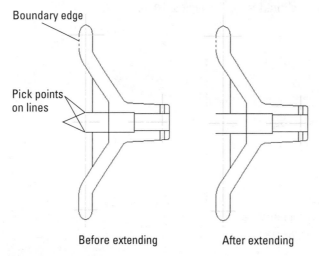

Boundary edge

Pick points on lines

Before extending   After extending

Figure 10-18: Extending two arcs to an implied intersection.

You can extend arcs, circles, elliptical arcs, lines, open polylines, rays, and splines. You can use polylines, arcs, circles, ellipses, lines, rays, regions, splines, text, or xlines as boundary edges.

To extend an object, choose Extend from the Modify toolbar. You cannot select objects before the command with Extend. AutoCAD displays the Select boundary edges: (Projmode = UCS, Edgemode = Extend) Select objects: prompt. In parentheses, AutoCAD lets you know the values of the two system variables that affect extending. Projmode is used only for 3D models. Edgemode is used for implied intersections. When Edgemode is set to 1 (Extend), AutoCAD extends to the implied intersection of the boundary edge and the object to be extended. At this prompt, pick the object(s) you want to use as the boundary edge(s). Press Enter to end object selection.

✦ If the extension will result in an actual intersection, at the <Select object to extend>/Project/Edge/Undo: prompt, select objects to extend. Be sure to pick each object at the end you want to extend. Press Enter to end object selection. AutoCAD extends the object(s).

✦ If you want to extend to an implied intersection, at the <Select object to extend>/Project/Edge/Undo: prompt, type **e** ↵. AutoCAD responds with the Extend/No extend <No extend>: prompt. Type **e** ↵. Then select the objects you want to extend at the <Select object to extend>/Project /Edge/Undo: prompt. Be sure to pick each object at the end you want to extend. Press Enter to end object selection. AutoCAD extends the object(s).

Use the Undo option if the results of the extension are not what you want. You can then continue to select objects to extend.

Tip

Generally, you pick the objects to be extended individually. You cannot use windows to select them. However, you can use the Fence object selection method. AutoCAD extends the side of the object that the fence line crosses.

Note

An object can be used as both a boundary edge and an object to be extended in the same extending process.

Step-by-Step: Extending Objects

On the CD-ROM

1. Open *ab10-e.dwg* from the CD-ROM.

2. Save it as *ab10-6.dwg* in your *AutoCAD Bible* folder. It looks like Figure 10-19.

3. Choose Extend on the Modify toolbar. At the `Select objects:` prompt, pick the line at ① in Figure 10-19, then press Enter.

4. At the `<Select object to extend>/Project/Edge/Undo:` prompt, pick the line at ② in Figure 10-19. Press Enter to finish selecting objects. AutoCAD extends the line.

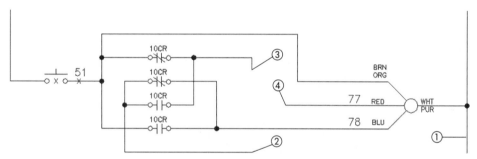

Figure 10-19: An electrical schematic.

5. Choose Extend on the Modify toolbar again. At the `Select objects:` prompt, pick the lines at ③ and ④ in Figure 10-19, then press Enter.

6. At the `<Select object to trim>/Project/Edge/Undo:` prompt, type **e** ↵ to select Edge. Type **e** ↵ again at the `Extend/No extend <No extend>:` prompt to choose the Extend option.

7. Pick lines ③ and ④ in Figure 10-19 again at the points shown. AutoCAD extends the lines to meet.

8. Save your drawing. It should look like Figure 10-20.

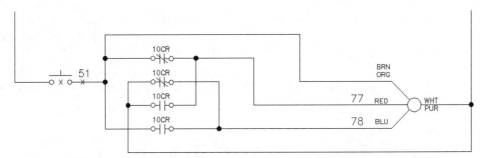

Figure 10-20: The completed electrical schematic.

Lengthening objects

The LENGTHEN command both lengthens and shortens. It works on open objects such as lines, arcs, and polylines, and also increases or decreases the included angle of arcs. (You can both change the length of an arc and change its included angle using LENGTHEN.) AutoCAD offers several ways of defining the new length or included angle. Use LENGTHEN when you want to lengthen or shorten an object but there is no available intersecting edge or boundary to use with TRIM or EXTEND.

Note

In the LENGTHEN command, the length of an arc is measured along its circumference. Don't confuse this with the Length of chord option of the ARC command, which refers to the length of a line stretched from one endpoint of the arc to the other endpoint.

To lengthen (or shorten) an object, choose Lengthen from the Modify toolbar. You cannot select objects before the command with LENGTHEN. AutoCAD responds with the `DElta/Percent/Total/DYnamic/<Select object>:` prompt. Choose one of the options as explained below.

✦ **Select object:** This is the default. However, its purpose is to display the current measurements of the object. This can help you to decide how to define the final length or angle of the object. The current length is displayed at the command line, followed by a prompt to choose one of the other options to specify the new length or angle you want.

✦ **DElta:** Type **de** ↵. Delta means the change, or difference, between the current and new length or included angle. AutoCAD responds with the `Angle/<Enter delta length (0.0000)>:` prompt. If you want to change an included angle, type **a** ↵ and then type in the change in the included angle. Otherwise, simply type in the change in the length of the object. A positive number increases the length or included angle. A negative number decreases the length or included angle.

✦ **Percent:** Type **p** ↵. At the Enter percent length <100.0000>: prompt, type in what percent of the original object you want the final object to be. Amounts over 100 lengthen the object. Amounts under 100 shorten the object. You cannot change an included angle using this option.

✦ **Total:** Type **t** ↵. At the Angle/<Enter total length (0.0000)>: prompt, you can either choose the Angle suboption, as described for the Delta option, or use the default total length option. Either way, you enter the total angle or length you want.

✦ **DYnamic:** Type **dy** ↵. This options lets you drag the endpoint of the object closest to where you picked it. You can use an object snap to specify the new endpoint.

Once you have used an option to specify the length you want, AutoCAD responds with the <Select object to change>/Undo: prompt. Here you select the object you want to change. Be sure to pick the endpoint of the object where you want to make the change.

AutoCAD then continues the same prompt so that you can pick other objects using the same length specifications. Choose Undo to undo the last change. Press Enter to end the command.

Step-by-Step: Lengthening and Shortening Objects

On the
CD-ROM

1. Open *ab10-f.dwg* from the CD-ROM.

2. Save it as *ab10-7.dwg* in your *AutoCAD Bible* folder. It is a capacitor symbol from an electrical schematic, as shown in Figure 10-21.

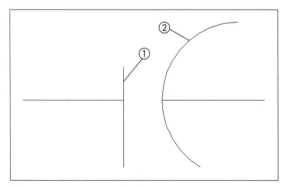

Figure 10-21: A poorly drawn capacitor symbol.

3. Choose Lengthen on the Modify toolbar and follow the prompts:

```
DElta/Percent/Total/DYnamic/<Select object>: Pick the line at ① in
Figure 10-21.
Current length: 0.200
DElta/Percent/Total/DYnamic/<Select object>: de ↵
Angle/<Enter delta length (0.000)>: .07 @e
<Select object to change>/Undo: Pick the line at ① in
Figure 10-21.
<Select object to change>/Undo: ↵
```

AutoCAD lengthens the line.

4. Choose Lengthen on the Modify toolbar and follow the prompts:

```
DElta/Percent/Total/DYnamic/<Select object>: Pick the arc at ② in
Figure 10-21.
Current length: 0.407, included angle: 150
DElta/Percent/Total/DYnamic/<Select object>: t ↵
Angle/<Enter total length (0.200)>: a ↵
Enter total angle <150>: 120 ↵
<Select object to change>/Undo: Pick the arc at ② in Figure 10-21.
<Select object to change>/Undo: ↵
```

AutoCAD shortens the arc.

5. Save your drawing. It should look like Figure 10-22.

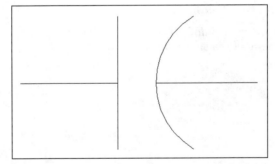

Figure 10-22: The completed capacitor symbol.

Stretching objects

The STRETCH command is generally used to stretch groups of objects. It can be used to enlarge a room in a floor plan, for example. You can also shrink objects. You can change not only the length of the objects but the angle as well. You use a crossing window to choose the objects to be stretched. All objects that cross the boundaries of the crossing window are stretched. All objects that lie entirely within the crossing window are merely moved. Successful stretching involves precise placement of the crossing window.

Figure 10-23 shows the process of stretching a conference room. Note that the walls that cross the boundaries of the crossing window are stretched. However, the objects that are entirely within the crossing window are just moved. This maintains the integrity of the model.

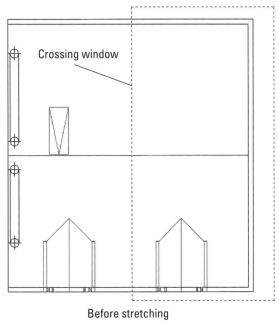

Figure 10-23: Stretching a garage.

Before stretching

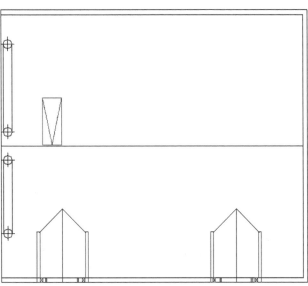

After stretching

You cannot stretch circles, text, or blocks. You can stretch arcs, although the result may not be what you expect.

The real power of the STRETCH command is in stretching a number of objects at once. However, you can also stretch one line. The results are similar to using the CHANGE command to change the endpoint of a line.

 To stretch objects, choose Stretch from the Modify toolbar. Alternatively, you can select the objects first and then the Stretch command, but be sure to use a crossing window. (You can also use a crossing polygon.)

If you choose the command first, AutoCAD responds with the Select objects to stretch by crossing-window or crossing-polygon... instruction and then the Select objects: prompt. Create the crossing window and select the objects you want to stretch. If you select objects first and then choose the command, AutoCAD explains Stretching selected objects by last window... and tells you how many objects it found.

Tip

After completing the crossing window, check to see which objects are highlighted. This helps you avoid unwanted results. You can use the object selection Remove option (type **r** ↵ at the command prompt) to remove objects that you don't want to stretch or move.

AutoCAD then displays the Base point or displacement: prompt. This part is just like moving objects. You can respond in two ways.

✦ Pick a base point. At the Second point of displacement: prompt, pick a second point. Object snaps are helpful for picking these points.

✦ Type a displacement, *without* using the @ sign. For example, to lengthen the objects by 6 feet in the 0-degree direction, type **6'<0** ↵. Then press Enter at the Second point of displacement: prompt.

AutoCAD stretches the objects.

Note

When specifying a displacement by typing at the keyboard, you can use both positive and negative distances. For example, 6'<180 is the same as -6'<0. Both would stretch the objects 6 feet to the left.

Tip

Usually, you want to stretch at an orthogonal angle. If you are going to stretch by picking, turn ORTHO on. Object snaps and snap modes are other helpful drawing aids for stretching.

Step-by-Step: Stretching Objects

On the CD-ROM

1. Open *ab10-g.dwg* from your CD-ROM.

2. Save it as *ab10-8.dwg* in your *AutoCAD Bible* folder. This drawing is the plan view of a garage, as shown in Figure 10-24.

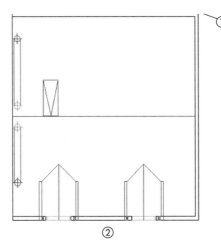

Figure 10-24: A plan view of a garage.

3. Choose Stretch from the Modify toolbar. At the `Select objects:` prompt, pick ① in Figure 10-24. At the `Other corner:` prompt, pick ②. AutoCAD notifies you that it found 32 objects. Press Enter to end object selection.

4. At the `Base point or displacement:` prompt, type **6'<0** ↵ to lengthen the garage by 6 feet. At the `Second point of displacement:` prompt, press Enter. AutoCAD ends the command.

5. Save your drawing. It should look like Figure 10-25.

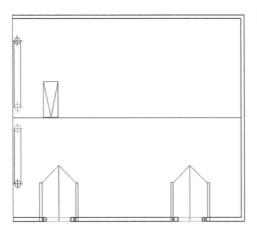

Figure 10-25: The longer garage.

Construction Commands

There are three additional commands that are commonly used in the process of constructing models. The BREAK command breaks objects at a point or points you specify. CHAMFER creates corners, and FILLET creates rounded corners.

Breaking objects

It is often much easier to draw a long line and then break it into two or more shorter lines. A common use for BREAK is to break a wall at a door or window in an architectural floor plan. You specify two points on the object and AutoCAD erases whatever is between those two points. Typically, you use object snaps to specify the points. Sometimes you can use TRIM to break an object, but if there is no convenient cutting edge, you may find BREAK more efficient.

You can break lines, polylines, splines, xlines, rays, circles, arcs, and ellipses.

 To break a line, choose Break from the Modify toolbar. You cannot select the object first and then the Break command. AutoCAD responds with the Select object: prompt. (Notice that you can only select one object to break.) At this prompt, you have two choices.

✦ Select the object at one of the break points you want to create. AutoCAD then responds with the Enter second point (or F for first point): prompt. Since you have already specified the first point, you can now specify the second point. AutoCAD breaks the object between the two points.

✦ Select the object using any method of object selection. AutoCAD then responds with the Enter second point (or F for first point): prompt. Type **f** ↲. At the Enter first point: prompt, pick the first break point. At the Enter second point: prompt, pick the second break point. AutoCAD breaks the object between the two points.

Tip

You can use BREAK to shorten an object. Pick one point on the object where you want the new endpoint to be. Pick the other point past its current endpoint. AutoCAD cuts off the object at the point you picked on the object.

Tip

Sometimes you may want to break an object into two pieces without erasing any part of it. The two new objects look the same as before on the screen until you select one of the objects. To do this, use the BREAK command and specify the same point for both the first and second points. You can specify the second point by typing @ ↲, which always signifies the last point entered. AutoCAD breaks the object at that point.

Step-by-Step: Breaking Objects

1. Open *ab10-h.dwg* from your CD-ROM.

2. Save it as *ab10-9.dwg* in your *AutoCAD Bible* folder. This is a site plan as shown in Figure 10-26.

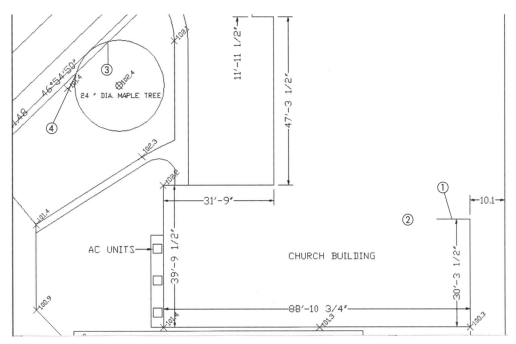

Figure 10-26: A site plan.

3. Choose Break from the Modify toolbar. At the `Select object:` prompt, pick the line at ①. At the `Enter second point (or F for first point):` prompt, pick ②. AutoCAD shortens the line.

4. Press Enter to repeat the BREAK command. At the `Select object:` prompt, pick the circle (it's a maple tree) anywhere along its circumference. At the `Enter second point (or F for first point):` prompt, type **f** ↵. At the `Enter first point:` prompt, pick the intersection at ③. At the `Enter second point:` prompt, pick the intersection at ④. AutoCAD breaks the circle.

Note

AutoCAD breaks circles counterclockwise. If you had picked ④, then ③, AutoCAD would have left only the smaller arc and erased the rest of the circle.

5. Save your drawing. It should look like Figure 10-27.

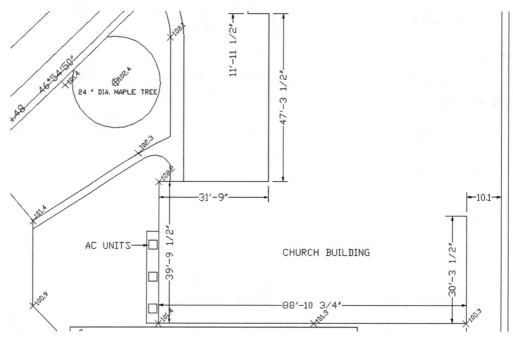

Figure 10-27: The edited site plan.

Creating corners with CHAMFER

The CHAMFER command creates corners from two nonparallel lines. You can also chamfer xlines, rays, and polylines. You can simply extend the lines to meet at an intersection, or create a beveled edge. If you create a beveled edge, you define the edge by either two distances or one distance and an angle relative to the lines you are chamfering. Figure 10-28 shows the elements of a chamfered corner.

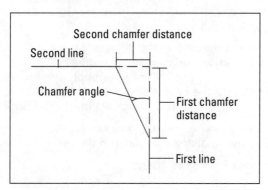

Figure 10-28: A chamfered corner.

Chamfering is a two-step process. First you define how you want to chamfer the corner, specifying either two distances or a distance and an angle. When you do this, AutoCAD ends the command. To actually chamfer, you need to start the command again and select the two lines you want to chamfer. AutoCAD chamfers them using the information you previously specified.

 To specify the chamfer information, choose Chamfer from the Modify toolbar. You cannot select objects before the command with Chamfer. AutoCAD responds with the `Polyline/Distance/Angle/Trim/Method/<Select first line>:` prompt. At the same time, AutoCAD lists the current distances or distance and angle, which are the last specifications you defined.

To define two distances, type **d** ↵. At the `Enter first chamfer distance <0 - 0 1/2 >:` prompt, type the first chamfer distance or press Enter to accept the default (which is the last distance you defined). At the `Enter second chamfer distance <0 -0 1/2 >:` prompt, type the second distance. The default for this is always the first chamfer distance, because equal chamfer distances are so common. AutoCAD ends the command.

To define a distance and an angle, type **a** ↵. At the `Enter chamfer length on the first line <0 -1 >:` prompt, enter a distance. This is the same as the first chamfer distance. At the `Enter chamfer angle from the first line <45>:` prompt, type the angle between the first line and the chamfer line. AutoCAD ends the command.

To extend two nonparallel lines to make a corner, set the chamfer distances to zero and then chamfer the lines. AutoCAD extends them to meet. If they already intersect, AutoCAD trims them to create a corner. The pick points on intersecting lines should be on the part of the lines you want to keep (not on the part of the lines you want to trim off).

To chamfer the two lines, start the CHAMFER command again. Your distances or distance and angle are displayed as you just specified them. At the `Polyline/ Distance/Angle/Trim/Method/<Select first line>:` prompt, select the first line. Unless you are creating a chamfer with equal distances, the order in which you select the lines is important. AutoCAD trims the first line selected by the first distance and the second line selected based on either the second distance or the angle. At the `Select second line:` prompt, select the second line. AutoCAD chamfers the lines.

By default, CHAMFER trims the original lines that it chamfers. If you want to keep the full original lines when you create a chamfer, choose the Trim option and choose No Trim.

 Choose the Polyline option to chamfer an entire polyline at once. (Polylines are covered in Chapter 16.) Chapter 24 discusses chamfering 3D models.

Step-by-Step: Chamfering Lines

On the
CD-ROM

1. Open *ab10-i.dwg* from your CD-ROM.

2. Save it as *ab10-10.dwg* in your *AutoCAD Bible* folder. This drawing is a very small section of a "porcupine" mixer, as shown in Figure 10-29.

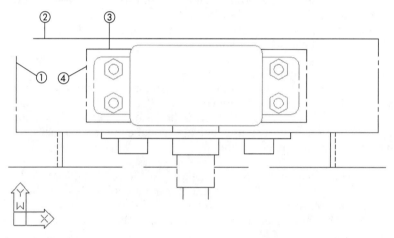

Figure 10-29: A mechanical drawing showing a small section of a "porcupine" mixer.

3. Choose Chamfer from the Modify toolbar. CHAMFER states the current mode and distances. If the distances are not zero, follow the prompts below. If they are already zero, skip to the next step.

```
Polyline/Distance/Angle/Trim/Method/<Select first line>: d ↵
Enter first chamfer distance <1/2>: 0 ↵
Enter second chamfer distance <0>: ↵
```

4. Press Enter to repeat the CHAMFER command. At the `Polyline/Distance/Angle/Trim/Method/<Select first line>:` prompt, pick ① in Figure 10-29. At the `Select second line:` prompt, pick ②. AutoCAD chamfers the two lines to make a corner.

5. Repeat the CHAMFER command. Follow the prompts:

```
Polyline/Distance/Angle/Trim/Method/<Select first line>: a ↵
Enter chamfer length on the first line <1>: 9/16 ↵
Enter chamfer angle from the first line <0>: 45 ↵
```

6. Repeat the CHAMFER command. At the `Polyline/Distance/Angle/Trim/Method/<Select first line>:` prompt, pick ③ in Figure 10-29. At the `Select second line:` prompt, pick ④. AutoCAD chamfers the two lines, as shown in Figure 10-30.

7. Save your drawing.

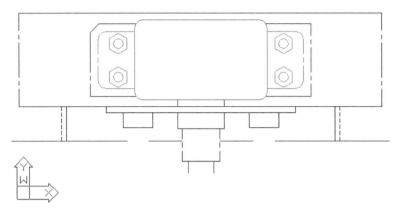

Figure 10-30: The edited drawing after using the CHAMFER command.

Creating rounded corners with FILLET

The FILLET command creates rounded corners, replacing part of two lines with an arc. Fillets are often used in mechanical drawings. In certain cases, you can use FILLET instead of the ARC command to create arcs. As with CHAMFER, you can fillet lines, xlines, rays and polylines — they can even be parallel. You can also fillet circles, arcs, and ellipses.

Chapter 24 discusses filleting 3D models.

You pronounce the *t* in Fillet. It's not pronounced like filet of fish!

The FILLET command defines the fillet arc by its radius, as shown in Figure 10-31.

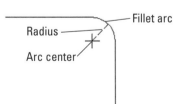

Figure 10-31: A fillet consisting of two lines and an arc.

Like chamfering, filleting is a two-step process. First you define the radius of the fillet arc. When you do this, AutoCAD ends the command. To actually fillet, you need to start the command again and select the two lines you want to fillet. AutoCAD fillets them using the information you previously specified.

 To specify the fillet information, choose Fillet from the Modify toolbar. You cannot select objects before the command with Fillet. AutoCAD responds with the Polyline/Radius/Trim/<Select first object>: prompt. Type **r** ↵ to choose the Radius option. At the Enter fillet radius <0.0000>: prompt, type the radius you want. The default is either zero or the last radius you specified.

To fillet two objects, start the FILLET command again. Your current radius is displayed as you just specified it. At the Polyline/Radius/Trim/<Select first object>: prompt, select the first object you want to fillet. At the Select second object: prompt, select the second object you want to fillet. AutoCAD creates the fillet.

By default, FILLET trims the original lines that it fillets. If you want to keep the full original lines when you create a fillet, choose the Trim option and choose No Trim.

 Choose the Polyline option to fillet an entire polyline at once. (Polylines are covered in Chapter 16.) Chapter 24 discusses filleting 3D models.

 Filleting with a zero radius gives the same results as chamfering with distances set to zero.

The order in which you select the two objects to be filleted is not important. However, *where* you pick the objects is quite important. If two objects intersect, AutoCAD keeps the objects on the same side of the intersection as your pick point and fillets them. Those parts of the objects on the far side of the intersection are erased.

When you fillet arcs and lines, if more than one fillet is possible, FILLET connects the endpoints closest to your pick points. Filleting circles and lines can result in unexpected results. Sometimes you need to experiment to find the proper pick points.

Step-by-Step: Filleting Objects

1. Open *ab10-i.dwg* from your CD-ROM.

2. Save it as *ab10-11.dwg* in your *AutoCAD Bible* folder. This is the same drawing used in the previous exercise. It is shown in Figure 10-32.

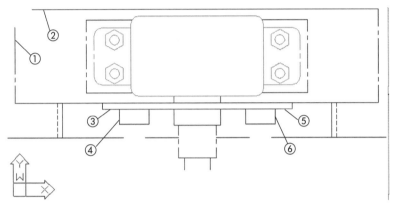

Figure 10-32: A mechanical drawing showing a small section of a "porcupine" mixer.

3. Choose Fillet from the Modify toolbar. At the `Polyline/Radius/Trim/ <Select first object>:` prompt, type **r** ↵. At the `Enter fillet radius <1/2>:` prompt, type **5/8** ↵. AutoCAD ends the command.

4. Press Enter to repeat the FILLET command. At the `Polyline/Radius/Trim/ <Select first object>:` prompt, pick the line at ① in Figure 10-32. At the `Select second object:` prompt, pick the line at ②. AutoCAD fillets the two lines.

5. Repeat the FILLET command. At the `Polyline/Radius/Trim/<Select first object>:` prompt, type **r** ↵. At the Enter fillet radius <5/8>: prompt, type **1/4** ↵.

6. Repeat the FILLET command. At the `Polyline/Radius/Trim/<Select first object>:` prompt, pick the line at ③ in Figure 10-32. At the `Select second object:` prompt, pick the line at ④. AutoCAD fillets the two lines. Repeat the command, this time picking at ⑤ and ⑥.

7. If you wish, you can connect the two loose lines that the fillets created and create some more fillets in the drawing.

8. Save your drawing. It should look like Figure 10-33.

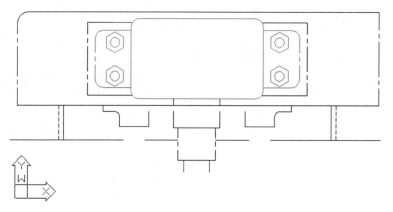

Figure 10-33: The filleted drawing.

Grips

Grips offer a whole new way to edit objects — without choosing commands. By using grips, you can quickly stretch, move, rotate, scale, and mirror objects. Grips were developed to more fully use the Windows graphical interface.

When you select an object without first choosing a command, the object appears highlighted with grips — small boxes at preset object snap points. (If you don't see grips, they may be turned off. See the section Customizing Grips later in this chapter to learn how to turn them back on.)

You can continue to select more objects in this way.

Tip

You can deselect an object by pressing Shift and clicking it. Other objects with grips continue to remain selected.

You then activate a grip by clicking it and use it to manipulate the object. When the grip is activated, it is filled in red (by default). An activated grip is also called a *hot* grip, shown in Figure 10-34. In some cases, you activate more than one grip at a time. To activate more than one grip, hold down Shift while you click the grips. If you activate a grip in error, click it again to deactivate it. Grips are so called because you can "hold on to" the object by dragging the grips with the mouse.

Release
14

Once you have activated a grip, right-click with the mouse to open the Grip short-cut menu listing all the grip options.

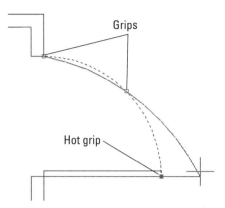

Grips

Hot grip

Figure 10-34: Stretching an arc. Grips appear at preset object snaps. A hot grip is used to manipulate an object.

You can also press Spacebar or Enter to cycle through the five possible commands on the command line. It takes a little time to get used to working with grips, but once you do, they are a quick way to make certain changes. As long as you are familiar with the STRETCH, MOVE, ROTATE, SCALE, and MIRROR commands, you can easily learn how to accomplish the same edits using grips because the prompts are so similar.

Once you have completed the edit, the object remains highlighted and the grips remain, so you can further edit the object. If you want to edit another object, press Esc once to remove the highlighting. The grips remain but you can ignore them. Then select another object or objects, or choose another command.

Tip

If the grips annoy you, press Esc a second time to remove them.

Stretching with grips

Stretching with grips involves understanding how the grip points relate to the object. For example, you cannot stretch a line from its midpoint — if you think about it, there's no way to define which way to stretch the line. Also, you cannot stretch a circle. (You can only scale it.) Aside from these limitations, anything goes.

Stretching one line

You can stretch one line. The result is similar to using the CHANGE command to change a line's endpoint. To stretch a line, select it. Click the grip at the endpoint you want to stretch. AutoCAD responds with:

```
** STRETCH **
<Stretch to point>/Base point/Copy/Undo/eXit:
```

STRETCH is the first grip editing command on the command line. The default is Stretch to point. Simply specify the new endpoint for the line, using any method of specifying a coordinate. AutoCAD stretches the line. The other options work as follows:

✦ **Base point:** Lets you define a base point — other than the activated grip — and a second point. Right-click to open the Grip shortcut menu and choose Base Point (or type **b** ↵). AutoCAD displays the `Base point:` prompt. Define a base point. AutoCAD responds with the original `<Stretch to point>/Base point/Copy/Undo/eXit:` prompt. Define the second stretch point to stretch the line.

✦ **Copy:** Puts you in Multiple mode. Right-click to open the Grip shortcut menu and choose Copy (or type **c** ↵). AutoCAD responds with the original `<Stretch to point>/Base point/Copy/Undo/eXit:` prompt. AutoCAD keeps the original line and creates a new line stretched as you specify. You can then continue to create new stretched lines.

✦ **Undo:** Undoes the last edit. Right-click to open the Grip shortcut menu and choose Undo (or type **u** ↵).

✦ **eXit:** Returns you to the Command prompt. Right-click to open the Grip shortcut menu and choose Exit (or type **x** ↵). Esc also returns you to the Command prompt.

Stretching multiple lines

Stretching more than one line at a time is similar to the most common use of the STRETCH command. However, it can also be somewhat confusing.

As explained earlier in this chapter for the STRETCH command, objects that cross the crossing window are stretched while objects entirely within the crossing window are moved. When you stretch multiple lines, activate endpoint grips to stretch lines and activate midpoint grips to move lines. Picking all those grips accurately can be difficult and time-consuming. Also, small objects close together create a lot of overlapping grips that are hard to select. For this reason, stretching multiple lines works best with simple models.

To stretch multiple lines, follow these steps:

1. Choose the objects you want to stretch. The objects are highlighted and display grips. You can use any method of choosing objects — you are not limited to crossing windows.

2. Hold down Shift and pick each grip that you want to stretch. If there are internal objects that you want to move with the stretch, select their grips too — the midpoints of the lines, centers of the circles, and all arc grips.

3. Release Shift and pick a grip to use as a base point. AutoCAD responds:

```
** STRETCH **
<Stretch to point>/Base point/Copy/Undo/eXit:
```

4. Specify a new stretch point. You can also use any of the other options.

At the end of the sections on grips, you have the opportunity to try them out in a Step-by-Step exercise.

Moving with grips

Moving is easy using grips. Choose all the objects you want to move. Click any grip to activate it. This becomes the base point. Right-click to open the Grip shortcut menu. Choose Move. AutoCAD responds:

```
** MOVE **
<Move to point>/Base point/Copy/Undo/eXit:
```

Use any method to specify the second point. Be sure to use @ if you are typing in relative coordinates. AutoCAD moves the selected objects. The other options work as follows:

✦ **Base point:** Lets you define a base point — other than the activated grip. Right-click to open the Grip shortcut menu and choose Base Point (or type **b** ↵). AutoCAD displays the `Base point:` prompt. Define a base point. AutoCAD responds with the original `<Move to point>/Base point/Copy/Undo/eXit:` prompt. Define the second move point to move the objects.

✦ **Copy:** Puts you in Multiple mode and lets you copy objects. Right-click to open the Grip shortcut menu and choose Copy (or type **c** ↵). AutoCAD responds with the original `<Move to point>/Base point/Copy /Undo/eXit:` prompt. AutoCAD keeps the original line and creates a new line where you specify. You can then continue to create new lines.

✦ **Undo:** Undoes the last edit. Right-click to open the Grip shortcut menu and choose Undo (or type **u** ↵).

✦ **eXit:** Returns you to the Command prompt. Right-click to open the Grip shortcut menu and choose Exit (or type **x** ↵). Esc also returns you to the Command prompt.

Rotating with grips

Rotating with grips is very similar to using the ROTATE command. Choose all the objects you want to rotate. Click any grip to activate it. This becomes the base point. Right click to open the Grip shortcut menu. Choose Rotate. AutoCAD responds:

```
** ROTATE **
<Rotation angle>/Base point/Copy/Undo/Reference/eXit:
```

Type in a rotation angle. AutoCAD rotates the objects. The other options work as follows:

✦ **Base point:** Lets you define a base point — other than the activated grip. Right-click to open the Grip shortcut menu and choose Base Point (or type **b** ↵). AutoCAD displays the `Base point:` prompt. Define a base point. AutoCAD responds with the original `<Rotation angle>/Base` `point/Copy/Undo/Reference/eXit:` prompt. Define the rotation angle to rotate the objects.

✦ **Copy:** Puts you in Multiple mode and lets you copy objects. Right-click to open the Grip shortcut menu and choose Copy (or type **c** ↵). AutoCAD responds with the original `<Rotation angle>/Base point/Copy/Undo /Reference/eXit:` prompt. AutoCAD keeps the original line and creates a new rotated line where you specify. You can then continue to create new lines.

✦ **Undo**: Undoes the last edit. Right-click to open the Grip shortcut menu and choose Undo (or type **u** ↵).

✦ **Reference:** Lets you specify a reference angle and a new angle. Right-click to open the Grip shortcut menu and choose Reference (or type **r** ↵). AutoCAD responds with the `Reference angle <0>:` prompt. Type an angle or pick two points to specify an angle. AutoCAD displays the `<New angle>/Base point/Copy/Undo/Reference/eXit:` prompt. Type an angle or pick a point. This works just like the Reference option for the ROTATE command. (See Chapter 9.)

✦ **eXit:** Returns you to the Command prompt. Right-click to open the Grip shortcut menu and choose Exit (or type **x** ↵). Esc also returns you to the Command prompt.

Scaling with grips

Scaling with grips is very similar to using the SCALE command. Choose all the objects you want to scale. Click any grip to activate it. This becomes the base point. Right-click to open the Grip shortcut menu. Choose Scale. AutoCAD responds:

```
** SCALE **
<Scale factor >/Base point/Copy/Undo/Reference/eXit:
```

Type a scale angle. AutoCAD scales the objects. The other options work as follows:

✦ **Base point:** Lets you define a base point — other than the activated grip. Right-click to open the Grip shortcut menu and choose Base Point (or type **b** ↵). AutoCAD displays the `Base point:` prompt. Define a base point. AutoCAD responds with the original `<Scale factor>/Base point/Copy/ Undo/Reference/eXit:` prompt. Define the scale factor to scale the objects.

✦ **Copy:** Puts you in Multiple mode and lets you copy objects. Right-click to open the Grip shortcut menu and choose Copy (or type **c** ↵). AutoCAD responds with the original `<Scale factor>/Base point/Copy/Undo/ eXit:` prompt. AutoCAD keeps the original line and creates a new scaled line where you specify. You can then continue to create new scaled lines.

✦ **Undo:** Undoes the last edit. Right-click to open the Grip shortcut menu and choose Undo (or type **u** ↵).

✦ **Reference:** Lets you specify a reference length and a new scale. Right-click to open the Grip shortcut menu and choose Reference (or type **r** ↵). AutoCAD responds with the `Reference length <0>:` prompt. Type a length or pick two points to specify a length. AutoCAD displays the `<New length>/Base point/Copy/Undo/Reference/eXit:` prompt. Type a length or pick a point. This works just like the Reference option for the SCALE command. (See Chapter 9.)

✦ **eXit:** Returns you to the Command prompt. Right-click to open the Grip shortcut menu and choose Exit (or type **x** ↵). Esc also returns you to the Command prompt.

Mirroring with grips

Mirroring with grips is very similar to using the MIRROR command. Choose all the objects you want to mirror. Click any grip to activate it. This becomes the first point of the mirror line. Right-click to open the Grip shortcut menu. Choose Mirror. AutoCAD responds:

```
** MIRROR **
<Second point>/Base point/Copy/Undo/eXit:
```

Specify the second point of the mirror line. AutoCAD mirrors the objects.

Caution

By default, AutoCAD erases the original objects. To keep the original objects, you must use the Copy option. This feature is the opposite of the MIRROR command, where the default is to keep the original objects.

The other options work as follows:

✦ **Base point:** Lets you define a base point — other than the activated grip — and a second point. Right-click to open the Grip shortcut menu and choose Base Point (or type **b** ↵). AutoCAD displays the `Base point:` prompt. Define a base point — that is, the first point of the mirror line. AutoCAD responds with the original `<Second point>/Base point/Copy/Undo/eXit:` prompt. Define the second point of the mirror line, and AutoCAD mirrors the objects.

✦ **Copy:** Puts you in Multiple mode and lets you keep the original objects. Right-click to open the Grip shortcut menu and choose Copy (or type **c** ↵). AutoCAD responds with the original `<Second point>/Base point/Copy /Undo/eXit:` prompt. AutoCAD keeps the original objects and creates new mirrored objects. You can then continue to create new mirrored objects.

✦ **Undo:** Undoes the last edit. Right-click to open the Grip shortcut menu and choose Undo (or type **u** ↵).

✦ **eXit:** Returns you to the Command prompt. Right-click to open the Grip shortcut menu and choose Exit (or type **x** ↵). Esc also returns you to the Command prompt.

Step-by-Step: Editing with Grips

On the
CD-ROM

1. Open *ab10-j.dwg* from the CD-ROM.

2. Save it as *ab10-12.dwg* in your *AutoCAD Bible* folder. This is a small section of a drive block, seen from above, as shown in Figure 10-35. ORTHO and OSNAP are on.

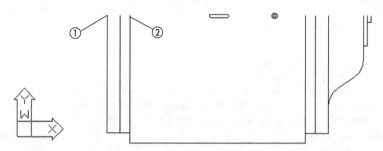

Figure 10-35: A small section of a drive block, seen from above, can easily be edited with grips.

3. Use a selection window to select the entire model. Now hold down Shift and place a selection window around the small circles and rectangle at the center of the model to deselect them.

4. Pick the grip at ① in Figure 10-35 to activate it. AutoCAD responds with the following prompt:

```
** STRETCH **
<Stretch to point>/Base point/Copy/Undo/eXit:
```

5. Right-click and choose Mirror from the shortcut menu. AutoCAD responds with the following prompt:

```
** MIRROR **
<Second point>/Base point/Copy/Undo/eXit:
```

6. Type **c** ↵ to choose the Copy option so that the original objects that you mirror are not deleted.

7. At the `<Second point>/Base point/Copy/Undo/eXit:` prompt, move the cursor to the right. You can see the mirror image of the model. Pick any point to the right (in the 0° direction) of the activated grip.

8. Type **x** ↵ to return to the command line. The original objects are still high-lighted.

9. Use a large selection window to select all the new objects including the small rectangle and circles in the middle. Everything should be highlighted and display grips.

10. Pick the grip at ② in Figure 10-35 to activate it. Right-click and choose Rotate from the shortcut menu. At the `<Rotation angle>/Base-point/Copy/ Undo/Reference/eXit:` prompt, type **90** ↵. AutoCAD rotates the model.

11. Pick the bottom right grip to activate it. Right-click and choose Scale from the shortcut menu. At the `<Scale factor>/Base point/Copy/Undo/ Reference/eXit:` prompt, type **.5** ↵. AutoCAD scales the model.

12. Pick the grip at the midpoint of the bottom line. Right-click and choose Move from the shortcut menu. At the `<Move to point>/Base point/Copy /Undo/eXit:` prompt, type **@0,-3** ↵. The model should look like Figure 10-36.

13. Press Esc twice to remove all grips. Define a crossing window by picking first at ①, then at ② (Figure 10-36).

14. Hold down Shift and pick all the grips. Then pick the grip at the middle of the bottom line. At the `<Stretch to point>/Base point/Copy/Undo/eXit:` prompt, type **@0,1** ↵. AutoCAD shrinks the model.

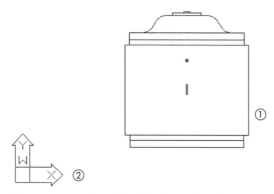

Figure 10-36: The drive block section, after several grip edits, looks a little like a cookie jar.

Note

If the stretch does not come out right, type **u** ↵ to undo the stretch and try again.

15. Save your drawing.

Customizing grips

You can turn grips on and off and customize their size and color. Choose Tools⇨Grips to open the Grips dialog box, as shown in Figure 10-37.

Figure 10-37: The Grips dialog box.

By default, grips are enabled (that is, turned on). Also by default, grips are turned off for blocks. Blocks are covered in Chapter 18. When grips are off for blocks, you see only one grip when you select a block — its insertion point. When grips are on, you see all the grips you would normally see for objects.

In the Grip Colors section, you can choose the colors you want for unselected and selected (hot) grips. Choosing the buttons in this section opens the Select Color dialog box, allowing you to choose a color.

The Grip Size section lets you drag the slider bar to set the size of the grips. Click OK when you have made the desired changes.

Groups

Groups lets you save a selection set of objects so you can easily select them whenever you need to edit them. If you have a certain set of objects that you need to edit as a group, and a busy drawing that makes their selection time-consuming, groups are for you.

Creating and modifying groups

To create or modify a group, choose Tools⇨Object Group to open the Object Grouping dialog box, as shown in Figure 10-38.

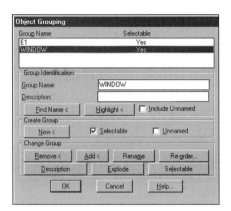

Figure 10-38: The Object Grouping dialog box.

Creating a new group

To create a new group, follow these steps.

1. Type a name in the Group Name text box. You can use a maximum of 31 characters with no spaces. You can use the hyphen (-) and underscore (_) anywhere in the name.

2. If you wish, type a description of up to 64 characters. The description can include spaces.

3. Click New. AutoCAD returns you to your drawing with the Select objects: prompt. Select the objects you want to be in the group. Press Enter to end object selection. AutoCAD returns you to the dialog box.

4. Click OK.

You can now use your group.

Note

An object can belong to more than one group.

The Group Identification section of the Object Grouping dialog box also has a Find Name button. Use this to find the name of the group to which an object belongs. AutoCAD lets you select an object and then lists the group's name or names.

The Highlight button highlights a group. First choose a group from the list in the Object Grouping dialog box. Click Highlight and AutoCAD returns to your drawing and highlights all the objects in your group. Click Continue to return to the dialog box. Use this when you are not sure which group you want to work with.

Changing a group

The Change Group section of the Object Grouping dialog box gives you a great deal of flexibility in managing groups. To change a group, click any existing group in the Group Name list at the top of the dialog box. The buttons in the Change Group section all become active. You can do the following:

✦ **Remove:** AutoCAD switches to the drawing area with the `Select objects to remove:` prompt. Select objects to remove and press Enter to end object removal. AutoCAD returns you to the dialog box. Click OK.

✦ **Add:** AutoCAD switches to the drawing area with the `Select objects to add:` prompt. Select objects to add and press Enter to end object selection. AutoCAD returns you to the dialog box. Click OK.

✦ **Rename:** Choose the group you want to rename. Change the name in the Group Name text box. Click Rename. The name changes in the Group Name list at the top of the dialog box. Click OK.

✦ **Re-order:** Each group in the object has a number, starting from zero. In rare cases, the order may be important to you, for example, if you are running a program that processes the members of a group. Choose the group you want to reorder. AutoCAD opens the Order Group dialog box. If you simply want to reverse the order of all the objects, click Reverse Order. Otherwise, click Highlight. AutoCAD opens a small Object Grouping message box with Next and Previous buttons. At the bottom right corner, the box displays Object: 0, and one of the objects in the group is highlighted. Click Next to move from object to object. If you are going to re-order the objects, you probably need to write down the number of each object. Click OK to return to the Order Group dialog box. Complete the text boxes described below.

   ✦ **Remove from position:** This is the position number of the object you want to move.

   ✦ **Replace at position:** This is the new position number you want for the object.

   ✦ **Number of objects:** This is the object number or range of numbers you want to re-order.

✦ **Description:** Updates a description for the group. Type in a new description in the Group Identification section of the dialog box. Then click Description.

✦ **Explode:** Removes the group entirely. All the objects remain in your drawing, but they are no longer grouped.

✦ **Selectable:** Toggles the selectability of the group. If a group is selectable, selecting one object of the group selects the entire group. If a group is not selectable, selecting one object of the group does not select the entire group. This option lets you temporarily work with one object in the group without having to explode the group.

Tip

When you choose Highlight from the Order Group dialog box, the Object Grouping message box opens in the middle of the screen, covering your objects. Drag it to one corner of the screen so you can see which objects are being highlighted.

Using groups

Using a group is very simple. If a group is selectable, just pick any object in the group to select all the objects in a group. You can then edit the objects in the group as a whole. If you need to temporarily edit one object in a group, change the group's selectable status to No as described in the previous section. Return the selectable status to Yes to work with the entire group again.

Tip

You can change the selectable status of all groups in your drawing by choosing Tools⊅Selection, which opens the Object Selection Settings dialog box. Deselect Object Grouping to disable object grouping entirely.

Step-by-Step: Using Groups

On the CD-ROM

1. Open *ab10-k.dwg* from your CD-ROM.

2. Save it as *ab10-13.dwg* in your *AutoCAD Bible* folder. This is a wiring diagram, as shown in Figure 10-39. ORTHO and OSNAP are on. A running object snap is set for Endpoint.

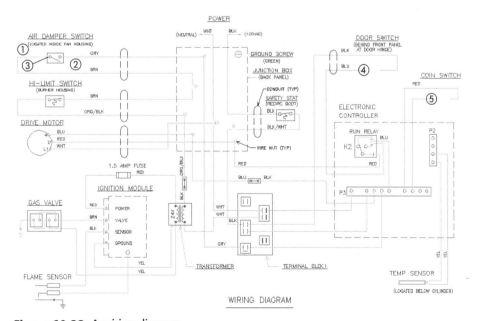

Figure 10-39: A wiring diagram.

3. Choose Tools⇨Object Group. In the Group Name box of the Object Grouping dialog box, type **switch**. Make sure that the Selectable box is checked. Choose New.

4. At the `Select objects:` prompt, use a window to select the AIR DAMPER switch, picking at ① and ② in Figure 10-39. AutoCAD tells you that four objects were found. Press Enter to end object selection. AutoCAD returns you to the Object Grouping dialog box. Click OK.

5. Choose COPY from the Modify toolbar. At the `Select objects:` prompt, pick anywhere on the switch. End object selection by pressing ↵.

6. At the `<Base point or displacement>/Multiple:` prompt, type **m** ↵. At the `Base point:` prompt, use the Endpoint object snap to pick ③. At the `Second point of displacement:` prompt, choose ④, then ⑤. Press Enter.

7. Save your drawing.

Selection Filters

Sometimes you need a more powerful way to select objects. For example, you may want to:

✦ Select all the lines in your drawing to change their color

✦ Check the arc radiuses of all your fillets

✦ Find short line segments that should be erased

Before selection filters, you had to write an AutoLISP program to accomplish these functions. (Sometimes an AutoLISP program is still the easiest way to go. See Chapters 34 and 35.) Now you can create fairly complex filters that select only the objects you want. You can save these filters for future use as well.

Note

Don't confuse object selection filters with point filters. Point filters are covered in Chapter 4.

Creating a single filter

To create a filter, type **filter** ↵ on the command line. AutoCAD opens the Object Selection Filters dialog box, as shown in Figure 10-40.

Tip

If you have already chosen a command, type **'filter** at the `Select objects:` prompt to create the selection filter transparently.

The box at the top of the dialog box lists the filters you have specified. Figure 10-40 shows a filter that selects only magenta-colored text.

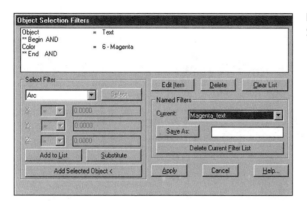

Figure 10-40: The Object Selection Filters dialog box.

Note

The selection filter only finds colors and linetypes of objects that have been set as such, rather than as part of a layer definition. Layers, colors, and linetypes are covered in Chapter 11.

Use the Select Filter section of the dialog box to specify a filter. The drop-down box lists all the possible filters. Click the arrow to drop down the list. There are several types of items — objects, object properties such as color or layer, object snaps such as arc center or circle radius, and logical operators such as AND, OR, and NOT. These logical operators combine filter specifications in various ways.

The first step is to choose a filter. In Figure 10-40, text was chosen from the drop-down list. If the item chosen does not need any further clarification, click Add to List. The filter appears in the box at the top of the dialog box. Notice that the Text filter appears as `Object = Text`.

Many filters require a value. There are two ways to enter a value:

✦ If you choose an object that can be listed, the Specify button becomes active. Click it and choose the value you want. For example, if you choose Color or Layer, you choose from a list of colors or layers.

✦ If you choose an object that can have any value, the boxes below the drop-down list box become active. They are labeled X, Y, and Z, but this is misleading. These boxes are used for X,Y, and Z coordinates only when you choose a filter requiring coordinates, such as Viewport Center. In most cases, you use the X box to give the filter a value. In this situation, the Y and Z boxes are not used. For example, if you choose Text Height, you type the height in the X box.

However, you don't always want to specify that a filter equals a value. Lets say you want to create a filter that selects all circles with a radius less than .75. When you choose Circle Radius, the X box becomes active. Click the arrow to drop down the list of relational operators and choose one. Table 10-1 lists the relational operators.

Table 10-1	
Relational Operators in the Object Selection Filters Dialog Box	
Operator	**Definition**
=	Equal to
!=	Not equal to
<	Less than
<=	Less than or equal to
>	Greater than
>=	Greater than or equal to
*	Equal to any value

In the example of a filter for all circles with a radius less than .75, you would choose < and then type **.75** in the text box. Choose Add to List to create the filter, as shown in Figure 10-41.

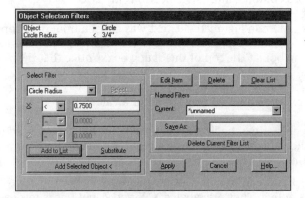

Figure 10-41: A filter that selects all circles with a radius less than .75.

Adding a second filter

To add a second filter, you first decide on the relationship between the first and the second filter, and then assign a logical operator. Logical operators always come in pairs — when you begin one you must also end it. The logical operators are at the end of the drop-down list of filter objects.

Note

When two or more filters are listed without logical operators, AutoCAD calculates them as if they were grouped with the AND operator. This means that AutoCAD only selects objects that meet all the criteria specified.

Table 10-2 explains the four logical operators. (AutoCAD calls them grouping operators because they group filter specifications together.) The example column explains the results of two filter specifications: Color = 1-Red and Object = Circle.

	Table 10-2	
	Logical (or Grouping) Operators Used for Selection Filters	
Operator	*Explanation*	*Example*
AND	Finds all objects that meet all criteria.	Finds red circles.
OR	Finds objects that meet any of the criteria.	Finds all red objects and all circles.
XOR	Finds objects that meet one criteria or the other but not both. Requires two criteria between Begin XOR and End XOR.	Finds red objects that are not circles and circles that are not red.
NOT	Excludes objects that meet the criteria. May only have one criteria between Begin NOT and End NOT.	If the NOT operator groups the Object = Circle filter, finds all red objects that are not circles.

Click Substitute and choose a saved filter to insert a saved filter into the filter you are currently defining. To add filters based on existing objects, choose Add Selected Object. AutoCAD adds all the properties of the object to the filter definition — which is often more than you want.

Naming and editing filters

Once you have completed the filter, you should save it. Even if you don't think you will use it again, you may make an editing error in the drawing while using it and have to go back to it. To save a filter, type a name in the Save As text box and click Save As.

You edit a listed filter using three buttons:

✦ **Edit Item:** Choose the line containing the item and click this button to edit the item. AutoCAD places the object name in the drop-down box and lets you specify new values for it.

✦ **Delete:** Choose Delete to delete a chosen item in a filter.

✦ **Clear List:** Choose Clear List to clear all the items in a filter and start over.

To choose a named filter to edit, choose it from the Current drop-down list.

Using filters

You can use filters in two ways. Most often you choose a command first and then realize that you need a filter to select the objects. Follow these prompts:

```
Select objects:  filter ↵
Define the filter in the Object Selection Filters dialog box. Click Apply.
Applying filter to selection.
Select objects: Type all ↵ or use a large selection window to select
all the objects you want to consider in the filter.
x found
y were filtered out
Select objects: ↵
Exiting filtered selection. x found
Select objects: ↵
```

AutoCAD continues with the command's usual prompts.

Alternately, you can start the FILTER command and define the filter. Click Apply. At the Select objects: prompt, type **all** or use a selection window. Press Enter to end object selection. Then start the editing command and use the Previous selection option to select the filtered objects.

Step-by-Step: Using Selection Filters

On the
CD-ROM

1. Open *ab10-k.dwg* from the CD-ROM.

2. Save it as *ab10-14.dwg* in your *AutoCAD Bible* folder. Notice that there are two lines of text in the middle of the drawing that are black instead of blue like all the other text. You want to check the color of all text and correct it if necessary.

3. Type **select** ↵. At the Select objects: prompt, type **'filter** ↵ to use filters transparently. The Object Selection Filters dialog box opens.

4. In the Select Filter drop-down list, choose Text. Click Add to List. At the top, the filter reads Object = Text.

5. From the Select Filter drop-down list, choose **Begin AND (this is towards the end of the list) and click Add to List.

6. From the Select Filter drop-down list, choose Color. In the drop-down list next to X: choose ! = (not equal). Choose Select. In the Select Color dialog box, choose BYLAYER. Click OK. In the Object Selection Filters dialog box, choose Add to List. The BYLAYER color number displays as 256. (Layers and colors are covered in the next chapter.)

7. From the Select Filter drop-down list, choose **End AND and click Add to List.

8. In the Save As text box, type **bad_text**. Click Save As. The Object Selection Filters dialog box should look like Figure 10-42.

9. Click Apply.

10. At the `Select objects:` prompt, type **all** ↵. AutoCAD tells you that two objects were found. Press Enter until you get the `Command:` prompt.

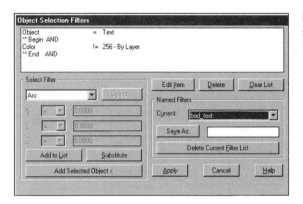

Figure 10-42: A filter that selects all text whose color is not BYLAYER.

11. Choose Properties from the Object Properties toolbar. At the `Select objects:` prompt, type **p** ↵. Press Enter. AutoCAD tells you that two objects were found.

12. In the Modify Text dialog box, choose Color. In the Select Color dialog box, choose BYLAYER. Click OK twice to return to your drawing. AutoCAD changes the color of the two text objects to BYLAYER — they turn blue like all the other text.

13. Save your drawing.

Summary

In this chapter you learned all the more advanced editing commands, including MIRROR, ARRAY, OFFSET, ALIGN, TRIM, EXTEND, STRETCH, LENGTHEN, and BREAK. CHAMFER and FILLET let you create square, beveled, and rounded corners.

Grips lets you edit objects without directly choosing commands. The grip options are Move, Mirror, Rotate, Scale, and Stretch. You can also use the Copy suboption to copy objects.

You can create named groups of objects that make it easy to select sets of objects. You can turn off the selectability of groups when you need to edit one of the objects within the group. You can also use selection filters as a powerful way to set selection criteria.

In the next chapter I cover layers, colors, and linetypes.

✦   ✦   ✦

Organizing Drawings with Layers, Colors, and Linetypes

Organizing Your Drawing

Until now you have drawn everything in black. Drawing everything in one color is not a very good way to draw — besides, it's boring! If everything is the same color, it is hard to distinguish the various elements of a drawing. If you have followed the exercises throughout this book, you have opened some drawings that used various colors and linetypes (such as dashed lines). For example, in some of the architectural drawings, you may have noticed that the walls are a different color than the fixtures (refrigerator, sink, and so on) in the kitchen. When you start to create text and dimensions, covered in Chapters 13, 14, and 15, you will almost always use a color that stands out from the main model you are drawing. This use of color and linetype helps to organize your drawings, making them easier to understand.

Most often, you assign color and linetype to a *layer*. A layer is simply an organizational tool that lets you organize the display of objects in your drawing. Every object must have a layer, and every layer must have a color and a linetype. You define layers that meet your drawing needs. Layer, color, and linetype are called *object properties*. You can easily change any object's properties. This chapter explains how to create and change these object properties to organize your drawing.

Working with Layers

The best way to organize your drawing into colors and linetypes is to use layers. Layers offer powerful features that enable you to distinguish all the various elements of your drawing. In an architectural drawing, for example, common layers are walls, doors, windows, plumbing, electrical, fixtures, structural elements, notes (text), dimensions, ceiling, insulation, posts, title block, and so on. Mechanical drawings might use center, hidden, hatch, object, and title block layers. Each discipline has its own conventions and you might have specific conventions where you work.

Creating layers is an important part of setting up a drawing, in addition to the setup features covered in Chapter 5. Layers can be created and saved in your templates so that they are available to you when you start to draw.

Layers give you many ways to organize your drawing.

+ You can assign different colors and linetypes to layers.

+ You can assign the various colors to different pens in a plotter, resulting in a drawing with varying colors or line widths.

+ You can control the visibility of layers. Making a layer invisible lets you focus on just the objects you need to draw or edit.

+ You can control which objects are plotted.

+ You can lock a layer so that objects on that layer cannot be edited.

Understanding layers

Every layer must have a name, a color, and a linetype. All drawings come with a default layer, called layer 0. Its color is black and its linetype is continuous. All the exercises in this book up to this point have used layer 0. To create a new layer, you must give it a name, a color, and a linetype. You can then start drawing on that layer.

Layers also have three types of *states*. These states control visibility, regeneration, and editability of layers.

+ **On/Off:** On layers (the default) are visible. Off layers are invisible but are regenerated with the drawing.

+ **Thawed/Frozen:** Thawed layers (the default) are visible. Frozen layers are invisible and not editable, but are not regenerated with the drawing. This saves time compared to turning layers off. However, when you thaw a frozen layer, it requires a regeneration.

✦ **Unlocked/Locked:** Unlocked layers (the default) are visible and editable. Locked layers are visible but cannot be edited. Use this when you want to refer to objects (you can see them and even snap to their object snaps) but want to ensure that they won't be changed.

Be careful when editing a drawing with frozen or off layers — it's easy to forget about them.

Both the Off and Frozen states make layers invisible. AutoCAD introduced the frozen and thawed layer states to reduce regeneration time — and that's the only difference between On/Off and Thawed/Frozen layer visibility options. However, today's computers are faster, and AutoCAD has since introduced several ways to avoid regeneration while panning and zooming — such as Aerial View, Zoom Dynamic, and real-time zooming and panning. Also, remember that thawing a layer causes a regeneration, whereas turning a layer back on only causes a redraw. If you have learned how to draw without causing regenerations, you might actually save a regeneration by using On/Off instead of Thawed/Frozen.

Creating new layers

To create a new layer, choose Layers from the Object Properties toolbar. AutoCAD opens the Layer & Linetype Properties dialog box with the Layer tab on top, as shown in Figure 11-1. This dialog box lists all current layers and their properties. You can also create new layers and modify current ones.

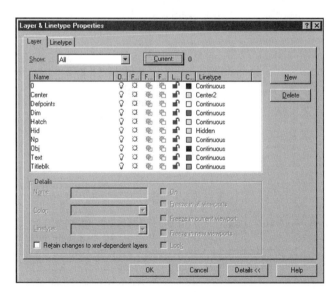

Figure 11-1: The Layer tab of the Layer & Linetype Properties dialog box after clicking Details to open the Details section of the dialog box.

The columns in the dialog box are as follows:

Name	The name of the layer
On/Off	Click to change the on/off state of a layer
Freeze/Thaw in all viewports	Click to change the freeze/thaw state of a layer in all viewports
Freeze/Thaw in current viewport	Click to change the freeze/thaw state of a layer in the current floating viewport
Freeze/Thaw in new viewports	Click to change the freeze/thaw state of a layer in the new floating viewports that you create
Lock/Unlock	Click to change the lock/unlock state of a layer
Color	Click to change the color of a layer
Linetype	Click to change the linetype of a layer

You can change the width of the columns in the Layer & Linetype Properties dialog box by placing the cursor over the line dividing two column headings and dragging. Double-click the same line to minimize the column width.

Naming the layer

Click New. A new layer appears, called Layer1, as shown in Figure 11-2. The name is highlighted so you can immediately type in a new name for the layer. Press Enter when you have typed the name. Notice that AutoCAD has assigned the default color and linetype. If you want the color to be black and the linetype to be continuous, you are finished.

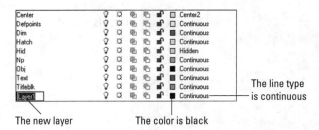

The new layer

The color is black

The line type is continuous

Figure 11-2: The new layer appears as Layer1 and is highlighted so you can enter the new layer name. AutoCAD assigns the default color and linetype.

Layer names can be up to 31 characters long and may not have spaces. You can use the hyphen (-) and underscore (_) to connect words. An example would be *no-plot* for a layer that you do not want to appear on the plotted output.

To create several new layers at once, simply click New as many times as you want. Then go back and name the layers. If you want a new layer to have the same color and/or linetype as an existing layer — which is very common — choose that existing layer and click New. The new layer will inherit the color and linetype of the selected layer. You can then make any changes you want.

Assigning a color

To change the default color, move the cursor to the black-colored box in the same row as the new layer. The ToolTip says Color. Click to open the Select Color dialog box, as shown in Figure 11-3.

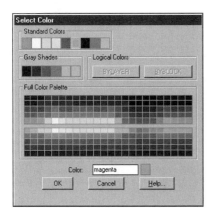

Figure 11-3: The Select Color dialog box.

Click the color you want. At the bottom of the dialog box, the color's name appears along with a sample of the color. Click OK to close the dialog box and return to the Layer & Linetype Properties dialog box.

Note that the Select Color dialog box offers you a choice of standard colors, gray shades, and a full palette of colors. The standard colors are the original colors AutoCAD offered, and they are the ones most often used, even today. Their advantage is that each color is easily distinguishable from the others. AutoCAD gives these colors both a name and a number, whereas other colors have only a number. The standard colors are yellow, cyan (turquoise), red, green, blue, white, and magenta.

Note

AutoCAD gives you a choice of drawing on a black or a white screen. In early versions of AutoCAD, the screen was black and the default color was white. When you work on a white screen, the default color appears black, but it is still called white. Therefore, if you choose the black color tile in the Select Color dialog box, AutoCAD lists the color as white. To change the screen color, choose Tools⇨Preferences⇨Display⇨Color.

Assigning a linetype

The default linetype is a continuous line. AutoCAD also provides many other *linetypes,* which are repeating patterns of dashes and/or dots and spaces. Linetypes can also include text and shapes. Linetypes are more fully covered later in this chapter.

To change the default linetype, move the cursor to the linetype in the same row as the new layer. Click to open the Select Linetype dialog box, as shown in Figure 11-4.

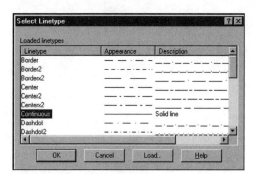

Figure 11-4: The Select Linetype dialog box.

If the linetype you want appears on the list, click the linetype and choose OK to close the dialog box. If the linetype does not appear, you need to load the linetype. Click Load to open the Load or Reload Linetypes dialog box, shown in Figure 11-5.

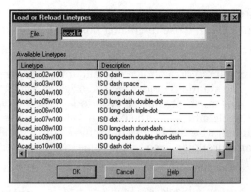

Figure 11-5: The Load or Reload Linetypes dialog box.

Linetypes are stored in text files with the filename extension *.lin*. AutoCAD's standard linetypes are stored in *acad.lin*. You can create your own linetypes and store them in *acad.lin* or another file with the extension *.lin*. Click File at the top of the dialog box if you want to load a linetype from a file other than *acad.lin*. Choose the linetype you want to load and click OK.

See Chapter 31 for a full discussion of creating your own linetypes.

To choose a range of linetypes to load, click the first linetype in the range, press Shift, and click the last linetype in the range. To choose more than one noncontiguous linetype, press Ctrl for each additional linetype you choose. To select all or clear all of the linetypes, right-click in the dialog box and choose from the shortcut menu.

Once you load a linetype and click OK, you return to the Select Linetype dialog box. The loaded linetype now appears on the list. Choose it and click OK.

You are now back in the Layer & Linetype Properties dialog box. Your new layer shows the color and linetype you have assigned to it. You are now ready to use the layer.

Note

The Details button on the Layer & Linetype Properties dialog box toggles the display of the bottom section of the dialog box. This section simply provides you with the same information about any selected layer as shown in the list, but in a different format. You can use this section to change a layer's name, color, and/or linetype without moving to another dialog box. The Details section is blank when no layer is selected.

On the CD-ROM

Step-by-Step: Creating a New Layer

1. Open *ab11-a.dwg* from the CD-ROM.

2. Save it as *ab11-1.dwg* in your *AutoCAD Bible* folder.

3. Choose Layers from the Object Properties toolbar to open the Layer & Linetype Properties dialog box.

4. Choose New. A new layer named Layer1 appears, highlighted. Type walls ø as the name for the new layer.

5. Click the black square in the Color column to open the Select Color dialog box. Choose the blue square from the standard colors and click OK.

6. Choose New again to create another new layer. Type **hidden** ↵.

7. If the Details section of the dialog box is not displayed, click the Details button. Click the Color drop-down box in the Details section and choose Magenta.

8. In the main layer listing, click Continuous in the same row as the *hidden* linetype. This opens the Select Linetype dialog box. Click Load to open the Load or Reload Linetypes dialog box. Scroll down until you see the Hidden linetype. Choose it and click OK. In the Select Linetype dialog box, choose Hidden and click OK. Click OK to close the Layer & Linetype Properties dialog box.

9. Click the Layer Control drop-down box to see the two layers you have just created listed there. Click again to close the box.

10. Save your drawing.

Using layers

To use a layer you have just created, click Current in the Layer & Linetype Properties dialog box. Then click OK to return to your drawing. Objects you create now are drawn on that layer and display its color and linetype.

AutoCAD puts all objects that you draw on the current layer. Once you have the layers you need, you need to switch from layer to layer as you draw. You can continue to choose Layers on the Object Properties toolbar, click the name of a layer, click Current, then click OK. But there is an easier way — the Layer Control drop-down list on the Object Properties toolbar, shown in Figure 11-6.

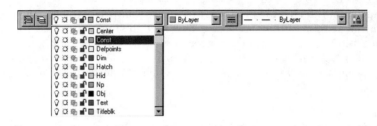

Figure 11-6: The Layer Control drop-down list.

The Layer Control drop-down list has two display modes.

✦ If no object is selected, it displays the current layer.

✦ If one or more objects are selected, it displays the layer of the selected object(s).

To check the current layer, make sure no object is selected. If necessary, press Esc to deselect any objects.

When objects on varying layers are selected, the Layer Control list goes blank, indicating that more than one layer is included in the selection.

To open the Layer Control drop-down list, click its arrow. You see a list of all your layers, including their states and colors. Pass the mouse over the items and a ToolTip tells you what they mean. The Layer Control drop-down list has three functions:

✦ It switches the current layer so you can draw on a new layer.

✦ It changes the current state of any specific layer on the list:
  • On/Off
  • Frozen/Thawed
  • Frozen/Thawed in Current (Floating) Viewport
  • Locked/Unlocked

✦ It changes the layer of a selected object.

Take the time to learn how to use this drop-down list; it can save you a great deal of time.

Switching the current layer

To switch the current layer, click the Layer Control drop-down list arrow and click the name of the layer you want to be current. Be careful to click only the name — otherwise, you may change the layer's state. Remember, this only works if no object is currently selected — so you may need to press Esc first to deselect all objects.

When you click a new layer name, the drop-down list automatically closes.

Changing a layer's state

Click any of the state icons to toggle a layer's state. For example, if you want to freeze a layer, click its sun and it switches to a snowflake. To access the Frozen/Thawed in Current Viewport state, you must have floating viewports. Floating viewports are covered in Chapter 17. Table 11-1 shows the icons for each state.

Table 11-1 Layer State Icons			
State	**Icon**	**State**	**Icon**
On	♀	Off	♀
Thawed	☼	Frozen	❋
Thawed in Current Viewport	🌣	Frozen in Current Viewport	❊
Unlocked	🔓	Locked	🔒

When you change a layer's state, the drop-down list stays open so that you can change the state of more than one layer at a time. Click the top of the list to close it.

Changing the layer of a selected object

Sometimes you need to change the layer of an object you have already drawn. You can do this easily in AutoCAD 14 by selecting one or more objects and clicking the layer name you want for the object in the Layer Control drop-down list. The list automatically closes.

Making an object's layer current

If you are adding an object, you usually want to draw on the same layer as an existing object. You could select the object to see what layer it's on, press Esc to deselect the object, and then choose that layer from the Layer Control drop-down list to make it current. However, AutoCAD has made this process even easier with the Make Object's Layer Current button on the Object Properties toolbar. Simply select an object and click the button. AutoCAD makes that object's layer current.

Step-by-Step: Working with Layers

1. Open *ab11-b.dwg* from the CD-ROM.

2. Save it as *ab11-2.dwg* in your *AutoCAD Bible* folder. This drawing is shown in Figure 11-7. The current layer is 0. OSNAP is on with running object snaps of Endpoint and Quadrant.

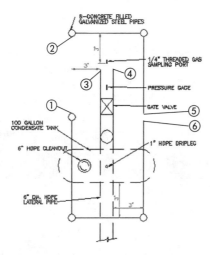

Figure 11-7: The gas extraction well plan drawing needs to be completed.

Credit: Thanks to the Army Corps of Engineers for this drawing.

3. Click the Layer Control drop-down list and click Pipes to change the current layer to Pipes.

4. Start the LINE command. Draw a line from ① to ② in Figure 11-7, using the Quadrant running object snap.

5. Click the Layer Control drop-down list and click Object to change the current layer to Object.

6. Click the Layer Control drop-down list and click the On/Off icon (the light bulb) of the Dim layer. Click again at the top of the list to close it.

7. Start the CIRCLE command. Type **2p** ↵ to use the two point option. Draw a circle from the endpoint of ③ to ④ in Figure 11-7 using the Endpoint running object snap.

8. Without changing the layer, start the CIRCLE command and again use the **2p** option. Draw a circle between the endpoints at ⑤ and ⑥ in Figure 10-7.

9. The last circle was drawn on the wrong layer. To change its layer, select the circle. Then click the Layer Control drop-down list and choose Pipes. Press Esc twice to remove the grips and see the result. The circle is now on the Pipes layer. Notice that the current layer is still Object in the Layer Control display.

10. Pick any red object (the Pipes layer). Choose Make Object's Layer Current from the Object Properties toolbar. Pipes is now the current layer. Draw a line from the right quadrant of the circle at ① to the left quadrant of the circle at ⑤ and ⑥ in Figure 11-7.

11. Pick any text to see what layer it is on. The Layer Control drop-down box changes to show the Text layer. Press Esc to deselect the text. Now choose the words *GAS EXTRACTION WELL PLAN* at the bottom of the drawing. Click the Layer Control drop-down box and choose Text. Press Esc twice to remove the grips.

12. Save your drawing. It should look like Figure 11-8.

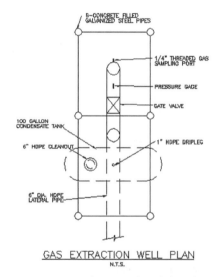

Figure 11-8: The completed drawing.

 Caution

It's easy to inadvertently change an object's layer. Make sure objects are not selected (press Esc) if you are about to use the Layer Control drop-down box just to change the current layer.

 On the CD-ROM

The CD-ROM includes an AutoLISP routine, Delayer, that erases all objects on any layer you choose. You can choose the layer name from a dialog box or select an object to determine the layer. This AutoLISP program creates a command called DELAYER. You can find it in the *\Software\Chap11\Delayer* folder.

I have also included an AutoLISP routine, Layonly, that turns off all layers except the one you pick. This can save a lot of time in a drawing with many layers. You can find it in the *\Software\Chap11\Layonly* folder.

Modifying layers

Sometimes you need to change the properties of a layer, such as its color or line-type. This is a powerful tool, because every object on that layer is automatically regenerated with the new properties. Other layer housekeeping tasks are renaming and deleting layers. You use the Layer & Linetype Properties dialog box for these functions.

Sorting columns

You can sort the layer listing in a drawing by any column, by clicking once on the column title. Click again to see the list in reverse order. This can be very helpful in quickly viewing which layers have been turned off, for example. If sorting by layer name does not appear to be working, increase the value for Maximum number sorted symbols in Tools⇨Preferences⇨General. Long layer names are truncated in the middle of the layer name, making it easy to distinguish between layers with names that differ only in the last few characters of their layer names.

Filtering the layer list

Some complex drawings may have dozens of layers. This can make it difficult to find the layer you want to change in the Layer & Linetype Properties dialog box. You can filter the layer list so you only see the layers you want. This makes it easy to change a group of layers at once. Click Show to drop down the filter choices and pick the filter you want.

If AutoCAD's standard filters don't meet your needs, you can create your own filter. Choose Set Filter Dialog from the list to open the Set Layer Filters dialog box, as shown in Figure 11-9.

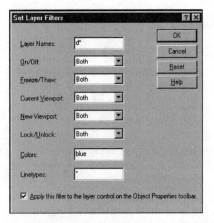

Figure 11-9: The Set Layer Filters dialog box.

You can set criteria by name, state (on/off, thawed/frozen, thawed/frozen for current and new floating viewports, unlocked/locked), color, and linetype. You can use *wildcards* to specify the name, color, and linetype. The two most common wildcards characters are * (asterisk), which replaces any number of characters, and ?, which replaces any single character. Figure 11-9 shows the layer name filter set to d*. The color is also specified as blue. Therefore only layers whose names start with the letter *d* and are blue are listed.

When you work with a large number of layers, think carefully about how you name them. It is common to name layers in groups. For example, if you have several text layers, you could name them t-title, t-notes, and t-table. A systematic layer-naming scheme makes it easy to filter the layers you need, which in turn makes it easy to make changes to groups of layers.

Changing a layer's color and linetype

To change a layer's color, choose Layers from the Object Properties toolbar. AutoCAD opens the Layer & Linetype Properties dialog box. There are two ways to change the color.

✦ Click Details if the lower section of the dialog box is not visible. Click the name of the layer you want to modify. In the Details section, click the Color drop-down list and choose the color you want. (If you don't want to choose one of the standard colors, choose Other to open the Select Color dialog box, choose a color and click OK.) When you have selected the color, click OK to close the Layer & Linetype Properties dialog box.

✦ Choose the color swatch of the layer you want to modify. AutoCAD opens the Select Color dialog box. Choose a color and click OK twice to return to your drawing.

To change a layer's linetype, follow the same procedure as for changing the color. The only difference is that the Details section doesn't let you load linetypes. If you need to choose a linetype that is not on the list, click the linetype of the layer to open the Select Linetype dialog box. There you can either choose a loaded linetype or load a linetype if necessary.

You can modify more than one layer at a time. In the Layer & Linetype Properties dialog box, right-click and choose Select All to choose all the layers. Choose Clear All to deselect all layers. You can choose a range of layers by clicking the first in the range, pressing Shift, and clicking the last in the range. Finally, you can choose individual layers by press Ctrl for each additional layer. Changes you make, such as color or linetype, now affect all the selected layers.

Renaming layers

It is best to carefully think out your layer naming scheme in advance. Many disciplines and offices have layer naming standards. However, sometimes you simply need to rename a layer. AutoCAD now makes it easier than ever to do so.

To rename a layer, chose Layers from the Object Properties toolbar to open the Layer & Linetype Properties dialog box. Click the name of the layer. A border appears, and the name is highlighted. Type the new name and press Enter.

You cannot rename layer 0.

Deleting layers

To delete a layer, chose Layers from the Object Properties toolbar to open the Layer & Linetype Properties dialog box. Click the name of the layer. Choose Delete and click OK.

You cannot delete the current layer or any layer that has objects on it. (Where would those objects go?) You also cannot delete layer 0, which is the default layer. There is also a layer that AutoCAD uses for defining dimensions, called DEFPOINTS, that you cannot delete. (Dimensions are covered in Chapters 14 and 15.) Finally, you cannot delete layers from external references (covered in Chapter 19).

Purging layers and linetypes

Layer and linetype definitions add to the size of your drawing because they are kept in the drawing's database. Therefore, it is worthwhile to eliminate layers and linetypes that you are not using. You can delete them, but sometimes it is hard to know which layers contain no objects. The PURGE command lets you delete many types of unused definitions, including layers and linetypes.

To purge layers and linetypes, type **purge** on the command line. AutoCAD responds with the Purge unused Blocks/Dimstyles/LAyers/LTypes/SHapes /STyles/Mlinestyles/All: prompt. To purge layers, type **la** ↵. To purge linetypes, type **lt** ↵.

Release 14 adds a great new feature to the PURGE command that lets you automatically purge all unused layers, linetypes, and so on without having to verify each one individually. At the Names to purge <*>: prompt, type in a name or press Enter to purge all. At the Verify each name to be purged? <Y> prompt, press Enter to be able to choose which items you want purged. AutoCAD lists the unused layers or linetypes and asks you if you want to purge them. Type **y** ↵ for each one you want to purge. However, if you know you want to purge all unused items, type **n** ↵. AutoCAD purges them all without further input from you.

Note The Incremental save % option in Tools⊅Preferences⊅Performance may prevent a Purge during a drawing session from removing all unreferenced layers or linetypes from the drawing. To avoid this, you can either set incremental save to zero, or save the drawing and reopen it and then immediately use the Purge command.

Step-by-Step: Modifying Layers

1. Open *ab11-c.dwg* from the CD-ROM.

2. Save it as *ab11-3.dwg* in your *AutoCAD Bible* folder. This drawing is shown in Figure 11-10.

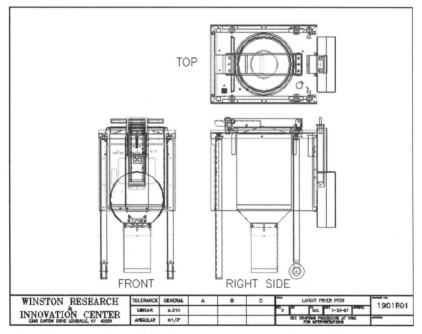

Figure 11-10: This drawing has 44 layers.

Credit: Thanks to Mary C. Redfern of Winston Research and Innovation Center, Easton, Pennsylvania, for this drawing.

3. Choose Layers from the Object Properties toolbar to open the Layer & Linetype Properties dialog box. From the Show drop-down list, choose Set Filter dialog. In the Layer Names box of the Set Layer Filters dialog box, type **m*** to list all layers starting with the letter *m*. Click OK. The Layer & Linetype Properties dialog box now looks like Figure 11-11.

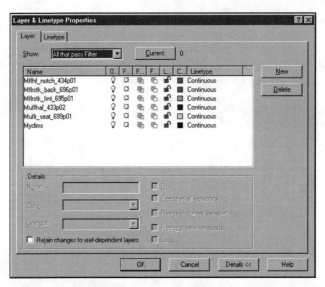

Figure 11-11: The Layer & Linetype Properties dialog box now shows only layers starting with the letter *m*.

4. Click the top layer. Press Shift and click the next-to-last layer. All the layers except for Mydims are selected. In the Details section (click Details if this section is not visible), click the Linetype drop-down list arrow and choose Dashed. Notice that all the selected layers now have a dashed linetype. Click OK to return to the drawing. AutoCAD regenerates the drawing with the new dashed linetypes.

5. Choose Layers from the Object Properties toolbar to open the Layer & Linetype Properties dialog box. Choose Mydims. Click it a second time so that a black border appears around the layer name. Type **titles** ↵. The name of the layer is changed. Notice that AutoCAD converted the first character to upper-case. Click OK.

6. Start the ERASE command and select any object on the title block (it is all one object) and the three labels FRONT, TOP, and RIGHT SIDE. Press Enter to end the command.

7. Choose Layers from the Object Properties toolbar to open the Layer & Linetype Properties dialog box again. Notice that the *titles* layer is not on the list because it no longer starts with the letter *m*. Click the Show drop-down list arrow and choose All. Scroll down the list of layers and choose *titles*. Click Delete. AutoCAD deletes the layer because it no longer has any objects on it.

8. Save your drawing.

Changing Color

You can change the color of an existing object or objects. You can also change the current color. When you change the current color, all future objects you draw have that color and are not drawn according to their layer's assigned color.

Changing an object's color

You can control an object's color using the Color Control drop-down list on the Object Properties toolbar, shown in Figure 11-12. As with the Layer Control drop-down list, the Color Control drop-down list shows the color of any selected object. When you create a layer, assign it a color, and draw with that layer, AutoCAD displays the color as *ByLayer*, as shown in Figure 11-13.

Figure 11-12: The Color Control drop-down list on the Object Properties toolbar.

The ByLayer color simply means that the color of the object is taken from the color of the object's layer. At the same time that you see the selected object's color in the Color Control drop-down list, you can look over to the Layer Control drop-down list and confirm the color assignment of the object's layer.

The best way to organize a drawing is to assign colors by layer. It can be confusing if related elements, such as centerlines in a mechanical drawing, appear in different colors. Also, if you see another line with the same color and linetype as most centerlines, you may assume it's a centerline in the wrong place. It is standard practice throughout the AutoCAD world to organize colors by layer.

Colors have a special significance because when you plot, you assign colors to pens. Therefore, color is the basis you use for plotting with various width pens (or color if you are plotting in color). You may want to temporarily change the color of an object to emphasize it in a plot or for some other reason. However, you should generally refrain from directly changing the color of objects.

Color Control drop-down list

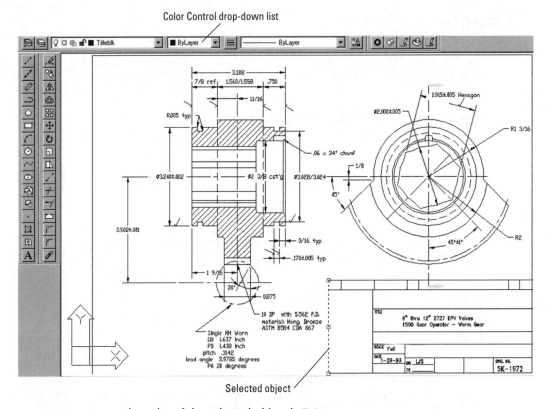

Selected object

Figure 11-13: The color of the selected object is ByLayer.

Credit: Thanks to Jerry Bottenfield of Clow Valve Company, Oskaloosa, Iowa, for this drawing.

If you need to change the color of an object, there are two ways to do it.

✦ To change just an object's color, select the object. Click the Color Control drop-down list and choose the color you want.

✦ If you want to change other properties at the same time, select the object and choose Properties from the Object Properties toolbar. AutoCAD opens a dialog box whose name and options depend on the object selected. Figure 11-14 shows the dialog box that opens when you choose a line. In this dialog box, you can change all the properties of the line. To change the color, choose Color to open the Select Color dialog box. Choose the color you want and click OK twice to return to your drawing.

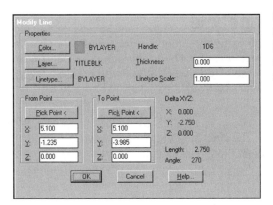

Figure 11-14: The Modify Line dialog box. If you select a circle, the dialog box is titled Modify Circle. If you select several varied objects, the dialog box is called Change Properties.

Tip

You can always change an object's color back to ByLayer, using the same Color drop-down list.

Changing the current color

When you change the current color, all future objects are drawn using that color, regardless of their layer. In general, you should do this only when you have a special need for two objects to be on one layer but have different colors. An example might be text in a title block. You might wish the text to have the same layer so that you can freeze it and thaw it (or turn it on and off) easily without having to remember that the text and title block are on two separate layers. If you also want part of the text to have a different color, change the current color before typing in that part of the text. Remember to change the current color back to ByLayer before drawing anything else.

To change the current color, click the Color drop-down list and choose the color you want. To change the current color back to Bylayer, click the Color drop-down list and choose ByLayer.

Cross-
Reference

You may also notice that there is a ByBlock color. The ByBlock color is discussed in Chapter 18.

You have an opportunity to do an exercise on changing colors after the next section.

Changing Linetypes

Linetypes work according to the same principles as colors. You can change the linetype of an existing object or objects. You can also change the current linetype. When you change the current linetype, all future objects you draw have that linetype and are not drawn according to their layer's assigned linetype.

Changing an object's linetype

You can control an object's linetype using the Linetype Control drop-down list on the Object Properties toolbar, shown in Figure 11-15. The Linetype Control drop-down list shows the linetype of any selected object. When you create a layer, assign it a linetype, and draw with that layer, AutoCAD displays the linetype as *ByLayer*, as shown in Figure 11-16.

Figure 11-15: The Linetype Control drop-down list on the Object Properties toolbar.

Linetype Control drop-down list

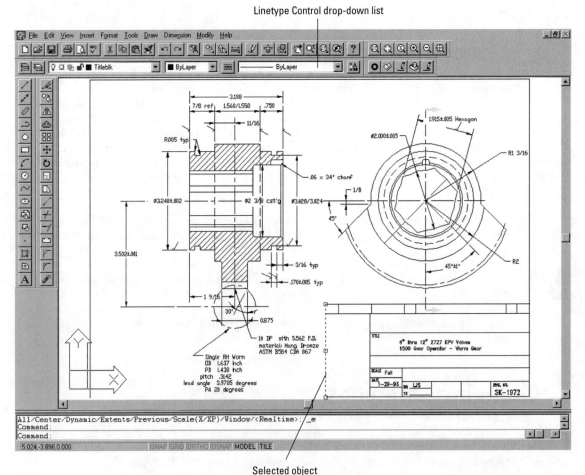

Selected object

Figure 11-16: The linetype of the selected object is ByLayer.

The ByLayer linetype simply means that the linetype of the object is taken from the linetype of the object's layer.

The best way to organize a drawing is to assign linetypes by layer. It can be confusing if related elements, such as plat borders in a surveyor's drawing, appear in different linetypes. Also, if you see another line with the same color and linetype as most plat borders, you may assume it's a plat border in the wrong place. It is common practice throughout the AutoCAD world to organize linetypes by layer.

If you need to change the linetype of an object, there are two ways to do it.

✦ To change an object's linetype, select the object. Click the Linetype Control drop-down list and choose the linetype you want.

✦ Select the object and choose Properties from the Object Properties toolbar. AutoCAD opens a dialog box whose name and options depend on the object selected. Using this method, you can change other properties at the same time. Figure 11-14 shows the dialog box that opens when you choose a line. In this dialog box, you can change all the properties of the line. To change the linetype, choose Linetype to open the Select Linetype dialog box. Choose the linetype you want and click OK twice to return to your drawing.

Tip

You can always change an object's linetype back to ByLayer, using the same Linetype Control drop-down list.

As discussed in the section, "Assigning a linetype," earlier in this chapter, you may need to load a linetype before you can use it. To load a linetype, choose Linetype from the Object Properties toolbar. This opens the same Layer & Linetype Properties dialog box that you worked with earlier in this chapter, but this time the Linetype tab is on top. Choose Load to open the Load or Reload Linetype dialog box, choose the linetype file (if not *acad.lin*), and choose the linetype you want to load. Click OK twice to return to your drawing.

Changing the current linetype

When you change the current linetype, all future objects are drawn using that linetype, regardless of their layer. In general, you should do this only when you have a special need for two objects to be on one layer but have different linetypes. An example might be a table containing notes in one corner of a drawing. You might wish the lines that make up the table to have the same layer so that you can freeze it and thaw it (or turn it on and off) easily without having to remember that the table is on two separate layers. If you also want some of the lines to have a different linetype, change the current linetype before adding those lines. Remember to change the current linetype back to ByLayer before drawing anything else.

To change the current linetype, click the Linetype drop-down list and choose the linetype you want, first making sure no objects are currently selected. To change the current linetype back to Bylayer, click the Linetype drop-down list and choose ByLayer.

Cross-Reference

You may also notice that there is a ByBlock linetype. The ByBlock linetype is discussed in Chapter 18.

On the CD-ROM

The CD-ROM includes a set of complex linetypes in the *pwrltype.lin* file. A few of these result in error messages and some have been included in Release 14, but there are still some very nice linetypes that you can use. Look in *\Software\Chap11\Pwrltype*.

Step-by-Step: Changing Colors and Linetypes

On the CD-ROM

1. Open *ab11-d.dwg* from the CD-ROM.

2. Save it as *ab11-4.dwg* in your *AutoCAD Bible* folder. This is an elevation view of a lavatory cabinet, shown in Figure 11-17.

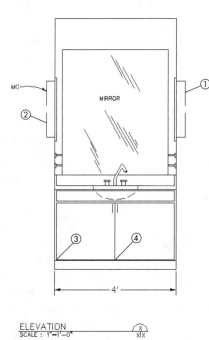

Figure 11-17: A lavatory cabinet.

Credit: Thanks to the Army Corps of Engineers for this drawing.

3. Pick one of the reflection lines in the mirror. Notice that the color is Red but the layer's color, as shown in the Layer Control drop-down list, is Magenta. Select all the reflection lines. Click the Color Control drop-down list and choose ByLayer from the top of the list. Press Esc twice to remove the grips and see the result.

4. Select the green dimension at the bottom of the cabinet. (The dimension is all one object.) To make it more visible, click the Color Control drop-down list and choose Red. Press Esc twice to see the result.

5. Pick the lines at ① and ② in Figure 11-17. Click the Linetype Control drop-down list and choose the Hidden linetype.

6. With grips still active for these lines, click the Color Control drop-down list box and choose Cyan to make it the current color. Press Esc twice to see the result.

7. Start the RECTANGLE command. Draw a rectangle inside the left cabinet. Use the COPY command to copy the rectangle to the right cabinet. (To copy, use an Intersection object snap at point ③ as the base point and ④ as the second point of displacement.) The rectangles are drawn in Cyan even though they are on the A-detl-lw10 layer.

8. Save your drawing. It should look like Figure 11-18.

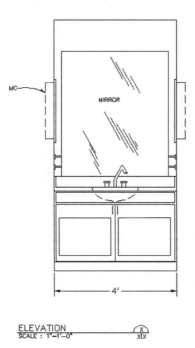

Figure 11-18: The finished cabinet.

Working with Linetype Scales

As mentioned earlier in this chapter, noncontinuous linetypes are created by repeating a defined pattern of dots, dashes, and spaces. (Linetypes can also include repeating text or shapes.) You may find that the linetype patterns in your drawing are too long or short for clarity. The linetype scale may even be so big or so small that the line looks continuous. How often the pattern is repeated is affected by three things:

- ✦ The linetype definition
- ✦ The global linetype scale
- ✦ The individual object's linetype scale

Changing linetype spacing by using a different linetype

One choice is to change the linetype. There are a number of linetypes that come in short, medium, and long variations, such as Dashed, Dashed2, and Dashedx2, shown in Figure 11-19.

Figure 11-19: A number of AutoCAD's standard linetypes come in three variations like the Dashed, Dashed2, and Dashedx2 linetypes.

AutoCAD's *acad.lin* contains a number of ISO linetypes that meet the specifications of the International Standards Organization. Your field or organization may require the use of these linetypes. If so, you should know that the ISO linetype patterns definitions are much longer than AutoCAD's other definitions. Figure 11-20 shows the ISO dash linetype and AutoCAD's dashed linetype. You may need to make adjustments to the linetype scale as a result.

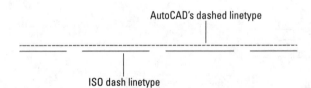

Figure 11-20: A comparison of the ISO dash linetype and AutoCAD's dashed linetype.

Changing linetype spacing by changing the global linetype scale

Another choice is to change the global linetype scale, which affects all noncontinuous linetypes in your drawing. AutoCAD multiplies the linetype definition by the global linetype scale to calculate the length of each repetition of the linetype. Linetype scales larger than 1 result in longer sections — and fewer repetitions of the linetype definition per unit. Linetype scales smaller than 1 result in shorter sections — and more repetitions of the linetype definition per unit. When you change the linetype scale, AutoCAD regenerates the drawing and changes all the linetypes. Figure 11-21 shows three versions of a drawing with linetypes at linetype scales of .5, 1, and 2. As you can see, a scale of 2 is too large and a scale of .5 is too small. A scale of 1 is just right. (Goldilocks would have been happy with it.)

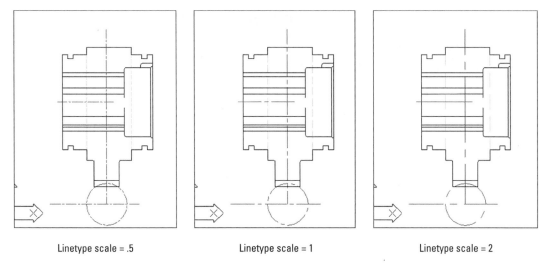

Linetype scale = .5   Linetype scale = 1   Linetype scale = 2

Figure 11-21: Three versions of a drawing, using linetype scales of .5, 1, and 2.

The global linetype scale is held in the LTSCALE system variable. You can change the linetype scale by typing **LTSCALE** at the command line and typing in a scale.

For purposes of drawing, you simply want to make sure that you can distinguish the linetype both when you can see the entire drawing on the screen and when you zoom in close. The main reason to scale linetypes is for plotting. A linetype scale that works for a drawing of a house on screen may appear continuous when you plot it at 1=96.

If you want the linetype to appear exactly according to its definition, use the scale factor for the linetype scale. Scale factors are covered in Chapter 5. However, since the entire drawing is so scaled down, it often works better to use a linetype scale of one-quarter to one-half the scale factor — in the 1=96 example, you might use a linetype scale of 24 or 48.

To change the linetype scale, choose Linetype from the Object Properties toolbar to open the Linetype tab of the Layer & Linetype Properties dialog box, shown in Figure 11-22. Make sure the lower portion of the dialog box is displayed, otherwise, click the Details button.

In the global scale factor text box, type the scale factor you want. Click OK. AutoCAD regenerates the drawing, changing the scale of every noncontinuous line-type in the drawing.

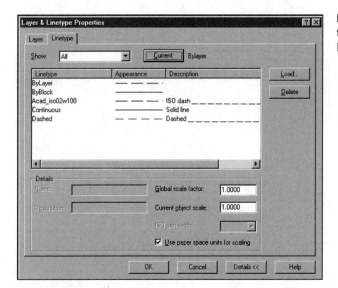

Figure 11-22: The Linetype tab of the Layer & Linetype Properties dialog box.

Changing linetype spacing by changing the object linetype scale

On occasion, you may want the linetype spacing to be different for one object — or a small group of objects — only. Perhaps the object is too small to show the linetype pattern or you want to set it off visually. AutoCAD also has a current object linetype scale that works like setting a current color or linetype — all objects drawn after you set the object linetype scale are drawn with the new linetype scale. In most cases, you want to make sure you change the current object linetype scale back to its default of 1 after using it for that one object or group of objects.

Note

The current object linetype scale is held in the CELTSCALE system variable. You can change the current object linetype scale by typing **CELTSCALE** at the command line and typing in a scale.

Changing the current object linetype scale

To change the current object linetype scale, choose Linetype from the Object Properties toolbar to open the Linetype tab of the Layer & Linetype Properties dialog box, shown in Figure 11-22. Make sure the lower portion of the dialog box is displayed; otherwise, click Details. In the Current object scale text box, type the scale factor you want. Click OK. Now all objects that you draw use the current object linetype scale.

If you have also set the global linetype scale to a value other than 1, AutoCAD multiplies the two linetype scales to calculate the final result. For example, if you have a global linetype scale of 12 and a current object linetype scale of .5, objects you draw will have a resulting linetype scale of 6.

Changing an existing object's linetype scale

It may be more common to draw an object without setting a special object linetype scale and then decide that you want to change its linetype scale. To change an object's linetype scale, select the object and choose Properties from the Object Properties toolbar. In the Linetype Scale text box of the dialog box, type in the new linetype scale. This linetype scale only affects the selected object. It does not affect the global linetype scale.

Step-by-Step: Working with Linetype Scales

On the CD-ROM

1. Open *ab11-e.dwg* from the CD-ROM.

2. Save it as *ab11-5.dwg* in your *AutoCAD Bible* folder. This is a bushing, shown in Figure 11-23. Notice that the linetype doesn't show clearly on the short line at ① and in the small circle at ②.

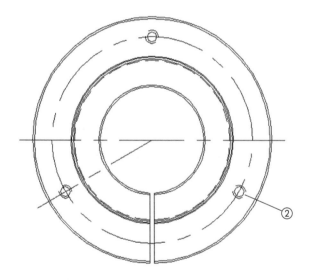
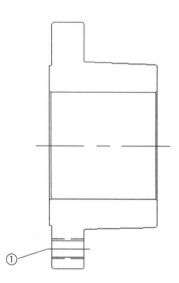

SECTION A–A

Figure 11-23: This drawing of a bushing has two noncontinuous linetypes.

Credit: Thanks to Robert Mack of The Dexter Company, Fairfield, Iowa, for this drawing.

3. Choose Linetype from the Object Properties toolbar. In the Linetype tab of the Layer & Linetype Properties dialog box, change the Global scale factor to .5. Click OK. AutoCAD regenerates the drawing. Note that the circles are better, but the short line at ① still looks like a continuous line.

4. Choose the line at ①. Choose Properties from the Object Properties toolbar. Change the Linetype Scale to .5. Choose OK. Notice the difference in the line, which now has a linetype scale of .5 (global) times .5 (object) = .25.

5. Save your drawing. It should look like Figure 11-24.

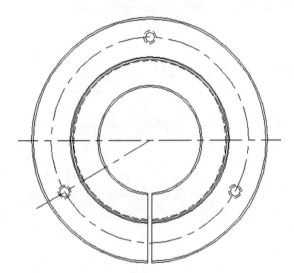
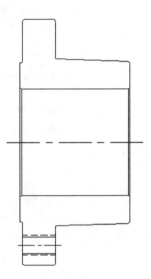

SECTION A—A

Figure 11-24: The drawing's noncontinuous lines are now more appropriate.

Matching Properties

You may be familiar with the Format Painter button available on the toolbars of many Windows 95 applications. With Release 14, AutoCAD has introduced a similar concept, at the same time allowing you to specify which properties you want to match. AutoCAD calls this process *matching properties*. It reminds me of Excel's Paste Special command, which lets you choose what properties you want to paste from what you copied to the Clipboard — everything, the formulas, values, formats, and so on.

An object can have so many properties that this could be a useful tool. To match properties, you need two objects, a source object and a destination object (or objects). Follow these steps to match properties.

1. Choose the object whose properties you want to match (the source object).

2. Choose Match Properties from the Standard toolbar. AutoCAD responds with the `Settings/<Select Destination Object(s)>:` prompt.

3. If you want to match all the object's properties, select the object(s) you want to receive the matching properties, that is, the destination object(s).

4. If you want to match only some of the object's properties, type **s** ↵ to open the Property Settings dialog box, shown in Figure 11-25. Uncheck all the properties you don't want to match and click OK. AutoCAD returns you to the same prompt as before. Select the object(s) you want to receive the matching properties, that is, the destination objects(s).

5. Press Enter to end object selection. AutoCAD matches the properties.

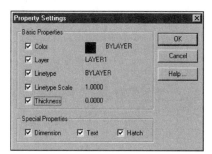

Figure 11-25: The Property Settings dialog box.

Note

You can choose Match Properties from the Standard toolbar first and then choose the source object.

Step-by-Step: Matching Properties

On the
CD-ROM

1. Open *ab11-f.dwg* from the CD-ROM.

2. Save it as *ab11-6.dwg* in your *AutoCAD Bible* folder. This is a drawing of a master bedroom suite plan, as shown in Figure 11-26.

3. Pick the wall at ① in Figure 11-26. Click Match Properties from the Standard toolbar. At the `Settings/<Select Destination Object(s)>:` prompt, use a crossing window to select all the folding closet doors on either side of the line you just selected. Press Enter to end object selection. AutoCAD matches the properties of the doors to the properties of the wall.

4. Pick the text *MASTER SUITE.* Choose Match Properties from the Standard toolbar. At the `Settings/<Select Destination Object(s)>:` prompt, type **s** ↵. In the Property Settings dialog box, deselect all the boxes except Text in the Special Properties section. Click OK.

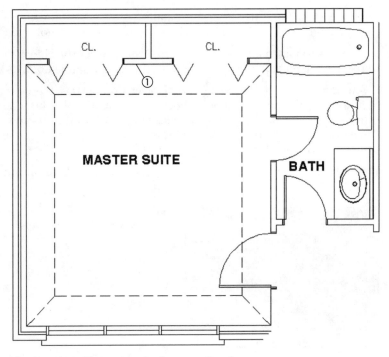

Figure 11-26: The master bedroom suite plan.

5. At the `Settings/<Select Destination Object(s)>:` prompt, choose the text *CL.* in both closets and press Enter to end the command. AutoCAD matches the text properties of the text. Notice that the *CL.* text becomes bold.

6. Save your drawing.

Summary

In this chapter you learned all about layers, colors, and linetypes. Layers help you organize your drawings by assigning the same properties to related objects. Each layer has a name, color, and linetype. You create new layers using the Layers & Linetype Properties dialog box. When you make a layer current, every new object is drawn on that layer. You can also change the layer of existing objects.

Layers can be assigned one of three states — On/Off, Thawed/Frozen, and Unlocked/Locked. You can change the properties of existing layers. You can also rename and delete them. To help you work with layers, you can filter the layer listing. In most cases, it is best to use layer definitions to assign color and linetype. Nevertheless, you can directly change the color and linetype of any object. When you make a color or linetype current, every new object is drawn with that color or linetype.

Linetype scales define how often a linetype pattern is repeated per unit. You can globally change the linetype scale. You can also change the current linetype scale, which affects the linetype scale of all new objects you draw. You can change the object linetype scale of existing objects as well.

The Match Properties command, which copies properties from one object to one or more destination objects, is new for Release 14.

✦　　✦　　✦

Getting Information from Your Drawing

✦ ✦ ✦ ✦

In This Chapter

Getting drawing-wide information

Getting information about objects

Measuring and segmenting objects

Using the calculator

✦ ✦ ✦ ✦

Your Intelligent Drawing

Your AutoCAD drawing is intelligent in many ways. Several commands can give you the details of each object. In addition, you can get listings that provide information about your drawing as a whole. I have mentioned system variables several times — you can list system variables and their current settings.

You can perform calculations on objects that may assist you in certain drawing tasks. For example, you can divide an object into any number of segments by placing point objects along the object or you can place point objects at a specified distance along the object. You can use AutoCAD's calculator, which not only does regular numerical calculations but also works with coordinates and geometric points on objects.

Drawing-Level Information

Some information applies to the drawing as a whole or even your computer system as a whole, rather than individual objects. This information can be important when there is a problem or when you simply need to find the status of system variables.

Listing the status of your drawing

The STATUS command provides a standard list of information that can be very helpful. To use the STATUS command, choose Tools⇨Inquiry⇨Status.

Figure 12-1 shows a sample status listing.

```
█ AutoCAD Text Window                                               _ □ ×
 Edit

Command: status
3520 objects in A:\9541mi_g.dwg
Model space limits are X:      0'-0"    Y:     0'-0"   (Off)
                       X:     90'-8"    Y:    58'-8"
Model space uses       X:      0'-0"    Y:     0'-0"
                       X:     90'-8"    Y:    58'-8"
Display shows          X:      0'-0"    Y:     0'-0"
                       X: 101'-9 35/64"  Y:    58'-8"
Insertion base is      X:      0'-0"    Y:     0'-0"   Z:    0'-0"
Snap resolution is     X:      0'-1"    Y:     0'-1"
Grid spacing is        X:      0'-0"    Y:     0'-0"

Current space:         Model space
Current layer:         TBLK
Current color:         BYLAYER -- 7 (white)
Current linetype:      BYLAYER -- CONTINUOUS
Current elevation:       0'-0"  thickness:       0'-0"
Fill on  Grid off  Ortho off  Qtext off  Snap off  Tablet off
Object snap modes:    Center, Endpoint, Intersection, Midpoint, Quadrant
Free dwg disk (A:) space: 1.2 MBytes
Free temp disk (D:) space: 22.8 MBytes
Free physical memory: 1.0 Mbytes (out of 15.5M).

Press RETURN to continue:                                  ◄ ►
```

Figure 12-1: A sample listing from the STATUS command.

As you can see, this is a big drawing, with 3,520 objects! Next AutoCAD lists the limits and extents of the drawing, as well as the extents of the current display on your screen. Other important items are the snap and grid spacing as well as the current layer, color, and linetype. You can see that Ortho and Fill are on but the other drawing aid settings are off. AutoCAD lists the running object snaps that have been set. Finally there is information about free disk space and free memory. (1.0 megabyte out of 15.5MB!)

Obviously, much of this information is available without using the STATUS command. The easiest to find are the current layer, color, and linetype, which are readily visible on the Object Properties toolbar. However, you would have to use a number of commands to obtain other information such as the snap and grid spacing and the drawing limits. STATUS puts it all together in one listing. Finally, the free disk and memory statistics provide valuable information not easily obtainable otherwise from within your drawing.

The most common use for STATUS is to troubleshoot problems. For example, if AutoCAD is crashing often, a listing such as the one shown in Figure 12-1 would suggest that insufficient memory is a possible cause. You could even send the listing to a colleague in another office who needs to work on the same drawing. Your colleague can then work more easily using the same settings you have used.

Listing system variables

In Chapter 5 I explained that AutoCAD stores settings in system variables. In the last chapter, for example, I mentioned that the global linetype scale is stored in the LTSCALE system variable and the object linetype scale is stored in the CELTSCALE system variable. You may want to know the settings of a group of related system variables. The SETVAR command provides a listing of all the system variables and their settings. It may be quicker to view system variable settings using the SETVAR command than typing each individual system variable on the command line.

There are too many system variables to show the entire listing here, but a few can convey the wealth of information available, as shown in Figure 12-2.

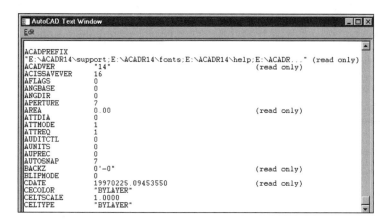

Figure 12-2: A partial SETVAR listing.

Note

Read-only system variables are for information only and cannot be changed. An example is ACADVER, which shows as 14 (meaning Release 14). Other system variables can be changed.

You can see, for example, that CELTSCALE is set to 1, but the LTSCALE is set to 24. (The drawing is an architectural floor plan of a house.) BLIPMODE, discussed in Chapter 5, is set to off. While some system variables allow any or a variety of values, many are either on or off. In general, a setting of 1 means on and 0 means off.

Cross-Reference

Appendix C lists the most useful system variables, including a brief explanation of each.

Most system variables do not need to be set directly. In Chapter 11, for example, you set the LTSCALE system variable using the Layer & Linetype Properties dialog box. However, there are a few system variables that can only be accessed by typing them on the command line.

You can use SETVAR to set system variables (that are not read-only) as well as to list them. In earlier releases of AutoCAD you had to use SETVAR to set system variables. However, you can now type them directly on the command line.

To list the system variables, choose Tools⇨Inquiry⇨Set Variable. At the `Variable name or ?:` prompt, type **? ↵**. At the `Variable(s) to list <*>:` prompt, press Enter to list all the system variables or type the name of a variable. (You can use the * and ? wildcards in the name.) AutoCAD either lists all the system variables or just the variable you typed.

If you type a variable, AutoCAD prompts you for a new value so you can change it. For example, if you type CELTSCALE, AutoCAD responds with the `New value for CELTSCALE <1.0000>:` prompt. You can then change the system variable by typing in a new value. You can simply press Enter to accept the current setting.

Tracking drawing time

You can track the time you spend working on a drawing. This feature is most often used for billing time to clients, or maybe your boss wants to see how much you're getting done.

To use the TIME command, choose Tools⇨Inquiry⇨Time. A typical listing is shown in Figure 12-3.

```
Command: time

Current time:                Tuesday, February 25, 1997 at 9:48:58:290 AM
Times for this drawing:
   Created:                  Tuesday, July 04, 1995 at 11:52:35:870 AM
   Last updated:             Sunday, February 23, 1997 at 9:15:46:580 PM
   Total editing time:       0 days 10:05:48.230
   Elapsed timer (on):       0 days 10:05:48.230
   Next automatic save in:   0 days 01:56:36.880

Display/ON/OFF/Reset:
```

Figure 12-3: A typical TIME listing.

Here's what the listing means.

Current time: The current date and time. The time is displayed to the nearest millisecond.

Created: The date and time the drawing was created.

Last updated: The date and time of the last save of the drawing.

Total editing time: Accumulates the time spent in the drawing, not including plotting time or time you worked on the drawing and quit without saving your changes.

Elapsed timer: Also accumulates time spent in the drawing, but you can turn this on and off and reset it.

Next automatic save in: Shows when AutoCAD will automatically save your drawing. Choose Tools➪Preferences➪General to set how often AutoCAD automatically saves your drawing.

Tip

Think of Total editing time as your car's odometer and Elapsed time as a timer (like the one some cars have) that lets you time a specific trip.

At the end of the listing, AutoCAD displays the `Display/ON/OFF/Reset:` prompt. The Display option redisplays the listing with updated times. ON and OFF turn the elapsed time on and off. The Reset option resets the elapsed time to zero.

Cross-Reference

Chapter 26, "Managing Drawings," explains how to keep a log file of your drawing activity.

Step-by-Step: Obtaining Drawing Information

On the CD-ROM

1. Open *ab12-a.dwg* from the CD-ROM.

2. Choose Tools➪Inquiry➪Status. Look at the listing to see how many objects it contains. Check the limits of the drawing. Look at the grid spacing. Read through any other items of interest to you. Press Enter to end the command.

3. Choose Tools➪Inquiry➪Set Variable. At the `Variable name or ?:` prompt, type **?** ↲. At the `Variable(s) to list <*>:` prompt, press Enter to accept the default. Look for the BLIPMODE setting. Check the location of the drawing (DWGPREFIX). Look for the global linetype scale (LTSCALE). Press Enter until you see the `Command:` prompt again.

4. Press Enter to start the SETVAR command again. At the `Variable name or ?:` prompt, type **blipmode** ↲. Type **0** ↲ to turn off blips.

5. Choose Tools➪Inquiry➪Time. Check the current time against your watch. (AutoCAD takes the time from your computer's clock.) Look at the Total editing time to see how long you have had this drawing open. Press Enter to end the command.

6. Do not save this drawing. Leave the drawing open if you are going on to the next exercise.

Object-Level Information

Several commands exist solely to provide information about the objects in your drawing.

Listing objects

The LIST command displays information about selected objects. The information displayed depends on the object. For example, the LIST command gives you the radius of a circle and the length of a line.

 To list an object, choose Tools⇨Inquiry⇨List or choose List from the Inquiry flyout of the Standard toolbar. If you use the Inquiry flyout, notice that the button you just selected from the flyout, List, now becomes the default button on the toolbar.

Figure 12-4 shows a typical listing for a line.

```
Command: list
1 found
                    LINE        Layer: A_ROOF
                                Space: Model space
                    Handle = 1210
             from point, X=61'-5 1/8"  Y=32'-4 5/8"  Z=    0'-0"
               to point, X=71'-9 51/64"  Y=32'-4 5/8"  Z=    0'-0"
       Length =10'-4 43/64".   Angle in XY Plane =        0
               Delta X =10'-4 43/64", Delta Y =       0'-0", Delta Z =      0'-
```

Figure 12-4: A typical listing for a horizontal line.

Here's what the listing means:

Layer: AutoCAD lists the object's layer. If the color and linetype are not ByLayer or ByBlock, AutoCAD lists these as well.

Space: AutoCAD tells you if the object is in model space or paper space. (Paper space is covered in Chapter 17.)

Handle: Every object in your drawing has a handle. AutoCAD uses handles to keep track of objects.

From point: Since AutoCAD is listing a line, it shows the start point.

To point: The end point of the line.

Length: The line's length.

Angle in XY Plane: The line's angle. This line is horizontal, so its angle is zero.

Delta X: The change in the X coordinate from the start point to the end point.

Delta Y: The change in the Y coordinate from the start point to the end point.

Release 14's new Object Properties toolbar now makes it easier than before to tell an object's layer, linetype, and color. Remember, when you select an object, its layer, linetype, and color appear in the Object Properties toolbar.

Calculating distances

AutoCAD makes it easy to calculate the distance between any two points. Choose Tools⇨Inquiry⇨Distance or choose Distance from the Inquiry flyout of the Standard toolbar. AutoCAD prompts you for two points. You can use any means of specifying a point, although object snaps or Snap mode are useful if you want to be sure which point you are specifying. Here is a typical display for a vertical line:

```
Distance = 19 -0 , Angle in XY Plane = 270, Angle from XY
Plane = 0
Delta X = 0 -0 , Delta Y = -19 -0 , Delta Z = 0 -0
```

You can use this information to check dimensions (covered in Chapter 14) or to make further calculations that you need for drawing.

The CD-ROM contains an AutoLISP routine called *ldtops.lsp* that provides distances in feet and inches, in decimal notation, in meters, and the angle. You can find it in the *\software\Chapter 12\ldtops* folder.

Finding coordinates

Finding a coordinate is even easier than calculating a distance. Choose Tools⇨Inquiry⇨ID Point or choose Locate Point from the Inquiry flyout of the standard toolbar. AutoCAD prompts you for a point. You can use any means of specifying a point, although object snaps or snap mode are useful if you want to be sure which point you are specifying. Here is a typical listing:

```
Point: X = 61 -5 1/8  Y = 32 -4 5/8  Z = 0 -0
```

You can use this information to specify or calculate an absolute coordinate.

Step-by-Step: Obtaining Object Information

1. Open *ab12-a.dwg* from the CD-ROM if it is not already open from the previous exercise. This is a civil engineering drawing showing several plots of land, as shown in Figure 12-5.

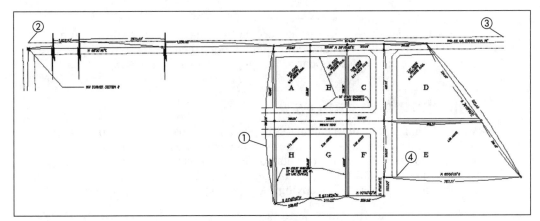

Figure 12-5: A civil engineering drawing of several plots of land.

 2. Choose List from the Inquiry flyout of the Standard toolbar. At the `Select objects:` prompt, pick at ① in Figure 12-5. The result is shown in Figure 12-6. Note the large scale that a civil engineering drawing uses and the surveyor's units.

Figure 12-6: The result of using the LIST command on an arc.

```
Select objects:
             ARC        Layer: 0
                        Space: Model space
              Handle = 7D3951
      center point, X= 7249.24  Y=  3753.29  Z=    0.00
      radius    1937.35
      start angle S 89d28'56" W
        end angle S 76d38'19" W
      length    434.28
```

3. Choose Distance from the Inquiry flyout of the Standard toolbar. At the `First point:` prompt, choose the endpoint at ② in Figure 12-5, using the Endpoint running object snap. At the `Second point:` prompt, choose the endpoint at ③. Here's the result:

```
2740.90, Angle in XY Plane = N 89d23 34  E, Angle from XY
Plane = E
Delta X = 2740.75, Delta Y = 29.05, Delta Z = 0.00
```

4. Choose Locate Point from the Inquiry flyout of the Standard toolbar. At the `Point:` prompt, pick the endpoint at ④ in Figure 12-5. Here is the result:

```
X = 6065.67 Y = 3450.58 Z = 0.00
```

5. Do not save this drawing. Leave the drawing open if you are going on to the next exercise.

Note

The precision set in the Units dialog box (Format⇨Units) affects the results of the LIST, DIST, and ID (Locate Point) commands.

Calculating area and perimeter

AutoCAD can also calculate the area and perimeter of any area.

 To start the AREA command, choose Tools⇨Inquiry⇨Area or choose Area from the Inquiry flyout of the Standard toolbar.

You can specify points bounding the area you want to calculate. The points do not have to be on an object. AutoCAD calculates the area and perimeter as if you had drawn lines between all the points. AutoCAD automatically closes the area if you don't close the area by picking the last point the same as the first point. This option is limited to areas with straight sides.

Instead of picking points, you can use the Object option to calculate the area of objects, which gives you the flexibility to use areas that include curves. Acceptable objects are circles, ellipses, splines, polylines, polygons, regions, and solids. (Splines, polylines, regions, and solids are covered in Chapter 16.) AutoCAD still calculates an area but adds a length instead of a perimeter. For a circle, you get a circumference. Although a polyline may have the exact same shape as an arc, if you try to calculate the area of an arc, AutoCAD replies: `Selected object does not have an area`. Polylines and splines can be open. AutoCAD calculates the area as if you had drawn a line from the endpoint to the start point but does not include that last imaginary line when calculating the length.

To calculate the area of irregular shapes, you can keep a running total by using the Add option. Start by specifying the first area. Then use the Add option and specify a second area. AutoCAD adds the two areas. You can continue to add areas. You can also use the Subtract option to subtract areas.

Figure 12-7 shows an example of calculating the open area in an office floor plan by picking points. The point objects show the points that were used to calculate the area and perimeter.

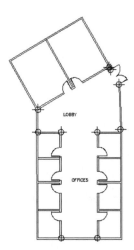

Figure 12-7: Calculating the area and perimeter for an office floor plan.

Tip

You can also use the BOUNDARY command to create one polyline or region from a complex area. (Boundaries and polylines are covered in Chapter 16.) You can then use the Object option of the AREA command instead of picking points. However, notice that BOUNDARY included the open doors in the area selected for the office floor plan, as shown in Figure 12-8.

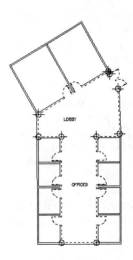

Figure 12-8: Using the BOUNDARY command to create on object for use with the AREA command. The boundary is indicated with a dashed line.

Step-by-Step: Using the AREA Command

On the
CD-ROM

1. Open *ab12-a.dwg* from the CD-ROM if it is not already open from the previous exercise.

2. Use ZOOM Window to zoom in on the parcels of land labeled D and E, as shown in Figure 12-9.

3. Choose Area from the Inquiry flyout of the Standard toolbar.

4. At the `<First point>/Object/Add/Subtract:` prompt, type **a** ↵ to start Add mode. At the `<First point>/Object/Subtract:` prompt, pick ① in Figure 12-9 using the Endpoint running object snap. At the `(ADD mode) Next point:` prompts, continue to pick ②, ③, ④, and ⑤. Press Enter. AutoCAD lists the area and perimeter. (Your figures may be somewhat different if you picked different points.)

   ```
   Area = 183399.88, Perimeter = 1884.62
   Total area = 183399.88
   ```

5. At the `<First point>/Object/Subtract:` prompt, pick ⑥ in Figure 12-9. At the `(ADD mode) Next point:` prompts, pick ⑦, ⑧, and ⑨. Press Enter to complete point selection. AutoCAD reports the area and perimeter of the

second area and adds the two areas together to give you the total area. Press Enter again to end the command.

```
Area = 123575.16, Perimeter = 1480.17
Total area = 306975.04
```

6. Do not save the drawing. Keep it open if you are continuing on to the next exercise.

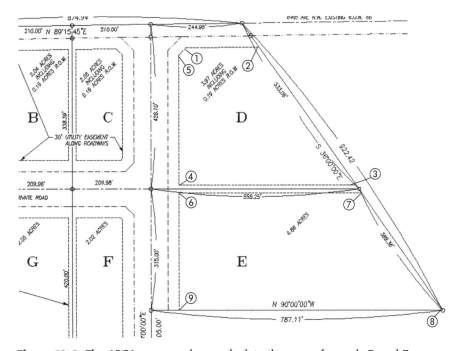

Figure 12-9: The AREA command can calculate the area of parcels D and E.

Note

The MASSPROP command is mostly used for 3D drawings, but it can also be used on regions, which are 2D solid surfaces, such as a shape cut from sheet metal. This command provides area and perimeter but also other engineering calculations, such as centroids, moments of inertia, the product of inertia, and so on. This command is covered further in Chapter 24.

Getting information from the Modify Object dialog box

You can also get information about an object by selecting it and choosing Properties from the Object Properties toolbar. Figure 12-10 shows the dialog box that opens when you select a line. You used this dialog box in Chapter 11 to change layer, color, and linetype properties. As you can see, the dialog box also lists the line's start and end points, delta (change) in X, Y, and Z, handle number, length, and angle — much like the LIST command.

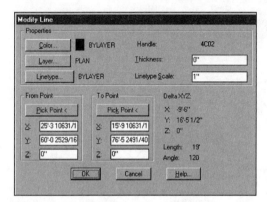

Figure 12-10: The Modify Object dialog box lists information about a selected object.

Measurement Commands

AutoCAD can make calculations on objects for you. The DIVIDE command divides an object into equally spaced sections. The MEASURE command divides an object into sections of a specified length. These commands are useful in many fields — you might need to space bolt holes evenly around the edge of a bushing, or place fence studs along the edge of a plot every five feet.

Dividing objects

The DIVIDE command divides an object into equally spaced sections. DIVIDE does not break the object — it simply places point objects along the object. You can then use the Node object snap if you wish to draw from those points.

To divide an object, choose Draw⇨Point⇨Divide. Select the object you want to divide. AutoCAD responds with the <Number of segments>/Block: prompt. Type in the number of segments you want to create. AutoCAD places the point objects and ends the command.

Remember that you can set the point display by choosing Format⇨Point Style. An easy-to-see point style is especially useful for the DIVIDE command. Specify the point style *before* using the command.

Remember that to create eight segments, for example, AutoCAD places seven point objects. If you have in your mind the number of point objects you want, add one when specifying the number of segments.

You can use the Block option to place a block of your choice along the object instead of a point object. Blocks are covered in Chapter 18. If you choose the Block option (by typing **b** ↵), AutoCAD responds with the `Block name to insert:` prompt. Type the name of the block. AutoCAD asks, `Align block with object? <Y>`. Answer Y or N depending on whether you want to align the block with the object.

Note

Aligning a block is appropriate for curved objects and blocks that are not completely symmetrical. Remember creating a polar array? (Arrays were covered in Chapter 10.) There, AutoCAD similarly asks if you want to rotate the objects as they are copied.

AutoCAD asks for the number of segments and you type the number that you want, as described earlier. Figure 12-11 shows an electrical schematic. Here you want to divide a line so you can evenly space wires entering the ignition module. Four wires need to come in so the line was divided into five segments, using an easy-to-see point object.

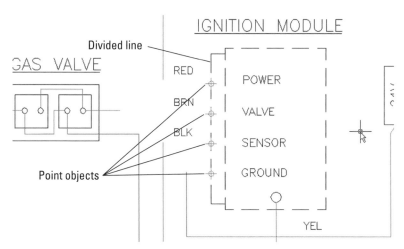

Figure 12-11: Dividing a line into five segments using point objects.

Credit: Thanks to Robert Mack of The Dexter Company, Fairfield, Iowa, for this drawing.

You can practice using the DIVIDE command after the next section.

Measuring objects

The MEASURE command is similar to the DIVIDE command except that you specify the distance between point objects instead of the total number of segments. AutoCAD starts measuring from the endpoint closest to where you pick the object. MEASURE does not break the object — it simply places point objects along the object. You can then use the Node object snap if you wish to draw from those points.

To divide an object, choose Draw⇨Point⇨Measure. Select the object you want to measure. AutoCAD responds with the `<Segment length>/Block:` prompt. Type the segment length you want. AutoCAD places the point objects and ends the command.

Tip

Remember that you can set the point display by choosing Format⇨Point Style. An easy-to-see point style is especially useful for the MEASURE command. Specify the point style *before* using the command.

Just as with the DIVIDE command, you can place a block along the object using the Block option. AutoCAD prompts you for the name of the block and lets you choose if you want to align the block with the object. AutoCAD asks for the segment length, and you type in the number of segments you want, as described earlier. Figure 12-12 shows a plot drawing with one side of a lot measured into 20-foot segments.

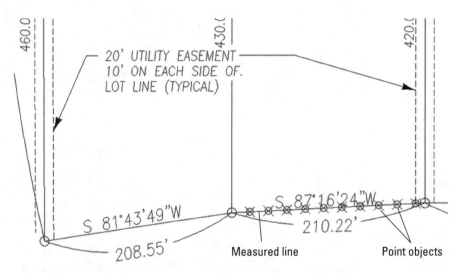

Figure 12-12: Measuring a line into 20-foot segments using point objects.

Credit: Thanks to Bill Maidment of Caltech, Inc, Fairfield, Iowa, for this drawing.

Step-by-Step: Using the DIVIDE and MEASURE Commands

1. Open *ab12-a.dwg* from the CD-ROM if it is not already open from the previous exercise.

2. If you didn't do the previous exercise, use ZOOM Window to zoom in to the parcels labeled D and E, as shown in Figure 12-13.

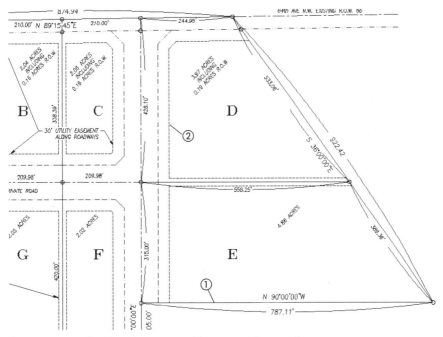

Figure 12-13: The site plan zoomed in to parcels D and E.

3. Choose Format⇨Point Style and choose the fourth style in the first row. Choose Set Size Relative to Screen and set the size to 5%. Click OK.

4. Choose Draw⇨Point⇨Divide. At the `Select object to divide:` prompt, choose ① in Figure 12-13. At the `<Number of segments>/Block:` prompt, type **3** ↵. AutoCAD places two points along the line, dividing it into three segments. (If you wish, draw lines from the points perpendicular to the opposite side of the parcel to divide it into three parcels.)

5. Choose Draw⇨Point⇨Measure. At the `Select object to measure:` prompt, choose ② in Figure 12-13. At the `<Segment length>/Block:` prompt, type **120** ↵ (10 feet). AutoCAD places two points along the line.

6. Do not save your drawing. Keep it open if you are continuing on to the next exercise.

AutoCAD's Calculator

AutoCAD's calculator is a geometric calculator that can not only calculate numbers like an ordinary calculator but also can calculate points and vectors. The calculator supports all the object snaps and has its own functions so that it is actually a simple programming language. In fact, you can even use AutoLISP variables in your expressions. Here I show you the basics of the calculator.

To start the calculator, type **cal** ↵ on the command line. If you are in the middle of a command, type **'cal** ↵.

Calculating numbers

Calculating numbers is quite straightforward and uses standard rules of precedence. The following illustrates this point:

```
Command: cal
> Expression: 3*(2+3)/5-1
2.0
```

Because the 2+3 sum is in parentheses, it is calculated first so that the expression multiplies 3 by 5 (which is 15), divides it by 5 (which is 3) and subtracts 1 (which is 2).

Using CAL in this way is just like having a hand-held calculator by your computer.

When you use CAL transparently, AutoCAD assumes you want the result to be a response to a prompt. Let's say you want to draw a horizontal line. You know it has to be the total of two other lines whose length you know. Follow the prompts:

```
Turn on ORTHO.
Start the LINE command.
From point: Pick the start point for the line.
Move the cursor to the right to draw at a zero-degree angle and so you
can use Direct Distance Entry.
To point:  cal ↵
> Expression: 3.953+6.8725 ↵
```

AutoCAD draws a line whose length is the sum of the two numbers.

You can add feet and inches as well. Use the format 6'5" or 6'-5". Don't put any spaces between the feet and inches. With the calculator, all inches must be marked with a double-prime ("), unlike regular AutoCAD command line usage. (See the sidebar "The ins and outs of feet and inches in CAL.")

Using coordinates

You can use coordinates in CAL expressions. Coordinates are enclosed in square brackets. Let's say you want to draw a line that is equal to the length of two other objects in your drawing that you happen to know are 3.953 and 6.8725 units long. You want the line to be at a 20-degree angle. At the To point: prompt, start CAL transparently.

```
> Expression: [@(3.953+6.8725)<20]
```

This uses a relative polar coordinate whose length is the sum of two numbers.

The ins and outs of feet and inches in CAL

Using fractional inches in CAL expressions is tricky. If you type 3'2-1/2" as a CAL expression, AutoCAD replies `Error: Invalid feet-inches format`. AutoCAD expects a hyphen only between feet and inches. Otherwise, it assumes a hyphen is a minus sign. To write out fractional inches, think of them as little division problems being added to the whole inches. Therefore, if you type the following expression, AutoCAD takes 3'2" and adds 1" divided by 2" to get 3'2-1/2". Similarly, in the second expression, AutoCAD adds 23" to 3" divided by 8" to get 23-3/8". Yes, it's slightly awkward.

```
(3 2 +1 /2 )+(23 +3 /8 )
61.875
```

If 3'-2" returns 38.0 as shown below (3' = 36" and 2 more inches is 38"), how do you subtract 2" from 3'?

```
> Expression: 3 -2
38.0
```

The answer is to put parentheses around the three feet so that AutoCAD doesn't assume the next expression is part of the same feet-inches expression, as shown below.

```
> Expression: (3 )-2
34.0
```

Here AutoCAD takes the three feet (36") and subtracts 2" to get 34.

Using object snaps

You can use the object snaps as part of CAL expressions. When you press Enter after completing the expression, AutoCAD prompts you for the objects for each object snap in the expression, one after another.

One of the most common uses for object snaps is to find the midpoint between two points. In Figure 12-14, you want to draw a line starting from the midpoint between the centers of two circles.

To accomplish this, start the LINE command and start CAL transparently at the `From point:` prompt. Then follow the prompts:

```
> Expression: (cen+cen)/2 ↵
> Select entity for CEN snap: Select the first circle.
> Select entity for CEN snap: Select the second circle.
```

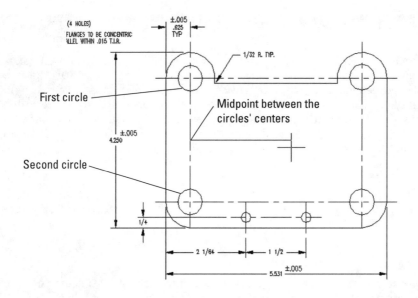

Figure 12-14: Drawing a line from the midpoint between the centers of the two circles.

In this expression, AutoCAD actually calculates the average between the coordinates of the centers of the two circles. If you subtract coordinates, as in the following expression, CAL gives you the change in X and Y, not the length between the two coordinates. In the following expression, two endpoints on a line were chosen:

```
> Expression: end-end
> Select entity for END snap:
> Select entity for END snap:
(-57.3212 -20.8632 0.0)
```

Compare this to using the DIST command as shown next. As you can see, the Delta X and Delta Y numbers match the CAL results:

```
Command:  _dist First point: Second point:
Distance = 61.0000, Angle in XY Plane = 20, Angle from XY
Plane = 0
Delta X = 57.3212, Delta Y = 20.8632, Delta Z = 0.0000
```

To calculate the length of the line, use the *abs* function from the list of mathematical functions in Table 12-1. The following expression shows how this works:

```
> Expression: abs(end-end)
> Select entity for END snap:
> Select entity for END snap:
61.0
```

You can easily use CAL as a substitute for the From object snap. For example, at the From point: prompt you can enter CAL and type **mid+[3,-2.5]** ↵. AutoCAD prompts you for the object for which you want the midpoint and starts the line (3,-2.5) units from there.

Using mathematical functions

CAL supports many mathematical functions typical of a scientific calculator. Table 12-1 lists these functions.

Table 12-1 CAL Mathematical Functions	
Function	**What It Does**
sin(angle)	Calculates the sine of the angle
cos(angle)	Calculates the cosine of the angle
tang(angle)	Calculates the tangent of the angle
asin(real)	Calculates the arc sine of the real number
acos(real)	Calculates the arc cosine of the real number
atan(real)	Calculates the arc tangent of the real number
ln(real)	Calculates the natural log of the real number
exp(real)	Calculates the natural exponent of the real number
exp10(real)	Calculates the base 10 exponent of the real number
sqr(real)	Calculates the square of the real number
sqrt(real)	Calculates the square root of the real number
abs(real)	Calculates the absolute value of the real number (the number not including its + or − sign), also used to calculate lengths
round(real)	Rounds the number to its nearest integer
trunc(real)	Truncates any decimal value leaving only the integer
r2d(angle)	Converts radian angles to degrees
d2r(angle)	Converts degree angles to radians
pi	Returns the constant pi

Note

A real number is any positive or negative number. Type large numbers without commas. AutoCAD restricts you to numbers between −32768 and +32767.

Using CAL's special functions

CAL has a set of special functions that you can use to find points. Table 12-2 lists most of these functions and what they do. You can find a complete list in the AutoCAD Command Reference.

Function	What It Does
Table 12-2 **Special CAL Functions**	
Function	*What It Does*
rad	Gets the radius of the selected object
cur	Gets any point that you pick
@	Gets the last point calculated
vec(p1,p2)	Calculates the vector from point p1 to point p2
vec1(p1,p2)	Calculates a one-unit vector from point p1 to point p2
pld(p1,p2,dist)	Calculates a point on the line from point p1 to point p2 that is *dist* units from point p1. If *dist* is .327, calculates the point .327 units from p1.
plt(p1,p2,t)	Calculates a point on the line from point p1 to point p2 that is *t* proportion from point p1. If *t* is .45, calculates the point .45 of the distance from p1 to p2 (or almost halfway between them).
dist(p1,p2)	Calculates the distance between point p1 and point p2
dpl(p,p1,p2)	Calculates the distance from point p to the line from point p1 to point p2
ang(p1,p2)	Calculates the angle between the X axis and the line from point p1 to point p2
ang(v)	Calculates the angle between the X axis and a vector you define. An example of a vector would be (end-end) where you pick the two endpoints of a line.
ang(apex,p1,p2)	Calculates the angle between the lines from apex to point p1 and apex to point p2. (The apex is the vertex of the angle.)
ill(p1,p2,p3,p4)	Calculates the intersection of two lines from p1 to p2 and from p3 to p4

Note

A vector is a direction. It is expressed as delta x, delta y.

Remember that these points can be specified in many ways, most commonly by object snaps. The *cur* function can be used to pick any point on the screen.

Step-by-Step: Using CAL

1. Open *ab12-a.dwg* from the CD-ROM if you do not have it open from the previous exercise.

2. Save the drawing as *ab12-1.dwg* in your *AutoCAD Bible* folder.

3. If you did not do the last exercise, use ZOOM Window to zoom in to the parcels labeled D and E, as shown in Figure 12-15.

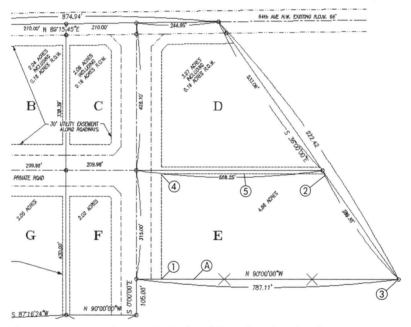

Figure 12-15: Parcels D and E in the civil engineering drawing.

4. In the Step-by-Step exercise on calculating area earlier in this chapter, you calculated a total area of 306975.04, in units of inches. To calculate what that is in square feet, type **cal** ↵. At the Expression: prompt, type **306975.04/144** ↵. AutoCAD calculates 2131.77.

5. In the Step-by-Step exercise on the DIVIDE command earlier in this chapter, you divided a line into three segments by placing two points on the line. You can use CAL to calculate the length of those segments. Type **cal** ↵. At the Expression: prompt, type **abs(end-end)/3** ↵. AutoCAD prompts you for the two endpoint snaps. Pick the two ends of the line at Ⓐ in Figure 12-15. AutoCAD calculates 262.37.

6. Suppose you want to draw a line *starting* from the intersection of two intersecting lines going from corner to diagonally opposite corner and *ending* perpendicular to the top line of the land parcel. Start the LINE command. At the From point: prompt, type **'cal** ↵. At the Expression: prompt, type **ill(end,end,end,end)** ↵. AutoCAD prompts you for four endpoints. Pick near ① and ② (in Figure 12-15) to define the first line, then near ③ and ④ to define the second line. AutoCAD starts the line at the intersection of the two lines. At the To point: prompt, choose the Perpendicular object snap and pick ⑤. Figure 12-16 shows the result.

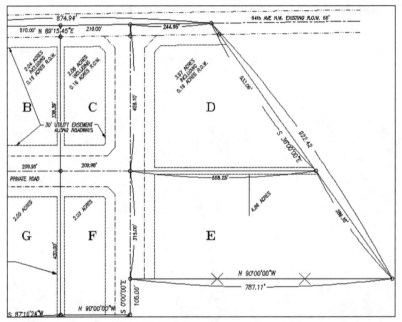

Figure 12-16: Using CAL, you can calculate the intersection of two lines without drawing the lines.

7. Save your drawing.

Summary

AutoCAD stores a great deal of information in each drawing. You can get a general status listing, list system variable settings, and track drawing time.

You can get information about individual objects using the LIST, DIST, and ID commands. You can also calculate area and perimeters. The Modify Object dialog box displays all of an object's properties.

You can divide and measure objects by placing point objects along them. AutoCAD's calculator lets you use calculated results as part of your command input.

✦   ✦   ✦

Creating Text

Annotating a Drawing

All drawings include some text that labels or explains the objects in the drawing. Such text is called *annotation*. AutoCAD has systematically improved the capabilities of its text objects so that you can now easily format and edit text to provide a professional appearance to your drawing. There is a wide array of font, alignment, and spacing options available. You can also import text from a word processor. This chapter tells you all you need to know about creating text in AutoCAD.

Creating Single-Line Text

Creating a single line of text using the defaults for font, height, and so on, is very simple. Choose Draw⇨Text⇨Single Line Text. This starts the DTEXT command. DTEXT stands for dynamic text because you can see the text on the screen as you type it. (There is also a TEXT command covered later in this chapter.) Follow the prompts:

```
Justify/Style/<Start point>: Pick a start point
for the text.
Height <0.2000>: Type a height, or press Enter to
accept the default.
Rotation angle <0>: Type a rotation angle, or
press Enter to accept the default.
Text: Type one line of text. Press Enter when you
are finished.
Text: Press Enter to end the command.
```

Note You must actually press Enter to end the command. You cannot use the Return button of the mouse.

The Justify option is covered in the next section. The Style option is discussed later in this chapter.

Single lines of text are very common in drafting. DTEXT continues to prompt you for lines of text so that you can type line after line. Unfortunately, you cannot control the spacing between the lines.

On the CD-ROM Respace creates a command, RS, that adjusts the spacing between existing lines of text. You can use it to fit text into a schedule or other chart in your drawing. Look in *\Software\Chap13\Respace* on the CD-ROM. Another routine, Context, prompts you to pick an existing line of text and continues below it with the same style, layer, height, justification, and line spacing of the existing text's style. You can find it in *\Software\Chap13\Context*.

One advantage of DTEXT is that each line of text is a separate object, making it easy to move or copy individual lines of text.

AutoCAD remembers the location of the last line of text even if you have used other commands in the meantime. To continue text below the last line of text you created, press Enter at the Justify/Style/<Start point>: prompt.

Cross-Reference You can also create text connected to arrows that point to objects, using the LEADER command. The LEADER command is covered in Chapter 14.

Justifying single-line text

When you pick a start point for text, the relationship between the start point and the actual letters is determined by the justification. The start point is also called the *insertion point.* When you want to refer to text using object snaps, you use the Insert object snap. If you select text without first choosing a command, the grip appears at the insertion point.

By default, text is left justified. To change the text's justification, type **j** ↵ at the Justify/Style/<Start point>: prompt. AutoCAD responds with this bewildering prompt:

    Align/Fit/Center/Middle/Right/TL/TC/TR/ML/MC/MR/BL/BC/BR:

Align and Fit offer two ways to fit text into a specified space. Both respond with the same next two prompts:

    First text line point:
    Second text line point:

Specify the beginning and the end of the text line. Align then prompts you for the text and then squeezes or stretches the text to fit within the text line. The height of the text changes accordingly to maintain the proportions of the font.

Fit adds the Height: prompt. Type in the height you want and then type the text. Fit also squeezes or stretches the text to fit within the text line but maintains the text height you specified, distorting the font letters to fit the space. Figure 13-1 shows an example of normal, fitted, and aligned single-line text.

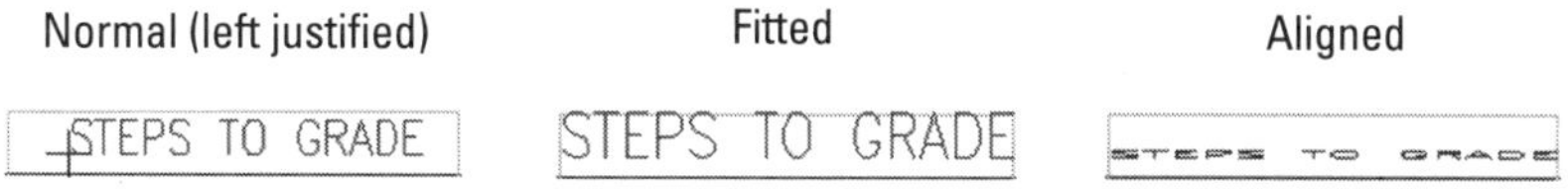

Normal (left justified)   Fitted   Aligned

Figure 13-1: Normal (left justified), fitted, and aligned text.

The other justification options specify the placement of the text's insertion point in relationship to the text line. They are shown in Table 13-1. Each insertion point is marked with a small ✕.

Table 13-1
Text Justification Options

Example	Option	Description
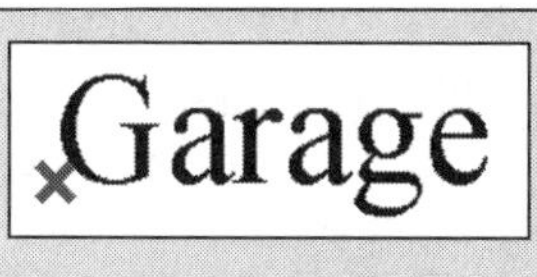 Garage	Left	Since this is the default justification, AutoCAD provides no suboption for left just-ification when you choose the Justify op-tion. The insertion point is on the baseline.
 Garage	Center	Text is centered around the insertion point. The insertion point is on the baseline.
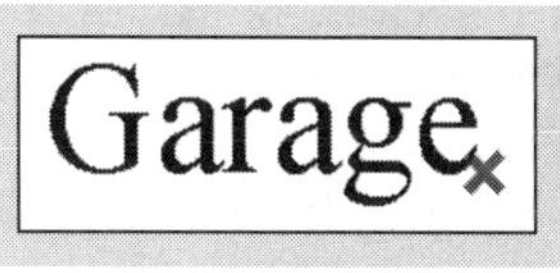 Garage	Right	Text is right justified from the insertion point. The insertion point is on the baseline.
 Garage	Middle	Text is centered both vertically and horizontally. Note that the vertical center point is measured from the baseline (not the bottom of the descending letters) to the top of the tallest letter.
 Garage	Top Left	Text is left justified and the insertion point is at the top of the highest possible letter. For some fonts the insertion point appears slightly above the highest letter; for others it appears exactly at the top.
 Garage	Top Center	Text is centered and the insertion point is at the top of the highest possible letter.

Example	Option	Description
Garage	Top Right	Text is right justified and the insertion point is at the top of the highest possible letter.
Garage	Middle Left	Text is left justified and centered vertically. Note that the vertical center point is measured from the baseline (not the bottom of the descending letters) to the top of the tallest letter.
Garage	Middle Center	Text is centered both horizontally and vertically. Note that the vertical center point is measured from the baseline (not the bottom of the descending letters) to the top of the tallest letter.
Garage	Middle Right	Text is right justified and centered vertically. Note that the vertical center point is measured from the baseline (not the bottom of the descending letters) to the top of the tallest letter.
Garage	Bottom Left	Text is left justified. The insertion point is below the lowest descending letter. For some fonts the insertion point appears slightly below the lowest letter; for others it appears exactly at the bottom.
Garage	Bottom Center	Text is centered. The insertion point is below the lowest descending letter.
Garage	Bottom Right	Text is right justified. The insertion point is below the lowest descending letter.

Tip

If you know the option abbreviation of the justification you want, you can use it at the `Justify/Style/<Start point>:` prompt.

If you choose a justification that centers or right justifies, the text does not appear with the proper justification until after you press Enter.

Setting the height

Setting the height of text is fairly straightforward. The default is .2 units but this is not suitable for all applications. The main point to consider is the scale factor. If you are drawing a house and plan to plot it at 1"=8' (1=96), you need to figure out how big to make the text so that when it is scaled down, you can still read it.

The formula is: specified height = final height × scale factor.

For example, if you want the text to be .2 units high and your scale factor is 96, your text needs to be 19.2 inches high (.2 × 96). On the other hand, if you are drawing a very small object such as a computer chip and your scale is .10, your text needs to be .02 inches high. The dimension text in Figure 13-2 is five inches high, but at a scale factor of 64, it plots at $5/64$ inches high.

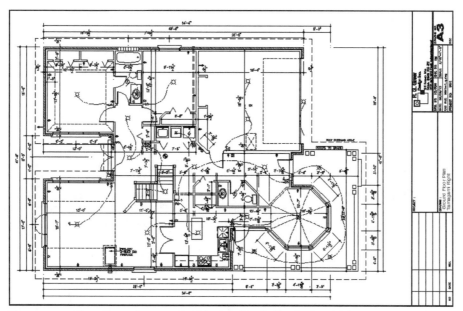

Figure 13-2: The dimension text in this drawing is five inches high.

AutoCAD calculates text height in units. Most word processors calculate text height in points. A point is $1/72$ of an inch. Therefore, 12-point text, a standard for most business letters, is about .17 inches high. The default of .2 units, if you are using inches as your unit, is just over 14 points, which is usually appropriate for annotating a drawing. (You don't usually hold a drawing as closely as you do a letter, so a larger point size is appropriate.)

Setting the rotation angle

The final prompt in DTEXT is the rotation angle. This angle applies to the entire line of text, not to individual characters. (You can specify slanted text—AutoCAD calls it obliqued text—using the STYLE command covered later in this chapter.) Figure 13-3 shows text rotated at 315 degrees.

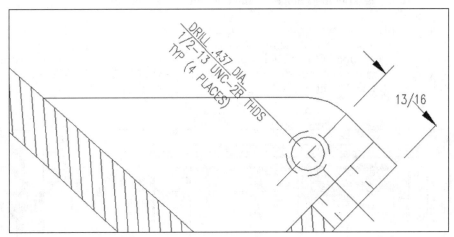

Figure 13-3: Text rotated at 315 degrees.

Adding special characters and formatting

The DTEXT command does not offer the same type of formatting options available for paragraph text (covered later in this chapter). Therefore, you have to use special codes to create special characters and formats. These codes are shown in Table 13-2.

These control codes work with standard AutoCAD text fonts only. They do not work with TrueType (supplied by Windows 95) or PostScript fonts.

Table 13-2	
Special Character Codes for AutoCAD Text Fonts	
Code	**Results**
%%o	Toggles overscore mode on/off
%%u	Toggles underscore mode on/off
%%d	Draws degree symbol (°)
%%p	Draws plus/minus tolerance symbol (±)
%%c	Draws circle diameter dimensioning symbol (Ø)

Figure 13-4 shows text using some of these codes, along with the entries that created them.

35.3 not 35.8   %%u35.3%%u not 35.8

Ø1.5   %%c1.5

±.002   %%p.002

Figure 13-4: Using special characters and formatting with AutoCAD text fonts.

Step-by-Step: Creating Text with DTEXT

1. Open *ab13-a.dwg* from your CD-ROM.

2. Save it as *ab13-1.dwg* in your *AutoCAD Bible* folder. This is a master bathroom plan drawing, as shown in Figure 13-5. Running object snaps are set for Endpoint, Midpoint, and Intersection.

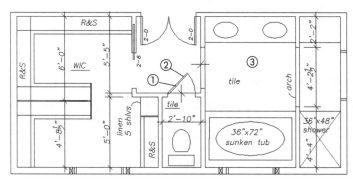

Figure 13-5: The master bathroom.

3. Choose Draw➪Text➪Single Line Text. Follow the prompts:

```
Justify/Style/<Start point>: j ↵
Align/Fit/Center/Middle/Right/TL/TC/TR/ML/MC/MR/BL/BC/BR: bc
↵ Bottom/center point: Use the Midpoint running object snap to pick
① in Figure 13-5.
Rotation angle <0>: Pick the endpoint at ②.
Text: 2-0 ↵
Text: ↵
```

4. Press Enter to start the DTEXT command again. Follow the prompts:

```
Justify/Style/<Start point>: j ↵
Align/Fit/Center/Middle/Right/TL/TC/TR/ML/MC/MR/BL/BC/BR: m ↵
Middle point: Pick ③. (This point doesn't have to be exact.)
Rotation angle <45>: 0 ↵
Text: %%UMASTER BATH ↵
Text: ↵
```

5. Save your drawing. It should look like Figure 13-6.

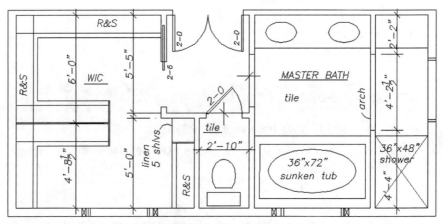

Figure 13-6: The master bathroom with added single-line text.

Using the TEXT command

The TEXT command is mainly used for customizing script files and menus (see Chapters 30 and 33). When you start customizing AutoCAD, you may find it helpful to be familiar with the prompts for this command.

TEXT is different from DTEXT in two ways:

✦ You do not see the characters on your screen until you finish the line of text and press Enter.

✦ TEXT does not prompt you for additional lines of text. To create a second line of text, you need to restart the command.

As with DTEXT, AutoCAD remembers the start point of the last line of text so you can continue to place text in a column.

Editing single-line text

As with any drawing object, the need often arises to edit your text. There are two ways to edit single-line text.

One way is to use the DDEDIT command. Choose Modify⇨Object⇨Text. At the `<Select an annotation object>/Undo:` prompt, select any text. Remember that each line of text created with DTEXT or TEXT is a separate object. AutoCAD opens the Edit Text dialog box with your text highlighted in an edit box, as shown in Figure 13-7. You can start typing to completely replace the text or click where you want to change part of the text and use standard Windows techniques to edit the text. Click OK to make the changes and return to your drawing.

Figure 13-7: The Edit Text dialog box.

The advantage of this method is that DDEDIT continues to prompt you for additional annotation objects to edit, making it very efficient for editing several lines of text at once.

 You can also change text using the Properties button on the Object Properties toolbar. Select any text object and click Properties to open the Modify Text dialog box, as shown in Figure 13-8. Here you can edit not only the text content but also every other conceivable property, including layer, linetype, color, insertion point, justification, rotation angle, and several other properties that I cover in the next section on text styles. Unfortunately, you can edit the contents of only one text object at a time this way.

The CD-ROM includes four routines for editing text:

On the CD-ROM

✦ **Mddedit** lets you select all the text objects in advance, then sequentially edit them. You can use it for both single-line and multiline text. Look in *\Software\ Chap13\Mddedit.*

✦ **Scltext** scales multiple text objects, each from its own insertion point. You can find it in *\Software\Chap13\Scltext.*

✦ **Textmod** edits multiple text objects at once. You can make global changes to the text height, style, rotation angle, obliquing angle, text width, and content. You can even mirror the text. To leave a property unchanged, press Enter at the prompt. You can find Textmod in *\Software\Chap13\Textmod.*

✦ **Ddchtext** changes layer, color, height, width, mtext frame width, rotation angle, obliquing angle, justification, and text style. Using a dialog box, you can change any number of text objects at once. It works on single and multi-line text as well as attributes. Look in *\Software\Chap13\Ddchtext.*

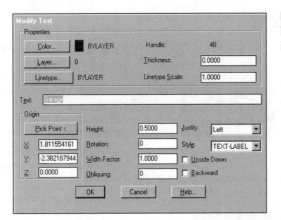

Figure 13-8: The Modify Text dialog box lets you edit all text properties, including text content, in one place.

Step-by-Step: Editing Text

On the CD-ROM

1. Open *ab13-b.dwg* from your CD-ROM.

2. Save it as *ab13-2.dwg* in your *AutoCAD Bible* folder. This is an air and vacuum release valve, shown in Figure 13-9.

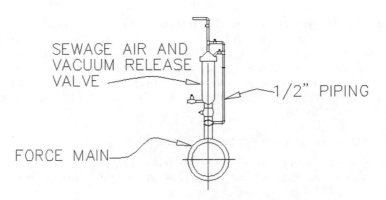

Figure 13-9: An air and vacuum release valve.

Credit: Thanks to the Army Corps of Engineers for this drawing.

3. Choose Modify⇨Object⇨Text. At the `<Select an annotation object>/Undo:` prompt, choose the text *1/2" PIPING.* The Edit Text dialog box opens. Highlight the text *1/2* and type **3/8**. Click OK. AutoCAD changes the text. Press Enter to end the command.

4. Choose Properties from the Object Properties toolbar. At the `Select objects:` prompt, select all the text in the drawing. AutoCAD opens the Change Properties dialog box. Choose Layer. In the Select Layer dialog box, choose TEXT and click OK. Click OK again to return to your drawing. All text is now on the TEXT layer.

5. Save your drawing.

Understanding Text Styles

You certainly do not always want to use AutoCAD's default font. AutoCAD allows you to create text styles that give you full creative control over the font, font style (bold, italic, or both), character width, obliquing angle, and text height. You can even design backward, upside-down, and vertical text. (Vertical text is like the text you occasionally see on the spine of a book. It goes down instead of to the right.)

Text styles are similar to layers, which you learned in Chapter 11. Like a layer, each text style:

   ✦ Has a name and several properties

   ✦ Is saved with the drawing

   ✦ Can be made current when you want to use it

   ✦ Can be renamed and deleted

Creating text styles is part of the typical drawing setup procedure. You should include text styles in your drawing templates.

Release 14 has improved support for TrueType fonts—the fonts used by most Windows applications—including bold, italic, and underscored text.

Creating a new text style

To create a new text style, choose Format⇨Text Style. This starts the STYLE command and opens the Text Style dialog box, shown in Figure 13-10.

When you choose the Format menu, you may notice that AutoCAD also offers dimension styles (see Chapter 15), point styles (see Chapter 7), and multiline styles (see Chapter 16).

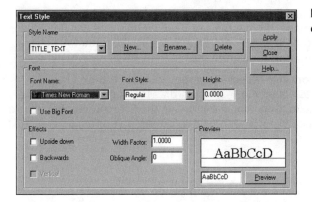

Figure 13-10: The Text Style dialog box.

Choose New to open the New Text Style dialog box, shown in Figure 13-11. Type the name of your new text style and click OK. Text style names follow the same rules as those for layers — a maximum of 31 characters and no spaces allowed. AutoCAD returns you to the Text Style dialog box where you define the new text style.

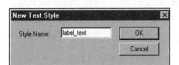

Figure 13-11: The New Text Style dialog box.

In the Font section of the Text Style dialog box, you specify the font, font style, and text height.

Font

Click the Font Name drop-down list arrow to see the list of fonts. Fonts with the double-T icon are TrueType fonts. The other fonts are AutoCAD's own fonts. AutoCAD fonts are defined in a shape file that has the filename extension *.shp* and are compiled into a file with the extension *.shx* for faster access.

Cross-Reference

You can create your own fonts. See Chapter 31.

Click a font to choose it. You can see a preview of the font in the Preview section of the dialog box. The Preview section also has an edit box. Type some characters and click Preview to see the preview of those characters.

Tip

AutoCAD includes a drawing named *truetype.dwg* in the sample folder. This drawing displays the alphabet for each TrueType font included with AutoCAD.

Archfont is a set of architectural fonts that look hand-drawn. You can find them in
\Software\Chap13\Archfont.

Font style

If the font you have chosen supports different styles, such as bold or italic, you can
choose one of them in the Font Style drop-down box. None of the AutoCAD fonts
supports font styles, but many of the TrueType fonts do.

Height

Type in the height you want for your font. Remember to take into account the scale
factor if necessary.

You can leave the height at zero if you want to be able to vary the text height within
that one style. If the height is zero, AutoCAD prompts you for a height whenever you
use DTEXT or TEXT.

If the text style being used has a specified height, AutoCAD does not display the
Height: prompt when you use DTEXT or TEXT.

In the Effects section, you specify the orientation, width, and oblique angle of the text
style.

Width factor

The default width of characters is set to 1. You can specify a smaller number to
compress text and a larger number to expand it, as shown in Figure 13-12.

Width = 1.5   Bearing   Housing
Width = .8   Bearing Housing

Figure 13-12: Text using different width factors.

Oblique angle

The oblique angle refers to the angle of the individual letters. It is generally used to
create an effect like italic text. Of course, it is not necessary if you are using a
TrueType font that supports italic text.

The angle used to define oblique text is different from the angle used for other objects.
Up and down text—that is, normal text—is a zero oblique angle. A positive angle
slants the text to the right—typical for italic text. A negative angle slants the text to
the left. Figure 13-13 shows text with a positive and negative oblique angle.

Oblique angle = –10   Bearing Housing

Oblique angle = 10   *Bearing Housing*

Figure 13-13: Text using differing oblique angles.

Text orientation

You can create text that is backward (like a mirror image) or upside down. Some fonts allow you to create vertical text. Figure 13-14 shows an example of each kind of text.

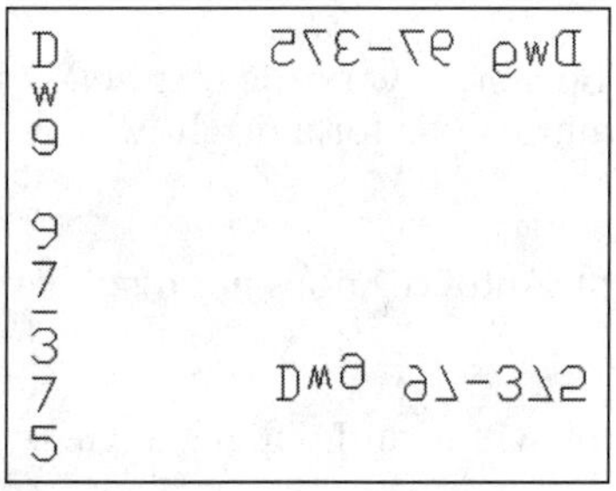

Figure 13-14: Vertical, backward, and upside-down vertical text.

Renaming and deleting text styles

You can rename and delete text styles easily. To rename a text style, start the STYLE command to open the Text Style dialog box. Choose Rename to open the Rename Text Style dialog box, shown in Figure 13-15. It works just like the New Text Style dialog box.

Figure 13-15: The Rename Text Style dialog box.

To delete a text style, choose it from the Style Name drop-down list of the Text Style dialog box and click Delete. AutoCAD asks you to confirm. Click Yes to delete the text style. You cannot delete a text style that is being used.

Step-by-Step: Creating Text Styles

1. Open *ab13-b.dwg* from your CD-ROM.

2. Save it as *ab13-3.dwg* in your *AutoCAD Bible* folder.

3. Choose Format⇨Text Style to open the Text Style dialog box. Click New. In the New Text Style dialog box, type **Notes** and click OK. From the Font Name drop-down list, choose *romans.shx*. In the Height text box, change the height to **1/16"**. In the Width Factor text box, change the width factor to **.95**. In the Oblique Angle text box, type **10**. Click Apply to make the new style current. Click Close.

4. Start the DTEXT command. At the Justify/Style/<Start point>: prompt, pick a start point at the lower left corner of the drawing. At the Rotation angle <0>: prompt, press Enter. At the Text: prompt, type **Note: Not drawn to scale.** ↵ Press Enter again to end the command.

5. Save your drawing. It should look like Figure 13-16. If you are going on to the next exercise, keep this drawing open.

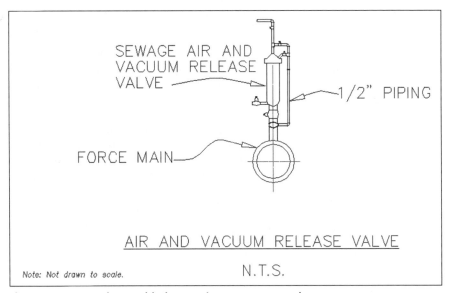

Figure 13-16: You have added text using a new text style.

Changing a text style

To change a style, choose Format⇨Text Style. From the Style Name drop-down list, choose the text style you want to change. Make changes in the same way you did when creating the style. Choose Apply, then Close. AutoCAD regenerates the drawing and changes all text that uses the style you changed. This is a powerful way to control the look of text in your drawing.

Note

Unfortunately, only changes to the font and orientation (upside down, backward, or vertical) change current text. Other changes, such as width factor, oblique angle, and height, are ignored. However, new text takes on these other changes.

Tip

To change a text's width factor, oblique angle, and height to conform to new text style properties, choose Properties from the Object Properties toolbar and select the text (only one text object at a time). In the Modify Text dialog box, re-choose the current text style in the Style drop-down list and click OK. AutoCAD updates the text.

To change existing text to another text style, choose Properties from the Object Properties toolbar and select the text. AutoCAD opens the Modify Text dialog box where you can choose a new text style in the Text Style drop-down list.

Making a style current

You choose the current style when you use one of the text commands. If you use DTEXT or TEXT, AutoCAD displays the Justify/Style/<Start point>: prompt. Type **s** ↵ for the Style name (or ?) <LABEL-TEXT>: prompt. (AutoCAD displays the current style in the angled brackets.)

If you know the name of the style you want to use, type it and press Enter. AutoCAD repeats the Justify/Style/<Start point>: prompt. You can choose the Justify option or pick a start point to continue the command.

If you don't know the name of the style you want to use, type **?** ↵. AutoCAD responds with the Text style(s) to list <*>: prompt. Type ***** ↵ and AutoCAD lists all the text styles with their properties and then repeats the Justify/Style/<Start point>: prompt. Here is a sample listing.

```
Text styles:
Style name: STANDARD        Font files: txt
    Height: 0.0000  Width factor: 1.0000  Obliquing angle: 0
    Generation: Normal
Style name: LABEL-TEXT        Font typeface: Arial
    Height: 0.5000  Width factor: 1.0000  Obliquing angle: 0
    Generation: Normal
Current text style: STYLE1
Justify/Style/<Start point>:
```

To change the current style, type **s** ↵ again and type in the style name from the list you just displayed. Then continue to use the Justify option or to pick a start point.

If you use MTEXT, the Multiline Editor opens, as explained in the next section. Choose the Properties tab and choose the text style you want from the Style drop-down list.

Step-by-Step: Changing Text Styles

On the
CD-ROM

1. If you have *ab13-3.dwg* open from the previous Step-by-Step exercise, continue to use it for this exercise. Otherwise, open *ab13-3.dwg* from the *Results* folder of your CD-ROM.

2. Save it as *ab13-4.dwg* in your *AutoCAD Bible* folder.

3. The note at the bottom left corner of the drawing uses the Notes text style. Choose Format⇨Text Style. In the Text Style dialog box, make sure NOTES is the Style Name listed, then choose *italic.shx* from the Style Name drop-down list. Choose Apply, then Close.

4. AutoCAD regenerates the drawing and changes the text's font.

5. Save your drawing.

Creating Multiline Text

Single-line text is awkward when you want to type quite a bit of text. The main disadvantage is that single-line text does not use word wrap, which wraps text to the next line to keep a neat right margin. Multiline text (also called paragraph text) solves this problem and also offers many more formatting options compared to single-line text. The entire paragraph of multiline text is one object.

Release
14

Release 14 offers a new editing box for creating multiline text. It more closely resembles Windows word processors—although the edit box is much smaller. You can use this box both to create and also to edit text and its properties. There is also new support for TrueType font families and character formatting, including bold, italic, and underscore character styles.

Using the Multiline Text Editor

A

To create paragraph text, choose Multiline Text from the Draw toolbar. This starts the MTEXT command. AutoCAD tells you the current style and text height. For example:

```
Current text style: ROMANS. Text height: 4 1/2
```

AutoCAD continues with the Specify first corner: prompt. Specify one corner of a bounding box to specify where to place the text. At the Specify opposite corner or [Height/Justify/Rotation/Style/Width]: prompt, specify the diagonally opposite corner of the bounding box. You can also choose one of the other options to specify the text properties before you type in the text. However, these options (explained later in this chapter) are also available in the Multiline

Text Editor, which opens once you have specified the bounding box. The Multiline Text Editor is shown in Figure 13-17.

Figure 13-17: The Character tab of the Multiline Text Editor.

Type your text in the large edit box. The Multiline Text Editor wraps the text to the next line when AutoCAD senses that the text has met the right side of the bounding box you specified. Although you have created a bounding box with four sides, AutoCAD only limits the text by the paragraph width, that is, the left and right margins. If you type too much text for the bounding box, AutoCAD expands the edit box, letting you increase the height of the bounding box.

The Character tab

Use the Character tab of the dialog box to format the characters of your text. The toolbar contains the following selections:

- ✦ **Font:** Choose any font from the Font drop down box.

- ✦ **Height:** Type a new height or choose one from the drop-down list.

- ✦ **Bold:** If Bold is supported for the font, select text and click Bold.

- ✦ **Italic:** If Italic is supported for the font, select text and click Italic.

- ✦ **Underline:** Select text and click Underline.

- ✦ **Undo:** Undoes the last editing option.

- ✦ **Stack/Unstack:** Toggles stacking and unstacking fractions. Figure 13-18 shows both stacked and unstacked fractions. Select the fraction and click Stack/Unstack.

- ✦ **Text Color:** Choose ByLayer or any color from the Font drop-down box.

- ✦ **Symbol:** Inserts the degree, plus/minus, or diameter symbol. Or choose Other to open the Windows Character Map to choose any of the available symbols.

In addition to the toolbar, you can click Import Text to open the Open dialog box (shown in Figure 13-19), which lets you choose a text (*.txt*) or Rich Text Format (*.rtf*) file to import. Find the file, choose it, and click OK. AutoCAD inserts it into the Multiline Text Editor. Other techniques for importing text are covered later in this chapter.

Note

Rich Text Format preserves formatting from application to application. Text-only documents retain no formatting.

$\frac{3}{8}$

3/8

Figure 13-18: Stacked and unstacked fractions.

Figure 13-19: Use the Open dialog box to choose a file to import into your drawing.

The Properties tab

Use the Properties tab to specify text style, justification, paragraph width, and rotation. These settings apply to the paragraph as a whole. The text you typed in the edit box remains visible, and you see the results of your formatting choices immediately. Text style, justification, and rotation have already been described. The width refers to the width of the paragraph, not the characters. A width of zero turns off word wrap, and you get a single line of text.

The Find/Replace tab

Release 14

Use the Find/Replace tab to find or replace specified text. This is similar to the Find and Replace commands available in word processors. If you want the search to match the case of the specified text, choose Match Case. If you want the search restricted to whole words that match the specified text, choose Whole Words. For example, if your specified text is *and,* choose the Whole Word check box to avoid finding *sand* and *random*.

Importing text

As mentioned earlier, you can import text from the Characters tab of the Multiline Text Editor. There are two other ways to import text:

✦ You can use drag-and-drop to insert text into a drawing. Open Windows Explorer and locate the file. It should be a text (*.txt*) or Rich Text Format (*.rtf*) file. Position the Explorer window so you can see the filename and your AutoCAD drawing at the same time. Click the file and drag it to your drawing. Close Windows Explorer and move the text to the desired location.

✦ You can copy text from another file to the Windows Clipboard. Open the other file, select the text, and choose Copy from the Standard toolbar. Return to your drawing by clicking the AutoCAD button on the Windows Taskbar. Choose Paste from the Standard toolbar. If you are in the Multiline Text Editor, you can paste the text directly into the editor. Right-click in the editor and choose Paste (or use Ctrl+V).

When importing Rich Text Format documents, the Editor is limited to files of no more than 16K in size.

Editing paragraph text

To edit paragraph text, choose Modify⇨Object⇨Text to start the DDEDIT command. AutoCAD responds with the `<Select an annotation object>/Undo:` prompt. You cannot select the text first. Select any multiline text to open the Multiline Text Editor.

If you choose single-line text created with TEXT or DTEXT, AutoCAD opens the Edit Text dialog box (refer to Figure 13-7).

Make your changes in the edit box. The techniques are similar to those in any word processor.

✦ Select text and press Del to delete the text.

✦ Click to move the insertion point to where you want to insert text and starting typing. (There is no overtype mode.)

✦ Use the Character and Properties menus to change character and paragraph formatting.

To change characters using the Character tab, you must first highlight the characters. This lets you make height or font changes to individual words or even letters. When changing paragraph properties from the Properties tab, you do not first highlight the characters because changes affect the entire paragraph. The following paragraph changes are immediately reflected in the Multiline Text Editor:

✦ Style

✦ Left, center, and right justification (but *not* top, middle, and bottom justification)

✦ Paragraph Width (if it affects word wrap)

You see the effect of top, middle, and bottom justification only when you click OK and return to your drawing. The same is true of rotation.

Right-click anywhere in the edit box to open a shortcut menu with Undo, Cut, Copy, Paste, and Select All options.

Click OK when you are done.

You can also choose Properties on the Object Properties toolbar to open the Modify Text dialog box. You can edit the text as well as its properties (layer, insertion point, and so on).

Step-by-Step: Creating Multiline Text

1. Open *ab13-c.dwg* from your CD-ROM.

2. Save it as *ab13-5.dwg* in your *AutoCAD Bible* folder. This is a plat drawing, as shown in Figure 13-20.

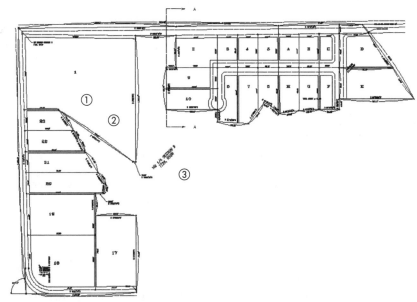

Figure 13-20: The plat drawing.

Credit: Thanks to Bill Maidment of Cantech, Inc., Fairfield, Iowa, for this drawing.

3. Choose Multiline Text from the Draw toolbar. At the prompts, pick points ① and ② in Figure 13-20. The Multiline Text Editor opens. In the Font Height box, change the text to **12.5**. In the main editing box, type the following:

   Containing 108.33 acres including 5.97 acres existing R.O.W. and 4.56 acres proposed R.O.W.

4. Highlight the text *108.33* and click Underline. Click the Properties tab. In the Justification drop-down list, choose Middle Left. Click OK. AutoCAD places the text.

On the
CD-ROM

5. Open Windows Explorer (Start➪Programs➪Windows Explorer). Find *ab13.txt* on your CD-ROM. Move the Windows Explorer window so that you can see both *ab13.txt* and ③ (see Figure 13-20) on your screen. Drag *ab13.txt* from the Windows Explorer window to point ③.

6. Choose Modify➪Object➪Text and choose the new text you imported to open the Multiline Text Editor. On the Properties tab, change the width to **500**.

7. Use ZOOM Window to zoom in on the new text. You can see how %%d became the degree symbol. This text was originally single-line text in an older AutoCAD drawing. You can see why you wouldn't want to retype it!

8. Choose Zoom Previous on the Standard toolbar to return to your original view. Save your drawing.

Managing Text

Text is a complex object type. Text greatly increases drawing size and adds redraw and regeneration time. The more complex fonts, such as the TrueType fonts, can have a huge impact on how long it takes to open and save a file. The three techniques described in this section help you to manage text and improve performance while editing your drawing. The last section introduces a way to control the mirroring of text objects.

Using Quicktext

The QTEXT command replaces all text with rectangles that approximate the placement of the original text, as shown in Figure 13-21. All text objects, including dimensions and attributes, are affected. To use QTEXT, type **qtext** ↵ on the command line. Type **on** ↵ to get the rectangles; Type **off** ↵ to return to regular text. Then type **regen** ↵ at the command line. Quicktext takes effect only after a regeneration.

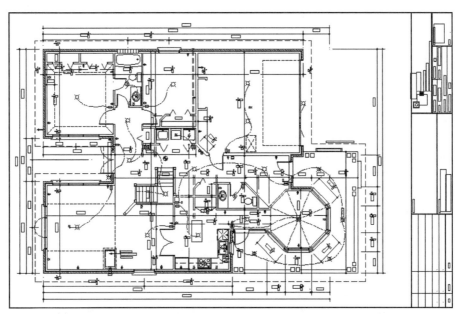

Figure 13-21: A drawing with QTEXT on. Rectangles have replaced all the text.

Credit: Thanks to Rod Greer of R. G. Greer Design Inc., Fergus, Ontario, Canada, for this drawing.

Using AutoCAD fonts

AutoCAD fonts are simpler than TrueType fonts, and some AutoCAD fonts are simpler than others. The simplest font is *txt.shx*, the font used by the default Standard text style. You can easily define a text style using an AutoCAD font and then change the font to something nicer just before plotting. AutoCAD immediately changes the font of all text using that style. Be aware that the text may take up more or less space than before.

When AutoCAD cannot find the specified font, it uses an alternate font. This may happen if you receive a drawing done by someone else that uses a custom or third-party font that you don't have. You can specify the alternate font by choosing Tools⇨Preferences and clicking the plus sign next to Text Editor, Dictionary, and Font File Names on the Files tab. Choose Alternate Font File to specify the alternate font, which is *simplex.shx* by default.

You can further control the fonts used by AutoCAD by customizing the Font Mapping File, which is *\support\acad.fmp* by default. The format is `current_font;font_to_substitute`. You need to use the actual filenames of the fonts. To substitute a simpler font for the Arial Black font, you could add the following line:

```
Ariblk.ttf;simplex.shx
```

To find the Windows TrueType fonts, look in the *Fonts* subfolder of your *Windows 95* folder.

Note

AutoCAD only reads the font mapping file when it opens a new drawing, so any changes you make are effective only once you start a new drawing.

Freezing text layers

Freezing text layers can help regeneration time dramatically—a good reason to give text its own layer. Don't forget to include dimension text, too. Dimensions are usually placed on a separate layer (see Chapter 14).

Using MIRRTEXT

When you mirror sections of your drawing that include text, by default the text is mirrored, resulting in backward text. Unless you are Alice going through the looking glass, you generally don't want this result. The MIRRTEXT system variable controls whether text is mirrored or retains its normal orientation.

To keep your mirrored text reading from left to right, type **MIRRTEXT** ↵. At the `New value for MIRRTEXT <1>:` prompt, type **0** ↵ to turn MIRRTEXT off. When you mirror text, it is copied but not turned backward.

Step-by-Step: Managing Text

On the CD-ROM

1. Open *ab13-d.dwg* from your CD-ROM.

2. Save it as *ab13-6.dwg* in your *AutoCAD Bible* folder. This is a small section of an electrical schematic, as shown in Figure 13-22. ORTHO and OSNAP are on, and running snaps are set for Endpoint, Midpoint, and Intersection.

3. Type **qtext** ↵. At the `ON/OFF <OFF>:` prompt, type **on** ↵. Type **regen** ↵. AutoCAD replaces the text with rectangles.

4. Type **qtext** ↵. At the `ON/OFF <OFF>:` prompt, type **off** ↵. Type **regen** ↵. AutoCAD redraws the original text.

5. Start the MIRROR command. Follow the prompts.

   ```
   Select objects: Start a crossing window by picking ① in Figure 13-22.
   Other corner: Pick ②. Press Enter to end object selection.
   First point of mirror line: Use the Midpoint running object snap to
   pick the midpoint at ③.
   Second point: Pick any point vertical to the first point.
   Delete old objects? <N> ↵
   AutoCAD mirrors the objects and the text. The text is
   backward.
   ```

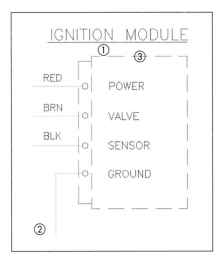

Figure 13-22: A section of an electrical schematic.

6. Choose Undo from the Standard toolbar.

7. Type **mirrtext** ↵. At the `New value for MIRRTEXT <1>:` prompt, type **0** ↵.

8. Repeat the mirror operation using the same instructions as in step 5. This time AutoCAD mirrors the objects, but the text reads properly, as shown in Figure 13-23.

9. Save your drawing.

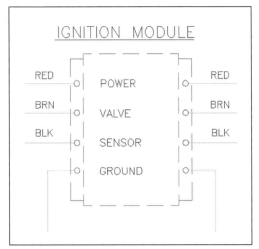

Figure 13-23: The text on the right was mirrored with MIRRTEXT set to 0.

Checking Your Spelling

Use the SPELL command to check your spelling. AutoCAD's spell checker acts just like the one in your word processor. Choose Tools⇨Spelling to open the Check Spelling dialog box, as shown in Figure 13-24.

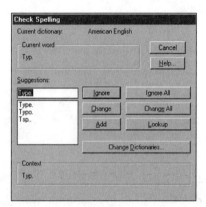

Figure 13-24: The Check Spelling dialog box.

AutoCAD prompts you to select objects. You can type **all** ↵ to spell check the entire drawing. You have the following options:

✦ **Ignore:** Choose Ignore to ignore the current instance of this word only.

✦ **Ignore All:** Choose Ignore All to ignore all instances of this word.

✦ **Change:** Select the suggested word you want and choose Change to change the current instance of the word to one of the suggested words.

✦ **Change All:** Select the suggested word you want and choose Change All to change all instances of the word to one of the suggested words.

✦ **Add:** Choose Add to add the word to the dictionary. The word will not appear again as misspelled.

✦ **Lookup:** Use this if you type a word in the Suggestion text box and want to check its spelling. Lists words similar to the word in the Suggestion text box.

AutoCAD automatically moves from word to word until you see the Spelling Check Complete message.

Customizing the spelling dictionary

You can change the main and custom spelling dictionaries. To change the spelling dictionaries, choose Change Dictionaries from the Check Spelling dialog box to open the Change Dictionaries dialog box, shown in Figure 13-25.

Figure 13-25: The Change Dictionaries dialog box.

Tip

Strangely enough, if you don't have any misspelled words in your drawing, you cannot open the Check Spelling dialog box. AutoCAD simply issues the `Spelling Check Complete` message. The trick is to insert a misspelled word and then use the SPELL command. You can erase or correct the word afterward.

The main dictionary is not customizable and comes with AutoCAD. You can choose from various languages depending on your version of AutoCAD. For example, my list lets me choose from American English, British English (ise), British English (ize), French with unaccented capitals, and French with accented capitals.

The custom spelling dictionary is the dictionary you add to when you click Add in the Check Spelling dialog box. It is a simple text file that includes words that you have added during spell checks, as well as a long list of AutoCAD-related words already included by AutoCAD. To see these words, scroll down the list in the Custom dictionary words section of the Change Dictionaries dialog box.

You can add words to the custom dictionary by typing them in the Custom dictionary words text box and clicking Add. This feature lets you add a number of words at one time.

Tip

Another way to edit the custom dictionary is to open the file directly with a text editor. The AutoCAD custom dictionary is in the AutoCAD folder's *support* subfolder and is called *sample.cus*.

Figure 13-26 shows *sample.cus* opened in Notepad, Windows 95's text editor. As you can see, AutoCAD has included every command, system variable, AutoLISP function, and so on. However, you might never use these words in a drawing.

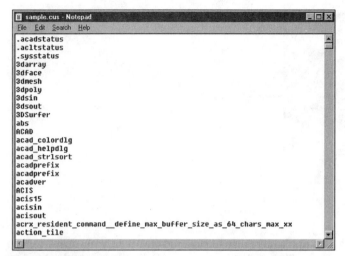

Figure 13-26: Opening *sample.cus* in Notepad so you can edit it directly.

You can use a different custom dictionary. It can be useful, for example, to use the same dictionary in AutoCAD as you use in your word processor. Follow the steps below to use the Microsoft Word dictionary:

1. Find Word's custom dictionary. If necessary, choose Start⇨Find and use Windows 95's Find dialog box to find the file. It has a filename extension of *.dic*. I found mine in the *d:\win95\msapps\proof,* but yours may be in a different location. It is called *custom.dic*. As with the AutoCAD custom dictionary, you can open it with Notepad and edit it directly.

2. Use Windows 95 Explorer to copy the file to the AutoCAD *support* folder. You can hold down Ctrl as you drag it from one folder to another or use the right mouse button to click the file, choose Copy, and then drag the copy to its new location.

3. Click *custom.dic* in the AutoCAD *support* folder to highlight it. Change its filename extension to *.cus.* (Windows 95 asks you if you are sure you want to do this. Click Yes.)

4. Open the Change Dictionaries dialog box. In the Custom dictionary text box, type in the name of the dictionary file, or choose Browse and find it.

5. Click OK to return to the Check Spelling dialog box, then Cancel to return to your drawing.

Summary

In this chapter you learned how to create, edit, and manage text. AutoCAD has three text creation commands, DTEXT, TEXT, and MTEXT. DTEXT and TEXT create single-line text. MTEXT creates paragraph text.

With text styles, you can organize text in much the same way that layers organize other objects. AutoCAD offers a wide range of formatting options for text. You can easily edit any text you have created. You can import text and Rich Text Format files into AutoCAD drawings. You can check your spelling. To make spell checks more accurate, you can edit and change custom dictionaries.

✦   ✦   ✦

Drawing Dimensions

Dimensioning a Drawing

Dimensions are an important part of most AutoCAD drawings. Dimensions indicate the measurement of the models you have created and are used in the manufacturing process. AutoCAD's dimensions offer a great deal of flexibility. In this chapter I cover the process of drawing dimensions. In the next chapter I explain how to customize the format of your dimensions using dimension styles.

Working with AutoCAD's Dimensions

Dimensioning is usually done once you have completed all or most of a drawing. Dimensioning a drawing all at once lets you create a unified, organized look for your dimensions. Before you can dimension, you need to understand the elements of a dimension and how to prepare for dimensioning.

Cross-Reference

In Chapter 17, I explain how to dimension a drawing in paper space.

The elements of a dimension

A dimension is a complex object, containing many parts. Understanding these parts and how they relate to the object you are dimensioning is an important first step. Figure 14-1 shows a typical linear dimension.

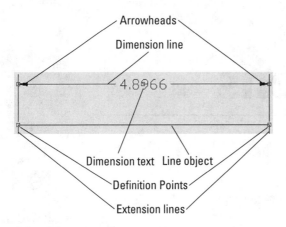

Figure 14-1: The parts of a dimension.

The parts of a dimension are:

✦ **Extension lines:** These extend from the dimensioned object to the dimension line and arrowheads. There is usually a small gap between the dimensioned object and the start of the extension lines. Extension lines visually clarify the extents of the object being dimensioned.

✦ **Dimension text:** This tells you the actual measurement of the dimensioned object. You can format this text in decimals, fractions, scientific units, and so on.

✦ **Dimension line:** This extends from the dimension text to the extension lines.

✦ **Arrowheads:** These mark the intersection of the dimension lines and the extension lines. They can take several forms, such as tick marks, open arrows, or dots.

✦ **Definition points:** These are invisible points that define the object being dimensioned. AutoCAD automatically creates a Defpoints layer when you create your first dimension in a drawing. This layer is not plotted. You can see them when you pick the dimension because grips appear at the definition points.

Dimensions have two interesting properties that you need to understand before you can successfully work with them.

✦ Dimensions are blocks. I have mentioned blocks before, and they are fully covered in Chapter 18. Blocks are groups of objects that you can manipulate as one object. As a result, if you pick a dimension, all parts of the dimension are selected.

✦ Dimensions are *associative*. This means that there is an association between the dimension and the object it dimensions. AutoCAD uses the definition points to make this association. If you change the size of the object, AutoCAD automatically adjusts the dimension.

All the parts of a dimension can be formatted individually. You generally format a dimension by creating a dimension style, which is a named set of formats for dimensions — just as a text style is a named set of formats for text. Dimension styles are the topic of the next chapter.

Preparing to dimension

Before starting to create dimensions, there are a few steps to take.

1. Create a layer for your dimensions. It is important that dimensions be easily distinguishable from the rest of your drawing. The color is usually a contrast to that of your models. For example, if your models are black (and you are working on a white screen), you might want your dimensions to be green, magenta, or cyan.

If you often turn layers on and off (or freeze and thaw them) you might want to create a separate dimension layer for each layer of drawing data. For example, if you dimension an Electrical layer that you turn off regularly, you can have a special Dim-elec dimension layer that you can turn off with the Electrical layer.

2. Create a text style for your dimensions.

Set the height of the text style to zero. You can then set the text height when you create the dimension style.

3. Choose Tools⇨Object Snap Settings and set the running object snaps you want. Endpoint and Intersection are a necessity. Add Center and Quadrant if you need to dimension arcs and circles. Double-click OSNAP on the status bar to turn it on.

4. Create a dimension style. Dimension styles are covered in the next chapter.

Save your dimension layer, dimension text style, dimension style, and running object snap settings in your drawing templates.

AutoCAD offers a Dimension toolbar that makes it easy to find the dimension commands quickly. New for Release 14 is a Dimension menu, which offers most of the same commands as the toolbar.

To display the Dimension toolbar, choose View⇨Toolbars and check Dimension from the Toolbars dialog box. Click Close to close the dialog box. The Dimension toolbar is shown in Figure 14-2.

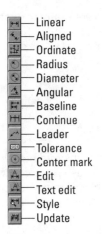

—Linear
—Aligned
—Ordinate
—Radius
—Diameter
—Angular
—Baseline
—Continue
—Leader
—Tolerance
—Center mark
—Edit
—Text edit
—Style
—Update

Figure 14-2: The Dimension toolbar.

Cross-Reference

You can dock the toolbar at the edges of the screen or leave it floating in the drawing area. You can also reshape it by pointing to its edge until you see a double arrow and dragging. See Chapter 3 for a discussion of managing toolbars.

Note

The dimensioning command names are generally long. For example, to draw a linear dimension, you would type **dimlinear** ↵. As briefly mentioned in Chapter 3, AutoCAD has shortcuts for many commands, including the dimensioning commands, contained in *acad.pgp*. Chapter 29 covers these shortcuts and how to create your own.

Drawing Linear Dimensions

Just as the most common objects are lines, the most common dimensions are linear dimensions.

Use linear dimensions for lines, a straight segment of a polyline, or a straight segment in a block. You can also draw a linear dimension for arcs and circles — you get the linear length of the arc (not its perimeter length) and the diameter of the circle.

Specifying the dimensioned object

To dimension a line, choose Linear Dimension from the Dimension toolbar. AutoCAD responds with the First extension line origin or RETURN to select: prompt. You can now either pick two extension line origin points or select an object for dimensioning.

Tip

Make it standard practice to use object snaps for choosing extension line origins. The point you pick specifies the definition point that determines the final measurement. Accurate dimensioning requires accurate drawings and then exact specification of the points you want to use for the dimensions.

If you are dimensioning more than one object, such as the distance from the endpoint of one line to the endpoint of another line, pick the first extension line origin. At the Second extension line origin: prompt, pick the second extension line origin. These two points define the length of the dimension.

If you are dimensioning one object, press Enter at the First extension line origin or RETURN to select: prompt. AutoCAD displays the Select object to dimension: prompt. Pick the object.

At the Dimension line location (Mtext/Text/Angle/Horizontal /Vertical/Rotated): prompt, pick a point for the location of the dimension line. As you move the mouse, you can see the results on your screen, as shown in Figure 14-3. If you want an exact location, you can type in a relative coordinate, such as **@0,.5** to specify that the dimension line should be .5 units above the object. Snap mode may also work well for you, depending on the drawing environment.

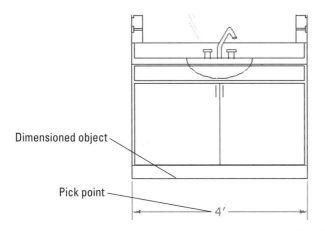

Figure 14-3: Picking a dimension line location for a linear dimension.

Release 14

Release 14's new Tracking feature makes it a snap to pick points for dimensioning. For example, if you are dimensioning a house, your first extension line origin may be the outside corner of the house, but the second extension line origin may be an inner wall. At the Second extension line origin: prompt, start Tracking and pick the inner wall endpoint as the first tracking point and the outer wall corner as the second tracking point. End tracking and AutoCAD places the dimension just where you need it.

Step-by-Step: Drawing Linear Dimensions

On the CD-ROM

1. Open *ab14-a.dwg* from your CD-ROM.

2. Save it as *ab14-1.dwg* in your *AutoCAD Bible* folder. This is the plan of a bedroom, as shown in Figure 14-4. ORTHO and OSNAP are on. Running object snaps are set for Endpoint, Midpoint, and Intersection. The current layer should be set to Dim.

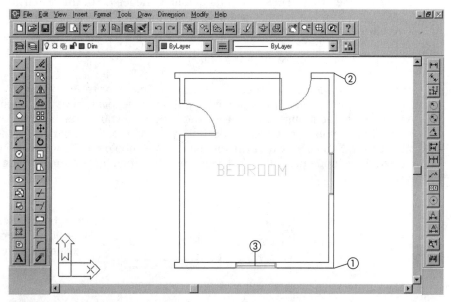

Figure 14-4: A bedroom plan.

3. To display the Dimension toolbar, choose View⇨Toolbars to open the Toolbars dialog box. Check Dimension and choose Close. If you wish, drag the toolbar over to the right side of your screen until it docks as shown in Figure 14-4.

4. Choose Linear Dimension from the Dimension toolbar. At the `First extension line origin or press ENTER to select:` prompt, pick ① in Figure 14-4. At the `Second extension line origin:` prompt, pick ②. At the `Dimension line location (Mtext/Text/Angle/Horizontal/Vertical/Rotated):` prompt, move the cursor to the right until you have sufficient space for the dimension text and click.

5. Press Enter to repeat the DIMLINEAR command. At the `First extension line origin or press ENTER to select:` prompt, press Enter. At the `Select object to dimension:` prompt, pick ③ (the window) in Figure 14-4. At the `Dimension line location (Mtext/Text/Angle/Horizontal/Vertical/Rotated):` prompt, move the cursor down until you have sufficient space for the dimension text and click.

6. Save your drawing. It should look like Figure 14-5.

Figure 14-5: The bedroom with two linear dimensions.

Using dimension options

You can also use one of the options offered at the command prompt to further control the final dimension.

Mtext

The Mtext option lets you replace the dimension text AutoCAD calculates or add a prefix or suffix to it. When you type **m** ↵ at the Dimension line location (Mtext/Text/Angle/Horizontal/Vertical/Rotated): prompt, AutoCAD opens the Multiline Text Editor, as shown in Figure 14-6.

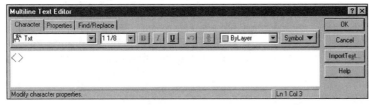

Figure 14-6: Changing the dimension text with the Multiline Text Editor.

The angle brackets represent the dimension text that AutoCAD automatically creates. The best use of the Mtext option is to add some text before or after the measurement, such as *TYP.* (for typical — used when one dimension applies to several objects) or *subject to final approval.* To add text before the measurement, place the cursor before the angle brackets. Similarly, to add text after the measurement, place the cursor after the angle brackets. Add the text and click OK.

If the measurement text itself does not appear the way you want it, you should change the annotation specifications in the dimension style. You can also specify a prefix or suffix (such as *mm*) for all dimensions, as explained in the next chapter.

Caution   You can delete the brackets and type your own dimension text, but you lose dimension associativity — the ability of the dimension to adjust to a change in its object.

Text

The Text option also lets you change dimension text but does not open the Multiline Text Editor. Instead, you can quickly retype the entire dimension text as you want it on the command line.

Angle

The angle of the text is specified in your dimension style. However, you can use this option to change the angle of the dimension text for a particular circumstance. Type **a** ↵ to get the `Enter text angle:` prompt. Type in an angle or pick two points to align the text with an existing object.

Horizontal/Vertical

Since Release 13, the DIMLINEAR command assumes you want a horizontal dimension if you select a horizontal object or two definition points running horizontally — ditto for a vertical dimension. Also, if you want to draw a vertical dimension of an object at an angle, you can specify this simply by moving the mouse cursor horizontally when specifying the dimension line location, as shown in Figure 14-7. If for some reason you need to force either a horizontal or vertical dimension, you can use the vertical or horizontal options.

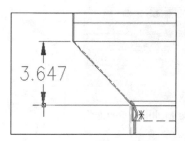

Figure 14-7: By simply dragging the mouse cursor to the left, you can create a vertical dimension for this angled line. The vertical dimension measures the change in the Y coordinates of the line, not the length of the line.

Rotated

Use a rotated linear dimension when the length you want to dimension is not parallel to the extension line origins. Just as the vertical dimension in Figure 14-7 does not measure the length of the line its extension lines extend to, a rotated linear dimension does not measure a specific object but the distance of an imaginary line parallel to the dimension line. Rotated dimensions are not very common, but when you need them they are the only way to get the dimension measurement you need.

To use a rotated dimension, start a linear dimension, pick the two extension line origins, and choose the Rotate option. At the `Dimension line angle <0>:` prompt, type the angle (or pick two points). AutoCAD draws the dimension.

Figure 14-8 shows a hexagonal stepping stone with a rotated linear angle. The extension lines of the dimension extend to a line at 104.5 degrees, but in this case you want to measure a length at an angle of 135 degrees. Note that AutoCAD has really dimensioned an imaginary line parallel to the dimension line, shown in the figure as a dashed line, rather than the side of the hexagon.

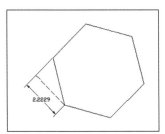

Figure 14-8: Drawing a rotated linear dimension for a hexagonal stepping stone.

Step-by-Step: Using Linear Dimension Options

On the
CD-ROM

1. Open *ab14-b.dwg* from your CD-ROM.

2. Save it as *ab14-2.dwg* in your *AutoCAD Bible* folder. This is a section of a plan of a house with an unusual-shaped ceiling, as shown in Figure 14-9. OSNAP is on, with running object snaps set to Endpoint and Intersection. If the Dimension toolbar doesn't appear, choose View➪Toolbars and check Dimension. Click Close.

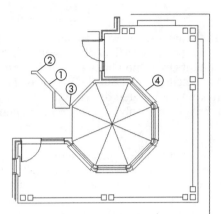

Figure 14-9: A house plan with an octagonal ceiling.

3. Choose Linear Dimension from the Dimension toolbar. Follow the prompts:

```
First extension line origin or press ENTER to select: ↵
Select object to dimension: Pick ① in Figure 14-9.
Dimension line location
(Mtext/Text/Angle/Horizontal/Vertical/Rotated): a ↵
Enter text angle:  Choose ② in Figure 14-9.
Second point: Choose ③ in Figure 14-9.
Dimension line location
(Mtext/Text/Angle/Horizontal/Vertical/Rotated): Position the
dimension line above the wall you dimensioned.
```

Note: You wouldn't actually dimension an architectural drawing in this style.

4. Repeat the DIMLINEAR command. Follow the prompts:

```
First extension line origin or press ENTER to select: ↵
Select object to dimension: Pick ④ in Figure 14-9.
Dimension line location
(Mtext/Text/Angle/Horizontal/Vertical/Rotated): m ↵
In the Multiline Text Editor move the cursor after the angled brackets and
type TYP. Choose OK.
Dimension line location
(Mtext/Text/Angle/Horizontal/Vertical/Rotated): Position the
dimension line above the window you dimensioned.
```

Notice that the text appears to the right of the dimension because it is now too long to fit between the extension lines.

5. Save your drawing. It should look like Figure 14-10.

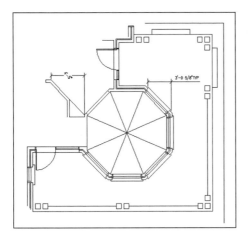

Figure 14-10: The dimensioned drawing.

Drawing Aligned Dimensions

When you want to dimension a linear object that is not orthogonal, use an aligned dimension. The dimension lines of an aligned dimension are always parallel to the object — unlike rotated dimensions. An aligned dimension measures the actual length of the object, not a vertical or horizontal distance that you dimension with a linear dimension. Therefore, your choice of linear, linear rotated, or aligned dimension depends on the distance you want to measure. Figure 14-11 shows several aligned dimensions.

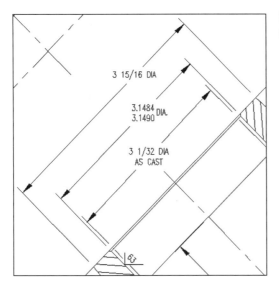

Figure 14-11: Three aligned dimensions.

Specifying the dimensioned object

 To create an aligned dimension, choose Aligned Dimension from the Dimension toolbar. This starts the DIMALIGNED command. AutoCAD responds with the First extension line origin or RETURN to select: prompt. You can now either pick two extension line origins or select an object.

If you are dimensioning more than one object, such as the distance from the endpoint of one line to the endpoint of another line, pick the first extension line origin. At the Second extension line origin: prompt, pick the second extension line origin. These two points define the length of the dimension.

If you are dimensioning one object, press Enter at the First extension line origin or RETURN to select: prompt. AutoCAD displays the Select object to dimension: prompt. Pick the object.

Because Figure 14-11 shows a cross-section view, there is no one object you can select. To create the aligned dimensions shown, you need to pick two extension line origins.

AutoCAD then displays the Dimension line location (Mtext/Text/Angle): prompt. Pick a point for the location of the dimension line. As you move the mouse, you can see the results on your screen. If you want an exact location, you can type in a relative coordinate, such as @2<45 to specify that the dimension line should be 2 units in a 45-degree direction from the extension line origins you specified.

Using the options

Once you have chosen what you want to dimension, you have three options — Mtext, Text, and Angle. These options were discussed in detail in the previous section.

Step-by-Step: Drawing Aligned Dimensions

On the CD-ROM

1. Open *ab14-b.dwg* from your CD-ROM.

2. Save it as *ab14-3.dwg* in your *AutoCAD Bible* folder. This is the same drawing used in the previous Step-by-Step exercise, as shown in Figure 14-12. OSNAP is on, with running object snaps set to Endpoint and Intersection. If the Dimension toolbar isn't visible, choose View⇨Toolbars and check Dimension. Click Close.

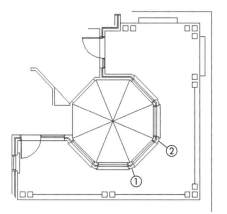

Figure 14-12: A section of a floor plan of a house.

3. Choose Aligned Dimension from the Dimension toolbar. Follow the prompts:

```
First extension line origin or press ENTER to select: Choose ① in
Figure 14-12.
Second extension line origin: Choose ② in Figure 14-12.
Dimension line location (Mtext/Text/Angle): m ↵
In the Multiline Text Editor, move the cursor to the right of the angled
brackets and type Typ. Click OK.
Dimension line location (Mtext/Text/Angle): Pick a location for the
dimension line.
```

4. Save your drawing. It should look like Figure 14-13.

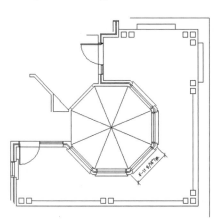

Figure 14-13: The house plan with an aligned dimension.

Creating Baseline and Continued Dimensions

Often, you want to create a whole series of attached, connected dimensions. AutoCAD offers two ways to accomplish this — baseline and continued dimensions.

✦ *Baseline dimensions* are a series of dimensions that all start from one point. The first extension line is the same for all the dimensions. The second dimension includes the first and an additional distance and so on.

✦ *Continued dimensions* are a series of dimensions that are all attached. The first extension line of the second dimension is the second extension line of the first and so on. Each dimension measures a different object or distance.

Figure 14-14 shows both baseline and continued linear dimensions. You can also create baseline and continued angular and ordinate dimensions.

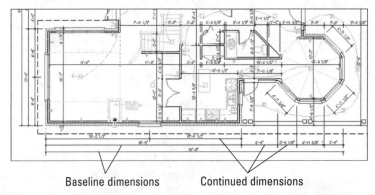

Baseline dimensions   Continued dimensions

Figure 14-14: A floor plan of a house using both baseline and continued dimensions.

Drawing baseline dimensions

To draw a baseline dimension, first create one linear, angular, or ordinate dimension in the regular way. (Angular and ordinate dimensions are covered later in this chapter.) Then choose Baseline Dimension from the Dimension toolbar. AutoCAD responds with the `Specify a second extension line origin or (<select>/Undo):` prompt.

If the previous dimension was a linear, angular, or ordinate dimension, AutoCAD uses its first extension line as the base for the new baseline dimension. Specify a new second extension line origin, and AutoCAD creates the baseline dimension with the same first extension origin as the original dimension and the new second extension origin you just specified.

If you don't want to work with the last dimension in the drawing, press Enter. AutoCAD responds with the Select base dimension: prompt. Be careful to pick the dimension closer to the side you want to use as the baseline. AutoCAD then prompts you to specify a second extension line origin. When you do so, AutoCAD creates the dimension.

AutoCAD continues to prompt you for second extension line origins so you can quickly create a chain of baseline dimensions. At each prompt you can type **u** ↵ to undo the last dimension. You can also press Enter at any time and select a different dimension to work from. Press Esc to end the command (or press Enter twice).

Drawing continued dimensions

Continued dimensions work similarly to baseline dimensions. To continue a dimension, first create one linear, angular, or ordinate dimension in the regular way. Then choose Continue Dimension from the Dimension toolbar. AutoCAD responds with the Specify a second extension line origin or (<select>/Undo): prompt.

If the previous dimension was a linear, angular, or ordinate dimension, AutoCAD uses its second extension line as the beginning of the new continued dimension. Specify a new second extension line origin, and AutoCAD creates the continued dimension.

If you don't want to continue from the last dimension in the drawing, press Enter. AutoCAD responds with the Select base dimension: prompt. Be careful to pick the dimension closer to the side you want to continue from. AutoCAD then prompts you to specify a second extension line origin. When you do so, AutoCAD creates the dimension.

AutoCAD continues to prompt you for second extension line origins so you can quickly create a chain of continued dimensions. At each prompt you can type **u** ↵ to undo the last dimension. You can also press Enter at any time and select a different dimension to work from. Press Esc to end the command (or press Enter twice).

Step-by-Step: Drawing Baseline and Continued Dimensions

1. Open *ab14-b.dwg* from your CD-ROM.

2. Save it as *ab14-4.dwg* in your *AutoCAD Bible* folder. This is the same drawing used in the last two exercises, as shown in Figure 14-15. OSNAP is on with running object snaps set to Endpoint and Intersection. If the Dimension toolbar isn't visible, choose View⇨Toolbars and check Dimension. Click Close.

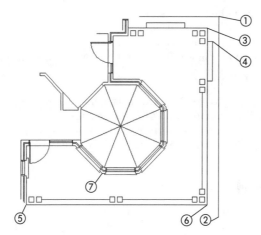

Figure 14-15: The house plan with the octagonal ceiling.

3. Turn on ORTHO.

4. Choose Linear Dimension from the Dimension toolbar. Follow the prompts:

```
First extension line origin or press ENTER to select: Use the
Endpoint object snap to pick ① in Figure 14-15.
Second extension line origin: Choose Tracking from the Standard
toolbar.
_tracking First tracking point: Choose the endpoint at ② in Figure
14-15.
Next point  (Press ENTER to end tracking): Choose the
intersection or endpoint at ③.
Next point (Press ENTER to end tracking): ↵
Dimension line location
(Mtext/Text/Angle/Horizontal/Vertical/Rotated): Pick a dimension
line location.
```

 5. Choose Continue Dimension from the Dimension toolbar. At the `Specify a second extension line origin or (<select>/Undo):` **prompt, choose Tracking. At the** `_tracking First tracking point:` **prompt, pick the endpoint at** ②. **At the** `Next point (Press ENTER to end tracking):` **prompt, pick the endpoint or intersection at** ④. **Press Enter to end tracking. AutoCAD places the continued dimension. Notice that AutoCAD uses a leader to place the text because there is not enough room between the extension lines.**

6. AutoCAD repeats the `Specify a second extension line origin or (<select>/Undo):` **prompt. Pick the endpoint at** ② **in Figure 14-15. AutoCAD places the dimension. Press Enter twice to end the command.**

7. Choose Linear Dimension from the Dimension toolbar. Follow the prompts:

```
First extension line origin or press ENTER to select: Choose
the endpoint at ⑤ in Figure 14-15.
Second extension line origin: Choose Tracking from the Standard
toolbar.
```

```
_tracking First tracking point: Pick the endpoint or intersection at
⑥.
Next point  (Press ENTER to end tracking): Pick the endpoint or
intersection at ⑦.
Next point  (Press ENTER to end tracking): ↵
Dimension line location
(Mtext/Text/Angle/Horizontal/Vertical/Rotated): Pick a dimension
line location fairly close to the line you dimensioned leaving just enough
room for the dimension text.
```

8. Choose Baseline Dimension from the Dimension toolbar. At the `Specify a second extension line origin or (<select>/Undo):` prompt, pick the endpoint or intersection at ⑥ in Figure 14-15. Press Enter twice to end the command.

9. Save your drawing. It should look like Figure 14-16.

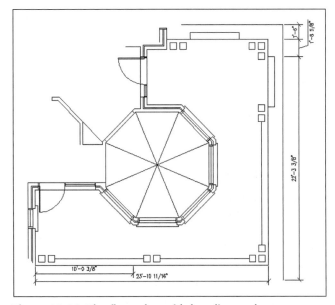

Figure 14-16: The floor plan with baseline and continued dimensions.

Dimensioning Arcs and Circles

When you dimension an arc or a circle, you measure its radius or diameter. It is also common to mark arc and circle centers to clarify what you are measuring. Arc and circle dimensions are most commonly used in mechanical drawings. AutoCAD's radius and diameter dimensions are easy to use.

Marking arc and circle centers

Circle and arc centers are often marked in mechanical drawings because the center is an important aspect of a circle or arc but is not obvious without a mark. You set the size and type of mark when you create a dimension style, as explained in the next chapter. You can use a center mark (a small cross) or center lines, as shown in Figure 14-17.

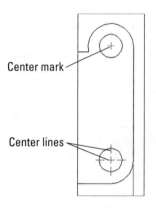

Figure 14-17: Circles marked with a center mark and with center lines.

Center mark

Center lines

Choose Center Mark from the Dimension toolbar. At the `Select arc or circle:` prompt, pick the arc or circle you want to mark. AutoCAD draws the mark or lines.

Creating radial dimensions

To dimension the radius of a circle or arc, choose Radius Dimension from the Dimension toolbar. AutoCAD responds with the `Select arc or circle:` prompt. Select an arc or circle. At the `Dimension line location (Mtext/Text/Angle):` prompt, pick where you want the dimension line to appear. AutoCAD automatically adds an *R* before the measurement to indicate the radius, as shown in Figure 14-18.

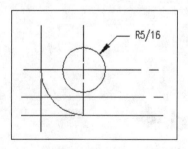

R5/16

Figure 14-18: This radius dimension uses a leader (a line and arrow pointing to the object) outside the circle because the circle is too small to place the dimension inside it.

You can also choose the Mtext, Text, or Angle option, as described in the section "Drawing Linear Dimensions."

Creating diameter dimensions

To dimension the diameter of a circle or arc, choose Diameter Dimension from the Dimension toolbar. AutoCAD responds with the `Select arc or circle:` prompt. Select an arc or circle. At the `Dimension line location (Mtext/Text/Angle):` prompt, pick where you want the dimension line to appear. AutoCAD automatically adds the diameter symbol before the measurement to indicate the dimension, as shown in Figure 14-19.

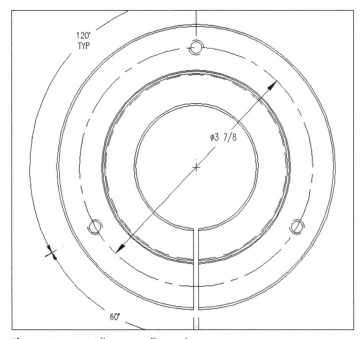

Figure 14-19: A diameter dimension.

You can also choose the Mtext, Text, or Angle option, as described in "Drawing Linear Dimensions."

Dimensioning Angles

AutoCAD offers several options for dimensioning angles. You may want to dimension the angular relationship between two lines, but the lines may intersect at their midpoints or may not intersect at all. Therefore, you need to be able to specify the vertex of the angle you want to dimension. Figure 14-20 shows an angular dimension with the points used to define it.

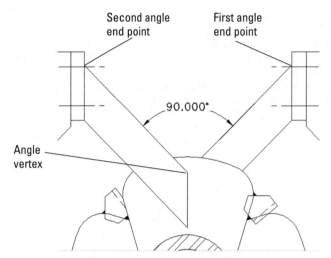

Second angle end point

First angle end point

90.000°

Angle vertex

Figure 14-20: An angular dimension.

Credit: Thanks to Mary Redfern of The Bethlehem Corporation, Easton, Pennsylvania, for this drawing.

 To create an angular dimension choose Angular from the Dimension toolbar. AutoCAD displays the `Select arc, circle, line, or RETURN:` prompt and responds differently depending on what you select.

✦ If you press Enter, AutoCAD asks for the angle vertex, the first angle endpoint, and the second angle endpoint. These three points define the angle.

✦ If you select an arc, AutoCAD dimensions the entire arc, using the arc's center as the angle vertex.

✦ If you select a circle, AutoCAD uses the pick point as the first angle endpoint and the circle's center as the angle vertex. AutoCAD then displays the `Second angle endpoint:` prompt. Pick a point on the circle.

✦ If you select a line, AutoCAD asks for a second line. AutoCAD measures the angle between the two lines. If the lines don't intersect, AutoCAD uses their implied intersection as the angle vertex.

Once you have defined the angle, AutoCAD responds with the `Dimension arc line location (Mtext/Text/Angle):` prompt. Pick a point for the dimension arc line — which is the same thing as a dimension line except that AutoCAD uses an arc for angular dimensions.

You can also choose the Mtext, Text, or Angle option, as covered in the "Drawing Linear Dimensions" section of this chapter.

Dimensioning minor, major, and supplemental angles

When two lines meet at an angle, they create two angles — the minor angle and the major angle. The angle that is less than 180 degrees is the minor angle. The major angle is always more than 180 degrees. AutoCAD also lets you measure the supplemental angle, which is the difference between 180 degrees and the minor angle. These angles are shown here.

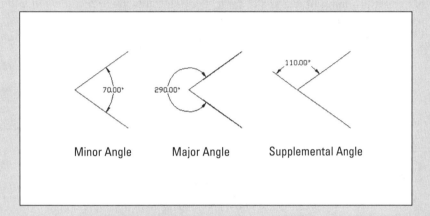

Minor Angle   Major Angle   Supplemental Angle

Here's how you create each type of dimension. Start the DIMANGULAR command. AutoCAD responds with the Select arc, circle, line, or RETURN: prompt.

To dimension the minor angle, select both lines. Then at the Dimension arc line location (Mtext/Text/Angle): prompt, place the dimension arc line inside the angle, as shown in the figure. (You can also press Enter, specify the angle vertex and the two lines, and place the dimension arc line inside the angle.)

To dimension the major angle, press Enter. (Do *not* select the lines.) At the prompts, specify the angle vertex and the two lines. At the Dimension arc line location (Mtext/Text/Angle): prompt, place the dimension arc line outside the angle, as shown in the figure.

To dimension the supplemental angle, select both lines. At the Dimension arc line location (Mtext/Text/Angle): prompt, place the dimension arc line outside the angle, as shown in the figure.

As you can see, how you specify the angle and where you place the dimension arc line determine which angle you measure.

Step-by-Step: Drawing Radial, Diameter, and Angular Dimensions

1. Open *ab14-c.dwg* from your CD-ROM.

2. Save it as *ab14-5.dwg* in your *AutoCAD Bible* folder. This is a view of a bearing housing for an industrial washing machine, as shown in Figure 14-21. OSNAP is on, with running object snaps set to Endpoint, Intersection, and Center. If the Dimension toolbar isn't visible, choose View➪Toolbars and check Dimension. Click Close.

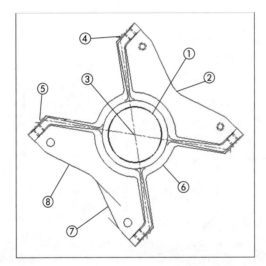

Figure 14-21: A bearing housing for an industrial washing machine.

3. Choose Center Mark from the Dimension toolbar. At the `Select arc or circle:` prompt, pick one of the four small circles at the corners of the model. Repeat the command for the other three circles.

4. Choose Diameter Dimension from the Dimension toolbar. At the `Select arc or circle:` prompt, choose the circle at ① in Figure 14-21. At the `Dimension line location (Mtext/Text/Angle):` prompt, pick a location for the dimension line.

5. Choose Radius Dimension from the Dimension toolbar. At the `Select arc or circle:` prompt, choose ② from Figure 14-21. At the `Dimension line location (Mtext/Text/Angle):` prompt, pick a location for the dimension line. The line may appear to the left of the angle; try moving the cursor until the dimension appears to its right.

6. Choose Angular Dimension from the Dimension toolbar. Follow the prompts:

```
Select arc, circle, line, or press ENTER: ↵
Angle vertex: Pick ③ in Figure 14-21.
First angle endpoint: Pick ④.
Second angle endpoint: Pick ⑤.
Dimension arc line location (Mtext/Text/Angle): Choose a
location for the dimension line.
```

7. Repeat the DIMANGULAR command. At the `Select arc, circle, line, or press ENTER:` prompt, pick the arc at ⑥. At the `Dimension arc line location (Mtext/Text/Angle):` prompt, pick a location for the dimension line.

8. Repeat the DIMANGULAR command. At the `Select arc, circle, line, or press ENTER:` prompt, pick ⑦ in Figure 14-21. At the `Second line:` prompt, pick ⑧. At the `Dimension arc line location (Mtext/Text/Angle):` prompt, pick a location for the dimension line to the left of the model.

9. Save your drawing. It should look like Figure 14-22.

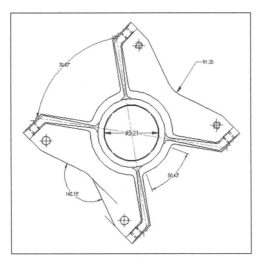

Figure 14-22: The bearing housing with center marks, radial and diameter dimensions, and angular dimensions.

Creating Ordinate Dimensions

Ordinate dimensions are used in mechanical drawing. They dimension an object by labeling X or Y coordinates based on a 0,0 coordinate placed somewhere on the model. Figure 14-23 shows a drawing with some ordinate dimensions.

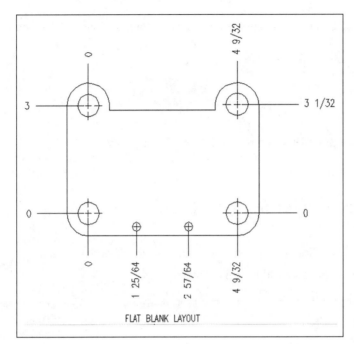

Figure 14-23: Ordinate dimensions in a mechanical drawing of a tension arm for a commercial dryer.

To place the 0,0 coordinate on the model, choose Tools⇨UCS⇨Origin. Pick a point on the model, using object snaps for an exact measurement. If you want to check the UCS, choose View⇨Display⇨UCS Icon⇨Origin. Also make sure On is checked. As long as there is room, the UCS icon moves to the new 0,0 coordinate.

 To create an ordinate dimension, choose Ordinate Dimension from the Dimension toolbar. At the `Select feature:` prompt, pick the part of the model that you want to dimension. Running object snaps with OSNAP turned on makes this an easy task.

At the `Leader endpoint (Xdatum/Ydatum/Mtext/Text):` prompt, pick the endpoint for the leader. AutoCAD generally decides whether to dimension the X coordinate (Xdatum) or Y coordinate (Ydatum) based on where you pick the leader endpoint. Pick the leader endpoint perpendicular from the coordinate's axis you want to measure — to measure an X coordinate, move up or down from the feature you selected. To measure a Y coordinate, move left or right to pick the leader endpoint.

Usually you work with ORTHO on to create straight lines. If you need to create bent lines to avoid previously drawn dimensions, turn ORTHO off. If you pick a leader endpoint at a nonorthogonal angle from the feature, you may need to force AutoCAD to measure the coordinate you want using either the Xdatum or Ydatum option.

Use the Mtext option to open the Multiline Text Editor and edit the dimension text. Use the Text option to change all the text on the command line.

Step-by-Step: Drawing Ordinate Dimensions

1. Open *ab14-d.dwg* from your CD-ROM.

2. Save it as *ab14-6.dwg* in your *AutoCAD Bible* folder. This drawing shows a simple sheet metal template, as shown in Figure 14-24. Snap is on and set to .25 units. If the Dimension toolbar isn't visible, choose View➪Toolbars and check Dimension. Click Close.

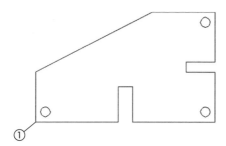

Figure 14-24: A sheet metal template.

3. Choose Tools➪UCS➪Origin. At the `Origin point <0,0,0>:` prompt, pick ① in Figure 14-24.

4. Choose Ordinate Dimension from the Dimension toolbar. At the `Select feature:` prompt, choose ① in Figure 14-24. At the `Leader endpoint (Xdatum/Ydatum/Mtext/Text):` prompt, pick a point .5 units to the left of ①, as shown in Figure 14-25. (Because Snap is on, this is easy. If necessary, press F6 until you get polar coordinates to display in the lower left area of the drawing screen.)

5. Press Enter to repeat the DIMORDINATE command. At the `Select feature:` prompt, choose ① in Figure 14-24. At the `Leader endpoint (Xdatum/Ydatum/Mtext/Text):` prompt, pick a point .5 units below ①.

6. Continue to dimension the drawing, using Figure 14-25 as a guide.

7. Save your drawing.

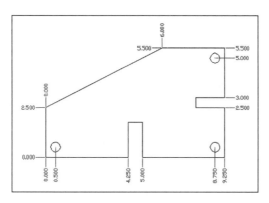

Figure 14-25: The dimensioned template.

Drawing Leaders

Leaders are lines pointing to objects. At the end of a leader, you place any text you want. Use leaders to label objects or provide explanatory text. Leaders are not associative; that is, no dimension text is calculated by AutoCAD. Figure 14-26 shows a good use of a leader.

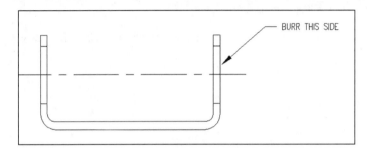

BURR THIS SIDE

Figure 14-26: Using a leader to point to an object and add explanatory text.

To create a leader, choose Leader from the Dimension toolbar. At the `From point:` prompt, pick the starting point of the leader, usually on or near the object the leader text labels or explains. AutoCAD continues with the `To point:` prompt. Usually you pick the endpoint of the leader.

AutoCAD displays the `To point (Format/Annotation/Undo)<Annotation>:` prompt. You have the following options:

✦ **To point:** You can pick another point to continue the leader. AutoCAD continues to repeat the same prompt until you press Enter. If the angle of the last segment of the leader is greater than 15 degrees, AutoCAD adds a short horizontal segment.

✦ **Annotation:** You can type **a** ↵ or press Enter to move on to the annotation. AutoCAD displays the `Annotation (or RETURN for options):` prompt. Since Annotation is the default, you can type your text immediately and press Enter. AutoCAD then responds with the `Mtext:` prompt. You can either press Enter to end the command or type an additional line of multiline text. AutoCAD continues the `Mtext:` prompt until you press Enter to end the command.

If you press Enter at the `Annotation (or RETURN for options):` prompt (instead of typing text), AutoCAD responds with the `Tolerance/Copy/Block/None/<Mtext>:` prompt. The suboptions are:

✦ **Tolerance:** Starts the same prompts as the TOLERANCE command, covered in the next chapter.

✦ **Copy:** Lets you select any text, block, or tolerance. AutoCAD automatically attaches it to the end of the leader.

✦ **Block:** Lets you specify a block and provides the usual block prompts.

✦ **None:** Ends the command without adding anything to the end of the leader.

✦ **Format:** You can type **f** ↵ to format the leader. AutoCAD responds with the `Spline/STraight/Arrow/None/<Exit>:` prompt. The format suboptions are:

✦ **Spline:** Creates a spline leader based on the points you specify. Splines are covered in Chapter 16.

✦ **Straight:** Creates a straight line leader. This is the default, but lets you return to a straight line leader after choosing the Spline option.

✦ **Arrow:** Creates a leader with an arrow pointing to the object. This is the default, but lets you draw a leader with an arrow if you have previously chosen the next option, None.

✦ **None:** Creates a leader with no arrow.

✦ **Exit:** Exits the Format suboptions.

✦ **Undo:** Type **u** ↵ to undo the last leader line segment.

Step-by-Step: Drawing Leaders

On the
CD-ROM

1. Open *ab14-e.dwg* from your CD-ROM.

2. Save it as *ab14-7.dwg* in your *AutoCAD Bible* folder. This is a drawing of a set of pulleys, as shown in Figure 14-27. If the Dimension toolbar isn't visible, choose View⇨Toolbars and check Dimension. Click Close. Running OSNAPs are not turned on.

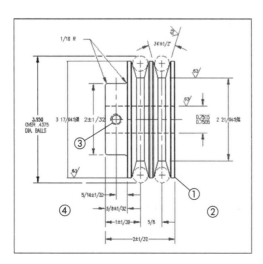

Figure 14-27: A set of pulleys.

3. Choose Leader from the Dimension toolbar. Follow the prompts:

```
From point: Pick ① in Figure 14-27.
To point: Pick ② in Figure 14-27.
To point (Format/Annotation/Undo)<Annotation>: ↵
Annotation (or press ENTER for options): ↵
Tolerance/Copy/Block/None/<Mtext>: ↵
In the Multiline Text Editor, type
BREAK EDGES ↵
TYP (8) PLACES
```

4. Click OK. AutoCAD places the leader.

5. Press Enter to repeat the LEADER command. Pick points ③ and ④ in Figure 14-27. At the `To point (Format/Annotation/Undo)<Annotation>:` prompt, press Enter. At the `Annotation (or press ENTER for options):` prompt, type **DRILL 'F' HOLE** ↵. At the `MText:` prompt, press Enter. AutoCAD places the leader.

6. Save your drawing. It should look like Figure 14-28.

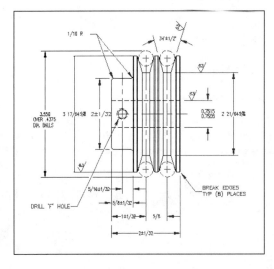

Figure 14-28: The pulleys with two leaders.

Editing Dimensions

Dimensions have many properties — text size, arrowhead size, text placement, and so on. You change most of these properties by changing the dimension style, either globally changing all dimensions using that style or overriding a dimension style setting for a particular dimension. Dimension styles are covered in the next chapter, but here I cover several other ways to edit dimensions.

Using the DIMEDIT command

 The DIMEDIT command offers four ways to edit dimensions. The advantage of this command is that you can change more than one dimension at a time. Choose Dimension Edit from the Dimension toolbar. AutoCAD responds with the `Dimension Edit (Home/New/Rotate/Oblique) <Home>:` prompt. The options are:

> ✦ **Home:** Moves dimension text to its default position as defined by the dimension style.
>
> ✦ **New:** Lets you type new text to replace the existing text. AutoCAD opens the Multiline Text Editor showing the angle brackets that represent the dimension text. You can use this option to add a suffix such as *TYP* (typical) to several dimensions.
>
> ✦ **Rotate:** Rotates the dimension text. This works like the rotation angle for text.
>
> ✦ **Oblique:** Angles the extension lines of the dimension. Use this when you have several dimensions close together that interfere with each other. Specify the final angle of the extension lines, *not* the rotation from the current angle.

The Oblique item on the Dimension menu executes the DIMEDIT command with the Oblique option.

Once you choose an option, DIMEDIT prompts you to select objects. You can select as many dimensions as you wish.

You have the opportunity to use the DIMEDIT command in a Step-by-Step exercise after the next section.

Using the DIMTEDIT command

 The DIMTEDIT command repositions dimension text. To start the command, choose Text Edit from the Dimension toolbar. Although its name gives the impression that you can edit the text content, you can only change its position. You can only edit one dimension at a time.

AutoCAD responds with the `Select dimension:` prompt. Select a dimension. Note the restrictions on the types of dimensions you can select in the list of options that follows.

At the `Enter text location (Left/Right/Home/Angle):` prompt, you can use the cursor to pick a text location. You can also choose one of the options listed here.

Left: Left-justifies the text of linear, radial or diameter dimensions.

Right: Right-justifies the text of linear, radial or diameter dimensions.

Home: Returns dimension text to its default position and angle.

Angle: Rotates dimension text. This option is equivalent to the Rotate option of the DIMEDIT command.

Step-by-Step: Using DIMEDIT and DIMTEDIT to Edit Dimensions

On the
CD-ROM

1. Open *ab14-f.dwg* from your CD-ROM.

2. Save it as *ab14-8.dwg* in your *AutoCAD Bible* folder. This is a civil engineering drawing whose dimensions need some editing. It is shown in Figure 14-29. If the Dimension toolbar isn't visible, choose View⇨Toolbars and check Dimension. Click Close.

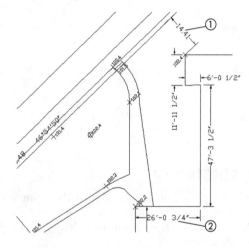

Figure 14-29: A dimensioned civil engineering drawing.

3. The dimension at ① in Figure 14-29 is not in the proper units because the text was entered explicitly as 14.41. To correct this, choose Dimension Edit from the Dimension toolbar. At the Dimension Edit (Home/New/Rotate /Oblique) <Home>: prompt, type **n** ↵. The Multiline Text Editor opens, showing the angle brackets. Since you want the original text, choose OK. At the Select objects: prompt, pick ①. Press Enter to end object selection. (You could correct several dimensions this way.) AutoCAD corrects the dimension, automatically creating the text in the current units.

4. The dimension text at ② in Figure 14-29 is too close to the dimension line of the vertical dimension that crosses it. Choose DimensionText Edit from the Dimension toolbar. At the `Select dimension:` prompt, pick ②. At the `Enter text location (Left/Right/Home/Angle):` prompt, type **r** ↵. AutoCAD moves the text to the right.

5. Save your drawing.

Using DDEDIT to edit dimension text

You can edit dimension text as you would any other multiline text object. Choose Modify⇨Object⇨Text. At the `<Select an annotation object>/Undo:` prompt, choose the dimension. AutoCAD opens the Multiline Text Editor. Using the Multiline Text Editor for dimension text has already been covered in this chapter under the Mtext option of the dimensioning commands.

Using DDMODIFY to edit dimensions

You can edit dimensions using the DDMODIFY command just as you can edit the properties of any other object. Choose Properties from the Object Properties toolbar and select one or more dimensions. If you select one dimension, the Modify Dimension dialog box opens, as shown in Figure 14-30. If you pick multiple dimensions, the dialog box allows only color, layer, and linetype changes.

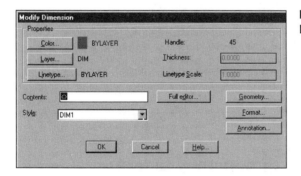

Figure 14-30: The Modify Dimension dialog box.

Parts of this dialog box make more sense once you have learned about dimension styles, which are covered in the next chapter. For example, the Geometry, Format, and Annotation buttons duplicate the buttons in the Dimension Styles dialog box, giving you full control over the selected dimension. You can also change the color, layer, and linetype. You can edit the text in this dialog box or click Full editor to open the Multiline Text Editor. The Style drop-down list lets you choose a different dimension style.

Using grips to edit dimensions

Grips are ideal for moving dimension lines and text. The grips at the dimension line endpoints and the text insertion point are quite useful for making adjustments in dimensions.

To move a dimension line closer or farther from the dimensioned object, pick the dimension to display the grips. Pick one of the grips at the endpoints of the dimension line to highlight it. The <Stretch to point>/Base point/Copy/ Undo/eXit: prompt appears. Drag the dimension line to the desired location. Press Esc twice to remove the grips.

To move dimension text, pick the dimension to display the grips. Pick the grip on the dimension text to highlight it. Drag the dimension text to its desired location.

Tip

Turn ORTHO on while trying to drag either the dimension line or the dimension text. If you drag at an angle, you move both the text *and* the dimension line at once.

Figure 14-31 shows the process of dragging a dimension to the right.

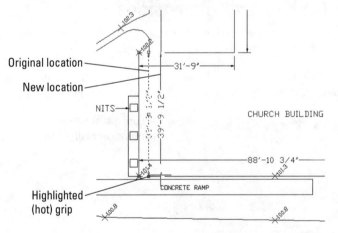

Figure 14-31: Using grips to relocate a dimension.

Credit: Thanks to Bill Maidment of Cantech Inc., Fairfield, Iowa, for this drawing.

Editing objects and dimensions together

Until now, you have not taken advantage of the associativity of AutoCAD's dimensions. This feature allows you to edit objects and have the dimensions automatically adjust to the new object measurements.

To edit objects and dimensions together, you must select both the object and its dimension. AutoCAD knows to adjust the dimension when its definition points change. The STRETCH command is usually the best way to accomplish this.

To stretch an object and its associated dimension, start the STRETCH command. Place the crossing window so that it selects both the object and the dimension.

Then pick the base point and a second point. Alternatively, type a displacement (without the @ sign) and press Enter at the `Second point of displacement:` prompt. AutoCAD adjusts both the object and the dimension. Figure 14-32 shows a house plan before and after stretching to move a window six inches to the left. The crossing window included the entire window, so it was simply moved. However, the crossing window crossed the walls on either side of the window and both dimensions so they were stretched six inches to the left. Notice the change in the dimension text, indicating the new measurements.

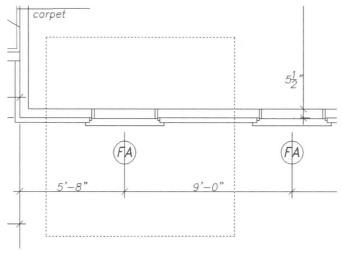

a) Before stretching

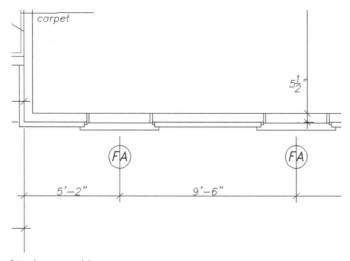

b) After stretching

Figure 14-32: Stretching objects and dimensions in one operation.

Step-by-Step: Using DDEDIT, DDMODIFY, Grips, and Stretching to Edit Dimensions

1. Open *ab14-g.dwg* from your CD-ROM.

2. Save it as *ab14-9.dwg* in your *AutoCAD Bible* folder. This is a cross-section of a nut, as shown in Figure 14-33.

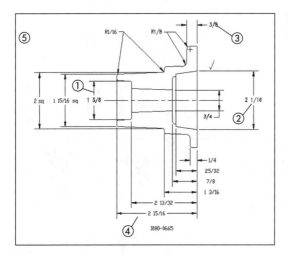

Figure 14-33: A dimensioned cross-section of a nut.

3. Choose Modify⇨Object⇨Text. At the `<Select an annotation object>/Undo:` prompt, choose the dimension at ① in Figure 14-33. The Multiline Text Editor opens with the cursor before the angle brackets. Click Symbols and choose Diameter. AutoCAD places the Unicode character equivalent of `%%c` before the dimension. Click OK.

4. AutoCAD repeats the `<Select an annotation object>/Undo:` prompt. Pick the dimension at ② in Figure 14-33 and make the same change you made in step 3. Press Enter to end the command.

5. Pick the dimension at ③ in Figure 14-33. Click the grip on the text to activate it. Drag it down slightly to place it closer to the object it is dimensioning.

6. Choose Stretch from the Modify toolbar. Follow the prompts:

```
Select objects: Pick at ④.
Other corner: Pick at ⑤.
30 found
Select objects: ↵
Base point or displacement: 5/8<180 ↵
Second point of displacement: ↵
```

AutoCAD stretches the nut and adjusts the two dimensions that crossed the crossing window.

Summary

AutoCAD's dimension features let you dimension almost anything. In this chapter I covered linear, radial, dimension, angular, and ordinate dimensions. You can also create leaders to label or annotate objects.

You also learned several techniques for editing dimension geometry and text.

In the next chapter I continue the subject of dimensions by explaining how to gain total control with dimension styles.

✦   ✦   ✦

Creating Dimension Styles and Tolerances

Understanding Dimension Styles

In Chapter 14 you drew many dimensions using AutoCAD's default style. However, you have a great deal of control over the way dimensions look. Now that you are familiar with dimensions, you can learn how to bend them to your will.

You should create your dimension styles before dimensioning. Some drawings have several dimension styles, although a drawing can look confusing if there are too many dimension styles. In general, you create a dimension style, save it in your template drawings, and (it is hoped) rarely have to deal with it again except to override a setting for a unique situation.

The various disciplines each have their own standards and customs regarding dimensions. AutoCAD's dimension styles are flexible enough to accommodate any type of dimensioning practice.

 To create a dimension style, choose Dimension Style from the Dimension toolbar to open the Dimension Styles dialog box, shown in Figure 15-1. The current dimension style is shown as STANDARD. The Standard dimension style is AutoCAD's default dimension style.

Figure 15-1: The Dimension Styles dialog box.

The Dimension Styles dialog box is the master control room where you manage dimensions. Here you name new dimension styles, create dimension families, and open the Geometry, Format, and Annotation dialog boxes to specify dimension settings.

The preset Standard dimension style that AutoCAD comes with is most appropriate for mechanical drafting. Whichever type of drafting you do, you will probably find the need to make some changes to the default dimension style. You do this by creating a new dimension style.

To create a new style, change the settings as explained throughout this chapter. Then type a new name in the Name text box and click Save. If you wish to name the style first, type the name in the Name text box and click Save. You have just made a copy of the Standard dimension style (or whichever dimension style was current). Now change the settings. Don't forget to click Save again before you leave the dialog box, or your new dimension style won't include the changes you made.

If you already have dimension styles and want to make a different one current, click the Current drop-down list and choose the dimension style you want. Click OK to return to your drawing.

You can also rename a dimension style. Use the Current drop-down list to choose the dimension style you want to rename. Highlight the name in the Name text box and type the new name. Click Rename.

The Family section of the dialog box is discussed later in this chapter.

Controlling Dimension Geometry

To start creating your new dimension style, make sure the setting for Family is Parent, and then click Geometry to open the Geometry dialog box, shown in Figure 15-2.

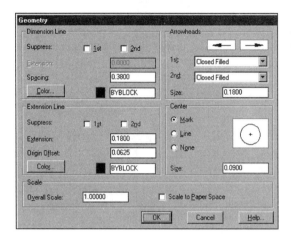

Figure 15-2: The Geometry dialog box controls dimension lines, extension lines, arrowheads, and center marks.

The Geometry dialog box is divided into five sections, which are explained below. (Depending on which Family option is selected, certain options in the Geometry dialog box will be disabled.)

Managing dimension lines

In Chapter 14, Figure 14-1, I illustrated the parts of a dimension. Refer to that figure if you need a refresher.

In some dimension styles, the dimension text splits the dimension line into two parts, as shown in Figure 15-3. This creates two dimension lines. You can suppress — that is, turn off — either the first or second dimension line by checking the appropriate box. The first line is nearest where you specified the first extension line origin. (If you selected an object instead of specifying two extension line origins, you may not be able to predict which dimension line is the first and which is the second. Experiment.) You would usually suppress dimension lines when they interfere with other dimensions or with objects in your drawing.

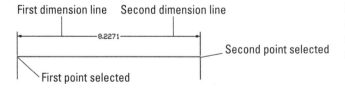

Figure 15-3: A typical mechanical dimension with text splitting two dimension lines.

The Extension text box determines how far the dimension lines extend past the extension lines. When you have arrowheads at the end of the dimension lines, the Extension option is unavailable. However, if you choose Architectural tick or

Oblique in the Arrowheads section of the dialog box, the Extension option becomes available. This type of extension is typical for architectural drafting. Figure 15-4 shows a dimension with an architectural tick and a .1-unit extension.

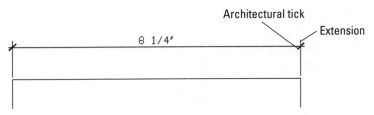

Figure 15-4: A typical architectural dimension showing the text above one dimension line, an architectural tick, and the dimension line slightly extending beyond the extension lines.

The Spacing text box determines the distance between successive dimension lines when you create baseline dimensions. AutoCAD uses this specification to create evenly spaced dimension lines.

Click Color to open the Color dialog box. You can pick a color for the dimension lines that differs from that of the rest of the dimension. Remember, dimensions are blocks. The default color is BYBLOCK so that dimensions take on the color of the current layer or color setting. In general, you should have a separate layer for dimensions. Then the entire dimension is the color set for that layer. Use this setting only if you want the dimension lines to be a different color from your dimension layer color. The arrowheads do not have a separate color setting and always follow the dimension line setting.

Managing arrowheads

The Arrowheads section of the Geometry dialog box controls the arrowheads that go at the ends of dimension lines. You do not actually have to use arrowheads, as shown in Figure 15-4. You can also set the first and second arrowheads individually. However, if you change the first arrowhead, the second one follows suit, assuming that you want both ends to look the same. To make them different, specify your choice in the first drop-down box, then in the second drop-down box.

You can create your own arrowhead. To do this, create the arrowhead you want with a unit size of 1. Make a block out of it. (See Chapter 18 for instructions.) For an arrow-shaped block, pick the point of the arrow for the insertion point and create it right-facing. You may have to experiment with the right insertion point or even create left- and right-handed blocks. In the first and second drop-down lists, choose User Arrow. The User Arrow dialog box opens, as shown in Figure 15-5. Type the name of the block and click OK. Figure 15-6 shows a dimension with a user arrow, a filled ellipse.

Figure 15-5: The User Arrow dialog box.

Figure 15-6: A dimension with an unusual user arrow, a filled ellipse.

Set the size of the arrowhead in the Size text box. As explained later in this section in the discussion of scale, you should use the final size you want to see when the drawing is plotted on paper.

Managing extension lines

You manage extension lines similarly to dimension lines. To suppress the first or second extension line so that it is not visible, click the appropriate box. (AutoCAD automatically suppresses extension lines when creating baseline and continued dimensions.) Figure 15-7 shows a dimension with the first extension line suppressed.

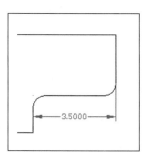

Figure 15-7: A dimension with the first extension line suppressed. You can just see the definition point.

Extension lines typically extend slightly past the dimension line, as you can see in some of the figures in this chapter. Use the Extension text box to specify this extension distance.

Extension lines typically do not actually touch the object they dimension, to make it easier to distinguish the dimension from the object. Use the Origin Offset text box to define the distance from the definition points — which are on the object being dimensioned — and the extension lines.

Click Color to open the Color dialog box. As with dimension lines, you can pick a color for the extension lines that differs from that of the rest of the dimension. The default color is BYBLOCK so that dimensions take on the color of the current layer or color setting.

Managing center marks

The Center section of the dialog box specifies how you want to mark the centers of arcs and circles when you choose Center Mark from the Dimension toolbar (the DIMCENTER command). Choose Mark to create a small cross or choose Line to create a cross plus four lines that cross. While it is common to use center lines for circles in mechanical drafting, center marks are usually used for arcs, as shown in Figure 15-8.

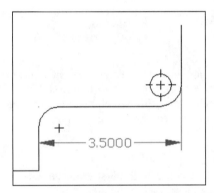

Figure 15-8: A circle with a center line and an arc with a center mark.

Specify the size of the center mark or line in the Size text box. For center marks, the size is the distance from the intersection of the two lines to their endpoints. If you use center lines, the size also specifies the distance from the circle quadrants to the end of the center lines.

Managing scale

The Scale section of the Geometry dialog box lets you specify the scale factor. The scale factor adjusts the size of dimension text, arrowheads, spacing, and so on. It has no effect on the content of dimension text — that is, it does not affect actual measurements. There are so many size options in a dimension style that you could spend all day trying to multiply each size option by the scale. Then, if you have to change the scale of the drawing, you would need to recalculate all the size specifications. Setting the Overall Scale factor makes your life easier because AutoCAD automatically multiplies every size specification by the scale factor.

Cross-
Reference

Scale factors are discussed in detail in Chapter 5. See Chapter 17 for a discussion of scaling dimensions to paper space.

After you make all the desired changes in the Geometry dialog box, click OK to return to the Dimension Styles dialog box.

Because the Standard dimension style is closest to mechanical drafting standards, in the following exercise (and others in this chapter), you create an architectural dimension style using the Standard style as a base. This requires you to make a maximum number of changes, thereby letting you become as familiar as possible with the dimension style settings.

Step-by-Step: Controlling Dimension Geometry

On the
CD-ROM

1. Open *ab15-a.dwg* from your CD-ROM.

2. Save it as *ab15-1.dwg* in your *AutoCAD Bible* folder. This drawing is an elevation of a garage, as shown in Figure 15-9. ORTHO and OSNAP are on. Running object snaps are set for Endpoint and Intersection. The Dim layer is current. If the Dimension toolbar is not visible, choose View⇨Toolbars and choose Dimension. Click Close.

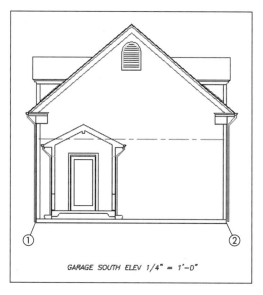

Figure 15-9: The garage elevation.

3. To see what the Standard dimension style looks like, choose Linear Dimension from the Dimension toolbar. At the `First extension line origin or press ENTER to select:` prompt, pick ① in Figure 15-9. At the `Second extension line origin:` prompt, pick ②. At the `Dimension line location (Mtext/Text/Angle/Horizontal/Vertical/Rotated):` prompt, pick a location for the dimension line below the line you dimensioned. The arrows and text are so small you cannot even see them.

4. Use a ZOOM Window to zoom in on ① and the left end of the dimension. Choose Zoom Previous from the Standard toolbar. Do another ZOOM Window to zoom in on the center of the dimension to see the text. (You may have to use ZOOM Window twice.) Choose Zoom Previous again. As you can see, this dimension needs some modification.

5. Choose Dimension Style from the Dimension toolbar. The current dimension style should be Standard. In the Name text box, type **Arch_48** and click Save to create a new dimension style based on the Standard dimension style.

6. Click Geometry. In the Arrowheads section, choose Oblique from the first drop-down list. The size should be 3/16". In the Dimension Line section, type **3/32** in the Extension text box. Since the drawing's scale is 1/4" = 1', or 1=48, type **48** in the Overall Scale text box. Click OK.

7. In the Dimension Styles dialog box, click Save, then click OK.

8. Choose Properties from the Object Properties toolbar. At the `Select objects:` prompt, choose the dimension you created in step 3. Click the right mouse button to end object selection. The Modify Dimension dialog box opens. In the Style drop-down list, choose ARCH_48. Click OK. The dimension now has the geometry settings you just made.

9. Save your drawing. It should look like Figure 15-10. Keep this drawing open if you are continuing on to the next exercise.

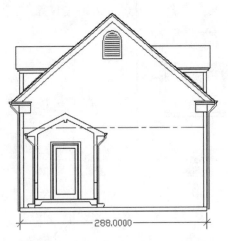

Figure 15-10: The garage elevation with one dimension. The Geometry settings have been changed.

Controlling Dimension Format

In the Dimension Styles dialog box, click Format to open the Format dialog box, as shown in Figure 15-11. This dialog box controls text justification and placement, as well as how AutoCAD fits a dimension when there is not enough space for all its elements.

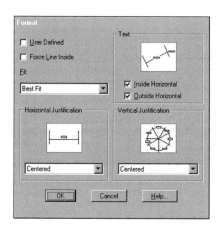

Figure 15-11: The Format dialog box.

Fitting dimensions into tight spaces

When there is not enough room to place the arrowheads, dimension line, and text between the extension lines, AutoCAD needs to place some elements of the dimension outside the extension lines. The following options in the Format dialog box let you specify how you want AutoCAD to handle this situation.

User Defined

The User Defined setting applies to the location of dimension text, which is generally controlled by the horizontal justification setting of the Format dialog box. When you check this box, AutoCAD places the text at the point you pick at the Dimension line location: prompt.

Force Line Inside

Check the Force Line Inside option to place a dimension line between the extension lines even when there isn't room for text or arrows, as shown in Figure 15-12.

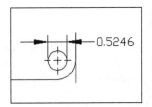

Figure 15-12: A dimension with a dimension line forced inside.

The Fit drop-down list

The Fit drop-down list offers options for how AutoCAD fits dimension elements when there is not enough room for everything. These are among the hardest of the dimension styles options to understand, yet they can greatly affect how your dimensions appear. The default is Best Fit.

The first option, Text and Arrows, keeps the text and arrows together — between the extension lines if there is enough room, outside the extension lines if not. The dimension line and the text cannot be moved separately. Figure 15-13 shows a dimension using this option.

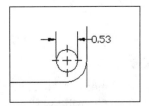

Figure 15-13: A narrow dimension using the Text and Arrows option.

The Text Only option splits up the text and the arrows. If there is not enough room for both between the extension lines, the text goes between them and the arrows go outside. The dimension line and the text cannot be moved separately. Figure 15-14 shows a dimension using this option.

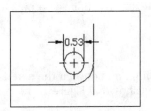

Figure 15-14: A narrow dimension using the Text Only option.

Arrows Only also splits up the text and the arrows. If there is not enough room for both between the extension lines, the arrows go between them and the text goes outside. The dimension line and the text cannot be moved separately. Figure 15-15 shows a dimension using this option.

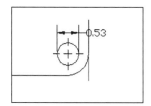

Figure 15-15: A narrow dimension using the Arrows Only option.

Best Fit puts whatever fits inside the extension lines. The arrowheads might fit inside and the text not, or the other way around. Or if there is not enough room for either, they both go outside the extension lines. The dimension line and the text cannot be moved separately. Figure 15-16 shows a dimension using this option.

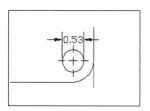

Figure 15-16: A narrow dimension using the Best Fit option.

The Leader option creates a leader when there is not enough space for the text. The advantage of this option is that is allows you more flexibility over text placement because the dimension line and the text can be moved separately. Figure 15-17 shows a dimension using this option. Figure 15-18 shows the text moved to a more suitable location where it does not cut across an object.

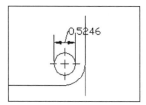

Figure 15-17: A narrow dimension using the Leader option.

Figure 15-18: The leader text has been moved to a better location.

No Leader fits the text between the extension lines if possible, with the arrows outside. If there is only enough room for the arrowheads, they go inside and the text goes above the dimension line but with no leader. If there is not enough space for either the text or the arrowheads, you can place the text anywhere, giving you maximum flexibility. Figure 15-19 shows a dimension using this option. This text is ideally placed, but you could move it independently of the dimension if you wished.

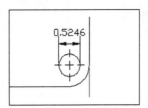

Figure 15-19: A narrow dimension using the No Leader option.

Controlling text alignment

The Text section of the Format dialog box affects whether text inside and outside of the extension lines is aligned with the dimension line or remains horizontal. Check the Inside check box to keep text between the extension lines horizontal. Check the Outside check box to keep text outside the extension lines horizontal. AutoCAD provides a useful visual confirmation of your choice.

Your choice in this section interacts with the vertical justification of the text. See the section "Controlling vertical justification" for further explanation.

Controlling horizontal justification

The Horizontal Justification section of the Format dialog box affects the placement of dimension text between the extension lines. Here again, AutoCAD provides a handy visual confirmation of your choice. Table 15-1 explains your choices.

Table 15-1	
Horizontal Justification Options for Dimensions	
Option	*Function*
Centered	This is the default. It centers text between the two extension lines.
1st Extension Line	Places the text next to the first extension line. The first extension line is always the first point you specified at the `First extension line origin or RETURN to select:` prompt. The picture and the words *Horizontal Justification* can be especially confusing for vertical dimensions. If you are not consistent in how you pick your dimensions, you can get some strange results. Figure 15-20 shows two vertical dimensions and two horizontal dimensions using a horizontal justification of 1st Extension Line. Because the lines were not picked consistently, the results are not satisfactory.
2nd Extension Line	Places the text next to the second extension line. The comments for the 1st Extension Line option apply to this option as well.

Option	Function
Over 1st Extension	Places the text over the first extension line. The comments for the 1st Extension Line option apply to this option as well.
Over 2nd Extension	Places the text over the second extension line. The comments for the 1st Extension Line option apply to this option as well.

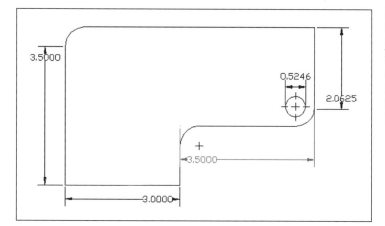

Figure 15-20: Using a horizontal justification other than centered can lead to unexpected results if you pick objects inconsistently.

Controlling vertical justification

The Vertical Justification section of the Format dialog box affects how text is justified relative to the dimension line. Table 15-2 lists the options.

Table 15-2 Vertical Justification Options for Dimensions	
Option	**Function**
Centered	Centers the text in the dimension line, breaking the dimension line into two. For nonhorizontal dimensions, the Inside Horizontal setting in the Text section affects the alignment of the text. To see the relationship, choose Centered in the Vertical Justification section. Then check and uncheck Inside Horizontal in the Text section, watching the visual change in the Vertical Justification section.
Above	Places text above the dimension line, as shown in Figure 15-21. Here too, the Inside Horizontal setting in the Text section affects the alignment of the text, as explained for the Centered option.

(continued)

Table 15-2 (continued)	
Option	**Function**
Outside	Places the text on the side of the dimension line that is farthest from the object you are dimensioning, as explained for the Centered option.
JIS	Places dimension text in conformation to the Japanese Industrial Standards rules, which vary the placement according to the angle of the dimension line, as explained for the Centered option.

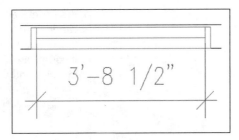

Figure 15-21: This dimension uses the Above option for vertical orientation. This is typical for architectural drawings.

When you have finished specifying your settings in the Format dialog box, click OK to return to the Dimension Styles dialog box.

Step-by-Step: Controlling Dimension Format

On the
CD-ROM

1. If *ab15-1.dwg* is open from the previous exercise, use it for this exercise as well. Otherwise, open *ab15-1.dwg* from the *Results* folder of the CD-ROM. ORTHO and OSNAP are on. Running object snaps are set for Endpoint and Intersection. The Dim layer is current. If the Dimension toolbar is not visible, choose View➪Toolbars and choose Dimension. Click Close.

2. Save it as *ab15-2.dwg* in your *AutoCAD Bible* folder.

3. Choose Dimension Style from the Dimension toolbar. The ARCH_48 style should be current. Choose Format to open the Format dialog box.

4. In the top left corner, check Force Line Inside. Architectural dimensions customarily place a line between the extension lines even if the text cannot fit. In the Fit drop-down list, choose No Leader. This lets you adjust the position of dimension text independently from the dimension line, which is useful for narrow dimensions.

5. In the Text section, uncheck Inside Horizontal and Outside Horizontal. While mechanical dimensions usually require horizontal text, architectural dimensions require that the text be aligned with the dimension line.

6. In the Vertical Justification section, choose Above from the drop-down list.

7. Click OK. In the Dimension Styles dialog box, click Save, then OK. The dimension automatically updates to include the changes.

8. Save your drawing. It should look like Figure 15-22.

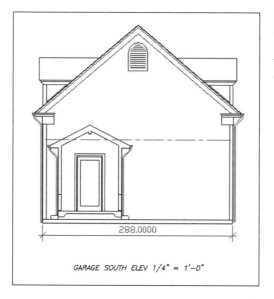

Figure 15-22: The garage elevation's dimension now has proper geometry and format, but the annotation settings are not correct.

Controlling Dimension Annotation

Click Annotation in the Dimension Styles dialog box to open the Annotation dialog box, shown in Figure 15-23. This dialog box sets the units used for dimensions, tolerance formatting, and text properties such as style, height, and color.

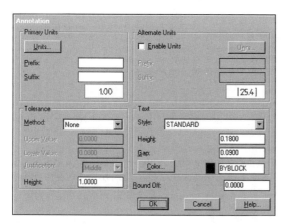

Figure 15-23: The Annotation dialog box.

Defining primary units

The first section of the Annotation dialog box is Primary Units. Start by clicking Units to open the Primary Units dialog box, shown in Figure 15-24. You should already be familiar with setting units. I discuss setting units for a drawing in Chapter 5. You must separately set your units for dimensions.

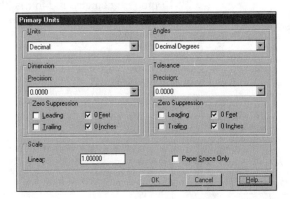

Figure 15-24: The Primary Units dialog box.

Units

In the Units section of the Primary Units dialog box, choose the type of units you want for your dimensions. You can choose from the following unit settings:

- ✦ Scientific
- ✦ Decimal
- ✦ Engineering
- ✦ Architectural (Stacked)
- ✦ Fractional (Stacked)
- ✦ Architectural
- ✦ Fractional
- ✦ Windows desktop

Tip

Stacked refers to fractions whose numbers are stacked on top of each other. When using one of the stacked unit types, you often find that the fractional numbers are too big compared to the whole numbers. It is a little-known fact that you can control the size of fractional numbers in AutoCAD. The height for tolerances — which you set in the Annotation dialog box — is used for fractions as well. Set the height to the *proportion* of the whole number size. Figure 15-25 shows a dimension with text set to ¼ units and the tolerance height set to ½. The whole numbers appear ¼ units high, and the fractions appear at ½ the height of the whole numbers.

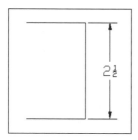

Figure 15-25: You can control the size of fractions relative to whole numbers by setting the tolerance height.

For the Windows desktop units setting, choose Start⇨Settings⇨Control Panel⇨Regional Settings to see the current setting. Click the Number tab. The Windows desktop setting does not give you as complete control over units as AutoCAD. However, if you need consistency with another Windows program, you might find this setting useful.

Angles

The Angles section of the Primary Units dialog box lets you format angular measurements. These choices are the same as for setting up units for a drawing. You can choose from Decimal Degrees, Deg/Min/Sec, Grads, Radians, and Surveyor.

Precision

Use the Precision section of the Primary Units dialog box to specify the level of precision. The format of the choices on the list depends on your choice in the Units section. In this section you also choose if you want to suppress leading and trailing zeros for decimal units. If you suppress leading zeros, a number like 0.375 appears as .375. If you suppress trailing zeros, a number like 3.7500 appears as 3.75.

For architectural units, you can choose to suppress 0 feet and 0 inches. If you suppress 0 feet, a number like 0'–8" becomes 8". If you suppress 0 inches, a number like 6'–0" becomes 6'.

Note   If you need different precision or tolerance levels for linear and angular dimensions, set these at the subfamily levels of a dimension style. Dimension families are discussed later in this chapter.

Tolerance

The Tolerance section of the Primary Units dialog box controls tolerance text. Choose the precision drop-down list to choose the precision you want for tolerances. You have the same zero suppression choices as you do in the Precision section of the dialog box, described in the preceding section.

Scale

You can set a scaling factor for linear dimensions, including radial and diameter dimensions. This factor changes the actual measurement text. For example, if you draw a line 2.5 units long and you specify a linear scale of .5, AutoCAD dimensions the object as 1.25 units. You could set this scale to 25.4 to use metric measurements on a drawing you have created with U.S. measurements — perhaps you are sending the same drawing to certain clients in the United States and other clients elsewhere in the world. You can also use this scale in conjunction with alternate units, as explained in the next section.

You can also set a linear scaling factor for paper space only.

When you have completed the Primary Units dialog box, click OK to return to the Annotation dialog box.

Defining alternate units

If you wish, you can show an alternate set of units in your dimensions. The most common use of this feature is to show millimeters and inches together. AutoCAD displays the alternate units in square brackets. To show alternate units, click Enable Units and choose Units in the Alternate Units section of the Annotation dialog box. The Alternate Units dialog box opens as shown in Figure 15-26.

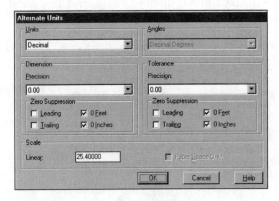

Figure 15-26: The Alternate Units dialog box.

As you can see, this dialog box is the same as the Primary Units dialog box, which I discussed in the previous section. Notice the default scale of 25.4 in the Linear text box. There are 25.4 millimeters to an inch. If your primary units are millimeters, you can set the linear scale to .03937, which is the number of inches to a millimeter. Of course, if your units are not inches but meters, miles, or something else, you need to make the appropriate calculations.

Figure 15-27 shows two dimensions with alternate units.

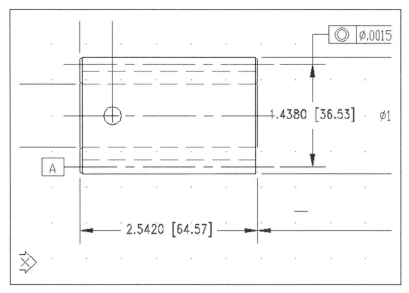

Figure 15-27: Dimensions showing both U.S. and metric measurements.

Credit: Thanks to Jerry Bottenfield of Clow Valve Company,
Oskaloosa, Iowa, for this drawing.

Specifying tolerances

Tolerances are used in mechanical drafting to specify how much deviation is
allowed from the exact measurement when the model is manufactured. Choose the
type of tolerance notation you want in the Tolerance section of the Annotation
dialog box.

Method

AutoCAD offers four tolerance methods from the Method drop-down list:

✦ *Symmetrical* tolerances have the same upper and lower amounts and are
   shown with a plus/minus sign, as shown in Figure 15-28. The Upper Value text
   box is active so you can type in the tolerance amount.

✦ *Deviation* tolerances can have different upper and lower amounts and are
   therefore shown after separate plus and minus signs, as shown in Figure
   15-29. When you choose a deviation tolerance, the Upper Value and Lower
   Value text boxes become active.

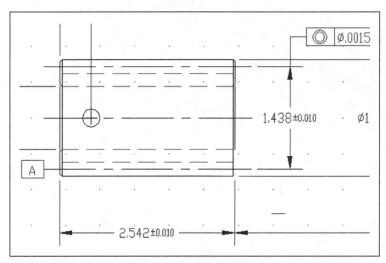

Figure 15-28: Symmetrical tolerances.

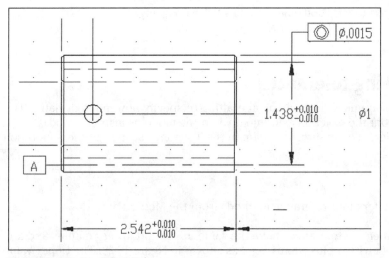

Figure 15-29: Deviation tolerances.

✦ *Limits* tolerances include the upper and lower tolerances in the measurement, as shown in Figure 15-30. Use the Upper Value and Lower Value text boxes to type in the upper and lower tolerance amounts.

✦ A *basic* dimension places the dimension in a box, as shown in Figure 15-31. The tolerance is created separately, using a geometric tolerance control frame, covered later in this chapter.

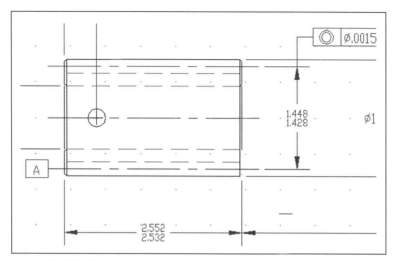

Figure 15-30: Limits tolerances.

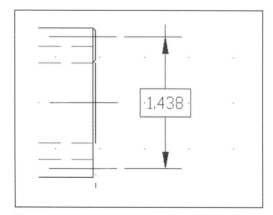

Figure 15-31: A basic dimension.

Justification

The Justification setting determines how the tolerance text is justified with the main measurement text. It is not available for limits and basic tolerances where there is no separate main and tolerance text. You can justify the tolerance text with the top, middle, bottom, or main text.

Tip

The Justification setting also applies to stacked fractions and determines how the fractions are justified with the whole number dimensions. However, if you choose architectural units, this option is not available. The trick is to choose any type of tolerance to make the Justification option available. Choose the option you want and then set the tolerance back to none.

Height

The Height setting determines the height of the tolerance text in relation to all regular dimension text. This setting is a proportion, so that a setting of 1.000 creates tolerance text equal in size to regular dimension text. A setting of .5000 creates tolerance text that is half the size of regular dimension text. This setting is also used to determine the size of numbers in stacked fractions.

Setting text properties

In the last section of the Annotation dialog box, you can set dimension text properties. You have full control over dimension text appearance, as you do over any other text in your drawing.

Choose a text style from the Style drop-down list. You may want to create a special text style such as DIMTEXT for dimension text to give you the flexibility to alter dimension text without changing other text in your drawing. Create the dimension text style before creating your dimension style.

Cross-Reference

See Chapter 13 for a discussion of text styles.

Choose the height for your dimension text. If your text style has a height of zero, you can set the height in this box. Otherwise, the text style height takes over. It's much easier to make all your dimension style adjustments in one place than to make changes in the text style as well.

Use the Gap text box to set the gap between the dimension text and the dimension line. If the dimension line is broken, the gap is the space between each side of the dimension text and the two dimension lines. If the dimension line is unbroken and the text is above the line, the gap is the space between the bottom of the text and the dimension line. The gap also controls the space between geometric tolerances and the text inside them.

When trying to fit dimension text, lines, and arrows in a narrow space, AutoCAD also uses the gap to calculate the minimum space required on either side of the dimension text. Reducing the gap can therefore help fit more of the dimension elements between the extension lines.

Click Color to open the Color dialog box. As with dimension lines, you can pick a color for the dimension text that differs from that of the rest of the dimension. Remember, dimensions are blocks. The default color is BYBLOCK so that dimensions take on the color of the current layer or color setting. In general, you should have a separate layer for dimensions. Then the entire dimension is the color set for that layer. Use this setting only if you want the dimension text to be a different color from your dimension layer color.

Rounding off dimension styles

Use the Round Off text box to round off dimension distances. (The Round Off feature does not apply to angular dimensions.) For example, you can round to the nearest .1 unit or 1/2 inch.

When you have completed your settings in the Annotation dialog box, click OK to return to the Dimension Styles dialog box. Don't forget to save the style you have created. Click OK to return to your drawing — you're ready to start dimensioning!

Step-by-Step: Controlling Dimension Annotation

On the CD-ROM

1. If *ab15-2.dwg* is open from the previous exercise, use it for this exercise as well. Otherwise, open *ab15-2.dwg* from the *Results* folder of the CD-ROM. ORTHO and OSNAP are on. Running object snaps are set for Endpoint and Intersection. The Dim layer is current. If the Dimension toolbar is not visible, choose View⇨Toolbars and choose Dimension. Click Close.

2. Save it as *ab15-3.dwg* in your *AutoCAD Bible* folder.

3. Choose Dimension Style from the Dimension toolbar. The ARCH_48 dimension style is current. Choose Annotation.

4. In the Annotation dialog box, choose Units from the Primary Units section. In the Primary Units dialog box, choose Architectural (stacked) from the Units drop-down list.

5. In the Precision drop-down list box, the precision should be 0'–0 1/8". In the Zero Suppression section, uncheck the 0 Inches check box, because architectural dimensions typically do show 0 inches. Click OK.

6. To format the stacked fractions in the Tolerance section, change the Height to 1/2". (Note: If you want to change the justification, you need to choose any tolerance method temporarily to make the Justification drop-down box active. Once you make the change, be sure to change the tolerance method back to None.)

7. In the Text section, choose ROMANS from the Style drop-down list box. Click OK.

8. Click Save, then click OK to return to your drawing. The dimension is automatically updated and now looks appropriate for an architectural drawing.

9. To see how the stacked fractions appear, create a linear dimension from ① to ② in Figure 15-32. If necessary, zoom in to see the dimension text clearly.

10. Return to the previous view if you zoomed in. Save your drawing. It should look like Figure 15-32. If you are continuing to the next exercise, leave the drawing open.

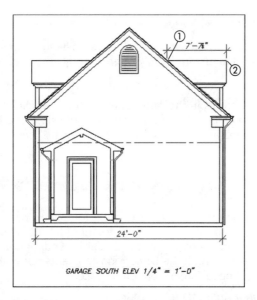

Figure 15-32: The dimension style is now complete.

Working with Dimension Families

You may find that you need to make slight adjustments in your dimension styles for certain types of dimensions. For example, you might want to use center lines for diameter dimensions but only center marks for radial dimensions. You may want to use different precision for angular dimensions than for linear dimensions. You can accomplish this using dimension families.

When you open the Dimension Styles dialog box, by default the Parent button in the Family section is selected. You should create and save the parent dimension style first. To create a child dimension style:

1. Choose the type of child you want. (Linear, Radial, Angular, Diameter, Ordinate, or Leader are your only choices.)

2. Make the changes by choosing Geometry, Format, and Annotation and specifying the new settings in the dialog boxes that open. Click OK to close each dialog box.

3. Back in the Dimension Styles dialog box, click Save.

4. Click OK to return to your drawing.

Caution

If you want to go back later and make further changes to the child dimension style, don't forget to make the parent style current in the Current drop-down list and then choose the child type before making your changes. Otherwise, your changes could be saved to the wrong parent style or child type.

Figure 15-33 shows an architectural drawing with angular and leader child styles that show different properties. Notice that the linear dimension, defined in the parent style, uses ticks to end the dimension lines, whereas the angular dimension uses right-angle arrows, and the leader uses closed arrows.

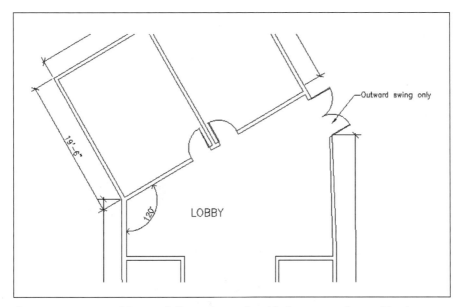

Figure 15-33: An architectural dimension style with linear, angular, and leader dimensions.

To see how AutoCAD stores the child styles, select a dimension created with a child style and choose Properties on the Object Properties toolbar. The Modify Dimension dialog box opens. Click the Style drop-down list. Here you see your child dimension styles listed according to the following codes:

$0	Linear
$2	Angular
$3	Diameter
$4	Radial
$6	Ordinate
$7	Leader

Figure 15-34 shows the Style list for the drawing in Figure 15-33, which had a parent dimension style named ARCH and angular and leader child styles.

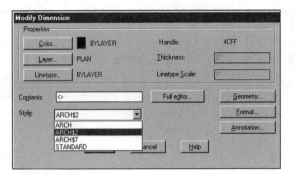

Figure 15-34: The Modify Dimension dialog box lists AutoCAD's codes for child dimension styles.

Step-by-Step: Creating Dimension Families

On the CD-ROM

1. If *ab15-3.dwg* is open from the previous exercise, use it for this exercise as well. Otherwise, open *ab15-3.dwg* from the *Results* folder of the CD-ROM. ORTHO and OSNAP are on. Running object snaps are set for Endpoint and Intersection. The Dim layer is current. If the Dimension toolbar is not visible, choose View⇨Toolbars and choose Dimension. Click Close.

2. Save it as *ab15-4.dwg* in your *AutoCAD Bible* folder.

3. Choose Dimension Style from the Dimension toolbar. The ARCH_48 dimension style is current. To create a child dimension style for angles, choose Angular in the Family section of the Dimension Styles dialog box.

4. Click Geometry. Oblique lines don't work very well for angular dimensions. In the Arrowheads section, choose Right-Angle from the 1st: drop-down list box. Right-Angle appears in the 2nd: field as well. Choose OK.

5. Choose Annotation, then choose Units. In the Dimension section, choose 0 from the Precision drop-down list. Click OK twice.

6. In the Dimension Styles dialog box, click Save. Now click Leader in the Family section. Choose Geometry.

7. In the Arrowheads section, choose Closed Filled from the 1st: drop-down list. Click OK.

8. Choose Format. In the Vertical Justification section, choose Centered from the drop-down list. This centers the text next to the end of the leader. Click OK.

9. Click Save, then OK to save the child dimension style and return to your drawing.

10. Choose Angular Dimension from the Dimension toolbar. Follow the prompts:

```
Select arc, circle, line, or press ENTER: ↵
Angle vertex: Choose ① in Figure 15-35.
```

```
First angle endpoint: Choose ②.
Second angle endpoint: Choose ③.
Dimension arc line location (Mtext/Text/Angle): Pick a point
below the garage window.
```

11. Choose Leader from the Dimension toolbar. Double-click ORTHO and OSNAP to turn them off. Follow the prompts:

```
From point: Pick ④ in Figure 15-35.
To point:   Pick ⑤.
To point (Format/Annotation/Undo)<Annotation>: ↵
Annotation (or press ENTER for options): To breezeway ↵
MText: ↵
```

12. Save your drawing. It should look like Figure 15-35.

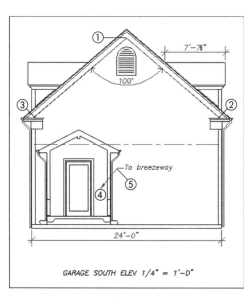

Figure 15-35: The garage with linear, angular, and leader dimensions.

Changing Dimensions

There are several ways to change dimensions in a drawing. You can choose a new dimension style, modify the characteristics of the dimension style in use, or override the dimension style with different dimension options for one dimension that you want to be an exception. You can also change current dimensions. Some dimension editing techniques were covered in the last chapter. This section explains how to make changes related to dimension styles.

Choosing a new current dimension style

To change dimension styles, or choose the child of a parent dimension style, follow these steps:

1. Choose Dimension Style from the Dimension toolbar.

2. Click the Current drop-down list and choose the style you want.

3. If you want a child, choose the child type.

4. Click OK.

Existing dimensions remain unchanged, but any new dimensions you add from this point forward will use the new current dimension style.

Modifying a dimension to use a new dimension style

You can choose Properties on the Object Properties toolbar and choose one dimension. In the Modify Dimension dialog box, you can choose a new dimension style for that dimension.

You can choose Match Properties on the Standard toolbar to match the properties of one dimension to those of another. Follow these steps:

1. Choose Match Properties.

2. At the `Select Source Object:` prompt, choose the dimension whose properties you want to copy.

3. At the `Settings/<Select Destination Object(s)>:` prompt, choose the dimension or dimensions you want to copy the properties to. (Use the Settings option if you only want to copy some of the properties.)

Modifying dimension styles

You can easily change a dimension style. The advantage of changing a dimension style is that all dimensions using that style are automatically updated. To change a style:

1. Choose Dimension Style from the Dimension toolbar.

2. Choose the dimension style you want to change from the Current drop-down list.

3. If you want to change a child dimension style, be sure to choose the child type from the Style drop-down list.

4. Open the Geometry, Format, and/or Annotation dialog boxes and make the changes you want. Click OK to close these dialog boxes and return to the Dimension Styles dialog box.

5. Choose Save.

6. Click OK.

AutoCAD automatically updates all dimensions using that parent or child dimension style.

Overriding a dimension style

Sometimes you want to make an exception to a style for one dimension. A good example is suppressing an extension line in a tight space. It is often not worthwhile to create a new dimension style for such a situation. To override a dimension style, simply change the style without saving it, following these steps.

1. Choose Dimension Style from the Dimension toolbar.

2. Choose the dimension style you want to change from the Current drop-down list.

3. If you want to change a child dimension style, be sure to choose the child type from the Style drop-down list.

4. Open the Geometry, Format, and/or Annotation dialog boxes and make the changes you want. Click OK to close these dialog boxes and return to the Dimension Styles dialog box.

5. Do *not* choose Save. Click OK to return to your drawing.

6. Create the dimension. You can create as many dimensions as you want using the unsaved changes in the dimension style.

To start creating dimensions with the saved dimension style again, choose Dimension Style from the Dimension toolbar and follow these steps.

1. Choose the style you want from the Current list. Often, this means rechoosing the current style.

2. AutoCAD opens an alert message asking you if you want to save the changes to the style, as shown in Figure 15-36. Choose No. AutoCAD displays a message at the bottom of the dialog box, Discarded changes.

3. Click OK to return to your drawing. New dimensions will conform to the original dimension style.

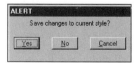

Figure 15-36: When you change a dimension style without saving it, and you choose the dimension style again, AutoCAD asks if you want to save the changes. Choose No if you made the changes only to override the dimension style.

Overriding the dimension style of an existing dimension

You may not realize that you need to override a dimension style until you have created the dimension. Rather than erasing the dimension or undoing the command then overriding the dimension style and starting over, you can easily change the properties of any current dimension. Follow these steps:

1. Select one dimension.

2. Choose Properties from the Object Properties toolbar. AutoCAD opens the Modify Dimension dialog box. (Or choose Properties first and then select the dimension.)

3. You see the same Geometry, Format, and Annotation buttons that you see in the Dimension Styles dialog box. Choose the one you want and make the change or changes.

4. Click OK to return to the Modify Dimension dialog box and click OK once more to return to your drawing. AutoCAD updates the dimension.

Updating a dimension style

 The Dimension toolbar includes an Update button. This command updates selected dimensions so that they use the current dimension style, including any overrides you may have just made. Use this when you realize that you want to include some existing dimensions in the overrides you have made.

You could also use the Modify Dimension dialog box to make the changes, but since you have already gone through the dimension style properties and made the changes you want, it is easier to choose Update.

After using Update, AutoCAD leaves a `Dim:` prompt at the command line. Press Esc to return to the regular command line prompt.

The `Dim:` prompt is a leftover from AutoCAD's original method of dimensioning, which used a `Dim:` subcommand prompt.

Using the DIMSTYLE command

You can use DIMSTYLE to compare a dimension style with the current dimension style. To do this, follow these steps:

1. Choose Styles from the Dimension toolbar and choose the dimension style you want to be current. Click OK.

2. Type **dimstyle** ↵. Then type **r** ↵ to choose the Restore option.

3. At the ?/Enter dimension style name or press ENTER to select dimension: prompt, type a tilde (~) followed by the name of the dimension style you want to compare with the current dimension style. For example, **~standard ↵**.

AutoCAD lists the dimension system variables that differ and shows their settings, as shown in Figure 15-37.

```
Command: dimstyle
dimension style: CIR
Dimension Style Edit (Save/Restore/STatus/Variables/Apply/?) <Restore>: r

?/Enter dimension style name or press ENTER to select dimension: ~standard

Differences between STANDARD and current settings:
            STANDARD            Current Setting
DIMCEN      0.0900             -0.0900
DIMEXE      0.1800              0.1250
DIMEXO      0.0625              0.1250
DIMTM       0.0000              0.0313
DIMTP       0.0000              0.0313
DIMTXT      0.1800              0.1000
```

Figure 15-37: Using DIMSTYLE to compare dimension styles.

Copying dimension styles from other drawings

With proper planning, dimension styles make dimensioning much easier and produce more uniform results. Although you can save dimension styles in your templates, sometimes you may need to work with someone else's drawing or an old drawing that does not contain the dimension styles you need. To copy dimensions styles from another drawing, follow these steps:

1. Choose Insert⇨Block to open the Insert dialog box.

2. Click File and use the Select Drawing File dialog box to locate the file that has the dimension styles you want.

3. Click Open to return to the Insert dialog box.

4. Verify that in the Options section of the Insert dialog box, Specify Parameters on Screen is checked. (This is the default.)

5. Click OK to return to your drawing.

6. Press Esc to cancel the Insert command. AutoCAD does not insert the drawing but inserts the dimension styles. (AutoCAD inserts all the layers and text styles, too!)

7. If this process inserts more than you want, use Purge to delete unused dimension styles, text styles, and layers.

Dimension system variables

I have already explained — mostly in Chapter 5 — that AutoCAD stores settings in system variables. All the settings you make in the Dimension Styles dialog box are stored in a large number of system variables devoted to dimensions.

Note: To get a list of the dimension variables, choose Help⇨AutoCAD Help Topics and click the Contents tab. Double-click Command Reference, then double-click System Variables. Click the D button. All the variables starting with DIM are dimension system variables.

Once upon a time the only way to manage dimensions was by knowing all the dimension system variables and individually setting each one. Today, the Dimension Styles dialog box makes managing dimensions much easier. However, if you want to create scripts or AutoLISP routines to manage your dimensions, you need to understand how the dimension system variables work, because scripts and AutoLISP routines cannot access dialog boxes.

You can also use the DIMSTYLE command to list all the system variable settings for a dimension style. To start the DIMSTYLE command, type **dimstyle** at the command line. The figure below shows a listing for an architectural dimension style, obtained using the STatus option. You can get a great education in dimension system variables by printing out and perusing this list.

```
Command: dimstyle
dimension style: ARCH
dimension style overrides:
        DIMSD1    On
        DIMSD2    On
Dimension Style Edit (Save/Restore/STatus/Variables/Apply/?) <Restore>: st

DIMALT    Off              Alternate units selected
DIMALTD   2                Alternate unit decimal places
DIMALTF   25.40            Alternate unit scale factor
DIMALTTD  2                Alternate tolerance decimal places
DIMALTTZ  0                Alternate tolerance zero suppression
DIMALTU   2                Alternate units
DIMALTZ   0                Alternate unit zero suppression
DIMAPOST                   Prefix and suffix for alternate text
DIMASO    On               Create associative dimensions
DIMASZ    1/4"             Arrow size
DIMAUNIT  0                Angular unit format
DIMBLK                     Arrow block name
DIMBLK1   _ARCHTICK        First arrow block name
DIMBLK2   _ARCHTICK        Second arrow block name
DIMCEN    0"               Center mark size
DIMCLRD   BYBLOCK          Dimension line and leader color
DIMCLRE   BYBLOCK          Extension line color
DIMCLRT   BYBLOCK          Dimension text color
DIMDEC    6                Decimal places
Press RETURN to continue:
DIMDLE    0"               Dimension line extension
DIMDLI    1/2"             Dimension line spacing
DIMEXE    1/4"             Extension above dimension line
DIMEXO    0"               Extension line origin offset
DIMFIT    1                Fit text
DIMGAP    0"               Gap from dimension line to text
DIMJUST   0                Justification of text on dimension line
DIMLFAC   1.00             Linear unit scale factor
DIMLIM    Off              Generate dimension limits
```

Dimension system variables (continued)

```
DIMLIM    Off                      Generate dimension limits
DIMPOST                            Prefix and suffix for dimension text
DIMRND    0"                       Rounding value
DIMSAH    On                       Separate arrow blocks
DIMSCALE  48.00                    Overall scale factor
DIMSD1    On                       Suppress the first dimension line
DIMSD2    On                       Suppress the second dimension line
DIMSE1    Off                      Suppress the first extension line
DIMSE2    Off                      Suppress the second extension line
DIMSHO    On                       Update dimensions while dragging
DIMSOXD   Off                      Suppress outside dimension lines
DIMSTYLE  ARCH                     Current dimension style (read-only)
DIMTAD    1                        Place text above the dimension line
Press RETURN to continue:
DIMTDEC   1                        Tolerance decimal places
DIMTFAC   0.75                     Tolerance text height scaling factor
DIMTIH    Off                      Text inside extensions is horizontal
DIMTIX    Off                      Place text inside extensions
DIMTM     0"                       Minus tolerance
DIMTOFL   On                       Force line inside extension lines
DIMTOH    Off                      Text outside horizontal
DIMTOL    Off                      Tolerance dimensioning
DIMTOLJ   0                        Tolerance vertical justification
DIMTP     0"                       Plus tolerance
DIMTSZ    0"                       Tick size
DIMTVP    0.00                     Text vertical position
DIMTXSTY  DIMTEXT                  Text style
DIMTXT    1/4"                     Text height
DIMTZIN   0                        Tolerance zero suppression
DIMUNIT   6                        Unit format
DIMUPT    Off                      User positioned text
DIMZIN    3                        Zero suppression
```

Notice that DIMSTYLE states the current dimension style, including the overrides at the start of the listing. Here, DIMSD1 and DIMSD2 are both on, meaning that both dimension lines 1 and 2 have been suppressed.

The other DIMSTYLE options are:

Save	Saves a dimension style.
Restore	Makes a dimension style current.
Variables	Lists dimension variables like the STatus option, but lets you first choose which dimension style you want to list the variables for. You can choose the dimension style by selecting a dimension in the drawing, which is very convenient.
Apply	Updates dimensions to the current style, including overrides. This is equivalent to choosing Update from the Dimension toolbar.
?	Lists all dimension styles in the drawing.

You can also create dimension style overrides on the command line, using the DIMOVER-RIDE command, which you must type at the command line. You need to know the name of the system variable and the setting code you want. AutoCAD offers the Dimension variable to override (or Clear to remove overrides): prompt. To create an override, type the system variable and its setting. Then select the dimensions for which you want to override dimension style settings. To clear all dimension style overrides, type **c ↵**. Then select the dimensions for which you want to remove overrides. This is a convenient way to remove overrides.

Step-by-Step: Changing Dimension Styles

1. Open *ab15-b.dwg* from your CD-ROM.

2. Save it as *ab15-5.dwg* in your *AutoCAD Bible* folder. This is a tension arm for a commercial dryer, as shown in Figure 15-38. ORTHO and OSNAP are on. Running object snaps are set for Endpoint, Intersection, and Center. The Dims layer is current. If the Dimension toolbar is not visible, choose View⇨Toolbars and choose Dimension. Click Close.

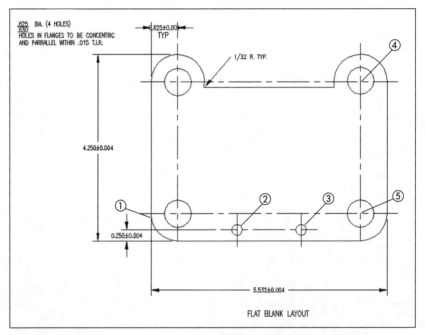

Figure 15-38: The tension arm needs some additional dimensions.

3. Choose Dimension Style from the Dimension toolbar. The current dimension style is CIR. Choose LIN from the Current drop-down list. Click OK.

4. Choose Linear Dimension from the Dimension toolbar. At the `First extension line origin or press ENTER to select:` prompt, choose the endpoint at ① in Figure 15-38. At the `Second extension line origin:` prompt, choose the intersection at ②. (Note: because ORTHO is on, AutoCAD dimensions a horizontal line even though the two points have different Y coordinates.) At the `Dimension line location (Mtext/Text/Angle/Horizontal/Vertical/Rotated):` prompt, choose an appropriate location above the bottom-most dimension.

5. Choose Dimension Style from the Dimension toolbar. Choose Annotation. Change the Tolerance Method to None. Click OK. Choose Geometry. In the

Extension Line section, check 1st to suppress the first extension line. Click OK. In the Dimension Styles dialog box, choose OK without saving the dimension style.

6. Choose Linear Dimension from the Dimension toolbar. At the First extension line origin or press ENTER to select: prompt, choose the intersection at ② in Figure 15-38. At the Second extension line origin: prompt, choose the intersection at ③. At the Dimension line location (Mtext/Text/Angle/Horizontal/Vertical/Rotated): prompt, pick the endpoint object snap at the right side of the previous dimension's dimension line in order to align the two dimensions.

7. The first dimension (the one you created in step 4) needs to be updated to remove the tolerance. Choose Update from the Dimension toolbar. At the Select objects: prompt, choose the first dimension. Press Enter to end object selection. Press Esc to exit the Dim: prompt. AutoCAD updates the dimension.

8. To list the overrides, type **dimstyle** ↵. Without choosing any option, press F2 to open up the AutoCAD Text Window. AutoCAD lists the overrides. Press F2 to return to the drawing window and press Esc to end the DIMSTYLE command.

9. To remove the overrides (no tolerance and the first extension line suppressed), choose Dimension Style from the Dimension toolbar. Notice that a plus symbol (+) appears in front of the current dimension style, indicating that overrides are present. From the Current drop-down list, choose LIN. AutoCAD displays the message, Save changes to current style? Choose No. Click OK.

10. Choose Linear Dimension from the Dimension toolbar. At the First extension line origin or press ENTER to select: prompt, choose the intersection at ④ in Figure 15-38. At the Second extension line origin: prompt, choose the intersection at ⑤. At the Dimension line location (Mtext/Text/Angle/Horizontal/Vertical/Rotated): prompt, pick an appropriate location to the right of the model.

11. To compare the CIR and LIN dimension styles, type **dimstyle** ↵. At the Dimension Style Edit (Save/Restore/STatus/Variables/Apply/?) <Restore>: prompt, type **r** ↵. At the ?/Enter dimension style name or press ENTER to select dimension: prompt, type **~cir** ↵. AutoCAD displays the listing shown in Figure 15-39. Press Enter twice to end the command.

```
Differences between CIR and current settings:
            CIR                Current Setting
DIMDEC    4                  3
DIMGAP    3/32               3/32
DIMTDEC   4                  3
DIMTIX    Off                On
DIMTM     1/32               0
DIMTOL    Off                On
DIMTP     1/32               0
DIMTXSTY  STANDARD           ROMANS
```

Figure 15-39: This listing compares the two dimension styles in this drawing.

12. Save your drawing. It should look like Figure 15-40.

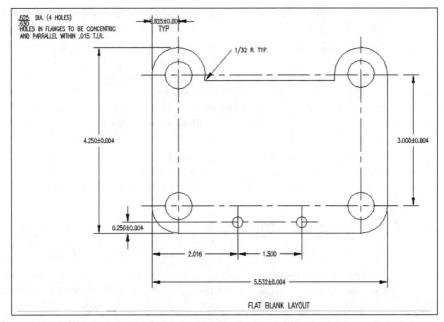

Figure 15-40: The correct dimensions have been added.

Creating Geometric Tolerances

Earlier in this chapter I explained how to format tolerances using dimension styles. AutoCAD offers another way to specify tolerances — geometric tolerances — using the TOLERANCE command. This command creates *feature control frames,* which define tolerances. This method of denoting tolerances is used to conform to international standards such as ISO (International Standards Organization), ANSI (American National Standards Institute), or JIS (Japanese Industrial Standard). Figure 15-41 shows a drawing using tolerance feature control frames.

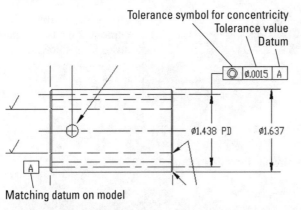

Tolerance symbol for concentricity
Tolerance value
Datum

Matching datum on model

Figure 15-41: An example of AutoCAD's tolerance feature control frames.

Credit: Thanks to Jerry Butterfield of Clow Value Company, Oskaloosa, Iowa, for this drawing.

Starting the tolerance frame

To start the frame, choose Tolerance from the Dimension toolbar, which opens the Symbol dialog box, as shown in Figure 15-42. Choose the symbol for the geometric characteristic you are tolerancing. (Table 15-3 explains these symbols.) Click OK. If you don't need any symbol, simply click OK.

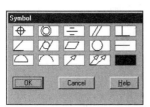

Figure 15-42: The Symbol dialog box.

	Table 15-3 Tolerance Symbols		
Symbol	**Name**	**Symbol**	**Name**
⊕	Position	▱	Flatness
◎	Concentricity	○	Circularity
≐	Symmetry	—	Straightness
∥	Parallelism	◠	Surface profile
⊥	Perpendicularity	◠	Line profile
∠	Angularity	⟋	Circular runout
⌀	Cylindricity	⟋⟋	Total runout

Building the frame

Once you choose a symbol from the Symbol dialog box and click OK, AutoCAD opens the Geometric Tolerance dialog box, shown in Figure 15-43.

Use this dialog box to build the frame. As you can see in Figure 15-43, the symbol you previously chose is already inserted into the frame in the Sym column — in this case, the concentricity symbol.

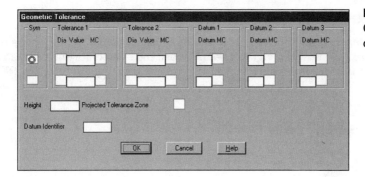

Figure 15-43: The Geometric Tolerance dialog box.

The frame allows you to create two tolerances, three datum references (for up to three dimensions), a projected tolerance zone value and symbol, and a datum identifier. You will rarely, if ever, use all the features in the frame.

Follow these steps to build the frame:

1. To insert a diameter symbol before the first tolerance, click the Dia box in the Tolerance 1 section.

2. Type the tolerance value in the Value box.

3. If you want to specify a material condition, click the MC box. AutoCAD opens the Material Condition dialog box, shown in Figure 15-44. Choose the symbol you want and click OK.

Figure 15-44: The Material Condition dialog box.

4. If desired, complete a second tolerance.

5. If desired, type a datum in the Datum box of the Datum 1 section, usually A.

6. If desired, add a material condition, using the same method described in step 3.

7. If desired, type in datum references in the Datum 2 and Datum 3 sections, usually B and C with material conditions.

8. If you need to specify a projected tolerance zone for a perpendicular part, type in the height. Then click the Projected Tolerance Zone box to insert the Projected Tolerance Zone symbol.

9. Finally, if you wish to specify a datum identifier, type the identifier letter in the Datum Identifier box.

10. Click OK to return to your drawing.

Tip

If you choose a material condition symbol and then change your mind, click the symbol to open the Material Condition dialog box and click the black empty box. Click OK to delete your symbol.

Inserting the tolerance frame

After you complete the frame, AutoCAD returns you to your drawing and offers the `Enter tolerance location:` prompt. Specify any point to insert the frame.

Tip

You can create a matching Datum reference to place on your model by creating a tolerance frame with no symbol and only the Datum letter.

Editing a tolerance frame

To edit a geometric tolerance, choose Modify⇨Object⇨Text, which starts the DDEDIT command. AutoCAD opens the Geometric Tolerance dialog box, and you can make any changes you need. Click OK to return to your drawing.

Step-by-Step: Creating Geometric Tolerances

On the CD-ROM

1. Open *ab15-c.dwg* from your CD-ROM.

2. Save it as *ab15-6.dwg* in your *AutoCAD Bible* folder. This drawing of a gear operator is shown in Figure 15-45. The Dim layer is current. If the Dimension toolbar is not visible, choose View⇨Toolbars and choose Dimension. Click Close.

3. Choose Tolerance from the Dimension toolbar. Choose the top left symbol (for position) in the Symbol dialog box and click OK.

4. In the Tolerance 1 section of the Geometric Tolerance dialog box, click the Dia box to insert the diameter symbol. In the Value box, type **.004**. Click the MC box. In the Material Condition dialog box, choose the first image tile (for Maximum material condition). Click OK.

5. In the Datum 1 section, type **B** in the Datum box. Click OK.

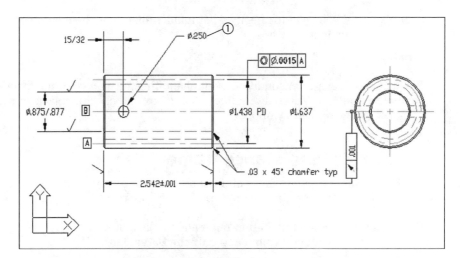

Figure 15-45: A mechanical drawing using geometric tolerances.

6. At the `Enter tolerance location:` prompt, pick ① in Figure 15-45. AutoCAD places the geometric tolerance.

7. Save your drawing. It should look like Figure 15-46.

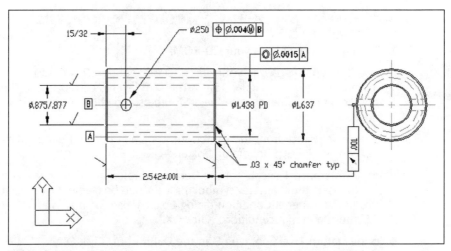

Figure 15-46: The drawing with the added geometric tolerance frame.

Summary

In this chapter you gained a thorough understanding of how to use dimension styles to organize your dimensions.

Use the Geometry, Format, and Annotation dialog boxes to define dimension styles. To further organize dimension styles, you can create families so that certain types of dimensions, such as angular or radial dimensions, can have their own set of properties.

You can change and override dimension styles. You can also copy dimension styles from other drawings.

Mechanical drawings usually require tolerance notation. You can create tolerances by defining them in a dimension style. You can also create geometric tolerances in tolerance frames to conform to international drafting standards.

✦   ✦   ✦

Drawing Complex Objects

AutoCAD's Complex Objects

AutoCAD offers a number of complex objects that can help you create accurate, professional drawings. Polylines are single objects that can combine line segments and arcs. Splines are mathematically controlled curves based on points you specify. Regions and boundaries create complex shapes from existing objects. Hatches create a solid or patterned fill. Multilines are sets of parallel lines. Sketching is a way to create freehand drawings. Digitizing with a tablet is a process that is used to reproduce an existing paper drawing. In this chapter I introduce you to these complex objects and explain how to use them.

Creating and Editing Polylines

Polylines are single objects that combine line segments and arcs. They are unique in that they can have a width, allowing you to make thick lines and arcs. In certain situations, it is useful to be able to edit an entire set of lines and arcs as one object. Polylines ensure that all the vertices of a closed area actually meet, which is very helpful if you want to hatch the area. They are also very useful for 3D drawing. In short, polylines are a neat, clean way to draw.

The RECTANG and POLYGON commands create polylines. Figure 16-1 shows a few examples of polylines.

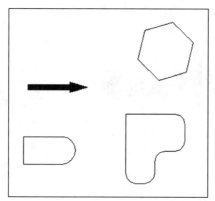

Figure 16-1: Some polylines.

Using the PLINE command

To draw a polyline, choose Polyline from the Draw toolbar. This starts the PLINE command. AutoCAD responds with the `Start point:` prompt. Specify the start point. Then AutoCAD responds with the `Arc/Close/Halfwidth/Length/Undo/Width/<Endpoint of line>:` prompt. It offers the following options:

✦ **Arc:** Lets you draw arcs. This option opens up a set of arc suboptions, which are explained later in this section.

✦ **Close:** Closes a polyline by drawing a line from the endpoint of the last line segment to the start point of the polyline.

✦ **Halfwidth:** Defines half the width of the polyline — the distance from the center of the polyline to its edge. AutoCAD asks you for the starting half-width and the ending half-width, letting you create polylines that are tapered.

✦ **Length:** Specifies the length of the next line segment. AutoCAD draws the line segment in the same direction as the last line segment or tangent to the last arc.

✦ **Undo:** Undoes the last line segment.

✦ **Width:** Defines the width of the polyline. AutoCAD asks you for the starting width and the ending width, letting you create polylines that are tapered.

✦ **Endpoint of line:** This is the default and lets you create a line segment.

Like the LINE command, PLINE continues to prompt you for more endpoints, repeating the entire prompt each time. When you are done, press Enter to end the command.

Note

When you create wide polylines, AutoCAD fills them if FILL is on — which it is by default. To turn FILL off, type **fill** ↵ and **off** ↵. You must regenerate the drawing to see the effect.

If you choose Arc, AutoCAD responds with the `Angle/CEnter/CLose/Direction/` `Halfwidth/Line/Radius/Second pt/Undo/Width/<Endpoint of arc>:` prompt. While this may seem overwhelming, most of the options are similar to the ARC command options. If you need a review, see Chapter 7. The arc options are:

✦ **Angle:** Specifies the included angle.

✦ **CEnter:** Specifies the arc's center.

✦ **CLose:** Closes the polyline by drawing a line from the endpoint of the last arc to the start point of the polyline.

✦ **Direction:** Specifies the direction of the arc from the start point.

✦ **Halfwidth:** Defines half the width of the polyline — the distance from the center of the polyline to its edge. AutoCAD asks you for the starting half-width and the ending half-width.

✦ **Line:** Returns you to the main polyline prompt so you can draw line segments.

✦ **Radius:** Specifies the arc's radius.

✦ **Second pt:** Specifies the second point of the arc.

✦ **Undo:** Undoes the last arc.

✦ **Width:** Defines the width of the polyline. AutoCAD asks you for the starting width and the ending width.

✦ **Endpoint of arc:** Specifies the endpoint of the arc. This is the default. AutoCAD creates an arc tangent to the previous arc (continuing in the same direction).

PLINE continues to display the arc submenu until you use the Line suboption or end the command by pressing Enter.

Generating linetypes on polylines

When you create a polyline with a noncontinuous linetype, you may find that the linetype does not appear properly along the polyline. One reason is that the segments of the poly-line may be too short to fit the entire linetype definition — in this case the polyline appears continuous even though it is defined with a dashed or other linetype. You can tell AutoCAD to generate the linetype continuously along the polyline instead of starting the linetype def-inition anew at each vertex. This results in a more normal looking linetype along the poly-line. To do this, you need to turn on the PLINEGEN system variable. By default it is off (set at 0). To turn on PLINEGEN, type **plinegen** ↵ then **1** ↵.

As explained in the section "Editing polylines with the PEDIT command," you can also mod-ify the PLINEGEN system variable for existing polylines.

Step-by-Step: Drawing Polylines

On the
CD-ROM

1. Open *ab16-a.dwg* from your CD-ROM.

2. Save it as *ab16-1.dwg* in your *AutoCAD Bible* folder. It shows a small section of a drive block, as shown in Figure 16-2. You need to complete part of the drawing. ORTHO and OSNAP are on. Running object snaps are set to Endpoint, Midpoint, and Intersection.

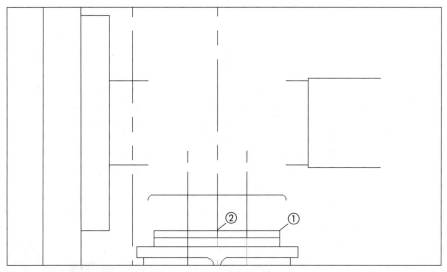

Figure 16-2: A small section of a drive block.

Credit: Thanks to Mary Redfern of Bethlehem Steel Corporation, Easton, Pennsylvania, for this drawing.

3. Make layer 3 current.

 4. Choose Polyline from the Draw toolbar. Follow the prompts:

```
From point: Choose the From Object Snap from the Object Snap
flyout.
Base point: Choose ① in Figure 16-2.
<Offset>: @-1/2,0 ↵ Arc/Close/Halfwidth/Length/Undo/
Width/<Endpoint of line>: Move the cursor in the 90-degree
direction and type 3/32 ↵.
```

5. Type **a** ↵ to continue with an arc. Follow the prompts:

```
Angle/CEnter/CLose/Direction/Halfwidth/Line/Radius/Second
pt/Undo/Width/<Endpoint of arc>: @3/16,3/16 ↵
```

6. Type **l** ⏎ to continue with a linear polyline segment. At the `Arc/Close/` `Halfwidth/Length/Undo/Width/<Endpoint of line>:` prompt, move the cursor in the 0-degree direction and type **11/32** ⏎.

7. Type **a** ⏎ to continue with an arc. At the prompt, type **@3/16,3/16** ⏎.

8. Type **l** ⏎ to continue with a linear polyline segment. At the prompt, move the cursor in the 90-degree direction and type **6-3/32** ⏎.

9. Type **a** ⏎ to continue with an arc. At the prompt, type **@-5/16,5/16** ⏎.

10. To create the last arc, type **r** ⏎. Follow the prompts:

```
Radius: 5-5/8 ⏎
Angle/<End point>: Choose the From object snap from the Object Snap
flyout.
Base point: Choose point ② in Figure 16-2.
<Offset>: @0,7-1/4 ⏎
```

11. Press Enter to exit the PLINE command. If you wish, you can mirror the polyline to complete the shape.

12. Save your drawing. It should look like Figure 16-3.

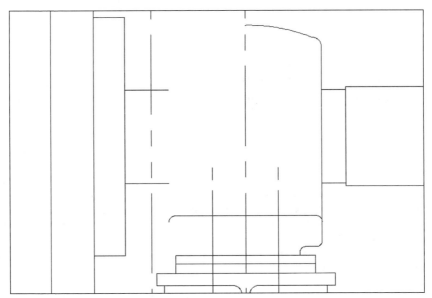

Figure 16-3: The completed polyline.

Editing polylines with the PEDIT command

Because polylines can be quite complex, AutoCAD has a special command to edit them, PEDIT. To edit a polyline, choose Modify⇨Object⇨Polyline. AutoCAD prompts you to select a polyline. Once you do so, AutoCAD responds with the `Close/Join/Width/Edit vertex/Fit/Spline/Decurve/Ltype gen/Undo/eXit <X>:` prompt. These options are:

✦ **Close:** Closes an open polyline. If necessary, it adds a segment to connect the endpoint to the start point. If the polyline is already closed, this prompt becomes Open. Open creates a break between the first and last segments of the polyline, but the polyline still appears closed.

✦ **Join:** Joins touching lines, arcs, or other polylines to the polyline.

✦ **Width:** Lets you specify one width for the entire polyline.

✦ **Edit Vertex:** Provides a set of suboptions for editing vertices. These are explained after this list.

✦ **Fit:** Turns the polyline into a curve that passes through the vertices.

✦ **Spline:** Creates a curve using the vertices as control points. The curve does not usually actually pass through the vertices. This is not the true mathematically exact spline that the SPLINE command produces (covered later in this chapter).

✦ **Decurve:** Returns a Fit or Spline curve to its original vertices.

✦ **Ltype gen:** Turns PLINEGEN on or off.

✦ **Undo:** Undoes the most recent edit.

✦ **eXit:** Exits the PEDIT command.

Tip

You can change any line or arc into a polyline. Start PEDIT and choose a line or arc. AutoCAD responds `Object selected is not a polyline. Do you want to turn it into one? <Y>`. Press Enter to accept the default. AutoCAD turns the object into a polyline. You can use this technique to turn a series of connected lines and arcs into a polyline. First, turn one of the objects into a polyline as just explained. Then use the Join option and select the other objects. When you finish object selection AutoCAD tells you how many segments were added to the polyline. In order to create a polyline in this way, the individual lines and arcs must connect exactly end to end.

When you choose the Edit Vertex option, AutoCAD offers a new set of suboptions, with the `Next/Previous/Break/Insert/Move/Regen/Straighten/Tangent/Width/eXit <N>:` prompt. You see an × at one of the vertices. This is the current vertex, which you can edit. The suboptions are as follows:

✦ **Next:** Moves you to the next vertex so you can edit it.

✦ **Previous:** Moves you to the previous vertex.

✦ **Break:** Lets you break the polyline. You can choose the Go suboption to break the polyline into two (although you can't see the break). You can move to another vertex using the Next or Previous suboptions and then choose Go. AutoCAD breaks the polyline between the original vertex and the vertex you moved to. Use the eXit suboption to return to the previous prompt. You could also use the BREAK command.

✦ **Insert:** Lets you insert another vertex. AutoCAD prompts you for its location.

✦ **Move:** Lets you move the vertex. AutoCAD prompts you for its location.

✦ **Regen:** Regenerates the polyline.

✦ **Straighten:** Deletes vertices. This works like the Break option with the same Next, Previous, Go, and eXit suboptions. Once you move to a new vertex, AutoCAD draws a straight line between it and the original vertex. If you don't move to a new vertex, this option only affects an arc, by changing it to a straight line segment.

✦ **Tangent:** Specifies a direction from the vertex. AutoCAD uses this if you choose the Fit option.

✦ **Width:** Lets you specify a starting and ending width of the segment starting with the current vertex. Use the Regen option after this command to see the effect.

✦ **eXit:** Exits this group of suboptions.

Caution You can make many changes during the PEDIT session. If you return to the command line and use the U or UNDO command, the entire session is undone. If you want to undo only part of the session, use the Undo options of the PEDIT command.

Note You can edit polylines with grips as well. A polyline has a grip at each vertex, making it easy to move vertices.

Editing polylines using the Modify Polyline dialog box

You can also edit polylines by choosing Properties on the Object Properties toolbar. Select a polyline and AutoCAD opens the Modify Polyline dialog box, as shown in Figure 16-4.

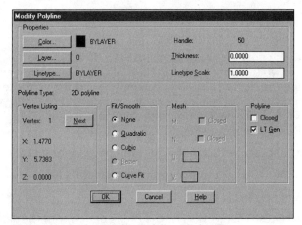

Figure 16-4: The Modify Polyline dialog box.

Notice that you can edit vertices by clicking Next in the Vertex Listing section of the dialog box. This is not as visually obvious as the × you see when you use the PEDIT command, but it could work with a simple polyline. The Fit/Smooth options let you choose the type of curve to create. Without the dialog box, you need to know the system variables and their settings to specify these options.

Note

The Mesh section only applies to 3D polylines.

Notice that you can close and open a polyline by checking and unchecking the Closed check box. You can also set PLINEGEN on by checking LT Gen. Of course, you can change the layer, color, linetype, and linetype scale as well. Choose OK when you have finished editing the polyline.

Step-by-Step: Editing Polylines

On the CD-ROM

1. Open *ab16-b.dwg* from your CD-ROM.

2. Save it as *ab16-2.dwg* in your *AutoCAD Bible* folder. This is a topological drawing as shown in Figure 16-5. The contours are polylines.

3. Choose Modify⇨Object⇨Polyline to start the PEDIT command. Select the polyline at ① in Figure 16-5.

4. At the `Close/Join/Width/Edit vertex/Fit/Spline/Decurve/Ltype gen/Undo/eXit <X>:` prompt, type **w** ↵. At the `Enter new width for all segments:` prompt, type **.5** ↵.

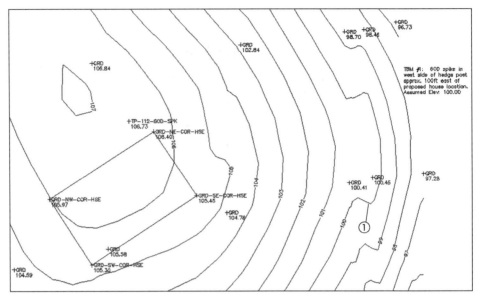

Figure 16-5: The topological drawing's contours are polylines.

Credit: Thanks to Henry Dearborn, AIA, of Fairfield, Iowa, for this drawing.

5. Type **e** ↵ to choose the Edit vertex option. At the `Next/Previous/Break/Insert/Move/Regen/Straighten/Tangent/Width/eXit <N>:` prompt, type **n** ↵ several times until the × mark is at ① in Figure 16-5. (There are many vertices—it's not important that you find the exact one.)

6. Type **m** to move the vertex. At the `Enter new location:` prompt, pick a point slightly above the existing vertex. Then type **x** ↵ to exit the Edit vertex submenu.

7. At the main PEDIT prompt, type **s** ↵. PEDIT smoothes out the polyline.

8. Type **x** ↵ to exit the PEDIT command.

9. Save your drawing.

Release 14 polylines are stored in the drawing more efficiently than in prior releases, which improves drawing performance and reduces the size of the drawing file. When a drawing from an earlier release is opened in Release 14, most types of polylines are automatically and transparently converted to the new format.

Using Splines

The SPLINE command draws a NURBS spline. If you care to know, that stands for nonuniform rational B-spline. Not to get too technical, a spline is a smooth curve that is defined by a series of points. The SPLINE command provides a more precise representation of a spline than the Spline option of the PLINE command. By default, the curve passes through each point you define. Figure 16-6 shows a bean bag chair created with two splines. By selecting the splines and pressing Esc just once, you can see both the chair and the grips that are on all the originally specified points.

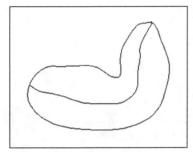

Figure 16-6: A bean bag chair created with two splines.

Drawing splines

To create a spline, chose Spline from the Draw menu. AutoCAD responds with the `Object/<Enter first point>:` prompt. Specify Object to convert a polyline that you have created with PEDIT's Spline option into a true spline. (It won't look any different, but its internal definition changes.) Otherwise, specify the first point for the spline.

If you choose a point, AutoCAD displays the `Enter point:` prompt so you can pick a second point. Once you do so, AutoCAD responds with the `Close/Fit Tolerance/<Enter point>:` prompt. Use these options as follows:

✦ **Close:** Closes the spline by connecting the last point with the first in a continuous (tangent) curve. AutoCAD asks for a tangent direction. You can specify a direction by picking a point (watch the spline image change as you move the cursor) or press Enter to accept the default tangent direction.

✦ **Fit Tolerance:** Specifies how closely the spline comes to the points you pick. The default, 0, creates a spline that passes through each point. If you want the curve to have a latitude of .5 units from the points, set the tolerance to .5.

✦ **Enter point:** The default is to continue to enter points. Press Enter to end point selection.

Once you have completed selecting points, AutoCAD prompts you for beginning and ending tangent directions. You can press Enter at both prompts to accept the tangents based on the curve's current shape. You can see the effect of other tangent points by moving the cursor and watching the image change.

Step-by-Step: Drawing Splines

On the
CD-ROM

1. Open *ab16-c.dwg* from your CD-ROM.

2. Save it as *ab16-3.dwg* in your *AutoCAD Bible* folder. This is a topological site map, shown in Figure 16-7. OSNAP is on with a running object snap set to Insert.

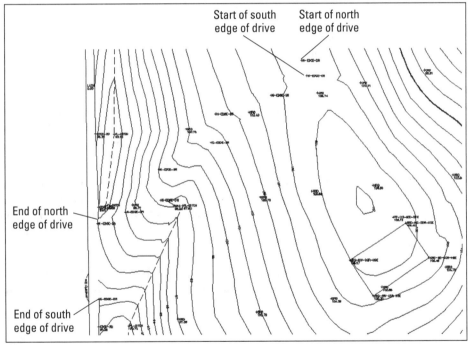

Figure 16-7: A topological site map. You need to complete the gravel road based on surveyor's data.

3. Use ZOOM Window to zoom in on the area near the start of the north edge of the drive. Choose Spline from the Draw toolbar.

4. At the `Object/<Enter first point>:` prompt, use the Insert object snap to pick the cross at the start of the north edge of the drive, as shown in Figure 16-7. Continue to pick the crosses marked N-EDGE-DR. Choose Pan from the Standard toolbar to do a real-time pan when you reach the edge of the display.

Press Esc. Continue picking points until you get to the end of the north edge of the drive, as shown in Figure 16-7. Press Enter to end point selection.

5. At the `Enter start tangent:` **and** `Enter end tangent:` **prompts, press Enter.**

6. Start the SPLINE command again and pick points for the south edge of the drive, from the start of the south edge of the drive to the end, as shown in Figure 16-7. Pan as necessary. Again, press Enter to accept the default directions for the start and end tangents.

7. If you wish, choose Zoom Previous on the Standard toolbar several times until you see the original view of the drawing. Save your drawing.

Editing splines

Like polylines, splines have their own editing command. To understand how to edit splines, you need to understand how AutoCAD stores them.

When you pick points to create the spline, AutoCAD stores these points as *fit points* (or data points). If the tolerance is zero, the curve lies on these fit points. When you select a spline at the command line, grips appear at these fit points. However, when you use the SPLINEDIT command, to see the fit points as grips, you must choose the Fit Data option first. Only then can you edit the fit points.

AutoCAD calculates *control points* based on the fit points. The spline is then calculated based on the control points, not the fit points. Most of the control points are not on the spline. When you use SPLINEDIT to edit a spline, and use the Move vertex option described below, AutoCAD displays the control points as grips and you can move the control points.

Figure 16-8 shows a spline created using point objects as the fit points — these were the points picked when creating the spline. Note that the spline passes through each fit point.

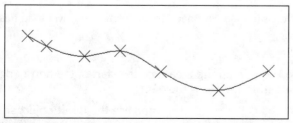

Figure 16-8: The point objects were used as the pick points. These are the fit points of the spline.

Figure 16-9 shows the same spline as in Figure 16-8 as it appears when selected with no command active. Notice that the grips are exactly on the fit points.

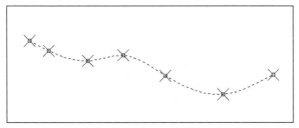

Figure 16-9: When you select a spline with no command active, you see grips on the fit points.

You can edit the fit points using grips, as shown in Figure 16-10.

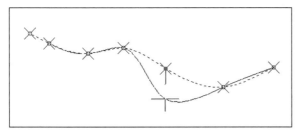

Figure 16-10: Editing fit points of a spline using grips.

Because AutoCAD calculates the spline based on the control points, it doesn't need the fit points to generate the spline. In fact, if you use the Move vertex or Refine options to move or edit a control point, AutoCAD now has to use only the control points to generate the spline and discards the fit point information so that you can no longer edit it. The Fit Data option also disappears from the prompt.

To edit a spline, choose Modify⇨Object⇨Spline to start the SPLINEDIT command. After you select the spline, AutoCAD responds with the Fit Data/Close/Move Vertex/Refine/rEverse/Undo/eXit <X>: prompt. Here's how to use these options:

✦ **Fit Data:** Fit data means the points you've chosen, their tolerance, and the tangents. Use this option to edit fit data. This option has its own list of suboptions that are explained after this list.

✦ **Close/Open:** If the spline is open, this option closes it by adding a continuous (tangent) curve from the last point to the start point. If the spline is closed, this option appears as Open. If the spline was originally closed, the spline Open removes the connection between the last and first points, although the spline looks the same. If the spline was originally open and you closed it, when you use the Open option, AutoCAD erases the curve that it added when you closed it.

✦ **Move Vertex:** This works like the Edit vertex option of PEDIT, except that here AutoCAD displays the points as grips and highlights them. You can use Next and Previous suboptions, select any point to move, and pick a new location for the highlighted vertex.

✦ **Refine:** Lets you refine the spline in three ways:

　✦ Add control points. This doesn't change the shape of the spline, but AutoCAD adjusts nearby control points slightly.

　✦ Elevate the order of the spline, which adds control points throughout the spline (but once you go up, you can't go down).

　✦ Change the weight of any control point. This is like the gravity they exert on the spline. Watch the spline inch toward the control point as you increase its weight.

✦ **rEverse:** Reverses the direction of the spline so that the start point becomes the end point and vice versa.

✦ **Undo:** Undoes the last edit operation.

✦ **eXit:** Closes the command.

When you use the SPLINEDIT command and select a spline, you see control points, not fit points. In Figure 16-11, the grips indicate the control points.

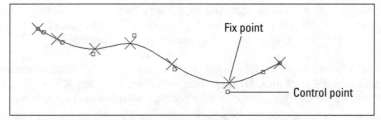

Fix point

Control point

Figure 16-11: When you choose the SPLINEDIT command and select a spline, the grips indicate the control points, which are not on the spline.

If you choose the Fit Data option, AutoCAD responds with the `Add/Open/Delete/Move/Purge/Tangents/toLerance/eXit <X>:` prompt. Descriptions of these options follow:

✦ **Add:** Adds fit data points to the curve. AutoCAD asks you to select a point and then automatically selects the next point as well, shown with highlighted grips. AutoCAD then prompts you for a new point, which must be between the two highlighted points. AutoCAD reshapes the spline accordingly.

✦ **Open/Close:** Opens or closes the spline using the fit points.

✦ **Delete:** Deletes a selected fit point.

✦ **Move:** Moves a fit point. You can use Next or Previous suboptions or the Select point option to select the point you want to move. Selected points appear as highlighted grips. AutoCAD prompts you for the new fit point location. You can also use grips to edit fit points.

✦ **Purge:** Deletes fit point information.

✦ **Tangents:** Lets you specify start and end tangents of open splines, or one tangent for closed splines. You can let AutoCAD calculate a default tangent.

✦ **toLerance:** Lets you specify the tolerance, which determines how closely the spline comes to the fit points.

✦ **eXit:** Exits the suboption menu.

Note

You can also use SPLINEDIT to edit 3D splines.

When you use SPLINEDIT and choose the Fit Data option, the grips appear on the fit points so you can edit them, as shown in Figure 16-12.

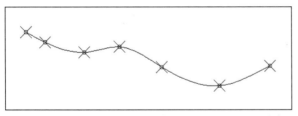

Figure 16-12: When you use the Fit Data option of the SPLINEDIT command, the grips appear on the fit points.

Note

You can choose Properties from the Object Properties toolbar and select a spline to open the Modify Spline dialog box. Here you can change only the layer, color, linetype, and linetype scale of the spline. However, the dialog box provides interesting coordinate information about the fit points (here called data points) and the control points. Click Next to cycle through the points. Click OK to return to your drawing.

Step-by-Step: Editing Splines

On the
CD-ROM

1. Open *ab16-3.dwg* from the *Results* folder of your CD-ROM. If you did the last exercise, you can open it from your *AutoCAD Bible* folder.

2. Save it as *ab16-4.dwg* in your *AutoCAD Bible* folder.

3. Use ZOOM Window to zoom in to the area shown in Figure 16-13.

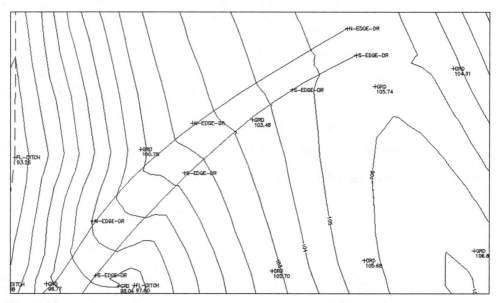

Figure 16-13: The topological site map with a gravel road created using the SPLINE command.

4. Use the MOVE command to move the S-EDGE-DR marker up and to the left slightly. You may find it helpful to turn off OSNAP.

5. Choose Modify⇨Object⇨Spline. At the `Select spline:` prompt, choose the spline that makes up the south edge of the drive. Note that the grips appear on the control points, which are different than the original points you selected to create the spline in the last exercise. Follow the prompts:

```
Fit Data/Close/Move Vertex/Refine/rEverse/Undo/eXit <X>: Type
f ↵ to edit the fit points. The grips move to the fit points.
Add/Close/Delete/Move/Purge/Tangents/toLerance/eXit <X>: Type
m ↵ to move a fit point.
Next/Previous/Select Point/eXit/<Enter new location> <N>: Type
s ↵ to select a point.
Select point: Pick the fit point nearest the S-EDGE-DR marker you
moved. AutoCAD highlights the grip.
```

```
Next/Previous/Select Point/eXit/<Enter new location> <N>: Turn
on OSNAP if you turned it off earlier. Pick the Insert object snap of the S-
EDGE-DR marker.
```

6. Type **x** ↵ three times to end the SPLINEDIT command.

7. Save your drawing.

Creating Regions

Regions are two-dimensional surfaces. They look like closed polylines, but
AutoCAD can calculate more information from regions than from polylines, such as
the centroid, moments of inertia, and other properties relating to mass. You can
also create complex shapes by combining, subtracting, and intersecting regions.
While these commands are most often used for 3D drawing, they are often used in
2D drawing as a preparation for 3D drawing.

You create a region from other objects. You can use closed polylines, closed
splines, circles, ellipses, and combinations of lines, arcs, and elliptical arcs that
create a closed shape. The shape cannot intersect itself like a figure "8."

Figure 16-14 shows a complex region. Although it looks like a circle with seven
circles inside it, it is actually a circular surface with seven holes in it. When you
select it, you can see that it is one object. The real proof of the pudding is when
you try to extrude it to create a 3D object out of it. You can then view it at an
angle, hide background lines, and clearly see the holes, as shown in Figure 16-15.

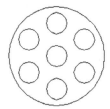

Figure 16-14: A complex region.

 To create a region, choose Region from the Draw toolbar. AutoCAD asks you to
select objects. Select all the objects and press Enter to end object selection. If all
the objects created a closed, nonintersecting shape, AutoCAD tells you.

```
1 loop extracted.
1 Region created.
```

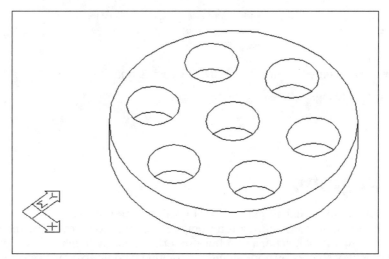

Figure 16-15: A region can be used to create a complex 3D object.

The original objects are deleted. If your objects aren't perfectly end to end, AutoCAD merely states:

```
0 loops extracted.
0 Regions created.
```

Note   If you want to keep the original objects, change the DELOBJ system variable to 0 (off) before you use the Region command.

Tip   In order to draw your original objects end to end, remember to use Endpoint object snaps. Also, don't forget that you can start a line or arc at the end of the last point drawn by pressing Enter at the first prompt. You can also use TRIM and EXTEND to clean up extraneous endpoints. The BOUNDARY command (see the next section) offers a way to create regions in situations where objects are not neatly drawn end to end.

If you had a hatch inside the objects, you lose hatch associativity. You can rehatch the region if you wish. When you create a region that is hatched, AutoCAD has no problem creating the region but doesn't quite know what to say about the hatch. Here's the response:

```
1 closed, degenerate or unsupported object rejected.
```

As mentioned earlier, you can combine, subtract, and intersect regions to create complex objects. The three commands to accomplish these functions are UNION, SUBTRACT, and INTERSECT. These commands are discussed in Chapter 24 because they are most often used in 3D drafting.

Step-by-Step: Creating Regions

1. Open *ab16-d.dwg* from your CD-ROM.

2. Save it as *ab16-5.dwg* in your *AutoCAD Bible* folder.

3. Choose Region from the Draw toolbar. At the `Select Objects:` prompt, use a selection window to select the entire model, which is shown in Figure 16-16. Press Enter to end object selection. AutoCAD responds with this message:

```
7 loops extracted.
7 Regions created.
```

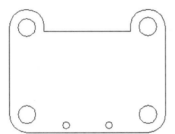

Figure 16-16: The outer profile and the six circles can all be turned into regions.

Creating Boundaries

The BOUNDARY command creates either polylines or regions from an enclosed area. This command has the capability of analyzing an area and ignoring intersecting lines that give the REGION command so much trouble. However, no spaces between objects are allowed. You may remember that in Chapter 12, I mentioned that you can use the BOUNDARY command to calculate the area of a closed space. Use the BOUNDARY command whenever you need to create a closed complex area.

To create a boundary, choose Draw⇨Boundary to open the Boundary Creation dialog box, as shown in Figure 16-17.

Figure 16-17: The Boundary Creation dialog box.

From the Object Type drop-down list, choose either Region or Polyline. Next, choose the boundary set. Usually, you can accept the default of From Everything on Screen. However, if you have a very complex drawing, choose Make New Boundary Set to temporarily return to your drawing. Specify a window around the area you want for the boundary. AutoCAD returns you to the dialog box. Now choose Pick Points. AutoCAD returns you to your drawing with the Select internal point: prompt. Pick any point inside the closed area you want for your boundary. AutoCAD starts to think as follows:

```
Selecting everything...
Selecting everything visible...
Analyzing the selected data...
Analyzing internal islands...
```

AutoCAD then prompts you for another internal point. If you want to create other boundaries, continue to pick internal points. Press Enter to end point selection. AutoCAD informs you how many regions or polylines it created and ends the command.

Note

By default, island detection is on. BOUNDARY detects enclosed areas that are totally inside the boundary area and creates polylines or regions of those enclosed areas as well.

When BOUNDARY creates a region or polyline, the original objects are not deleted. You end up with a region or polyline on top of your original objects.

Step-by-Step: Creating Boundaries

On the CD-ROM

1. Open *ab16-e.dwg* from your CD-ROM.

2. Save it as *ab16-6.dwg* in your *AutoCAD Bible* folder. This is a bushing, shown in Figure 16-18.

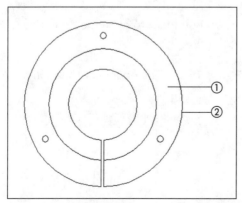

Figure 16-18: A bushing.

3. Choose Draw⇨Boundary. In the Boundary Creation dialog box, choose Region as the object type.

4. Choose Pick Points.

5. At the `Select internal point:` prompt, choose ① in Figure 16-18.

6. Press Enter to end internal point selection. AutoCAD responds:

```
4 loops extracted.
4 Regions created.
BOUNDARY created 4 regions
```

7. To see the new region, start the MOVE command. At the `Select objects:` prompt, pick ②. Move the region to the right—the exact distance is not important. You see both the new region and the original objects.

8. Save your drawing.

Hatching Areas

Hatches are patterns that fill in an area. Most types of drafting make use of hatching. In architectural drafting, hatched areas are used to indicate materials such as insulation or grass. In mechanical drafting, hatching often indicates hidden areas or certain materials. AutoCAD provides a large number of hatch patterns. Hatches are created from repeating patterns of lines.

Chapter 31 explains how to create your own hatch patterns.

In Release 14 you can create solid fills in the same way you create hatch patterns. Also, although it doesn't affect how you work, Release 14 drawings store hatch patterns in a more efficient way, using less memory and resulting in smaller drawings.

Figure 16-19 shows a drawing with a simple hatch pattern. Here the cross-section shows solid metal hatched to distinguish it from the holes.

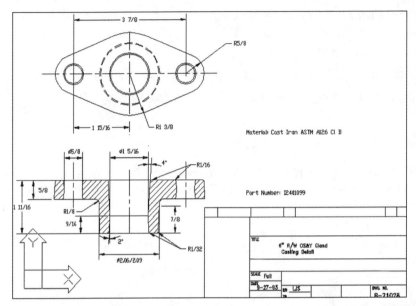

Figure 16-19: Hatch patterns help you distinguish between different materials or textures.

Credit: Thanks to Jerry Bottenfield of Clow Valve Company, Oskaloosa, Iowa, for this drawing.

Understanding hatch patterns

Hatch patterns have two special qualities:

✦ They are blocks. This means that all the lines that fill in an area are one object. Blocks are covered in Chapter 18.

✦ They are associative. If you edit the object that is hatched, the hatch automatically adjusts to fit the new shape of the object.

These two qualities make hatch patterns similar to dimensions.

There are several ways to specify exactly what area you want to hatch. In order to properly hatch an area, AutoCAD tries to find closed boundaries. Often, the key to successful hatching lies in how you construct the area you want to hatch. You can use the BOUNDARY and REGION commands covered in previous sections of this chapter to create complex closed areas that AutoCAD can easily find and hatch.

AutoCAD stores hatch pattern definitions in the *acad.pat* file. If you create your own hatch patterns, you can put them in another file with the filename extension *.pat*.

Tip

Create a separate layer for hatch patterns. You may want to turn off or freeze your hatch layer to reduce visual clutter or assist in selecting objects. Hatches are also typically a different color than the model you are hatching.

Creating a hatch

To hatch an area, choose Hatch from the Draw toolbar. This starts the BHATCH command. AutoCAD opens the Boundary Hatch dialog box, shown in Figure 16-20.

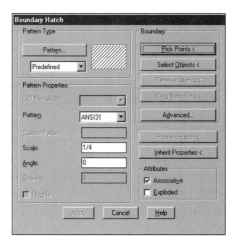

Figure 16-20: The Boundary Hatch dialog box.

This dialog box has several sections in which you choose and specify the hatch pattern, then define the area you want to hatch.

Pattern Type

The drop-down list in the Pattern Type section has three choices:

✦ **Predefined:** Lets you select one of AutoCAD's provided hatch patterns.

✦ **User-defined:** Lets you define your own hatch pattern by specifying the angle and spacing, using the current linetype.

✦ **Custom:** Lets you choose a pattern you have created in your own *.pat* file.

In this section, you can also click Pattern to open the Hatch pattern palette, which lets you choose the hatch patterns from a list or from image tiles, as shown in Figure 16-21.

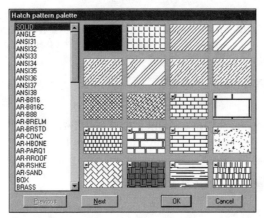

Figure 16-21: The Hatch pattern palette.

In the palette, click Next to see the next set of image tiles until you get to the end. Click either the image tile or the name on the list to choose a hatch pattern and click OK. The palette is simply another method of choosing the hatch pattern. You can also choose the pattern using the drop-down list in the Pattern Properties section of the dialog box.

Pattern Properties

This section lets you choose the hatch pattern and specify certain of its properties. If you have already chosen your pattern in the Pattern Type section, its name appears in the Pattern drop-down box. Otherwise, click the list arrow and choose the pattern you want. Either way, a picture of the pattern appears in the image tile in the Pattern Type section.

The ISO Pen Width box is available only for ISO standard hatch patterns. If you scroll down the Pattern drop-down list, you see several patterns that start with ISO. AutoCAD adjusts the scale of the pattern according to the pen width you specify. Notice that when you choose a pen width from the drop-down box, the scale shown in the Scale box automatically changes to be equal to the pen width. Note that you still have to separately set the width of your plotter pens when you plot your drawing.

The Custom box is available only if you have chosen Custom as the pattern type. Here you type in the name of your custom hatch pattern.

Use the Scale text box to type the scale of the hatch pattern. AutoCAD scales the hatch pattern proportionately to its definition. A scale of 1 (the default) creates the hatch as defined. A scale of .5 shrinks it by one-half. Figure 16-22 shows two hatch patterns using the ANSI31 pattern. The left one uses a scale of 1 and the right one uses a scale of .5.

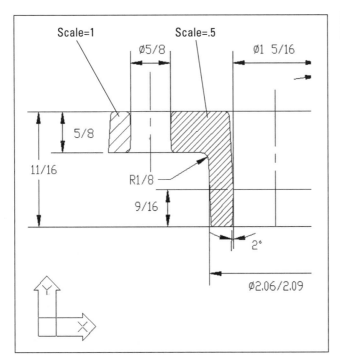

Figure 16-22: You can scale the hatch pattern to your needs.

 Note   If you choose a user-defined hatch pattern, you cannot scale it. Instead, use the Spacing text box to achieve the same effect.

Use the Angle text box to set the angle of the hatch pattern. Watch out here — many of the patterns are already defined at an angle. The hatch pattern in Figure 16-22 uses a 0-degree angle because ANSI31 is defined as diagonal lines.

The Spacing box is available if you choose a user-defined hatch pattern. Follow the steps below to define a user-defined hatch pattern. Figure 16-23 shows a user-defined double hatch with an angle of 45 degrees and .1 unit spacing.

1. Choose Hatch from the Draw toolbar to open the Boundary Hatch dialog box.

2. In the Pattern Type section, choose User-Defined.

3. In the Angle box, type an angle. When creating a user-defined hatch, you need to specify the actual angle you want to see.

4. In the Spacing box, enter the spacing between the lines. If you type .5, AutoCAD creates a hatch pattern with lines .5 units apart.

5. If you want to cross-hatch so that the parallel lines are crossed by an equal number of perpendicular lines, choose Double.

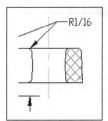

Figure 16-23: A user-defined hatch uses the current linetype and creates a hatch based on the spacing and angle you specify.

In the next section I explain how to place the hatch.

Determining the hatch boundary

The hardest part of hatching is placing the hatch, not defining it. Hatching an entire object is the simplest way to place a hatch. But often the area you want to hatch is fairly complex, and AutoCAD needs to do some calculations to determine it.

The Boundary Hatch dialog box offers two ways to specify the hatch boundary — you can pick points inside an area and let AutoCAD try to find an enclosed boundary, or you can select objects.

If you want to hatch an entire object, choose Select Objects. AutoCAD returns you temporarily to your drawing. Select all the objects you want to hatch. You can use all the standard object selection options to select objects. Remove and Add are especially helpful. When you are done, click the right mouse button (or press Enter) to end object selection and return to the dialog box. If you are sure about your hatch and its boundary, click Apply. AutoCAD creates the hatch and closes the dialog box.

Tip

It's usually worthwhile to click Preview Hatch before applying it. AutoCAD returns you to your drawing so you can see what the hatch will look like. The Continue button lets you return to the dialog box to either apply the hatch or make some changes. (For some reason, the Continue button usually obscures the objects you are trying to look at. Just drag it out of the way.)

If the area you want to hatch does not neatly fit into one or more objects, choose Pick Points. AutoCAD handles this task in the same way it handles the BOUNDARY command, also covered in this chapter. AutoCAD temporarily returns you to your drawing and displays the following:

```
Select internal point: Selecting everything...
Selecting everything visible...
Analyzing the selected data...
Select internal point:
```

AutoCAD is determining the *boundary set,* which is simply everything visible on the screen. At the `Select internal point:` prompt, pick a point that is inside the boundary you want to hatch. You can continue to pick internal points to hatch adjoining areas. AutoCAD helpfully highlights the boundaries it finds. Press Enter to return to the dialog box. Click Apply to create the hatch or Preview Hatch if you want to try it before you apply it.

Click View Selection if you want to temporarily return to your drawing and check which objects you have selected.

Choose Inherit Properties to use the hatch type, pattern, angle, scale, and/or spacing of an existing hatch. AutoCAD returns you to your drawing, and you pick a hatch pattern. You then return to the Boundary Hatch dialog box.

Islands

Islands are enclosed areas entirely inside a hatch boundary. Islands make hatching more difficult because sometimes you don't want to hatch the inside of the island. Figure 16-24 shows a top view of a 3-inch operating nut, which is a good example of enclosed areas with islands.

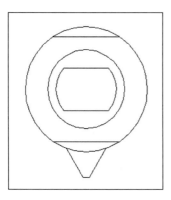

Figure 16-24: A model that includes islands can be more challenging to hatch.

Credit: Thanks to Jerry Bottenfield of Clow Valve Company, Oskaloosa, Iowa, for this drawing.

Note

Text is counted as an island, allowing you to hatch areas that contain text without hatching over the words.

Managing islands when you select objects to hatch

When you choose the hatching boundary by selecting objects, you must also select the islands. If you can select the entire area by window, you automatically include the internal islands. If you need to pick individual objects, you must also pick the islands individually.

In Release 14, if you later erase an island, AutoCAD retains hatch associativity and regenerates the hatch so it covers the entire outer boundary.

The resulting hatch depends on the boundary *style*. To specify the boundary style, in the Boundary Hatch dialog box, click Advanced to open the Advanced Options dialog box, shown in Figure 16-25.

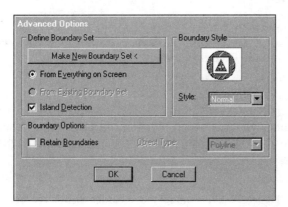

Figure 16-25: The Advanced Options dialog box is used to refine the hatching process.

There are three boundary styles that affect how islands are hatched:

✦ **Normal:** Hatches alternating areas so that the outer area is hatched, the next inner island is not hatched, the next inner is hatched, and so on.

✦ **Outer:** Hatches only the outer area and does not hatch any inner islands.

✦ **Ignore:** Ignores islands and hatches everything from the outside in.

Figure 16-26 shows three copies of the nut hatched in the three styles. To hatch this model, I selected the entire model except the spout at the bottom with a window, then used the Remove selection option to remove the two horizontal lines.

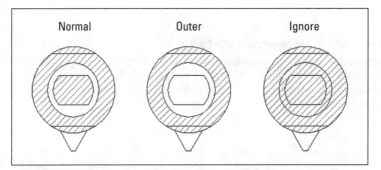

Figure 16-26: Hatching islands using the three boundary styles.

Managing islands when you pick points to specify the hatch

When you pick points instead of selecting objects, you do not need to select the islands. AutoCAD detects islands by default. Once you pick points, the Remove Islands button becomes available and you can select the islands to remove them from consideration. For example, if you remove all the islands shown in Figure 16-26, the result is the same as using the Ignore style — everything inside the outside boundary is hatched.

If you don't want AutoCAD to detect islands when you pick points, click Advanced. In the Advanced Options dialog box, uncheck Island Detection.

Other advanced options

In the Advanced Options dialog box you can also specify a smaller boundary set than the objects visible on screen. Use this only when you are picking points and have such a complex drawing that AutoCAD takes a long time to analyze the visible objects.

When you pick points to determine the hatch boundary, AutoCAD uses the same mechanism as the BOUNDARY command to temporarily create a boundary for hatching. Check Retain Boundary in the Advanced Options dialog box if you want to keep the boundary and specify if you want it to be a region or a polyline. Otherwise, AutoCAD discards the boundary once it completes the hatch. For more information, see the discussion of the BOUNDARY command earlier in this chapter.

Editing hatches

To edit a hatch pattern, choose Modify⇨Object⇨Hatch. AutoCAD prompts you to select a hatch object and then opens the Hatchedit dialog box, shown in Figure 16-27.

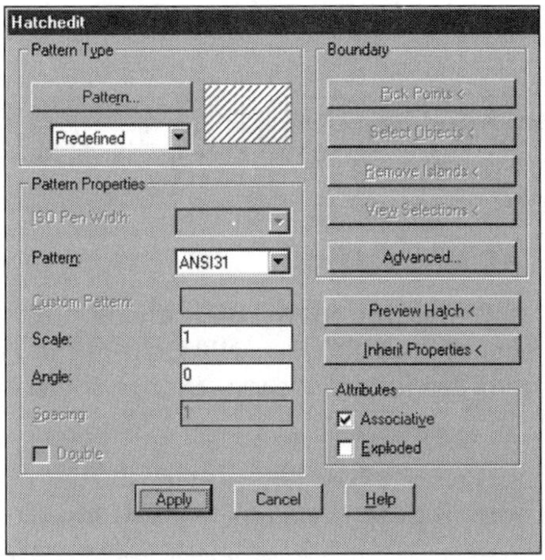

Figure 16-27: The Hatchedit dialog box.

As you can see, this dialog box is exactly the same as the Boundary Hatch dialog box, except that not all of the options are available. You can use this dialog box to change any of the hatch properties, however. You can choose Advanced to change the boundary style. You can also preview the hatch. You can change the hatch from associative to exploded. An exploded hatch is not a block — each line becomes a separate object.

When you have made your changes, click Apply to return to your drawing.

Because hatches are associative (unless you explode them), when you edit their boundaries, they adjust to fit the new boundary. However if the new boundary is no longer closed, or you erase an island, the hatch can no longer adjust and loses its associativity. AutoCAD warns you with the Hatch boundary associativity removed message.

To move or stretch a hatched boundary, you can select the hatch along with the boundary. However, say you want to change the boundary's layer. You may find it difficult to select the boundary without the hatch, especially if the hatch is tightly spaced. If you are at a Select objects: prompt, use a window to select the boundary and the hatch together, then use Remove to pick the hatch. Another option is to turn off the hatch's layer. Finally, you can zoom in enough so that you can pick the boundary without the hatch lines.

You may find it difficult to select solid fill hatches. In some locations, you can pick the solid hatch while at other points, you get the Other corner: prompt, meaning that AutoCAD didn't find anything. Try a crossing window. If necessary, try a crossing window at the edge of the hatch. This always selects the solid hatch but also selects the boundary. Hatches have a grip at their center. If you can find the grip and include it in the window, you can easily select the solid hatch.

Note   When you create hatches — solid fill or lines — AutoCAD displays them if FILL is on, which it is by default. To turn FILL off, type **fill** ↵ and **off** ↵. You must regenerate the drawing to see the effect.

Step-by-Step: Creating and Editing Hatches

On the
CD-ROM

1. Open *ab16-f.dwg* from your CD-ROM.

2. Save it as *ab16-7.dwg* in your *AutoCAD Bible* folder.

3. Choose Hatch from the Draw toolbar. In the Boundary Hatch dialog box, choose Pattern in the Pattern Type section and choose ANSI35 from the Hatch pattern palette. Click OK. In the Pattern Properties section, change the scale to .5. Choose Select Objects.

4. AutoCAD returns you to your drawing. Pick the two large circles in Figure 16-28 and press Enter to end object selection. Choose Preview Hatch. AutoCAD

returns you to your drawing again. Click Continue. In the Boundary Hatch dialog box, choose Apply to create the hatch and end the BHATCH command.

5. Again choose Hatch from the Draw toolbar. In the Pattern Type section, choose User-defined from the drop-down list. In the Pattern Properties section, set the angle to 135 and the spacing to .05.

6. Choose Pick Points. In your drawing, pick points ①, ②, ③, and ④ in Figure 16-28. Press Enter to end internal point selection. Choose Preview Hatch. AutoCAD returns you to your drawing again. Click Continue. In the Boundary Hatch dialog box, choose Apply to create the hatch and end the BHATCH command.

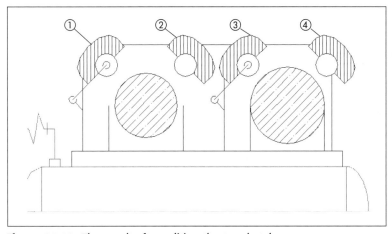

Figure 16-28: The result after editing the two hatches.

7. Click the circumference of the left large circle. Pick the top grip to make it hot. At the `<Stretch to point>/Base point/Copy/Undo/eXit:` prompt, type **@0,-.0667** ↵.

8. Choose Modify⇨Object⇨Hatch. At the `Select hatch object:` prompt, choose one of the hatches at the top of the model. Notice that AutoCAD selects all of them because they were created with one command. Change the angle to 90 and the spacing to .04. Choose Apply. Your drawing should look like Figure 16-28.

9. Save your drawing.

AutoCAD also has a command, SOLID, that creates solidly filled areas. (It is not at all related to 3D solids.) In general, BHATCH is much more flexible now that it can create solid fills. However, although the SOLID command is a 2D command, it is sometimes used in 3D drawing. When you create a 2D solid and give it thickness, it creates surfaces with tops and bottoms. See Chapter 24 for a description of how to use the SOLID command to create 3D models.

SOLID is used to create straight-edged shapes. If FILL is on, AutoCAD fills in the shape with a solid fill (that's why it's called SOLID).

To draw a solid, type **solid** ↵. AutoCAD prompts you for first, second, third, and fourth points. You *must* specify these points in zigzag order, not around the perimeter of the shape. So if you are drawing a rectangular shape, the third point must be under the first point, not under the second point. After the fourth point, AutoCAD continues to prompt for third and fourth points, which you can use to add to the solid. Press Enter to end the command.

Creating and Editing Multilines

Multilines are sets of parallel lines that you draw with one command. You can specify how far apart they are, and each line can have its own color and linetype. Multilines are ideal for drawing architectural plans where you need to draw an inner and outer wall. To draw a multiline, you first define, save, and load a multiline style. Then you can use the multiline style to draw multilines. There is a separate command for editing multilines that lets you break multiline intersections, as you would for the doors and windows in a floor plan. Figure 16-29 shows a floor plan for an apartment drawn using multilines.

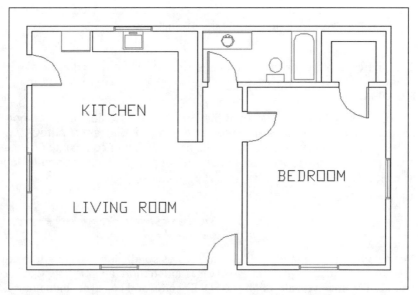

Figure 16-29: A floor plan of an apartment drawn using multilines.

Credit: Thanks to Bill Wynn of New Windsor, Maryland, for this drawing.

Creating a multiline style

The first step in drawing multilines is to design the multiline style. To create a multiline style, choose Format⇨Multiline Style to open the Multiline Styles dialog box, as shown in Figure 16-30.

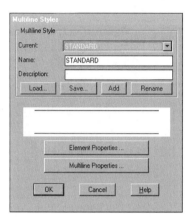

Figure 16-30: The Multiline Styles dialog box.

Like text styles and dimension styles, multiline styles group a set of properties under one name. AutoCAD provides a default multiline style called Standard that defines two lines 1 unit apart. Multiline styles have two parts: element properties and multiline properties. The element properties define each individual line element. The multiline properties define properties that apply to the multiline as a whole.

Defining element properties

To start defining the multiline style, type a new name in the Name text box and then choose Element Properties to open the Element Properties dialog box, shown in Figure 16-31.

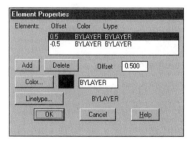

Figure 16-31: The Element Properties dialog box.

The Elements box lists the current elements of the multiline. Elements are simply the lines that make up the multiline. The offset defines the distance of the line from the start point when you start to draw. An offset of zero places the line on the start line. As you can see, the Standard multiline style has two elements, each .5 units from the start point. Figure 16-32 shows the Standard multiline style as it appears in relation to the start point you pick.

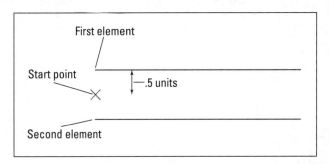

Figure 16-32: The Standard multiline style places two lines on either side of the start point.

Note   You can also change the relationship of the start line and the element lines by using the Justification option when you draw the multiline.

To define the element lines of a multiline style, follow these steps:

1. In the Elements box, highlight the first element. Even if you typed a new name for the multiline style, the elements listed are the same as the current multiline style.

Tip   When creating a new multiline style, first set as current the multiline style that is the most similar to the one you want to create.

2. In the Offset box, type the offset you want. The offset should be zero if you want the line to appear on your pick points, a positive number (in units) if you want the line to appear above your pick points, and a negative number (in units) if you want the line to appear below your pick points.

Tip   When defining the multiline style elements, think of the multiline as being drawn horizontally to the right to help you visualize what above and below mean.

3. Choose Color to choose a color for the line element.

4. Choose Linetype to choose a linetype for the line element.

5. Choose Add to add a new element or Delete to delete a listed element.

6. To define the next element, select the second element in the Elements box and repeat steps 2– 4. Continue to define elements until you are done.

7. Click OK to return to the Multiline Styles dialog box.

Note

A multiline style can have up to 16 elements. You can create some very useful and complex multiline styles by using varying linetypes.

Defining multiline properties

Choose Multiline Properties in the Multiline Styles dialog box to open the Multiline Properties dialog box, as shown in Figure 16-33.

Figure 16-33: The Multiline Properties dialog box.

Use this box to set the overall properties of the multiline. Figure 16-34 shows the effects of all the possible choices in this box.

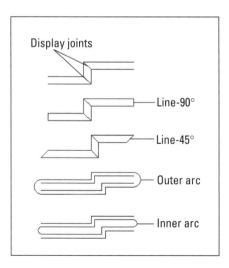

Figure 16-34: The options in the Multiline Properties dialog box.

You can also turn FILL on or off and choose a color to add a solid fill to the multiline. When you have made your choices, click OK to return to the Multiline Styles dialog box.

Saving a new multiline style

Before you can use the multiline style, you must save it. AutoCAD saves multiline styles in a file with the filename extension *.mln*. When you click Save, AutoCAD opens the Save Multiline Style dialog box, as shown in Figure 16-35.

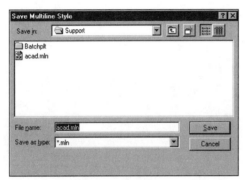

Figure 16-35: Saving a multiline style.

In general, you can save your multiline styles in the default file, which is *acad.mln*. Click Save to return to the Multiline Styles dialog box.

Loading a multiline style

Like linetypes, multiline styles must be loaded before you can use them. Choose Load to open the Load Multiline Styles dialog box, shown in Figure 16-36. Choose the style you created from the list and click OK.

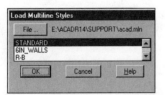

Figure 16-36: The Load Multiline Styles dialog box.

AutoCAD returns you to the Multiline Styles dialog box. You are now ready to use the multiline style. Click OK to return to your drawing.

You can also use the Multiline Styles dialog box to rename multiline styles and make another multiline style current.

Step-by-Step: Creating a Multiline Style

On the CD-ROM

1. Open *ab16-g.dwg* from your CD-ROM.

2. Save it as *ab16-8.dwg* in your *AutoCAD Bible* folder. This is a site plan, shown in Figure 16-37.

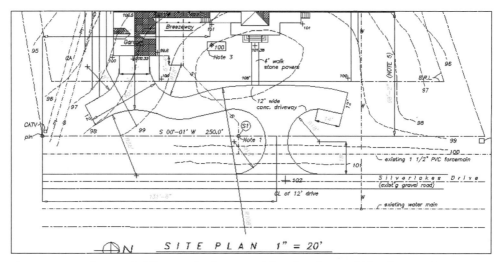

Figure 16-37: The parallel lines at the bottom of the site plan could be drawn using a multiline.

3. Choose Format⇨Multiline Style to open the Multiline Styles dialog box. In the Name text box, type **siteplan**. Choose Save.

4. Choose Element Properties. With the top element highlighted, change the offset to 0, the color to black (it lists as white), and the linetype to dashdot.

5. Highlight the second element. Change the offset to −132 (11' times 12"), the color to magenta, and the linetype to continuous.

6. Click Add. Change the offset to −180 (15' times 12"), the color to red, and the linetype to center.

7. Click Add. Change the offset to −228 (19' times 12"), the color to magenta, and the linetype to continuous.

8. Click Add. Change the offset to −360 (30' times 12"), the color to black, and the linetype to dashdot.

9. Click Add. Change the offset to −480 (40' times 12"), the color to red, and the linetype to center.

If you are using someone else's computer, check with the owner before saving the linestyle to *acad.mln.* You can't do any damage, but the owner may not want to have your multiline style there. You can change the name in the File Name text box to something else, like *my_mls.mln.*

10. In the Save Multiline Style dialog box, you should see *acad.mln* in the File Name text box. You can also type a new *.mln* file name. Choose Save.

11. Choose Load in the Multiline Styles dialog box. In the Load Multiline Styles dialog box, find the SITEPLAN multiline style, highlight, and choose Load. Choose OK.

12. Save your drawing. If you are continuing on to the next exercise, keep the drawing open.

Drawing multilines

Defining a multiline style is the hard part. Once the style is defined, saved, loaded, and made current, you can draw with it. You may find you need some practice to get the hang of it since you are drawing more than one line at once. To draw a multiline, choose Multiline from the Draw toolbar to start the MLINE command. AutoCAD responds with the `Justification/Scale/STyle/<From point>:` prompt. AutoCAD also displays the current justification and scale. The default is to pick a point. From there you get the `<To point>:` prompt. After the first segment, you get the `Undo/<To point>:` prompt, and after the second segment, the `Close/Undo/<To point>:` prompt. Actually, these are the same options you have with the LINE command except that the MLINE command makes the prompts explicit. Here is how to use the options:

✦ **Justification:** You can choose Zero, Top, or Bottom.

✦ **Zero** places the zero offset in the multiline definition at the pick point. You do not need to have a line at zero offset, as is the case with the Standard multiline style. The top example in Figure 16-38 shows the Standard multiline style with zero justification.

✦ **Top** places the line with the highest positive offset at the pick point. The middle example in Figure 16-38 shows the Standard multiline style with top justification.

✦ **Bottom** places the line with the highest negative offset at the pick point. The bottom example in Figure 16-38 shows the Standard multiline style with bottom justification.

Figure 16-38: Drawing a multiline using the Standard multiline style in zero, top, and bottom justification.

✦ **Scale:** Multiplies the offset values in the multiline definition by the scale. The Standard multiline style places two lines one unit apart. A scale of 6 would place them 6 units apart.

✦ **Style:** Lets you specify the current multiline style. Type **?** ↵ to get a list of the available multiline styles.

As you draw a multiline, whenever you create a corner by changing direction, AutoCAD creates a clean corner with no intersecting lines.

On the CD-ROM

Step-by-Step: Drawing Multilines

1. Continue from the previous exercise. (If you didn't do the previous exercise, you should do it to create the multiline style.)

2. Choose Multiline from the Draw toolbar. AutoCAD displays the following message:

   ```
   Justification = Top, Scale = 1.00, Style = SITEPLAN
   ```

3. At the `Justification/Scale/STyle/<From point>:` prompt, choose the From object snap. At the `_from Base point:` prompt, choose ① in Figure 16-39 (press Tab until you get the Intersection object snap). At the `<Offset>:` prompt, type **@0,-10'** ↵.

4. At the `<To point>:` prompt, type **255'** ↵. If you wish, you can experiment by drawing other line segments. Press Enter to end the command. The drawing should look like Figure 16-39.

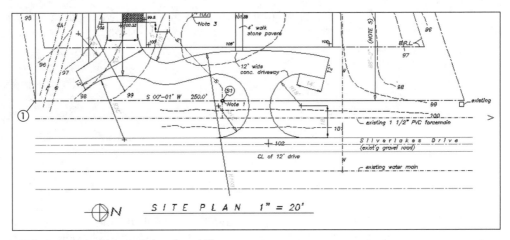

Figure 16-39: The completed multiline.

5. Save your drawing.

Editing multilines

The entire multiline — no matter how many segments it contains — is one object.
Many editing commands simply do not work with multilines. Table 16-1 shows the
editing commands and whether they work with multilines.

Table 16-1			
Using Editing Commands with Multilines			
Command	*Usable with Multilines*	*Command*	*Usable with Multilines*
ARRAY	yes	FILLET	no
BREAK	no	LENGTHEN	no
CHAMFER	no	MIRROR	yes
COPY	yes	MOVE	yes
ERASE	yes	ROTATE	yes
EXPLODE	yes	SCALE	yes
EXTEND	no	STRETCH	yes

You can also use grips to stretch, move, copy, mirror, and rotate multilines.

AutoCAD provides a special multiline editing command, MLEDIT. To start MLEDIT, choose Modify⇨Object⇨Multiline to open the Multiline Edit Tools dialog box, shown in Figure 16-40.

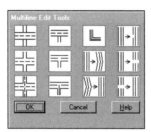

Figure 16-40: The Multiline Edit Tools dialog box.

The purpose of this dialog box is to let you edit multiline intersections and corners. You can also add or delete a vertex. Click one of the images, and its name appears at the bottom of the dialog box.

The first column manages crossing intersections. To edit a crossing intersection, choose one of the tiles in the first column and click OK. AutoCAD prompts you to pick a first multiline and then a second multiline. MLEDIT always cuts the first multiline you pick. The second one may be cut if called for by the edit type.

Note

Although AutoCAD prompts you to pick two multilines, they can actually be two parts of the same multiline, as in Figure 16-41. Figure 16-41 shows the results of using the three crossing intersection edits.

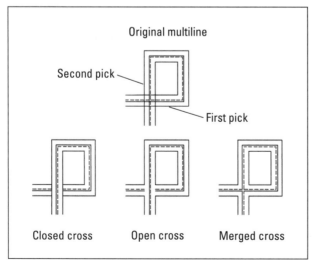

Figure 16-41: Creating a closed cross, an open cross, and a merged cross.

The second column manages tee-shaped intersections. To edit a crossing intersection, choose one of the tiles in the second column and click OK. AutoCAD prompts you to pick a first multiline and then a second multiline. MLEDIT always cuts the first multiline you pick. The second one may be cut if called for by the edit type and depending on the shape of the multiline. Figure 16-42 shows the results of using the three tee intersection edits.

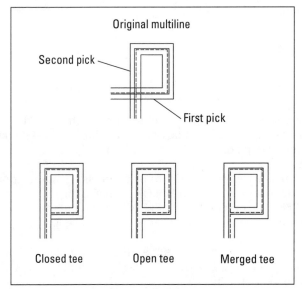

Figure 16-42: Creating a closed tee, an open tee, and a merged tee.

The third column manages corners and vertices. The top tile creates a corner. Figure 16-43 shows the result of using the corner edit.

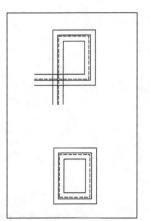

Figure 16-43: Creating a corner.

The second tile adds a vertex, and the third deletes a vertex. Choose the edit you want and click OK. AutoCAD prompts you to select a multiline. Be careful — the point you pick is the location at which AutoCAD adds or deletes the vertex. To see the current vertices, pick the multiline with no command active to see the grips. Figure 16-44 shows the result of adding and deleting a vertex. The grips show the vertices clearly.

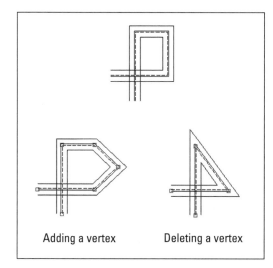

Adding a vertex   Deleting a vertex

Figure 16-44: The results of adding and deleting a vertex. The multiline with the added vertex was then stretched using grips.

The last column of the dialog box makes cuts through multilines and welds them back together again.

✦ Use the top tile to make a cut through one element of a multiline.

✦ Use the middle tile to cut through all the elements of a multiline.

In both cases, AutoCAD prompts you to select a multiline and then a second point. Be careful — the point you use to select the multiline is the first point of the cut. For a single cut, the pick point of the multiline also determines which element AutoCAD cuts.

✦ Use the bottom tile to remove the cuts. AutoCAD calls this *welding*.

For all of these editing tools, AutoCAD continues to prompt you for further edits. Press Enter to end selection.

Step-by-Step: Editing a Multiline

On the CD-ROM

1. Open *ab16-h.dwg* from your CD-ROM.

2. Save it as a*b16-9.dwg* in your *AutoCAD Bible* folder. This is a simple layout of two rooms using the Standard multiline style, as shown in Figure 16-45.

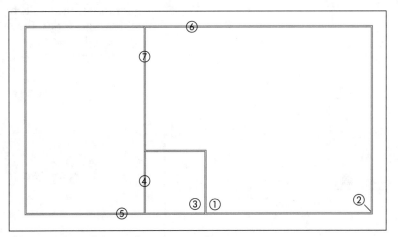

Figure 16-45: A layout of two rooms.

3. Choose Modify⇨Object⇨Multiline. In the Multiline Edit Tools dialog box, choose Delete Vertex and click OK. Note: Click once on each icon to see its label in the lower left corner of the dialog box.

4. At the `Select mline:` prompt, choose the multiline at ① in Figure 16-45. Press Enter to end multiline selection.

5. Pick the multiline again and click the grip at ②. At the `<Stretch to point>/Base point/Copy/Undo/eXit:` prompt, move the cursor in the 90-degree direction and type **4'** ↵.

6. Pick the multiline at ③ and click the grip at ③ in Figure 16-45. At the `<Stretch to point>/Base point/Copy/Undo/eXit:` prompt, move the cursor in the 180-degree direction and type **4'** ↵.

7. Choose Modify⇨Object⇨Multiline. In the Multiline Edit Tools dialog box, choose Corner Joint and click OK. At the `Select mline:` prompt, pick the multiline at ④ and ⑤ in Figure 16-45. Press Enter to end multiline selection.

8. Choose Modify⇨Object⇨Multiline. In the Multiline Edit Tools dialog box, choose Cut All and click OK. At the `Select mline:` prompt, pick the multiline

at ⑥. (The exact point doesn't matter.) At the `Select second point:` prompt, type **@3',0** ↵. At the `Select mline(or Undo):` prompt, pick the multiline near ⑦ in Figure 16-45. At the `Select second point:` prompt, type **@0,-3'** ↵. Press Enter to end multiline selection.

9. Save your drawing. It should look like Figure 16-46.

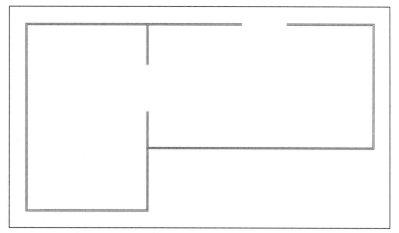

Figure 16-46: The edited multilines.

AutoCAD also has an old command, TRACE, that draws lines with width. In general, you can use polylines or multilines instead to create the same effect.

Note

Multiline styles are stored with the drawing, so that they can be updated and viewed, even if the multiline style file containing the multiline definition is not available.

Sketching

The SKETCH command lets you draw freehand in AutoCAD. Freehand drawing is useful for contour lines in architectural or civil engineering drawings, for illustrative effects, and for when you are feeling artistic. Although you may get best results if you have a digitizer and a stylus pen, you can sketch with a mouse or puck as well. Figure 16-47 shows some contour lines created with SKETCH.

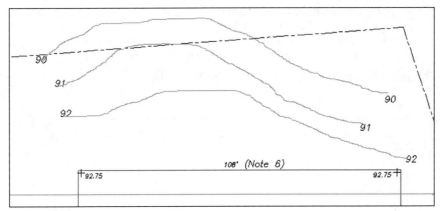

Figure 16-47: Contour lines drawn with SKETCH.

Sketch can create lines or polylines. Polylines are probably easier to work with if you need to edit the sketch later — you can use the PEDIT command. To specify whether SKETCH creates lines or polylines, set the SKPOLY system variable. A value of zero creates lines, and a value of one creates polylines.

Start the SKETCH command by typing **sketch** ↵. AutoCAD places you in a special sketch mode and displays a special menu on the command line.

```
Record increment <0.1000>:
Sketch.  Pen eXit Quit Record Erase Connect
```

Type the record increment, which is the length of the line or polyline segment you want to create. If the increment is too big, small movements do not create a segment at all and the sketch line appears jagged instead of smooth. However, you need to take into account the scale of your drawing and your zoom factor.

The pick button is equivalent to typing **p** and toggles the pen up and down. Follow these steps to start sketching:

1. Place the cursor where you want to start drawing.

2. Press the pick button. AutoCAD responds with the <Pen down> message. You can now draw.

3. Without holding down the pick button, move the mouse or stylus to create the shape you want. SKETCH creates a temporary, green line.

4. When you have finished, click the pick button again to see the <Pen up> message.

5. Move the mouse to the starting point of your next line or polyline. Continue in this manner until you have finished sketching.

6. Type **r** to record the sketch. AutoCAD tells you what you have created. The sketch changes to the color of the current layer and becomes permanent. For example,

```
4 polylines with 238 edges recorded.
```

7. Type **x** to exit Sketch mode.

Here are the other options:

✦ **Quit:** Quits Sketch mode without saving your sketch. The temporary line disappears.

✦ **Erase:** Erases temporary lines before you record them.

✦ **Connect:** Lets you continue drawing from the end of the last sketch. Use this when the pen is up. Type **c** and move to the endpoint of the last temporary sketch.

✦ **. (Period):** Lets you draw straight line segments from the endpoint of the last sketch. While the pen is up, type a period and move the cursor to the location of the endpoint of the line segment you want to draw.

Step-by-Step: Sketching

On the
CD-ROM

1. Open *ab16-i.dwg* from your CD-ROM.

2. Save it as *ab16-10.dwg* in your *AutoCAD Bible* folder. It shows the front elevation of a house. You will add the sketched path and contours, as shown in Figure 16-48.

3. Type **skpoly** ↵. Set SKPOLY to 1 and press Enter.

4. Type **sketch** ↵. At the `Record increment <0 -0 >:` prompt, type **1** ↵ and set the record increment to 1".

5. At the `Sketch. Pen eXit Quit Record Erase Connect:` prompt, move the cursor to ① in Figure 16-48. Click the pick button to put the pen down and draw the first line of the path. Click the pick button to put the pen up.

6. Use the same technique to draw the other lines in Figure 16-48. If you make a mistake, type **q** ↵ to quit and then start again.

7. When you are done, type **r** ↵ to record the lines.

8. Type **x** ↵ to end the SKETCH command.

9. Save your drawing.

Figure 16-48: A sketched path and contours.

Digitizing Drawings

In Chapter 3, I explained how you can use a digitizer to execute AutoCAD commands. One important use for a digitizer is to copy paper drawings into AutoCAD. Many companies have used this technique to copy old drawings that were drafted by hand so they could be edited using AutoCAD. Digitizing can also be used to copy artwork and logos into a drawing.

To digitize a paper drawing, use a special digitizing mode that turns the entire digitizer into a drawing tablet. To start the TABLET command, choose Tools⇨Tablet.

If you have been using the digitizer to execute commands, you need to reconfigure it to eliminate the command areas and enlarge the drawing area. Use the Configure option of the TABLET command and reconfigure the digitizer for 0 tablet menus. Respecify the screen pointing area so that the fixed screen pointing area covers the entire digitizing area.

Attach the paper drawing securely to the digitizer so it won't move as you work.

To set up the digitizing mode, start the TABLET command and choose the Calibrate option. AutoCAD prompts you to pick two points on the paper drawing and specify which coordinates they represent. To do this you need to mark two points on the paper drawing: take out a ruler and measure their distance. If the drawing has a title block, two corners of the title block are distinctive points to mark and measure. If the drawing is drawn to a scale — and it probably is — the coordinates you type should be the distance in real life, not the measurement. In other words, if the two horizontal points are one inch apart and one inch represents 48 inches (a scale of 1=48), you could enter 0,0 for the first point and 48,0 for the second point. However, it is usually useful to choose points over a wider area of your drawing. You can calibrate more than two points if you wish.

Note

If your drawing is distorted or uses a perspective view that you want to straighten out, you can calibrate additional points and choose either Affine or Projective calibration to account for the distortion. Affine calibration requires at least three points and scales the X and Y axes separately. Projective calibration requires at least four points and stretches the coordinates to adjust for the perspective view. You can provide up to 31 calibration points.

When you have finished specifying calibration points and coordinates, press Enter. Now your entire tablet can be used only for picking points. You can press F12 to use a menu or toolbar and press F12 to return to picking points, or type commands on the command line.

Note

You can turn Tablet mode on and off by starting the TABLET command and choosing the ON and OFF options. On some systems Ctrl+T also toggles Tablet mode on and off. Tablet calibration settings are lost when you close the drawing session.

Choose the command you need and pick points along the paper drawing. When you are done, turn off Tablet mode and do any editing and cleanup necessary.

If you have a digitizer, you can try this exercise. Otherwise, skip it.

Step-by-Step: Digitizing Drawings

1. Start a new drawing using *acad.dwt* as your template.

2. Save it as *ab16-11.dwg* in your *AutoCAD Bible* folder. This is a sheet metal template as shown in Figure 16-49.

3. Make a photocopy of Figure16-49 and tape it to the active area of your digitizer.

4. Choose Tools⇨Tablet⇨Calibrate. Follow the prompts:

```
Digitize point #1: Pick ① in Figure 16-49.
Enter coordinates for point #1: 0,0 ↵
Digitize point #2: Pick ② in Figure16-49.
Enter coordinates for point #2: 7,5 ↵
Digitize point #3 (or RETURN to end): ↵
```

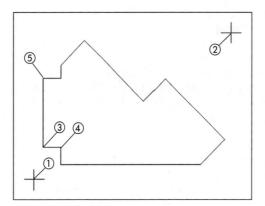

Figure 16-49: An unfolded sheet metal template.

5. Type **tablet** ↵ and **on** ↵.

6. Type **line** ↵.

7. In Figure16-49, pick ③ with the digitizer, then ④, then each line endpoint in turn counterclockwise around the figure.

8. When you've reached ⑤, do not digitize point ① again. Instead, type **c** ↵ to close the figure exactly.

9. Type **tablet** ↵. Type **off** ↵ to return the digitizer to screen pointing mode.

10. Save your drawing.

Summary

Several types of complex objects add greatly to AutoCAD's capabilities. Polylines can combine lines, segments, and arcs of any width into one object. Splines are mathematically calculated smooth curves fit to points you specify. Regions are two-dimensional surfaces. The BOUNDARY command can create regions or polylines from complex areas. Hatches fill in an area with lines or a solid fill. Multilines let you draw complex parallel lines at one time.

You can draw freehand using the SKETCH command, creating either lines or polylines. When you need to copy a paper drawing into AutoCAD, you use a digitizer in Tablet mode.

✦   ✦   ✦

Plotting and Printing Your Drawing

CHAPTER

17

Putting It on Paper

Most drawing jobs are not complete until you see the final
result on paper. Traditionally, drawings are plotted on a
plotter. However, you can also print a drawing on a regular
computer printer. There are many printers and plotters
available that can handle a wide range of drawing sizes and
paper types. In this chapter I explain the process of preparing
a drawing for plotting, including laying it out in paper space.
Finally I explore the actual process of specifying plotting
parameters.

Preparing a Drawing for Plotting or Printing

Once you have completed your drawing, there are often some
details to finish. If you did not start with a title block, you
may need to insert one. Even if you have a title block, you
may need to complete some of its annotation — such as the
date you completed the drawing. If there are layers you do
not want to appear on paper, you should freeze them.

Many architectural and mechanical drawings show several
views of the model. Now is the time to check that the views
are pleasingly laid out with enough space between them for
dimensions and annotation.

Doing a draft plot

You may want to do a draft plot, either to check the drawing itself or to be sure it will print out properly. Although you can preview the plot, sometimes the results are not what you want, and it pays to test the plot on inexpensive paper before plotting on expensive vellum. Draft plots for checking purposes can often be done on a printer. Some companies have ink-jet printers that accept 17" × 22" paper and are used exclusively for check plots. Even if the final plot will be all in black, color printers are a good choice for check plots because you can easily check the layer scheme.

Laying Out a Drawing in Paper Space

If you are using several views of your model, you should consider using paper space. Although paper space was designed for the needs of 3D drawings, it can be useful for 2D layout as well. For example, if you want to show views of your model at different scales, paper space is indispensable. Paper space is a tool specifically for laying out several views of a drawing. It is analogous to creating a sheet of paper the size you will plot on and placing views on the paper. You place the views by means of floating viewports.

Cross-Reference

AutoCAD also offers tiled viewports, which are discussed in Chapter 8.

Entering paper space

You draw in model space. Paper space is used to lay out a drawing. When you are in paper space, you can only view your drawing through floating viewports. In order to enable paper space, you must turn Tile mode off, so that you can use floating viewports instead of tiled ones.

Entering paper space is easy. Double-click TILE on the status bar. The TILE button is grayed. Your screen goes blank, and MODEL changes to PAPER on the status bar. If you click the View menu, you see a check next to the Paper Space item. There is also a new UCS icon, as shown in Figure 17-1.

To switch back to model space, double-click TILE again.

Using MVSETUP

MVSETUP is an AutoLISP routine that functions like any AutoCAD command. It helps automate the process of laying out a drawing in paper space. While you may eventually want to lay out your drawings on your own, MVSETUP is a great way to get started using paper space.

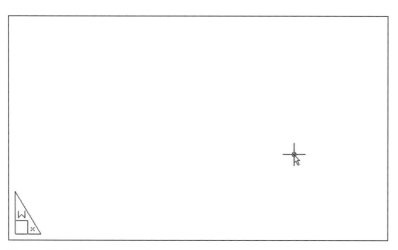

Figure 17-1: The screen when you enter paper space.

To use MVSETUP, follow these steps:

1. Double-click TILE on the status bar to enter paper space.

2. Type **mvsetup** ↵.

3. At the Align/Create/Scale viewports/Options/Title block/Undo: prompt, type **o** ↵ to choose the Options option. Choose the LImits suboption to tell MVSETUP to set the limits to the extents of the drawing. Choose Layer to set the current layer. The Units option sets the units. You can also choose to have the title block inserted or created as an external reference. (External references are covered in Chapter 19.) Press Enter to return to the original prompt.

4. Choose the Title block option and select a title block. You can easily insert your own title blocks by naming them identically to the choices in this option and placing them in AutoCAD's *Support* folder.

5. Use the Create option to create viewports. You have a choice of the number of viewports and their placement.

6. Use the Scale viewports option to create a scale for each viewport or all the viewports.

7. If necessary, use the Align option to align views in various viewports to each other.

8. At each step you can use the Undo option to undo the last operation.

9. Press Enter to exit the command.

Step-by-Step: Using MVSETUP in Paper Space

1. Open *ab17-a.dwg* from your CD-ROM.

2. Save it as *ab17-1.dwg* in your *AutoCAD Bible* folder.

3. Double-click TILE on the status bar. The Tile button is grayed, the Model button changes to display Paper, you see the paper space UCS icon, and your drawing disappears.

4. Type **mvsetup** ↵. At the `Align/Create/Scale viewports/Options/Title block/Undo:` prompt, type **o** ↵ to choose the Options option.

5. At the `Choose option to set   Layer/LImits/Units/Xref:` prompt, type **li** ↵. At the `Set drawing limits? <N>:` prompt, type **y** ↵. This tells MVSETUP to set the limits to the drawing extents once you insert a title block.

6. MVSETUP repeats the `Choose option to set   Layer/LImits/Units/Xref:` prompt. Type **l** ↵. At the `Layer name for title block or . for current layer <.>:` prompt, type **titleblk** ↵.

7. Press Enter again to return to the `Align/Create/Scale viewports/Options/Title block/Undo:` prompt. Type **t** ↵ to choose the Title block option.

8. At the `Delete objects/Origin/Undo/<Insert title block>:` prompt, press Enter to accept the default option. AutoCAD lists all the available title block options. Type **7** ↵ to insert the ANSI-A Size (in) title block.

9. To create a viewport, follow the prompts:

```
Align/Create/Scale viewports/Options/Title block/Undo: c ↵
Delete objects/Undo/<Create viewports>: ↵
Available Mview viewport layout options:
        0:      None
        1:      Single
        2:      Std. Engineering
        3:      Array of Viewports
Redisplay/<Number of entry to load>: 1 ↵
Bounding area for viewport(s). First point: Pick the top left of
the left viewport shown in Figure 17-2.
Other point: Pick the bottom right of the left viewport shown in Figure
17-2.
```

10. Again choose the Create option and repeat the prompts in step 9 to create the right viewport in Figure 17-2.

11. Save your drawing. It should look like Figure 17-2.

    Note

    You would still need to scale and pan the model to get the views you want in each viewport. You can also use the Scale viewports option to scale the objects, but you will still need to pan them to center them in the viewports.

Laying out a drawing in paper space on your own

Now that you have used MVSETUP once, you can try it on your own. Follow the same basic steps. First enter paper space.

In Release 14 you can use real-time and transparent pans and zooms in paper space. Also, zooms and pans do not require a regeneration as they did before.

Limits

Since you are now on a virtual sheet of paper, you should set the paper size using the LIMITS command. When you plot from paper space, you always plot at 1=1 scale. The upper right limits should be the actual size of the paper.

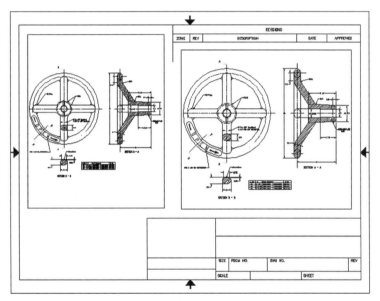

Figure 17-2: Using MVSETUP to create paper space viewports.

Layers

If necessary, create the layers you need. If you want to insert a title block, create a separate layer for it. The actual viewports should also be on their own layer, since it is common to freeze that layer so the rectangles do not show.

Title block

Insert the title block. You can have a file that contains just the title block. You can use a block or external reference.

Floating viewports

In order to see your drawing, you need to create floating viewports. Floating viewports have the following properties:

✦ Unlike tiled viewports, they are actual objects that you can erase, move, and stretch. They can — and should — be on separate layers, so that you can turn off the visibility of the viewport frames when desired. They do not need to take up the entire screen. You can define their size and location freely.

✦ In paper space, the crosshairs are not limited to one floating viewport.

✦ In paper space, the UCS icon (if set to On) appears only once, not in each floating viewport.

✦ You can create as many viewports as you want, but it's best to keep the drawing uncluttered.

✦ Whatever you draw in paper space does not affect your models — it is only in paper space and disappears when you return to model space.

✦ Once you have created floating viewports, you can switch to model space and work on your models. In model space, floating viewports are similar to tiled viewports — only one can be active at a time.

✦ You can save and restore viewport configurations.

To create floating viewports, choose View⇨Floating Viewports. You have the following submenu items:

✦ **1 Viewport:** This is the equivalent of the Fit option. It creates one viewport that fits the entire screen.

✦ **2 Viewports:** Creates two floating viewports. You can choose a horizontal or vertical configuration. You can choose Fit to fit them to the entire screen or pick diagonal points. The diagonal points define the combined two viewports, not each viewport.

✦ **3 Viewports:** Creates three floating viewports. You can choose from several configurations. You can choose Fit to fit them to the entire screen or pick diagonal points. The diagonal points define the combined three viewports, not each viewport.

✦ **4 Viewports:** Creates four floating viewports. You can choose Fit to fit them to the entire screen or pick diagonal points. The diagonal points define the combined four viewports, not each viewport.

✦ **Restore:** Uses a configuration you saved for tiled viewports, but applies it to floating viewports. Saving tiled viewport configurations is covered in Chapter 8.

✦ **Viewports On:** Turns on a floating viewport; displays the model in the viewport.

✦ **Viewports Off:** Turns off a floating viewport; does not display the model in the viewport.

✦ **Hideplot:** Instructs AutoCAD to hide lines during plotting. Hiding lines is covered later in this chapter and in Chapter 25. It is used for 3D models.

Start by choosing the number of viewports you want and choose either Fit or specify two diagonal points. You can now see your drawing in the viewport(s).

Viewport scale

The next step is to set the zoom for each viewport to exact scale. To do this, double-click PAPER on the status bar to return to model space. You can now access your models. Working with floating viewports in model space is quite similar to working with tiled viewports. Click a floating viewport to make it active. It shows a dark border. Now choose Zoom Scale from the Zoom flyout of the Standard toolbar. You need to use the inverse of the scale factor with the xp option of the ZOOM command. If you have an architectural drawing at a scale of 1:48, type **1/48xp** ↵. Each viewport can have its own scale.

Viewport layout

Once you have scaled each viewport, you need to go back and pan until you see what you want in the viewport. If you can't get it perfectly, don't worry — you can also change the size of the viewport itself.

Viewport size and placement

Now return to paper space by double-clicking MODEL on the status bar. You cannot access your models any more but now you can move and resize the viewports if necessary. You can use grips to stretch and move them or use the STRETCH and MOVE commands.

Layers

If you wish, you can individually set layer visibility in floating viewports. For example, you might have some annotation that appears in more than one floating viewport but there is no need to show it more than once. Or you may not want to use hatching in one of the viewports. You must be in model space. To freeze a layer in a viewport, click it to make it active. Click the Layer Control drop-down list on the Object Properties toolbar. Find the layer you want to freeze in that viewport and place the mouse cursor over the third column. The ToolTip says *Freeze/Thaw in current viewport.* Click the icon, then click the top of the drop-down list to close it. That layer disappears in the active viewport.

Note

You can also freeze/thaw layers in new viewports — meaning viewports that you have not yet created. Choose Layers from the Object Properties toolbar to open the Layers and Linetypes dialog box. The fourth column of icons freezes or thaws layers for new viewports. Click the icon for the layer you want and choose OK to close the dialog box.

Text

In general, text that relates directly to the model is created in model space — dimensions, leaders, section lines, and so on. However, annotation that applies to the entire drawing, title block text, or whatever, can be, and often is, created in paper space. Change to a text layer and use the DTEXT or MTEXT command as usual.

Dimensions

Dimensioning is usually done in model space but you can dimension in paper space as well. There as several advantages to dimensioning in paper space:

✦ You don't have to worry about the size of the dimensions. If you plot from paper space you plot at 1:1 scale.

✦ You can place the dimensions outside the border of the floating viewport, which may make it easier to fit the dimensions.

✦ You can easily dimension just one view of the model. If you dimension in model space, you see the dimensions in all the viewports unless you freeze that layer in some of the viewports.

However, dimensions in paper space are not associative. Also, you have to change the Linear Scale to reflect the viewport scale — otherwise, the dimension numbers come out wrong by the scale factor!

To dimension in paper space:

1. Open the Dimension Styles dialog box and choose Geometry. Check Scale to Paper Space. Click OK.

2. Choose Annotation, then Units. Set the Linear Scale to the inverse of the viewport scale. For example, if the viewport is scaled at 1/4XP, set a linear scale of 4.

3. You can now dimension objects in that viewport.

Tip

If you plan to plot at varying scales, remember to check Scale to Paper Space in the Geometry dialog box when creating your dimension style. This lets AutoCAD automatically adjust the size of your dimensions (arrows, text, and so on) to the scale of each floating viewport. As a result, all the dimensions appear the same size on your final plot.

In the next exercise you lay out the same drawing used in the previous exercise.

Step-by-Step: Laying Out a Drawing in Paper Space

On the CD-ROM

1. Open *ab17-a.dwg* from your CD-ROM.

2. Save it as *ab17-2.dwg* in your *AutoCAD Bible* folder.

3. Double-click TILE on the status bar to enter paper space.

4. Choose Format⇨Drawing Limits. Set the limits to **0,0** and **11,8-1/2**. This lets you plot to a printer if you don't have a plotter available.

5. Click the Layer Control drop-down list arrow. Choose the Titleblk layer to make it current.

On the CD-ROM

6. Choose Insert⇨Block to open the Insert dialog box. Click File. Choose *ab-a-blk.dwg* from the CD-ROM and click Open. In the Options section of the dialog box, uncheck Specify Parameters on Screen. At the bottom, check Explode. Click OK. AutoCAD inserts the title block, as shown in Figure 17-3.

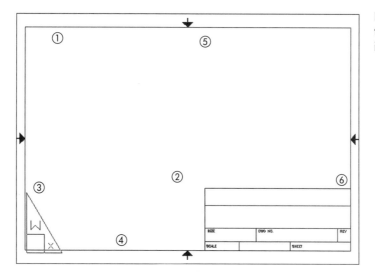

Figure 17-3: The title block inserted into paper space.

7. Click the Layer Control drop-down list. Choose the np layer to make it current.

8. Choose View⇨Floating Viewports⇨1 Viewport. At the First Point: prompt, choose ① in Figure 17-3. At the Other corner: prompt, choose ② in Figure 17-3.

9. Click the right mouse button to repeat the MVIEW command. At the First Point: prompt, choose ③ in Figure 17-3. At the Other corner: prompt, choose ④ in Figure 17-3. Again repeat the command and choose ⑤ and ⑥ in Figure 17-3. You now see the drawing in the three viewports.

10. Double-click PAPER on the status bar. It changes to MODEL and you return to model space. Click the top left viewport. Choose Zoom Scale from the Zoom flyout of the Standard toolbar. At the prompt, type **.4xp** ↵. Do the same for the top right viewport.

11. Click the bottom viewport. Choose Zoom Scale from the Zoom flyout of the Standard toolbar. At the prompt, type **.5xp** ↵.

12. Click each viewport in turn and pan until you see the view shown in Figure 17-4. It doesn't have to match exactly.

13. Return to paper space. Click the Layer Control drop-down arrow. Click the icon in the third column (Freeze/Thaw in current viewport) next to the np layer. Click the top of the drop-down box to close it.

14. Change the current layer to Text. Choose Draw⇨Text⇨Single Line Text. Complete the text in the title block at the default height as shown in Figure 17-4.

15. Save your drawing.

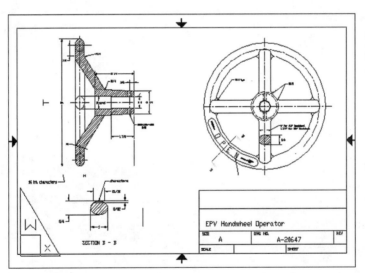

Figure 17-4: The completed drawing layout is now ready for plotting.

Note

The PTLTSCALE system variable controls linetype scaling in paper space viewports. By default, it is set to 1 so that the viewport scale controls the scale of any noncontinuous linetypes. This lets you have viewports of differing scales but display linetypes identically. When you set PTLTSCALE to 0, linetype scales are based on the drawing units where the object was created (in either model space or paper space). Linetypes are still scaled by the LTSCALE factor.

When you either change PSLTSCALE or change the zoom scale in a viewport with PSLTSCALE set to 1, you need to do a REGEN to update the linetype scales in each viewport.

Plotting a Drawing

Once you have laid out your drawing, you are ready to plot it. The first step is to check the plotter or printer — it should be on, connected to your computer, and have the appropriate paper in it. Your drawing should appear on the screen.

Plotter configuration is covered in Appendix A.

To start plotting, choose Print from the Standard toolbar to open the Print/Plot Configuration dialog box, as shown in Figure 17-5.

Although most AutoCAD users refer to plotting not printing, Microsoft Windows standards require that this button say Print. However, clicking it starts the PLOT command.

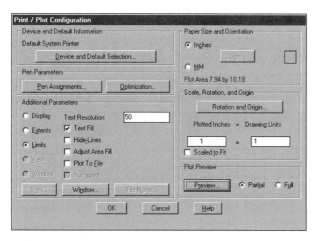

Figure 17-5: The Print/Plot Configuration dialog box.

Use this dialog box to set up your plot parameters. Many of these settings have defaults that you specify when you configure your plotter/printer. To configure a plotter/printer, choose Tools⇨Preferences.

Choosing a plotter/printer

Use the Device and Default Information section to choose a plotter/printer. Many companies have several output devices available, especially if they are networked. You may also use a printer for check/draft plots and a plotter for final plots. Choose Device and Default Selection to open the Device and Default Selection dialog box, shown in Figure 17-6.

Choose the plotter/printer you want from the list, then click OK. You can also use this dialog box to show and change certain device configuration parameters.(See the sidebar "Saving and using plot configurations.")

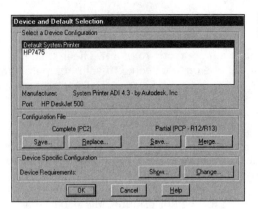

Figure 17-6: The Device and Default Selection dialog box.

When you have finished using the Device and Default Selection dialog box, click OK.

Saving and using plot configurations

Since there are so many options related to plotting, you can save your plotting parameters in a configuration file. You can then reuse this configuration so that you don't need to reset the plot configuration. You might want to do this if you commonly use different devices for draft and final plots or if you have certain drawings that require special settings.

There are two types of configuration files. Partial configuration files were used in Releases 12 and 13. They contain plot settings that are not related to your specific device and have the filename extension *.pcp.* You can use them if you exchange drawings with people who use Release 12 or 13. Release 14 introduces complete configuration files which have the extension *.pc2.* These files include settings specific to your plotter/printer and can be used for Release 14's new batch plot utility.

To save either type of configuration file, choose Print from the Standard toolbar and specify all the settings you want. Choose Device and Default Selection. Choose Save under Partial (PCP-R12/R13) or Complete (PC2). In the Save to . . . dialog box, choose a location for the file (the *Support* folder is probably a good idea), enter a filename that describes the configuration, and choose OK.

To use a saved configuration, open the Device and Default Selection dialog box.

✦ To choose a complete configuration file (*.pc2*), choose Replace. The Replace from PC2 File dialog box opens. Choose the configuration file you want to use. Click Open. Provide a unique description in the Describe Device dialog box. Click OK.

✦ To choose a partial configuration file (*.pcp*), choose Merge. The Merge from PCP File dialog box opens. Choose the configuration file you want to use. Click Open.

The saved configuration replaces the current one.

Assigning pen parameters and optimization settings

For any multi-pen device, you need to assign pens. Even a laser or inkjet plotter may make use of pen assignments for determining shades of gray or line widths. To assign pens, choose Pen Assignments from the Print/Plot Configuration dialog box to open the Pen Assignments dialog box, shown in Figure 17-7.

In AutoCAD, you assign pens according to color. If you are plotting in color, you may want to match each pen's color to the color you see on your screen, if possible. If you are plotting in black only, you match the pen's width to a color. For example, everything in black may be drawn with a .3mm-wide pen, and everything in red may be drawn with a .7mm-wide pen. The plotter assigns a number to each pen. You assign pen numbers to colors and then make sure the right pens are in the right holders in the plotter's carousel.

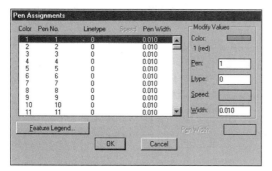

Figure 17-7: The Pen Assignments dialog box.

To change a pen assignment, click the color in the list box. Use the Modify Values section to change the pen, linetype, speed, or width.

In practice, you never set the linetype because you create linetypes in your drawing. You rarely set the speed, although if you have a multi-pen plotter you may need to adjust the speed of certain pens on certain types of paper.

The pen width setting is used only for solid filled areas and for the Adjust Area Fill option of the Plot Configuration dialog box. AutoCAD uses the pen width setting to calculate how far to move over each time it creates a line for the solid fill. Adjust this only if you are not getting good results with the default on your solid fills, and make sure to enter the pen width value in AutoCAD units — if you are plotting in inches, convert the actual pen width from millimeters to inches.

When setting pen assignments, you can select more than one color at a time. Use this if you want to set a new pen width for all your pens, for example.

When you are finished setting pen assignments, click OK.

In the Plot Configuration dialog box choose Optimization to open the Optimizing Pen Motion dialog box. Only those options applicable to your plotter/printer are available. Each successive option is added onto the previous option (except for the No optimization option), so that choosing the last option selects all the previous ones. Optimization options are techniques that AutoCAD uses to minimize pen movement and therefore speed up your plot. You can usually accept the default, but there's no harm in trying out a higher level of optimization. Printers with no pens do not need any optimization. Click OK when you are done.

Deciding what to plot and other options

In the Additional Parameters section of the Print/Plot Configuration dialog box, you have five choices of what to plot.

✦ **Display:** Plots the current viewport. If you are in model space and have not defined any tiled viewports, the whole screen is the current viewport. If you are in paper space, this option plots the entire screen.

✦ **Extents:** Plots the extents of your drawing. Objects that are on layers that are turned off are still considered part of the drawing extents.

✦ **Limits:** Plots the limits you have set using the LIMITS command. Being able to use this option is one good reason to use the LIMITS command.

✦ **View:** If you have saved a view, choose the View button at the bottom of the Additional Parameters section to open the View Name dialog box. Choose the view you want and choose OK. The View radio button then becomes available and selected.

✦ **Window:** To specify a window to plot, choose the Window button at the bottom of the Additional Parameters section to open the Window Selection dialog box. You can type in coordinates, but it is usually easier to choose Pick, which returns you to your drawing to pick two corners of a window. Choose OK in the dialog box. The Window radio button then becomes available and selected.

There are several other options in the Additional Parameters section.

✦ **Text Resolution:** Sets a resolution for text. In most cases, the default is satisfactory.

✦ **Text Fill:** For TrueType and PostScript fonts, unchecking this option plots text as outlines instead of filled in.

✦ **Hide Lines:** Hides lines in 3D drawings that you would normally not see in a realistic 3D view because they are behind another object or in back. Used in model space only. For paper space viewports, use the Hideplot option of the MVIEW command.

✦ **Adjust Area Fill:** For solidly filled areas, makes the plotter adjust for pen width so that the edges don't go past the area's boundary. This is generally used for printed circuit board drawings that require a very high degree of accuracy.

✦ **Plot to File:** Sends the plot data to a file instead of to a plotter/printer. The File Name button at the bottom of the section becomes active. Click it to open the Create Plot File dialog box, shown in Figure 17-8. Change the folder as necessary and enter a filename. Choose Save.

✦ **Autospool:** Plots to a given filename. You use this when queuing a drawing to plot on a shared plotter or printer. You must plot to a file.

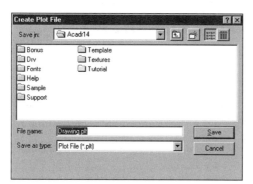

Figure 17-8: The Create Plot File dialog box.

Specifying paper size

In the Paper Size and Orientation section of the Print/Plot Configuration dialog box, first select whether you want to use inches or millimeters for all plot measurements. When you configure your printer, you can set sizes for inches or millimeters, and most users do not need to change this setting. Of course, if you sometimes draft in inches and sometimes in millimeters, you need to pay attention to this setting.

To choose the paper size, choose Size to open the Paper Size dialog box, shown in Figure 17-9. This dialog box lists the possible sizes your device can handle. You can also type in your own user sizes. The maximum size does not include the *hard clip* area, which is the area that a plotter/printer needs to leave around the edge of a sheet of paper. Choose OK.

To choose the paper size for System printers, choose Device and Default Selection, then Change next to Device Requirements.

The Paper Size dialog box also lets you know the current paper orientation, landscape or portrait. However, you cannot change the orientation in this dialog box.

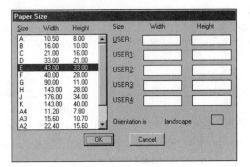

Figure 17-9: The Paper Size dialog box.

Specifying scale, rotation, and origin

In the Scale, Rotation, and Origin section, specify the scale in the format `plotted inches/millimeters = drawing units`. Chapter 5 explains drawing scales in detail. Choose Scale to Fit if you want AutoCAD to fit the drawing onto the paper. This results in odd scales but can be useful for a draft plot.

Choose Rotation and Origin to open the Plot Rotation and Origin dialog box, shown in Figure 17-10.

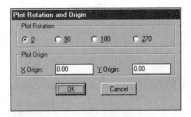

Figure 17-10: The Plot Rotation and Origin dialog box.

In order to determine the rotation, you need to understand where your plotter or printer places the 0,0 point. For most plotters, the default of 0 degrees is the most useful setting. However, on a regular printer that is set up for printing in portrait orientation, you often need a rotation of 270 degrees. Usually, AutoCAD knows the proper orientation for your output device and sets it appropriately.

Setting the origin to 0,0 (the default) is most common. However, if this does not give the proper results, you can adjust the origin to move the plot in any direction on the paper. You can sometimes nicely center a plot on a sheet of paper by changing the origin.

If you are not sure how your plotter or printer determines the 0,0 point and the X and Y axes, you should look in the plotter or printer manual. If that is not available, try changing the origin and previewing the plot. By changing the origin to 3,3 for example, and seeing in which direction the plot moves, you can determine the 0,0 point.

Previewing your plot

Release 14 adds a Print Preview button on the Standard toolbar just like the one you have in your Windows word processor. When you choose Print Preview, you see a preview of your plot using current plot parameters. In addition, you can right-click to open a shortcut menu that lets you plot, zoom, pan, or exit the preview.

You can also preview your drawing from the Print/Plot Configuration dialog box. Choose Plot Preview to preview your plot. You can choose a partial or complete preview. While the complete preview takes more time, it is much more helpful. Figure 17-11 shows a partial preview. The red rectangle (larger rectangle in Figure 17-11) indicates the paper size. The blue rectangle (smaller rectangle in Figure 17-11) indicates the area the plot uses. The small triangle indicates the 0,0 corner of your drawing. If AutoCAD detects any problems, they are displayed in the Warnings box.

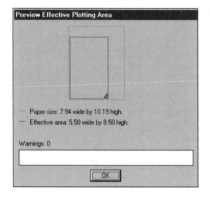

Figure 17-11: A partial plot preview.

Figure 17-12 shows a complete preview for the same drawing.

Right-click during any preview to zoom or pan. This doesn't change the zoom of your drawing but simply lets you see any part of the preview more clearly. Press Esc or Enter to exit the preview.

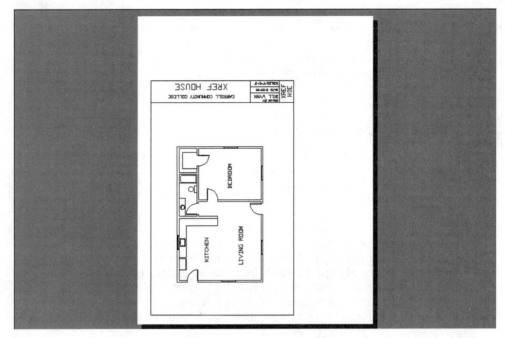

Figure 17-12: A complete plot preview.

I have covered previewing a plot last because it should be the last step before you actually plot. However, it can also be the first step, helping you to determine what settings you need.

When you insert objects (called OLE objects) or raster images from other applications, AutoCAD may not plot them as it would regular AutoCAD objects. Chapter 27 provides more information about these objects.

Creating the plot

To start the plotting process, simply click OK from the Print/Plot Configuration dialog box.

If you have a printer or plotter available, you can follow the next exercise. Because of the wide variety of devices available, you need to determine some of the settings yourself. Even if you do not have a printer or plotter available, you can follow all the steps except clicking OK in step 8. Just click Cancel to close the Print/Plot Configuration dialog box.

Step-by-Step: Plotting a Drawing

On the
CD-ROM

1. Open *ab17-2.dwg* from the *Results* folder of your CD-ROM. If you completed the last exercise, you can open it from your *AutoCAD Bible* folder.

2. Choose Print from the Standard toolbar to open the Print/Plot Configuration dialog box.

3. Choose Device and Default Information. If the printer/plotter you want to use is not selected, select it and click OK.

4. If you have a multi-pen plotter, choose Pen Assignments. Usually the default setup, created during initial plotter configuration, is acceptable. If not, you may have to make some adjustments. Choose OK.

5. In the Additional Parameters section, choose Limits.

6. In the Paper Size and Orientation section, if the Size button is active, choose it and select a size A drawing.

7. In the Scale, Rotation, and Origin section, deselect Scaled to Fit if necessary. In the Plotted Inches box, type **1**. In the Drawing Units box, type **1**.

8. In the Plot Preview section, choose Full and click Preview. Press Esc to exit preview mode. If the drawing is okay, choose OK to plot. If not, you may need to choose Rotation and Origin and rotate the drawing. The plot should look like Figure 17-4.

9. Do not save the drawing.

Batch plotting

Release
14

Release 14 includes a new Extended Batch Plot Utility (I'll call it BPU for short) that lets you choose a group of drawings to plot in a batch. It's great for plotting a whole slew of draft plots on your printer overnight.

To specify a different configuration for all drawings or to use a different configuration for different drawings, save *.pc2* or *.pcp* files as explained earlier in this chapter. Now you're ready to batch plot.

You must start outside of AutoCAD because Batch Plot Utility opens AutoCAD for you. (However, you could have BPU open a second session of AutoCAD so you can work while plotting.)

To start BPU, choose Start⇨Programs⇨AutoCAD R14⇨Batch Plot Utility. Wait while BPU loads AutoCAD and opens the AutoCAD Batch Plot Utility dialog box, shown in Figure 17-13.

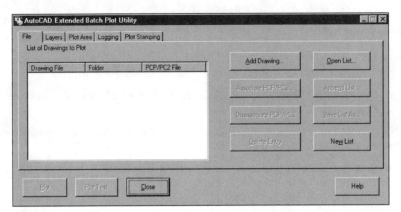

Figure 17-13: The File tab of the AutoCAD Extended Batch Plot Utility dialog box.

The File tab

Choose Add Drawing to open the Add Drawing File dialog box. Choose any drawing and click Open. Continue to do this until you have chosen all the drawings you want to print. You can choose a contiguous group of drawings by choosing the first, pressing Shift, and choosing the last. You can select noncontiguous drawings by pressing Ctrl as you choose each one.

To associate a *.pc2* or *.pcp* file with a drawing, choose the drawing and choose Associate PCP/PC2. This opens the Associate PCP/PC2 dialog box, where you find and choose a configuration file. Choose OK.

Tip

You can select as many drawings as you want to quickly associate a *.pc2* or *.pcp* file with all of them.

To save the list to a batch plot list file (a file with a filename extension of *.bp2*) for future use, choose Save List As. Choose a location and a name. (The *batchplt* folder seems a good location.) Choose OK. Figure 17-14 shows a sample *bp2* file created using this process. If you have already saved a list, choose Open List to choose the list.

You have several other options:

✦ **Delete Entry:** Deletes a file from the batch list.

✦ **Drawings and Configuration files list:** Displays the current batch list.

✦ **Append List:** Opens the Open Batch Plot List dialog box, letting you choose a batch plot list file (*.bpl*) to use for batch plotting. BPU adds this list to the current list.

Figure 17-14: A batch plot list file.

The Layers tab

Use the Layers tab, shown in Figure 17-15, to turn layers on and off for individual drawings. Choose a drawing and BPU loads it. You then see the layers and their status on the right. You can choose a layer and choose either the On or Off button. These layer changes are not saved to the drawing but are used only for the batch plot. The Refresh button rereads the layers from the drawing, returning the layer list to its status as found in the drawing.

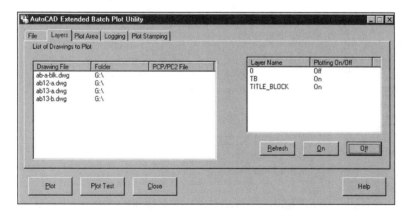

Figure 17-15: The Layers tab of the AutoCAD Extended Batch Plot Utility dialog box.

Tip

Because BPU needs to load each drawing individually, making layer changes to individual drawings can be a slow process. Therefore, use the Layers tab sparingly and prepare your drawings' layers as you want them plotted when you save the drawings.

The Plot Area tab

The Plot Area tab, shown in Figure 17-16, lets you set the area and scale for each drawing. You can also choose to plot either model space or paper space. If the drawing has named views, you can choose one to plot. The viewport drop-down list lists the viewports in the drawing. A paper space viewport is always considered the first viewport, so the viewport is listed as 2 if the drawing has only model space.

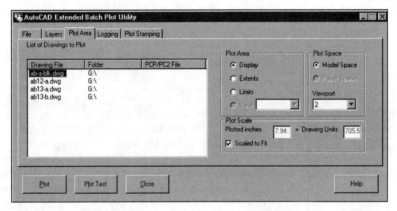

Figure 17-16: The Plot Area tab of the AutoCAD Extended Batch Plot Utility dialog box.

Choose the drawing you want to set the plot area for first. BPU loads the drawing, reading the extents, limits, named views, type of space, and so on. By default, the plot area is set to Display, the plot space is set to the drawing's last saved space and viewport, and the plot scale is set to Scaled to Fit.

If you have associated the drawing with a configuration file, the settings are according to that file. However, any changes you make on this tab override the configuration file's settings.

The Logging tab

The Logging tab, shown in Figure 17-17, lets you create a log file when you batch plot. The log file helps you troubleshoot batch plot failures. Since most batch plotting is done unattended, you have no other way to figure out what went wrong at 2:00 A.M. when you return to the office at 8:00 A.M.

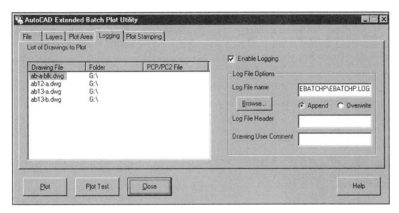

Figure 17-17: The Logging tab of the AutoCAD Extended Batch Plot Utility dialog box.

You can specify the log filename, which should have a file extension of *.log*. Choose Append to add the log file contents to the end of an existing log file. Choose Overwrite to erase the existing log file and create a new one. You can add a log file header, which is simply a line of text that BPU saves as the first line of the log file. You can use this to document the location of the drawings you are plotting, when you started the batch plot, your name, and so on. You can also add a drawing user comment, which is the first line for each drawing in the log file. You create a drawing user comment for each drawing.

The Plot Stamping tab

The Plot Stamping tab, shown in Figure 17-18, lets you place text at one corner of each plot. Common uses for plot stamping are placing the drawing name, the date and time saved, or the date and time plotted on each plot.

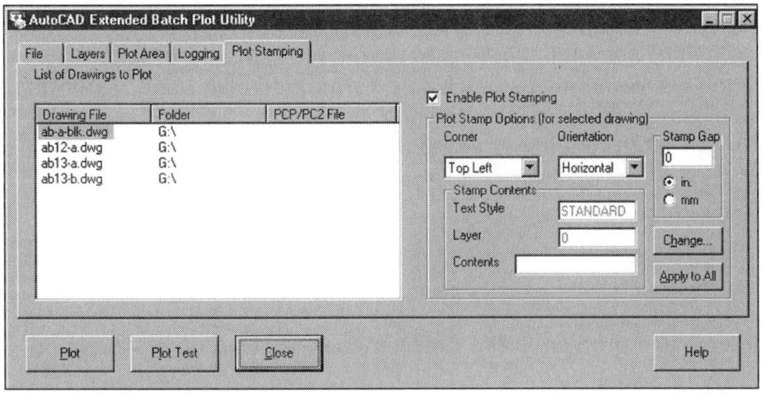

Figure 17-18: The Plot Stamping tab of the AutoCAD Extended Batch Plot Utility dialog box.

Check Enable Plot Stamping if you want to plot stamp. Then choose the corner that is relative to the position of the drawing on the plotted page. You can choose either horizontal or vertical as the orientation. You can specify a stamp gap of up to one inch (or 25.4 mm), which indents the stamp from the corner by the amount of the gap.

The Stamp Contents section determines the text style, layer, and contents of the stamp. To change these, choose Change to open the Plot Stamp Contents dialog box, shown in Figure 17-19.

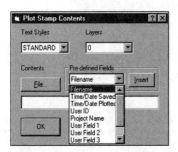

Figure 17-19: The Plot Stamp Contents dialog box.

Use the drop-down boxes to choose a text style and layer. For the content, you can choose a file, but the maximum stamp content length is 50 characters. You can also choose one of the predefined fields. Alternately, you can enter the stamp content in the Contents text box.

You can use system variables in the format &(SYSVAR). For example, &(DWGPREFIX) inserts the drawing path. You can place a system variable within text, as in Archive Plot of &(DWGPREFIX) &(DWGNAME).

When you have completed specifying the stamp, click OK.

Doing a plot test

When you have completed specifying the batch plot parameters, you may want to do a plot test by clicking Plot Test at the bottom of the dialog box. This test checks that all the required components, such as external references and raster images, are available. Figure 17-20 shows an example of plot test results. You can append the results to the batch plot log or save it as a separate file.

Note

The message

```
WARNING: Xref file <xlg filename> not accessible, xref
checking cannot be verified
```

does not indicate any problem if the drawing does not contain any xrefs.

Of course, if the plot test does indicate problems, you should resolve them before beginning the batch plot.

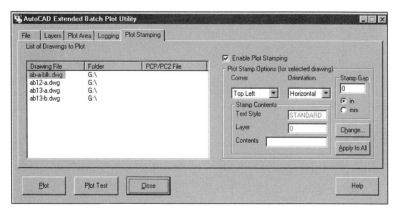

Figure 17-20: The plot test results.

Starting the batch plot

You are now ready to start the batch plot. Check that any printers/plotters you
need to use are on and ready. Choose Plot to start the batch plot. When the batch
plot is done, choose Close to close BPU and AutoCAD.

Note

If AutoCAD issues any messages, you may have to move the BPU window to see
them, but you'll hear a beep to alert you of the message.

Summary

In this chapter you learned how to lay out and plot a drawing. In many cases, you
can lay out the entire drawing in model space. However, if you are using different
views or scales, using paper space is a definite advantage.

You can use MVSETUP to automate laying out a drawing in paper space. To lay out
a drawing in paper space, switch to paper space, set your limits, and insert a title
block. Create the floating viewports you need. In model space, adjust the view of
each viewport. In paper space, make any necessary adjustments to the size and
placement of the viewports and add any text you need.

You use the Print/Plot Configuration dialog box to set up a drawing for printing or
plotting. The basic steps include choosing a printer/plotter; assigning pens;
deciding what part of your drawing to plot; specifying paper size, scale, rotation,
and origin; and previewing the drawing. Release 14's new Batch Plot Utility lets you
plot any number of drawings at one time.

✦   ✦   ✦

Working with Data

Part III covers the various ways you work with data in your drawings. This part brings you to a new level of sophistication in terms of automation and interfacing with other drawings and data. Chapter 18 covers blocks and attributes, which allow you to work repetitively with objects and text. Chapter 19 explains how to refer to other drawings. Chapter 20 describes how to connect external databases to objects in your drawings.

Working with Blocks and Attributes

Working with Repetitive Objects

A common drawing task is placing the same group of objects several times in a drawing. An architect needs to place windows and doors many times in a plan layout of a house. An electrical engineer places electrical symbols in a drawing over and over again. A mechanical model may include many nuts, bolts, surface finish symbols, and the like many times in a drawing. *Blocks* are groups of objects that you save and name so that you can insert them in your drawing whenever you need them. A block is one object regardless of the number of individual objects that were used to create it. Because it is one object, you can easily move, copy, scale, or rotate it. However, if necessary, you can *explode* a block to obtain the original individual objects.

One advantage of blocks is that they reduce the size of the drawing file. AutoCAD stores the composition of a block only once, along with a simple reference to the block each time it is inserted, rather than storing each individual object in each block in the drawing database.

Once you have a block in a drawing, you can work with it as with any other object. You can snap to object snaps of the individual objects within blocks even though you can't edit the individual objects. For example, you can draw a line from the midpoint of a line in a block.

Many fields use *parts libraries* that may consist of thousands of items. These are saved and inserted using the block feature of AutoCAD. You can save blocks in a drawing or as a separate file so that you can insert them in any drawing you wish.

AutoCAD lets you attach *attributes* to blocks. Attributes are simply labels that are associated with a block. Attributes have two main uses — to label objects and to create a simple database.

This chapter explains how to make the most of blocks and attributes.

Combining Objects into Blocks

Any object or set of objects can be saved as a block. It is easy to create a block, but a little planning in advance makes using it much simpler. Before you create a block you need understand how blocks are inserted and how you want to use the specific block that you are creating.

Understanding base points and insertion points

Figure 18-1 shows the legend for a plat drawing. Each legend symbol is a block that is then inserted in the drawing as needed. The first symbol has been selected, and you can see that it has one grip at the *base point.* The base point is the point you use to insert the block. Every block must have a base point. When you insert the block, the base point is placed at the coordinate you specify for inserting the block — the *insertion point.* All the objects of the block are then inserted in their proper place relative to that insertion point.

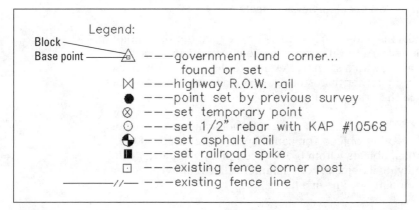

Figure 18-1: Each legend symbol is a block. Every block has a base point.

The base point does not have to be on the object, but it should be in a location that makes it easy to insert the block. Figure 18-2 shows a different sort of block — a title block. In this case, the base point is usually inserted at 0,0 of the drawing. By placing the base point at the lower-left corner of the border, you can easily place this block in any drawing.

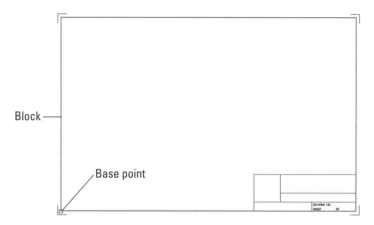

Figure 18-2: This title block is a block. Its base point is at the lower-left corner.

Creating a block

To create a block, first create the objects just as you want to save them. You may include other blocks as objects in your block. (A block within a block is called a *nested* block.) After you have created the objects for your block, follow these steps:

1. Choose Make Block from the Draw toolbar to start the BMAKE command and open the Block Definition dialog box, shown in Figure 18-3. The dialog box, new for Release 14, makes it easy to define a block.

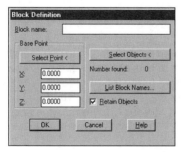

Figure 18-3: The Block Definition dialog box.

2. In the Block name text box, type a name for the block (31 characters maximum with no spaces). You can also use the dollar sign ($), hyphen (-), and underscore (_) characters anywhere in the block name.

3. Click Select Objects. AutoCAD returns you to your drawing temporarily. Use any selection method to select the objects you want in your block. Press Enter to end selection and return to the Block Definition dialog box.

4. Choose a base point. By default, the base point is 0,0 (or 0,0,0 for 3D drawings). To define any other point, such as an object snap on any of the objects in the block, click Select Point. AutoCAD temporarily returns you to your drawing. At the Insertion base point: prompt, specify a point. AutoCAD returns you to the dialog box.

Caution
For precision, you should always use an object snap when defining the base point. If the base point you need to use is not on any object, you can use the From object snap, tracking, or some other means of specifying a precise coordinate.

5. If you want to keep the objects that you selected to make the block in your drawing, check Retain Objects (the default). If you created the objects to insert them elsewhere and do not need the original objects uncheck Retain Objects.

6. Click OK to return to your drawing.

The definition of the block is now stored in the drawing, ready for you to insert as many times as needed. If you unchecked Retain Objects, your objects also disappear. You can retrieve them by the one AutoCAD command with a sense of humor — OOPS. OOPS unerases the last object you erased — whether by using the ERASE command or by creating a block, even if you used some other command in the meantime.

Tip
If you create a number of block definitions that you do not end up using in the drawing, you can use the PURGE command to delete them. This reduces the size of the drawing file.

Redefining a block

One advantage of not retaining the objects is that their disappearance confirms that you selected the right objects. If you make a mistake, or if you want to change the block in some way, you can redefine it. If you just created the block, use UNDO and make any changes necessary. If you created the block earlier, insert the block and explode it. (Exploding is covered later in this chapter.) Simply repeat the process of defining the block, using the same name for the block. When you complete the process, AutoCAD asks if you want to redefine the block. Click Yes. If you redefine a block that has been inserted in your drawing, AutoCAD updates all the blocks. This is a powerful technique to control your drawing. If you have repetitive symbols in your drawing, it is worthwhile to make blocks out of them just so that you can make this type of global change if necessary.

Step-by-Step: Creating a Block

On the
CD-ROM

1. Open *ab18-a.dwg* from the CD-ROM.

2. Save it as *ab18-1.dwg* in your *AutoCAD Bible* folder. This is a small portion of an electrical schematic drawing, as shown in Figure 18-4. OSNAP is on, and running object snaps are set for Endpoint, Quadrant, and Intersection.

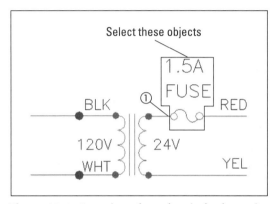

Figure 18-4: A portion of an electrical schematic.

3. To make a block of the 1.5 amp fuse, choose Make Block from the Draw toolbar.

4. In the Block Name text box of the Block Definition dialog box, type **1-5ampfuse**.

5. Click Select Objects to return to the drawing temporarily.

6. Select the objects shown in Figure 18-4: the two lines of text, the two circles, and the two arcs. Press Enter to end selection and return to the dialog box. Under the Select Objects button, AutoCAD displays Number found: 6.

Tip

You can also select the objects first and then choose Make Block.

7. Click Select Point in the Base Point section of the dialog box.

8. In the drawing, use the Quadrant object snap to pick ① in Figure 18-4.

9. In the dialog box, uncheck Retain Objects. Click OK to return to your drawing. AutoCAD erases the objects that made up the block.

10. To check that the block has been created, choose Make Block from the Draw toolbar. Choose List Block Names. The Block Names In This Drawing dialog box lists your block, as shown in Figure 18-5. Click OK.

11. Save your drawing.

Figure 18-5: The Block Names In This Drawing dialog box lists the blocks you have created.

Note

Besides the blocks you have created, the list of blocks can include externally referenced files (discussed in Chapter 19), blocks from those externally referenced files, and unnamed blocks. Hatching and dimensioning generally create unnamed blocks. (Remember that hatches and dimensions are blocks.) AutoCAD automatically assigns its own names to these blocks.

Saving blocks as files

To use a block in another drawing, you need to save it as a separate drawing file. Parts and symbol libraries are made up of many individual drawing files, one for each part or symbol. Such libraries are a powerful aid to drawing more efficiently.

To save a block as a file, follow these steps:

1. Type **wblock** ↵. (WBLOCK stands for write block. Writing to a file is another expression for saving to a file.)

2. In the Create Drawing File dialog box, choose the location (drive and folder) for the file.

3. In the File Name text box, type the name of the file you want to create. If you have already created the block in your drawing, you should generally use the same name as the block to avoid confusion.

4. At the Block name: prompt, choose one of four options:

   ✦ Type the name of an existing block.

   ✦ Type = (an equal sign) to use the name of the block as the filename.

   ✦ Type * to save the entire drawing as a new file.

   ✦ Press Enter to return to your drawing and define a block. AutoCAD prompts you for a base point and to select objects.

The last two options let you create the block just for the file you are creating. No block is created in the drawing. However, the objects you selected are deleted. As with regular blocks, you can use OOPS to bring them back.

Tip   When you save a drawing to use as a block, use the BASE command to create the insertion point. By default the base point is 0,0,0. By setting the base point to another point in the drawing you can control how that drawing is inserted.

Replacing an existing file

If you make a mistake when selecting objects to write to a file with WBLOCK, or wish to change the objects in the file, you can replace the file. Start WBLOCK and type the name of the block file you want to change. Be sure to choose the same file location. When you click Save, AutoCAD asks if you want to replace the existing file. Click Yes. Then continue to define the block as you normally would.

Tip   Once you find the file's location, the filename appears in the Create Drawing File dialog box. You can choose it instead of typing the name again. Then click Save.

Step-by-Step: Saving a Block to a File

On the CD-ROM

1. Open *ab18-b.dwg* from the CD-ROM.

2. Save it as *ab18-2.dwg* in your *AutoCAD Bible* folder. This is a large title block as shown in Figure 18-6. OSNAP is on, and a running object snap is set for Endpoint.

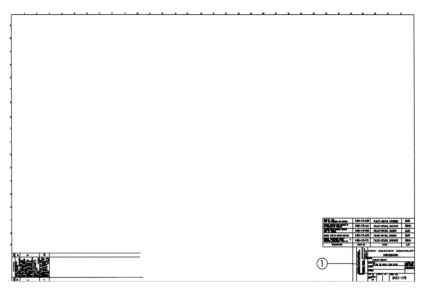

Figure 18-6: A title block can be saved as a file and inserted into any other drawing.

3. Type **wblock** ↵. In the Create Drawing File dialog box, set the Save in drop-down box to your *AutoCAD Bible* folder. In the File name text box, type **tb-f**. Click Save.

4. At the `Block name:` prompt, type * ↵ (an asterisk). AutoCAD saves the drawing as a new file with the name *tb-f.dwg.*

5. Press Enter to repeat the WBLOCK command. The Create Drawing File dialog box should already be set to your *AutoCAD Bible* folder. In the File name text box, type **notes-tol**. Click Save.

6. At the `Block name:` prompt, press Enter. At the `Insertion base point:` prompt, use Zoom Window to zoom in on the text at the bottom right corner of the title block. AutoCAD resumes the WBLOCK command.

7. Use the Endpoint object snap to pick the bottom left corner of the box containing the text at a 90-degree angle, marked as ① in Figure 18-6. Using this base point lets you easily place the text in the box at any time.

8. At the `Select objects:` prompt, select all the text at ①. Include the lines that make up the text bracket. (You may have to zoom in again to see the objects clearly.) Press Enter to end selection. AutoCAD saves the block as a file.

9. Type **oops** ↵ to bring back the text.

10. Choose Zoom Extents from the Zoom flyout of the Standard toolbar. Save your drawing.

Inserting Blocks and Files into Drawings

Blocks that are defined in a drawing and separate files are inserted in the same way. Once you choose the location, AutoCAD lets you change the size and rotation of the block. This capability is ideal for parts libraries. Parts may be created at the size of one unit and then scaled or rotated as needed. Figure 18-7 shows a window block inserted at various scales and rotation angles.

To insert a block or file, follow these steps:

1. Choose Insert Block from the Draw toolbar to start the DDINSERT command. AutoCAD opens the Insert dialog box.

2. Choose Block or File.

   ✦ If you choose Block, AutoCAD opens the Defined Blocks dialog box. Choose any block and click OK.

   ✦ If you choose File, AutoCAD opens the Select Drawing File dialog box. Locate the file's drive and folder, then choose the file. A preview appears to the right. Click Open.

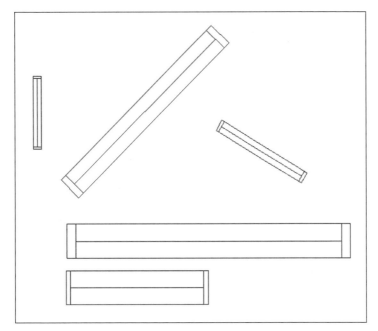

Figure 18-7:
A block of a window inserted at various rotation angles and scales.

3. In the Options section of the Insert dialog box, uncheck Specify Parameters on Screen if you want to specify the insertion point, scale, and rotation angle in the dialog box. Then specify the parameters in the dialog box.

4. Check the Explode check box if you want to insert the block as individual objects instead of as one block object.

5. Click OK to close the Insert dialog box.

6. If Specify Parameters on Screen was checked, AutoCAD prompts you for the parameters. At the `Insertion point:` prompt, specify the insertion point. If you are dragging the block on the screen and want to see how it looks at a specific scale or rotation angle, you can use one of the options in Table 18-1.

7. At the `X scale factor <1> / Corner / XYZ:` prompt, press Enter to accept the default scale factor of 1 or type in another scale. The `Corner` option lets you define a square box whose side defines the scale factor. A side of 1 unit results in a scale factor of 1. The `XYZ` prompt lets you separately define the scale factor of the X, Y, and Z axes.

8. If you specify the X scale factor, AutoCAD now prompts you for the Y scale factor. The default is the same scale as X, but you can specify a different one.

9. At the `Rotation angle <0>:` prompt, type in a rotation angle. You can also pick a point, and AutoCAD uses the angle from the insertion point to the point you picked as the rotation angle. This is useful for aligning a block with an existing object.

A negative scale factor for any of the axes creates a mirror image of the block or file. When you specify a negative X scale axis, the block is mirrored around the Y axis. When you specify a negative Y scale axis, the block is mirrored around the X axis. Figure 18-8 shows a door block inserted with negative scale factors. The rotation angle of all of the blocks is 0 degrees. By combining negative and positive scale factors with rotation angles, you can get any door configuration you want.

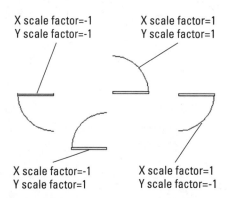

X scale factor=-1
Y scale factor=-1

X scale factor=1
Y scale factor=1

X scale factor=-1
Y scale factor=1

X scale factor=1
Y scale factor=-1

Figure 18-8: A door block inserted at various positive and negative scale factors, creating mirror images in different directions.

When you are dragging a block on the screen to specify an insertion point, it may be helpful to see the block at the scale and rotation angle you want. The problem is that the prompts for scale and rotation come after the prompt for the insertion angle. AutoCAD therefore lets you preset the scale and rotation angle at the Insertion point: prompt, using the options shown in Table 18-1. To use one of these options, type its abbreviation (the capitalized letter or letters) at the Insertion point: prompt.

Table 18-1
Insertion Point Prompt Options for Inserting Blocks

Option	Use
Scale	Specifies the scale factor
Xscale	Specifies the X scale factor
Yscale	Specifies the Y scale factor
Zscale	Specifies the Z scale factor
Rotate	Specifies the rotation angle
PScale	Specifies the preliminary scale factor for the display of the block as you drag it and prompts you again for the scale so you can change it
PXscale	Specifies the preliminary X scale factor for the display of the block as you drag it and prompts you again for the scale so you can change it

Option	Use
PYscale	Specifies the preliminary Y scale factor for the display of the block as you drag it and prompts you again for the scale so you can change it
PZscale	Specifies the preliminary Z scale factor for the display of the block as you drag it and prompts you again for the scale so you can change it
PRotate	Specifies the preliminary rotation angle for the display of the block as you drag it and prompts you again for the scale so you can change it

Step-by-Step: Inserting Blocks and Files

On the CD-ROM

1. Open *ab18-c.dwg* from the CD-ROM.

2. Save it as *ab18-3.dwg* in your *AutoCAD Bible* folder. This is the floor plan of the first floor of a house, as shown in Figure 18-9. Many of the doors need to be inserted. OSNAP is on, with a running object snap set for Endpoint. The current layer is Door.

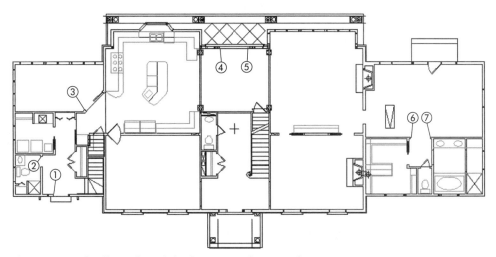

Figure 18-9: The floor plan of the house needs some doors.

3. Use Zoom Window to zoom in on the left third of the house.

 4. Choose Insert Block from the Draw toolbar. In the Block section of the Insert dialog box, click Block. In the Defined Blocks dialog box, choose DOOR and click OK. Specify Parameters on Screen should be checked. Click OK to close the Insert dialog box.

Tip

If you make a mistake while inserting a door, press Esc if you are in the middle of the prompts. If you have completed the command, click Undo on the Standard toolbar or Erase the door and start over.

5. As you move the cursor, you can see the dragged image of a door. This image shows you the block at an X and Y scale of 1 and a 0-degree rotation angle. Follow the prompts:

```
Insertion point: Use the Endpoint object snap to pick ① in Figure 18-9.
X scale factor <1> / Corner / XYZ: -1 ↵
Y scale factor (default=X): 1 ↵
Rotation angle <0>: 270 ↵ (You could also specify -90 degrees.)
```

6. Repeat the DDINSERT command. The Insert dialog box already shows the Door block. Click OK. Follow the prompts. You'll probably want to use Zoom Window to zoom closely into the area of ② in Figure 18-9.

```
Insertion point: Pick ② in Figure 18-9.
X scale factor <1> / Corner / XYZ: 2/3 ↵
Y scale factor (default=X): 2/3 ↵
Rotation angle <0>: 180 ↵
```

7. Return to the previous view using Zoom Previous. Zoom in to the area around ③ in Figure 18-9. Choose Insert Block from the Draw toolbar. Click OK. Follow the prompts:

```
Insertion point: Pick ③ in Figure 18-9.
X scale factor <1> / Corner / XYZ: -3/4 ↵
Y scale factor (default=X): 3/4 ↵
Rotation angle <0>: 315 ↵
```

8. Use Zoom Dynamic to zoom in to the area around ④ and ⑤ in Figure 18-9. Choose Insert Block from the Draw toolbar. Click OK. Follow the prompts.

```
Insertion point: Pick ④ in Figure 18-9.
X scale factor <1> / Corner / XYZ: -1 ↵
Y scale factor (default=X): 1 ↵
Rotation angle <0>: 270 ↵
```

9. Repeat the DDINSERT command and click OK. Follow the prompts:

```
Insertion point: Pick ⑤ in Figure 18-9.
X scale factor <1> / Corner / XYZ: 1 ↵
Y scale factor (default=X): ↵ (to accept the default)
Rotation angle <0>: 90 ↵
```

10. Use Zoom Dynamic to zoom in on the area around ⑥ and ⑦ in Figure 18-9. Start the DDINSERT command and click OK. This time you want to preset the scale and rotation. Follow the prompts:

```
Insertion point: s ↵ (for scale)
```

```
Scale factor: 2/3 ↵
Insertion point: r ↵ (for rotate)
Rotation angle: 270 ↵
Insertion point: Pick ⑥ in Figure 18-9.
```

11. Repeat the DDINSERT command and click OK. This time you want to tentatively pre-set the scale and rotation. Follow the prompts:

```
Insertion point: px ↵
X scale factor: -2/3 ↵
Insertion point: py ↵ (for PYscale)
Y scale factor: 2/3 ↵
Insertion point: pr ↵ (for PRotate)
Rotation angle: 90 ↵
Insertion point: Pick ⑦ in Figure 18-9.
X scale factor <1> / Corner / XYZ: -2/3 ↵
Y scale factor (default=X): 2/3 ↵
Rotation angle <0>: 90 ↵
```

12. Do a Zoom Extents and save your drawing.

AutoCAD also has a MINSERT command that lets you insert blocks in a rectangular array. Type **minsert** ↵. MINSERT prompts you for an insertion point, scale factors, and rotation angle using the same prompts as the DDINSERT command, without the dialog box. It then starts the same prompts as the ARRAY command, asking for the number of rows and columns and the distance between them. The value of MINSERT is that it reduces the size of your drawing because AutoCAD saves the array as one block object. The disadvantage is that you cannot edit the individual blocks in the array or the array as a whole in any way. If you need to edit them, erase the entire array of blocks, redefine the single block, if necessary, and start over, this time using DDINSERT and ARRAY separately. You cannot explode a minserted block.

Managing Blocks

There are several factors that require care when working with blocks. Large libraries of blocks need to be well managed so you can find the block you need quickly.

Working with layers

You may want a block to take on the current layer when inserted or to retain its original layer. AutoCAD lets you manage block layers and their color and linetype properties to obtain the desired result. There are four ways to define a block in order to determine what layer, color, and linetype properties it will use when it is inserted, as shown in Table 18-2. Each method has different results when the block is inserted, although some of the differences are minor.

Table 18-2 — Properties of Block Component Objects and Insertion Results	
Properties of Component Objects	*Insertion Results*
On any layer (except layer 0), with color and linetype set to ByLayer	Block keeps properties of that layer. If you insert block into another drawing without that layer, AutoCAD creates the layer. If you insert block into another drawing with that layer, but the layer has different color and linetype properties, block takes on properties of the layer that are different from those you created it on. If you insert block on a different layer, the block keeps the properties of the layer on which it was created, but the DDMODIFY command (choose Properties on the Object Properties toolbar) reports the block as being on the layer on which it was inserted because it reports the layer of the insertion point, not the block objects.
On any layer (except 0), with color and linetype set explicitly	Block keeps the color and linetype properties that were explicitly set. If you insert block into another drawing, AutoCAD creates the layer on which original objects were made.
On any layer (except layer 0), with color and linetype set to ByBlock	Block takes on the layer and properties of the current layer. If you insert block into another drawing, AutoCAD creates the layer on which original objects were made. Note: If you retain objects when creating the block in a drawing, the block is always shown with black/white color and a continuous linetype.
On layer 0 (with color and linetype set to ByBlock or ByLayer)	Block takes on the layer and properties of the current layer it is inserted on. If you insert block into another drawing, no layers are created.

As you can see, careful planning of the layers you use when creating a block is essential. As Table 18-2 makes clear, two of the methods (setting the objects to ByBlock and creating them on layer 0) create chameleon blocks that take on the properties of the current layer. The other two methods are used when you want the block to retain its properties regardless of the current layer.

Tip

If you can, creating blocks on layer 0 is the simplest. If you want the blocks to have a specific color and linetype, create a layer for them and switch to that layer before inserting the blocks. You can also change the layer of a block once it is inserted in the same way that you change the layer of any object.

Step-by-Step: Working with Blocks and Layers

On the CD-ROM

1. Open *ab18-d.dwg* from the CD-ROM.

2. Save it as *ab18-4.dwg* in your *AutoCAD Bible* folder. This is a portion of an electrical schematic, as shown in Figure 18-10. OSNAP is on, with running object snaps set for Endpoint, Intersection, Quadrant, and Midpoint.

3. Choose Make Block from the Draw toolbar. In the Block name text box of the Block Definition dialog box, type **hlswitch**. Choose Select Objects. Use a selection window to select the entire hi-limit switch box. Don't include any of the electrical wire. Press Enter to end selection. Choose Select Point in the Base Point section of the dialog box. Use the Quadrant object snap to pick the left quadrant of the left circle in the switch, at ① in Figure 18-10. The Retain objects check box should be checked. Click OK. The objects in this block are on the Object layer, which is red with a continuous linetype. The color and linetype are set to ByLayer.

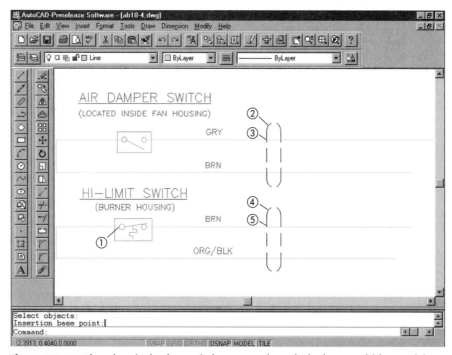

Figure 18-10: The electrical schematic has several symbols that would be useful as blocks.

4. Use a selection window to select the air damper switch. Don't include any of the electrical wire. (The objects are currently on the Object layer, which is red with a continuous linetype.) Click the Color Control drop-down list box and choose ByBlock. Click the Linetype Control drop-down list box and choose ByBlock. The switch turns black (or white if you are using a black screen). The objects are still selected.

5. Choose Make Block again from the Draw toolbar. In the Block name text box, type **switch**. The dialog box says `Number found: 4`. Choose Select Point. Use the Quadrant object snap to pick the left quadrant of the left circle in the switch. Click OK.

6. Use a selection window to select the top conduit at ② in Figure 18-10 (it is four objects). (It is currently on the Conduit layer, which is black and has a linetype of Hidden2.) Use the Color Control drop-down list box to set the color to green. Use the Linetype Control drop-down list box to set the linetype to Hidden2. Choose Make Block from the Draw toolbar. In the Block name text box, type **topconduit**. The dialog box tells you that AutoCAD has found four objects. Choose Select Point. Use the Intersection object snap to pick ③. Click OK. The conduit appears green with the Hidden2 linetype.

7. Use a selection window to select the bottom conduit at ④. (It is currently on the Conduit layer, which is black and has a linetype of Hidden2.) Use the Layer Control drop-down list box to set the layer to 0. Choose Make Block from the Draw toolbar. In the Block name text box, type **botconduit**. The dialog box tells you that AutoCAD has found four objects. Choose Select Point. Use the Intersection object snap to pick ⑤. Click OK. The conduit appears black with a continuous linetype.

8. Type **wblock** ↵. In the Create Drawing File dialog box, choose your *AutoCAD Bible* folder. Type **hlswitch** in the File Name box and click Save. At the `Block name:` prompt, type = ↵ (an equal sign). Press Enter to repeat the WBLOCK command and do the same for the *switch*, *topconduit*, and *botconduit* blocks.

9. Save your drawing. Choose New from the Standard toolbar. In the Create New Drawing dialog box, choose Start from Scratch. The default setting should say English. Click OK. AutoCAD opens a new drawing. This drawing has only one layer, layer 0. (Click the Layer Control drop-down list to check, if you wish.)

10. Choose Insert Block from the Draw toolbar. In the Insert dialog box, choose File. Locate your *AutoCAD Bible* folder and choose *hlswitch.dwg*. Click Open. In the Insert dialog box, click OK. Follow the prompts to insert the file anywhere in the drawing, using a scale factor of 3. The block retained its original color and linetype but is listed as being on layer 0. Select the block and look at the Layer Control drop-down list to verify these properties.

11. Now check the Layer Control drop-down list. There are two new layers, Object and Line. Object is the layer that the original objects were on and Line was simply the current layer at the time *hlswitch.dwg* was created.

12. Again choose Insert Block from the Draw toolbar. In the Insert dialog box, choose File. Locate your *AutoCAD Bible* folder and choose *topconduit.dwg*.

Click Open. In the Insert dialog box, click OK. Follow the prompts to insert the file anywhere in the drawing, using a scale factor of 3. Again, the object retains its properties of green color and Hidden2 linetype but is listed as being on layer 0. Click the Layer Control drop-down list to see that the Conduit layer has been added to the drawing.

13. Choose Layers from the Object Properties toolbar and click New in the Layer and Linetype Properties dialog box. Name the new layer **4** and set its color to Cyan. Click OK.

14. In the Layer Control drop-down list, choose layer 4 to make it current.

15. Again choose Insert Block from the Draw toolbar. In the Insert dialog box, choose File. Locate your *AutoCAD Bible* folder and choose *switch.dwg.* Click Open. In the Insert dialog box, click OK. Follow the prompts to insert the file anywhere in the drawing, using a scale factor of 3. The object has the properties of layer 4 and is listed on layer 4.

16. Again choose Insert Block from the Draw toolbar. In the Insert dialog box, choose File. Locate your *AutoCAD Bible* folder and choose *botconduit.dwg.* Click Open. In the Insert dialog box, click OK. Follow the prompts to insert the file anywhere in the drawing, using a scale factor of 3. The object has the properties of layer 4 and is listed on layer 4.

17. Do not save this new drawing.

Exploding blocks

You can *explode* blocks into their original objects. You may need to do this to edit a block. If you wish, you can then redefine the block as explained earlier in this chapter. To explode a block, choose Explode from the Modify toolbar. (You can select objects before or after choosing the command.) You can also explode polylines, dimensions, hatches, regions, multilines, and certain 3D objects (bodies, 3D meshes, 3D solids, polyface meshes, and polygon meshes) into simpler types of objects. (Drawing in 3D is covered in Part IV.) When you explode a block with nested blocks, AutoCAD only explodes the top level block. You need to use EXPLODE again to explode the next level of blocks.

When you explode blocks that were created on layer 0 or with BYBLOCK objects, the objects return to their original status and appear black with a continuous linetype again.

If you insert a block with different X and Y scales, AutoCAD does its best to create objects based on their new shapes. For example, if you have a block that includes a circle and insert it with an X scale of 1 and a Y scale of 2, you see an ellipse. Therefore, when you explode the block, AutoCAD creates an ellipse from what used to be a circle.

Using the XPLODE command

The XPLODE command is a version of the EXPLODE command that you can use to control the final layer, color, and linetype of the objects. If you select more than one object, you can set the properties for all the objects you select at once, that is, *globally*, or for each object individually.

To xplode an object, type **xplode** ↵. (XPLODE is actually an AutoLISP program.) At the Select objects: prompt, select one or more blocks. If you select more than one object, XPLODE displays the XPlode Individually/<Globally>: prompt. Type **i** ↵ to get prompts for each block individually. Press Enter to accept the Globally default option. If you choose the Individually option, XPLODE highlights each block in turn so you know which block you are referring to as you respond to prompts.

At the All/Color/LAyer/LType/Inherit from parent block/<Explode>: prompt, choose whether you want to specify color, layer, linetype, or all three. The Inherit from parent block option works only for blocks created on layer 0 whose color and linetype were also set to BYBLOCK. These BYBLOCK objects then retain their color and linetype after you explode them.

Note

Xplode cannot explode blocks whose X and Y scale factors have unequal absolute values. That means an X scale of 1 and a Y scale of -1 is okay, but not an X scale of 2 and a Y value of -3.

Step-by-Step: Exploding and Xploding Blocks

On the
CD-ROM

1. Open *ab18-e.dwg* from the CD-ROM.

2. Save it as *ab18-5.dwg* in your *AutoCAD Bible* folder. This is the same electrical schematic used in the previous exercise, except that the objects are now blocks that have been inserted. It is shown in Figure 18-11. OSNAP is on, with running object snaps set for Endpoint, Intersection, Quadrant, and Midpoint. The current layer is Object.

3. Choose Explode from the Modify toolbar. At the Select objects: prompt, choose the air damper switch at ① in Figure 18-11. Press Enter to end selection. The switch turns black or white (the opposite of your screen color) because it was created from objects whose color and linetype were set to ByBlock.

4. Choose Undo from the Standard toolbar.

5. Type **xplode** ↵. At the Select objects: prompt, choose the air damper switch again. Press Enter to end selection. At the All/Color/LAyer/LType/ Inherit from parent block/<Explode>: prompt, type **la** ↵. At the XPlode onto what layer? <OBJECT>: prompt, press Enter to accept the default of OBJECT, the current layer. AutoCAD informs you, Object exploded onto layer OBJECT.

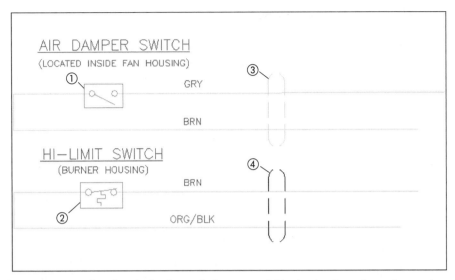

Figure 18-11: The electrical schematic has several blocks that have been inserted.

6. Choose the hi-limit switch at ②. Choose Explode from the Modify toolbar. AutoCAD explodes the block onto the Object layer because these objects were created on that layer with their color and linetype set to ByLayer.

7. Type **xplode** ⏎. The top conduit was created from objects set explicitly to green color and hidden2 linetype. The bottom conduit was created from objects set to layer 0. Follow the prompts.

```
Select objects: Choose the conduits at ③ and ④. End selection.
2 objects found.
XPlode Individually/<Globally>: ⏎ to accept the default.
All/Color/LAyer/LType/Inherit from parent block/<Explode>:
la ⏎
XPlode onto what layer? <OBJECT>: conduit ⏎
Objects exploded onto layer conduit.
```

8. Save your drawing.

Editing blocks

I have already discussed how you can redefine blocks. Here are a few additional points that can help you work with blocks.

Editing blocks with grips

To a certain extent, you can use grip editing with blocks. By default, when you select a block, only one grip — at the base point — is displayed. However, you can show the grips of all the objects by choosing Tools⇨Grips and clicking Enable grips within blocks in the Grips dialog box. Figure 18-12 shows the results of both settings.

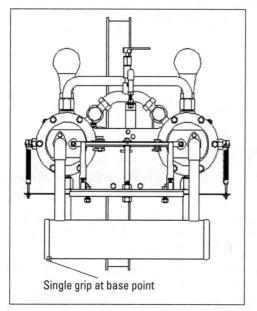
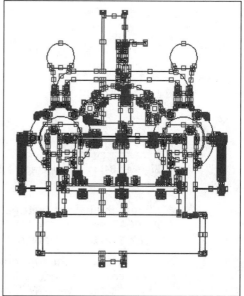

Figure 18-12: By default, AutoCAD displays only one grip at the base point for a block. You can also choose to display the grips for all the component objects.

Credit: Thanks to Sid Herbage of Mississauga, Ontario, Canada, for this drawing of the engine of a quadricycle.

As a general rule, you don't want to enable grips for blocks when working with such complex blocks. However, you can turn them on to use grips to mirror, rotate, move, or scale the block if you want to use the grip of a component object as a base point for the edit.

Updating blocks

As I mentioned earlier in the chapter, when you redefine a block, all instances of that block are automatically updated. However, if you inserted a file to use as a block in a drawing and then changed the file, AutoCAD has no way of knowing of the change in that drawing. (Use an external reference instead to solve this problem. See Chapter 19.) To update blocks that came from inserting files, you can reinsert the file. Follow these steps:

   1. Choose Insert Block.

2. Click File.

3. Choose the file you have changed and click OK.

4. AutoCAD asks if you want to redefine the block because that block already exists in the drawing. Choose Yes.

5. Press Esc to avoid actually inserting a new copy of the block.

AutoCAD updates all the instances of the block with the new file.

Substituting blocks

You can also substitute a different file. There are three reasons for doing this:

✦ If you have many instances of complex blocks, you may find that regen times are slow. You can create a simple block, WBLOCK it and substitute it for the original blocks until plotting time. This is similar to using QTEXT to replace text with rectangles. (See Chapter 13.)

✦ Another use for substitution is to create more than one version of a drawing, for example, an office layout with various kinds of desks. You can create the drawing with one type of desk, inserting files of the desks. Substitute a file of another type of desk and you have a new office layout design.

✦ Another common reason to substitute blocks is when your office switches to a different standard for a part.

To substitute blocks, follow these steps:

1. Choose Insert Block from the Draw toolbar.

2. Choose File. Find and choose the file you want to put into your drawing.

3. In the Block text box, type or choose the name of the block you want to replace. You now have both a file and a block listed. The file will replace the block currently in the drawing.

4. Click OK.

5. AutoCAD tells you that the block with this name already exists and asks if you want to redefine it. Choose Yes.

6. Press Esc to avoid actually inserting a new copy of the new file.

AutoCAD replaces the current blocks with the file you inserted.

Caution

Usually when you insert a file into a drawing, the block name and filename are the same. Likewise, when you WBLOCK a block, you usually name the file with the name of the block. Be aware that when you use block substitution you have a block in your drawing that is the same as a file of a different name. For example, if you have a block in your drawing called *smalldesk* and substitute a file called *bigdesk*, you now have a block called *smalldesk* that is actually the same as the file *bigdesk*. This can get confusing, so use block substitution with care.

The *AutoCAD 14 Bible* CD-ROM contains two programs that can help you work with blocks:

✦ Sclblock.lsp is an AutoLISP routine that scales any number of selected blocks at their respective insertion points. Look in *Software**Chapter 18**Sclblock*.

✦ Blkarray.lsp uses its BLOCKARRAY command to create arrays of blocks like the minsert command, but you can choose to create them as separate, editable blocks or even as exploded blocks. To create an array of standard, separate blocks, precede the block name with one asterisk when prompted. To create an array of exploded blocks, precede the block name with two asterisks. Using the block name without any asterisks performs the standard MINSERT command. Look in the *Software**Chapter 18**Blkarray* folder.

Organizing blocks

Parts or symbol libraries may take two forms — individual files for each part or symbol, or drawings that include many parts or symbols. You have already worked with individual files in this chapter. One technique that works well for some applications is to create 1-unit by 1-unit blocks. You can then easily insert them at any X or Y scale without much calculation.

You can also create files that include many parts or symbols to simplify the number of files you have to keep track of. To further simplify matters, you can label the blocks and print out the drawing to use as reference. When you need a part or symbol, follow these steps:

1. Choose Insert Block.

2. Click File.

3. Choose the file containing your parts and choose OK.

4. In the Insert dialog box, choose OK.

5. At the `Insertion point:` prompt, press Esc.

If you choose Insert Block and click Block, you see all the blocks in the part library listed. You can now insert the one you need.

This method inserts many blocks that you never actually use, which increases drawing file size. If you wish, use PURGE to eliminate any unused blocks.

If your part library file uses a long filename that includes spaces, AutoCAD informs you that the block name must be less than 32 characters and have no spaces when you are inserting it. Change the block name to any valid name. In this case the actual name doesn't make any difference, because you do not actually insert the block.

An important part of managing blocks is the maintenance of a block book with each block file or library file printed out and labeled. Insertion points should be marked. This can be done by choosing a visible point style and placing a point on each block using the Node object snap.

A consistent naming scheme is essential. Keep in mind that block names cannot have spaces, even though Windows 95 files can. Also, you may have some applications that don't accept long filenames such as e-mail, compression (zipping), and encoding/decoding programs. Once you know the limitations of your naming scheme, choose names that are both meaningful and consistent throughout.

Organizing a folder (directory) scheme for block and library files is equally important. Your block book should include the location of each block or library file and an overall diagram of the folder scheme. If you use a separate file for each block, you may have hundreds or even thousands of files to keep track of. Find logical categories so you can place related blocks together.

Finally, make sure you keep the book updated as you add and change blocks and libraries.

On the CD-ROM The *AutoCAD 14 Bible* CD-ROM contains a number of block collections that you may find useful:

✦ Acadarch includes 79 drawings of architectural details for office floor plans, such as conference tables, several types of chairs, a bookcase, file cabinets, panels, pedestals, a storage cabinet, a sofa, square and round tables, desks, a wardrobe closet, and a work surface. Many items come in several sizes. If you can't figure out what a drawing represents (for example, the bookcase is just a rectangle), use the LIST command on the text *Description*. This is an attribute definition which describes the object. You can use the attributes for facilities management. Look in the *\Software\Chap18\Acadarch* folder.

✦ Acadart1 contains 87 drawings of electronic and electrical symbols for schematics. It also includes some great isometric drawings of connectors, some interesting grids, and other tidbits. Look in the *\Software\Chap18\Acadart1* folder.

✦ Disney is a drawing of Mickey, Minnie, Donald, and Goofy having a good time. Just for fun! Look in *\Software\Chap18\Disney*.

✦ Elec-001 contains 39 drawings of electronic parts and electrical symbols, such as a capacitor, crystal, resistor, and so on. Look in *\Software\Chap18\ Elec-001*.

✦ Elect-002 is part 2 of the electrical symbol library, with 21 drawings. Look in *\Software\Chap18\Elec-002*.

✦ Elect-003 is part 3 and contains electronic components. Look in *\Software\Chap18\Elec-003*.

✦ Libeltr is a drawing that contains a library of electronic and electrical symbols. Look in *\Software\Chap18\Libeltr.*

✦ Epdxf001 contains 48 DXF files with parts for creating electrical schematics. To open a DXF file, start a new drawing in AutoCAD, click Open on the Standard toolbar, choose DXF (*.dxf) from the Files of type drop-down list, and choose the file you want to open. Then click Open. Look in *\Software\Chap18\Epdxf001.*

✦ Nuts is a block library consisting of 97 drawings of nuts, screws, bolts, and washers of various types and sizes, based on standard military hardware. Look in *\Software\Chap18\Nuts.*

✦ Pipesym1 and Pipesym2 are two collections of blocks for creating flow chart diagrams of piping systems. Pipesym2 has a helpful *Pleg.dwg,* which contains a legend of the symbols. Look in *\Software\Chap18\Pipesym1* and *Pipesym2.*

✦ Screwit is a comprehensive library of 32 drawings of screws shown in two views. Look in *\Software\Chap18\Screwit.*

✦ Sharelib contains two drawings of architectural symbols — one for plan view and the other for elevation view. The elevation view drawing is mostly doors. The plan view drawing contains doors, appliances, and fixtures. Look in *\Software\Chap18\Sharelib.*

✦ MPE-arch is a library of mechanical, plumbing, and electrical symbols for architectural drawings, mostly lights and outlets. *Mpe.dwg* contains all the symbols and can be used as a legend. Look in *\Software\Chap18\Mpe-arch.*

✦ Archsym is a collection of architectural symbols, mostly for floor plans. It includes fixtures (sinks, tub, and so on), appliances, and other symbols. Look in *\Software\Chap18\Arch-sym.*

Using the Windows Clipboard and drag-and-drop

In the foregoing discussion on part and symbol libraries, you may have thought that these libraries are somewhat like clipart files. Clipart files include many individual pieces of clipart. You "clip" one piece of clipart by selecting it, copying it to the Windows Clipboard, returning to your original document, and pasting the clipart into your document. Alternately, you set up your screen so you can see both the clipart and your document and drag the clipart into your document. Actually, you can do the same in AutoCAD. In fact, you can sometimes use these methods instead of creating blocks.

Manipulating objects with the Windows Clipboard

You are probably familiar with cutting or copying data in other Windows applications and then pasting it, either within a file or from file to file. Table 18-3 compares copying, using blocks, and using the Clipboard (CUTCLIP, COPYCLIP, and PASTECLIP).

Table 18-3 Comparison of Methods of Moving/Copying Objects	
Method	**Features**
MOVE/COPY	Precise placement of objects, only works within a drawing
BMAKE/WBLOCK/INSERT	Precise placement of objects; can scale and rotate; creates block definition; can insert many times even after other commands; can insert files (other drawings) that you save permanently
CUTCLIP/COPYCLIP/PASTECLIP	No precise placement of objects (uses bottom-left corner of extents of object(s) you copy); creates anonymous block in file with a name like A$CE314; can scale and rotate; can both move and copy objects; can insert (paste) many times but only until you copy something else to the Clipboard; can copy from drawing to drawing or to other Windows applications

In general, for one-time moving or copying with a drawing, you should use the MOVE or COPY command. If you want to copy an object several times over a period of time, use a BLOCK command. Use the Clipboard when you want to insert objects into another drawing one or more times without saving the objects. Also, the Clipboard is indispensable for copying objects to other applications.

To place objects on the Clipboard, first select them. To move them, choose Cut to Clipboard on the Standard toolbar. To copy them, choose Copy to Clipboard. If you want to paste them in another drawing, open it. Choose Paste to Clipboard on the Standard toolbar. AutoCAD uses the same prompts as for inserting a block or file.

Chapter 27 covers moving and copying objects to other applications.

Using drag-and-drop

Windows' drag-and-drop feature lets you drag another drawing file into your drawing. Then AutoCAD prompts you as it would if you inserted the file using the DDINSERT command. You need to open either My Computer or Windows Explorer. In the steps below, I use Windows Explorer. To insert a drawing file using drag-and-drop, follow these steps:

1. Open Windows Explorer (Start⇨Programs⇨Windows Explorer).

2. In the All Folders window, click the folder containing the drawing file you want to insert.

3. Locate the drawing file.

   a. If the AutoCAD window is visible, drag the drawing file into the AutoCAD window.

   b. If the AutoCAD window is not visible, drag the drawing file onto the AutoCAD button on the taskbar, wait for AutoCAD to open, and then drag the file into the AutoCAD window.

4. Respond to the prompts as you would for inserting a block or file.

Figure 18-13 shows dragging the file *window.dwg* from Windows Explorer into an open AutoCAD drawing.

Drag-and-drop is easy to use. It is very helpful if you aren't sure where the file you want is located, because it is easier to navigate with Windows Explorer than from the Select Drawing File dialog box.

Tip

If you really don't know where the file is, or are not even sure of its name, use the Windows Find feature. Choose Start⇨Find⇨Files or Folders. In the Find dialog box, set the criteria for the file. For example, you could find all drawings starting with the letter C by typing **c*.dwg** in the Named text box. From the resulting list, choose the drawing you want and drag it onto your drawing using the same steps listed above.

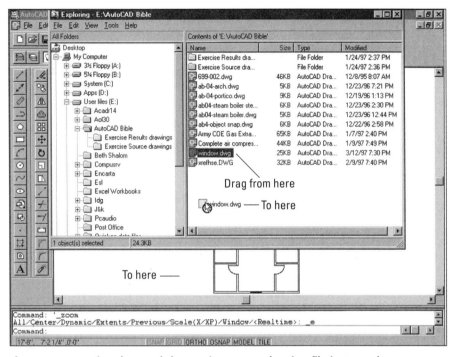

Figure 18-13: Using drag-and-drop to insert one drawing file into another.

Step-by-Step: Using the Windows Clipboard and Drag-and-Drop

On the
CD-ROM

1. Open *ab18-f-1.dwg* from the CD-ROM. This is a set of office furniture, as shown in Figure 18-14.

Figure 18-14: A set of office furniture.

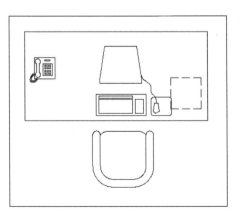

2. Pick the chair, which is a block, and choose Copy to Clipboard from the Standard toolbar.

3. Choose Open from the Standard toolbar. Do not save changes to *ab18-f-1.dwg.* AutoCAD opens the Select File dialog box. Open *ab18-f-2.dwg* from the CD-ROM. This is the plan of an office building, as shown in Figure 18-15.

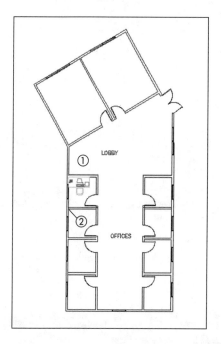

Figure 18-15: The office plan.

4. Save the drawing as *ab18-6.dwg* in your *AutoCAD Bible* folder.

5. Choose Paste from Clipboard from the Standard toolbar. At the Insertion point: prompt, pick ① in Figure 18-15. Press Enter three times to accept the defaults for X and Y scale and rotation. AutoCAD inserts the armchair in the lobby.

6. From the taskbar menu, choose Start⇨Programs⇨Windows Explorer. Locate *ab18-f-1.dwg* on the CD-ROM. If necessary, resize the Exploring window so that you can see some of the AutoCAD window.

7. Drag *ab18-f-1.dwg* from its listing in Windows Explorer onto the AutoCAD drawing area and release the mouse button.

8. At the Insertion point: prompt, pick ②. Use ZOOM Window first to zoom in.

9. Press Enter three times to accept the defaults. AutoCAD inserts the entire drawing.

10. Save your drawing. It should look like Figure 18-16.

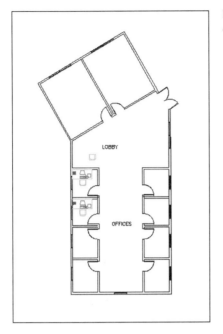

Figure 18-16: The office plan with added chair and office furniture.

As you can see, copying to the Clipboard is ideal when you want to insert part of an existing drawing into another drawing. Drag-and-drop is also a simple way to insert an entire drawing.

Working with Attributes

Your drawings do not exist in a vacuum. The objects in your drawing represent real objects. These objects have characteristics that you cannot visually represent in a drawing, such as cost, manufacturer, date purchased, and so on. You may keep this data in a separate database. Using *attributes,* you can attach such data to blocks. You can then extract the data and import it into a database program or spreadsheet.

You can also access and link outside databases from within AutoCAD. See Chapter 20 for more information on external databases.

Attributes can also be used to place text relative to blocks. A common example is to use attributes for completing title block information such as the drawing name, drawing number, date, scale, revision number, drafter, and so on. In this case, your plan is not to extract the data at all — you just use the attributes to help you place the text in the title block.

Attributes have several limitations. They can only be attached to blocks. However, you can create a dummy block that contains only attributes. Also, the extraction process is somewhat awkward. Nevertheless, attributes are quite useful for simple database needs as well as for placing text.

Defining an attribute essentially creates a template into which you can place values when you insert the block. You define a *tag,* which is equivalent to a field or category in a database. When you insert the block, AutoCAD prompts you for the tag's *value.* For example, if your tag is COST, the value may be 865.79.

Creating attributes

The first procedure when working with attributes is to draw the individual objects that are to make up the block. The exception is when you want to create attributes without creating any block. You might do this to extract attributes that apply to the drawing as a whole.

Tip

If the block already exists, explode it and then define the attributes.

Once you have the objects, choose Draw⇨Block⇨Attributes to start the DDATTDEF command. AutoCAD opens the Attribute Definition dialog box, shown in Figure 18-17.

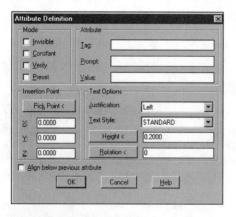

Figure 18-17: The Attribute Definition dialog box.

Mode section

In the Mode section of the dialog box, you set the attribute's properties, as shown in Table 18-4.

Table 18-4 Attribute Modes	
Mode	*Explanation*
Invisible	The attribute values you set are not displayed in the drawing. Use this for attributes that you want to extract into a database but do not want to see in the drawing. Examples would be model numbers, purchase dates, cost, and so on. If you are using attributes to place text in a drawing, of course you want it to be visible.
Constant	Sets a constant value for an attribute. AutoCAD automatically inserts the attribute value you set (in the Attribute section of the dialog box) and does not prompt you for a value. You might use this for the first three digits of employees' telephone numbers that are always the same. You cannot edit constant attribute values.
Verify	When you insert an attribute, AutoCAD asks you to verify the value. Use this if you have a preset default set.
Preset	AutoCAD automatically inserts a default value that you specify. For example, if the most common manufacturer of a chair is American Interiors, you can specify this as a preset value. As you insert the block, this default is inserted for you and you have to type a value only if it differs from the default.

Note

You can insert attributes either in a dialog box or on the command line. By default, you insert them on the command line. To use a dialog box, set the system variable ATTDIA to 1. You would use the command line to automate the insertion of attributes using an AutoLISP routine, menu item, or script file. When you use a dialog box, the Verify and Preset modes have no real meaning.

Attribute section

In the Attribute section of the dialog box, specify the Tag, which is the name of the attribute. You use this tag when you extract the attributes. A tag is equivalent to a field in a database. When you import the data into a spreadsheet, for example, the tags would be the column heads. The tag name cannot include spaces.

The Prompt is simply a plain-English version of the tag. AutoCAD uses the prompt to ask you for the value of the attribute. If the tag is PUR_DATE, you may define the prompt as Date Purchased.

The Value is used for setting a default value. You can use this if the value is usually the same.

You can use the value to make clear a format that should be followed when entering information. For example, you could set the value of a date to dd/mm/yy so that users know how to format the date.

Text Options section

Use the Text Options settings to format the text. Choose a justification and text style from the drop-down text boxes. When you set the height, be sure to take into account the scale factor. You can also set a rotation angle for the text.

Insertion Point section

In the Insertion Point section, choose Pick Point to place the attribute. If you are using the attributes to place text in a schedule or title block, obviously the placement is very important. If you are inserting invisible attributes, simply place them near the block. If you are creating more than one attribute for a block, place the attribute so there is room for the other attributes underneath. When you have placed the attribute and completed the entire dialog box, click OK to end the DDATTDEF command.

By default, the insertion point is 0,0. Use this for title blocks that you want to insert into a drawing.

If you are creating a block for a table or an electrical symbol, you don't want the insertion point to be 0,0. Instead, you want an insertion point near the block. If you forget to pick a point and click OK to close the dialog box, AutoCAD automatically places the insertion point at 0,0. If 0,0 isn't visible on the screen, you don't see the attribute — it seems to disappear! You can choose Undo from the Standard toolbar and create a new attribute in the right location or move the attribute as explained in the section on editing attributes later in this chapter.

Once you have defined one attribute, the Place below previous attribute check box is active. Click this to line up succeeding attributes under the first one.

Now is the time to check that the attributes are the way you want them. You can edit attributes before they have been placed into a block in three ways:

✦ Choose Properties on the Object Properties toolbar, choose one attribute, and edit all the properties of an attribute, such as the tag, value, prompt, and modes (DDMODIFY command).

✦ Choose Modify⇨Object⇨Text and change the tag, the prompt, and the default (DDEDIT command).

✦ Use the CHANGE command — press Enter at the `Properties/<Change point>:` prompt and step through the prompts.

If you are creating many blocks with similar attributes, you can copy just the attributes, modify them as just described, place them near other objects and then create the blocks. This way you don't have to define all the attributes from scratch.

Creating the block

Once you have created the objects and their attributes you generally create a block. Choose Make Block from the Draw toolbar. Select the objects and the attributes in the block.

If the order of the attribute prompts is important, don't use a window to select the attributes — select them in the order in which you want the prompts to appear. You can then use a crossing or window box to select the rest of the objects to be included in the block.

Name the block and define the block's insertion point as you would normally. Generally, you want to uncheck Retain objects since you have no need for the block with the attribute tags in your drawing.

Don't forget to pay attention to the layer of the attributes just as you would the layer of the block objects. The same layer rules apply to attributes as to blocks.

There is one exception to creating a block with attributes. If you want to insert the objects and the attributes as a file instead of as a block, you don't need to create a block at all. Create a drawing containing just the block and its attributes. Use the BASE command to change the base point of the drawing (usually 0,0) to the desired insertion point of the block. Then save the drawing. When you insert the drawing, AutoCAD prompts you for the attributes as usual. Use this technique for blocks and attributes that you use for more than one drawing, such as a title block.

Once you create the block, you cannot edit the attributes by choosing Properties on the Object Properties toolbar. I cover other techniques for editing attributes later in this chapter.

Step-by-Step: Creating Attributes

1. Open *ab18-g.dwg* from the CD-ROM. This is a plan of an office building zoomed in to one office. A file containing one set of office furniture has been inserted, as shown in Figure 18-18.

2. Save the drawing as *ab18-7.dwg* in your *AutoCAD Bible* folder.

3. Choose Explode from the Modify toolbar and select the furniture in the office. This block has nested blocks. Choose the chair and explode it again to get its component objects.

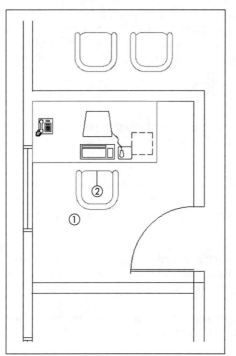

Figure 18-18: An office with a set of office furniture.

4. Choose Draw⇨Block⇨Define Attributes. In the Attribute Definition dialog box, check Invisible in the Mode section.

5. In the Attribute section enter the following:

```
Tag: mfr
Prompt: Manufacturer
Value: American Office Furniture
```

6. Click Pick Point to temporarily return to the drawing. Pick point ① in Figure 18-18. Leave the Text Options as they are. Click OK to end the command.

7. Repeat the DDATTDEF command. Click Align below previous attribute. Enter the following:

```
Tag: pur_date
Prompt: Date purchased
Value: 3/91
```

8. Click OK.

 9. Choose Make Block from the Draw toolbar. In the Block Name text box, type **armchair**. Click Select Objects. Select the entire chair plus the two attributes. End selection. In the dialog box, AutoCAD notes that it found 18 objects. Choose Select Point. Use the Endpoint object snap to choose ② as the base point. Uncheck Retain Objects. Click OK.

10. AutoCAD asks if you want to redefine the block. Choose Yes. AutoCAD displays this message because there is already a block definition with the same name in the drawing.

11. Save your drawing. If you are continuing on to the next Step-by-Step exercise, leave the drawing open.

Inserting blocks with attributes

Once you have defined a block with attributes, you insert it as you would any block. AutoCAD automatically senses the existence of the attributes and prompts you for their values.

As mentioned earlier, set the ATTDIA system variable to 1 if you want to enter attributes in a dialog box.

Step-by-Step: Inserting Blocks with Attributes

On the
CD-ROM

1. Use *ab18-7.dwg* if you have it open from the previous exercise. Otherwise, open it from the *Results* folder of the CD-ROM.

2. Save the drawing as *ab18-8.dwg* in your *AutoCAD Bible* folder. ATTDIA is set to 1.

3. Choose Insert Block from the Draw toolbar. Click Block. Chose ARMCHAIR and click OK twice to specify the insertion point.

4. Pick a point in front of the desk (double-click OSNAP if AutoCAD snaps to the endpoint of the desk). Press Enter three times to accept the X and Y scale and rotation defaults. AutoCAD opens the Enter Attributes dialog box, as shown in Figure 18-19. The values that were entered when the attributes were defined are displayed, but you can change them.

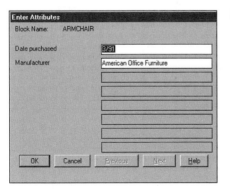

Figure 18-19: The Enter Attributes dialog box.

5. The reason for the default values is that most of the furniture was purchased at one time when the office was opened. However, let's assume that this chair was purchased a year later. Change the purchase date to **3/92**. Click OK. Since the attributes are invisible, you see only the chair, but the values are there in the drawing database.

6. Save the drawing.

Editing attributes

As mentioned earlier, you can edit the properties of the attribute tags before you create the block, using DDMODIFY (choose Properties from the Object Properties toolbar), DDEDIT (choose Modify⇨Object⇨Text), or CHANGE (press Enter at the Change point default option and step through the prompts). Once you have created the block, use one of three commands to edit attributes: DDATTE, ATTEDIT, and ATTREDEF, described in this section.

Caution

If you explode a block with attribute values, you lose the attribute values.

Changing an attribute value

Once you have inserted a block and given values to its attributes, you can change the attribute values. Choose Modify⇨Object⇨Attribute⇨Single to start the DDATTE command. Once you select a block that contains attribute values, AutoCAD opens the Edit Attributes dialog box so that you can change the attribute values, as shown in Figure 18-20.

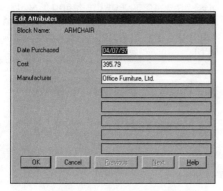

Figure 18-20: The Edit Attributes dialog box.

Making attribute display and global changes

Another command (with a very similar name) for editing attributes is the ATTEDIT command. To change attribute display, you must use the `Edit attributes one at a time` option. Attribute display edits include changing the value, position, height, angle, text style, layer, and color. If you answer No to the `Edit attributes one at a time` option, you can make global changes to attribute values — for example, change all instances of *A-* in your part numbers to *B-*.

Here's how you use ATTEDIT to edit attributes one at a time.

1. To start the ATTEDIT command, choose Modify➪Object➪Attribute➪Global. (It's probably quicker to type **attedit**.) AutoCAD responds with the `Edit attributes one at a time?` `<Y>` prompt. To edit one attribute at a time, press Enter.

2. At the `Block name specification <*>:` prompt, press Enter to leave open the option to edit any block, or type in the name of the block whose attributes you want to edit.

3. At the `Attribute tag specification <*>:` prompt, you usually press Enter to allow you to modify all attribute tags, but you can limit it to a particular tag.

4. At the `Attribute value specification <*>:` prompt, you usually press Enter to allow you to modify all attribute values, but you can limit it to a particular value.

5. At the `Select Attributes:` prompt, pick each attribute you wish to modify. To use a window, you must type **w** ↵ or **c** ↵ first. Press Enter to end selection. If you include other objects or blocks that do not fit the block name, attribute tag, or attribute value specifications you made, AutoCAD does not select them. AutoCAD informs you how many attributes were selected.

6. At the `Value/Position/Height/Angle/Style/Layer/Color/Next <N>:` prompt, choose the type of change you want to make.

7. If you choose Value, AutoCAD responds with the `Change or Replace? <R>:` prompt. Choose Change if you want to specify a specific text string (any consecutive text) to change. AutoCAD then asks for the new string. For example, if you want to change each instance of *Ltd.* to *Co.* in a supplier's name, you could use Change and avoid having to retype in the entire name of the supplier. Choose Replace when you need to retype the entire prompt.

The other option prompts are straightforward.

Using ATTEDIT to make global changes is similar to using the Change option when you individually change the value of an attribute (see step 7 just previous). To use ATTEDIT to make global changes, follow these steps:

1. Start the ATTEDIT command.

2. At the Edit attributes one at a time? <Y> prompt, type **n** ↵.

3. At the Edit only attributes visible on screen? <Y> prompt, answer **y** or **n** ↵, as desired. Answer **n** to edit invisible attributes, but you must know the attribute text string you want to change since it's invisible. You can use DDATTE to view an attribute first.

4. At the Block name specification <*>: prompt, you can type a block name to limit the changes to one block or press Enter to let you select any block.

5. At the Attribute tag specification <*>: prompt, you can type a tag to limit the changes to one tag type or press Enter to let you select any tag.

6. At the Attribute value specification <*>: prompt, you can type a value to limit the changes to one value or press Enter to let you select any value.

7. If you chose to edit only attributes visible on screen, AutoCAD responds with the Select Attributes: prompt. (If not, skip to step 8.) Pick each attribute you wish to modify. To use a window, you must type **w** ↵ or **c** ↵ first. Press Enter to end selection. If you include other objects or blocks that do not fit the block name, attribute tag, or attribute value specifications you made, AutoCAD does not select them. AutoCAD informs you how many attributes were selected.

8. At the String to change: prompt, type the text string (any consecutive text) you want to change.

9. At the New string: prompt, type the text string you want to replace the old string.

If you chose to edit attributes not visible on the screen, AutoCAD regenerates the drawing and lists the changes it made.

Redefining attributes

You can redefine a block with attributes to include different objects and attributes, using the ATTREDEF command. Follow these steps:

1. Explode one of the blocks with attributes. If there are nested blocks that you want to change, explode them, too.

2. If you want to add attributes, define and place them.

3. Type **attredef** ↵.

4. At the Name of Block you wish to redefine: prompt, type the name of the block.

5. At the Select objects for new Block... prompt, select the objects and the attributes you wish to include. Do not include any existing attributes that you wish to delete.

6. At the Insertion base point of new Block: prompt, pick the base point for the block.

Here's how AutoCAD handles the changes:

✦ If you created new attributes, AutoCAD places them for all existing blocks and gives them their default values.

✦ Any attributes that you did not change retain their old values for all existing blocks.

✦ Any attributes that you did not include in the new block definition are deleted from existing blocks.

Mddatte.lsp allows you to edit any number of block attributes one after the other without having to use the DDATTE command for each block. Look in the *\Software\Chap18\Ddatte* folder.

Step-by-Step: Editing Attributes

1. Use *ab18-h.dwg* from the CD-ROM.

2. Save it as *ab18-9.dwg* in your *AutoCAD Bible* folder. This is a portion of an office building plan layout, shown in Figure 18-21.

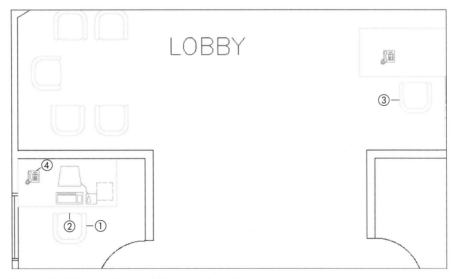

Figure 18-21: An office building plan layout.

3. Choose Modify⇨Object⇨Attribute⇨Single to start the DDATTE command. At the `Select block:` prompt, pick the chair at ① in Figure 18-21. In the Edit Attributes dialog box, change the date purchased to **4/97** and click OK. Notice that the manufacturer is American Office Furniture. Since these attributes are invisible, you can't see the result in the drawing.

4. Choose Modify⇨Object⇨Attribute⇨Global to start the ATTEDIT command. Follow the prompts:

```
Edit attributes one at a time? <Y> n ↵
Global edit of attribute values.
Edit only attributes visible on screen? <Y> n ↵
Drawing must be regenerated afterwards.
Block name specification <*>: armchair ↵
Attribute tag specification <*>: ↵
Attribute value specification <*>: ↵
6 attributes selected.
String to change: American ↵
New string: Acme ↵
Acme Office Furniture
Acme Office Furniture
Acme Office Furniture
Regenerating drawing.
```

5. Choose Explode from the Modify toolbar and select the chair at ① in Figure 18-21. The attributes reappear. Choose Draw⇨Block⇨Define Attributes. Create an invisible attribute with a tag and prompt of **Color** and a value of **Dusty Blue**. Click Pick Point and pick a point underneath the other two attributes of the armchair. (Exact placement is not important.) Choose OK.

6. Type **attredef** ↵. Follow the prompts:

```
Name of Block you wish to redefine: armchair ↵
Select objects for new Block... Use a window to select the chair
and the three attributes. Press Enter to end selection.
Insertion base point of new Block: Use an Endpoint object snap to
pick the endpoint at ②.
```

The armchair block disappears.

7. Choose Insert Block. In the Insert dialog box, type **armchair** in the Block text box and click OK. Insert the chair at ② and accept the default scale and rotation. In the Enter Attributes dialog box, click OK to accept the values.

8. To see that AutoCAD has redefined the block elsewhere, type **ddatte** ↵. Select the block at ③. Notice that the Color tag has been added with a value of Dusty Blue. Click OK to accept the values.

9. Use a Zoom Window to zoom in closely to the telephone at ④ in Figure 18-21. The telephone has a visible attribute of the phone number. The number is so small that it cannot usually be seen and so does not interfere with the drawing.

10. Choose Modify⇨Object⇨Attribute⇨Global. Follow the prompts:

```
Edit attributes one at a time? <Y> ↵
Block name specification <*>: ↵
Attribute tag specification <*>: ↵
Attribute value specification <*>: ↵
Select Attributes: Pick the attribute (the four-digit number in the
rectangle).
Select Attributes: ↵
1 attributes selected.
Value/Position/Height/Angle/Style/Layer/Color/Next <N>: p ↵
Enter text insertion point: Pick a point in the middle of the
rectangle to move the attribute to the right. (If OSNAP is on, turn it off.)
AutoCAD moves the attribute.
Value/Position/Height/Angle/Style/Layer/Color/Next <N>: v ↵
Change or Replace? <R>: r ↵
New attribute value: 7925 ↵
Value/Position/Height/Angle/Style/Layer/Color/Next <N>: ↵
```

AutoCAD replaces the attribute with the new phone number.

11. Choose Zoom Previous from the Standard toolbar. Save the drawing.

Extracting a database from attributes

Once you have inserted all your blocks and attributes, you can extract the data
using the DDATTEXT (for attribute extraction) command. First you need to tell
AutoCAD which data to extract and in what format. You do this by creating a
template file, a plain-text (ASCII) file, with a text editor such as Windows 95
Notepad. AutoCAD uses this template file to create the *output* file, which contains
the data you have requested.

You can also use almost any word processor for the template file and save it as a
Text Only or MS-DOS Text file.

The template file

The template file contains two columns. The first is the name of the attribute tag.
The second is a format code that tells AutoCAD if the data is a character or
number, how many spaces to allow for the data, and the decimal precision to use.
The format code uses the following syntax:

```
Twwwppp
```

where T is the data type — either N for numeral or C for character, www is the width
including commas and decimal points, and ppp is the precision. For integers and
all character data, use 000 as the precision.

For example, you would use N006002 for costs that range up to $999.99. The N
means the data is numeric, 006 means that you will have up to six spaces including

the decimal point, and the 002 means that you have precision of two decimal places.

In addition to information from your attributes, AutoCAD lets you extract certain standard fields from the drawing's database. This can add to the usefulness of your final report. Table 18-5 lists these fields. The fields all start with BL: followed by the name of the field. The table also includes the format code information you need to know to create the format code for the template file.

Table 18-5
Standard Extraction Fields

Field	Format	Explanation
BL: LEVEL	Nwww000	Block nesting level
BL: NAME	Cwww000	Block name
BL: X	Nwwwppp	X coordinate of block insertion point
BL: Y	Nwwwppp	Y coordinate of block insertion point
BL: Z	Nwwwppp	Z coordinate of block insertion point
BL: NUMBER	Nwww000	Block counter
BL: HANDLE	Cwww000	Block handle
BL: LAYER	Cwww000	Block insertion layer name
BL: ORIENT	Nwwwddd	Block rotation angle
BL: XSCALE	Nwwwddd	X scale factor
BL: YSCALE	Nwwwddd	Y scale factor
BL: ZSCALE	Nwwwddd	Z scale factor
BL: XEXTRUDE	Nwwwddd	X component of Block's extrusion direction
BL: YEXTRUDE	Nwwwddd	Y component of Block's extrusion direction
BL: ZEXTRUDE	Nwwwddd	Z component of Block's extrusion direction

The block number is a number given to the blocks you select when extracting the data. The block handle is a unique alphanumeric code given to all objects in your drawing. To see a block's handle, choose List from the Inquiry flyout on the Standard toolbar and select the block. AutoCAD includes the block's handle. Handles are used for referring to objects when you write AutoLISP or other programming code. The extrusion data is used for 3D drawing. See Chapter 24 for an explanation of extrusion.

Template files are quite finicky. Here are some of the rules:

✦ You must include at least one attribute tag in your template.

✦ Each row must be unique. You can't include the same attribute more than once.

✦ You must use only spaces to line up the two columns — no tabs! (You don't have to line up the two columns; it just makes it easier to read.)

✦ End each line with a return, including the last line.

✦ Don't put any extra spaces after any line or any extra returns after the last line of text.

Each row in the template file becomes a column in the resulting output file. If you choose space-delimited form for the output file, AutoCAD doesn't automatically put spaces between the columns, resulting in output files that are hard to read. This is especially true for numerical data where you specify only the number of spaces required to line up the numbers. You can place dummy rows in the template file for the purpose of creating spaces in the resulting columns. A typical dummy row would look like this:

```
DUMMY1       C002000
```

Because each row must be unique, if you need another dummy row, call it DUMMY2. This row would create a blank column in the output file of two spaces.

Figure 18-22 shows a typical template file. Here a Facilities Manager uses attributes to track the company division, as well as the furniture's manufacturer, purchase date, cost, and color.

Figure 18-22: A template file.

Tip

If you have forgotten the exact name of your tags, you can use the LIST command on the block. After listing the block information, the LIST command lists the properties of any attributes, including the tag name.

Step-by-Step: Creating an Attribute Template File

1. From the Windows 95 taskbar, choose Start⇨Programs⇨Accessories⇨Notepad to open Notepad.

2. Type the following. Remember to put a return after each line, including the last line. Don't use any tabs, only spaces, to line up the columns.

```
BL:NAME      C010000
BL:X         N007002
DUMMY1       C002000
BL:Y         N007002
DUMMY2       C002000
BL:ORIENT    N003000
DUMMY3       C002000
MFR          C026000
PUR_DATE     C008000
COLOR        C015000↵
```

3. Choose File⇨Save. Save the file as *ab18-1.txt* in your *AutoCAD Bible* folder. It should look like Figure 18-23. Close Notepad.

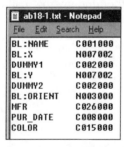

Figure 18-23: The template file.

Attribute extraction

Once you have created the template file, you can extract the data. Type **ddattext** ↵. AutoCAD opens the Attribute Extraction dialog box, shown in Figure 18-24.

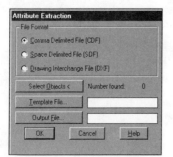

Figure 18-24: The Attribute Extraction dialog box.

Use the File Format section of the dialog box to choose the format of the output file you will create. You have three choices:

✦ Comma Delimited File (CDF) creates a file with commas between the fields (columns).

✦ Space Delimited File (SDF) creates a file with spaces between the fields (columns).

✦ Drawing Interchange File (DXF) creates a file in the format used by AutoCAD's DXF format but includes only the data from the blocks you select. You do not create a template file for this format.

Cross-Reference

See Chapter 27 for more on the DXF format.

Your choice of format depends on how you plan to use the output file. Will you import it into a mainframe database or use a PC-based spreadsheet? Most database programs can accept both comma- and space-delimited files, as do most spreadsheets. However, one format is often much easier to work with than the other. Check with the documentation of the application you will use with the output file to see what formats it can accept.

Choose Select Objects to select the blocks you want to include in the output file. AutoCAD returns you temporarily to your drawing. Press Enter to end object selection and return to the dialog box.

Choose Template File to specify the template file you have created. If you know its name and location, you can type it in.

Choose Output File to create an output file. The output file's name should be different than the template file's name. Otherwise, if they are in the same folder, the output file will overwrite the template file!

When you have specified the file format, selected objects, and specified the template and output files, click OK to create the output file.

If there are any mistakes in the template file, AutoCAD issues a message on the command line. In most cases, AutoCAD does not complete the output file. If you get the message ** Field overflow in record n, it means that an attribute was too long for its column. AutoCAD completes the output file but truncates the attribute value.

Note

You can also use the ATTEXT command to extract attribute data without a dialog box.

Step-by-Step: Extracting Attribute Data

On the
CD-ROM

1. Open *ab18-i.dwg* from the CD-ROM. This is the same office building plan you used earlier in this chapter, shown in Figure 18-25.

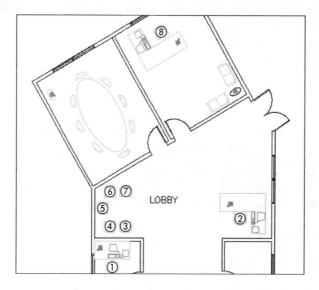

Figure 18-25: The office building plan includes several blocks of armchairs with invisible attributes.

2. Type **ddattext** ↵ to open the Attribute Extraction dialog box.

3. Choose Space Delimited File (SDF).

4. Choose Select objects. Pick the chairs marked ① through ⑧ in Figure 18-25.

On the
CD-ROM

5. Choose Template File. Choose *ab18-1.txt* in your *AutoCAD Bible* folder if you did the last exercise. Otherwise, locate it in the *Exercise Results* folder of the CD-ROM.

6. Choose Output File. In the Output File dialog box, choose your *AutoCAD Bible* folder and name the file *ab18-2.txt.* Choose Save.

7. Click OK in the Attribute Extraction dialog box. AutoCAD creates the file. AutoCAD ends with the message 8 records in extract file.

8. To view the output file, from the Windows 95 taskbar choose Start⇨Programs⇨Accessories⇨WordPad. (Notepad doesn't line up the columns for you.) Choose File⇨Open and locate the *ab18-2.txt* file in your *AutoCAD Bible* folder. Click Open. It should look like Figure 18-26.

9. Do not save your drawing.

Figure 18-26: The output file that results from extracting the attributes in the office building plan.

Importing an attribute database into a spreadsheet

You can't do very much with the database in WordPad. However, if you import it into a database management or spreadsheet application, you can manipulate the data as you wish. If you import it into a word processing program, you can include the data in a report. In this section I explain how to import the text into Microsoft Excel as an example.

Note

You can open the Multiline Text Editor and click Import Text to import the output file into your drawing. You can also open the output file, copy it to the Clipboard, and paste it into your drawing. The Import Text method lets you format the text as you would any multiline text but takes some experimenting to set up in the proper columns. You cannot format the text you import using the Clipboard method, but it is nicely lined up in columns.

Version 7.0 of Excel uses a wizard to import text files. You can use either comma- or space-delimited files.

Step-by-Step: Importing Attribute Output Files into Microsoft Excel

On the CD-ROM

1. Open Microsoft Excel. Choose File⇨Open. In the Open dialog box, choose Text files from the Files of type drop-down list. Open *ab18-2.txt* in your *AutoCAD Bible* folder if you did the last exercise. Otherwise, open it from the *Results* folder on the CD-ROM.

2. Excel opens the Text Import Wizard, as shown in Figure 18-27, and decides correctly that your file is a Fixed Width file, meaning that the data is aligned in columns with spaces between each field. Click Next.

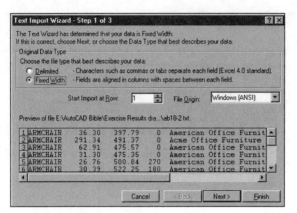

Figure 18-27: Excel's Text Import Wizard.

3. In the next frame of the wizard, you format the columns. Use the horizontal scroll bar until you see the part of the report shown in Figure 18-28. As you can see, Excel has created columns in the middle of the manufacturer and color columns. Double-click the two incorrect columns in the manufacturer column and the incorrect column in the color column to delete them. Click Next.

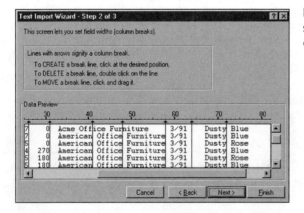

Figure 18-28: The next frame shows column breaks, which can be edited.

4. The third frame of the wizard sets the data format. By default, the columns are set to the General format, which converts numeric values to numbers, date values to dates, and everything else to text. This suits most situations. Click Finish. Excel imports the text. Figure 18-29 shows the result after adding headings and adding some simple formatting.

5. Save the Excel file as *ab18-2.xls* in your *AutoCAD Bible* folder.

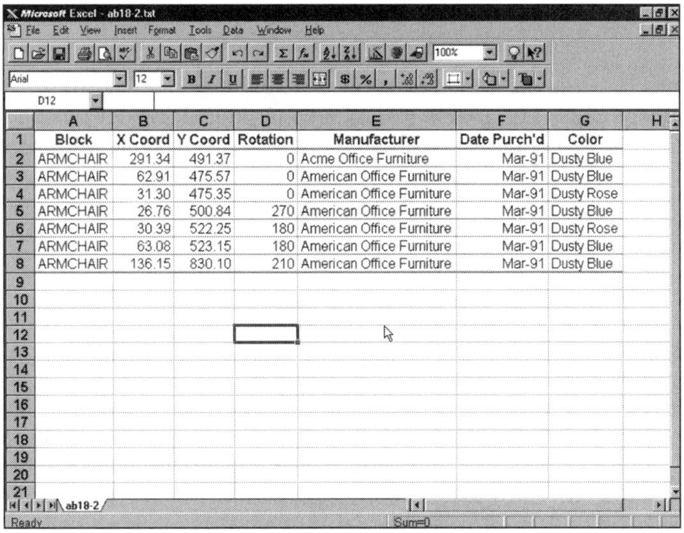

Figure 18-29: The result of importing the attribute data into Excel.

You can also import comma-delimited files into Excel — in fact, it's easier than importing space-delimited data. For Lotus 1-2-3, comma-delimited files are almost a necessity. See the sidebar "Here's how to import extracted attribute files into Lotus 1-2-3."

Here's how to import extracted attribute files into Lotus 1-2-3

If you want to import an extraction file into Lotus 1-2-3, you should extract the data as a comma-delimited file. Then follow these steps:

1. Choose File⇨Open to display the Open dialog box.

2. In the Files of type drop-down list, choose Text.

3. Choose the output file you created using DDATTEXT and click Open. 1-2-3 displays the text File Options dialog box.

4. Select the first option (Start a new column at each) and choose Comma from the drop-down list.

5. Click OK. 1-2-3 creates a new workbook with the data.

(Thanks to John Walkenbach, a spreadsheet guru and author of numerous books on 1-2-3 and Excel, for these steps.)

Summary

In this chapter I covered all the ways you can use blocks and attributes in your drawings. You can combine objects into blocks in your drawings so that you can edit them as a unit. You can also easily insert them at any scale and rotation.

To use a block in any drawing, save it as a file. You can create symbol or part libraries to use for all your drawings.

You can also copy objects using the Windows Clipboard. This is ideal for copying part of another drawing and inserting it into your current drawing. You can import files using drag-and-drop.

Attributes are text attached to blocks. Attributes have two main uses: to place text and to create simple databases. Once you create the attributes, you make a block that includes the objects and attributes together. Then you insert the block into your drawing. AutoCAD automatically prompts you for the attribute values. There are several commands that let you edit attributes both before and after including them in blocks.

Once you have the blocks and their attributes inserted, you can extract them into one of three formats. If you want to create comma- or space-delimited files, you need to create a template file first. Then you extract the attribute data. Once you have the attribute output file, you can import it into a database management program, a spreadsheet, a word processor, or even back into your drawing.

✦   ✦   ✦

Referencing Other Drawings

Understanding External References

Sometimes you need to refer to another AutoCAD drawing without inserting it. You may want to use part of another drawing as an example for your current drawing or see how the model in your drawing fits in with models in other drawings. Before AutoCAD offered external references, you had to print out the other drawing to refer to it while in a current drawing or perhaps print out both drawings and lay one on top of the other to compare them.

External references (commonly called *xrefs*) let you view any drawing as a reference while in your current drawing. The external drawing is not part of your current drawing. The current drawing keeps track of the location and name of external reference so you can always reference it easily. As with blocks, you can snap to objects in the external reference, thereby using it as a reference for the drawing process. You can also change the visibility settings of the xref's layers.

There are several advantages of xrefs over blocks:

+ Xrefs keep your drawing smaller than blocks. The externally referenced drawing doesn't become part of your drawing. Your drawing only maintains a reference (name and location) to the other drawing.

+ You always have the most updated version of the xref. Each time AutoCAD loads your drawing, it loads the current copy of the xref. By contrast, you would need to reinsert a file inserted as a block to see the most updated version.

CHAPTER

19

✦ ✦ ✦ ✦

In This Chapter

Understanding external references

Attaching and overlaying external references

Clipping external references

Using demand loading with spatial and layer indexes

Using the new Xref Manager

Managing external references

✦ ✦ ✦ ✦

✦ In a team project, several people can use the same drawing as an xref, each having access to the latest changes.

✦ You may not want the xref to be part of your drawing. If you are only using the xref for reference, you may detach it before plotting. Xrefs can be attached and detached easily for maximum flexibility, or overlaid for temporary use.

Release 14 introduces several new xref features, which are covered in this chapter.

Attaching an external reference

The first step is to attach the external reference, which is just another drawing, to your current drawing. When working with xrefs, you may find it useful to use the Reference toolbar. To open the Reference toolbar, choose View⇨Toolbars (or right-click any toolbar currently displayed) and check Reference. Click Close on the Toolbars dialog box.

To attach an xref, follow these steps:

1. Choose External Reference from the Reference toolbar or choose Insert⇨ External Reference. AutoCAD opens the External Reference dialog box, shown in Figure 19-1, your one-stop shopping mall for external references.

This dialog box, new for Release 14, lets you manage all your xrefs in one place.

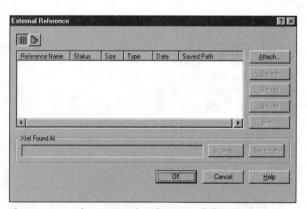

Figure 19-1: The External Reference dialog box.

2. If you don't have any xrefs in use in a drawing, the External Reference dialog box is blank. This screen shows your current external references. To attach an external reference, choose Attach to open the Select file to attach dialog

box. This dialog box is like any Open dialog box. Choose the file you want to attach and click Open. AutoCAD opens the Attach Xref dialog box, shown in Figure 19-2. The Xref Name section displays the file you chose along with its path (location).

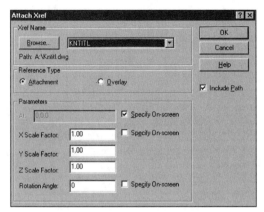

Figure 19-2: The Attach Xref dialog box.

3. Choose the type of xref in the Reference Type section:

   ✦ **Attachment:** when you attach a drawing, any xrefs in that drawing also appear. In other words, you can see nested layers of xrefs.

   ✦ **Overlay:** when you overlay a drawing, you only see that drawing. Any xrefs in that drawing are not shown in your current drawing. In other words, you cannot see nested layers of xrefs.

Tip Use overlays when you don't want the complication of nested xrefs or just want to see another drawing temporarily. Otherwise, use attachments.

4. Use the Parameters section to specify the insertion point, X and Y scale factors, and rotation angle either in the dialog box or on screen. These prompts are the same ones you use when inserting a block or file.

5. Check Include Path if you want AutoCAD to save not only the xref's name but its location. You want to include the path if the drawing is not in the Support Files or Project Files search path. You can set these search paths by choosing Tools⇨Preferences⇨Files.

6. When you have completed the dialog box, click OK.

AutoCAD attaches the xref. If your current view does not show the extents of the xref, do a ZOOM Extents to see the entire xref.

Spotlight on AutoCAD Users
Using xrefs for electrical designing

Wing T. Duong works for Pacific Engineering Associates, an electrical engineering firm in Oakland, California. He mostly creates floor plans for power distribution and lighting fixtures layout.

When he starts a new project, if he is dealing with a new architect, he meets with the CAD people to review the basic setup—layer names, fonts, colors, and so on, to make sure there is no conflict between standards. This process also involves the mechanical, structural, and civil engineers. Then he gets a set of drawings from the architect. He calls them architectural backgrounds because he uses them as xrefs in his electrical drawings. The xrefs are the base plans that he uses to create his electrical designs. If the architectural plans change, he gets new drawings from the architect, copies these files over the old drawings, and then his drawings automatically display the newest version of the xref. You see here a typical architectural design of the type Wing uses.

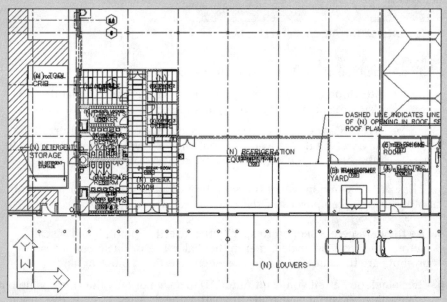

Credit: Thanks to Kent Hetherwick of Kava Massih Architects, Berkeley, California, for this drawing.

On a typical project, Wing's set of drawings include a cover sheet that contains a symbol list, abbreviations, general notes, and a drawing list. He adds a site plan that shows the outlines and locations of the related buildings and the surrounding landscape with power and site lighting fixtures layout. He includes one or two sheets containing the power plan—all the electrical device locations as well as the branch circuitry so the electrical contractor knows how to connect them together, and the same for the lighting plan(s). An example is shown here.

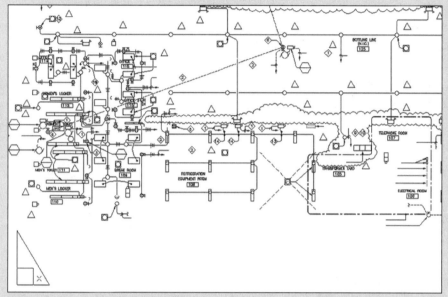

Credit: Thanks to Wing Duong of Pacific Engineering Associates, Oakland, California, for this drawing.

Other pieces of the puzzle include a detail sheet showing various devices or lighting fixtures, what they look like and their mounting methods, a single-line diagram that shows all the electrical panels and their relationships, a panel schedule sheet containing data imported from a spreadsheet, and possibly other items depending on the project.

All these drawings are submitted several times—for the schematic design review, the building permit, the final submittal, and to update the project whenever there are changes (and there always are). When the project is finally built, a set of final drawings, called the as-built drawings, are created. Here you see his power plan with the architectural plan visible as an xref.

(continued)

Once you have the xref in your drawing, you can start to work. The xref is like a block, but you cannot explode or edit it. To edit an xref, you return to that file and edit it there. However, you can use object snaps on all the objects in an xref, just as you can with blocks. This lets you use the xref as a basis for your own drawing.

Viewing xref relationships

To see what type of xrefs you have in your drawing, choose Insert⇨External Reference. The external references are listed in the External Reference dialog box. You can choose one of two views:

✦ **List View** lists all the xrefs along with their status, size, type, date and time saved, and the saved path, if any.

✦ **Tree View** lists all the xrefs in a graphical view that shows their relationships. This is great for understanding nested xrefs.

Tip You can change the width of the columns in List View by placing the cursor on a column dividing line until it changes to a two-headed arrow. Then drag in either direction.

Click any xref and the Xref Found At box displays the location of the xref.

Step-by-Step: Attaching Xrefs

On the CD-ROM

1. Open *ab19-a.dwg* from the CD-ROM. This is the floor plan for a house.

2. Open Windows Explorer (right click Start on the Taskbar and choose Explore). Copy *ab19-b.dwg* from the CD-ROM to your *AutoCAD Bible* folder.

3. Choose Insert⇨External Reference. Click Attach. In the Select file to attach dialog box, choose *ab19-b.dwg*. Choose Open.

4. In the Attach Xref dialog box, you see the filename displayed. Leave the other defaults and click OK. AutoCAD displays *ab19-b.dwg,* which is a title block, in *ab19-a.dwg.*

5. Save the drawing as *ab19-1.dwg* in your *AutoCAD Bible* folder.

6. Start a new drawing using *acad.dwt* as the template. Choose Format⇨Units and choose Architectural. Choose OK. Save it as *ab19-2.dwg* in your *AutoCAD Bible* folder.

7. Choose Insert⇨External Reference. Click Attach. In the Select file to attach dialog box, choose *ab19-1.dwg,* which you just saved in your *AutoCAD Bible* folder. Choose Open.

8. In the Attach Xref dialog box, you see the filename displayed. Leave the other defaults and click OK. AutoCAD displays *ab19-1.dwg,* which includes both the title block and the floor plan of the house, in your new drawing. The title block drawing (*ab19-b.dwg*) is a nested xref in the floor plan (*ab19-1.dwg*) xref. AutoCAD tells you this with the following message:

```
Attach Xref AB19-1: C:\AutoCAD Bible\ab19-1.dwg
AB19-1 loaded.
Attach Xref AB19-B: E:\AutoCAD Bible\ab19-b.dwg
AB19-B loaded.
```

9. To help you visualize the relationships among the three drawings, choose Insert⇨External Reference again. The External Reference dialog box lists both drawings. Click Tree View at the top of the dialog box. AutoCAD now lists the two xrefs in a tree structure, showing their relationship more clearly, as shown in Figure 19-3.

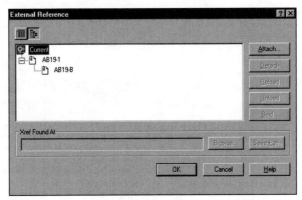

Figure 19-3: Tree view shows nested xrefs clearly.

10. Choose Zoom Extents from the Zoom flyout of the Standard toolbar. Save your drawing. It should look like Figure 19-4.

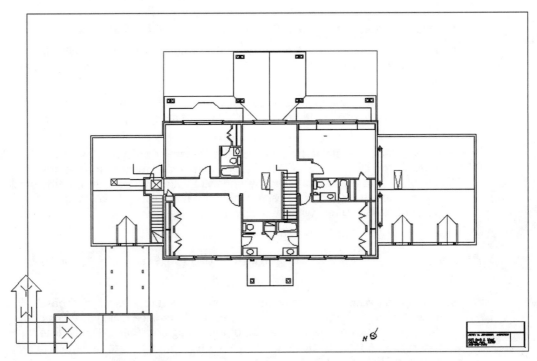

Figure 19-4: The current drawing is blank but displays an xref of a house plan that has a nested xref of a title block.

Controlling Xref Display

You can control the display of xref layers so that you see only those layers you need. Release 14 has added several new features to control the process of displaying xrefs, making it easier to see only part of an xref and speeding up the display of very large xrefs.

Xrefs and dependent symbols

Dependent symbols are named items in a drawing, such as layers, text styles, dimension styles, and so on. When you attach an xref, these symbols are listed in your current drawing. For example, the Layer Control drop-down list displays the layers of the xref. Xref symbols have the format `xref_name|symbol_name`. This system distinguishes xref symbols from those of your current drawing and ensures that there are no duplicate symbols.

Xrefs and layers

You can turn on and off, or freeze and thaw, xref layers. You can also change an xref layer's properties in the Layer and Linetype Properties dialog box. By default these changes are temporary. The next time you open the drawing or reload the xref, the original settings are restored. However, you can set the VISRETAIN system variable to 1 to retain these changes.

Objects created on layer 0 do not take on the typical xref layer name format, but stay on layer 0. If objects in the xref are on layer 0 with the color and linetype set to ByLayer, they take on the color and linetype properties of the current layer in the current drawing. If color and linetype are set to ByBlock, objects assume the current properties when the xref is attached. If you explicitly set color and linetype, objects retain those settings.

The XBIND command

Symbols are the various properties of objects that are saved in a drawing, such as layers, dimension styles, text styles, and so on. You can use the XBIND command to import only the symbols you want from the external reference into the current drawing. This makes it easy to work with a consistent set of symbols in the current drawing and the xrefs. For example, you can choose to import the titleblk layer and the dec dimension style. Type **xbind** ↵ on the command line. AutoCAD opens the Xbind dialog box, which lists each xref in the drawing and its symbols in a Windows 95 Explorer-like display, as shown in Figure 19-5.

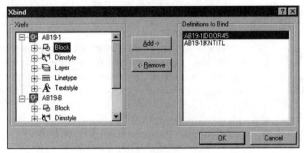

Figure 19-5: Using the XBIND command to import symbols such as layers, text styles, and so on.

Click the plus sign next to any symbol type to open a list of symbols. Click the one you want and choose Add to add it to the Definitions to Bind list. Click OK when you are done.

Circular references

If drawing *a* includes drawing *b* as an xref and drawing *b* includes drawing *a* as an xref, you have a circular reference. Circular references can exist among three or more xrefs as well as when you have nested xrefs. Release 14 now detects circular references and loads as much as it can instead of leaving out an entire branch. If you try to load an xref in such a situation, AutoCAD gives you the following message:

```
Warning: Circular reference from XREF to current drawing.
(AutoCAD inserts the actual name of the xref.)
Circular reference(s) have been found. Continue? <N> Type y
to continue to load the xref.
Breaking circular reference from XREF to current drawing.
```

Clipping xrefs

You may want to see only part of an xref. This option is especially important when you are using very large xref drawings. Although clipping xrefs was introduced in Release 13, Release 14 has a new command, XCLIP, which makes clipping easier and more practical.

To clip an xref, choose Modify➪Object➪Clip or choose External Reference Clip from the Reference toolbar. AutoCAD prompts you to select objects. Pick the xref you want to clip. Note that any nested xrefs are clipped with the main xref you select.

Table 19-1 explains the options of this command.

Table 19-1
XCLIP Options

Option	How to Use It		
ON	Turns the clipping boundary on, displaying only the portion of the xref inside the clipping boundary. By default, the clipping boundary is on. Use this after you have turned it off, to see only the clipped portion again.		
OFF	Turns the clipping boundary off, displaying the entire xref. The clipping boundary is still retained. This is somewhat like turning off a layer. You may want to see the entire xref for a while, for example, while redefining the boundary. Then you can turn the boundary back on (using the ON option) when you need only the clipped portion again.		
Clipdepth	This is used for 3D drawings only. After you set a clipping boundary, you can set front and back planes parallel to the boundary. AutoCAD displays only the portion of the xref within that three-dimensional space. You create the front and back planes by specifying a distance from the clipping boundary. The Remove suboption removes the clipping planes.		
Delete	Deletes the clipping boundary. The boundary is no longer retained in the drawing.		
Generate Polyline	Creates a polyline from the clipping boundary, using the current layer, color, and linetype. If you want to change the clipping boundary, you can edit the polyline using PEDIT and redefine the boundary with the new polyline.		
New boundary	This is the default option. Press Enter to get the suboptions.		
		Select polyline	Lets you specify the clipping boundary by selecting an existing polyline. AutoCAD decurves fit-curved or arc portions of the polyline when creating the boundary.
		Polygonal	Lets you specify a polygonal area—like a polyline with straight edges. AutoCAD creates a rubber-band line as you pick points, keeping the polygon closed. You can use this option to create an irregularly shaped area that includes only the portion of the xref you wish to see.
		Rectangular	Lets you pick two points on diagonally opposite corners of a rectangle, just like creating a selection window.

Note

You can also clip blocks.

Tip

To see the clipping boundary (if you haven't used an existing polyline to define it), change the value of the XCLIPFRAME system variable to 1.

Figure 19-6 shows an xref clipped with a polygonal boundary. XCLIPFRAME has been turned on so you can clearly see the specified boundary. Compare this to Figure 19-4, which shows the entire xref.

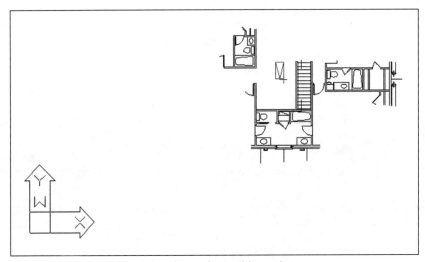

Figure 19-6: An xref clipped with a polygonal boundary.

Speeding up the display of large xrefs

Release
14

Release 14 introduces *demand loading*, which lets AutoCAD load only the objects necessary to display the xref in your drawing. Demand loading works with two other new features: spatial and layer indices.

✦ The spatial index is created when you save a drawing. AutoCAD uses this index when you have enabled demand loading and attach a clipped xref that was saved with a spatial index. AutoCAD uses the index to determine how much of the xref needs to be read to display it.

✦ The layer index is also created when you save a drawing. AutoCAD uses this index when you have enabled demand loading and attach an xref with frozen or turned off layers that was saved with a layer index. AutoCAD uses the index to determine how much of the xref needs to be read to display it.

The purpose of demand loading and the spatial and layer indices is to speed up display of huge xrefs, such as those used in GIS or 3D drawings.

To make it perfectly clear, you need all of the following to use this new feature:

✦ Demand loading must be enabled in the current drawing.

✦ The xref must have been saved with a spatial or layer index.

✦ The xref must either be clipped (for a spatial index) or have layers that are frozen or turned off (for a layer index).

Demand loading

You turn on demand loading in your current drawing. To turn on demand loading, choose Tools➪Preferences➪Performance. In the External reference file demand load drop-down list, choose Enabled. Others on a networked system cannot then edit the original drawing while you are referencing it. To let others edit the original drawing, choose Enabled with copy. AutoCAD then uses a copy of the referenced drawing for your xref. Click OK. You can turn on demand loading just before you attach an xref. It is not necessary to keep demand loading on all the time.

Spatial indices

You save a spatial index for a drawing that you expect to use as an xref. AutoCAD creates an index of all the objects in the drawing. The saving process takes a little longer, but you save time at the other end when you load a clipped xref or clip an xref for the first time. To create a spatial index, choose File➪Save As to open the Save Drawing As dialog box. Choose Options to open the Export Options dialog box, shown in Figure 19-7.

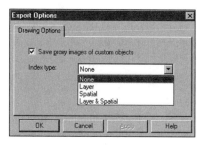

Figure 19-7: The Export Options dialog box.

From the Index type drop-down list, choose Spatial or Layer & Spatial. Click OK twice.

Tip

If you want to create an index for an existing drawing, click OK once to return to the Save Drawing As dialog box. Click Cancel. In other words, you don't have to actually save the drawing to set up the index, which is controlled by the INDEXCTL system variable.

Once you have created a spatial index, each time you save the drawing, AutoCAD displays this message:

```
Updating Indexes for block *MODEL_SPACE
```

To stop saving the index, choose File⇨Save As. Choose Options. In the Export Options dialog box, choose None from the Index type drop-down list. Click OK once, then Cancel.

Layer indices

You save a layer index for a drawing that you expect to use as an xref. AutoCAD creates an index of all the objects in the drawing. The saving process takes a little longer, but you save time at the other end when you load an xref with frozen or turned off layers. To create a layer index choose File⇨Save As to open the Save Drawing As dialog box. Choose Options to open the Export Options dialog box, shown in Figure 19-7.

From the Index type drop-down list, choose Layer or Layer & Spatial. Click OK twice.

Once you have created a layer index, each time you save the drawing, AutoCAD displays this message:

```
Updating Indexes for block *MODEL_SPACE
```

To stop saving the index, choose File⇨Save As. Choose Options. In the Export Options dialog box, choose None from the Index type drop-down list. Click OK once, then Cancel.

Step-by-Step: Controlling Xref Display

On the
CD-ROM

1. Open *ab19-1.dwg* from your *AutoCAD Bible* folder if you did the previous exercise.

   Note: If you didn't do the previous exercise, first use Windows Explorer to find *ab19-a.dwg* and *ab19-b.dwg* in the root of the CD-ROM and *ab19-1.dwg* and *ab19-2.dwg* in the *Results* folder of the CD-ROM. Copy all four files to your *AutoCAD Bible* folder. In Windows Explorer, right click each file and choose Properties. Uncheck the Read-only option and click OK. If *ab19-1.dwg* gives you a message that it cannot find its xrefs (*ab19-a.dwg* and *ab19-b.dwg*), choose Tools⇨Preferences and click Project Files Search Path on the Files tab. Click Add and add your *AutoCAD Bible* folder. You can click Browse to choose the folder from a dialog box.

2. Choose File⇨Save As. Choose Options. In the Export Options dialog box, choose Layer & Spatial. Click OK. (It may already be set for these indexes.) Click Cancel.

3. Choose Save from the Standard toolbar. Note the message on the command line that AutoCAD is updating the indexes.

On the CD-ROM

4. Open *ab19-2.dwg* from your *AutoCAD Bible* folder. This drawing has an attached xref of a house plan and a nested xref of a title block, as shown in Figure 19-8.

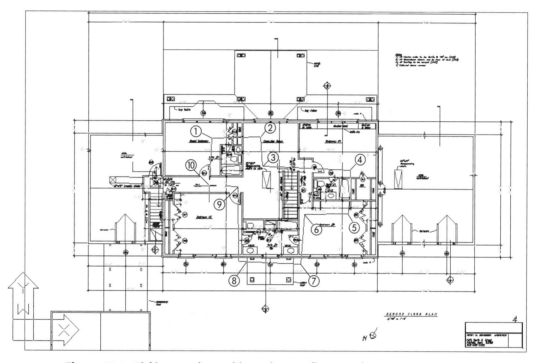

Figure 19-8: Picking a polygonal boundary to clip an xref.

5. Save it as *ab19-3.dwg* in your *AutoCAD Bible* folder.

6. Choose Tools➪Preferences➪Performance. In the External reference file demand load drop-down list, choose Enabled. (It may already be set to Enabled.) Click OK.

7. Click the Layer Control drop-down list. Click the On/Off icon next to the Ab19-1|notes layer to turn the layer back on. Click the top of the drop-down list box to close it. AutoCAD displays the notes layer.

8. Choose External Reference Clip from the Reference toolbar or choose Modify➪Object➪Clip to start the XCLIP command. Follow the prompts:

```
Select objects: Pick anywhere on the xref in Figure 19-8.
Select objects: ↵
ON/OFF/Clipdepth/Delete/generate Polyline/<New boundary>: ↵
Specify clipping boundary:
Select polyline/Polygonal/<Rectangular>: p ↵
```

```
First point: Pick ① in Figure 19-8.
Undo/<Next point>: Pick ②.
Undo/<Next point>: Pick ③.
Undo/<Next point>: Pick ④.
Undo/<Next point>: Pick ⑤.
Undo/<Next point>: Pick ⑥.
Undo/<Next point>: Pick ⑦.
Undo/<Next point>: Pick ⑧.
Undo/<Next point>: Pick ⑨.
Undo/<Next point>: Pick ⑩.
Undo/<Next point>: ↵
```

AutoCAD clips the xref.

9. Turn off the Ab19-1|notes layer again.

10. Save your drawing. It should look like Figure 19-9. Keep the drawing open if you are continuing on to the next exercise.

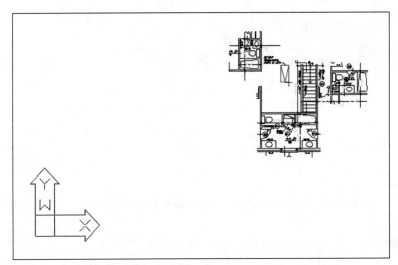

Figure 19-9: The clipped xref.

Managing Xrefs

If you have many xrefs in a drawing, you need a way to keep track of them and their relationships to your drawing. AutoCAD offers several techniques for managing xrefs.

Tip

This may be obvious, but the first principle of managing xrefs is to keep them simple. Overly complex nested configurations are hard to manage, no matter what you do.

The Xref Manager

Release
14

Release 14's new External Reference dialog box is designed to let you manage xrefs from one place. This Xref Manager has the following features, explained in Table 19-2.

Table 19-2
External Reference Dialog Box Features

Feature	What It Does	
Attach	Opens the Attach Xref dialog box and lets you specify an xref to attach to your drawing, as explained earlier in this chapter.	
Detach	Detaches an xref. The xref is not displayed, and the xref definition is no longer saved in the drawing.	
Reload	Reloads the xref. AutoCAD automatically reloads the xref when you open the drawing or plot. Use this whenever the xref has changed during a session (because someone else on a networked system has edited the xref drawing) or after unloading an xref. AutoCAD then loads the most recent version of the xref.	
Unload	Unloads the xref without detaching it. The xref is not displayed, but the xref definition is still saved in the drawing. You can then use Reload to display the xre f again.	
Bind	Changes the xref to a block. Opens the Bind Xrefs dialog box, which lets you choose to either bind or insert the xref.	
	Bind	When creating a block from the xref, changes named layers, text styles, dimension styles, and so on (called symbols) from the format `xref_name|symbol_name` to `drawing_name$#$symbol_name`, where # is zero if the same name does not exist in the current drawing, 1 if it already exists. In this way, AutoCAD makes sure no symbol names are duplicated. This method lets you keep track of where the symbols came from.
	Insert	When creating a block from the xref, removes the xref_name| portion of symbol names. For example, if a layer of that name already exists in your drawing, objects on that layer take on the properties of that layer as defined in your drawing. The same applies to text styles, dimension styles, and so on. This method removes the complexity that arises with the xref naming of the se symbols.
Xref Found At	Specifies where the xref was actually found, which may be different from the saved path. You can then click Save Path to save the current path. If the location of an xref is changed and is not in the *Support Files* or *Project Files* search path, AutoCAD lists the status of the xref as Not Found. Use the Browse button to find and open the xref and click Save Path. Click OK and AutoCAD automatically reloads the xref.	

Note   You cannot bind or detach nested xrefs.

The Xref log file

If you set the XREFCTL system variable to 1 (by default it is set to 0), AutoCAD makes a copy of all xref activity in an ASCII text file. You can read the log to troubleshoot problems that may occur. Figure 19-10 shows part of an xref log file. AutoCAD places the log file in the same folder as your drawing and uses your drawing name with the *.xlg* filename extension.

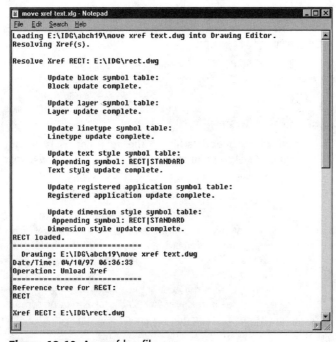

Figure 19-10: An xref log file.

Tip   The whole first section of the file in Figure 19-10 is simply a record of loading the xref. As you can see, this file can get long! In addition, whenever you work on the drawing, AutoCAD appends the messages to the file. Therefore, once in a while, you should delete all or part of the file.

Step-by-Step: Managing Xrefs

On the CD-ROM

1. Use *ab19-3.dwg* from your *AutoCAD Bible* folder if you did the previous exercise. Otherwise, open it from the *Results* folder of the CD-ROM.

2. Save it as *ab19-4.dwg* in your *AutoCAD Bible* folder.

3. Choose Modify➪Object➪Clip. At the `Select objects:` prompt, pick the xref anywhere. Press Enter. At the `ON/OFF/Clipdepth/Delete/generate Polyline/<New boundary>:` prompt, type **d** ↵. AutoCAD deletes the clip and restores the entire view of both xrefs.

4. Choose Insert➪External Reference. Click Tree View. Choose *ab19-b*, the nested xref. Choose Unload and click OK. AutoCAD unloads *ab19-b* and it disappears.

5. Repeat the XREF command. Choose *ab19-b* again. Choose Reload and click OK. AutoCAD reloads the xref and it reappears.

6. Again repeat the XREF command. This time choose *ab19-1*. Choose Bind. In the Bind Xref dialog box, choose Insert and click OK twice. AutoCAD inserts both xrefs (*ab19-1* and *ab19-b*) as blocks. (Click the Layer Control drop-down list to see that there are no xref-type layer names.)

7. Save your drawing.

Summary

In this chapter I covered the techniques you need to know to work with xrefs. Xrefs are especially helpful when working in a team, networked environment. You can choose either to attach or to overlay xrefs. Release 14 offers several new xref features including easier clipping, demand loading, spatial and layer indexes, and an easy-to-use Xref Manager.

In the next chapter I cover AutoCAD's SQL Environment, which lets you access outside databases.

✦   ✦   ✦

Using External Databases

Using the AutoCAD SQL Environment

The AutoCAD SQL Environment (ASE) lets you communicate with an external database from within AutoCAD.

ASE is a powerful way to link drawing objects with data and is more flexible than using block attributes. With ASE, you can link data in an external database to any object in a drawing. In this chapter I show you that ASE does not have to be as difficult as it often sounds.

Many AutoCAD users maintain databases separately from their drawings. Now you can work directly with your data by linking the rows of the database tables to objects in your drawings. The drawing objects thus become intelligent and carry these links with them in the drawing. You can also change data, such as a price or a part number, from within AutoCAD and have that change automatically applied and available in all drawing objects that are linked to that database item.

Understanding ASE Concepts

The linking of databases and AutoCAD drawings is referred to as *external database access.* The main purpose of external database access is to let you:

  ◆ Create links between AutoCAD drawing objects and the external data

✦ View data in external databases

✦ Edit data in external databases

✦ Display external database data in your drawing

ASE provides an easy-to-use, consistent dialog box interface to databases. It supports the new database standard, ISO SQL2. ASE works with the following databases:

✦ dBASE III+

✦ Open Database Connectivity (ODBC) compliant (32-bit) databases such as Excel, Access, FoxPro, and dBASE IV

✦ Oracle 7 (Windows)

Understanding basic database concepts

A *database* is a set of related information, usually maintained by a database management system (DBMS), that is, an application that manages databases. A database is stored in the form of a *table* that contains *rows* and *columns.* A row, also called a record, contains one element of data, such as the information for one desk. A column, also called a field, contains the attribute for that row, such as the desk's price.

Table 20-1 shows the first three rows of the database used as an example in this chapter.

Table 20-1 A simple database table				
Part No.	**Description**	**Dwg Size**	**Bought/Pur**	**Units**
8665-023-012	Welding Wire — .030 Stainless	B	P	FT
8665-023-013	Weld Rod — .045 Dia Stainless Steel	B	P	FT
8665-023-014	Welding — Rod .045 Dia S.S.	B	P	FT

A *relational database* is a type of database that contains a collection of tables. Each *table* represents a set of data for a defined use.

Structured Query Language *(SQL* — pronounced "sequel" or "S-Q-L") was created to provide users with a database language that would be applicable across multiple platforms and database management programs. AutoCAD supports SQL2, which is a new international standard that introduces the terms *environment, catalog,* and *schema.*

In the SQL2 standard, environments, catalogs, schemas, and tables create a hierarchy of *database objects*. A *database object* is simply the term used to specify any of the following SQL2 objects: Environment, Catalog, Schema, Table.

✦ *Environment* means the entire database system — the DBMS, the databases it can access, the users, and the programs that can access those databases.

✦ A *catalog* is a collection of schemas and is named by the folder path name where the database is located.

✦ A *schema* is a set of tables and other database components and is named by the catalog subfolder where the database tables reside.

Let's say you have a database in Microsoft Access. You keep the Access database in *C:\databases\drawing info*. The environment might be called Access. The catalog is *c:\databases,* which might contain several folders besides *drawing info*. The schema is *drawing info*. The folder *drawing info* contains the actual tables of the database.

ODBC catalogs also require at least one schema called the *information schema*. This schema is a table that describes all the catalogs in the environment, any schemas in the current catalog, and the tables in each schema (if any).

Preparing ASE

The basic steps for working with ASE are as follows:

1. Make sure you have installed the External Database feature of AutoCAD.

2. Arrange your database tables into schemas (subfolders) and catalogs (folders) appropriate for your application.

3. Use the External Database Configuration Program provided with AutoCAD to define the environment and register the catalog and schema.

4. Start the ASE Administration command.

5. Set the Environment to the correct database management software (DBMS) driver.

6. Establish a user access name and password, if necessary.

7. Set the catalog and schema.

8. Register the table by establishing a Link Path Name.

9. Link database rows to objects in your drawing.

Installing ASE

ASE is not part of the Typical AutoCAD installation. To use ASE you must either do a Full installation or a Custom installation. If you do a Custom installation, choose `External Db (External Database tools and support files)` in the Custom Components dialog box.

If you are not sure whether you installed ASE, open the Tools menu. If External Database is not disabled (you can choose it), you installed ASE.

If you did not install ASE and wish to, follow these steps:

1. Insert the AutoCAD CD-ROM in your CD-ROM drive. If the CD-ROM doesn't automatically run, choose Start➪Run@ and type your CD-ROM drive in the text box (for example, **d:**). Choose OK. Then double-click `Setup.exe`.

2. Choose Next in the first screen.

3. In the second screen, choose Add.

4. In the next screen, check `External Db`.

5. Continue to follow the onscreen instructions to install ASE.

Creating the catalog/schema structure

AutoCAD comes with a default environment, catalog, and schema already set up for a dBaseIII database. In this Step-by-Step exercise, you create a similar structure within the *AutoCAD Bible* folder that you have been using to save your exercise drawings. (Instructions for creating this folder were given in Chapter 1.) In order to define a catalog and a schema, you need at least a folder with a subfolder. If you want, you can create the folder in the root drive and place a subfolder inside it. The catalog is the folder where you keep all your different types of databases. The schema contains the actual tables that you want to use with AutoCAD.

Note

In this chapter, you cannot do the later exercises without doing the previous ones. The later exercises depend on the setup and configuration you create in the earlier exercises. You should therefore leave enough time to do all the exercises in this chapter at one sitting — perhaps an hour or two.

Step-by-Step: Creating the Structure for the Catalog and Schema

1. Right-click Start on the taskbar. Choose Explore to open the Windows Explorer.

2. If your *AutoCAD Bible* folder is not displayed in the All Folders window, click the plus sign (+) next to the drive containing the *AutoCAD Bible* folder.

3. Click the *AutoCAD Bible* folder and choose File⇨New⇨Folder. A new folder appears in the right window, called *New Folder*. Type **Databases** ↵ to rename the folder.

4. If necessary, in the All Folders window, click the plus sign to open the *AutoCAD Bible* folder. You should see the new *Databases* folder.

5. Click the *Databases* folder and choose File⇨New⇨Folder. A new folder appears in the right window, called *New Folder*. Type **dbf** ↵.

On the
CD-ROM

6. From the CD-ROM, copy *ab20-prt.dbf* to the *dbf* folder you just created. Be sure to choose the *ab20-prt.dbf* file, not the *ab20-prt.xls* file. The *.dbf* file is a database of parts. Figure 20-1 shows this database as it appears when opened in Microsoft Excel.

7. Because this file is coming from a CD-ROM, it may be read only. Still in Explorer, right-click *ab20-prt.dbf* and choose Properties from the menu. If Read-only is checked, click it to uncheck it and check Archive. Click OK.

8. Click the Close button of Explorer to close it.

	A	B	C	D	E
1	PART_NO	DESCRIPT	DWG_SIZE	BOUGHT_PUR	UNITS
2	8665-023-012	WELDING WIRE - .030 STAINLESS	B	P	FT
3	8665-023-013	WELD ROD - .045 DIA STAINLESS STEEL	B	P	FT
4	8665-023-014	WELDING - ROD .045 DIA S.S.	B	P	FT
5	8665-023-015	WELDING ROD - 1/16 DIA TYPE 312 SS	B	P	FT
6	8665-023-016	WELDING ROD	B	P	FT
7	8665-023-017	WELD ROD - .052 MS (60# COIL)	B	P	FT
8	8665-073-042	NIPPLE - 1.2 X 2 1/2 (NOT GALV)	C	P	EACH
9	8685-079-000	TAPE	A	P	IN
10	8685-092-000	TAPE - TEFLON	A	P	IN
11	8685-097-002	TAPE	B	P	IN
12	8685-097-003	TAPE	B	P	IN
13	8685-097-004	TAPE - STRAPPING	B	P	IN
14	8685-117-001	TAPE		P	IN
15	8685-118-001	TAPE - DUCT	A	P	FT
16	8685-119-001	TAPE - FOAM, DBL. SIDE ADHESIVE	B	P	IN
17	8688-003-000	PIN - DOWELL	A	P	EACH
18	8697-003-000	GAUGE - PRESSURE	A	P	EACH
19	8711-001-001	TRANSFORMER	B	P	EACH
20	8711-002-001	TRANSFORMER - CONTROL	C	P	EACH
21	8711-002-002	TRANSFORMER - CONTROL	C	P	EACH

Figure 20-1: The dBASEIII database in Excel.

Credit: Thanks to Gary Morris of The Dexter Company, Fairfield, Iowa, for this database.

Tip

You can open dBASEIII files in Excel, and you can save Excel worksheets to dBASEIII (*.dbf*) format.

Defining the AutoCAD SQL Environment

To start working with external databases, you must define the environment (including the catalogs and schemas) in the Windows registry, using the External Database Configuration program. This method of defining the environment is new with Release 14. AutoCAD provides a default setup that refers to sample files provided in the *\sample\dbf* subfolder. Use the External Database Configuration program to change, add, or delete environment, catalog, or schema information.

To start the program choose Start⇔Programs⇔AutoCAD⇔External Database Configuration to open the External Database Configuration dialog box, shown in Figure 20-2.

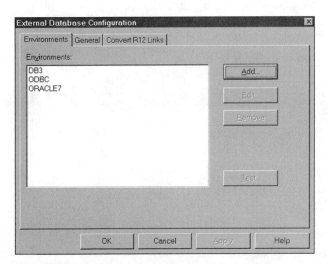

Figure 20-2: The External Database Configuration dialog box.

The configuration utility has three tabs that apply to all supported database drivers:

✦ The Environments tab adds, edits, and removes database environments.

✦ The General tab updates paths and languages used by ASE.

✦ The Convert R12 Links tab converts AutoCAD Release 12 ASE links in a drawing to Release 14 format.

The instructions to set up the database vary according to the drivers you use. The AutoCAD online help contains extensive help on all three drivers, and special notes on using ODBC drivers for different applications.

This section provides instructions for using a dBASE III driver to work with a dBASE III (*.dbf*) table. See the sidebar "Using ASE with Excel" for information about configuring an ODBC driver.

To configure a new external database environment, follow these steps:

1. In the External Database Configuration dialog box, choose the Environments tab. You can choose the DBMS you want from the three available listings and select Edit, or you can choose Add to open the Select DBMS for new Environment dialog box and create a new DBMS Environment, shown in Figure 20-3.

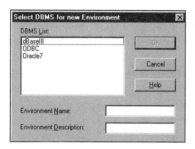

Figure 20-3: The Select DBMS for new Environment dialog box.

2. From the DBMS List, choose the DBMS you want to use.

3. For the Environment Name, enter a name that describes the DBMS, for example **db3** or **access**. Enter a description. Click OK.

4. AutoCAD opens the Environment dialog box, which lists the new environment name in the title bar, as shown in Figure 20-4. In the Catalog section, type a name for your catalog. It can be the same as the folder you have created for the catalog. For the path, click Browse and find the catalog folder in the Browse dialog box. Make sure that the path shows correctly at the top of the dialog box and click OK. Click New to register the catalog.

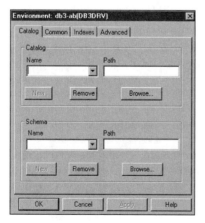

Figure 20-4: The Environment dialog box.

5. In the Schema section, type a name for your schema. It can be the same as the folder you have created for the schema. For the path, click Browse and find the catalog folder in the Browse dialog box. Make sure that the path shows correctly at the top of the dialog box and click OK. Click New to register the schema.

6. AutoCAD returns you to the External Database Configuration dialog box. Choose Test to see if you configured everything correctly.

7. The Login dialog box opens. Fill in the user name and password if required by your driver. (The dBASEIII and ODBC drivers don't require these.) Click Connect.

8. If you completed everything correctly, the Connection test passed dialog box appears. You see a listing of the SQL features supported by the driver you chose, as shown in Figure 20-5. Click Done.

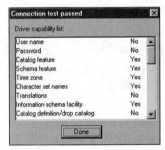

Figure 20-5: The Connection test passed dialog box.

Note If an error message appears, you did not complete the steps correctly. Repeat the above procedure after making sure you have the necessary drivers installed and the overall configuration is correct. Also, don't forget to click New each time after specifying the catalog and schema.

9. Choose OK to close the External Database Configuration dialog box.

You are now ready to start ASE and establish a connection between a database and an AutoCAD drawing.

The Environment dialog box also has three other tabs:

✦ The Common tab lets you choose a language (such as Afrikaans_ South Africa, the first language on the list) and define a default catalog and schema.

✦ The Indexes tab lets you associate an index with a table. An index is used to uniquely define each row (record) in the table.

✦ The Advanced tab lets you specify the use of long filenames, configure multiuser settings, and specify a date format for indexes.

This Step-by-Step exercise requires that you completed the steps in the previous exercise.

Step-by-Step: Defining the ASE Environment

1. From the taskbar, choose Start⇨Programs⇨AutoCAD R14⇨External Database Configuration.

2. In the External Database Configuration dialog box, click Add to open the Select DBMS for New Environment dialog box.

3. Choose dBASEIII from the DBMS List. In the Environment Name text box, type **ab-db3**. In the Environment Description text box, type **dBASE III database for AutoCAD Bible**. Click OK.

4. AutoCAD opens the Environment dialog box. In the Catalog Name box, type **databases**. Click Browse to open the Browse dialog box. The Directories listing probably reads c:\acadr14 or something similar. You can double-click the drive at the top of the box to return to the root if necessary. From there find your *AutoCAD Bible* folder and double-click. Now find the *Databases* subfolder and double-click. The Directories listing at the top should read c:\AutoCAD Bible\Databases (or as appropriate for your system). Click OK.

5. Click New in the Environment dialog box.

6. In the Schema Name box, type **dbf**. Click Browse and use the same procedure as for Step 4 to find the *dbf* subfolder you created. Click OK in the Browse dialog box.

7. Click New in the Environment dialog box.

8. Click the Advanced tab and choose ON in the Use Long Filenames drop-down list box. Click OK to close the Environment dialog box.

9. In the External Database Configuration dialog box, click Test. Click Connect in the Login dialog box.

10. AutoCAD opens the Connection test passed dialog box, listing the environment's features. Click Done, then OK. You have now configured the ASE environment, catalog, and schema.

Using ASE with Excel

The most common DBMSs on PCs — for example Access and Excel — use the ODBC driver. Unfortunately, they are harder to set up with ASE. Here I try to make it as painless as possible, using Excel as an example.

Before you start to configure the databases, you must install and configure the 32-bit ODBC Administrator and a 32-bit ODBC driver.

To check if the ODBC 32-bit Administrator is installed on your computer, open the Control Panel. There should be an icon called ODBC or 32-bit ODBC.

To check if you have the required drivers installed, double-click the ODBC icon. In the Data sources dialog box, choose Drivers. In the Drivers dialog box, select the driver you want to use, and choose About. You should see a dialog box like this.

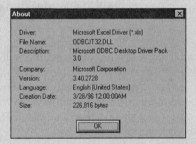

Make sure that the filename contains the number 32. If it says 16, then you have an older 16-bit driver and need to install the newer 32-bit drivers.

If you don't have the ODBC 32-bit Administrator, you need to install the Microsoft ODBC Driver Pack version 2.5 (or later). The ODBC Driver Pack 3.0 is free from Microsoft's Web site, *www.microsoft.com*. On the site, choose Products, then ODBC. Look for *wx1220.exe* or *wx1335.exe*.

To install either of these files, copy it to a new folder, perhaps called *ODBC*. In Explorer, double-click the file to extract all the compressed files it contains. Now you have the ODBC Administrator.

Since setting up the ODBC Administrator also includes configuring the DBMS and table you want to use, you first need to set up the Excel structure properly. Follow these steps:

1. Follow the steps in the Step-by-Step exercise Creating the Structure for the Catalog and Schema, but in step 5, name the folder *excel* instead of *dbf*. In step 6, copy the *ab20-prt.xls* file instead of the *.dbf* file.

2. At the same time copy the *infsch.xls* file. The ODBC driver requires an *information schema* that defines the structure of the database environment. The *infsch.xls* file creates the information schema.

3. If you are just installing the ODBC Driver Pack, double-click *setup.exe* in the folder where you placed it. Choose Custom installation and accept the default folder. In the Options list, choose Desktop Drivers and ODBC components. AutoCAD opens the Data Sources dialog box.

4. If you already have the ODBC Driver Pack, double-click the ODBC icon in the Control Panel to open the Data Sources dialog box, shown here.

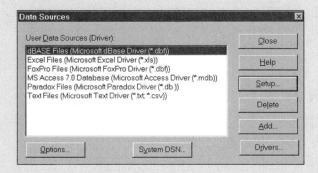

5. Choose the Excel driver and choose Add. (If you wish, you can select the others if you don't need them and choose Delete.)

6. In the Add Data Source dialog box, choose the Microsoft Excel driver and click OK.

7. In the ODBC Microsoft Excel Setup dialog box type **ODBC_Excel** as the Data Source Name. You will use this later as the database environment in AutoCAD's External Database Configuration program. (If you wish, type a description.)

8. Click Select Workbook. Use the Select Workbook dialog box to choose the *AutoCAD Bible\databases\excel\infsch.xls* worksheet. Click OK twice.

9. Click Close in the Data Sources dialog box.

10. To configure the database environment, choose Start⇨AutoCAD R14⇨External Database Configuration.

11. With the Environments tab on top, choose Add.

12. In the Select DBMS for New Environment dialog box, choose ODBC.

13. For the Environment Name, type **ODBC_Excel**. Choose OK. AutoCAD displays the General tab of the Environment ODBC (ODBC_Excel) dialog box.

14. Click Browse to choose the *AutoCAD Bible\databases\excel\infsch.xls* worksheet as the information schema.

15. Choose Apply. Click OK. Click Test to test the environment configuration. Click OK.

Using ASE with Excel (continued)

16. In the next Step-by-Step exercise, Connecting a Database to a Drawing, in step 4, choose ODBC_Excel. Skip step 5.

17. For step 6, Schema is automatically selected. Choose the schema in the Database Objects box.

18. For step 7, the database object is called parts. Choose it.

You can continue the rest of the exercises without change.

To work with your own Excel worksheets, you need to customize *infsch.xls*. Open this worksheet and read the instructions there.

Working with ASE

Before starting to use ASE, you should think about the relationship between the drawing and the database. For example, you should decide:

✦ If the data is to be in one database with many tables or in several separate databases

✦ Which data you want to link to which drawing objects

✦ If several drawing objects will be linked to one row or only one object will be linked to a row

✦ If you want a drawing object linked to more than one row, table, or database

✦ Which column(s) will identify unique records

You are now ready to connect your database to your drawing.

Connecting a database to a drawing

When working with ASE commands in AutoCAD, you may find it helpful to open the External Database toolbar. Right-click any toolbar, choose External Database and close the Toolbar dialog box.

The ASEADMIN command lets you create the connection to the external database.

Follow these steps to connect an external database to a drawing:

1. Open the drawing you want to use with ASE.

 2. Choose Administration from the External Database toolbar to open the Administration dialog box, as shown in Figure 20-6. Any environments that you configured using the External Database Configuration program are listed.

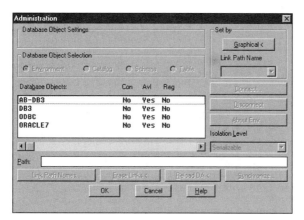

Figure 20-6: The Administration dialog box.

3. In the Database Objects list, choose the environment you want. The Environment radio button is automatically selected. Click Connect.

4. The Connect to Environment dialog box appears, requesting a user name and password. (Not all drivers support user names and passwords, in which case you can leave these fields blank.) Just choose OK. The driver is now connected, which loads it into memory. The Con (Connect) column next to the environment you chose changes from No to Yes.

5. If the Catalog button is available, choose Catalog. Choose a catalog object listed in the Database Objects box.

6. If the Schema button is available, choose Schema. Choose a schema object listed in the Database Objects box.

7. Choose Table and highlight the actual database file you want in the Database Objects list box. The table also appears in the Path text box, confirming that the connection was made.

The entire database structure is now connected, and you can now view and work with the database data within AutoCAD.

The next exercise depends on the completion of the previous two exercises.

Step-by-Step: Connecting a Database to a Drawing

On the
CD-ROM

1. Open *ab20-a.dwg* from the CD-ROM.

2. Save it as *ab20-1.dwg* in your *AutoCAD Bible* folder. If the External Database toolbar is not open, right-click any toolbar, choose External Database and close the Toolbars dialog box.

The External Database toolbar fits nicely to the right of the Standard toolbar.

3. Choose Administration from the External Database toolbar.

4. Choose AB-DB3. Click Connect. Click OK in the Connect to Environment dialog box. The Con column in the Database Objects listing changes to Yes.

5. Choose Catalog in the Database Object Selection section. The Database Objects box lists the DATABASE catalog. Choose it.

6. Choose Schema in the Database Object Selection section. The Database Objects box lists the DBF schema. Choose it.

7. Choose Table in the Database Object Selection section. The Database Objects box lists the *ab20-prt* table. Choose it. You have now connected the table to the drawing. Click OK to close the Administration dialog.

8. Save the drawing. Keep it open. Continue to the next Step-by-Step exercise.

Creating link path names

A *link path* is a named reference to a table row. You define both the link path and link path name (LPN) by choosing Link Path Names in the Administration dialog box. The purpose of a link path is to let you connect an object to a row of data in a database table.

Key columns

In order to link a drawing object to a row in a table, you need to be able to specify one row value that is unique. You do this by choosing a column heading ASE uses when searching for a row. ASE looks down the column identified by the column heading and finds the row containing the value you specify. This column heading is called a *key*. By choosing a key, that is, a column, that contains no duplicates, you can be sure to find only one row of data.

If you want to use a column that has some equal values, you should combine that column with another column to give unique keys.

If ASE finds two rows with the same data, it accesses the first row. It makes sense, therefore, to be careful to choose a column that contains no duplicate values. Most DBMS systems offer a feature to create an index field that ensures that each row is unique.

Note

LPNs are like layer names — they cannot contain spaces or be longer than 32 characters. All the LPNs in one drawing should be unique.

You cannot work with a database until you have defined a link path name. Once you define the link path name, the `Reg` column in the Administration dialog box changes from No to Yes.

Creating a link path name

To create a link path name, follow these steps:

1. In the Administration dialog box, choose Link Path Names. (This button only becomes available after you have specified a table.)

2. The Link Path Names dialog box appears, as shown in Figure 20-7. All the columns in the table are listed. Choose a column, then choose On. As explained above, the ideal column is one that has no duplicate row values.

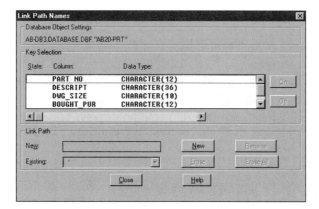

Figure 20-7: The Link Path Names dialog box.

3. Enter a name for the link path name in the New text box. Use a descriptive name so you can identify the columns in the LPN later.

4. Choose New. The message `Registered Successfully` appears at the bottom of the dialog box.

5. Repeat steps 3 and 4 if you want to add another column. Then choose Close.

   The completed Database Object Settings area in the Administration dialog box now states the complete database configuration in the form `environment.catalog.schema.table(LPN)`. This is the way that you specify the complete and unique path to the external database.

6. Choose OK to close the Administration dialog box.

The database configuration is saved in the current drawing, and you don't need to retrace these steps again for this drawing.

You are now ready to start working with the database and drawing objects.

Tip

A drawing can contain multiple LPNs from one or more databases. Keep the management of your tables and drawings as simple as possible by creating a new LPN only when you really need to access your data in a different way. Many of the ASE commands only work with one LPN at a time.

The following exercise requires that you have completed the previous exercises in this chapter.

Step-by-Step: Creating a Link Path Name

On the CD-ROM

1. Continue with *ab20-1.dwg* from the previous exercise. Choose Administration from the External Database toolbar.

2. Choose Link Path Names.

3. In the Key Selection box, choose PART_NO. This column contains no duplicate rows. Click On.

4. In the New text box of the Link Path section, type **part_no**. Click New.

5. Click Close to return to the Administration dialog box. Notice that the AB-DB3 environment is now registered (the REG column displays Yes). The complete database configuration is also listed in the Database Object Settings section, as shown in Figure 20-8.

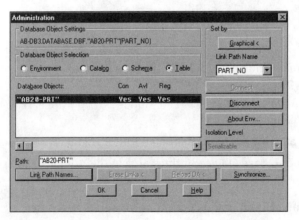

Figure 20-8: The Administration dialog box with a completely registered database.

6. Click OK to return to the drawing. Save your drawing. Leave it open to continue with the next exercise.

You are now ready to link drawing objects to your database.

Using ASE Commands

You can work with external databases in several ways. You can:

✦ Create links between the database records and drawing objects. (These links are stored in the drawing file as Link Path Names, which can be accessed in later sessions with ASE.)

✦ Create *displayable attributes* in the drawing that contain values of a linked row as text.

✦ Use ASE to modify the contents of a database from inside AutoCAD, without even starting the DBMS. ASE's commands let you add, delete, or modify the external database rows.

ASE is loaded the first time you use one of the ASE commands, such as ASEADMIN, or when you open a drawing that already contains ASE Link Path Name (LPN) information. You can also load it by typing **(arxload "ase")** and pressing Enter.

There are three ways to access the ASE commands:

✦ From the ASE toolbar

✦ By choosing Tools⇨External Databases. The commands appear in a submenu.

✦ At the command line

A summary of the ASE commands and their functions is shown in Table 20-2.

Table 20-2 The ASE Commands	
Command	**Function**
ASEADMIN	Lets you specify and register the database and create link paths.
ASEEXPORT	Creates text files in space-delimited, comma-delimited, or native database formats containing link information for selected objects.
ASELINKS	Manages link information.
ASEROWS	Lets you display and edit database records, creates links and selection sets.
ASESELECT	Creates a selection set of objects linked to data.
ASESQLED	Executes SQL statements from AutoCAD or a file.

The ASEROWS command

Once you have defined an LPN between a table and a drawing, you use the ASEROWS command to:

✦ View data

✦ Modify data

✦ Create links with drawing objects

 To start the command, choose Rows from the External Database toolbar. The Rows dialog box is shown in Figure 20-9.

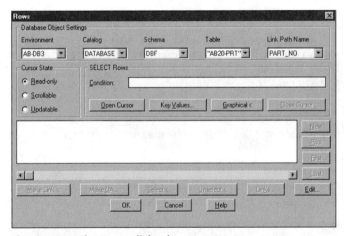

Figure 20-9: The Rows dialog box.

The Database Object Settings area of the dialog box contains the same information as the Administration dialog box, but you can switch between tables and LPNs by choosing them from the list box. You must use the Administration dialog box to connect a driver (that is, connect an environment), but once connected you can switch between catalogs, schemas, tables, and LPNs from this dialog box.

Viewing data

To access the data in a table, you need to set the Cursor State and then open a cursor. The three types of cursor states control what you can do with the database and how you view the current table.

✦ **Read-only:** Lets you view rows only, not edit them.

✦ **Scrollable:** Lets you view rows only, not edit them, but you can use all four access options (Next, Prior, First, Last) to view the table rows.

✦ **Updatable:** Lets you edit the current row, but you can only use the Next access option to view rows.

The SELECT Rows area lets you filter the rows you view in three ways:

✦ Use the Condition text box to define an SQL statement to limit the rows you see. If you want to view all the rows, leave the Condition box blank.

✦ Choose Key Values to open the Select Row by Key Values dialog box. Type the value of the row in the Value text box and press Enter. Click OK to show the row matching the value you entered.

✦ Click Graphical to pick an AutoCAD object and link a row to the object. If there is more than one link, you can pick the one you want from the Links dialog box.

Note

To specify a SQL condition, if you are looking for data in a character field, you must enclose the text in single quotes (' ') and get the case of the entry exactly right. An example is `part_no = 9003-232-001` . Type this in the Condition text box and press Enter to view the row whose PART_NO value is 9003-232-001.

Modifying a database from AutoCAD

One of the most important features of ASE is that you can edit a database from inside AutoCAD.

Note

You cannot use ASE to change the structure of a database, such as adding or renaming columns.

Use the Rows dialog box to access the database data from inside ASE. To modify a database, set the Cursor State to Updatable. With the Updatable cursor, you can only work with one row at a time. However, you can specify a Key value or specify a condition to go directly to the desired row, instead of scrolling through the table with the Next button.

Once you locate the row you want, choose Edit to modify the record. AutoCAD opens the Edit Row dialog box, shown in Figure 20-10.

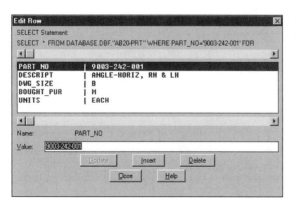

Figure 20-10: The Edit Row dialog box.

From the Edit Row dialog box, you can do the following:

✦ To edit a value, highlight its column and type a new value in the Value text box. Press Enter. AutoCAD automatically highlights the next column. Click Update. Click Close to make the change permanent. (You can always change the value back again.)

✦ To create a new row, choose Insert. This places default values in the row. Highlight the first column and type the new value in the Value text box. Press Enter. Continue to type values for all the columns.

✦ To delete a row, click Delete, then Close to make the change permanent.

Caution
You should not use the DBMS to edit a database separately while it is connected to AutoCAD. If you do edit the database table outside of AutoCAD during an ASE connection, you may get system crashes or corrupted data. If you need to edit the database using the DBMS, make sure you disconnect the environment using ASEADMIN first.

Creating links

A link is the relationship between a drawing object and an external database. The links are stored in the AutoCAD drawing, and you can only modify the links when you load the drawing file. ASE offers two types of links: a *drawing object* link and a *displayable attribute* link. I cover displayable attributes later in this chapter.

Caution
If you create a link between a drawing object and a row and in a later session of AutoCAD edit that object without starting ASE, the link information may become corrupted.

To create a link, follow these steps:

1. Select the record that you want as described earlier.

2. Choose Make Link in the Rows dialog box. AutoCAD returns you to your drawing temporarily and prompts you to select objects.

3. Select the object or objects that you want to link to the record. Press Enter when you are finished to return to the Rows dialog box.

You can link a drawing object to as many records in a database as you want, and you can link one database record to several drawing objects.

The ASESELECT command

The ASESELECT command lets you create selection sets of objects based on linked objects, selection filters that you specify, and graphical selection (picking the objects in the drawing). You can then use the results as a previous selection set with other commands. For example, you can start the COPY command, type **p** ↵ to use the Previous option, and get the selection set.

Note Since ASESELECT works with linked objects, you need to create the links using ASEROWS first.

 Start the ASESELECT command by choosing Select Objects from the External Database toolbar to open the Select Objects dialog box, shown in Figure 20-11.

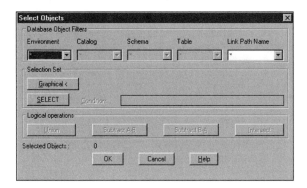

Figure 20-11: The Select Objects dialog box.

Here's how you create the selection set:

1. First filter the linked objects by choosing an environment, catalog, schema, table, and/or link path name in the Database Object Filters section of the dialog box. When you open the dialog box, these drop-down list boxes show an asterisk (*) to indicate that no filters are set and the selection set will be based on linked objects in every registered table in all the registered schemas, catalogs, and environments. Use the drop-down list boxes to limit the selection set of linked objects to the tables you want. You can choose a link path name to automatically fill in the entire database configuration of the LPN and limit the selection set to the one table containing that LPN.

2. In the Selection Set section of the dialog box, choose either Graphical to temporarily return to your drawing and select objects, or SELECT to create a SQL condition in the Condition text box.

3. If you want to combine selection sets, choose a logical operator.

4. Use either Graphical or SELECT to create a second selection set for the operator to work on.

5. Click OK. AutoCAD returns you to your drawing with the selected objects highlighted with grips. You can now use the selection set with any command as explained earlier.

Note You must choose the logical operator after using either Graphical or SELECT to create your first selection set. After using the logical operator, you then use Graphical or SELECT to create the second selection set. The logical operator then operates on the two selection sets.

Tip   Once you have used a logical operator on two selection sets, that result becomes the first selection set of subsequent selection sets. That is, you can then use another logical operator and again create a selection set. You can do this as many times as you like.

Table 20-3 shows how the logical operators work.

Table 20-3	
Logical Operators for Selection Sets in ASE	
Operator	**Function**
Union	Combines all objects meeting search criteria
Subtract A-B	Subtracts the second set of objects from the first
Subtract B-A	Subtracts the first set of objects from the second
Intersect	Selects only objects that match both sets of criteria

The ASELINKS command

The ASELINKS command tells you if a drawing object is linked to one or more external database rows. To use the ASELINKS command, choose Links from the External Database toolbar. AutoCAD displays the `Select object:` prompt, allowing you to select one object, and then opens the Links dialog box, shown in Figure 20-12. The dialog box displays all links associated with the selected object.

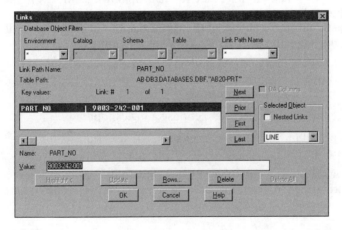

Figure 20-12: The Link dialog box.

Step-by-Step: Using ASE Commands

1. Continue with *ab20-1.dwg* from the previous exercise. Choose Rows from the External Database toolbar to open the Rows dialog box.

2. Choose Scrollable in the Cursor State section and click Open Cursor to see the first row (record) of the database. This lets you scroll through the entire database. Click Next to see the next record. Click Last to see the last record. Click First to return to the first record. Click Close Cursor.

3. Choose Updatable in the Cursor State section and click Key Values. In the Value text box at the bottom of the Select Row by Key Values dialog box, type **9003-242-001** ↵. When you press Enter, the value appears in the box above. Click OK. The row containing the part number 9003-242-001 appears in the Rows dialog box.

4. Choose Edit to open the Edit Row dialog box. Click the MADE_PUR line. In the Value text box, type **B** ↵. At the bottom of the dialog box, AutoCAD displays the message Row is updated. Click Update. Choose Close to change the database.

5. In the Rows dialog box, choose Make Link. In the drawing, zoom into the area of ① in Figure 20-13.

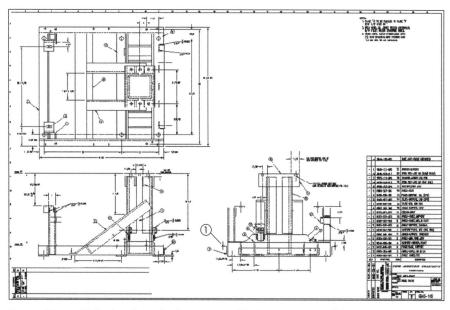

Figure 20-13: This drawing of a base assembly for a commercial washing machine has objects that can be linked to the database of parts.

Credit: Thanks to Robert Mack of The Dexter Company, Fairfield, Iowa, for this drawing.

6. Select all the objects that make up the angle indicated by the balloon labeled ②, as shown in Figure 20-14. Include the two cyan hidden lines representing the hole, but *not* the yellow center line. Press Enter to end selection. Click OK to close the Rows dialog box.

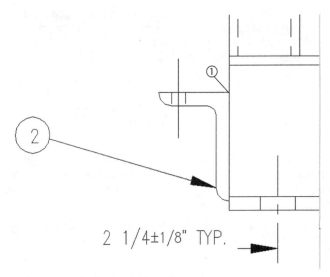

2 1/4±1/8" TYP.

Figure 20-14: The horizontal angle.

 7. To see one way of using the object selection feature of ASE, choose Select Objects from the External Database toolbar. In the Link Path Name drop-down list, choose PART_NO.

8. Click SELECT. Since you have only created one set of links and want them all, you do not need to specify a condition. AutoCAD selects all the linked objects in the angle. Click Union.

9. Click Graphical. In the drawing, select the yellow center line. Press Enter to end selection. You now have a selection set consisting of the objects linked to PART_NO 9003-242-001 and the additional line. Click OK.

10. All the objects now have grips. Choose Make Block on the Draw toolbar. In the Block Name text box, type **horiz_angle**. Notice that the objects are already selected. Choose Select Point. In the drawing, use the Endpoint object snap to choose ① in Figure 20-14. In the dialog box, click OK. You now have made the angle into a block.

 11. Choose Links from the External Database dialog box. At the Select object: prompt, select the angle block. AutoCAD opens the Links dialog box, listing the part's number and letting you know that the entire block is still linked to the database properly.

12. Click OK to close the dialog box. Keep the drawing open for the next exercise.

Creating displayable attributes

A *displayable attribute* (DA) is an unnamed AutoCAD block containing text that is linked to a row in your database. The data in the row appears as text in the drawing, like a block attribute. Although DAs look like attributes, you cannot extract them to a file.

Figure 20-15 shows a displayable attribute in a drawing.

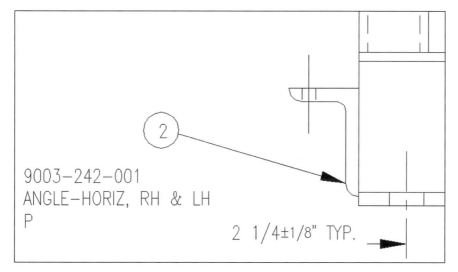

9003-242-001
ANGLE-HORIZ, RH & LH
P

2 1/4±1/8" TYP.

Figure 20-15: A displayable attribute showing some of the data linked to the object.

To create a displayable attribute, follow these steps:

1. Choose Rows from the External Database toolbar. (You should already have specified the link path name.)
2. Display the record you want to use for the displayable attributes. You can scroll through the database, set a condition, or use Key Values.
3. Choose Make DA to open the Make Displayable Attribute dialog box, shown in Figure 20-16.
4. From the Table Columns list, choose each column you want to display and click Add. You can also use the Remove, Add All, or Remove All buttons.
5. In the Format section, define the way that the DA text appears on screen with the Justification, Text Style, Height, and Rotation options.
6. Choose OK.

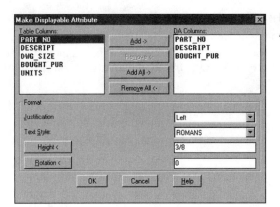

Figure 20-16: The Make Displayable Attribute dialog box.

7. AutoCAD prompts you for a text insertion point based on the justification you chose and returns you to the Rows dialog box.

8. Click OK. The text appears in the drawing.

A Displayable Attribute Link is like any other link in your drawing. To view it, choose Links from the External Database toolbar, select the DA text at the `Select objects:` prompt, and AutoCAD displays the link information in the Links dialog box. Choose Rows in the Links dialog box to see the entire row of linked row data.

Choose DA Columns in the Links dialog box to view all the columns used to create a DA. The column names appear in the DA columns list box. When DA Columns is not checked, ASE only displays the key columns used in the link path name.

You cannot edit DAs using DDATTE, ATTEDIT, or DDEDIT. To change the columns a DA uses, first erase the DA. Repeat the steps you used to create the DA. Remove columns you don't want and/or add new columns. When you return to your drawing, AutoCAD immediately creates the new DA.

If you change your data using the database application, choose Reload DA in the Administration dialog box. You can then see the new data when you load the drawing.

If you use the Rows dialog box to edit the data in your database, AutoCAD automatically updates the DA.

Step-by-Step: Creating Displayable Attributes

1. Continue with *ab20-1.dwg* from the previous exercise. Choose Rows from the External Database toolbar to open the Rows dialog box.

2. Choose Key Values and set the value to **9003-242-001**. Press Enter, then click OK. The data appears in the Rows dialog box.

3. Choose Make DA. Choose PART_NO and click Add. Do the same for DESCRIPT and MADE_PUR.

4. Set the Text Style to Romans. Leave the other settings the same. Click OK.

5. At the Left point: prompt in the drawing, choose a point below and to the left of the ② balloon in Figure 20-15.

6. Click OK in the Rows dialog box. AutoCAD places the attributes.

Using ASEEXPORT

The ASEEXPORT command is used to create database tables that list your linked objects and their handles. *Handles* are unique names that AutoCAD gives to each object in the drawing. You can export the reports in the same format as your database (called the native format) or in space- or comma-delimited formats. You can use these reports to keep track of how many objects are linked to a row, for example.

To use the ASEEXPORT command, choose Export Links from the External Database toolbar. AutoCAD prompts you to select objects.

Tip You can select the entire drawing, and AutoCAD finds just the linked objects.

When you complete object selection, AutoCAD opens the Export Links dialog box, shown in Figure 20-17.

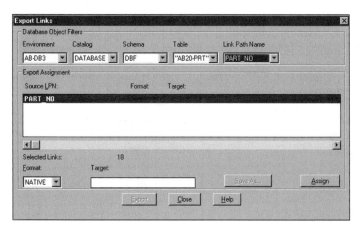

Figure 20-17: The Export Links dialog box.

The top of the dialog box is the same as the top of the Links dialog box. Use it to filter the tables that AutoCAD searches for the linked information.

Choose the LPN you want from the Source LPN list. You can then select a format from the Format drop-down list. If you choose CDF (comma-delimited file) or SDF (space-delimited file), you can choose Save As to open the Export to File dialog box where you can navigate to the location you want. For the native format, you can type in a target. Otherwise, AutoCAD defaults to the schema's path. Choose Export to create the file.

Querying with SQL statements

You can use SQL statements to gather more information about the elements in the drawing and database files. The ASESQLED command lets you issue SQL statements from an edit box or from existing files that can view or modify database tables.

If you don't know SQL, you won't be using the SQL Editor very much, and it is beyond the scope of this book to cover SQL. However, a few examples can give you a sense of the possibilities.

Using SQL you can do the following:

- ✦ Query the contents of a database
- ✦ Create indexes or index files
- ✦ Directly manipulate data as it relates to other tables in a database
- ✦ Work with multiple rows simultaneously
- ✦ Access all the tables in one schema with a series of SQL commands
- ✦ Modify the structure of your tables, to create new tables and to create views of the table data
- ✦ Combine SQL queries with graphical selection methods and show the results on screen with the ASESELECT command

You can also create an external file that contains several SQL statements and execute them sequentially like a batch file.

 To open the SQL Editor, choose SQL Editor from the External Database toolbar. To execute a SQL statement, either type it in the SQL Statement box or click File to choose a file containing SQL statements. Then choose Execute.

Creating SQL statements

While a full coverage of SQL syntax is beyond the scope of this book, there are a few rules that you may find helpful.

✦ Text data must be enclosed in single quotation marks ('B').

✦ Column names are not case-sensitive, but column values *are*.

✦ There are certain SQL keywords that are used in the program. You cannot use these as table or column names. Examples are: CHAR, GROUP, SQL, TABLE, USER, and CURRENT.

✦ In most standard SQL syntax you need to end each statement with a semicolon (;) — however, this is not necessary in ASE.

✦ You cannot use AutoCAD or DOS wildcard characters such as ? or * in column values or names.

✦ When specifying a table, you only need to specify the schema and table — you can omit the environment and catalog.

✦ To name more than one specification, separate each one by commas.

The SELECT statement is probably the most common SQL statement. The SELECT statement can retrieve a subset of the rows in one or more tables, retrieve a subset of the columns in one or more tables, or link rows in two or more tables to retrieve common data to both tables.

The following shows the syntax of the SQL SELECT statement, including modifying statements that instruct the DBMS exactly which rows to select.

```
SELECT  <select list>
FROM <table name>  [{,<table name>}...]
[WHERE <search condition>]
[GROUP BY <column spec>[{,<column spec>}...]
[HAVING <search condition>]
[ORDER BY <sort spec> [{,<sort spec>}...]
```

Note

In the above syntax, square brackets indicate optional elements, an ellipsis (three periods) indicates that the statement may be repeated, and curly brackets mean that the elements are listed in sequence.

Here is the meaning of the statement functions:

✦ The SELECT statement specifies the columns to retrieve.

✦ The FROM clause specifies the tables containing the specified columns.

    ✦ The WHERE clause specifies the rows you want to retrieve in the tables.

    ✦ The GROUP BY clause divides a table into groups. Groups are designated by a column name or by the results of computed numeric data type columns.

    ✦ The ORDER BY clause sorts results into one or more columns in either ascending (ASC) or descending (DESC) order.

Here are some examples:

```
SELECT part_no, descript FROM ab20-prts WHERE part_no =
9003-242-001
SELECT part_no, dwg_size FROM ab20-prts WHERE dwg_size =  C
SELECT descript, bought_pur FROM ab20-prts WHERE made_pur =
B  ORDER BY part_no
```

Summary

Using external databases to store textual information about drawing objects can reduce the size of drawings, simplify reporting, make data accessible to all users on a network, and let you edit a database from inside AutoCAD. Using the AutoCAD SQL Environment (ASE) involves configuring the database environment, connecting a drawing to a database environment, creating links between drawing objects and rows in the database, and then accessing the external data.

This chapter ends Part III, Working with Data. In Part IV, you start to draw in three dimensions.

✦   ✦   ✦

Drawing in Three Dimensions

✦   ✦   ✦   ✦

Part IV introduces you to three-dimensional drawing. AutoCAD creates three types of 3D objects, also called models — wireframes, surfaces, and solids. Wireframes, as the name implies, look like models created with wire. They do not have real surfaces or solidity. However, they are useful for creating shapes that you can turn into surfaces or solids. Surfaces, unlike wireframes, can hide objects behind them. They are especially useful for creating unusually shaped objects. Solids are defined as the entire volume of space they enclose. You can add and subtract solids from each other, creating realistic objects.

In Chapter 21 I explain the basics of 3D drawing, including specifying 3D coordinates, using the User Coordinate System for 3D drawing, and creating objects with elevation and thickness. Chapter 22 explains the techniques for viewing 3D objects. Chapter 23 covers surface models. Chapter 24 covers true solids. Chapter 25 explains how to create photorealistic views of your 3D drawings, including many new features in Release 14.

Specifying 3D Coordinates

Understanding 3D Drawings

Until now, you have worked with two axes, X and Y. When you work in three dimensions, you add the Z axis. Once you have a drawing with 3D objects, you can view it from any angle. The view you have been using in 2D drawings is like looking at a house from the top. Just as an architect calls this a plan view or a floor plan, AutoCAD calls this Plan View. From this view, even a 3D drawing looks 2D. But when you look at a 3D drawing from an angle, you can see that there's more to it than met the eye at first. Figure 21-1 shows the plan view of an office building. Figure 21-2 shows the same drawing viewed in a perspective view from the front.

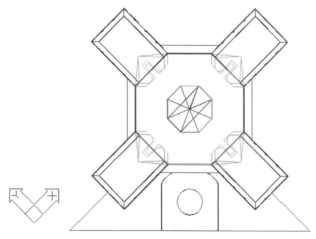

Figure 21-1: An office building in plan view.

Credit: Thanks to Roger Cusson of Interface Architectural Software, Montreal, Canada, for this drawing.

Figure 21-2: The same office building viewed from the front.

Although this drawing is quite complex, you can easily get started by working on simpler models. Three-dimensional drawing is not as difficult as it seems at first. This chapter first explains how to work with 3D coordinates. I also cover wireframe models and 3D surfaces created with thickness and elevation. These are essentially 2D objects placed in 3D space and are therefore a good place to start when learning about drawing in 3D.

Working with 3D Coordinates

All the 2D methods of specifying coordinates have their 3D counterparts. Just as you can draw a line by specifying a start point of 3,4 and an end point of 5,7, you can draw a 3D line by specifying a start point of 3,4,2 and an end point of 5,7,6. Absolute coordinates are the same in 3D — you just add a Z coordinate. In the same way, you can specify relative coordinates. In 3D drawings, you can use two new types of coordinates that are 3D counterparts of polar coordinates — *cylindrical* and *spherical*. Figure 21-3 shows the three axes X, Y, and Z. The arrows show the positive direction of the axes. Note that the UCS is set to display at the origin. Working with the UCS is essential in 3D work.

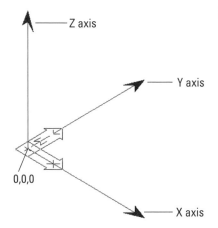

Figure 21-3: The three axes in 3D drawing.

Cross-Reference

If you are not familiar with the User Coordinate System (UCS), review it in Chapter 8.

However, most 2D commands accept 3D coordinates (that is, a coordinate that includes a Z value) only on the first point. After that you must omit the Z coordinate because AutoCAD requires that it be the same as that of the first point. For example, if you draw a rectangle, you can specify its first corner as 2,3,8 but the second corner must be specified without the Z value, as in 6,7. The Z value for all other points is automatically 8.

The LINE command is an exception. It is a true 3D command, so you can specify X, Y, and Z values at all points.

Absolute and relative Cartesian coordinates in 3D

You don't use absolute coordinates more in 3D than you do in 2D — maybe less. But understanding absolute coordinates are important to understanding the Cartesian coordinate system that AutoCAD uses to define every point in your drawing. Figure 21-4 shows a wireframe model of a square and a triangle drawn with absolute coordinates, viewed from above (plan view) and from the *southeast* view (above, to the right, and in front). The square is drawn in 2D — which means that the Z coordinates are all zero — to be a reference point for visualizing the 3D points of the triangle.

You can use relative coordinates in the same way, by including the change in coordinates. For example, to draw the line from (3,2,1) to (6,4,3), shown in Figure 21-4, you could start with the absolute coordinate (3,2,1) and then specify @3,2,2 because that's the difference between (6,4,3) and (3,2,1).

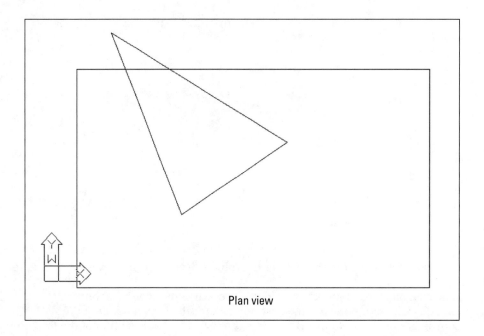

Plan view

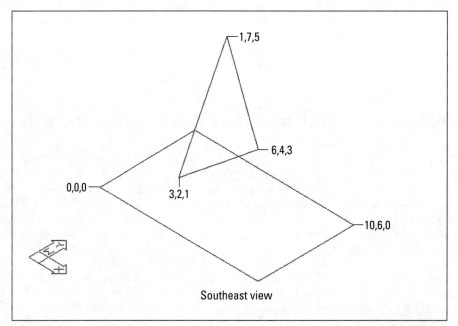

Southeast view

Figure 21-4: A rectangle and triangle viewed from plan view and southeast view.

Cylindrical and spherical coordinates

Just as polar coordinates are often more useful than Cartesian coordinates in 2D, cylindrical and spherical coordinates can be more useful in 3D. Here's how they work.

Cylindrical coordinates have the format (@)distance<angle,distance. The first distance is the number of units in the XY plane from the origin (for absolute coordinates) or your last point (for relative coordinates). The angle is the number of degrees from the X axis in the XY plane. The second distance is the number of units along the Z axis. Cylindrical coordinates can be absolute or relative. Add the @ for relative coordinates. When you draw a line using cylindrical coordinates, neither distance you specify is the length of the line. In essence, you are defining the lengths of two sides of a triangle to draw the hypotenuse. Figure 21-5 shows an example of a line drawn with cylindrical coordinates. The line was drawn from 0,0,0 to @5<30,3, which results in a line 5.8310 units long. (The @ wasn't necessary since the line was drawn from 0,0,0.)

Note

The two sides of the triangle are 5 and 3 units long. To calculate the length of the hypotenuse, use the Pythagorean theorem, which says that $a^2 + b^2 = c^2$ where a and b are the two sides of the triangle and c is the hypotenuse. Therefore, the hypotenuse is the square root of 25+9 or 34, which is 5.8310. Of course, you can use the DIST or LIST command to check it out.

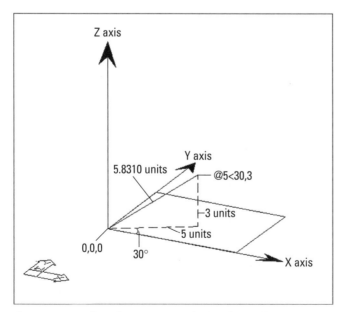

Figure 21-5: A line drawn using cylindrical coordinates.

Spherical coordinates have the format (@)distance<angle<angle. The first distance is the total number of units from the origin (for absolute coordinates) or your last point (for relative coordinates). The first angle is the number of degrees from the X axis in the XY plane. The second angle is the number of degrees from the XY plane in the Z direction. Spherical coordinates can be absolute or relative. Add the @ for relative coordinates. When you draw a line using spherical coordinates, the first distance is the actual length of the line. Figure 21-6 shows an example of a line drawn with spherical coordinates.

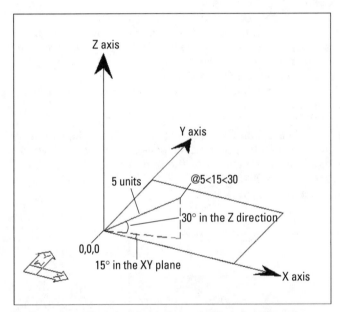

Figure 21-6: A line drawing using spherical coordinates.

Using editing commands with 3D wireframes

Certain 2D editing commands work well in 3D. Others have special 3D versions. Since wireframes are simply 2D objects placed in 3D space, you can generally use the familiar editing commands. For example, to move an object 3 units in the positive Z axis direction, type **0,0,3** at the Base point or displacement: prompt.

You need to be careful when selecting objects for editing. For example, if you draw two identically sized rectangles at different Z coordinates, you only see one rectangle when you look at them from plan view. How do you know which rectangle you are selecting?

You need to change the angle from which you view your drawing (fully covered in the next chapter). Once you can see all the parts of the drawing, you can select objects easily.

Cross-Reference

Multiple tiled viewports in which you view your drawing from different viewpoints can be very helpful in 3D drawing. Tiled viewports are covered in Chapter 8.

In this exercise you draw a simple wireframe piano bench and practice using 3D coordinates for both drawing and editing commands. You also view the drawing from two different angles.

Step-by-Step: Using 3D Coordinates

On the CD-ROM

1. Open *ab21-a.dwg* from the CD-ROM.

2. Save it as *ab21-1.dwg* in your *AutoCAD Bible* folder.

3. Choose Rectangle from the Draw toolbar. At the `Chamfer/Elevation/Fillet/Thickness/Width/<First corner>:` prompt, type **0,0,19** ⏎. At the `Other corner:` prompt, type **39,15** ⏎. This creates a rectangle 39 units long by 15 units wide that is 19 units above the plane created by the X and Y axes. Notice that you omit the Z coordinate for the second corner.

4. Start the COPY command. To copy the rectangle 2 units above the original rectangle, follow the prompts:

```
Select objects: Pick the rectangle.
Select objects: ⏎
<Base point or displacement>/Multiple: 0,0,2 ⏎
Second point of displacement: ⏎
```

You now have two rectangles, but because you are looking from the top, you see only one.

5. Choose SE Isometric View from the View flyout of the Standard toolbar. Now you can see the two rectangles, as shown in Figure 21-7.

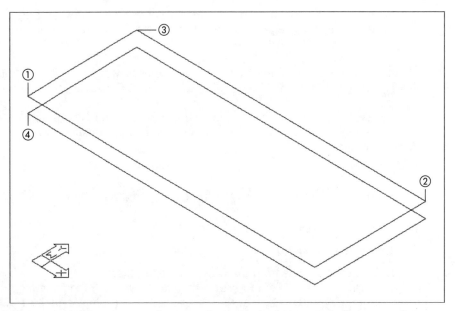

Figure 21-7: The two rectangles, seen from Southeast Isometric View.

6. Double-click OSNAP. Set a running object snap for Endpoints.

7. Start the LINE command. Follow the prompts:

```
From point: Pick the endpoint at ① in Figure 21-7.
To point: 0,0,0 ⏎
To point: 1,0,0 ⏎
To point: 1,0,21 ⏎
To point: ⏎
```

8. Start the COPY command. At the Select objects: prompt, select the three lines you just drew. End object selection. At the <Base point or displacement>/Multiple: prompt, type **38,0,0** ⏎. At the Second point of displacement: prompt, press Enter. AutoCAD copies the three lines. Since the bench is 39 units long and the legs are 1 unit wide, copying the leg 38 units in the X direction places the copy in the right location.

9. Do a ZOOM Extents so you can see the entire drawing.

10. Repeat the COPY command. Use two separate crossing windows to select the first leg, then the second leg. AutoCAD should find three objects each time. End object selection. At the <Base point or displacement>/Multiple: prompt, type **0,15,0** ⏎ to copy the legs 15 units in the Y direction. Press Enter at the Second point of displacement: prompt. AutoCAD copies the legs to the back of the bench.

11. To draw an open cover for the piano bench, start the LINE command. Start it at the endpoint at ② in Figure 21-7. At the `To point:` prompt, type **@15<90<45** ↵. You know the length of the line because the cover is the same as the width of the piano bench. At the `To point:` prompt, turn on ORTHO, move the cursor parallel to the length of the bench and type 39. At the `To point:` prompt, use the Endpoint object snap to pick ③. End the LINE command. Zoom out so you can see the entire bench.

12. To draw some bracing inside the bench, repeat the LINE command. At the `From point:` prompt, choose the endpoint at ④. At the `To point:` prompt, type **@15<90,2** ↵. End the LINE command. Here, cylindrical coordinates are ideal because you don't know the length of the line but you know the change in the X and Z coordinates (the width and the height of the bench's body respectively).

13. Save your drawing. It should look like Figure 21-8.

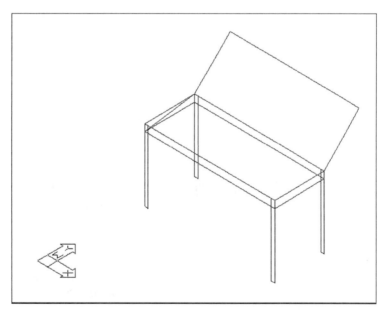

Figure 21-8: The completed wireframe piano bench.

Using point filters, object snaps, and grips in 3D

As mentioned earlier, it is often hard to tell which point you are picking in 3D. On a flat screen, you can only be sure of two dimensions. The other dimension is, so to speak, coming out of the screen — it could be X, Y, or Z depending on the angle you are using to look at the drawing. That dimension is the one that is hard to pick on the screen. In AutoCAD you use point filters, object snaps, and grips to be sure you have the right point in 3D drawing.

Point filters

In Chapter 4 I discussed point filters from a 2D point of view. They work the same way in 3D. You usually use point filters together with object snaps. For example, for the X coordinate you might pick the endpoint of a line. Often point filters are the only way to define a 3D point that is not on an existing object. The point filters for 3D drawings are .xy, .xz, and .yz. For example, if you want to pick a point 3 units in the Z direction from the endpoint of an existing line, you can use the .xy point filter to choose the endpoint of the line. AutoCAD then asks you for the Z coordinate, which you can specify as a number or using an object snap.

Object snaps

Object snaps are essential for 3D work. Using Release 14's new OSNAP setting with running object snaps makes 3D drawing even easier than before. Object snaps ensure that you are specifying the point you want. However, don't forget that in 3D drawings, you can have two lines, one on top of the other. Use a view that lets you see the two lines separately so you can pick the object snap you want. The Apparent Intersection object snap is especially useful for 3D work. You can use it to specify points that look as if they intersect from your viewpoint, even though in true 3D they would not intersect.

Grips

You can use grips to edit 3D objects as well. Again, it is important to choose a view that makes the editing easy. You cannot use grips to stretch solids; other than that, there is no difference between 2D and 3D editing when you use grips.

Step-by-Step: Using Point Filters and Object Snaps with 3D Wireframe Objects

1. Open *ab21-b.dwg* from the CD-ROM.

2. Save it as *ab21-2.dwg* in your *AutoCAD Bible* folder. This drawing has a running object snap for endpoints, and OSNAP is on. This is the same piano bench drawn in the last Step-by-Step exercise, but without the cover. In this exercise, you use the bench to create a chair.

3. Choose Stretch from the Modify toolbar. Use a crossing window to select the right side of the bench. AutoCAD should find eight objects. At the Base point or displacement: prompt, use the Endpoint running snap to pick ① in Figure 21-9. At the Second point of displacement: prompt, type **@-15,0** ↲.

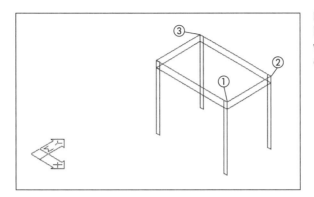

Figure 21-9: The piano bench after being shrunk with the STRETCH command.

4. Use Pan Realtime to move the chair to the bottom of your screen.

5. Start the LINE command. Follow the prompts:

```
From point: Choose ② in Figure 21-9.
To point: .xy ↵
of Pick ②.
(need Z): 45 ↵
To point: .yz ↵
of Pick the endpoint of the line you just drew.
(need X): Pick ③.
To point: Pick ③.
To point: ↵
```

6. Repeat the LINE command. Choose the Midpoint object snap from the cursor menu (Shift+right-click) to draw a line from the midpoint of the left side of the back of the chair back to the midpoint of the right side.

7. Choose Fillet from the Modify toolbar. At the `Polyline/Radius/Trim/ <Select first object>:` prompt, type **r** ↵. At the `Enter fillet radius <0.5000>:` prompt, type **1** ↵.

8. Repeat the FILLET command. At the `Polyline/Radius/Trim/<Select first object>:` prompt, pick ① in **Figure 21-10**. At the `Select second object:` prompt, pick ②.

9. Repeat the FILLET command and pick ② and ③ for the two lines.

10. Save the drawing of the chair. It should look like Figure 21-10.

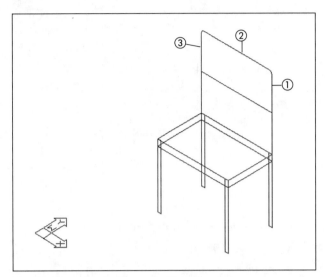

Figure 21-10: A wireframe model of a chair.

Creating 3D polylines

You have already created 3D lines by specifying 3D coordinates for the endpoints. The LINE command is a true 3D command because it accepts 3D coordinates. However, many commands cannot accept 3D coordinates. For example, you cannot place the center of a circle on one Z coordinate and the circumference on another. The whole circle must be on the same XY plane. Later in this chapter I explain how to change the UCS to get around this restriction.

This doesn't mean that you can't use circle in 3D work. You can always create a circle in one XY plane and then use that circle as a base for a cylinder, for example. The point is that the CIRCLE command itself is only a 2D command.

One command that has a 3D counterpart is PLINE. The 3D command is called 3DPOLY. The 3DPOLY command is like the PLINE command with a few differences:

- ✦ You cannot draw arcs.
- ✦ You cannot give it a width.
- ✦ You cannot use a noncontinuous linetype.

The 3DPOLY command can accept all 3D coordinates. You can also edit it with the PEDIT command, although there are fewer options.

Tip

If you want to create curved shapes in 3D space, you can use 2D polylines with a width and then add a thickness, as explained in the next section.

Using Elevation and Thickness

Wireframes have a number of limitations. As you saw in Figure 21-10, the chair you drew in the last exercise, you can see the back leg through the seat of the chair. Also, creating the detail of a real chair would be tedious by means of individual lines or 3D polylines. Finally, wireframes don't have any surface or solid properties. You can't display them in any realistic fashion or calculate properties such as area, mass, and so on.

Creating surfaces with thickness

You can create simple surfaces by adding *thickness* to 2D objects. When you add thickness to a 2D object, AutoCAD *extrudes* it. For example, a circle becomes a cylinder and a rectangle becomes a box. Figure 21-11 shows some objects created using thickness.

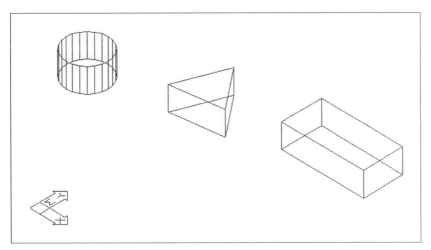

Figure 21-11: 3D surfaces created by adding thickness to 2D objects.

Surfaces created by adding thickness are sometimes called $2^{1}/2$D objects. Although they have three dimensions, the third dimension can only be a straight side perpendicular to the 2D object at the base.

The parallel lines on the cylinder are called *tessellation* lines. AutoCAD uses them to help you visualize curved surfaces. They are not actually part of the cylinder — you cannot use object snaps on them, for example.

You can add thickness to a 2D object in several ways:

✦ If you have already drawn a 2D object, choose Properties on the Object Properties toolbar and select the object. (You can also select the object first.) In the dialog box that opens, change the number in the Thickness text box and click OK.

✦ For existing objects, you can use the CHANGE command with the Properties option or the CHPROP command on the command line. Type **t** ↵ for the Thickness option and enter the new thickness.

✦ You can also change the current thickness. To do so, use the ELEV command (which also changes the current elevation, discussed in the next section) by typing it on the command line. The ELEV command prompts you for the current elevation and the current thickness. To change the current thickness, type a number. In most cases, you use a positive number, which extrudes objects in the positive direction of the Z axis. However, you can use a negative number to extrude objects in the negative direction of the Z axis. Once you change the current thickness, all objects you draw have that thickness.

Since it is easy to forget the current thickness, unless you are drawing a number of objects with the same thickness, it is usually safer to draw objects with no thickness and then use the Properties button to change the thickness. If you do change the current thickness, don't forget to change it back to zero when you are finished creating the 3D objects.

The RECTANG command has new prompts for Release 14. You can now specify elevation and thickness as options to the command. These specifications continue for all subsequent rectangles drawn.

Using the HIDE command

Because objects with thickness are surfaces, not wireframes, you can use the HIDE command to hide lines that would normally be hidden from view in real life. AutoCAD calculates which lines are behind surfaces from the current viewpoint you are using and hides them. Figure 21-12 shows the same objects as Figure 21-11 after using the HIDE command. You may notice that the cylinder has a top but the triangular prism and the box don't. For a further explanation, see the sidebar "Do objects with thickness have tops and bottoms?"

To return to the wireframe display, use the REGEN command.

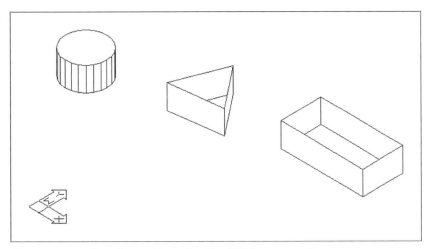

Figure 21-12: 3D surfaces after using the HIDE command.

Note

The word *wireframe* is used in two senses in AutoCAD. First, it means 3D objects that are created using only lines and 3D polylines. These objects have no surfaces or solidity. Second, it means surfaces and solids that are displayed as if they are created with lines and 3D polylines, like the models in Figure 21-11. This can get confusing. In this book, I usually distinguish between wireframes and wireframe display. If the subject is surfaces and solids, then the term *wireframe* generally means wireframe display.

Do objects with thickness have tops and bottoms?

If you look carefully at Figure 21-12, you see that the cylinder has a top but the triangular prism and the box don't. AutoCAD puts top and bottom surfaces on some objects with thickness, but not others.

When you add a thickness to objects created with the SOLID command (a 2D command), circles, and wide polylines, AutoCAD treats them as surfaces with tops and bottoms.

However, if you draw a closed polyline, for example with the RECTANG or POLYGON command, and give it a thickness, AutoCAD does not give it a top or a bottom surface. The same is true for a closed figure you draw with the LINE command.

Therefore, if you want a top and bottom, use the SOLID or REGION commands, draw a polyline with a width greater than zero, or draw a circle. (Hatching a closed figure with a solid fill does not have the same effect as the SOLID command.) These objects create opaque horizontal surfaces. You can also use the 3DFACE command, covered in Chapter 23. You can see the difference when you use the HIDE command.

AutoCAD ignores text when you hide a drawing unless you give it a thickness. If you want to hide text, give it a very small thickness, such as .001 units.

Adding elevation to objects

Until now, all of your 3D objects were based on 2D objects that were on the XY plane. In other words, their Z coordinate was zero. Although you generally don't want objects to float in the air, you certainly may want to place one object on top of another. To do this, you need to start the object above the XY plane. (You can also place objects below the XY plane.) To do this, you give an object *elevation*, which is its Z coordinate.

To give elevation to an object, you can use one of several methods:

✦ For existing objects, use the CHANGE command by typing it on the command line. Choose the Properties option and the Elev suboption.

✦ For existing objects, move the object(s) with the MOVE command in the Z direction.

✦ For new objects, change the current elevation with the ELEV command.

Note

For some objects, you can choose Properties on the Object Properties toolbar, select the object, and change the Z coordinate. This works for circles, lines, arcs, and ellipses, but not for polylines.

When you change the current elevation, all objects that you create are drawn on that elevation. Remember to change the elevation back to zero when you want to draw on the XY plane again.

Step-by-Step: Working with Elevation, Thickness, and the HIDE Command

1. Start a new drawing using *acad.dwt* as the template.

2. Save it as *ab21-3.dwg* in your *AutoCAD Bible* folder.

3. Start the CIRCLE command. Specify the center as 6,6 and the radius as 18.

4. Choose Properties from the Objects Properties toolbar. Select the circle and end object selection. In the Modify Circle dialog box, change the thickness in the Thickness text box to 3.000. Click OK.

5. Type **elev** ↵. At the New current elevation <0.0000>: prompt, type **3** ↵. Since you just changed the existing circle's thickness to 3, you set the elevation to 3 to place an object on top of the circle. At the New current thickness <0.0000>: prompt, type **24** ↵.

6. Start the CIRCLE command again. Choose Center from the Object Snap flyout of the Standard toolbar to pick the center of the existing circle as the center of the new circle. Set the radius to 3.

7. Type **elev** ↵. At the New current elevation <0.0000>: prompt, type **27** ↵. At the New current thickness <0.0000>: prompt, type **3** ↵. This places any new object on top of the two circles you just drew.

8. Start the CIRCLE command. Specify the center as 6,6 and the radius as 18. Because you don't specify a Z coordinate, AutoCAD uses the current elevation.

9. Choose SE Isometric View from the Viewpoint flyout of the Standard toolbar. You can now see the three circles.

10. Type **hide** ↵. You can now see the cable spool clearly.

11. Save your drawing. It should look like Figure 21-13.

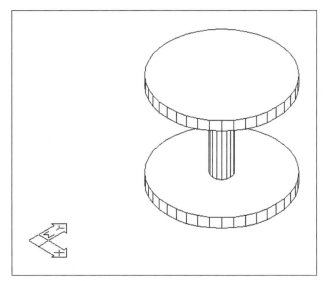

Figure 21-13: A cable spool created by drawing 2D circles with thickness and elevation.

On the CD-ROM   Flatten is a program that changes the z coordinate of lines, polylines, circles, arcs, text, blocks, points, and solids (created with the SOLID command) to 0. Look in the \Software\Chap21\Flatten folder.

Working with the UCS

Cross-Reference   I covered the User Coordinate System (UCS) in Chapter 4. If you are unfamiliar with the UCS, you should review that chapter. Here I offer a brief review of UCS features that are particularly useful for 3D drawing.

Except for certain true solids, much of 3D work starts with a 2D shape. However, the 2D drawing commands can only be drawn on, or parallel to, the XY plane. The spool in Figure 21-13, for example, consists of three circles, all parallel to the XY plane. How do you draw a circle, or any other 2D object for that matter, that is not parallel to the XY plane?

The answer is to change the UCS, thereby changing the definition of the XY plane. You can move the UCS to any location and orientation to define the XY plane any way you wish. Once you have done so, you can draw a 2D object at any angle.

Using the UCS icon

Although you may have found the UCS icon an annoyance in 2D work, you should display it when working in 3D. Otherwise, it is easy to lose track of which direction is which. Remember, you can also choose the Origin option, which displays the UCS icon, if possible, at the origin.

UCSs and viewpoints

When you look at a drawing from different viewpoints, you are seeing the viewpoints relative to the current UCS. A plan view of the World UCS (the default) is different from the plan view of a UCS that you have created by rotating the UCS around the X axis, for example. The UCS defines the orientation and origin of the X, Y, and Z axes. The viewpoint shows you your drawing from different angles without changing the orientation or origin of the axes. It is important to understand the difference between the UCS and viewpoints.

The broken pencil

When you choose a viewpoint that shows your drawing from the front, back, or one side instead of the top or an angle, you are looking straight at the XY plane. This is like looking at a table (which represents the XY plane) by kneeling down so your eyes are exactly at the same height as the surface of the table. From this vantage point, you cannot easily pick objects on the XY plane. A circle looks like a line. In such a situation, AutoCAD replaces the UCS icon with a broken pencil to warn you that you are looking at the XY plane of the current UCS edge on.

Figure 21-14 shows the same drawing from three viewpoints: plan view, the SE Isometric view (one of AutoCAD's preset viewpoints), and the front view. From the front view, AutoCAD displays the broken pencil icon. Notice that the plan (top) view displays even less detail of the drawing and would also make it difficult to select objects. The middle version uses the SE Isometric preset view, which displays the drawing from above and to one side. This view displays the drawing most clearly.

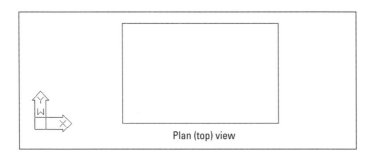

Plan (top) view

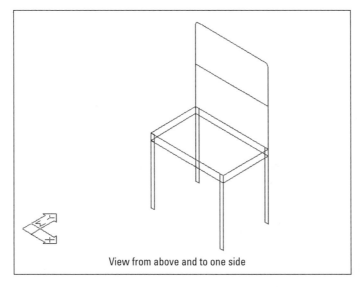

View from above and to one side

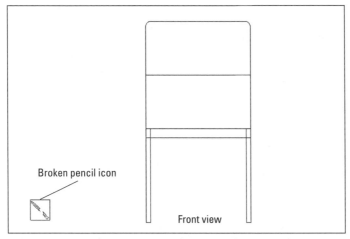

Broken pencil icon

Front view

Figure 21-14: Looking at a drawing from different viewpoints. When you are looking at the XY plane edge on, AutoCAD displays the broken-pencil icon.

UCS options

To change the UCS, choose Tools⇨UCS and choose one of the options. The following UCS options are useful for 3D drawing.

OBject

You can align the UCS with any existing object. Because AutoCAD orients the UCS differently for different objects, this option can sometimes be confusing. However, to modify some objects you must be on its XY plane — a good time to use the OBject option. The overall principle is that AutoCAD leaves the UCS's XY plane parallel to the previous UCS, except for 3Dface objects. Table 21-1 explains how AutoCAD aligns the UCS for various kinds of objects.

Table 21-1 UCS Orientation with the Object Option	
Object	**UCS Orientation**
Line	The endpoint nearest your pick point is the origin. The line lies on the X axis.
2D Polyline	The endpoint of the polyline nearest your pick point is the origin. The first segment of the polyline lies on the X axis.
Dimension	AutoCAD places the origin at the midpoint of the dimension text. The X axis is parallel to the X axis that you used when you created the dimension.
Text	AutoCAD places the origin at the insertion point and aligns the X axis with the rotation angle of the text. The same applies to attributes.
Block	AutoCAD places the origin at the insertion point and aligns the X axis with the rotation angle of the block.
Circle	The origin is at the circle's center. The X axis is aligned with your pick point.
Arc	The origin is at the circle's center. The X axis is aligned with the endpoint closest to your pick point.
Point	The origin is at the point. The X axis may be difficult to determine in advance.
Solid	AutoCAD uses the first point you specified for the origin and the first and second points to align the X axis.
3Dface	AutoCAD uses the first point for the origin. The X axis is aligned with the first two points. The Y axis is aligned with the first and fourth points. The new UCS may not be parallel to the prior UCS.

View

The View option aligns the X and Y axes with the current view. AutoCAD retains the current origin. The View option is most often used for creating text that you want to appear flat from your viewpoint of a 3D view of the drawing.

Origin

The Origin option creates a UCS parallel to the current UCS but with a new origin that you specify. You can use the Origin option for working at a new elevation, instead of changing the current elevation.

Z Axis Vector

The Z Axis Vector option lets you define an origin and then a point on the positive side of the Z axis. You can keep the previous origin to twist the UCS around its origin.

3Point

The first point you specify is the origin, the second point indicates the positive direction of the X axis, and the third point indicates the positive direction of the Y axis.

X Axis Rotate

The X Axis Rotate option maintains the current origin and rotates the Y and Z axes around the current X axis at the rotation angle you specify. The most common rotation is 90 degrees or a multiple of 90 degrees, but you can specify any angle.

Y Axis Rotate

The Y Axis Rotate option keeps the current origin and rotates the X and Z axes around the current Y axis. You specify the angle.

Z Axis Rotate

The Z Axis Rotate option keeps the current origin and rotates the X and Y axes around the current Z axis. You specify the angle.

Step-by-Step: Creating UCSs

On the CD-ROM

1. Open *ab21-c.dwg* from the CD-ROM.

2. Save it as *ab21-4.dwg* in your *AutoCAD Bible* folder. This drawing contains some center lines based on measurements of a chair. OSNAP is on, with running object snaps set for Endpoint and Quadrant. The UCS icon is set at the origin.

3. Choose Circle from the Draw toolbar. Use the From object snap to specify the center at @2,0 from ① in Figure 21-15. Set the radius to .5.

4. Choose Properties from the Object Properties toolbar and select the circle you just drew. In the Modify Circle dialog box, change the thickness to 16. Click OK.

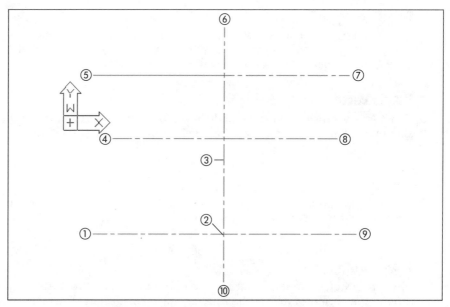

Figure 21-15: These center lines are the basis for drawing a chair.

5. Double-click ORTHO on the status bar to turn it on. Choose Mirror from the Modify toolbar. Select the circle. Specify the endpoint at ② for the first point of the mirror line. Specify any point vertical to ② for the second point of the mirror line.

6. Repeat the MIRROR command. Select the two circles. Choose the Midpoint object snap from the cursor menu (Shift+right-click) and pick the midpoint of the line at ③ for the first point of the mirror line. Pick any point horizontal to the first point for the second point of the mirror line. There are now four legs.

7. Type **elev** ↵. Change the elevation to 16 and the thickness to 1.

8. Choose Polyline from the Draw toolbar. At the From point: prompt, choose the From object snap, use the Center object snap of the circle near ①, and an offset of @-2,0. Continue to pick points ④ through ⑩. Then type **c** ↵ to close the polyline.

9. Choose Modify⇨Object⇨Polyline (or type **pedit** ↵). Select the polyline. At the prompt, type **f** ↵ to fit the polyline. Type **x** ↵ to end the command.

10. To see the result, choose SE Isometric View from the Viewpoint flyout of the Standard toolbar. Then type **hide** ↵. Remember that the polyline has no top or bottom surface. Imagine your model as a glass-bottomed chair. It should look like Figure 21-16.

11. Choose List from the Inquiry flyout of the Standard toolbar. Select the front left leg at ① in Figure 21-16. The center (of the circle at the bottom of the leg) is X= 3.5000 Y= -7.0000 Z= 0.0000.

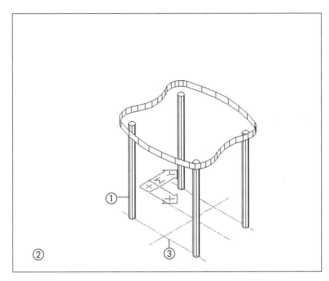

Figure 21-16: Part of a 3D chair.

12. To see the effect of a different UCS option, choose Tools⇨UCS⇨XAxis Rotate. To rotate the UCS around the X axis, type **90** ↵. Again, choose List from the Inquiry flyout of the Standard toolbar and select the same leg of the chair. Now the center is X = 3.5000 Y= 0.0000 Z= 7.0000. Look at the UCS icon (which is at 0,0,0) and try to visualize why the coordinates are as AutoCAD lists them.

13. Since you know the center of the circle of the front leg, you can move the UCS there. Type **ucs** ↵. Type **o** ↵ to choose the Origin option. At the Origin point <0,0,0>: prompt, type **0,0,7** ↵. This places the X axis through the center of the circle.

14. Repeat the UCS command. Choose the View option. AutoCAD places the UCS parallel to your current view. Choose Draw⇨Text⇨Single-Line Text. Start the text at ②. Set the height to 1.0 and the rotation to 0. Type **A glass-bottomed chair.** Press Enter twice to end the command.

15. Start the UCS command. Choose the OBject option. Pick the line at ③. Repeat the UCS command with the Origin option. Type **0,0,17** as the origin to place the UCS at the top of the seat.

16. Repeat the UCS command with the X option. Rotate the UCS around the X axis by −10. The UCS rotates. This lets you create the back of the chair at a 10-degree angle. Type **plan** ↵ and press Enter again to accept the default. (This command is covered in the next chapter.) It lets you view your drawing from plan view, in this case relative to the current UCS.

Tip

Although it's not necessary for this exercise, this would be a good UCS to save (choose Tools⇨UCS⇨Save).

17. Type **elev** ↵. Set the elevation to 17 and the thickness to 16.

18. Start the CIRCLE command. Choose a Center object snap and choose the top-left circle inside the chair's seat for the center of the circle. Accept the default radius of .5. Use the same technique to draw a circle at the corresponding right circle.

19. Change the elevation to 28 and the thickness to -5. Type **hide** ↵ so you can see the circles you just created more clearly.

20. Start the ARC command. The start point should be at the left quadrant of the left circle. The second point is the intersection of the vertical center line and the top horizontal center line. The endpoint is the right quadrant of the right circle.

21. Start the UCS command. Press Enter to accept the default World option. Choose SE Isometric View from the Viewpoint flyout of the Standard toolbar. Then type **hide** ↵ to see the final result.

22. Save your drawing. The chair should look like Figure 21-17.

A glass-bottomed chair

Figure 21-17: The completed glass-bottomed chair.

Summary

This chapter introduced you to 3D drawing, including wireframe models and surfaces you create by giving objects thickness and elevation. I covered 3D coordinates and how to use the UCS command in 3D.

In the next chapter I explain how to work with viewpoints in 3D drawings.

✦   ✦   ✦

Viewing 3D Drawings

Different Points of View

Once you start to work in three dimensions, you need to be
able to see the drawing from different angles. By combining
various UCSs and different viewpoints, you can draw any
object in 3D.

Your basic point of reference is plan view in the World
Coordinate System (WCS). This is the way you draw in 2D, so
it is familiar. Plan view is the view from the top. For a
building, the top is obvious. However, for a bushing, which
view is the top? The answer is that *you* decide which view is
easiest and most intuitive for you. Figure 22-1 shows a 2D
drawing of a bushing. Figure 22-2 shows the 3D version. As
you can see, the left view of Figure 22-1 is the plan view, and
the right view is a side view. The drawing was created this
way because it is easier to extrude a circle than to turn a
polygon into a circular model.

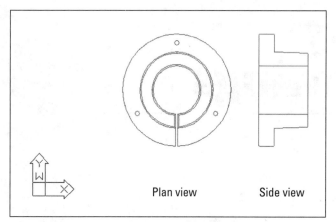

Figure 22-1: The left view is the plan view, looking down from the top.

Credit: Thanks to Robert Mack, The Dexter Company, Fairfield, Iowa, for this drawing.

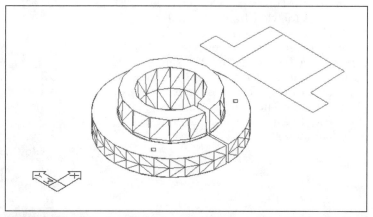

Figure 22-2: A 3D view of the bushing after using the HIDE command.

When working in 3D, you can use many of the familiar 2D techniques for viewing your drawing:

✦ You can use ZOOM Previous to display the previous viewpoint.

✦ You can save views so that you can easily return to them.

✦ You can use real-time zoom and pan as well as all the other ZOOM options.

Working with the Standard Viewpoints

AutoCAD offers ten standard viewpoints on the Viewpoint flyout of the Standard toolbar. These viewpoints are useful and easy to use because they are the most commonly used viewpoints. You can do a lot of your work just using these viewpoints. The standard viewpoints show viewpoints relative only to the WCS, not the current UCS. Therefore they are most useful when you are using the WCS.

To use a preset viewpoint you can choose it from the Viewpoint flyout of the Standard toolbar. You can also choose View⊃3D Viewpoint and choose the viewpoint you want from the submenu.

Using the VPOINT command

The standard viewpoints from the Viewpoint flyout actually use the VPOINT command with preset X, Y, and Z vectors. The VPOINT command was the original, command-line method of setting viewpoints. Now it is generally used for scripts and AutoLISP routines that need a way to set a viewpoint from the command line.

The VPOINT command defines a viewpoint using X, Y, and Z vectors. The vectors are based on a maximum of one unit. Imagine a model of the three axes floating out in space. You are Superman and can fly around the model from any angle. When you are over the Z axis, you can define the Z vector from 0,0,0 to your position as 1. The other vectors are zero because you are right over them, so 0,0,1 defines the top, or plan, view.

You would define a viewpoint using vectors in a script file or AutoLISP program. The next section shows the vector equivalents for the standard viewpoints to give you a feel for the vector system.

The VPOINT command also has a Rotate option that is the command-line equivalent of the DDVPOINT command's Viewpoint Presets dialog box. Using this option, you define a viewpoint by the angle from the X axis in the XY plane and then the angle from the XY plane.

Looking at a drawing from the standard viewpoints

It is easier to show than to describe the viewpoints. Here I show a 3D house from all ten standard viewpoints.

Top view

The top view is the plan view. You are looking at the model from a bird's eye perspective, suspended over the model. The VPOINT equivalent is 0,0,1. Figure 22-3 shows a house from the top.

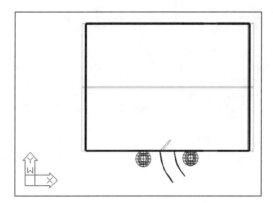

Figure 22-3: The top viewpoint of a 3D house.

You can also get this view by typing PLAN on the command line. The PLAN command has three options:

✦ **Current UCS** shows you plan view of the current UCS.

✦ **UCS** lets you choose a UCS that you have saved and named.

✦ **World** displays the plan view of the World Coordinate System.

Note that the PLAN command does not change the UCS even though you choose to see the plan view of a different UCS. This actually makes it very flexible — you can see what your drawing looks like from a different UCS without actually changing the UCS.

Bottom view

The bottom view is the plan view for groundhogs. It's not very useful for buildings, but may be very useful for 3D mechanical drawings. The VPOINT equivalent is 0,0,–1. Figure 22-4 shows the house from the bottom. Notice the direction of the UCS icon.

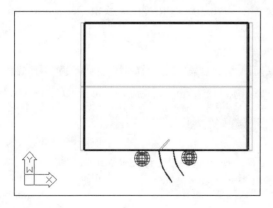

Figure 22-4: The bottom viewpoint of the 3D house.

Left view

The left view shows you your model from the side — the left side, of course. In architecture it would be one of the elevation views. The VPOINT equivalent is –1,0,0. Figure 22-5 shows the house from the left view. Notice the backward text. The text was drawn from the right view. Notice the broken-pencil icon.

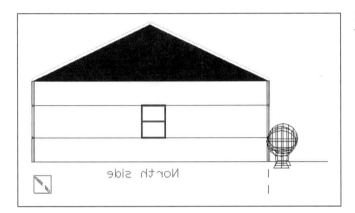

Figure 22-5: The left view of the 3D house.

Right view

The right view shows you your model from the right side. Like left view, right view is an elevation view. The VPOINT equivalent is 1,0,0. Figure 22-6 shows the house from the right view. Notice that the text now appears correctly, because it was drawn from this view.

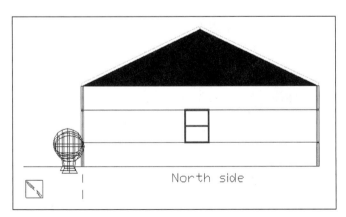

Figure 22-6: The right view of the 3D house.

Front view

The front view, another elevation view, shows your model from the front. The VPOINT equivalent is 0,-1,0. Figure 22-7 shows the house from the front. The text, stating that the front faces the east, doesn't represent any rule in AutoCAD. It simply helps you see the differences in the sides of the house.

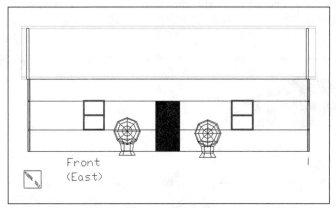

Figure 22-7: The front view of the 3D house.

Back view

The back view, another elevation view, shows your model from the back, as shown in Figure 22-8. Here you see the text of the front of the house, shown backward. The VPOINT equivalent is 0,1,0.

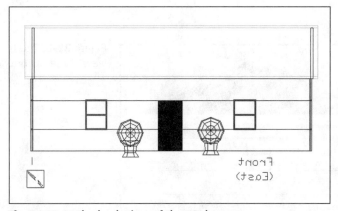

Figure 22-8: The back view of the 3D house.

SW isometric view

The SW (southwest) isometric view shows you your model from a diagonal viewpoint in all three dimensions (Figure 22-9). Notice how one corner of the house is closest to you (the corner between the left and front views), and you are also looking at the house from a view halfway between a side view and the top view. The isometric views are excellent for viewing all the 3D objects in a drawing. As you can see, many more objects are visible than with the top view or any of the side views. The VPOINT equivalent is -1,-1,1.

Don't get confused with the house's direction — the front facing east. From AutoCAD's point of view, east is 0 degrees when looking from the top view, and 0 degrees faces to the right.

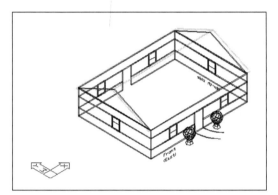

Figure 22-9: The SW isometric view of the 3D house.

SE isometric view

The SE (southeast) isometric view also shows your model from a diagonal viewpoint in all three dimensions. Here you are looking at the house at the corner between the right and front views, as well as halfway between a side view and the top view. You see the same objects as you do in SW isometric view. However, in a drawing not as symmetrical as the house, one view may bring certain objects to the front so that you can select them. The VPOINT equivalent is 1,-1,1. Figure 22-10 shows the house from the SE isometric view.

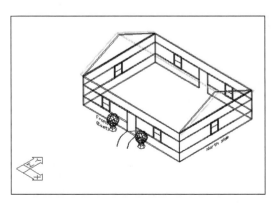

Figure 22-10: The SE isometric view of the 3D house.

NE isometric view

The NE isometric view shows your model from the corner between the right and the back views, as well as halfway between a side view and the top view. The VPOINT equivalent is 1,1,1. Figure 22-11 shows the house from the NE isometric view.

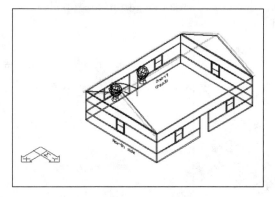

Figure 22-11: The NE isometric view of the 3D house.

NW isometric view

The NW isometric view shows your model from the corner between the left and the back views, as well as halfway between a side view and the top view. The VPOINT equivalent is -1,1,1. Figure 22-12 shows the house from the NW isometric view.

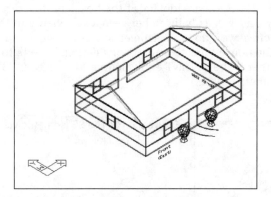

Figure 22-12: The NW isometric view of the 3D house.

Using DDVPOINT

If the standard views are not sufficient for your needs, the easiest alternative is using DDVPOINT. To use this command, choose View⇨3D Viewpoint⇨Select to open the Viewpoint Presets dialog box, shown in Figure 22-13. This dialog box lets you set the view to a great degree of accuracy.

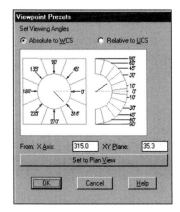

Figure 22-13: The Viewpoint Presets dialog box.

The left side of the dialog box determines the angle from the X axis, in the XY plane. These angles work as follows:

270	Front view
0	Right view
90	Back view
180	Left view

Other angles result in viewpoints between these views. For example, an angle of 315 degrees lets you look at your drawing from a view between front and right. If you're thinking that this is similar to the SE isometric view, you are right.

The right side of the dialog box determines the angle from the XY plane, in the Z direction. A zero-degree angle lets you look at your drawing from the front, back, or one side — depending on the setting on the left part of the dialog box. Often you want to look at your drawing from above. A 90-degree angle shows you plan view. An angle between 0 and 90 gives you a slanted view from the top — like one of the isometric standard views. (Actually, the isometric views set the angle from the XY plane to 35.3 degrees.)

Tip
There's an art to using the two dials to set the view angle you want. If you click the inside border of either one, close to the indicator needle, AutoCAD sets the angle based on exactly where you clicked. This results in uneven degrees, such as 47.6. However, if you click the outside border of either image, or the numbers themselves, AutoCAD rounds the angle to the value in the segment.

When you open the dialog box, the black needles indicate the angles for the current view. When you change the angles, the black needles move to the new angle but are replaced by red needles that indicate the current angle. This lets you constantly see the current angles for reference.

Beneath the dials are text boxes that reflect your choices. You can simply type the angles you want in the text boxes.

There's a very handy Set to Plan View button at the bottom of the dialog box. This lets you quickly return to plan view when you get a little dizzy from flying around your model.

You can set the viewing angles either based on the WCS or relative to a different UCS that you are using. It can get confusing if you have several different UCSs and start viewing them from several different viewpoints. As a result, the default is to view the drawing based on the WCS. However, sometimes you need to see your drawing relative to a UCS you have created. To do so, click Relative to UCS.

Tip   Keep the number of UCSs to the minimum necessary and save them. When possible, use a new viewpoint instead of creating a new UCS.

Click OK when you have completed making your changes.

Step-by-Step: Using Standard Viewpoints and DDVPOINT

On the CD-ROM

1. Open *ab22-a.dwg* from the CD-ROM.

2. Save it as *ab22-1.dwg* in your *AutoCAD Bible* folder. It shows the same house used in the earlier figures in this chapter from the SE isometric view.

3. Choose Top View from the Viewpoint flyout of the Standard toolbar.

4. Choose Bottom View from the Viewpoint flyout of the Standard toolbar. Notice the difference in the UCS icon.

5. Choose Front View from the Viewpoint flyout of the Standard toolbar. You see the front of the house with the two strange bushes.

6. Choose Right View from the Viewpoint flyout of the Standard toolbar. You see the text `North side`.

7. Choose NW Isometric View from the Viewpoint flyout of the Standard toolbar. You are looking at the back of the house.

8. Choose SW Isometric View from the Viewpoint flyout of the Standard toolbar. You are looking at the front of the house. If you wish, try the rest of the standard viewpoints.

9. Choose View⇨3D Viewpoint⇨Select to open the Viewpoint Presets dialog box. Set the left dial (angle from X axis) to 315 degrees by clicking on the number `315`. Set the right dial (angle from XY plane) to 60 degrees by clicking the second to top segment pointed to by the number 60. Click OK. You see a view somewhat like the SE isometric view, but from much higher up.

10. Repeat the DDVPOINT command. In the left image, click between 225 and 270 (click within the circle in the center). In the XY Plane text box, type **10**. Click OK. You get a view from slightly off the ground, much as you might see it if you were walking up to the house.

11. Type **hide** ↵. Notice that you can see the windows on the far side through the windows on your side of the house.

12. Choose View➪Named Views and click New. In the Define New View dialog box, type the name of the view, **walk-up.** Click Save View. Click OK to return to your drawing.

13. Save the drawing. It should look like Figure 22-14.

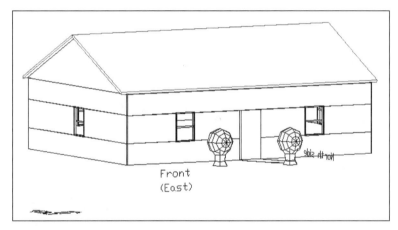

Figure 22-14: The final view of the house.

Note You cannot save a hide. When you restore the view, you see it as a wireframe display. You can, however, make a slide of the view. Slides are covered in Chapter 30.

Working with the Tripod and Compass

You can choose another method of defining views, using the VPOINT command. To start this command, choose View➪3D Viewpoint➪Tripod. AutoCAD displays the tripod and compass, as shown in Figure 22-15.

If you type the VPOINT command, or press Enter to repeat the command, press Enter at the Rotate/<View point> <0 -2 15/16 ,-0 -2 3/4 ,0 -1 9/16 >: prompt to see the compass and tripod. (The numbers show the current viewpoint.)

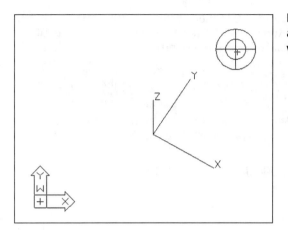

Figure 22-15: The VPOINT tripod and compass is used to define viewpoints in 3D.

Move the cursor about and two things happen. The cursor moves within the compass, and the axes dynamically shift position.

Imagine that you take a tangerine and make a large cross-shaped cut at the very bottom. Then you open out the bottom and remove the peel from the tangerine. Flatten the peel on the table. This is the concept of the compass, except that the outer edge is round. (The tangerine peel would have the shape of the cuts on its outer edge.) The very center of the compass — or the peel — is like the North Pole. When you are over the North Pole, you are looking straight down at your model — or the tangerine. The inner circle of the compass is where the middle of the tangerine was — at the equator. From the equator, you are looking sideways at your model. The outer circle of the compass represents the South Pole. From over the South Pole, you are looking at the bottom of your model — or the tangerine.

All of this is equivalent to the right image in the Viewpoint Presets dialog box that you use with the DDVPOINT command — it determines your view relative to the XY plane:

✦ At the center of the compass, you are right on top. This is a plan view.

✦ At the inner circle, you are on the side, looking at the XY plane on its edge.

✦ At the outer circle, you are beneath the XY plane.

The cross that goes through the compass represents the X and Y axes. If you place the cursor on the positive (right) side of the X axis, you are looking at the tanger-ine from its right side — this is equivalent to a right view. The position of the cursor relative to the X and Y axes is equivalent to the left image in the Viewpoint Presets dialog box that you use with the DDVPOINT command — it determines your view relative to the X axis in the XY plane. To summarize, going clockwise:

✦ The positive X axis gives you a right view.

✦ The negative Y axis is equivalent to a front view.

✦ The negative X axis gives you a left view.

✦ The positive Y axis gives you a back view.

When you have the cursor at the desired location, simply click. AutoCAD displays your drawing with the viewpoint you specified.

You cannot get an exact viewpoint this way. However, some people find this method of defining a viewpoint more intuitive. You can also look at the tripod as the axes move about — but be careful — sometimes it's difficult to see if an axis is coming toward you or going away from you.

Along with the tripod and compass, AutoCAD includes the current UCS icon based on the current viewpoint to help you get your bearings. Figure 22-16 shows a cursor location that results in the viewpoint shown in Figure 22-17. This is very close to the SE isometric view.

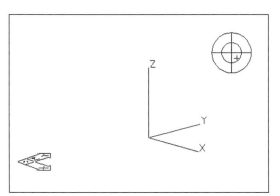

Figure 22-16: This cursor location results in the viewpoint shown in Figure 22-17.

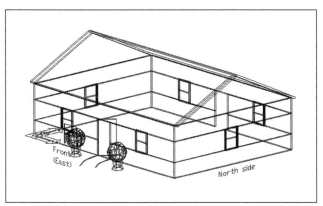

Figure 22-17: This viewpoint results from the cursor location on the compass shown in Figure 22-16.

Spotlight on AutoCAD Users Visualizing Sound
Tim Garrison of Michael Garrison Associates, Fresno, CA

Michael Garrison Associates designs acoustics, sound, house and stage lighting, and video IMAG (Image magnification) systems. While most architects may do a rendering or walk-through after the schematic and design development stage is completed, Michael Garrison Associates creates the rendering as part of a complete architectural solution.

Michael Garrison explains, "For our projects, we often get the 2D plans and partial sections of a performance space (usually a church). We have found that our customers—the project owners—want to participate in design decisions but have difficulty with visualization when working with 2D architectural plans. Using 3D rendered drawings, we can offer solutions in a way that the owner can comprehend what the final product will look like. This is also great for our interests because the shapes and designs we come up with are often non-standard, and to convey these with only 2D drawings can give a harsh impression and scare people off." Here you see one of the 2D drawings that Michael Garrison Associates worked on, Southeast Christian Church in Louisville, Kentucky.

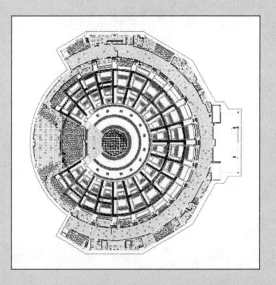

"We are very concerned with line of sight requirements as well as space requirements, often in ceilings. We also use other 3D computer design packages for acoustical and sound system design, such as CADP2, by JBL Professional, Northridge, California (800-852-5776 or www.jblpro.com). We start most projects by building a 3D model from information provided by the architect." An example is shown here, based on the 2D drawing above. This process revealed several conflicts with both the location of loudspeakers and house and stage lighting.

"We work out the sound and lighting system solutions in 3D and then quickly render an image using Accurender (Robert McNeel & Associates, Seattle, Washington at 800-677-0600 or `www.mcneel.com`) and present ideas usually in either A or B size color prints or computer files. Often this is the first time the owner (and architect) get a real feel for the space they are building. This has often made us the hit of the meeting and puts us in a nice place to steer the project in the direction which we believe is in the best interest of the owner—who is after all building this building to get the best results for both sight and sound. We are all trying for the goal of "form follows function" and can do our best when the function is incorporated into the form from the beginning of the process."

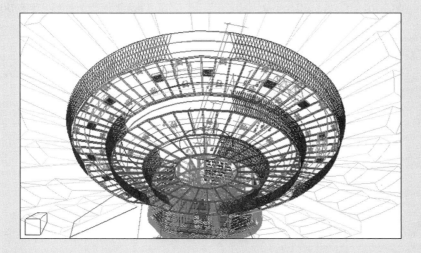

Here you see one of the final renderings. As you can see, it is much easier to visualize what the actual building will look like.

Getting a Quick Plan View

The PLAN command is a quick way to return to plan view. Type **plan** ↵. This command has three options:

- ✦ **<Current UCS>:** This is the default. You get the plan view of the current UCS.
- ✦ **UCS:** The UCS option lets you choose a named UCS. Type **?** ↵ to get a list of the named UCSs. Otherwise, type in the name of a UCS.
- ✦ **World:** This option gives you the plan view of the WCS. If your current UCS is the WCS, there is no difference between this option and the Current UCS option.

Figure 22-18 shows a sample UCS listing. Note that the units are architectural.

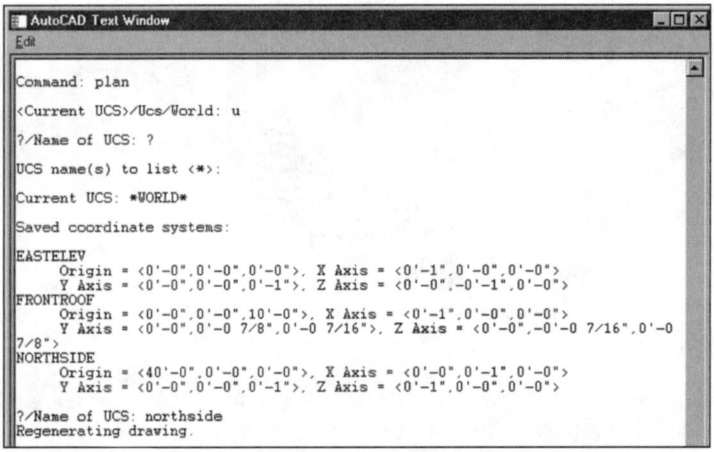

```
AutoCAD Text Window
Edit

Command: plan

<Current UCS>/Ucs/World: u

?/Name of UCS: ?

UCS name(s) to list <*>:

Current UCS: *WORLD*

Saved coordinate systems:

EASTELEV
     Origin = <0'-0",0'-0",0'-0">, X Axis = <0'-1",0'-0",0'-0">
     Y Axis = <0'-0",0'-0",0'-1">, Z Axis = <0'-0",-0'-1",0'-0">
FRONTROOF
     Origin = <0'-0",0'-0",10'-0">, X Axis = <0'-1",0'-0",0'-0">
     Y Axis = <0'-0",0'-0 7/8",0'-0 7/16">, Z Axis = <0'-0",-0'-0 7/16",0'-0
7/8">
NORTHSIDE
     Origin = <40'-0",0'-0",0'-0">, X Axis = <0'-0",0'-1",0'-0">
     Y Axis = <0'-0",0'-0",0'-1">, Z Axis = <0'-1",0'-0",0'-0">

?/Name of UCS: northside
Regenerating drawing.
```

Figure 22-18: A listing of saved UCSs.

Returning to plan view when you change the UCS

If you like plan views, you'll love UCSFOLLOW. UCSFOLLOW is a system variable that tells AutoCAD to return to plan view whenever you change the UCS. It's for those of you who like to get your bearings in plan view first before going on to change the viewpoint in another UCS.

Most 2D objects that you use in 3D drawings can only be drawn and edited in plan view since they don't interpret the Z coordinate. Therefore, returning to plan view is helpful in many situations.

The default value is zero (off), which means that AutoCAD does not return to plan view. In other words, your display remains unchanged when you change the UCS. Type **ucsfollow** ↵ and change the value to 1 to turn UCSFOLLOW on. From then on, AutoCAD automatically displays the plan view when you change the UCS.

Step-by-Step: Using the Compass and Tripod and the PLAN command

1. Open ab22-b.dwg from the CD-ROM. This is the same house used in the previous Step-by-Step exercise.

2. Choose View⇨3D Viewpoint⇨Tripod. Pick the point shown at ① in Figure 22-19. You see the result in Figure 22-20.

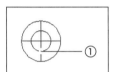

Figure 22-19: Picking a front viewpoint on the compass.

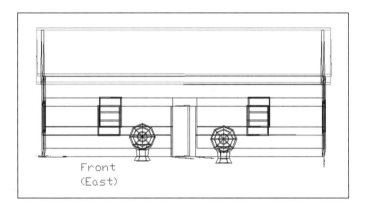

Figure 22-20: The front viewpoint. Notice that it is not exact.

3. Press Enter twice to repeat the VPOINT command and display the tripod and compass. Pick the point shown by the cross in Figure 22-21. Use the HIDE command to clearly see the results, as shown in Figure 22-22.

Figure 22-21: Picking a back left viewpoint from beneath the house.

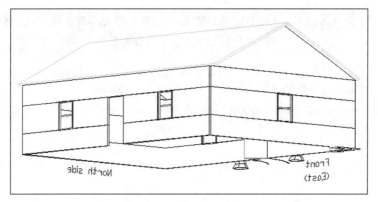

Figure 22-22: The resulting viewpoint. Notice that the house doesn't have a floor!

4. Type **vpoint** ↵. Press Enter once. Pick the point shown in Figure 22-23. Do a hide to see the results. This time you get an above-ground view from the front left corner.

Figure 22-23: The pick point for step 4.

5. Type **plan** ↵. Press Enter to accept the default option. AutoCAD displays the plan view of the house.

6. Do not save this drawing.

Using Tiled Viewports

As you learned in Chapter 8, you can create multiple viewports to view your drawing at different zooms and pans. Tiled viewports are very helpful in 3D drawings as well. Although you can, and should, save UCSs and views, if you find yourself switching back and forth between two to four viewpoints, try creating two to four viewports with the different viewpoints in them. The only disadvantage is that you have less real estate on your screen for each viewport.

Cross-
Reference

Refer to Chapter 8 for a full explanation of viewports.

Defining a Perspective View

AutoCAD offers a feature that lets you define views with true perspective from any angle and distance. These views differ from the viewpoints covered in this chapter in the following ways:

✦ A perspective view is more realistic, especially at a distance. Everyone is familiar with the concept of drawing parallel railroad tracks so that they merge in the distance. Perspective views create this effect of distance.

✦ You can look in any direction. While a viewpoint always looks at your model, in a perspective view, you can look from your model to the outside. For example, you can place yourself in a house and create a view looking out a window. (You won't see anything unless you've drawn some trees or other buildings outside.)

✦ Perspective views use the metaphor of a camera. There is a camera point — here you are standing — and a target point — what you are looking at. By defining these two points, you can create either close-up or distance views, much as you would with the zoom or panoramic lens of a camera.

The DVIEW command creates both parallel and perspective views. Figure 22-24 shows a parallel view. Notice the side brackets. Figure 22-25 shows a perspective view of the same model. The side brackets approach each other as they move to the back.

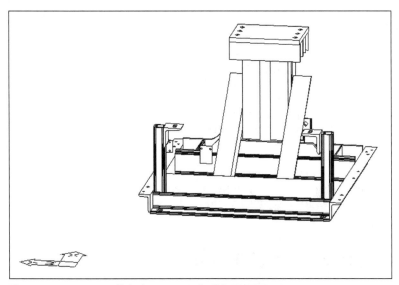

Figure 22-24: A parallel view created with DVIEW.

Credit: Thanks to Robert Mack of The Dexter Company, Fairfield, Iowa, for this drawing, a base housing for an industrial washing machine.

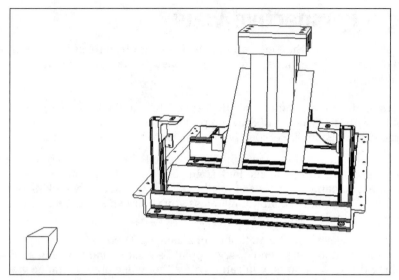

Figure 22-25: A perspective view of the same model.

Using DVIEW

To create a perspective view, choose View⇨3D Dynamic View to start the DVIEW command. At the `Select objects:` prompt, select the objects you want to include in the process of defining the perspective view.

Tip

You should select as few objects as you need to visualize the final result if you have a complex drawing. If you want to select the entire drawing, type **all** ↵ if the current view doesn't display the entire drawing.

Press Enter if you don't want to choose any objects. AutoCAD substitutes a block called *dviewblock,* which is a simple house. You can use the house to set your perspective view.

Note

If you wish, you can create your own block and name it *dviewblock.* Create it with X, Y, and Z dimensions of 1. When you press Enter at the `Select objects:` prompt, AutoCAD looks for *dviewblock* and uses it to display the results of the perspective view settings.

Understanding the DVIEW options

Once you select objects or press Enter, you see the following prompt:

```
CAmera/TArget/Distance/POints/PAn/Zoom/TWist/CLip/Hide/Off/Und
o/<eXit>:
```

You use these options to define the perspective view, as explained in the following sections.

CAmera

Use the Camera option to specify the angle of the camera, which represents where you are standing. You need to specify the angle from the X axis in the XY plane and the angle from the XY plane. This is very similar to the way you specify a view using the DDVPOINT command, explained earlier in this chapter.

When you choose this option, by typing **ca** ↵, you see the following prompt:

```
Toggle angle in/Enter angle from XY plane <90.0000>:
```

The default angle is based on the current view when you start DVIEW. (The 90-degree default means that the view was a plan view.) If you know the angle from the XY plane, you can just type it in. You can also move the cursor vertically to dynamically see the results. The view constantly changes as you move the cursor, moving up over your objects as you move the cursor up, and down as you move the cursor down. Move the cursor in one direction and then keep it still for a second to see the full effect.

However, moving the cursor horizontally changes the angle from the X axis in the XY plane. It can be confusing to change both angles at once, so AutoCAD lets you limit the effect of your cursor movement to one angle. You do this with the Toggle suboption.

Type **t** ↵ to see the next prompt of the Camera option:

```
Toggle angle from/Enter angle in XY plane from X axis
<-90.00000>:
```

Now, your cursor only affects the angle from the X axis. Move the cursor horizontally to see your objects rotate around you at a constant altitude. Press Enter when you like what you see, or you can type in an angle.

Tip
If you want to set the angle in the XY plane first and limit the effect of cursor movement to that change, you need to use the Toggle suboption to get to the `Enter angle in XY plane from X axis:` prompt. Once you set the angle in the XY plane, the suboption ends. Start the Camera option again to set the angle from the XY plane.

TArget

The Target option (type **ta** ↵) works exactly like the Camera option except that it defines the angles for the target of your viewpoint — what you would see through the camera lens. However, the angles are relative to the camera position. If you have already set the camera angles, the target angles default to those created by drawing a straight line from the camera angle through 0,0,0.

As with the Camera option, use the Toggle suboption to switch between the two angles you need to specify.

Distance

The Distance option is very important because using it turns on perspective mode. Before you use this option, the views you see are parallel views. When you use the Distance option, you see a slider bar at the top of the screen, as shown in Figure 22-26. AutoCAD also replaces the UCS icon with the perspective mode icon.

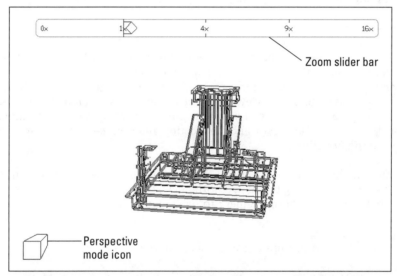

Figure 22-26: Using the Distance option turns on perspective mode and displays a slider bar.

AutoCAD displays the `New camera/target distance <1.0000>:` prompt. You can type a distance from the camera to the target or use the slider bar. Move the cursor to the right to zoom out. Moving the cursor to 4x is equivalent to using the ZOOM command and typing **4x** ↵. Move the cursor to the left of 1x to zoom in. The zoom factor is relative to the current display so that 1x leaves the zoom unchanged.

You can also type a distance in drawing units.

POints

You can use the Points option (type **po** ↵) to define the camera and target. AutoCAD displays the `Enter target point <26.8900, 61.0851, -11.8438>:` prompt. The default target point, which is different for each drawing, is the center of the current view. AutoCAD places a rubber-band line from the target point, which you can use to get your bearings when choosing a new target point. You can also type a coordinate.

At the `Enter camera point <26.8900, 61.0851, 63.1563>:` prompt, pick or type a point. AutoCAD keeps the rubber-band line from the target so you can visualize the camera and target points.

Because it is difficult to know what 3D points you are picking, you should use an object snap or XYZ point filters to pick points.

Tip

While it is common to choose a target point on one of the objects in your drawing, often you want the camera point to be off the objects, so that you are looking at the objects from a certain distance and angle. To pick the camera point, choose Format⇨Point Style (before starting DVIEW) and choose an easily visible point style. Decide what elevation you want, type **elev** ↵ and set a new elevation. From plan view, choose Point from the Draw toolbar and pick a point. The point is created on the current elevation. Then use the Node object snap to snap to the point when specifying the camera point in the Points option.

Even though the Points option sets both distance and angle for the camera and target points, you still need to use the Distance option to turn on perspective mode.

PAn

You cannot use the regular PAN or ZOOM commands within DVIEW, so DVIEW has its own Pan and Zoom options. At the `Displacement base point:` prompt, pick any point. At the `Second point:` prompt, pick the point to which you want the first point to pan. The model moves the distance and direction indicated by an imaginary line from the base point to the second point.

Zoom

The Zoom option displays the same slider bar you see with the Distance option, explained previously. If perspective mode is not on, you see the `Adjust zoom scale factor <1>:` prompt, which works like the Distance option slider bar. If perspective mode is on, you see the `Adjust lenslength <50.000mm>:` prompt. A shorter lens length, such as 35mm, zooms you out, giving a wider angle view. A longer lens length, such as 70mm, zooms you in, giving a narrower angle view.

Note

Although the prompt shows a default in the form `50.000mm`, you can only type in a number. Omit the `mm`.

TWist

The Twist option turns your objects around in a circle parallel to the current view you have defined. The default is zero degrees, which is no twist. Assuming your current view looks at the objects right side up, 180 degrees turns the objects upside down, as if you had turned the camera in your hands upside down. AutoCAD displays a rubber-band line from the center of the view, which you can use to pick a twist point, or you can type in an angle.

CLip

The Clip option lets you create front and back planes that clip off the view. Objects in front of the front clipping plane or behind the back clipping plane are not displayed. You can use the front clipping plane to clip off a wall in front of the camera, letting you see through the wall to the objects beyond — a kind of AutoCAD x-ray vision. Use the back clipping plane when you want to exclude objects in the distance from your perspective view. The clipping planes are always perpendicular to the line of sight, so you only need to set their distance from the target point.

Compare Figure 22-27 to Figure 22-25. In Figure 22-27, the front posts and brackets have been clipped so that they no longer obscure the rest of the model.

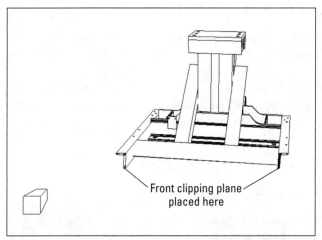

Front clipping plane
placed here

Figure 22-27: This model has a front clipping plane that hides the front of the model. Compare it to Figure 22-25.

When you choose the Clip option, you see the `Back/Front/<Off>:` prompt. Choose Back or Front to set the back or front clipping planes. Choose Off to turn off all previously defined clipping planes.

Note

When you use the Distance option to create a perspective view, AutoCAD automatically turns on a front clipping plane at the camera point.

When you choose the Front suboption, AutoCAD responds with the `Eye/<Distance from target> <2.5680>:` prompt. Choose Eye to set the clipping plane at the camera point. You can define the clipping plane by typing in a distance or using the slider bar that appears at the top of your screen. As you move the cursor on the slider bar, stop to let the drawing redraw to see the result.

When you choose the Back suboption, AutoCAD displays the `ON/OFF/<Distance from target> <0.0000>:` prompt. Choose On or Off to turn the clipping plane on or off, or specify the distance as for the front clipping plane.

Hide

The Hide option performs a hide, just like the HIDE command, letting you clearly see the results of the view you have created.

Off

The Off option turns off perspective mode and returns you to a parallel view. Otherwise, when you leave DVIEW after going into perspective mode, AutoCAD retains the perspective view until you change the view — for example, with DDVPOINT or VPOINT. Until then, you cannot pick points on the screen or use object snaps, which can be very frustrating. This option lets you exit from DVIEW in the normal viewing mode.

Undo

The Undo option undoes the effect of the last DVIEW option. You can undo through all the changes you have made in DVIEW.

eXit

Use Exit to exit DVIEW. If you are in perspective mode, AutoCAD retains your perspective view until you change the view.

Step-by-Step: Creating Perspective Views

On the
CD-ROM

1. Open *ab22-c.dwg* from the CD-ROM.

2. Save it as *ab22-2.dwg* in your *AutoCAD Bible* folder. This is a portion of a 3D house in plan view, as shown in Figure 22-28. OSNAP is on with a running object snap set for Endpoint.

3. You want to create a perspective view from approximately ① to ② in Figure 22-28. You can see right away that the wall near ① will need clipping. To get the distance of the clipping plane from the target, choose Distance from the Inquiry flyout of the Standard toolbar and pick ③ and ④. The pertinent information is `Distance = 12 -5 9/16`. You may get a slightly different distance. To see the distance information, press F2 to open the Text window.

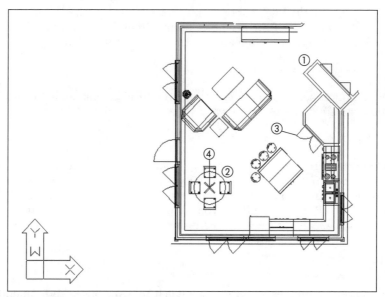

Figure 22-28: A 3D house in plan view.

Credit: Thanks to Andrew Wilcox of Virtual Homes, Inc., Hammonds Plains, Nova Scotia, Canada, for this drawing. I have used only a small portion of it.

4. Choose NE Isometric View from the Viewpoint flyout of the Standard toolbar. The result is as shown in Figure 22-29. This is a quick approximation and helps you plan your camera and target points. To test for endpoints, start the LINE command. Place the cursor at ① in Figure 22-29. The Endpoint Snap Tip and marker appear. Place the cursor at ②, the top of the table leg. You should see the Endpoint Snap Tip and marker. Press Esc to cancel the LINE command.

5. Choose View➪3D Dynamic View. At the `Select objects:` prompt, type **all** ↵. Press Enter to end object selection.

6. At the main DVIEW prompt, type **po** ↵. At the `Enter target point <14 -5 15/16 , 21 -9 3/8 , 6 -1 1/4 >:` prompt, pick the endpoint at ② in Figure 22-29. At the `Enter camera point <14 -6 15/16 , 21 -10 3/8 , 6 -2 1/4 >:` prompt, pick the endpoint at ①.

7. Type **d** ↵ for the Distance option. At the `New camera/target distance <20 -7 7/8 >:` prompt, move the cursor to 4x on the slider bar. Take your hand off the mouse to let the drawing redraw until you can see the result. Click at the 4x mark. Notice the perspective view icon.

8. To move the camera point, type **ca** ↵. At the `Toggle angle in/Enter angle from XY plane <11.7278>:` prompt, type **8** ↵ to lower the camera point slightly. At the `Toggle angle from/Enter angle in XY plane from X axis <47.11071>:` prompt, move the cursor close to ③ in Figure 22-29 (relative to the screen, not the model).

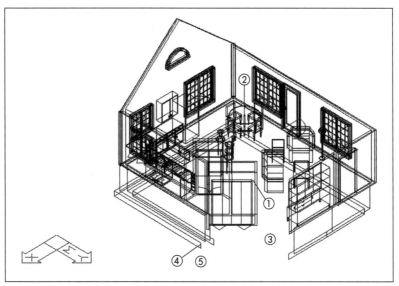

Figure 22-29: The NE isometric view of the house.

9. Type **z** ↵ for the Zoom option. At the `Adjust lenslength <35.000mm>:` prompt, type **60** to zoom in slightly.

10. Type **cl** ↵. Type **f** ↵ to set the front clipping plane. At the `Eye/<Distance from target> <15 -0 >:` prompt, type **13'** ↵. AutoCAD hides the front walls blocking the view.

11. Type **pa** ↵ to pan. At the `Displacement base point:` prompt, pick ④ in Figure 22-29. At the `Second point:` prompt, pick ⑤. The display moves down.

12. Type **h** ↵ to hide the drawing. Your drawing should look approximately like Figure 22-30.

Figure 22-30: The final perspective view.

13. After all that work, you should save the view. Choose View⇨Named Views. In the View Control dialog box, click New. In the Define New View dialog box, type **persp-1** in the New Name text box. Click Save View. Click OK to return to your drawing.

14. Save your drawing.

Laying out 3D Drawings

AutoCAD offers three AutoLISP routines that help you lay out your 3D drawing in paper space — SOLVIEW, SOLDRAW, and SOLPROF. You can find them on the Solids toolbar.

Using SOLVIEW to lay out paper space viewports

SOLVIEW automates the process of creating floating viewports and orthogonal views — views at right angles from each other.

 To start SOLVIEW, choose Setup View from the Solids toolbar. SOLVIEW has five options:

✦ **UCS** lets you choose the UCS to work from as well as set the scale, center, and clipping corners of a floating viewport. Use this option first. After you choose a UCS, type in a scale. You can change this later if you want. Then SOLVIEW prompts you for the center of the view. Pick a point and wait until the 3D model regenerates. SOLVIEW continues to prompt you for a view center, letting you pick points until you like what you see. Press Enter to continue the prompts. The clipping corners are the corners of the viewport. At the `View name:` prompt, type a name. SOLVIEW creates the first viewport.

 View names cannot have spaces. Choose a view name that describes the view, such as Top or Front. This helps you when you start creating orthogonal views.

✦ **Ortho** creates orthogonal views. At the `Pick side of viewport to project:` prompt, pick one of the edges of the first viewport. Again, choose a view center and clip the corners to create the viewport. Type a name for this new view.

 If you don't see the model properly when you pick the view center, continue with the prompts, picking clipping corners where you want them. Then pick the viewport (in model space with tile off) and do a ZOOM Extents. You can then pan and zoom as you wish. This problem can happen when you have several separate 3D objects in your drawing.

✦ **Auxiliary** creates inclined views. At the `Inclined Plane s 1st point:` prompt, pick a point in one of the viewports. At the `Inclined Plane s 2nd point:` prompt, pick another point in the same viewport. The two points are usually at an angle to create the inclined view. At the `Side to view from:` prompt, pick a point. You then pick a view center, clipping corners and specify a view name.

✦ **Section** creates cross-sections. At the `Cutting Plane s 1st point:` prompt, pick a point in a viewport. At the `Cutting Plane s 2nd point:` prompt, pick a point on the opposite side of the model, to create a cross-section. You then pick a side to view from, enter the view scale, a view center, clipping corners, and a view name.

✦ **eXit** exits the command. You can either exit the command after using an option and restart the command to use another option, or use all the options and then exit the command at the end.

Figure 22-31 shows an example with a top view, an orthogonal view from one side, an auxiliary view, and a section.

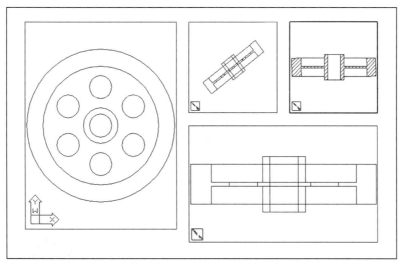

Figure 22-31: An example of using SOLVIEW.

Using SOLDRAW to create hidden lines and hatching

SOLDRAW uses the views created by SOLVIEW and creates 2D profiles that include solid and hidden lines to represent the profiles and hatching for sectional views. You must use SOLVIEW before using SOLDRAW.

To use SOLDRAW, choose Setup Drawing from the Solids toolbar. SOLDRAW puts you into paper space and prompts you to choose objects, which means floating viewports. You can select all of them if you want. SOLDRAW then proceeds to automatically create the profile views. Figure 22-32 shows an example of the hatching created for a sectional view.

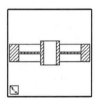

Figure 22-32: The result of using SOLDRAW on a sectional view.

SOLDRAW uses hatch pattern defaults to define the hatch. You may have to change these settings using HATCHEDIT.

SOLVIEW creates a whole set of new layers in your drawing. SOLDRAW freezes your original layers, leaving visible only the layers needed to display the profile in that paper space viewport. SOLVIEW creates a special layer that you can use for dimensioning — one for each view you create. For a view named front, the layer is named front-dim. You can use these dimensioning layers to create dimensions in paper space.

Using SOLPROF to create profiles

The SOLPROF command creates profiles like SOLDRAW, but you don't need to use SOLVIEW first. In addition, SOLPROF is more interactive than SOLDRAW. To start the command, choose Setup Profile from the Solids toolbar. SOLPROF prompts you to select objects.

When you start SOLPROF, you must have already created a floating viewport and you must be in model space.

At the `Display hidden profile lines on separate layer? <Y>:` prompt, type **Y** or **N**. By choosing Yes, you give yourself the capability of freezing or turning off the layer containing hidden parts of the model. You can also hide other 3D objects behind the one you are profiling.

At the `Project profile lines onto a plane? <Y>:` prompt, type **Y** or **N**. If you choose Yes, SOLPROF creates 2D objects. If you choose No, SOLPROF creates 3D objects.

At the `Delete tangential edges? <Y>:` prompt, type **Y** or **N**. A tangential edge is the meeting of two contiguous faces. Most drafting application do not require you to show tangential edges.

Figure 22-33 shows the result of SOLPROF after freezing the layer containing the original object — SOLPROF creates its own layers for the profile.

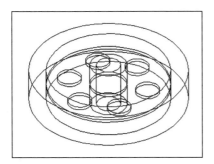

Figure 22-33: A profile created with SOLPROF.

Figure 22-34 shows the result of SOLPROF after also freezing the layer that SOLPROF created containing the hidden parts of the model. In this case, the layer was named Ph-2d0. Look for the *h*, which stands for hidden. The last part of the layer name is the handle of the object you are profiling and so differs for each object.

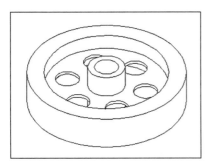

Figure 22-34: A profile created with SOLPROF after freezing the layer containing the hidden parts of the model.

You can combine viewports created with SOLPROF and viewports created with SOLVIEW and SOLDRAW. For example, you can create two orthogonal views with SOLVIEW and SOLDRAW and then add a viewport and use SOLPROF to create another view.

Once you have a separate layer for the hidden portion of the model, you can modify that layer's color and/or linetype to show the hidden lines in a contrasting color or linetype.

Summary

In this chapter I covered all the ways to view your 3D drawing. You can use the standard viewpoints on the Viewpoint flyout for a quick look, the DDVPOINT command to specify exact angles, and the tripod and compass for flexibility. The PLAN command quickly returns you to plan view. Another way to work in 3D is to set up two or more tiled viewports, each showing a different view.

The DVIEW command lets you create parallel and perspective views. You set the camera and target. You can create front and back clipping planes. Generally, once you have created the perspective view, you save it.

In the next chapter I explain how to create 3D surfaces.

✦   ✦   ✦

Creating 3D Surfaces

Working with AutoCAD Surfaces

In this chapter you learn to create all types of surfaces, also called *meshes*. Surfaces have a great advantage over 3D wireframe models because you can hide back surfaces and create shaded images for easier visualization of your models. Surfaces also allow you to create unusual shapes, such as for topological maps or freeform objects. Figure 23-1 shows a lamp created using surfaces.

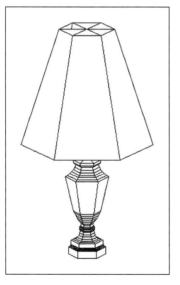

Figure 23-1: A lamp created with surfaces.

You cannot obtain information about physical properties, such as mass, center of gravity, and so on, from surfaces — such information can be obtained only from 3D solids, which are covered in the next chapter.

AutoCAD approximates curved surfaces by creating a mesh of planes at varying angles. You see the planes because AutoCAD displays them using a web of intersecting lines. AutoCAD defines the mesh by its vertices — where the lines intersect. Figure 23-2 shows a mesh with its vertices.

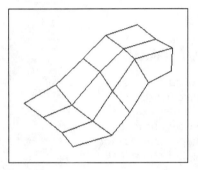

Figure 23-2: A surface mesh.

When working with surfaces you may want to display the Surfaces toolbar, shown in Figure 23-3. To open the toolbar, choose View⇨Toolbars to open the Toolbars dialog box and choose Surfaces. Click Close to close the Toolbars dialog box. You can also right-click any open toolbar to open the Toolbars dialog box.

Figure 23-3: The Surfaces toolbar.

Drawing Surfaces with 3DFACE

Two-dimensional objects are often used to create three-dimensional models. I have already discussed in Chapter 21 how you can use 2D solids (the SOLID command), wide polylines, and circles to make horizontal surfaces when you add a thickness to them. In fact, the SOLID command is so useful in 3D that you can find its icon on the Surfaces toolbar.

You can also use regions in 3D drawings. While regions are 2D objects and cannot be given a thickness, when you use the HIDE command, AutoCAD converts the region to a surface. When the drawing is regenerated to a wireframe display, the region turns back into a wireframe, too, losing its surface properties.

Another option is to use 3DFACE, which is a true 3D command. 3DFACE creates three-or four-sided surfaces that can be in any plane. You can place surfaces together to make a many-sided surface. While AutoCAD draws lines between these surfaces, you can make the lines invisible to create the effect of a seamless surface. You define the surface by specifying the points that create the corners of the surface. As a result, a 3D face cannot have any curves. 3DFACE only creates surfaces — you cannot give a thickness to a 3D face. However, you can create a 3D solid from a 3D face using the EXTRUDE command. 3D solids are covered in the next chapter.

Using the 3DFACE command

To create a 3D face, choose 3D Face from the Surfaces toolbar. AutoCAD prompts you for first, second, third, and fourth points. You must specify points clockwise or counterclockwise, not in the zigzag fashion required by the 2D SOLID command. When creating a 3D face:

✦ Press Enter at the `Fourth point:` prompt to create a three-sided surface. Then press Enter again to end the command.

✦ To create a four-sided surface, specify a fourth point. AutoCAD repeats the `Third point:` prompt. Press Enter to end the command.

✦ To create surfaces of more than four sides, continue to specify points. AutoCAD repeats the `Third point:` and `Fourth point:` prompts until you press Enter — twice after a third point or once after a fourth point.

As you continue to add faces, the last edge created by the third and fourth points becomes the first edge of the new face so that adding a face only requires two additional points.

Tip

It often helps to prepare for a complex 3D face by creating 2D objects for some or all of the faces. You can then use Endpoint object snaps to pick the points of the 3D face.

Making 3D face edges invisible

Making edges invisible makes a series of 3D faces look like one 3D face. Figure 23-4 shows three 3D faces with and without internal seams.

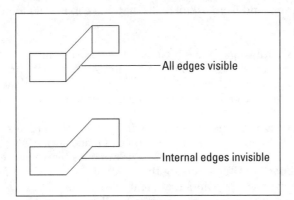

All edges visible

Internal edges invisible

Figure 23-4: You can make internal edges of a 3D face invisible.

There are several ways to control the visibility of 3D face edges.

Controlling visibility during 3D face creation

While you are drawing the 3D face, you can type **i** ↵ before each edge. Then specify the next point. However, it is sometimes difficult to predict exactly where to indicate the invisible edge. If the 3D faces are complex, it can even be difficult to predict where the edge will be.

Using the EDGE command

After creating the entire 3D face, you can use the EDGE command. The purpose of the EDGE command is solely to make 3D face edges visible and invisible and is probably the easiest way to control the visibility of 3D face edges.

Choose Edge from the Surfaces toolbar. At the `Display/<Select edge>:` prompt, select a visible edge that you want to make invisible. AutoCAD repeats the prompt so you can select additional edges. Press Enter to make the edges invisible. Although a visible edge might actually be two edges belonging to two adjacent 3D faces, EDGE makes them both invisible.

To make invisible edges visible, choose the Display option. AutoCAD displays all the edges in dashed lines and shows the `Select/<All>:` prompt. Press Enter to display all the edges or use the Select option to select 3D faces (you can use windows for selection). Either way, you see the edges of the 3D face you want to edit. AutoCAD then repeats the `Display/<Select edge>:` prompt. You can now select the edge you want to make visible. Press Enter to end the command and make the edge visible.

Using the Modify 3D Face dialog box

After creating one or more 3D faces, you can also choose Properties from the
Object Properties toolbar and select one 3D face. This opens the Modify 3D Face
dialog box, shown in Figure 23-5.

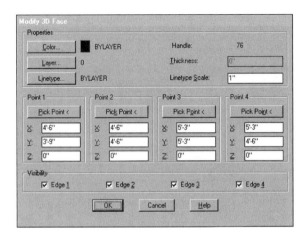

Figure 23-5: You can use the Modify 3D Face dialog box to change the visibility of 3D Face edges.

There are two difficulties with using this dialog box to edit 3D face edge visibility.
First, there is no easy way to know which edge is which. The dialog box only labels
them Edge 1, 2, 3, and 4. Second, while the EDGE command makes both edges of
adjacent 3D faces visible or invisible, the Modify 3D Face dialog box does not. You
need to use the dialog box for each adjacent face.

Tip

Use the EDGE command to control visibility of 3D face edges.

Using the SPLFRAME system variable

Setting the SPLFRAME system variable to 1 and then regenerating the drawing
makes all 3D face edges visible. (The SPLFRAME system variable also affects the
display of spline-fit polylines, hence its name.) To return edges to their original
setting, set SPLFRAME to 0 and do a REGEN.

**On the
CD-ROM**

The CD-ROM contains a small routine, Stairs, that creates a 3D staircase with 3D
faces. Look in *\Software\Chap23\Stairs.*

In the following Step-by-Step exercise, you draw a kitchen cabinet.

Step-by-Step: Drawing 3D Faces

1. Open *ab23-a.dwg* from the CD-ROM.

2. Save it as *ab23-1.dwg* in your *AutoCAD Bible* folder. This is a blank drawing with architectural units. ORTHO is on. OSNAP is on and running object snaps are set for endpoints and midpoints. If the Surfaces toolbar is not displayed, right-click any toolbar, scroll down until you see Surfaces and check the check box. Close the Toolbars dialog box.

3. Choose 3D Face from the Surfaces toolbar. Follow the prompts:

```
First point: 6,6 ↵
Second point: @20,0 ↵
Third point: @0,2' ↵
Fourth point: @-20,0 ↵
Third point: ↵
```

4. Start the COPY command. Follow the prompts:

```
Select objects: Select the 3D face.
Select objects: ↵
<Base point or displacement>/Multiple: m ↵
Base point: Pick any point.
Second point of displacement: @0,0,1.5' ↵
Second point of displacement: @0,0,3' ↵
Second point of displacement: ↵
```

You don't see any difference because you are looking at the three 3D faces in plan view and one is on top of the other.

5. Choose SE Isometric View from the Viewpoints flyout of the Standard toolbar. Your drawing should look like Figure 23-6. You now have the top, bottom, and shelf of the cabinet.

6. Start the 3DFACE command again. Follow the prompts:

```
First point: Pick the endpoint at ① in Figure 23-6.
Second point: Pick the endpoint at ②.
Third point: Pick the endpoint at ③.
Fourth point: Pick the endpoint at ④.
Third point: Pick the endpoint at ⑤.
Fourth point: Pick the endpoint at ⑥.
Third point: Pick the endpoint at ⑦.
Fourth point: Pick the endpoint at ⑧.
Third point: ↵
```

7. To draw the door of the cabinet, change the current layer to Const. Start the LINE command and draw a line from ② in Figure 23-6 to @18<225. End the LINE command. Now start the COPY command and copy the line from ② to ①. These two construction lines frame the door.

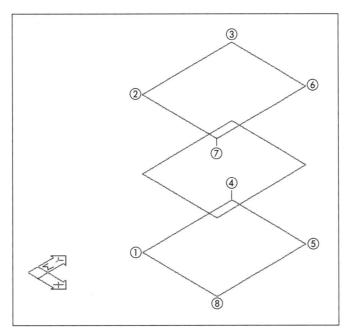

Figure 23-6: The three 3D faces from an isometric viewpoint.

8. To make it easier to work on the door, choose Tools⊅UCS⊅3 Point. Follow the prompts:

```
Origin point <0,0,0>: Pick the left endpoint of the bottom
construction line.
Point on positive portion of the X-axis <0'-1",0'-0",0'-0">:
Pick ① in Figure 23-6.
Point on positive-Y portion of the UCS XY plane <0 -0 ,0 -
1 ,0 -0 >: Pick the left endpoint of the top construction line.
```

9. Start the LINE command again. Follow the prompts:

```
From point: Choose the From object snap.
Base point: Pick the left endpoint of the top construction line.
<Offset>: @3,-3 ↵
To point: Move the cursor to the right and type 12 ↵.
To point: Move the cursor down and type 30 ↵.
To point: Move the cursor to the left and type 12 ↵.
To point: c ↵
```

Your drawing should look like Figure 23-7.

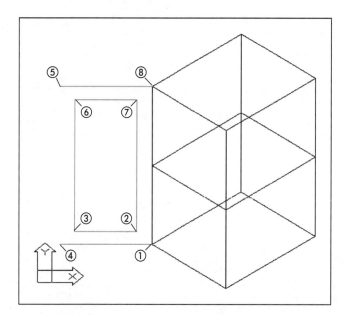

Figure 23-7: The partially completed cabinet.

10. Change the current layer to 0. Choose 3D Face from the Surfaces toolbar. Follow the prompts:

```
First point: Pick the endpoint at ① in Figure 23-7.
Second point: Pick the endpoint at ② in Figure 23-7.
Third point: Pick the endpoint at ③.
Fourth point: Pick the endpoint at ④ in Figure 23-7. Notice the edge
lines between ① and ② and between ③ and ④.
Third point: i ↵ Pick the endpoint at ⑤ in Figure 23-7.
Fourth point: Pick the endpoint at ⑥.
Third point: i ↵ Pick the endpoint at ⑦.
Fourth point: Pick the endpoint at ⑧.
Third point: Pick the endpoint at ① in Figure 23-7.
Fourth point: Pick the endpoint at ②.
Third point: ↵
```

11. Choose Edge from the Surfaces toolbar. At the `Display/<Select edge>:` prompt, pick the edge between ① and ② and then the edge between ③ and ④. (A midpoint marker and Snap Tip appear.) Press Enter. The edges disappear.

12. Start the UCS command and press Enter to return to the WCS. Choose View⇨3D Viewpoint⇨Select to open the Viewpoint Presets dialog box. Set the From: X Axis angle to about 200 degrees. Set the XY Plane angle to about 35 degrees. Choose OK.

13. Type **hide** ↵ to see the result. You can clearly see through the cabinet door's window.

14. Save your drawing. It should look like Figure 23-8.

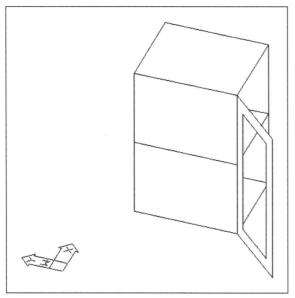

Figure 23-8: The completed kitchen cabinet, including a window in the door.

Drawing Surfaces with PFACE

PFACE draws surfaces called polyface meshes, which are a type of polyline. However, you cannot edit them with PEDIT. The best way to edit them is with grips. AutoCAD designed PFACE for the creation of surfaces using AutoLISP routines or other automated methods. Consequently, the input for polyface meshes is somewhat awkward. However, polyface meshes have the following advantages:

✦ You can draw surfaces with any number of sides, unlike 3D faces, which can only have three or four sides.

✦ The entire surface is one object.

✦ Sections that are on one plane do not show edges so you don't have to bother with making edges invisible.

✦ You can explode polyface meshes into 3D faces.

✦ If you create a polyface mesh on more than one plane, each plane can be on a different layer or have a different color. This can be useful for assigning materials for rendering or other complex selection processes.

On the other hand, polyface meshes are difficult to create and edit. Figure 23-9 shows two polyface meshes — one on one plane and the other on three planes.

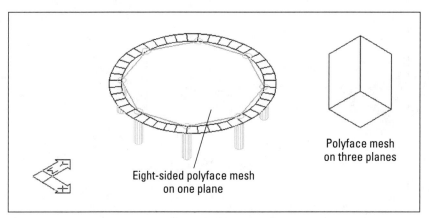

Eight-sided polyface mesh
on one plane

Polyface mesh
on three planes

Figure 23-9: You can create many-sided polyface meshes on one plane, or on several different planes. After a hide, the polyface mesh hides objects behind it.

The prompts for PFACE are divided into two phases. The first phase simply asks for vertices. The second phase asks you to specify which vertex makes up which face (or plane). The second phase is fairly meaningless for polyface meshes on one plane, but you have to specify the vertices anyway. Here's how to do it:

1. Type **pface** ↵.

2. At the Vertex 1: prompt, specify the first vertex.

3. Continue to specify vertices at the Vertex 2:, Vertex 3: (and so on) prompts. Press Enter when you have finished.

4. At the Face 1, Vertex 1: prompt, type which vertex starts the first face of the polyface mesh. It is usually vertex 1, so you type **1** ↵.

5. At the Face 1, Vertex 2: prompt, type which vertex comes next on the first face. Continue to specify the vertices for the first face.

   If you are drawing a polyface mesh on one plane, continue to specify all the vertices in order and press Enter twice when you are done to end the command.

   If you are drawing a polyface mesh on more than one plane, continue to specify the vertices on the first face (that is, plane) and press Enter. At the Face 2, Vertex 1: prompt, type the first vertex of the second face (plane) and continue to specify vertices for the second face. Press Enter. Continue to specify vertices for all the faces. Press Enter twice to end the command.

Tip   In order to easily draw a polyface mesh with PFACE, draw 2D objects as a guide for picking vertices. Then you can use object snaps to pick the vertices. Also, for polyface meshes on more than one plane, draw a diagram that numbers the vertices. This helps you specify which vertices make up which face.

During the second phase of the prompts, when PFACE asks you to define the faces, you can specify the next face. Then specify the vertices that are to be on that layer or color.

In the following Step-by-Step exercise, you draw a hexagonal night table with polyface meshes.

Step-by-Step: Drawing Polyface Meshes

1. Open *ab23-b.dwg* from the CD-ROM.

2. Save it as *ab23-2.dwg* in your *AutoCAD Bible* folder. Two hexagons have been drawn, one 24 inches above the other, on the Const layer, as shown in Figure 23-10.

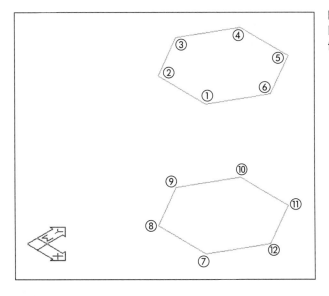

Figure 23-10: The two hexagons are the basis for a night table.

3. Type **pface** ↵. Follow the prompts. First you specify all the vertices. Then you specify the top hexagon, then the five sides (the front is open), and finally the bottom hexagon. Unfortunately, if you make a mistake, you must start over.

```
Vertex 1: Pick ① in Figure 23-10.
Vertex 2: Pick ② in Figure 23-10.
Vertex 3: Pick ③ in Figure 23-10.
Vertex 4: Pick ④ in Figure 23-10.
Vertex 5: Pick ⑤ in Figure 23-10.
Vertex 6: Pick ⑥ in Figure 23-10.
Vertex 7: Pick ⑦ in Figure 23-10.
Vertex 8: Pick ⑧ in Figure 23-10.
Vertex 9: Pick ⑨ in Figure 23-10.
```

```
Vertex 10: Pick ⑩ in Figure 23-10.
Vertex 11: Pick ⑪ in Figure 23-10.
Vertex 12: Pick ⑫ in Figure 23-10.
Vertex 13: ↵
Face 1, vertex 1: 1 ↵
Face 1, vertex 2: 2 ↵
Face 1, vertex 3: 3 ↵
Face 1, vertex 4: 4 ↵
Face 1, vertex 5: 5 ↵
Face 1, vertex 6: 6 ↵
Face 1, vertex 7: ↵
Face 2, vertex 1: 12 ↵
Face 2, vertex 2: 6 ↵
Face 2, vertex 3: 5 ↵
Face 2, vertex 4: 11 ↵
Face 2, vertex 5: ↵
Face 3, vertex 1: 5 ↵
Face 3, vertex 2: 11 ↵
Face 3, vertex 3: 10 ↵
Face 3, vertex 4: 4 ↵
Face 3, vertex 5: ↵
Face 4, vertex 1: 10 ↵
Face 4, vertex 2: 4 ↵
Face 4, vertex 3: 3 ↵
Face 4, vertex 4: 9 ↵
Face 4, vertex 5: ↵
Face 5, vertex 1: 3 ↵
Face 5, vertex 2: 9 ↵
Face 5, vertex 3: 8 ↵
Face 5, vertex 4: 2 ↵
Face 5, vertex 5: ↵
Face 6, vertex 1: 8 ↵
Face 6, vertex 2: 2 ↵
Face 6, vertex 3: 1 ↵
Face 6, vertex 4: 7 ↵
Face 6, vertex 5: ↵
Face 7, vertex 1: 7 ↵
Face 7, vertex 2: 8 ↵
Face 7, vertex 3: 9 ↵
Face 7, vertex 4: 10 ↵
Face 7, vertex 5: 11 ↵
Face 7, vertex 6: 12 ↵
Face 7, vertex 7: ↵
Face 8, vertex 1: ↵
```

4. Type **hide** ↵ to see the final result.

5. Save your drawing. It should look like Figure 23-11.

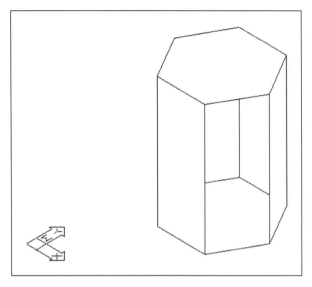

Figure 23-11: The completed hexagonal night table.

Creating Polygon Meshes with 3DMESH

The 3DMESH command creates polygon meshes (not to be confused with the polyface meshes created by PFACE). The 3DMESH command is used for creating irregular surfaces, vertex by vertex. The great advantage of polygon meshes is that AutoCAD considers them to be polylines and they can therefore be edited with the PEDIT command — although in a limited manner. Figure 23-12 shows two surfaces created with 3DMESH. The surface on the right has been smoothed using PEDIT.

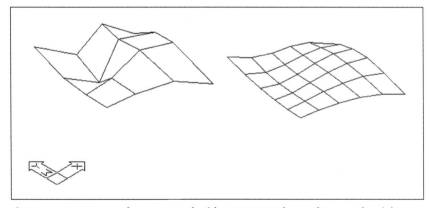

Figure 23-12: Two surfaces created with 3DMESH. The surface on the right has been smoothed using the Smooth option of PEDIT.

To use 3DMESH, choose 3D Mesh from the Surfaces toolbar. AutoCAD then asks you for the Mesh M size and Mesh N size. M is the number of vertices going in one direction. N is the number of vertices going in the other direction. Figure 23-13 shows a 3D Mesh with an M size of 5 and an N size of 3.

Once you set the size of the 3D Mesh, you need to specify each vertex. For example, the 3D Mesh in Figure 23-13 has 15 vertices that you need to specify. AutoCAD prompts you for each vertex in order, starting with (0,0). Vertex (0,1) is the second vertex in the first column. Vertex (1,0) is the first vertex in the second column, starting from the bottom. It's a little confusing because AutoCAD starts the counting from zero, not one. For the 3D Mesh in Figure 23-13, the last vertex is (4,2).

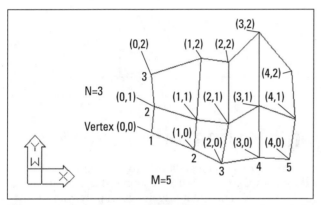

Figure 23-13: A 3D Mesh with an M size of 5 and an N size of 3, showing the vertex designations.

In Figure 23-13, the 3D Mesh is five vertices wide and three vertices high as you look at it in plan view. However, you do not have to specify the vertices in the same direction. For the 3D mesh in the figure, I started at the bottom left, continued to move up for (0,1) and (0,2), then moved to the right. However, you could start at the bottom left and move to the right for (0,1) and (0,2), then go back to the left either above or below (0,0) — resulting in a 3D mesh that is three vertices wide and five vertices high as you look at it in plan view. In other words, M and N can be in any direction, which is appropriate for a 3D surface.

3D meshes are especially suitable for AutoLISP routines; in fact, AutoCAD supplies several. These are discussed in the next section.

To smooth a polygon mesh, start the PEDIT command and select the polygon mesh. AutoCAD responds with the Edit vertex/Smooth surface/Desmooth/ Mclose/Nclose/Undo/eXit <X>: prompt. Table 23-1 explains how to use these options:

Table 23-1
PEDIT Options for 3D Polygon Meshes

Option	Description
Edit vertex	Displays the `Vertex (0,0). Next/Previous/Left/Right/ Up/Down/Move/REgen/eXit <N>:` prompt. Use the Next, Previous, Left, Right, Up, and Down suboptions to move the X marker that displays the current vertex. When you are at the vertex you want to move, use the Move suboption. REgen regenerates the 3D mesh. Use eXit to return to the original prompt.
Smooth surface	Smoothes the surface according to one of three possible sets of equations — Quadratic, Cubic, or Bezier. Bezier results in the smoothest surface. Use the SURFTYPE system variable to set the type of smoothing. Set SURFTYPE to 5 to create a quadratic b-spline surface, 6 to create a cubic b-spline surface, or 7 to create a Bezier surface. Cubic (6) is the default setting. To smooth a 3D Mesh, there must be *more* than three vertices in both the M and N directions.
Desmooth	Removes the smoothing on the 3D mesh surface.
Mclose	Closes the surface in the M direction by connecting the last edge to the first edge.
Nclose	Closes the surface in the N direction by connecting the last edge to the first edge.
Undo	Undoes the last option.
eXit	Exits PEDIT

Tip

You can use 3DMESH to create 3D topological surfaces. You may have a surveyor's drawing marking measurement points. Open a new drawing, using the surveyor's drawing as an xref. In plan view, create a polygon mesh. For the vertices, simply pick the surveyor's measurement points. (You'll need to count them first to determine a regular grid for the M and N sizes.) When you finish, select the polygon mesh to display its grip points. Select each grip in turn, and at the `<Stretch to point>/Base point/Copy/Undo/eXit:` prompt, type **@0,0,100.78** ↵ where the last coordinate is the height of the plot at the measurement point. When you are done, look at the surface in any nonplanar viewpoint to see the result.

Drawing Standard 3D Shapes

AutoCAD includes several AutoLISP routines that use the 3DMESH command to create some standard shapes. These shapes all have icons on the Surfaces toolbar. You can also choose Draw➪Surfaces➪3D Surfaces to open the 3D Objects dialog box, as shown in Figure 23-14.

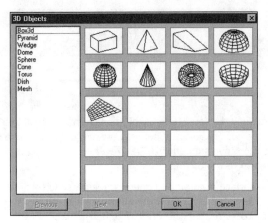

Figure 23-14: The 3D objects dialog box.

Note   On the command line, you can type **3d** ↵ and choose the shape you want to draw from the command options. You can also type **ai_** followed by the name of the shape, such as **ai_box**.

Box

Figure 23-15 shows a box from the SE Isometric viewpoint after using the HIDE command.

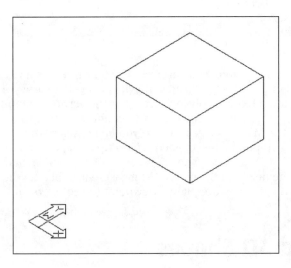

Figure 23-15: A box from an isometric viewpoint after using the HIDE command.

Here's how to draw one:

1. Choose Box from the Surfaces toolbar.

2. At the `Corner of box:` prompt, specify the lower left corner of the base of the box.

3. At the `Length:` prompt, specify the length of the box along the X axis.

4. At the `Cube/<Width>:` prompt, specify the width of the box along the Y axis. If you choose the Cube option, AutoCAD creates a cube with a width and height the same as the length you just specified and you don't see the Height prompt.

5. At the `Height:` prompt, specify the height of the box along the Z axis.

6. At the `Rotation angle about Z axis:` prompt, specify an angle. AutoCAD rotates the box in the XY plane. There is no default of zero degrees, so you must type **0** ↵ even if you do not want to rotate the box. You can also use the Reference suboption, which works like the Reference option of the ROTATE command.

Note

As you define the box, AutoCAD draws a temporary image in yellow to show you the result of your specifications. There is also a rubber-band line from the box corner so you can pick the side dimensions with the mouse. However, if you are drawing in plan view, AutoCAD uses the length of the rubber-band line to determine the dimensions, not the point you pick. Figure 23-16 shows what happens when you use the rubber-band line to pick the width. The cursor shows the pick point, but the top-right corner of the square shows the result. Because of this, in plan view it's easier to type in the lengths of the sides. On the other hand, if you use a nonplanar view such as SE Isometric view, you can pick the ends of each side without problem.

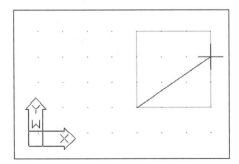

Figure 23-16: AutoCAD uses the length of the rubber-band line to determine the width, not the pick point.

Wedge

Figure 23-17 shows a wedge. The prompts are the same as for the box, except that there is no Cube option. A wedge is half of a box.

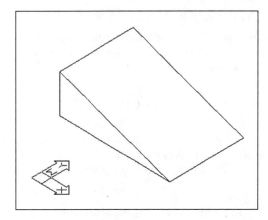

Figure 23-17: A wedge from an isometric viewpoint after the HIDE command.

Here's how to draw a wedge:

 1. Choose Wedge from the Surfaces toolbar.

2. At the `Corner of box:` prompt, specify the lower left corner of the base of the wedge.

3. At the `Length:` prompt, specify the length of the wedge along the X axis.

4. At the `Width:` prompt, specify the width of the wedge along the Y axis.

5. At the `Height:` prompt, specify the height of the wedge along the Z axis.

6. At the `Rotation angle about Z axis:` prompt, specify an angle. AutoCAD rotates the wedge in the XY plane. There is no default of zero degrees, so you must type **0** ↵ even if you do not want to rotate the wedge. You can also use the Reference suboption, which works like the Reference option of the ROTATE command.

Pyramid

You can draw pyramids with three- and four-sided bases. A pyramid with a three-sided base creates a four-sided object called a tetrahedron. You can top the pyramid with a point, a flat top, or for four-sided bases, a ridge. Figure 23-18 shows the various types of pyramids you can draw.

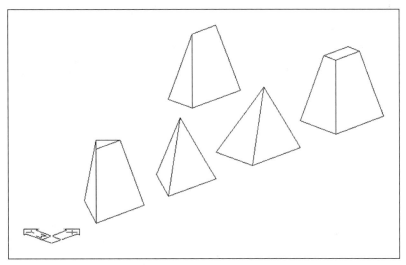

Figure 23-18: You can draw all these pyramidal shapes.

Here's how to draw the pyramids:

 1. Choose Pyramid from the Surfaces toolbar.

2. At the `First base point:` prompt, specify the first point (any point) on the base.

3. At the `Second base point:` prompt, specify the second point on the base.

4. At the `Third base point:` prompt, specify the third point on the base.

5. At the `Tetrahedron/<Fourth base point>:` prompt, specify the fourth point on the base or choose the Tetrahedron option (creates a pyramid with a base of three points).

At the `Top/<Apex point>:` prompt, if you chose the Tetrahedron option, specify the apex (top point) or choose the Top option. AutoCAD prompts you for three top points.

At the `Ridge/Top/<Apex point>:` prompt, if you specified a fourth base point, specify the apex (top point) or choose the Ridge or Top options. If you choose the Ridge option, specify the two points for the ridge. If you choose the Top option, specify the four top points.

Tip Specifying the apex or ridge can be tricky unless you know the absolute coordinates you want. You can't change viewpoints during the command. However, you can easily change the points later using grips. Another trick is to start any drawing command, such as LINE, before starting the pyramid. At the `From point:` prompt, pick the point you want to use for the first base point of the pyramid.

Then press Esc to cancel the command. This leaves that point as the last point specified. Now define the base of the pyramid, using the same point as the first base point. When you need to specify the apex or ridge, you can use relative coordinates from the first base point. For example, to create an apex two units directly over the first base point, specify **@0,0,2** for the apex. When you use the Top option AutoCAD provides a rubber-band line from each of the base corners in turn, letting you use relative coordinates from the base corners.

Cone

You can create full or partial cones. Figure 23-19 shows both types, as displayed after using the HIDE command.

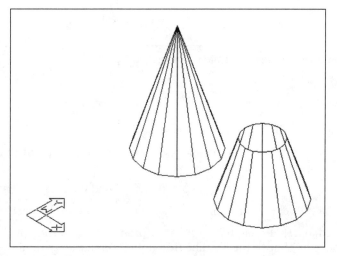

Figure 23-19: You can draw full or partial cones.

Here's how to create cones:

 1. Choose Cone from the Surfaces toolbar.

2. At the `Base center point:` prompt, pick the center for the circle that makes the base of the cone.

3. At the `Diameter/<radius> of base:` prompt, specify the radius for the circle at the base or choose the Diameter option to specify the diameter.

4. At the `Diameter/<radius> of top <0>:` prompt, specify the radius of the top or choose the Diameter option and specify the diameter. If you accept the default of zero, you get a complete cone. If you specify a radius or diameter, you get a truncated cone.

Note

You can specify the base's size to be larger than the top's size, resulting in an inverted cone.

5. At the Height: prompt, specify the height.

6. At the Number of segments <16>: prompt, specify the number of mesh segments. A higher number results in a smoother looking cone.

Sphere

Drawing a sphere is quite easy — you just specify the center and radius. Figure 23-20 shows a sphere after using the HIDE command.

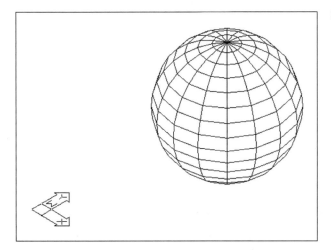

Figure 23-20: A sphere.

Here's how to do it:

  1. Choose Sphere from the Surfaces toolbar.

2. At the Center of sphere: prompt, specify a point.

3. At the Diameter/<radius>: prompt, specify the radius, or choose the Diameter option to specify the diameter.

4. At the Number of longitudinal segments <16>: prompt, type the number of north-south lines you want. A higher number results in a smoother looking sphere.

5. At the Number of latitudinal segments <16>: prompt, type the number of east-west lines you want. A higher number results in a smoother looking sphere.

The only tricky point with spheres is remembering that the center point is the center in all three dimensions. If you want to draw a ball on a table, it's easy to specify the center on the plane of the table top — but you end up with a ball that's half beneath the table. So plan ahead.

Dome

A dome is the top half of a sphere, as shown in Figure 23-21. The prompts are very similar to those for a sphere.

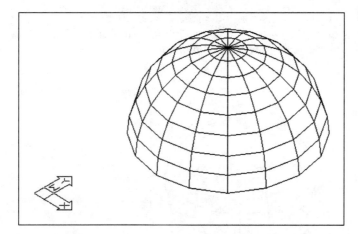

Figure 23-21: A dome.

Here's how to draw a dome:

1. Choose Dome from the Surfaces toolbar.

2. At the `Center of dome:` prompt, specify the center point of the circle that makes up the base of the dome.

3. At the `Diameter/<radius>:` prompt, specify the radius or use the Diameter option to specify the diameter.

4. At the `Number of longitudinal segments <16>:` segments, type the number of north-south lines you want. A higher number results in a smoother looking dome.

5. At the `Number of latitudinal segments <8>:` prompt, type the number of east-west lines you want. A higher number results in a smoother looking dome. Notice that the default is 8 instead of 16 as for the sphere, because you are drawing only half a sphere.

Dish

A dish is the bottom half of a sphere, as shown in Figure 23-22. Actually, a bowl would be a better name for it. The prompts are very similar to those for a sphere.

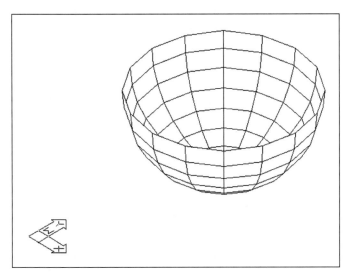

Figure 23-22: A dish.

Here's how to draw a dish:

1. Choose Dish from the Surfaces toolbar.

2. At the `Center of dish:` prompt, specify the center point of the circle that makes up the base of the dish.

3. At the `Diameter/<radius>:` prompt, specify the radius or use the Diameter option to specify the diameter.

4. At the `Number of longitudinal segments <16>:` segments, type the number of north-south lines you want. A higher number results in a smoother looking dish.

5. At the `Number of latitudinal segments <8>:` prompt, type the number of east-west lines you want. A higher number results in a smoother looking dish. Notice that the default is 8 instead of 16 as for the sphere, because you are drawing only half a sphere.

As with spheres, remember that the center point is the center of the top of the dish, not its base.

Torus

A torus is a 3D donut, as shown in Figure 23-23.

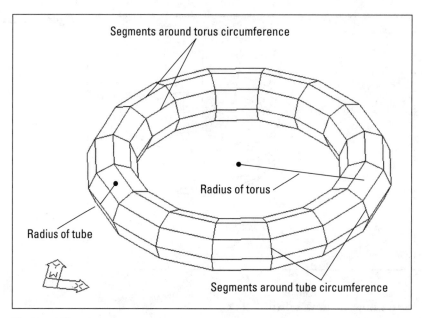

Figure 23-23: A torus.

Follow these steps to create a torus:

1. Choose Torus from the Surfaces toolbar.

2. At the `Center of torus:` prompt, specify the center of the torus.

3. At the `Diameter/<radius> of torus:` prompt, specify the radius of the torus, as shown in Figure 23-23, or use the Diameter option to define the diameter.

4. At the `Diameter/<radius> of tube:` prompt, specify the radius of the tube, as shown in Figure 23-23, or use the Diameter option to define the diameter.

5. At the `Segments around tube circumference <16>:` prompt, specify the number of segments around the tube, as shown in Figure 23-23.

6. At the `Segments around torus circumference <16>:` prompt, specify the number of segments around the torus, as shown in Figure 23-23.

As with a sphere, a torus is half above and half below the center point in the Z direction.

Mesh

The 3D command has a Mesh option that does not appear on the Surfaces toolbar, but you can type **3d** ↵ and choose the Mesh option or choose it from the 3D Objects dialog box. (Choose Draw➪Surfaces➪3D Surfaces.)

The Mesh option creates a 3D mesh. All you have to do is pick the four corners and the M and N mesh sizes. Of course, this option does not give you the flexibility of the 3DMESH command, but it's a lot easier!

Specify the four corner points in clockwise or counterclockwise order. Then specify the M and N mesh sizes. Figure 23-24 shows a mesh with M=8 and N=4.

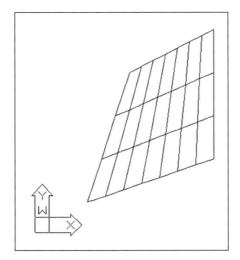

Figure 23-24: A mesh with M=8 and N=4.

Step-by-Step: Drawing 3D Polygon Meshes

On the
CD-ROM

1. Open *ab23-c.dwg* from the CD-ROM.

2. Save it as *ab23-3.dwg* in your *AutoCAD Bible* folder. The drawing is in architectural units. OSNAP is on with running object snaps set for Endpoint and Midpoint. The Surfaces toolbar should be displayed. If it isn't, right-click any toolbar and choose Surfaces from the Toolbars dialog box.

3. Choose Box from the Surfaces toolbar. Follow the prompts to make the tabletop:

```
Corner of box: 1,1,30 ↵
Length: 4' ↵
Cube/<Width>: 3' ↵
Height: 1 ↵
Rotation angle about Z axis: 0 ↵
```

4. Do a ZOOM Extents to see the entire box. You are in plan view so it looks like a rectangle.

5. Choose Box from the Surfaces toolbar again. Follow the prompts to make a leg:

```
Corner of box: 1,1 ↵
Length: 1 ↵
Cube/<Width>: 1 ↵
Height: 30 ↵
Rotation angle about Z axis: 0 ↵
```

6. Mirror the leg from the midpoint of one side of the table to the midpoint of the opposite side. Then mirror the two legs in the other direction (from the other two midpoints) so that you have four legs.

7. Choose Dish from the Surfaces toolbar. Follow the prompts to create a bowl on the table:

```
Center of dish: 2',2',35-1/2 ↵
Diameter/<radius>: d ↵
Diameter: 9 ↵
Number of longitudinal segments <16>: ↵
Number of latitudinal segments <8>: ↵
```

The dish's diameter is 9, so its height is half that, or 4-1/2. The bottom of the dish is at height 35-1/2 because the table top is at 31 (31+4-1/2=35-1/2).

8. Type **elev** ↵. Change the elevation to 31. Leave the thickness at zero.

9. Choose Cone from the Surfaces toolbar. Follow the prompts to create a salt-shaker:

```
Base center point: 2',1'6 ↵
Diameter/<radius> of base: 1 ↵
Diameter/<radius> of top <0>: .5 ↵
Height: 4 ↵
Number of segments <16>: 8 ↵
```

10. Choose Sphere from the Surfaces toolbar. Follow the prompts to draw an orange in the bowl:

```
Center of sphere: 2',2',32-1/2 ↵
Diameter/<radius>: d ↵
Diameter: 3 ↵
Number of longitudinal segments <16>: 8 ↵
Number of latitudinal segments <16>: 8 ↵
```

11. Choose Cone from the Surfaces toolbar. Follow the prompts to make a plate:

Note

It may not seem logical to use a cone to make a flat plate. Actually, it's not logical — I just thought of it and it worked well. It works because you can create a truncated cone upside down and very shallow. It's an unusual but interesting use for the CONE command.

```
Base center point: 1',1' ↵
Diameter/<radius> of base: 2 ↵
Diameter/<radius> of top <0>: 5 ↵
Height: 1/2 ↵
Number of segments <16>: ↵
```

12. Choose SE Isometric View from the Viewpoints flyout of the Standard toolbar to get a view of what you have already drawn.

13. Choose Wedge from the Surfaces toolbar. Follow the prompts to make a wedge of cheese on the plate:

```
Corner of wedge: 10,10 ↵
Length: 5 ↵
Width: 2 ↵
Height: 2 ↵
Rotation angle about Z axis: 30 ↵
```

14. Choose Pyramid from the Surfaces toolbar. Follow the prompts to draw a pyramidal pepper shaker:

```
First base point: 2'6,2'6 ↵
Second base point: @1,0 ↵
Third base point: @0,1 ↵
Tetrahedron/<Fourth base point>: @-1,0 ↵
Ridge/Top/<Apex point>: t ↵
First top point: @1/4,1/4,3 ↵
Second top point: @-1/4,1/4,3 ↵
Third top point: @-1/4,-1/4,3 ↵
Fourth top point: @1/4,-1/4,3 ↵
```

15. Type **hide** ↵. You can now visualize the drawing better.

16. Save your drawing. It should look like Figure 23-25. If you look carefully, you'll see that the edge of the cheese wedge goes through the plate slightly.

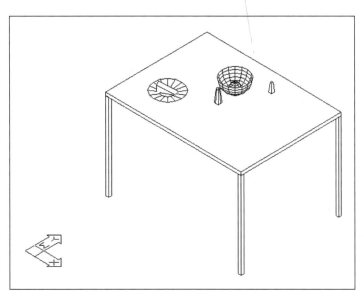

Figure 23-25: The table with a plate, wedge of cheese, bowl, orange, and nonmatching salt and pepper shakers.

Drawing a Revolved Surface

The REVSURF command takes an outline, or profile — which AutoCAD calls a *path curve* — and revolves it around an axis, creating a 3D polygon mesh. Figure 23-26 shows two examples of revolved surfaces.

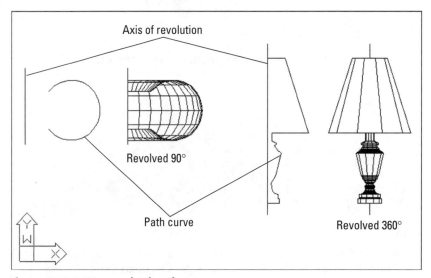

Figure 23-26: Two revolved surfaces.

The path curve must be one object — a line, arc, circle, polyline, ellipse, or elliptical arc. It can be open, like the path curves shown in Figure 23-26, or closed. A closed path curve creates a model that is closed in the N direction.

Tip

Remember that you can use PEDIT to change lines and arcs to polylines and to join them together.

Determining the angle of rotation

You can start the angle of rotation at any angle; it doesn't have to start on the plane of the path curve. You can rotate the path curve to any angle. Of course, rotating the path curve 360 degrees closes the model (in the M direction of the mesh).

When you rotate the path curve less than 360 degrees, you need to know which way to rotate. You can specify a positive (counterclockwise) or negative (clockwise) angle.

The point at which you pick the axis of rotation object affects the positive direction of rotation. Then you use the *right-hand rule* to determine which way the path curve will rotate around the axis. To do this, point your right thumb along the axis in the opposite direction from the endpoint closest to where you pick the axis. The direction in which your other fingers curl is the positive direction of rotation. Figure 23-27 shows the same model revolved in different directions. In the left model, the line of the axis was picked near the bottom endpoint. In the right model, the line of the axis was picked near the top endpoint.

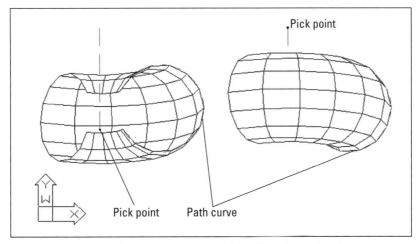

Figure 23-27: From the viewer's point of view, the left revolved surface was rotated back 125 degrees and the right revolved surface was rotated forward 125 degrees.

Setting the number of segments

You use the SURFTAB1 and SURFTAB2 system variables to determine how AutoCAD displays the mesh.

✦ SURFTAB1 affects how the M direction — the direction of revolution — is displayed.

✦ SURFTAB2 affects how the N direction — the path curve — is displayed.

The higher the setting, the more lines AutoCAD uses to display the model. However, if the path curve is a polyline with straight segments, AutoCAD just displays one line at each segment vertex.

In Figure 23-27, SURFTAB1 is 6 and SURFTAB2 is 12. Figure 23-28 shows the same model with SURFTAB1 at 20 and SURFTAB2 at 5 to show the contrast between the two.

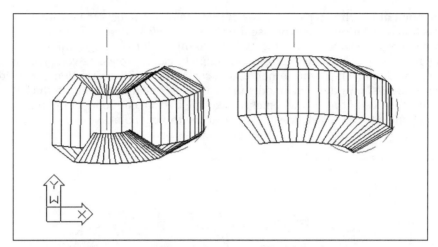

Figure 23-28: The same model re-created with SURFTAB1=20 and SURFTAB2=5.

To set these system variables, type them and specify the new value you want.

Using the REVSURF command

To create a revolved surface, follow these steps:

1. First create the path curve, which must be one object.

2. Then draw the axis of revolution, usually a line.

 3. Choose Revolved Surface from the Surfaces toolbar.

4. At the `Select path curve:` prompt, select the path curve object.

5. At the `Select axis of revolution:` prompt, select the axis of revolution object.

6. At the `Start angle <0>:` prompt, press Enter to accept the default of zero or type in a start angle.

7. At the `Included angle (+=ccw, -=cw) <Full circle>:` prompt, press Enter to revolve the surface 360 degrees or type in a positive or negative angle.

Cross-Reference

You may need to create the path curve and axis in a different plane than the one you use when revolving them. You can draw the path curve and axis in one UCS and use REVSURF in another. Another option is to rotate the entire object when completed. Rotating objects in 3D is covered in the next chapter.

Tip

REVSURF retains the original path curve and axis objects. It helps to draw them in a different layer and color so you can easily erase them afterward. Otherwise, they are hard to distinguish from the revolved surface. Having them on a separate layer also helps if you need to redo the revolved surface — you can easily avoid erasing them when you erase the revolved surface so you can use them again.

Step-by-Step: Drawing Revolved Surfaces

On the CD-ROM

1. Open *ab23-d.dwg* from the CD-ROM.

2. Save it as *ab23-4.dwg* in your *AutoCAD Bible* folder. The path curve and axis are already drawn in a UCS revolved around the X axis of the WCS by 90 degrees.

3. Choose Revolved Surface from the Surfaces toolbar.

4. At the `Select path curve:` prompt, select the polyline to the right.

5. At the `Select axis of revolution:` prompt, select the line.

6. At the `Start angle <0>:` prompt, press Enter. At the `Included angle (+=ccw, -=cw) <Full circle>:` prompt, press Enter to revolve the path curve in a full circle.

7. Choose Tools⇨UCS⇨World to return to the WCS.

8. Type **plan** ↵ and press Enter to return to plan view of the WCS.

9. Choose SE Isometric View from the Viewpoint flyout of the Standard toolbar.

10. Type **hide** ↵ to see the shape more clearly.

11. Save your drawing. It should look like Figure 23-29.

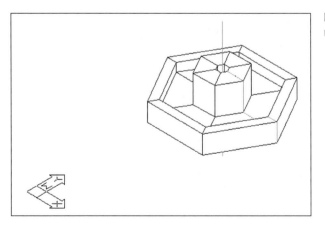

Figure 23-29: The revolved surface.

Drawing an Extruded Surface

To *extrude* means to thrust out. In AutoCAD, it refers to creating a 3D object from a 2D object. The TABSURF command takes an outline, or profile, which AutoCAD calls a *path curve,* and extrudes it along a vector that defines the direction and distance of the extrusion. TABSURF creates a 3D polyline mesh. The type of surface created is called a *tabulated surface.* Figure 23-30 shows two examples of extruded surfaces.

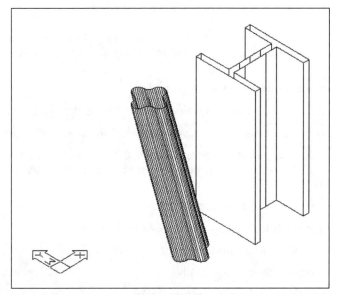

Figure 23-30: Two extruded surfaces created using TABSURF.

For the I-beam, you could have simply given the 2D polyline profile a thickness and achieved a similar result. However, the extruded surface on the left could only have been created with TABSURF because the extrusion is not perpendicular to the XY plane that contains the 2D polyline profile. TABSURF can extrude a shape in any direction.

When you select the vector object, your pick point determines the direction of the extrusion. AutoCAD starts the extrusion from the end of the vector closest to the pick point.

You use SURFTAB1 to control the number of lines AutoCAD uses to display the curve. If the curve is made up of polyline segments, AutoCAD displays one line at each segment vertex.

Note

Look at the I-beam in Figure 23-30. Notice that there are extra tabulation lines along the middle section. They are there because the I-beam was created by mirroring half the I-beam shape and then it was stretched to alter the dimensions. Then the separate polylines were joined. However, they remained as separate segments in the polyline definition. If you want a clean look, you need to draw clean. In this case, you could have used the original shape as a guide to draw a new polyline on top of the old one, then erased the original. TABSURF would have then created an I-beam without the extraneous lines.

Tip

You should use a nonplanar view when using TABSURF to check that you have accurately defined the extrusion vector into the third dimension.

To draw an extruded surface, follow these steps:

1. Draw the object to extrude — a line, arc, circle, polyline, ellipse, or elliptical arc. This is the path curve.

2. Draw the vector, usually a line. If you use a 2D or 3D polyline, AutoCAD uses an imaginary line from the start point to the endpoint to determine the vector.

 3. Choose Tabulated Surface from the Surfaces toolbar.

4. At the Select path curve: prompt, select the path curve object.

5. At the Select direction vector: prompt, select the line you are using for the vector.

Step-by-Step: Drawing Tabulated Surfaces

On the CD-ROM

1. Open *ab23-e.dwg* from the CD-ROM.

2. Save it as *ab23-5.dwg* in your *AutoCAD Bible* folder. You see a tabletop drawn at a Z height of 30. The current elevation is 30. You are looking at the table from the SE Isometric view. OSNAP is on, with running object snaps for endpoints, midpoints, and centers. The current layer is Const. The drawing is shown in Figure 23-31.

3. Start the CIRCLE command. Follow the prompts:

```
3P/2P/TTR/<Center point>: Choose the From object snap.
  _from Base point: Pick the endpoint at ① in Figure 23-31.
<Offset>: @-1,3 ↵
Diameter/<Radius>: .75 ↵
```

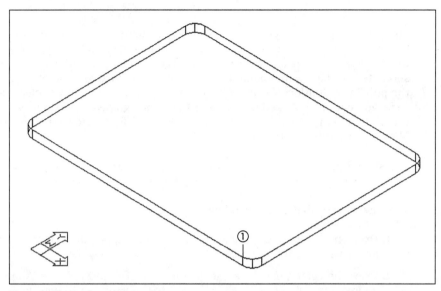

Figure 23-31: The tabletop.

4. Start the LINE command. At the `From point:` prompt, choose the Center object snap of the circle you just drew. At the `To point:` prompt, type **@3,-3, -30** ↵ to draw a line flaring out from the circle and going down to the floor. End the LINE command.

5. Choose Tabulated Surface from the Surfaces toolbar. At the `Select path curve:` prompt, select the circle. At the `Select direction vector:` prompt, select the line. (You can only see the top part of the line, but that's the part you need to pick.) AutoCAD creates the tabulated surface.

6. Start the MIRROR command. Select the entire leg. Choose the midpoint of the bottom edge of both long sides of the table for the two points of the mirror line.

7. Repeat the MIRROR line and select both legs. Mirror them using the midpoints of the bottom edge of the short sides of the table for the two points of the mirror line.

8. Do a ZOOM Extents to see the entire table.

9. Save your drawing. It should look like Figure 23-32.

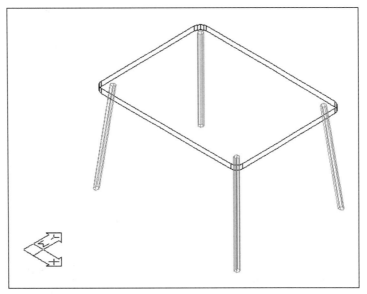

Figure 23-32: The completed table.

Drawing Ruled Surfaces

Use the RULESURF command to create a surface that extends between two objects. The objects can be lines, polylines (2D or 3D), circles, ellipses, elliptical arcs, splines, and points. The two objects must either be both open or both closed. Only one of the two can be a point.

Use the SURFTAB1 system variable to control the number of lines AutoCAD uses to display the surface. Figure 23-33 shows some ruled surfaces.

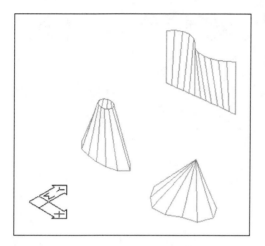

Figure 23-33: Ruled surfaces.

The pick points of the two objects affect the resulting curve. If you pick them both on the same side, you get the type of curves shown in Figure 23-33. If you pick them on opposite sides, the curve intersects itself, as shown in Figure 23-34.

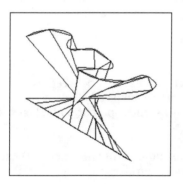

Figure 23-34: A self-intersecting ruled surface.

Follow these steps to draw a ruled surface:

1. Draw the two objects for the ruled surface.

2. Choose Ruled Surface from the Surfaces toolbar.

3. At the Select first defining curve: prompt, choose the first object.

4. At the Select second defining curve: prompt, choose the second object.

Step-by-Step: Drawing Ruled Surfaces

On the CD-ROM

1. Open *ab23-f.dwg* from the CD-ROM.

2. Save it as *ab23-6.dwg* in your *AutoCAD Bible* folder. You see a spline, as shown in Figure 23-35. In this exercise, you use the spline to draw some drapes.

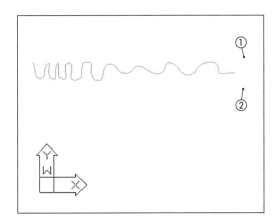

Figure 23-35: A spline.

3. Mirror the spline. For the mirror line, turn on ORTHO and use ① and ② as shown in Figure 23-35.

4. Start the COPY command and select both splines. At the `<Base point or displacement>/Multiple:` prompt, type **0,0,73** ⏎ to copy the splines 73 units in the positive Z direction. Press Enter at the `Second point of displacement:` prompt.

5. Choose SE Isometric Viewpoint from the Viewpoints flyout of the Standard toolbar.

6. Choose Ruled Surface from the Surfaces toolbar. At the `Select first defining curve:` prompt, choose the top right spline near its right endpoint. At the `Select second defining curve:` prompt, choose the bottom right spline near its right endpoint.

7. Repeat the RULESURF command. At the `Select first defining curve:` prompt, choose the top left spline near its left endpoint. At the `Select second defining curve:` prompt, choose the bottom left spline near its left endpoint.

8. Save your drawing. It should look like Figure 23-36.

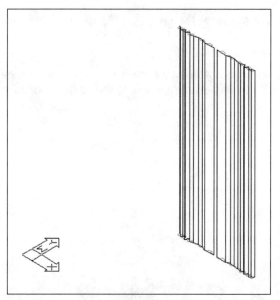

Figure 23-36: The completed drapes.

Drawing Edge Surfaces

You can use the EDGESURF command to create unusual surfaces bound by four touching objects. The objects can be lines, arcs, splines, or polylines (2D or 3D). EDGESURF creates a polygon mesh that looks like a Coons surface patch — a surface defined by four edges. Figure 23-37 shows an edge surface.

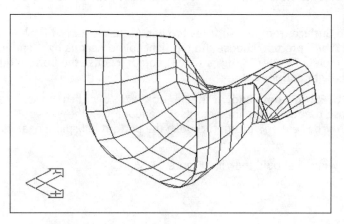

Figure 23-37: An edge surface created with the EDGESURF command.

Use the SURFTAB1 and SURFTAB2 system variables to vary the displayed lines in each direction.

Follow these steps to create an edge surface:

1. Draw the four objects to create a boundary for the surface. They must touch, so use endpoint object snaps to create them or to move them into place.

 2. Choose Edge Surface from the Surfaces toolbar.

3. AutoCAD prompts you to select edges one through four. You can select them in any order.

Tip Creating the four edges involves moving from UCS to UCS since they are all in 3D. It helps to create a bounding box for your object using the AI_BOX command. You can then use the corners of the box to define your UCSs.

Step-by-Step: Drawing Edge Surfaces

 On the CD-ROM

1. Open *ab23-g.dwg* from the CD-ROM.

2. Save it as *ab23-7.dwg* in your *AutoCAD Bible* folder. You see four curves in a bounding box, as shown in Figure 23-38. In this exercise, you use the curves to draw a dustpan.

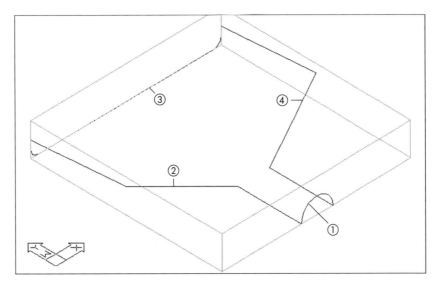

Figure 23-38: The four curves are the basis for creating an edge surface.

3. Freeze the Const layer.

4. Choose Edge Surface from the Surfaces toolbar. At the prompts, select ①, ②, ③, and ④ in Figure 23-38.

5. Type **hide** ↵ to see the result.

6. Save your drawing. It should look like Figure 23-39. It's either a dustpan or a starship.

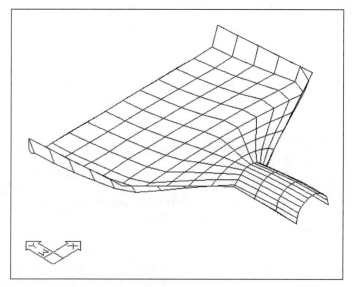

Figure 23-39: The completed dustpan — or starship.

Summary

In this chapter you learned all about 3D surfaces. AutoCAD offers many ways to create surfaces, including 3D faces, polyfaces, and 3D polygon meshes. AutoCAD provides routines to draw the basic geometric shapes: box, pyramid, wedge, dome, sphere, cone, torus, and dish.

You can also create complex surfaces by revolving a profile around an axis, extruding a curve, stretching a ruled surface between two curves, and creating an edge surface enclosed inside four curves.

In the next chapter you learn how to create true solids (well, true electronic ones at least) as well as how to edit in 3D.

✦   ✦   ✦

Creating Solids and Editing in 3D

Working with AutoCAD Solids

Although you can create great-looking models with surfaces, if you want truly realistic models, you need to create solids. After all, in real life, objects have solidity. Even a thin object like a wastepaper basket or a drape has some thickness. Solids let you create much more realistic models than surfaces. You can also combine or subtract solids and get information about their physical properties. Figure 24-1 shows a complex model created using solids.

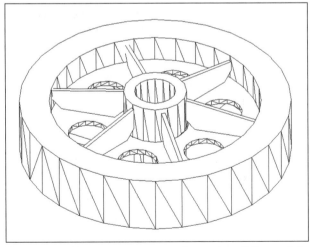

Figure 24-1: You can create complex and realistic models using solids.

Credit: Thanks to Hans-Joachim Fach, Bremen, Germany, for this drawing.

To work with solids, display the Solids toolbar by right-clicking any toolbar and choosing Solids from the Toolbars dialog box. You can also access all the solids commands by choosing Draw⇨Solids and then choosing the specific command from the submenu that opens.

Drawing Standard Shapes

As with surfaces, AutoCAD makes it easy to create most standard geometrical shapes. The prompts are similar to the surface commands, but there are some slight differences.

Controlling the display of solids

Curved surfaces are drawn using segments. When you draw a surface sphere, AutoCAD prompts you for the number of lines to draw. The display of all curved solids in a drawing is controlled by the ISOLINES system variable. The default, 4, provides a bare minimum of curved lines to let you view the outlines of the curve, and results in the quickest display. Increasing the ISOLINES value improves the visual result but slows down the drawing display. Generally, you can find a happy medium based on the size of your drawing, the speed of your computer, and your personal preferences. The ISOLINES variable affects wireframe display only — it has no effect when you use the HIDE command. Figure 24-3 shows the effect of varying the ISOLINES setting.

The FACETRES system variable is the 3D version of VIEWRES and determines the display of curved surfaces and solids when using the HIDE, SHADE, or RENDER commands. You can set FACETRES from 0.01 to 10.0. Here you see a hidden sphere at FACETRES settings of .05 (left) and 5.0 (right). The default is .5, which is generally a happy medium.

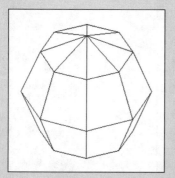
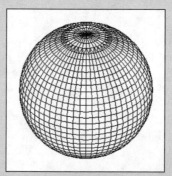

THE DISPSILH system variable determines whether AutoCAD creates a silhouette of a model based on the current viewpoint. The effect is most noticeable after a hide. The left model below shows the result of setting DISPSILH to 0 (the default) after a hide. The right model shows the results of setting DISPSILH to 1 (on) after a hide. You can see that the right model provides a very uncluttered display. When you set DISPSILH to 1 in wireframe display, AutoCAD adds silhouette lines. For complex objects, you may find that DISPSILH slows down your display. This is a complicated matter for AutoCAD to compute. So, you may want to set DISPSILH back to zero after doing a hide, depending on the models you are working with.

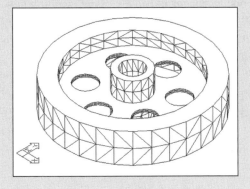 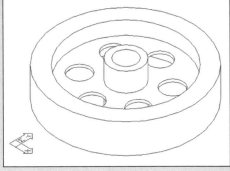

Tip When you change the ISOLINES value, do a regen to see the result on existing objects.

Drawing a box

Figure 24-2 shows a solid box after a hide. Visually, it looks the same as a surface box.

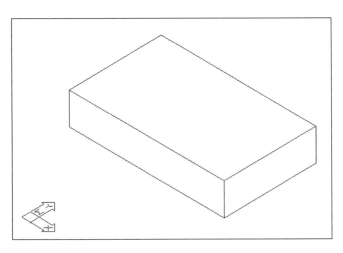

Figure 24-2: A solid box.

To draw a box, follow these steps:

1. Choose Box from the Solids toolbar.

2. At the `Center/<Corner of box> <0,0,0>:` prompt, specify any corner of the box or type **c** ↵ and use the Center option to specify the 3D center of the box.

3. If you specify the corner (the default), you then see the `Cube/Length/<other corner>:` prompt.

   a. The default is to pick the opposite corner in the XY plane. AutoCAD then asks you for the height in the Z direction. This completes the box.

   b. If you specify the Length in the XY plane, AutoCAD asks you for a width and a height.

   c. If you use the Cube option, AutoCAD asks for one length and completes the box.

4. If you specify the center, you see the `Cube/Length/<corner of box>:` prompt.

   a. If you pick the corner of the box, AutoCAD completes the box by calculating the length, width, and height from the two points—the center and the corner.

   b. If you specify the length, AutoCAD then asks for a width and a height.

   c. If you use the Cube option, AutoCAD asks for a length and completes the box.

You can specify a negative length, width, or height to build the box in the negative direction. If you specify the center of the cube, don't forget that the center's Z coordinate is different from the corner's Z coordinate. AutoCAD always creates the box parallel to the XY plane.

Drawing a sphere

Figure 24-3 shows two solid spheres. The left sphere uses the default ISOLINE value of 4. The right sphere uses an ISOLINE value of 8.

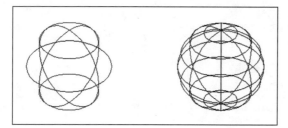

Figure 24-3: Two solid spheres, with ISOLINES set at 4 (left) and 8 (right).

To draw a sphere, follow these steps:

1. Choose Sphere from the Solids toolbar.

2. At the `Center of sphere <0,0,0>:` prompt, specify the center of the sphere. If you want the sphere to lie on the XY plane, the Z coordinate of the center should be equal to the radius of the sphere.

3. At the `Diameter/<Radius> of sphere:` prompt, type the radius or use the Diameter option to specify the diameter.

Drawing a cylinder

Figure 24-4 shows four solid cylinders. You can draw cylinders with circular or elliptical bases. By separately specifying the center of the top of the cylinder, you can draw them at an angle.

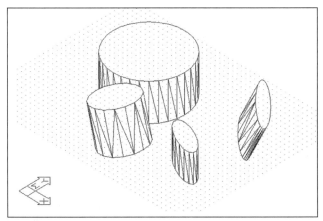

Figure 24-4: Some solid cylinders. The grid helps you visualize the XY plane.

Here's how to draw a cylinder:

1. Choose Cylinder from the Solids toolbar.

2. At the `Elliptical/<center point> <0,0,0>:` prompt, specify the center point for a circular cylinder or choose the Elliptical option to define an ellipse as a base.

   a. If you specified a center point, at the `Diameter/<Radius>:` prompt, specify a radius or use the Diameter option to specify the diameter.

   b. If you chose the Elliptical option, use the standard ELLIPSE prompts to define the elliptical base.

3. At the `Center of other end/<Height>:` prompt, specify the height or use the Center of other end option to specify the center of the top of the cylinder.

Drawing a cone

You can draw cones with circular or elliptical bases. By specifying a negative height, you can create an inverted cone (like an ice cream cone). By specifying the apex, you can draw cones on an angle from the XY plane. Figure 24-5 shows some cones.

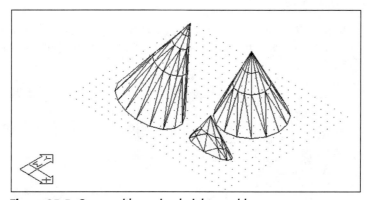

Figure 25-5: Cones with varying heights and bases.

Follow these steps to draw a cone:

1. Choose Cone from the Solids toolbar.

2. At the `Elliptical/<center point> <0,0,0>:` prompt, specify the center of the base if you want a circular cone. Otherwise, use the Elliptical option to define an elliptical base.

   a. If you specified a center point, at the `Diameter/<Radius>:` prompt, specify a radius or use the Diameter option to specify the diameter.

   b. If you chose the Elliptical option, use the standard ELLIPSE prompts to define the elliptical base.

3. At the `Apex/<Height>:` prompt, specify the height or use the Apex option to specify the coordinate of the apex.

Drawing a wedge

A wedge is a box sliced in half. The prompts are exactly the same as the Box command. Figure 24-6 shows two wedges.

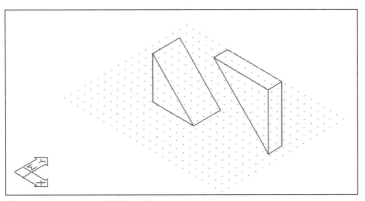

Figure 24-6: Two solid wedges.

 1. Choose Wedge from the Solids toolbar.

2. At the `Center/<Corner of wedge> <0,0,0>:` prompt, specify any corner of the wedge or type **c** ↵ and use the Center option to specify the 3D center of the wedge.

3. If you specify the corner (the default), you then see the `Cube/Length/<other corner>:` prompt.

    a. The default is to pick the opposite corner in the XY plane. AutoCAD then asks you for the height in the Z direction. This completes the wedge.

    b. If you specify the Length in the XY plane, AutoCAD asks you for a width and a height.

    c. If you use the Cube option, AutoCAD asks for one length and completes the wedge.

4. If you specify the center, you see the `Cube/Length/<corner of wedge>:` prompt.

    a. If you pick the corner of the wedge, AutoCAD completes the wedge by calculating the length, width, and height from the two points — the center and the corner.

    b. If you specify the length, AutoCAD then asks for a width and a height.

    c. If you use the Cube option, AutoCAD asks for a length and completes the wedge.

Drawing a torus

A torus is a 3D donut. Figure 24-7 shows some examples. You can make some unusual shapes by varying the torus and tube radii. If the torus radius is negative and the tube radius is larger than the absolute value of the torus radius (for example, –2 and 3), you get the lemon. If the tube radius is larger than the torus radius, you get the puckered ball.

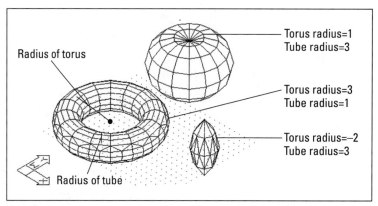

Figure 24-7: Torus examples.

To create a torus, follow these steps:

 1. Choose Torus from the Solids toolbar.

2. At the `Center of torus <0,0,0>:` prompt, specify the center of the torus (the center of the hole).

3. At the `Diameter/<Radius> of torus:` prompt, specify the radius of the entire torus or use the Diameter option to specify the diameter.

4. At the `Diameter/<Radius> of tube:` prompt, specify the radius of just the tube or use the Diameter option to specify the diameter.

Step-by-Step: Drawing Standard 3D Solids

1. Start a new drawing using *acad.dwt* as the template.

2. Save it as *ab24-1.dwg* in your *AutoCAD Bible* folder. If the Solids toolbar is not displayed, right-click any toolbar, choose Solids from the Toolbars dialog box, and close the Toolbars dialog box. Turn on OSNAP and set running object snaps for Endpoint, Midpoint, and Center.

3. Choose Box from the Solids toolbar. Follow the prompts:

```
Center/<Corner of box> <0,0,0>: 3,3 ↵
Cube/Length/<other corner>: 1 ↵
Length: 3 ↵
Width: 2 ↵
Height: 1 ↵
```

4. Choose Cylinder from the Solids toolbar. Follow the prompts:

```
Elliptical/<center point> <0,0,0>: Choose Tracking from the Object
Snap flyout of the Standard toolbar.
First tracking point: Pick the midpoint of the right side of the box.
```

```
Next point  (Press ENTER to end tracking): Pick the midpoint of
the bottom side of the box.
Next point  (Press ENTER to end tracking): ↵
Diameter/<Radius>: .5 ↵
Center of other end/<Height>: 1 ↵
```

5. To see the result, choose SE Isometric Viewpoint from the Viewpoints flyout of the Standard toolbar. Then choose Zoom Out from the Zoom flyout.

6. Choose Cone from the Solids toolbar. At the `Elliptical/<center point>` `<0,0,0>:` prompt, type **7,5** ↵. At the `Diameter/<Radius>:` prompt, type **1** ↵. At the `Apex/<Height>:` prompt, type **−4** ↵.

7. Choose Sphere from the Solids toolbar. At the `Center of sphere <0,0,0>:` prompt, use the Center object snap to pick the center of the cone's base. At the `Diameter/<Radius> of sphere:` prompt, type **1** ↵.

8. Type **isolines** ↵. Set the new value to **8**. Do a regen to see the result.

9. Choose Zoom Extents from the Zoom flyout of the Standard toolbar.

10. Do a hide.

11. Save your drawing. It should look like Figure 24-8.

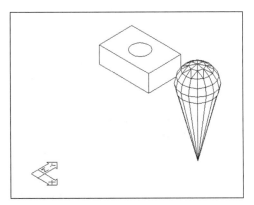

Figure 24-8: The four solids.

Creating Extruded Solids

The EXTRUDE command creates solids from closed 2D objects. The result is similar to adding thickness to a 2D object (discussed in Chapter 21) or using the TABSURF command (see Chapter 23) except that you get a solid instead of a surface.

You can extrude closed 2D polylines, circles, ellipses, closed splines, donuts, and regions. You can use the REGION command to create one object from several for this purpose. You can select several objects and extrude them at one time. Figure 24-9 shows several extruded solids.

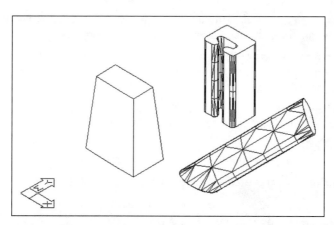

Figure 24-9: Some extruded solids.

Tip

The DELOBJ system variable determines whether objects used by EXTRUDE to make other objects are retained. By default, they are deleted. Therefore, when you use a 2D object to make a solid, the 2D object is deleted. If you make a mistake during extrusion and notice it later — after it's impractical to undo several commands you want to keep — when you erase the solid, you have no 2D object to use to recreate the solid. (You can put such objects on a layer that can be turned off, in case you need them again.) Set DELOBJ to zero to keep objects used to create other objects. On the other hand, if you are sure about what you are doing, keeping DELOBJ at 1 avoids having to erase unwanted 2D objects in your drawing.

When you extrude an object, by default you extrude it perpendicular to the object. However, you can also taper the extrusion, as in the left solid in Figure 24-9. The angle is measured so that a positive angle tapers the object inward. A negative angle tapers the object outward so it gets wider as it extrudes.

Note

Don't taper the object too much. If the taper angle would result in the object coming to a point before its full height, AutoCAD cannot create the solid.

You can extrude the object along a path. A path can be a line, circle, arc, ellipse, elliptical arc, polyline, or a spline. The path object must be in a different plane than the original object. Figure 24-10 shows a circle extruded along an arc.

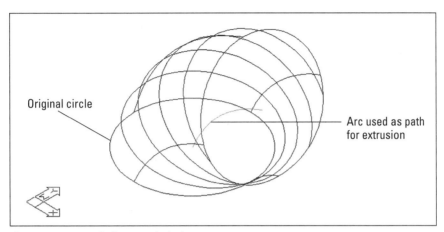

Figure 24-10: A circle extruded along an arc.

Caution   Not all paths are suitable for extruding objects. In the following situations, the extrusion may not work. The path should not be:

✦ Too close to the original object's plane

✦ Too complex

✦ Too tightly curved or bent for the size of the original object

Here are the steps for creating an extruded solid:

1. Draw the object you want to extrude. If you want to extrude along a path, draw the path object.

2. Choose Extrude from the Solids toolbar.

3. Select the object or objects to extrude.

4. At the `Path/<Height of Extrusion>:` prompt, specify the height of extrusion or use the Path option to extrude along a path object.

    a. If you specified a height, at the `Extrusion taper angle <0>:` prompt, press Enter to extrude with no taper angle or specify a taper angle.

    b. If you chose the Path option, at the `Select path:` prompt, select the path object.

Step-by-Step: Creating Extruded Solids

On the
CD-ROM

1. Open *ab-24-a.dwg* from the CD-ROM.

2. Save it as *ab24-2.dwg* in your *AutoCAD Bible* folder. If the Solids toolbar is not displayed, right-click any toolbar, choose Solids from the Toolbars dialog box, and close the Toolbars dialog box. OSNAP is on, and running object snaps are set for Endpoint and Midpoint. This is a small mounting angle, shown in a side view.

3. The angle is made up of lines and arcs. To extrude it, you need to change it into a polyline or region. To change it into a polyline, type **pedit** ↵. Follow the prompts:

```
Select polyline: Select any object on the angle.
Object selected is not a polyline
Do you want to turn it into one? <Y> ↵
Close/Join/Width/Edit vertex/Fit/Spline/Decurve/Ltype gen/Undo/
eXit <X>: j↵
Select objects: Use a window to select all the objects in the
angle.
Select objects: ↵
6 segments added to polyline
Open/Join/Width/Edit vertex/Fit/Spline/Decurve/Ltype gen/Undo/
eXit <X>: x ↵
```

4. Choose Extrude from the Solids toolbar. Select the angle, and then press Enter to end object selection. At the Path/<Height of Extrusion>: prompt, type **3** ↵. At the Extrusion taper angle <0>: prompt, press Enter to accept the default.

5. Choose SE Isometric View from the Viewpoints flyout to see the result.

6. Do a hide.

7. Save your drawing. It should look like Figure 24-11.

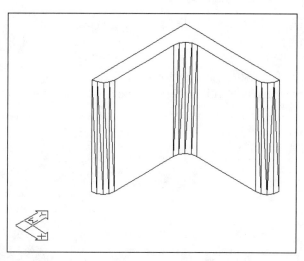

Figure 24-11: The completed mounting angle.

The mounting angle should have two holes in it. You create the holes using the SUBTRACT command, which is covered later in this chapter.

Drawing Revolved Solids

The REVSURF command, which creates surfaces, revolves an open profile around an axis. The REVOLVE command creates solids from closed profiles only. You can revolve closed 2D polylines, circles, ellipses, closed splines, and regions. You can only revolve one object at a time.

The DELOBJ system variable affects whether the original objects are deleted. The default setting is 1 (delete objects). Set DELOBJ to zero to retain the original objects.

Figure 24-12 shows a solid created by revolving a rectangle around a line. You could also create this solid by drawing two circles and extruding them and then subtracting the smaller circle from the larger one — it just depends on which technique you're more comfortable with.

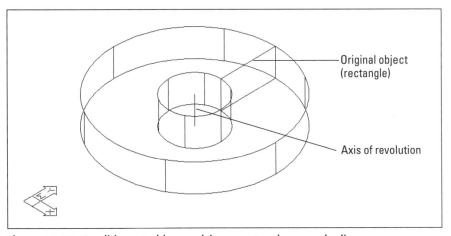

Original object (rectangle)

Axis of revolution

Figure 24-12: A solid created by revolving a rectangle around a line.

To create a revolved solid, follow these steps:

1. Choose Revolve from the Solids toolbar.

2. At the `Select objects:` prompt, select one closed object.

3. At the `Axis of revolution - Object/X/Y/<Start point of axis>:` prompt, you can pick two points to create an axis of revolution. You can also select an object as an axis — use a line or one segment of a polyline. Use the X or Y options to revolve the object around the X or Y axes.

4. At the `Angle of revolution <full circle>:` prompt, press Enter to revolve the object 360 degrees or type an angle, either positive or negative.

As with the REVSURF command, you need to determine the positive direction of rotation if you are revolving less than 360 degrees. (Of course, it may be quicker to try one way and just do it the other way if it doesn't turn out right.) Here's how to figure it out:

1. First determine the positive direction of the axis. If you specify start and end points, the positive axis direction goes from the start point to the endpoint. If you pick an object, the positive axis direction goes from the pick point to the other endpoint. If you choose the X or Y axis, the positive direction is obvious.

2. Point your thumb in the positive direction of the axis.

3. Look at the curl of your fingers on that hand. That's the positive direction of the axis.

Creating Complex Solids

To create realistic objects, you usually need to edit the simple shapes I have covered in this chapter. You can create complex solids by adding them, subtracting them, or intersecting them. These processes are called *Boolean* operations, which in this context means using logical functions such as plus or minus on objects.

Adding solids

You use the UNION command to add two solids together, making one solid.

 Tip   You can also use the UNION command with 2D regions.

Figure 24-13 shows the union of two solids after a hide.

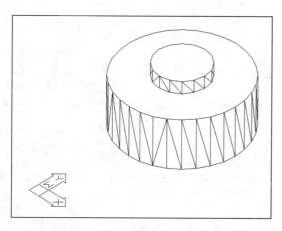

Figure 24-13: The results of UNION on two solids — shown after a hide.

To start the UNION command, type **union** ↵. (You can also open the Modify II toolbar and choose Union, or choose Modify⇨Boolean and use the submenu.) At the Select objects: prompt, select the objects you want to unite.

Caution   When you create complex solids, the original solids are not retained. Setting the DELOBJ system variable to zero doesn't work because the original solids have been changed. If you wish, you can copy the original objects to another location in the drawing in case you need to use them again. You can also use UNDO if the result is not what you expected.

Subtracting solids

You use the SUBTRACT command to subtract one solid from another. This command is most commonly used to create holes. Figure 24-14 shows the result of subtracting a small cylinder from a larger one and performing a hide.

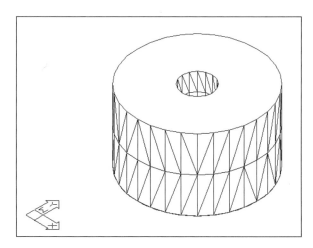

Figure 24-14: You can create holes using the SUBTRACT command.

To subtract solids, follow these steps:

  1. Type **subtract** ↵.

   2. At the following prompt, choose the solid (or region) that you want to subtract from (the one you want to keep).

    Select solids and regions to subtract from...
    Select objects:

   3. At the following prompt, choose the solid (or region) that you want to subtract (the one you want to get rid of).

    Select solids and regions to subtract...
    Select objects:

Creating a solid from the intersection of two solids

You can also create a solid from the volume that two solids have in common. This volume is called their intersection. Figure 24-15 shows two solids before and after using the INTERSECT command. The solid on the right is shown after a hide.

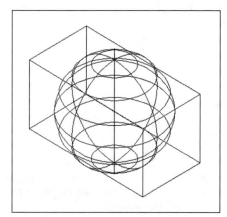 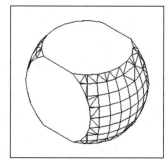

Figure 24-15: A box and a sphere before and after using the INTERSECT command.

As you can see, you can create some very unusual models this way.

 To use the INTERSECT command, type **intersect** ↵ or choose Intersect from the Modify II toolbar. Just select the objects in any order, and AutoCAD creates the new solid.

Creating a new solid using INTERFERE

INTERFERE is similar to INTERSECT except that the original solids remain. AutoCAD creates a third solid from the volume that the two solids have in common. The INTERFERE command can also be used to highlight the common volume of several pairs of solids. Figure 24-16 shows a solid created using INTERFERE, after it was moved away from its original location. As you can see, the original solids remain intact.

INTERFERE is useful when you have a number of interfering solids. This command lets you divide the selection set of solids into two sets so you can compare one against the other. For example, you can compare a box with three other solids by putting the box in one set and the other three solids in the other set. INTERFERE highlights each pair of interfering solids in turn so you can easily visualize your drawing.

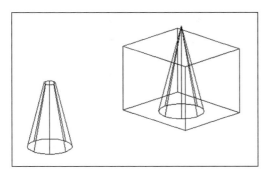

Figure 24-16: When you use INTERFERE, the original solids remain intact.

Tip

INTERFERE can be used for troubleshooting and visualizing a complex drawing. For example, you can use INTERFERE to determine which solids need to be subtracted from which other solids. The new objects are created on the current layer. You can change the current layer before using INTERFERE to help you more clearly distinguish the new solid you create.

To use INTERFERE, follow these steps:

1. Choose Interfere from the Solids toolbar.

2. At the Select the first set of solids: prompt, select objects. If you want to compare only two objects, you can put them both in the first set. Otherwise, select solids for the first set and press Enter to end object selection.

3. At the Select the second set of solids: prompt, select the second set of objects and press Enter to end object selection. If you don't want a second set, press Enter. AutoCAD displays the number of solids and sets and how many interfering pairs it finds.

4. At the Create interference solids ? <N>: prompt, press Enter if you don't want to create a new solid. Type **y** ↵ if you do.

5. At the Highlight pairs of interfering solids ? <N>: prompt, press Enter if you don't need to see each pair of interfering solids highlighted. Type **y** ↵ if you want AutoCAD to highlight the pairs. If you choose Yes, AutoCAD highlights the first pair of solids that interfere.

6. At the eXit/<Next pair>: prompt — which only appears if there is more than one pair — press Enter to see the next pair highlighted. Continue to press Enter to cycle through the interfering pairs. Type **x** ↵ to exit the command.

Step-by-Step: Creating Complex Solids

1. Open *ab-24-b.dwg* from the CD-ROM.

2. Save it as *ab24-3.dwg* in your *AutoCAD Bible* folder. OSNAP is on, with running object snaps set for Endpoint, Midpoint, and Center. This drawing is measured in millimeters. The solids have been created by drawing circles, using EXTRUDE, and moving the solids to the proper Z coordinate. The result is shown in Figure 24-17.

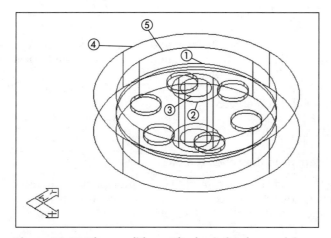

Figure 24-17: These solids are the basis for the model.

3. Display the Modify II toolbar by right-clicking any toolbar and choosing Modify II. Close the Toolbars dialog box.

4. To create the six holes arrayed around the center plate, choose Subtract from the Modify II toolbar. Follow the prompts:

```
Select solids and regions to subtract from...
Select objects: Select the central plate at ① in Figure
24-17.
Select objects: ↵
Select solids and regions to subtract...
Select objects: Select the six circles arrayed around the plate. Press
Enter to end selection.
```

5. To create the central tube, choose Subtract from the Modify II toolbar. Follow the prompts:

```
Select solids and regions to subtract from...
Select objects: Select the outer tube at ②.
Select objects: ↵
Select solids and regions to subtract...
Select objects: Select the inner tube at ③. Press Enter to end
selection.
```

6. To "carve out" the central disk, choose Subtract from the Modify II toolbar. Follow the prompts:

```
Select solids and regions to subtract from...
Select objects: Select the outer circle at ④.
Select objects: ↵
Select solids and regions to subtract...
Select objects: Select the inner circle at ⑤. Press Enter to end
selection.
```

7. Do a hide to see the result. This lets you check the effects of the subtraction operations. Your drawing should look like Figure 24-18.

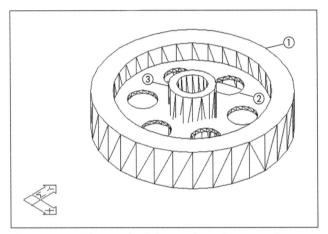

Figure 24-18: The result of three subtraction operations.

8. Choose Union from the Modify II toolbar. Select the three solids at ①, ②, ③ in Figure 24-18.

9. Do a hide again to see the result.

10. Save your drawing. It should look like Figure 24-19. If you are continuing on to the next exercise, leave it open.

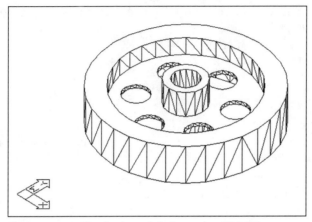

Figure 24-19: The final model after using UNION to create one object from three.

Sectioning and Slicing Solids

The SECTION and SLICE commands are both used to create cross-section views of your 3D models.

Using the SECTION command

The SECTION command creates a 2D region from a cross-section of a 3D model along a plane you specify. The original objects are left untouched. Figure 24-20 shows a region created using the SECTION command.

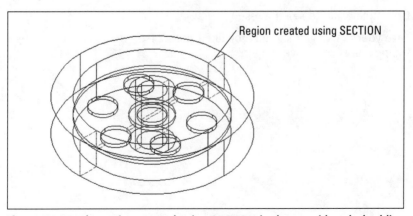

Region created using SECTION

Figure 24-20: The region created using SECTION is shown with a dashed line.

Tip The SECTION command creates the region on the current layer. Make the current layer color different from the object so that the region is clearly visible.

To use the SECTION command, choose Section from the Solids toolbar. Select the object you want to section. AutoCAD displays the `Section plane by Object/Zaxis/View/XY/YZ/ZX/<3points>:` prompt. Use these options to define the plane of the cross-section. Table 24-1 explains how to use the options.

	Table 24-1 **SECTION Options**	
Option	**Description**	
Object	Choose a circle, ellipse, arc, spline, or 2D polyline.	
Zaxis	Lets you define the plane by defining a Z axis. The sectioning plane is then the XY plane perpendicular to the Z axis you defined. You define the Z axis by first specifying a point on the sectioning plane. This point is the 0,0,0 point (for purposes of this command only) where the sectioning plane and the Z axis meet. Then you pick a point on the Z axis.	
View	Define the section plane parallel to the current view at the intersection of a point you specify.	
XY	Define the section plane parallel to the XY plane at the intersection of a point you specify.	
YZ	Define the section plane parallel to the YZ plane at the intersection of a point you specify.	
ZX	Define the section plane parallel to the ZX plane at the intersection of a point you specify.	
3points	This is the default. Specify three points to define the section plane. It's a good idea to use object snaps.	

You can move the region you create and view it separately to spot errors in your models.

Using the SLICE command

The SLICE command slices a solid into two parts along a plane. The original solids are modified but can be reunited with UNION. You can delete either part or keep both. Figure 24-21 shows the result of slicing a model, after one-half of the model has been deleted. This can help to identify problems in the construction of the model. For example, this slice reveals a fault with the model — the flat disk continues through the central tube — not the desired result.

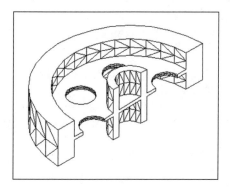

Figure 24-21: The result of slicing a solid and retaining one of the resulting pieces.

To use the SLICE command, choose Slice from the Solids toolbar. Select the object you want to slice. AutoCAD displays the `Slicing plane by Object/Zaxis/ View/XY/YZ/ZX/<3points>:` prompt. Use these options to define the plane of the cross-section. Table 24-2 explains how to use the options. (They are the same as for the SECTION command.)

	Table 24-2 SLICE Options	
Option	**Description**	
Object	Choose a circle, ellipse, arc, spline, or 2D polyline.	
Zaxis	Lets you define the plane by defining a Z axis. The slicing plane is then the XY plane perpendicular to the Z axis you defined. You define the Z axis by first specifying a point on the slicing plane. This point is the 0,0,0 point (for purposes of this command only) where the slicing plane and the Z axis meet. Then you pick a point on the Z axis.	
View	Define the slicing plane parallel to the current view at the intersection of a point you specify.	
XY	Define the slicing plane parallel to the XY plane at the intersection of a point you specify.	
YZ	Define the slicing plane parallel to the YZ plane at the intersection of a point you specify.	
ZX	Define the slicing plane parallel to the ZX plane at the intersection of a point you specify.	
3points	This is the default. Specify three points to define the slicing plane. It's a good idea to use object snaps.	

Step-by-Step: Slicing Solids

On the CD-ROM

1. If you have *ab24-3.dwg* open from the last exercise, use it. Do a regen to remove the hidden view. If you don't have it open, open it from your *AutoCAD Bible* folder or from the *Results* folder of the CD-ROM. OSNAP is on, with running object snaps set for Endpoint, Midpoint, Quadrant, and Center. If you don't have the Solids toolbar open, right-click any toolbar, choose Solids from the toolbar list, and close the Toolbars dialog box. The drawing is shown in Figure 24-22.

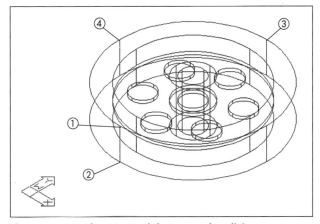

Figure 24-22: The 3D model you use for slicing.

2. Save your drawing as *ab24-4.dwg* in your *AutoCAD Bible* folder.

3. Choose Slice from the Solids toolbar. Follow the prompts:

```
Select objects: Select the solid model.
Select objects: ↵
Slicing plane by Object/Zaxis/View/XY/YZ/ZX/<3points>: Pick the
quadrant at ① in Figure 24-22.
2nd point on plane: Pick the quadrant at ②.
3rd point on plane: Pick the quadrant at ③.
Both sides/<Point on desired side of the plane>: Pick the model
at ④.
```

4. As mentioned earlier, the slicing reveals an error — the disk cuts through the central tube, as shown in Figure 24-23. To fix the error now, choose Zoom Realtime from the Standard toolbar and zoom in so the model takes up the entire screen.

5. Start the CIRCLE command. At the `3P/2P/TTR/<Center point>:` prompt, pick the midpoint at ① in Figure 24-23. At the `Diameter/<Radius>:` prompt, pick the endpoint at ②.

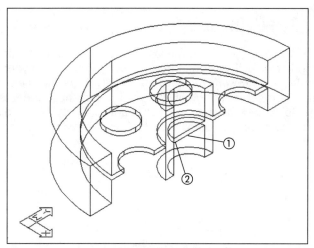

Figure 24-23: The solid after slicing and deleting one half.

6. Choose Extrude from the Solids toolbar. Select the new circle. Set the height of extrusion to 16 and accept the default taper angle of zero.

7. Type **subtract** ↵. At the Select solids and regions to subtract from... Select objects: prompt, select the large solid and press Enter to end object selection. At the Select solids and regions to subtract... Select objects: prompt, select the new extruded circle you just drew and press Enter. AutoCAD subtracts the extruded circle from the larger model.

8. Erase the original circle and do a hide. Your drawing should look like Figure 24-24.

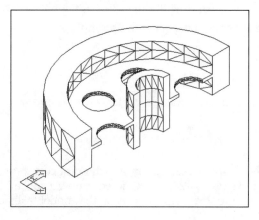

Figure 24-24: The solid after subtracting the extruded circle and doing a hide.

9. Save your drawing. If you are continuing on to the next Step-by-Step exercise, keep the drawing open.

Note The error could have been avoided by subtracting the inner tube from the outer tube as the last step, instead of doing it earlier. If you wanted to correct the entire model, you could subtract out the circle as you just did in the exercise, mirror the entire model, and use UNION to make the two halves whole. Mirroring in 3D is covered in the next section. You could also undo the slice as soon as you saw the error and make the correction on the entire model.

Editing in 3D

There are a number of editing commands that are exclusively for 3D or have special 3D options. In this section I explain these special commands and options.

Table 24-3 lists most of the editing commands and how they are used in 3D drawings.

Table 24-3 Editing Commands in 3D	
Command	*Use in 3D Drawings*
ERASE	Same as for 2D.
COPY	Same as for 2D.
MIRROR	Can be used on 3D objects as long as the mirror line is in the XY plane. Otherwise, use MIRROR3D.
OFFSET	Can be used in 3D space but only on 2D objects.
ARRAY	Can be used on 3D objects in the XY plane. Otherwise, use 3DARRAY.
MOVE	Same as for 2D.
ROTATE	Can be used on 3D objects in the XY plane. Otherwise, use ROTATE3D.
SCALE	Can be used on 3D objects. Scales all three dimensions.
STRETCH	Can be used in 3D space but only on 2D objects, wireframes, and surfaces. The results may not be what you expect because it is hard to visualize the direction of the stretch.
LENGTHEN	Can be used in 3D space but only on 2D objects.
TRIM	Has special options for 3D but only works on 2D objects such as lines.
EXTEND	Has special options for 3D but only works on 2D objects such as lines.
BREAK	Can be used in 3D space but only on 2D objects.

(continued)

Table 24-3 (continued)

Command	Use in 3D Drawings
CHAMFER	Has special options for 3D.
FILLET	Has special options for 3D.
EXPLODE	Works on 3D objects — solids explode to surfaces, and surfaces explode to wireframes. You can also explode blocks containing 3D objects.
ALIGN	Works on 3D objects.

You can use grips on 3D objects, although it is sometimes difficult to visualize in which plane you are moving or stretching an object. You cannot stretch solids, but you can stretch surfaces and wireframes. (If you try to stretch a solid, AutoCAD just moves it.)

Mirroring in 3D

If the mirror line is on the XY plane, you can mirror any 3D object with the regular MIRROR command. If you want to mirror in any other plane, use MIRROR3D.

To use MIRROR3D, follow these steps:

1. Choose Modify⇨3D Operation⇨Mirror 3D.

2. Select the object or objects you want to mirror.

3. At the `Plane by Object/Last/Zaxis/View/XY/YZ/ZX/<3points>:` prompt, choose one of the options to define the mirroring plane. These are the same options described in Tables 24-1 and 24-2 for the SECTION and SLICE commands. The only new option is Last, which uses the last defined mirroring plane.

Step-by-Step: Mirroring in 3D

On the
CD-ROM

1. If you have *ab24-4.dwg* open from the last exercise, use it. Do a regen to remove the hidden view. If you don't have it open, open it from your *AutoCAD Bible* folder or from the *Exercise Results* folder of the CD-ROM. OSNAP is on, with running object snaps set for Endpoint, Midpoint, Quadrant, and Center. If you don't have the Solids toolbar open, right-click any toolbar, choose Solids from the toolbar list, and close the Toolbars dialog box. The drawing is shown in Figure 24-25.

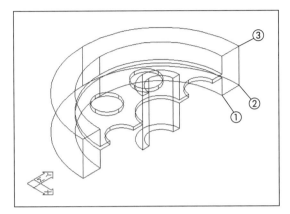

Figure 24-25: This 3D model was sliced and can now be mirrored.

2. Save your drawing as *ab24-5.dwg* in your *AutoCAD Bible* folder.

3. Choose Modify⇨3D Operation⇨Mirror 3D. Follow the prompts:

```
Select objects: Select the solid.
Plane by Object/Last/Zaxis/View/XY/YZ/ZX/<3points>: Pick ① in
Figure 24-25.
2nd point on plane: Pick ②.
3rd point on plane: Pick ③.
Delete old objects? <N> ↵
```

4. Select Union from the Modify II toolbar or type **union** ↵. Select both solids. AutoCAD unites them.

5. Save your drawing.

Arraying in 3D

You can array any 3D object using the ARRAY command as long as you define the array in the current XY plane. The 3DARRAY command lets you create a rectangular array with the normal rows and columns but adding levels in the Z direction. For a 3D polar array, you define an axis of rotation instead of the 2D point used in the ARRAY command.

Creating 3D rectangular arrays

To create a 3D rectangular array, follow these steps:

1. Choose Modify⇨3D Operation⇨3D Array to start the 3DARRAY command.

2. Select the objects you want to array.

3. At the `Rectangular or Polar array (R/P):` prompt, type **r** ↵.

4. At the `Number of rows (---) <1>:` prompt, type the number of rows you want to create. Rows are parallel to the X axis.

5. At the `Number of columns (|||) <1>:` prompt, type the number of columns you want to create. Columns are parallel to the Y axis.

6. At the `Number of levels (...) <1>:` prompt, type the number of levels you want to create. Levels are parallel to the Z axis.

7. At the `Distance between rows (---):` prompt, type a unit distance or pick two points.

8. At the `Distance between columns (|||):` prompt, type a unit distance or pick two points.

9. At the `Distance between levels (...):` prompt, type a unit distance or pick two points.

Step-by-Step: Creating a Rectangular Array in 3D

On the
CD-ROM

1. Open *ab24-c.dwg* from the CD-ROM.

2. Save it as *ab24-6.dwg* in your *AutoCAD Bible* folder. This is a drawing showing a sphere, a bead-like shape sometimes used for table legs. In this exercise you create a 3D rectangular array to create four table legs.

3. Choose Modify⇨3D Operation⇨3D Array. Follow the prompts:

```
Select objects: Select the bead.
Rectangular or Polar array (R/P):   r ↵
Number of rows (---) <1>: 2 ↵
Number of columns (|||) <1>: 2 ↵
Number of levels (...) <1>: 20 ↵ (The bead is 1.5 inches high and
the leg should be 30 inches high.)
Distance between rows (---): 26 ↵ (This is the narrower distance
between the legs.)
Distance between columns (|||): 36 ↵ (This is the wider distance
between the legs.)
Distance between levels (...): 1.5 ↵ (You want the beads to touch
along the leg.)
```

4. Do a ZOOM Extents to see the result. (Now you would create the table top.)

5. Save your drawing. It should look like Figure 24-26.

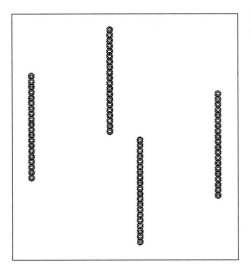

Figure 24-26: The four legs of a table, created using a 3D rectangular array.

Creating 3D polar arrays

To create a 3D polar array, follow these steps:

1. Choose Modify⇨3D Operation⇨3D Array to start the 3DARRAY command.

2. Select the objects you want to array.

3. At the `Rectangular or Polar array (R/P):` prompt, type **p** ↵.

4. At the `Number of items:` prompt, type the total number of items you want.

5. At the `Angle to fill <360>:` prompt, press Enter to array around a full circle or type any lesser angle.

6. At the `Rotate objects as they are copied? <Y>:` prompt, press Enter to accept the default or type **n** ↵ if you don't want to rotate the objects as they are arrayed.

7. At the `Center point of array:` prompt, specify the center point of the array. This is also the first point of the axis of rotation.

8. At the `Second point on axis of rotation:` prompt, specify any other point on the axis of rotation.

If you rotate less than a full circle, you need to determine the positive angle of rotation. The positive direction of the axis goes from the first point you specify (the center point) to the second point. Point your thumb in the positive direction and follow the curl of the fingers of that hand to determine the positive angle of rotation.

Step-by-Step: Creating 3D Polar Arrays

On the CD-ROM

1. Open *ab24-d.dwg* from the CD-ROM.

2. Save it as *ab24-7.dwg* in your *AutoCAD Bible* folder. You see part of a lamp, as shown in Figure 24-27.

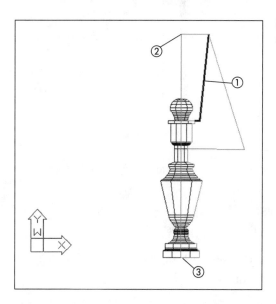

Figure 24-27: A partially completed lamp.

3. To array the bracket that supports the lampshade, choose Modify⇨ 3D Operation⇨3D Array. Follow the prompts:

```
Select objects: Select the support at ① in Figure 24-27.
Select objects: ↵
Rectangular or Polar array (R/P): p↵
Number of items: 3 ↵
Angle to fill <360>: ↵
Rotate objects as they are copied? <Y>: ↵
Center point of array: Pick the endpoint at ②.
Second point on axis of rotation: Pick the endpoint at ③.
```

4. One of the three supports cannot be seen in this view. To see all three, choose View⇨3D Viewpoint⇨Select. Type **290** in the X Axis text box and **75** in the XY Plane text box. Click OK.

5. Choose Top View from the Viewpoint flyout of the Standard toolbar to return to plan view and save your drawing.

Rotating in 3D

You can rotate 3D objects in the XY plane with the ROTATE command. Use ROTATE3D when you need to rotate objects in any other plane. The ROTATE3D options are shown in Table 24-4.

<table>
<tr><td colspan="2" align="center">Table 24-4
ROTATE3D Options</td></tr>
<tr><td>**Option**</td><td>**Description**</td></tr>
<tr><td>Object</td><td>Choose a line, circle, arc, spline, or 2D polyline. If you choose a circle or arc, AutoCAD rotates around a line that starts at the object's center and extends perpendicular to the object.</td></tr>
<tr><td>Last</td><td>Uses the last defined axis of rotation.</td></tr>
<tr><td>View</td><td>Define the axis of rotation parallel to the current view at the intersection of a point you specify.</td></tr>
<tr><td>Xaxis</td><td>The axis of rotation is parallel to the X axis and passes through a point you specify.</td></tr>
<tr><td>Yaxis</td><td>The axis of rotation is parallel to the Y axis and passes through a point you specify.</td></tr>
<tr><td>Zaxis</td><td>The axis of rotation is parallel to the Z axis and passes through a point you specify.</td></tr>
<tr><td>2points</td><td>This is the default. Specify two points to define the axis. It's a good idea to use object snaps.</td></tr>
</table>

Tip

Sometimes it is easier to create an object in the XY plane and then rotate it afterward. In other words, you may create an object in the wrong plane on purpose and use ROTATE3D later to properly place it.

To use ROTATE3D, follow these steps:

1. Choose Modify⇨3D Operation⇨Rotate 3D.

2. Select the object or objects you want to rotate.

3. At the `Axis by Object/Last/View/Xaxis/Yaxis/Zaxis/<2points>:` prompt, select one of the options, explained in Table 24-4, and define the axis according to the option prompts.

4. At the `<Rotation angle>/Reference:` prompt, specify a positive or negative rotation angle or choose the Reference option. (The reference option works like the Reference option for ROTATE. See Chapter 9.)

You need to determine the positive direction of rotation. Point your thumb in the positive direction of the axis and follow the curl of your fingers. If you pick two points, the positive direction of the axis goes from the first point to the second pick point.

Step-by-Step: Rotating in 3D

On the
CD-ROM

1. Open *ab24-e.dwg* from the CD-ROM.

2. Save it as *ab24-8.dwg* in your *AutoCAD Bible* folder. You see the same lamp used in the previous Step-by-Step exercise, but it has now been completed, as shown in Figure 24-28.

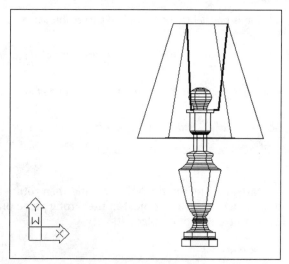

Figure 24-28: The completed lamp.

3. To insert the lamp in a plan view drawing of a house, you need to see it in plan view from the WCS. In other words, you should be looking down at the lamp. To do this, you need to rotate the lamp around the X axis. To visualize this, look at the UCS icon and imagine rotating the top of the lamp towards you around the horizontal (X) axis. To rotate the lamp, choose Modify➪3D Operation➪Rotate 3D. Follow the prompts:

```
Select objects: Use a crossing window to select the entire lamp.
Other corner: Pick the other corner.
Select objects: ↵
Axis by Object/Last/View/Xaxis/Yaxis/Zaxis/<2points>: x ↵
Point on X axis <0,0,0>: ↵
<Rotation angle>/Reference: 90 ↵
```

4. Choose Zoom Extents from the Zoom flyout of the Standard toolbar to see the entire lamp. The lamp is now rotated 90 degrees around the X axis in relation to the UCS, and you are looking at it from the top.

5. To get a better view, choose SE Isometric View from the Viewpoints flyout of the Standard toolbar. Then hide the drawing. It should look like Figure 24-29. Of course, looking at the lamp from a different viewpoint does not change the orientation of the lamp relative to the UCS.

Figure 24-29: The lamp is now ready to place in a 3D drawing of a house.

6. Save your drawing.

Aligning in 3D

I have already covered the ALIGN command in Chapter 10. When you work in 3D, you can use the ALIGN command to move, rotate in the XY plane, and rotate in the Z direction — all in one command.

In this Step-by-Step exercise, you practice using ALIGN in 3D.

Step-by-Step: Rotating in 3D

On the
CD-ROM

1. Open *ab24-f.dwg* from the CD-ROM.

2. Save it as *ab24-9.dwg* in your *AutoCAD Bible* folder. You see part of the base assembly for an industrial washer, as shown in Figure 24-30. One sidebar needs to be moved and rotated into place. OSNAP is on, with a running object snap set for Endpoint.

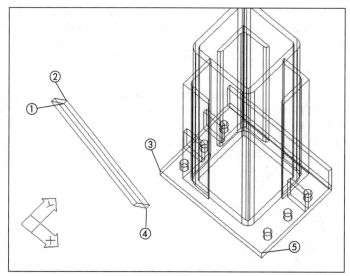

Figure 24-30: Part of a base assembly for an industrial washer with a sidebar that needs to be moved and rotated into place.

Credit: Thanks to Robert Mack of The Dexter Company, Fairfield, Iowa, for this drawing.

3. Notice that it's hard to tell which way the sidebar is facing because it is displayed in wireframe. Do a hide. This tells you that ① in Figure 24-30 is facing away from you. Do a regen.

4. You need to know the width of the sidebar (the smallest dimension) so you can specify its placement. Choose Distance from the Inquiry flyout of the Standard toolbar. At the First point: prompt, pick the endpoint at ①. At the Second point: prompt, pick the endpoint at ②. AutoCAD tells you that the distance is .3750. This information is used in the next step.

5. Choose Modify⇨3D Operation⇨Align.

```
Select objects: Select the sidebar.
Select objects: ↵
Specify 1st source point: Pick ① in Figure 24-30.
Specify 1st destination point: Pick ③.
Specify 2nd source point: Pick ④.
Specify 2nd destination point: Pick ⑤.
Specify 3rd source point or <continue>: Pick ②.
Specify 3rd destination point: Choose the From object snap from
the Object Snap flyout on the Standard toolbar.
_from Base point: Pick ③.
<Offset>: @0,.3750 ↵. Here you tell AutoCAD to place ② at a Y
distance of .3750 from the corner at ③. This rotates the sidebar so it
rises perpendicular from the base.
```

6. AutoCAD aligns the sidebar. Save your drawing. It should look like Figure 24-31.

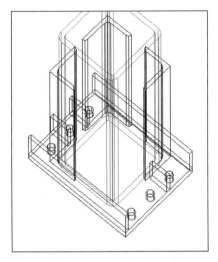

Figure 24-31: The sidebar has been aligned with the rest of the model.

 Tip

The trick when aligning is to properly visualize the parts. Hiding the drawing first, as you did in the exercise, helps. Also, take the time to find a UCS and a viewpoint that makes the points you are specifying easy to see and pick.

Trimming and extending in 3D

 Cross-Reference

The TRIM and EXTEND commands are covered in Chapter 10. Review that discussion if necessary. Here I explain how to use them in 3D.

You cannot trim or extend surfaces or solids, but you can trim or extend 2D objects in 3D space. AutoCAD provides the Project option for working in 3D space. The Project option has three suboptions:

✦ **None:** AutoCAD only trims or extends objects that actually intersect or can intersect in 3D space.

✦ **UCS:** This is the default. AutoCAD projects objects onto the XY plane of the current UCS. Therefore, if two lines are on different Z coordinates, you can trim and extend one of them with reference to the other, even though they do not and cannot actually meet in 3D space.

✦ **View:** This projects objects parallel to the current view. Objects are trimmed or extended based on the way they look on the screen. They need not (and probably won't) actually meet in 3D space.

You can also use the Extend option to trim or extend to implied intersections, as explained in Chapter 10.

In the following Step-by-Step exercise, you extend objects in 3D. Trimming works the same way.

Step-by-Step: Extending Objects in 3D

1. Open *ab24-g.dwg* from the CD-ROM.

2. Save it as *ab24-10.dwg* in your *AutoCAD Bible* folder. You see a bushing, in 2D and 3D, as shown in Figure 24-32. The 3D bushing has been exploded into simple geometry — otherwise you wouldn't be able to use it to extend the 2D lines.

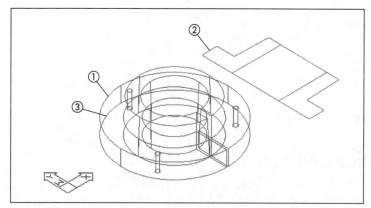

Figure 24-32: A bushing in 2D and 3D. The 3D bushing has been exploded but still looks the same. It can now be used to extend lines.

3. Choose Extend from the Modify toolbar. Follow the prompts.

```
Select boundary edges: (Projmode = UCS, Edgemode = No extend)
Select objects: Pick the 3D bushing at ① in Figure 24-32.
Select objects: ↵
<Select object to extend>/Project/Edge/Undo: p ↵
None/Ucs/View <Ucs>: v ↵
<Select object to extend>/Project/Edge/Undo: Pick the 2D bushing
at ②.
<Select object to extend>/Project/Edge/Undo: ↵
```

4. Pick Top View from the Viewpoint flyout of the Standard toolbar. You can now see that the 2D line doesn't actually meet the 3D bushing. By using the View option, you only extended the line in that view.

5. Choose Zoom Previous from the Zoom flyout.

6. Again, choose Extend from the Modify toolbar. Follow the prompts:

```
Select boundary edges: (Projmode = View, Edgemode = No
extend)
Select objects: Pick the bottom edge of the 3D bushing at ③.
Select objects: ↵
<Select object to extend>/Project/Edge/Undo: p↵
None/Ucs/View <Ucs>: n ↵
<Select object to extend>/Project/Edge/Undo: Pick the same line
you picked before, but this time pick it closer to the 3D bushing, on the
new length you created by extending it.
<Select object to extend>/Project/Edge/Undo: ↵
```

7. Choose Top View from the Viewpoint flyout of the Standard toolbar. You can now see that the 2D line now actually meets the 3D bushing.

8. Click Undo on the Standard toolbar twice to undo the viewpoint change and the extend operation.

9. Use a window to select the entire 3D bushing. Choose Move from the Modify toolbar. At the `Base point or displacement:` prompt, type **0,0,2** ↵. Press Enter again to end the command. If you miss any of the objects, pick them and move them too. This moves the entire 3D bushing 2 units in the Z direction.

10. Choose Extend from the Modify toolbar. Follow the prompts:

```
Select boundary edges: (Projmode = View, Edgemode = No
extend)
Select objects: Pick the 3D bushing at ③ (the bottom ring).
Select objects: ↵
<Select object to extend>/Project/Edge/Undo: p ↵
None/Ucs/View <None>: u ↵
<Select object to extend>/Project/Edge/Undo: Pick the same line
you extended before, closer to its left endpoint.
<Select object to extend>/Project/Edge/Undo: ↵
```

11. Choose Top View from the Viewpoint flyout of the Standard toolbar. It looks as if the 2D line now actually meets the 3D bushing.

12. Choose Front View from the Viewpoint flyout of the Standard toolbar. Now you can see that the 2D line doesn't meet the 3D bushing.

13. Save your drawing. It should look like Figure 24-33.

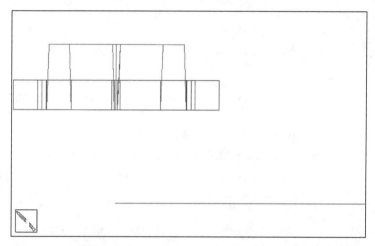

Figure 24-33: When you use the UCS option, the line seems to touch its boundary edge when you look at it from the top, but they can have different Z coordinates.

Filleting in 3D

You can fillet solids but not wireframes or surfaces. Figure 24-34 shows a 3D mechanical drawing with several filleted edges.

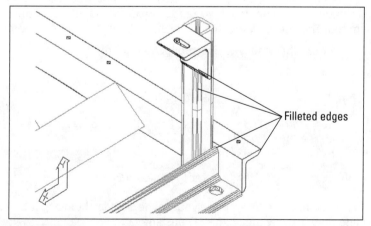

Figure 24-34: Filleted edges are common in 3D mechanical drawings.

Here's how to use the FILLET command for solids:

1. Choose Fillet from the Modify toolbar.

2. At the `Polyline/Radius/Trim/<Select first object>:` prompt, select the edge of the solid that you want to fillet. You cannot deselect this edge, so you must select the solid at the proper edge. Ignore the other options.

3. AutoCAD senses that you have selected a solid and responds with the `Enter radius <0.5000>:` prompt. Press Enter to accept the default of .5 or type a new radius.

4. At the `Chain/Radius/<Select edge>:` prompt, press Enter if you only want to fillet the one edge you have already selected. You can also select other edges of the same solid. Press Enter to end selection of edges. AutoCAD fillets the edge or edges you selected. You can also change the Radius at this prompt.

5. Use the Chain option to fillet a set of attached edges. AutoCAD responds with the `Edge/Radius/<Select edge chain>:` prompt. Continue to pick edges that are attached to the previous edge you picked. Press Enter to end selection of edges. AutoCAD fillets the entire chain of edges.

Note You can select different radii for different edges. At the first `Enter radius <0.5000>:` prompt, specify the radius for the edge you just selected. After that, use the Radius option to set the desired radius before you select the edge.

Step-by-Step: Filleting Solids

On the CD-ROM

1. Open *ab24-h.dwg* from the CD-ROM.

2. Save it as *ab24-11.dwg* in your *AutoCAD Bible* folder. This is a mounting angle, as shown in Figure 24-35. It needs to be filleted.

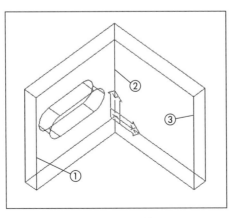

Figure 24-35: The mounting angle needs filleting.

3. Choose Fillet from the Modify toolbar.

4. At the `Polyline/Radius/Trim/<Select first object>:` prompt, pick the edge at ① in Figure 24-35.

5. At the `Enter radius <0.5000>:` prompt, type **.25** ↵.

6. At the `Chain/Radius/<Select edge>:` prompt, pick ②.

7. At the `Chain/Radius/<Select edge>:` prompt, pick ③. Press Enter to end the command. AutoCAD fillets all three edges.

8. Save your drawing. It should look like Figure 24-36.

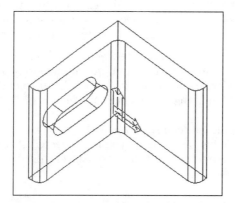

Figure 24-36: The filleted mounting angle.

Chamfering in 3D

You can chamfer solids but not wireframes or surfaces. Figure 24-37 shows a solid with chamfered edges. (You can see this solid in the wheel shown at the beginning of this chapter in Figure 24-1.)

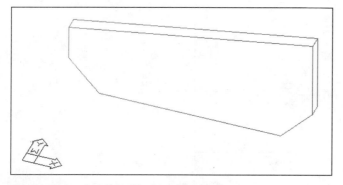

Figure 24-37: A solid with chamfered edges.

To chamfer a solid, follow these steps:

1. Choose Chamfer from the Modify toolbar.

2. At the `Polyline/Distance/Angle/Trim/Method/<Select first line>:` prompt, select the edge you want to chamfer. The edge is displayed as a line between two surfaces. AutoCAD highlights one of the surfaces that touches the edge you selected.

3. At the `Select base surface: Next/<OK>:` prompt, press Enter to accept the highlighted surface as the base surface. You need to define the base surface in case the two chamfering distances are not equal. Type **n** ↵ to highlight the next surface. (There are only two surfaces that touch the edge you selected.) Press Enter when the desired surface is highlighted.

4. At the `Enter base surface distance <30.0000>:` prompt, type the chamfering distance for the first surface. This is the amount you want to cut off from that surface. (The default is the last distance you specified.)

5. At the `Enter other surface distance <30.0000>:` prompt, type the chamfering distance for the other surface. (The default is the last distance you specified.)

6. At the `Loop/<Select edge>:` prompt, select the edge you want to chamfer. This may seem superfluous, but you need to do it. You can also use the Loop option. AutoCAD then prompts you to select the edge loop. Select the surface, and AutoCAD chamfers all the edges of that surface.

7. AutoCAD continues to prompt you to select edges or edge loops. Press Enter to end selection when you are finished.

Step-by-Step: Chamfering Solids

On the
CD-ROM

1. Open *ab24-i.dwg* from the CD-ROM.

2. Save it as *ab24-12.dwg* in your *AutoCAD Bible* folder. This is a simple box with dimensions of 233 × 102 × 12 millimeters, as shown in Figure 24-38.

3. Choose Chamfer from the Modify toolbar. Follow the prompts:

```
Polyline/Distance/Angle/Trim/Method/<Select first line>: Pick
the edge at ① in Figure 24-38.
Select base surface: Next/<OK>: ↵
Enter base surface distance <0.5000>: 30 ↵
Enter other surface distance <0.5000>: 30 ↵
Loop/<Select edge>: Pick ①.
Loop/<Select edge>: ↵
```

You can't properly see the chamfer because of the viewpoint. You change the viewpoint at the end of the exercise.

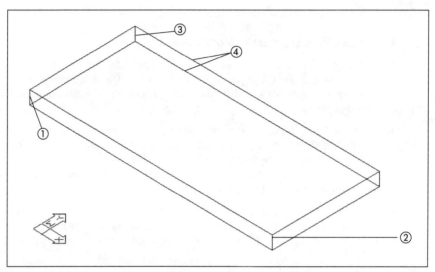

Figure 24-38: You can chamfer this solid box to create a new shape.

4. Repeat the CHAMFER command. Do the exact same operation as in step 3, but pick ②.

5. Repeat the CHAMFER command. Follow the prompts:

```
Polyline/Distance/Angle/Trim/Method/<Select first line>: Pick
the edge at ③.
Select base surface: Next/<OK>: ↵ Make sure the surface indicated
by ④ is highlighted. If not, type n ↵. Then press Enter again.
Enter base surface distance <30.0000>: 233 ↵
Enter other surface distance <30.0000>: 40 ↵
Loop/<Select edge>: Pick ③.
Loop/<Select edge>: ↵
```

6. Choose Top View from the Viewpoints flyout on the Standard toolbar. This shows you the shape in profile.

7. Save your drawing. It should look like Figure 24-39.

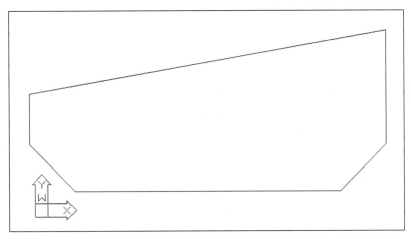

Figure 24-39: The completed solid. Compare it to the model in Figure 24-1.

Exploding 3D objects

The EXPLODE command has a particular effect on 3D objects. Table 24-5 lists the effects of exploding 3D objects.

Table 24-5 Using EXPLODE on 3D Objects	
Object	*Result*
Solids	Flat surfaces become regions. Curved surfaces become bodies.
Bodies	Curved surfaces become single-surface bodies. Flat bodies become regions or curves.
Polyface Meshes	3D faces
Polygon Meshes	3D faces
Polylines with thickness	Lines

Note

A *body* is a freeform solid. You cannot directly create a body. AutoCAD uses bodies when 3D models do not fit into any other object type.

ACIS and lithography (*.stl*) are two file formats especially applicable to 3D models. Chapter 27 explains how to export drawings in these formats.

Listing Solid Properties

The MASSPROP command provides information about regions and solids that is useful for engineering applications. The bounding box, for example, is an imaginary box that contains the solid. The calculations are based on the relationship of the solid to the UCS. If you rotate the solid or change the UCS, you get different results. For example, after running MASSPROP to find the center of gravity (centroid) and axes of your model, move the UCS to the centroid and then run MASSPROP again to identify the moments of inertia.

For 2D regions, the area moment of inertia that MASSPROP generates can be used to calculate bending and twisting stresses. You could generate a 2D region of a solid model using the SECTION command, and then use the UCS command with the OBJECT option to set the UCS coplanar to the region. The MASSPROP command would then report the area moment of inertia.

AutoCAD assumes a density of 1 for all solids. You can then apply material density multipliers on the values that get reported. Figure 24-40 shows the results of MASSPROP on a solid.

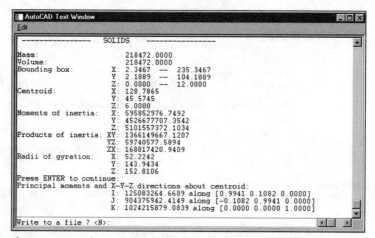

Figure 24-40: The results of the MASSPROP command.

To list a solid's properties, choose Mass Properties from the Inquiry flyout of the Standard toolbar. Select the object you want to list. AutoCAD opens the Text Window to display the calculations. At the `Write to a file?` prompt, press Enter to accept the No default or type **y** ↵. AutoCAD prompts you for a filename and copies the data to that file.

Summary

In this chapter you learned how to create solids. AutoCAD provides several standard shapes that you can quickly draw. You can also create extruded and revolved solids from 2D profiles. To create more complex shapes, use the UNION, SUBTRACT, and INTERSECT commands. You can also use the INTERFERE command to see the volume of interference between solids. To help visualize solids, use the SECTION and SLICE commands.

This chapter also covered 3D editing. Some special 3D editing commands are MIRROR3D, 3DARRAY, and ROTATE3D. The TRIM, EXTEND, FILLET, and CHAMFER commands have special options for 3D editing. You can explode solids into surfaces and surfaces into 2D objects.

AutoCAD can calculate a number of engineering functions on solids using the MASSPROP command.

In the next chapter, I cover shading and rendering 3D models.

✦　　✦　　✦

Shading and Rendering in 3D

Visualizing 3D Drawings

While 3D drawings are more realistic than 2D ones, they nevertheless look very artificial — they lack realistic color, shading, lighting, and so on. Shading and rendering let you display a 3D drawing more realistically. You can shade and render 3D surfaces or solid models.

 Release 14 has added a great deal to the rendering process. Capabilities that were previously part of AutoVision, a separate Autodesk product, have now been included in AutoCAD. These include creating shadows, making objects transparent, and *mapping,* which is the projection of a 2D image on the surface of a 3D model. Figure 25-1 shows a scene that includes these features.

Figure 25-1: This cog has been rendered with shadows and a background of clouds.

Because so many features have been added to Release 14, this chapter cannot hope to cover every aspect of the rendering process. It does, however, give you a fairly detailed overview of the entire process and gets you started rendering on your own.

Shading 3D Models

Shading is a much simpler version of rendering. You can use shading to get a quick visualization of your drawing. Shading is based on one default light source that AutoCAD automatically places behind the viewer and which shines on the model. However, you can control shading through two system variables — SHADEDGE and SHADEDIF.

SHADEDGE controls shading of edges, using the settings shown in Table 25-1.

Table 25-1 SHADEDGE Settings	
Setting	**Effect**
0	Shades faces without highlighting edges
1	Shades faces and highlights edges in background color
2	Leaves faces unshaded and highlights edges in object color
3	Shades faces in object color and edges in background color. This is the default.

SHADEDIF controls the amount of diffuse reflective light — light that reflects off the model — as a percentage of ambient light — light that comes from all around the model. The default is 70, which means that 70 percent of the light is diffuse reflective light and 30 percent is ambient light. If you reduce the SHADEDIF value too much, you increase the ambient light, resulting in a drawing that is too light with not enough contrast.

Once you have set these two system variables, choose Shade from the Render toolbar or type **shade** ↵. Depending on the drawing and the speed of your computer, you may have to wait a short while.

Note

To open the Render toolbar, right-click any toolbar, choose Render from the Toolbars dialog box, and close the dialog box.

You cannot work on your model once you have shaded it. Do a regen to return to the wireframe display.

Tip

Objects in color shade better than those in black and white.

You cannot save or print the shaded view, but you can make a slide of it. Slides are covered in Chapter 33.

Two new system variables, HIDEPRECISION and FACETRATIO, affect hiding, shading, and rendering. HIDEPRECISION is set to zero by default, which calculates hides and shades with single precision. You can set it to 1 to calculate with double precision, although this uses more memory and may increase the time AutoCAD needs to complete the hide or shade. FACETRATIO affects the mesh density created for cylindrical and conic solids. By default, it is set to zero, which creates the normal mesh density. Set it to 1 to increase the mesh density. This should improve the quality of rendered and shaded cylindrical and conic solids.

Step-by-Step: Shading a Drawing

1. Open *ab25-a.dwg* from the CD-ROM.

2. Save it as *ab25-1.dwg* in your *AutoCAD Bible* folder. If the Render toolbar is not displayed, right-click any toolbar, choose Render, and close the Toolbar dialog box.

3. Type **shadedge** ↵ and set it to 1, or accept the default if it is already 1.

4. Type **shadedif** ↵ and set it to 60.

5. Choose Shade from the Render toolbar. Wait while AutoCAD shades the drawing.

6. Save your drawing. It should look like Figure 25-2.

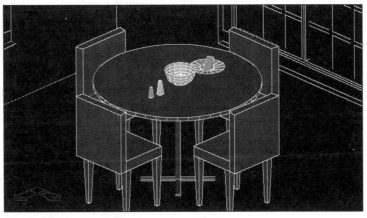

Figure 25-2: A shaded scene.

Understanding Rendering

Rendering is a much more sophisticated means of visualizing a drawing than shading. Now that Release 14 has incorporated the features of AutoVision, it is even more useful than before — more complicated, too! AutoCAD now offers three kinds of rendering — *Render, Photo Real,* and *Photo Raytrace.*

✦ **Render** is AutoCAD's original rendering tool and provides the fewest options but the fastest results.

✦ **Photo Real** creates images line by line, can display bitmaps, create transparent materials, and make volumetric and mapped shadows.

✦ **Photo Raytrace** traces rays of light to generate reflections, refraction, and precise ray-traced shadows.

Learning the steps

Rendering is a many-step process. It generally requires a good deal of trial and error before you get the exact results you want. Here are the steps:

1. Start with trial rendering using the default settings. The results let you know what settings need to be changed.

2. Create lights. AutoCAD has four types of lights: ambient, distant, point, and spotlight. These are explained in the section on lights later in this chapter.

3. Create scenes. Scenes are simply views with lights.

4. Load materials from the materials library. You can create your own materials. Materials are surface characteristics and include color and/or pattern, ambient light, reflection, roughness, transparency, refraction, and bump map. These characteristics are explained in the section on materials.

5. Attach materials to the objects in your drawing. You can attach materials by object, color, or layer.

6. Add a background or fog effect.

7. Set your rendering preferences, if desired.

8. Render the drawing.

The order of the steps is flexible. For example, you can create scenes after you have attached materials. Also, after you render you will probably see some room for improvement so you may go back and change the lights, scenes, and/or materials.

Doing a default rendering

It often helps to do a default rendering. The results help you decide what materials and lights need to be created and reveals any problems with the models themselves. When you render, you should open the Render toolbar, which contains most of the tools you need. Right-click any toolbar, choose Render from the Toolbars dialog box, and click Close. Figure 25-3 shows the Render toolbar.

Figure 25-3: The Render toolbar.

 To render a drawing using the default settings, choose Render from the Render toolbar to open the Render dialog box, shown in Figure 25-4.

Figure 25-4: The Render dialog box.

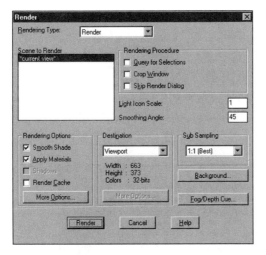

I cover this dialog box completely later in the chapter, but there are a couple of things you can do when you are trying to get a quick rendering.

You can save time by rendering only some of the objects in the view. To do this, use the Rendering Procedure section of the dialog box.

✦ Check **Query for Selection** to tell AutoCAD to display the `Select objects:` prompt before rendering.

✦ Check **Crop Window** to tell AutoCAD to prompt you to specify a window before rendering.

✦ In the Rendering Options section, check **Render Cache** if you plan to render the same scene several times, as is often the case when you are working on a rendering. AutoCAD saves the rendering data in a file and uses it for subsequent renderings — saving the time needed for AutoCAD to analyze the drawing each time.

Click Render to render the drawing.

Step-by-Step: Creating a Default Rendering

On the
CD-ROM

1. Open *ab25-a.dwg* from the CD-ROM.

2. Save it as *ab25-2.dwg* in your *AutoCAD Bible* folder. If the Render toolbar is not displayed, right-click any toolbar, choose Render, and close the Toolbar dialog box.

3. Choose Render from the Render toolbar. In the Rendering Procedures section, check Crop Window. In the Rendering Options section, check Render Cache.

4. Click Render.

5. At the Pick crop window to render: prompt, pick a window similar to that shown in Figure 25-5. Wait until AutoCAD renders the drawing.

6. Save your drawing. It should look like Figure 25-5. As you can see, the rendering is too dark and the objects need realistic materials.

Figure 25-5: An initial rendering using default options and a crop window.

Creating Lights

When you render using the default options, AutoCAD uses one light source from behind the viewer, which falls on the objects in the view. However, that is rarely enough — nor is it realistic. AutoCAD offers four types of lights to give you a great deal of flexibility in creating a realistic scene. With the new capability of casting shadows, the proper placement of lights is more important than ever.

 To create lights, choose Lights from the Render toolbar to open the Lights dialog box, shown in Figure 25-6.

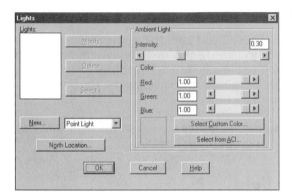

Figure 25-6: The Lights dialog box.

Assigning color to a light

The process of assigning a color to a light applies to all types of lights. Light colors are somewhat different than pigment colors. Pigment colors are more familiar. You know that there are three primary colors — red, yellow, and blue — and you know what colors you get when you mix them. The three primary light colors are red, green, and blue. Their mixtures are different as well — for example, red and green make yellow. White light is the sum of all colors of light together. Black is the absence of any colors of light.

An addition to the RGB light color system is the HLS system (hue, lightness, saturation). Instead of mixing primary colors, you choose the color from a range of hues and then vary its lightness (brightness) and saturation (purity).

There are three options for choosing a color for a light:

✦ **RGB:** The RGB (red-green-blue) system lets you define colors by the amount of each primary light color. You can use the slider bars or type in a number from zero to one. When all three are set to one, you get white light, the default.

✦ **Windows:** Choose Select Custom Color to open the Windows Color dialog box, which lets you select colors either by an RGB or an HLS system. An HLS system determines color by hue, lightness, and saturation settings. Hue is the color; lightness — or brightness — is the amount of white the color contains. Saturation is the amount of black the color contains.

✦ **ACI:** Choose Select from ACI to use the AutoCAD Color Index system. AutoCAD opens the Select Color dialog box so you can choose a color.

In most cases, white light is fine. You can get some unexpected results when using colored lights on colored objects.

Setting the North location

Setting the North location is important if you want to use the Sun Angle Calculator to create a distant light and if you will create shadows. By default, North is the positive Y direction in the World Coordinate System. To change it, type a new angle in the Angle box or use the slider bar. The Y axis is 0 degrees, the positive X axis is 90 degrees, and so on clockwise.

If you have saved a UCS, you can choose it from the list on the right side. AutoCAD uses the Y axis in that UCS as the default North direction.

Setting the ambient light

Ambient light is background light that has no source or target. It illuminates all surfaces in your drawing equally. It can, however, have a color. By default, ambient light is set at .30. Use the Intensity slide bar to change the setting or type a number from zero to one. Making ambient light too high results in a rendering that looks like an overexposed image. Use a lower setting for night scenes.

Creating a point light

A point light is equivalent to a light bulb. It comes from a specific location and radiates in all directions. A point light *attenuates,* meaning that the intensity becomes less the farther away you are from the light's source.

To create a new point light, choose Point Light from the drop-down list next to the New button. Then click New to open the New Point Light dialog box, shown in Figure 25-7.

Name

In the Light Name text box, type a name for the light.

Use a name that makes it clear that the light is a point light. Keep the name short. A simple sequence of P1, P2 is often sufficient. However, you could also use P-overhead and P-door or something similar.

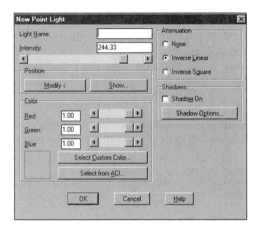

Figure 25-7: The New Point Light dialog box.

Attenuation

Set the Attenuation, which is the manner in which the light loses intensity as the distance from its source increases. You have three choices:

✦ **None:** The light doesn't lose intensity.

✦ **Inverse Linear:** The light loses intensity in a linear manner, so that at 2 units from its source the light is half as intense and at 4 units away the light is one quarter as intense. This is the default.

✦ **Inverse Square:** The light loses intensity at the square of the distance, so that at 2 units from its source the light is one quarter as intense and at 4 units away the light is one sixteenth as intense. Setting the attenuation to inverse square means that the intensity of the light drops off very quickly.

Intensity

Set the intensity, or brightness, of the light in the Intensity text box or use the slider bar. AutoCAD sets the maximum brightness based on the attenuation and the drawing extents.

✦ If you chose inverse linear attenuation, the maximum intensity is half the distance from the lower left corner to the upper right corner of the extents of the drawing.

✦ If you chose inverse square attenuation, the maximum intensity is half the square of the distance from the lower left corner to the upper right corner of the extents of the drawing.

✦ If you chose no attenuation, the maximum intensity is 1.

Tip

Set the intensity to zero to turn a light off. You can use this technique to switch a scene from a day view to a night view or to experiment with different lights without having to delete them.

Position

The position of the light is quite important, especially if you decide to create shadows. If you set the XY coordinates in plan view, be sure to set the proper Z coordinate as well. In an architectural drawing, you don't want your lights to be coming from the floor! However, in a mechanical drawing, it might be appropriate to light your model from any angle.

Release 14 also lets you set the transparency of materials. If you create an opaque lampshade and place a light inside it, light will get out only through the top and bottom.

Choose Show to see the current position. Choose Modify to temporarily return to your drawing to pick a position.

Use object snaps or point filters to specify the position of your lights. If there are no objects available, work out the position in advance and place easily visible point objects there. You can then snap to the point objects using the Node object snap.

Color

Set the color of the light. Setting light color has already been discussed in the section "Assigning color to a light."

Shadows

Shadows are new for Release 14. I cover shadows in a separate section at the end of the discussion on lights. Check Shadows On if you want to create shadows. Choose Shadow Options to set the type of shadows you want and set shadow map size and softness. Creating shadows adds significantly to rendering time.

When you are done creating the point light, click OK.

Creating a spotlight

A spotlight differs from a point light in that it has a direction. As a result, you not only specify its location, but its target — two coordinates instead of one. In addition, a spotlight has a brighter center, called the hot spot. Outside the bright center is a ring of lesser brightness called the falloff. Figure 25-8 shows the same scene used previously in this chapter with one overhead spotlight.

Falloff area

Figure 25-8: A rendering with one spotlight overhead.

To create a new spotlight, choose Spotlight from the drop-down list next to the New button in the Lights dialog box. Then click New to open the New Spotlight dialog box, shown in Figure 25-9.

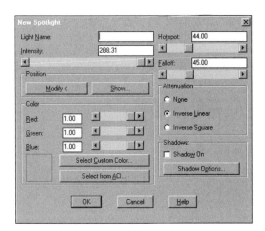

Figure 25-9: The New Spotlight dialog box.

Name

In the Light Name text box, type a name for the light.

Tip

Use a name that makes it clear that the light is a spotlight. Keep the name short. A simple sequence of S1, S2 is often sufficient. However, you could also use S-overhead and S-door or something similar.

Hotspot and Falloff

Set the hotspot and falloff angles. These angles emanate from the spotlight in the direction of the light's target. The maximum angle for both is 160. If the hotspot and falloff angles are the same, there is no falloff — the entire spotlight is bright. The defaults are 44 degrees for the hotspot and 45 degrees for the falloff. This does not leave very much falloff area. You may need to experiment to get the desired result.

To set the hotspot and falloff angles, type the angles in the text boxes or use the slider bars.

The rest of the options for spotlight are the same as for a point light. Set the attenuation, intensity, position, color, and shadows. When you are done creating the spotlight, click OK.

Creating a distant light

A distant light is equivalent to the sun. Its rays come from so far away that for all practical purposes they are parallel. A distant light does not attenuate (unless you're drawing a model on Pluto).

To create a new distant light, choose Distant Light from the drop-down list next to the New button in the Lights dialog box. Then click New to open the New Distant Light dialog box, shown in Figure 25-10.

Name

In the Light Name text box, type a name for the light.

Tip

Use a name that makes it clear that the light is a distant light. Keep the name short.

Intensity

Set the intensity, or brightness, of the light in the Intensity text box or use the slider bar. The intensity can range from zero to one.

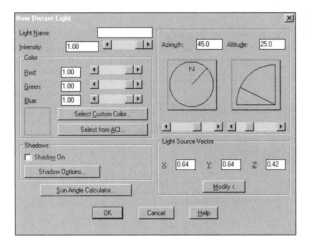

Figure 25-10: The New Distant Light dialog box.

Tip

Set the intensity to zero to turn the distant light off. You can use this technique to switch a scene from a day view to a night view or to experiment with different lights without having to delete them.

Position

The position of the light is quite important, especially if you decide to create shadows. If you set the XY coordinates in plan view, be sure to set the proper Z coordinate as well. Generally, you position a distant light at the extents of your drawing.

There are three ways to specify the position of a distant light.

Azimuth and Altitude

The azimuth is the angle in the XY plane — North is located at 0 degrees. Use a positive angle to move clockwise from North and a negative angle to move counterclockwise from North. Values can range from –180 to 180. (Both –180 and 180 would represent South.) The altitude is the angle from the XY plane. The slider bar lets you enter angles from 0 to 90, or you can type in angles from –90 to 90. (An altitude of –90 would mean the light was coming from beneath the model.)

Light Source Vector

Click Modify to return temporarily to your drawing. AutoCAD prompts you to enter the light direction to and from. This only sets the direction of the light. AutoCAD places the light outside the model.

Sun Angle Calculator

Click Sun Angle Calculator to open the Sun Angle Calculator dialog box, shown in Figure 25-11. The Sun Angle Calculator is new in Release 14. (It was previously a part of AutoVision, a separate Autodesk product.)

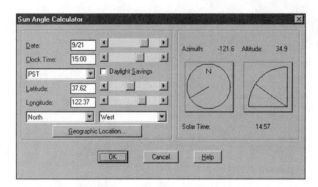

Figure 25-11: The Sun Angle Calculator dialog box.

Use the Sun Angle Calculator when you are using a distant light to simulate the sun. The calculator locates the sun based on the latitude and longitude of the model's location and the time of day. Naturally, you would use this for architectural or surveying drawings. It's fun to use, too.

You use the left side of the dialog box to specify the information that Render needs to calculate the position of the sun. Follow these steps to complete the dialog box.

1. Type the date or use the slider bar.

2. Type the time using 24-hour format or use the slider bar.

3. Choose the time zone from the drop-down list. Check Daylight Savings if applicable.

4. Specify the Latitude and Longitude by typing them in or using the slider bars. Latitude goes from 0 degrees (the equator) to 90 degrees (the North or South pole). Longitude goes from 0 degrees in Greenwich, England, to 180 degrees around the opposite side of the globe.

5. Specify the hemispheres — North or South and East or West.

6. If you don't know the latitude and/or longitude, click Geographic Location to open the Geographic Location dialog box, shown in Figure 25-12.

   a. Choose the continent from the drop-down list above the map. The appropriate map appears. (Try choosing various continents — it's a great way to travel.)

   b. Check Nearest Big City if your model is in a big city. Then click on the map. If Nearest Big City is checked, the blue crosshairs jump to the nearest big city. You can also choose from the City list, and the blue crosshairs move to the proper location on the map.

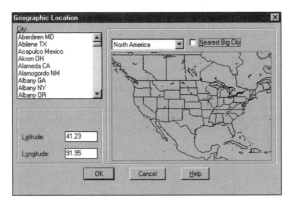

Figure 25-12: Use the Geographic Location dialog box to determine latitude and longitude for specific locations.

   c. When you are done, click OK.

7. In the Sun Angle Calculator dialog box, click OK to return to the New Distant Light dialog box.

Note

If you forgot to set the North location, choose North Location now. None of the sun calculations work properly if North is not properly defined.

Color

Set the color of the light. Setting light color has already been discussed in the section "Assigning color to a light."

Shadows

Check Shadows On if you want to create shadows. Choose Shadow Options to set the type of shadows you want and set shadow map size and softness. I cover shadows in the next section.

When you have finished defining the distant light, click OK to return to the Lights dialog box.

Release
14

Creating shadows

Shadows are new for Release 14. They add greatly to the realism of your rendered image. They also add greatly to the rendering time.

Tip

For your practice renderings while you are creating lights and materials, turn shadows off in the Render dialog box. When you are satisfied with the results, turn shadows on.

Types of shadows

AutoCAD creates three different types of shadows. Table 25-2 compares these types of shadows.

Table 25-2 Shadow Characteristics			
Type	**Which Renderer to Use**	**Description**	**Characteristics**
Volumetric	Photo Real or Photo Raytrace	Based on volume of space cast by object's shadow	Hard edges, outlines are approximate, affected by color of transparent objects
Maps	Photo Real or Photo Raytrace	Based on a map size that you set	Soft edges, which you can adjust, not affected by the color of transparent objects
Raytraced	Photo Raytrace	Calculated by tracing the path of rays from a light	Hard edges, accurate outlines, affected by color of transparent objects

Choose the type of shadows you want based on their characteristics and your needs.

Shadow settings

To create shadows, you need to turn on shadows in two places. When you create a new light, you check Shadows On in the dialog box you use to create the new light. In addition, you need to check Shadows in the Rendering Options section of the Render dialog box. This shadows option is only available if you choose Photo Real or Photo Raytrace as the type of rendering in the Render dialog box.

You set shadow settings when you create or modify a light source. Click Shadow Options to open the Shadow Options dialog box, shown in Figure 25-13.

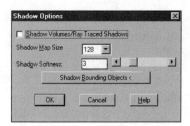

Figure 25-13: The Shadow Options dialog box.

Check Shadow Volumes/Raytrace Shadows to create volumetric shadows with Photo Real rendering and raytraced shadows with Photo Raytrace rendering. The shadow map settings are disabled.

If you uncheck Shadow Volumes/Raytrace Shadows, you can create a shadow map.

You can set the shadow map size from 64 to 4,096 pixels. Larger map sizes are more accurate but take longer to render.

Set the shadow softness from 1 to 10 pixels. This means the number of pixels at the edge of the shadow that are blended into the rest of the image, creating the soft effect. AutoCAD recommends using a setting from 2 to 4.

Choose Shadow Bounding Objects to temporarily return to the drawing to select objects that create a bounding box that AutoCAD uses to clip the shadow maps.

Step-by-Step: Creating Lights and Shadows

On the
CD-ROM

1. Open *ab25-a.dwg* from the CD-ROM.

2. Save it as *ab25-3.dwg* in your *AutoCAD Bible* folder. If the Render toolbar is not open, right-click on any toolbar and choose Render and then close the Toolbar dialog box.

3. Choose Lights from the Render toolbar. Choose Point Light from the drop-down list next to the New button. Click New to open the New Point Light dialog box.

4. Type **P1** in the Name text box. Click Modify. AutoCAD returns you to your drawing. Click Pan Realtime and pan to the right a couple of times until you see the floor lamp as shown in Figure 25-14. Press Esc to exit Pan mode. At the Enter light location <current>: prompt, pick the endpoint shown in Figure 25-14. AutoCAD returns you to the New Point Light dialog box.

5. Set the intensity to 250. In the Color section, click Select Custom Color and choose the yellow box in the first row. Click OK. Notice that AutoCAD adjusts the RGB settings.

6. Click Shadow On. Click OK to return to the Lights dialog box.

7. Choose Spotlight from the drop-down box and click New. Type **S1** in the Name text box. Click Modify. At the Enter light target <current>: prompt, pick an endpoint at the top of the bowl on the table. At the Enter light location <current>: prompt, type **@0,0,5'** to place the light directly over the table like a light hanging from the ceiling.

8. Set the Falloff to 55.00 and click Shadow On. Click OK to return to the Lights dialog box.

9. Choose Distant Light from the drop-down box and click New. Type **D1** in the Name text box. Click Shadow On.

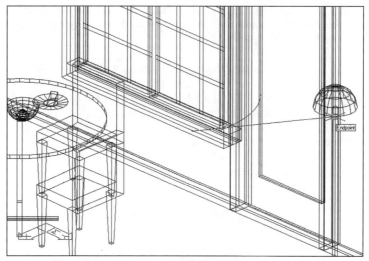

Figure 25-14: Picking the point light location.

10. Click Sun Angle Calculator. Set the date to 9/21. Set the time to 8:00 in the morning. (You're having breakfast.) Set the time zone to CST. Click Daylight Savings. Set the latitude to 41.00 and the longitude to 91.57. The two drop-down list boxes below should read North and West. Click Geographic Locator to see where you ended up. (If you typed in the right latitude and longitude, the blue cross should be in southeast Iowa.) Click OK until you return to the Lights dialog box.

11. In the Lights dialog box, click North location. Type **90** degrees in the text box. Click OK twice to return to your drawing.

12. Choose Named Views from the Viewpoint flyout of the Standard toolbar. Choose Render1, click Restore, and click OK.

13. Choose Render from the Render toolbar. Change the Light Icon Scale to 24 so you can see the icons that AutoCAD creates at the location of each light you have created. (You should use the drawing scale factor.) In the Rendering Type drop-down list, choose Photo Real. Click Render. The rendering should take less than a minute. It should look like Figure 25-15. There is more than enough light this time — but remember you wouldn't normally eat breakfast with all the lights on. Notice the effect of the yellow point light.

14. Choose Render again. Check Shadows in the Rendering Options section. Click Render. Notice that the rendering takes much longer. Wow! Lots of shadows. This rendering also makes it clear that no light is coming through the windows. In the next section you learn how to make materials transparent. The rendering should look like Figure 25-16.

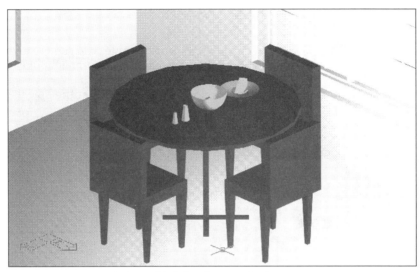

Figure 25-15: A rendering with lights but no shadows.

Figure 25-16: The same rendering with shadows.

15. Save your drawing. If you are continuing on to the next exercise, keep this drawing open.

Creating Scenes

Scenes help you manage lights and views. For example, you can create two scenes — one with only a distant light to mimic the effect of natural light only and another with no distant light and only point lights and spotlights to create a nighttime effect. You can also change the view so that you can look at the objects from different vantage points.

 To create a scene, choose Scenes from the Render toolbar to open the Scenes dialog box, shown in Figure 25-17.

Figure 25-17: The Scenes dialog box.

This dialog box lists your scenes and lets you create, modify, and delete scenes.

To create a new scene, follow these steps:

1. Click New to open the New Scene dialog box, shown in Figure 25-18. The New Scene dialog box lists all the saved views and all the lights you have created.

Figure 25-18: The New Scene dialog box.

2. Type a name in the Scene Name text box.

3. Choose a view. You can only choose one.

4. Choose the lights you want. Press Ctrl to choose more than one light. Press Shift to choose a range of lights. You can also choose *ALL* to quickly choose all the lights for the scene.

5. Click OK.

Your scene is now listed in the Scenes dialog box. Click OK again to return to your drawing. When you render the drawing, you can choose this scene from the Render dialog box.

Step-by-Step: Creating a Scene

On the
CD-ROM

1. If you have *ab25-3.dwg* open, use it. Otherwise, open it from your *AutoCAD Bible* folder or the *Results* folder of the CD-ROM.

2. Save it as *ab25-4.dwg* in your *AutoCAD Bible* folder. If the Render toolbar is not open, right-click any toolbar and choose Render, and then close the Toolbar dialog box.

3. Choose Scenes from the Render toolbar. Click New in the Scenes dialog box to open the New Scene dialog box.

4. Type **morning** in the Scene Name text box.

5. Choose RENDER1 from the Views list.

6. Choose D1 and P1 from the Lights list, using the Ctrl key to select each one.

7. Click OK twice to return to the drawing.

8. Save the drawing. If you are continuing on to the next Step-by-Step exercise, keep it open.

Working with Materials

Working with materials involves two steps — adding them to the drawing and attaching them to objects. Designing appropriate materials is an important part of the rendering process and greatly affects the results. Materials interact with lights. For example, shiny materials reflect light differently than dull materials because they create highlights. The object's color affects how light appears on it as well.

Adding materials

AutoCAD comes with a large selection of materials. You can modify these to create your own materials. To add materials to the drawing, choose Materials Library from the Render toolbar to open the Materials Library dialog box, shown in Figure 25-19.

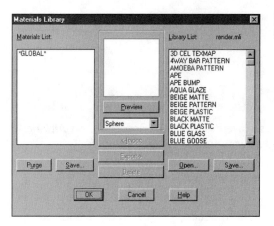

Figure 25-19: The Materials Library dialog box.

Working with lists of materials

Materials are saved in a file with the extension *.mli* (materials library). The default materials library is *render.mli*.

✦ You can save the entire library list in another file by clicking Save on the right side of the dialog box.

✦ You can also save the list of materials in the drawing that is open in another file by clicking Save on the left side of the dialog box.

✦ Click Open to open a different library list and use its materials.

✦ Click Purge to delete all the materials in the list from the drawing.

Importing and previewing materials

Release 14 has added many new materials to the materials library. To add materials to your drawing, follow these steps:

1. Choose a material from the library list at the right side of the dialog box.

2. Click Import.

3. Choose the material from the Materials List.

4. From the Preview drop-down list, choose the preview type of either Cube or Sphere, based on whether the object you want to use the material for is flat or curved.

5. Click Preview to see a sample of the material.

6. Continue steps 1 through 5 until you have all the materials you want.

7. Click OK.

Tip

If you don't find the exact material you want, import the closest one you can find. You can then create a new material based on that material.

You can choose a range of materials by holding down Shift and clicking the first and last materials in the range. You can choose any nonconsecutive materials by holding down Ctrl and clicking the materials you want.

If you don't like a material that you have imported, highlight it and click Delete. Use the Export option to save materials you have created in the drawing to the materials library file. If you make changes to the materials library file, when you click OK to close the Materials Library dialog box, AutoCAD asks you if you want to save the changes to the file. Save the changes to update the file.

Step-by-Step: Importing Materials

On the CD-ROM

1. If you have *ab25-4.dwg* open from the last exercise, use it. Otherwise, open it from your *AutoCAD Bible* folder (if you did the exercise) or the *Results* folder of the CD-ROM.

2. Save it as *ab25-5.dwg* in your *AutoCAD Bible* folder. If the Render toolbar is not open, right-click on any toolbar and choose Render. Click Close in the Toolbar dialog box.

 3. Choose Materials Library from the Render toolbar. Hold down Ctrl and scroll as necessary to choose Beige Plastic, Green Glass, Light Wood Tile, Pink Marble, Stitched Pattern, White Matte, Wood — Med. Ash, Wood White Ash, and Yellow Plastic. Click Import.

4. From the left list, choose Pink Marble. Choose Cube from the Preview drop-down list and click Preview to see the result. Do the same with Stitched Pattern.

5. Preview Green Glass with the Sphere.

6. Click OK. Save your drawing. If you are continuing to the next Step-by-Step exercise, keep the drawing open.

Creating your own materials

Once you have imported materials from the materials library, you can modify them to create your own materials. Choose Materials from the Render toolbar to open the Materials dialog box, shown in Figure 25-20.

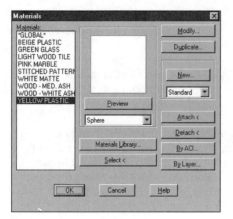

Figure 25-20: The Materials dialog box.

Notice that you can click Materials Library in this dialog box to open the Materials Library dialog box. You can therefore use the Materials dialog box to manage the entire process of importing, creating, and attaching materials. You can preview imported materials in this dialog box as well.

When you create a new material, you have three choices:

- ✦ You can modify an existing material.

- ✦ You can duplicate an existing material and then make modifications to the copy, leaving the original material intact.

- ✦ You can start from scratch and create an entirely new material.

The dialog box that AutoCAD opens when you choose one of the above options depends on your choice in the drop-down list below the New button. You have four choices. The marble, granite, and wood options are new for Release 14.

- ✦ **Standard** creates a standard material.

- ✦ **Marble** creates a material that mimics marble. In this dialog box you specify turbulence and sharpness of the veins as well as the scale of the veins to the entire object of marble.

- ✦ **Granite** creates a material that mimics granite. In this dialog box you can specify up to four colors and their sharpness (distinctness) as well as the scale of the texture relative to the entire granite object.

- ✦ **Wood** creates a material that mimics wood. In this dialog box you specify the light/dark ratio of the grain, the ring density and width, and the scale of the rings relative to the entire wood object.

When you choose a method of creating a new material, whether by modifying, duplicating, or creating from scratch, AutoCAD opens the dialog box appropriate for the material you have chosen. Figure 25-21 shows the New Standard Material dialog box.

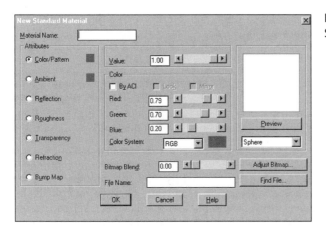

Figure 25-21: The New Standard Material dialog box.

Unless you are modifying an existing material, you first give the material a name in the Material Name text box.

You use this dialog box by choosing the attributes listed on the left side one by one, specifying the values for each attribute from the choices on the right for each one.

Color/Pattern

The color is the basic color of the object. The reflection of light off the object (called diffuse reflection) is determined by this color. You set the color in the Color section of the dialog box, using one of four methods:

✦ By ACI (AutoCAD Color Index) lets you set the color to the color of the object in the drawing. You must uncheck this to choose one of the three other methods.

✦ Choose RGB from the Color System drop-down list to specify the color using the Red-Green-Blue system. These are the three primary light colors. You can type in values from zero to one or use the slider bars. When all three are set to one, you get white light, the default.

✦ Choose HLS from the Color System drop-down list to specify the color using the Hue, Lightness, and Saturation system. Hue is the color; lightness — or brightness — is the amount of white the color contains; saturation is the amount of black the color contains.

✦ Click the color swatch to open the Windows Color dialog box, letting you specify a color using either the RGB or the HLS system.

In addition to setting the color, you set the value. The value affects the surface finish and interacts with the Reflection value. For example, AutoCAD recommends using a color value of .7 and a reflection value of .3 for a dull finish and reversing the values for a shiny finish. You can type a value or use the slider bar.

If you choose a bitmap file, the color becomes a pattern. See the sidebar on "Mapping" for more information.

Ambient

The Ambient color and value affect the color reflected by ambient light. Remember that you set the amount of ambient light when you created lights. You can click Lock in the Color section of the dialog box to lock the ambient and reflection colors to the main color. (You cannot use Lock if you checked By ACI as the color.)

Reflection

The Reflection setting affects highlights created by light that shines on the object. To create a shiny object, you can use a reflection value of .7 with a color value of .3. Shiny objects often create a white highlight — for this effect, set the color to white by setting red, green, and blue to 1. You can also choose a bitmap file to create a reflection map. See the sidebar on "Mapping" for more information.

Roughness

Roughness has no color setting — you only set a value. A rough surface produces smaller highlights. Use a lower value to create smaller highlights. If you chose a zero value for reflection, the roughness setting is not used.

Transparency

The transparency setting, new for Release 14, lets you create transparent or translucent materials. You set the value from zero to one. Higher values mean greater transparency. Using transparency increases rendering time. You can choose a bitmap to create an opacity map. See the sidebar on "Mapping" for more information.

Refraction

Refraction only applies to Photo Raytrace rendering when you have a transparent (or translucent) material. Refraction is the bending of a light wave when it passes through an object to an object of another density. A higher value increases the refraction.

Bump Map

Bump maps create the effect of varying heights on the surface of the object — in other words, bumps. You use the bottom part of the dialog box to choose the bump map and for bump map settings. See the sidebar "Mapping" for more information about bump maps.

As you complete the dialog box, you can press Preview and see the result as a sphere or cube at any time. When you like the results, click OK.

Mapping

Release 14 lets you project a 2D image onto the surface of a 3D object. This is called mapping. You must use the Photo Real or Photo Raytrace rendering types to render with mappings. The 2D images are bitmap files that can be in several file formats, such as *TGA, BMP, TIF,* and *JPEG.* AutoCAD provides a large number of *TGA* files in the Textures subfolder.

Note: You need to do a full or custom installation of AutoCAD to get all the texture maps.

You can actually place up to four bitmaps onto an object. When you create a material, you can add bitmaps to the Color/Pattern, Reflection, Transparency, and Bump Map characteristics of a material.

There are four kinds of maps that correspond to the four characteristics:

✦ Texture maps place a pattern of colors onto the object. When you include a bitmap in the Color/Pattern definition, you turn a plain color into a pattern.

✦ Reflection maps place a scene on the surface of a reflective object, in the same way that you can see yourself reflected in a pool of water. Add a bitmap to the Reflection definition.

✦ Opacity maps mimic areas of opacity and transparency. Add a bitmap to the Transparency definition.

✦ Bump maps create the effect of varying heights. Choose Bump Maps and choose a bitmap file.

AutoCAD comes with a number of materials that include maps. In the Materials Library dialog box, check out the Bumpywhite stone and Checker textures, for example. As their names make clear, the first material is a bump map and the second a texture map. Import and preview them to see how they look. Using these materials saves you the task of specifying a bitmap file.

Bitmap Blend determines how much the bitmap is used. The values range from zero to 1. For example, a 1.0 value for a bump map gives you the full value of the bumps. A lower value creates lower bumps.

Choose Adjust Bitmap to open the Adjust Material Bitmap Placement dialog box. Here you set the offset of the origin of the bitmap and the scale. The scale is the number of times the bitmap fits onto the object. If you are unfamiliar with the bitmap, you'll need to experiment. You can try various options and click Preview to see the results. Bitmapping uses U and V axes, which are like X and Y axes but can have any direction and origin. Click Maintain Aspect Ratio to keep the U and V scales equal.

By default, bitmaps are tiled, which means that if the scale is less than 1, AutoCAD repeats the pattern to cover the entire object. You can also crop, which creates a decal effect — the pattern is placed just once on the object.

Step-by-Step: Creating Materials

On the
CD-ROM

1. If you have *ab25-5.dwg* open from the last exercise, use it. Otherwise, open it from your *AutoCAD Bible* folder (if you did the exercise) or the *Results* folder of the CD-ROM.

2. Save it as *ab25-6.dwg* in your *AutoCAD Bible* folder. If the Render toolbar is not open, right-click any toolbar, choose Render, and close the Toolbar dialog box.

3. Choose Materials from the Render toolbar. The materials that were imported in the last Step-by-Step exercise are listed on the left. Choose Yellow Plastic and click Duplicate.

4. In the Material Name text box of the New Standard Material dialog box, type **Yellow Cheese**.

5. With Color/Pattern selected from the Attributes section of the dialog box, click the color swatch to the right of the Color System drop-down list. In the Color dialog box, pick the yellow box in the top row. Click OK.

6. Choose Ambient from the Attributes section. Click Lock in the Color section. The color changes to the same yellow as the Color/Pattern swatch.

7. Choose Reflection. Change the value to 0.10, since cheese isn't very shiny. Click Lock here as well.

8. Choose Roughness. Change the value to 0.75.

   You can omit transparency, since its default value is zero. Refraction is irrelevant without a transparency setting.

9. Omit this step if you don't have a Full installation or a custom installation that includes textures. Preview the yellow cheese on a cube. Choose Bump Map from the Attributes section. Choose Find File at the bottom right of the dialog box. In the Bitmap File dialog box, find the *Textures* folder inside the main *AutoCAD* folder and double-click. Choose *bmps.tga* and click Open. Click Preview again to see the difference. Note that the bumps are too big.

10. Click Adjust Bitmap. In the Adjust Bitmap Material Placement dialog box, check Maintain Aspect Ratio. Change the scale to 2 and click Preview using the cube. The bumps are smaller now. Click OK three times to return to your drawing.

11. Save your drawing. Leave it open if you are continuing to the next exercise.

Attaching materials

Once you have imported, created, and modified the materials you need, you attach them to objects. AutoCAD lets you attach materials by object, layer, or color. To attach any material, follow these steps:

1. Choose Materials from the Render toolbar.

2. Choose the material from the list of materials.

3. Use one of these methods to attach the material:

   a. Click Attach to attach a material by selecting the object or objects. AutoCAD temporarily returns you to your drawing.

   b. Click By ACI (AutoCAD Color Index) to attach a material by its color in the drawing. AutoCAD opens the Attach by AutoCAD Color Index dialog box, which lets you choose a color, or colors by their numbers.

   c. Click By Layer to attach a material by layer. AutoCAD opens the Attach by Layer dialog box, which lets you choose a layer or layers.

Tip

Attaching materials by layer can be a very efficient method. It requires some planning in advance. For example, if you have a block that is a chair, if you create it so that the legs are on one layer and the seat and back are on a second layer, you can easily attach a wood-like material to the legs and a nice pattern to the seat and back.

Note

You can assign a material to an object, its layer, and its color — which would mean that the object has three materials. AutoCAD gives priority to direct attachments by object, then to attachments by color, and finally to attachments by layer.

Step-by-Step: Attaching Materials

On the CD-ROM

1. Open *ab25-b.dwg* from the CD-ROM.

2. Save it as *ab25-7.dwg* in your *AutoCAD Bible* folder. If the Render toolbar is not open, right-click any toolbar and choose Render, then close the Toolbar dialog box. This is the same drawing used earlier in the chapter, but all the materials have been imported and modified and some materials have been attached to objects. Also, the table and chairs have been separated into appropriate layers.

3. Choose Materials from the Render toolbar. Click By Layer. In the Attach By Layer dialog box, choose PINK MARBLE from the Select a Material list. Choose TABLE_TOP from the Select Layer list. Click Attach. The PINK MARBLE material appears next to the TABLE_TOP layer.

4. Choose STITCHED PATTERN from the left list and CUSHIONS from the right list and click Attach. In the same way, attach WOOD-WHITE ASH to the LEGS layer. Click OK.

5. In the Materials dialog box, choose GREEN GLASS and click Attach. AutoCAD finds the bowl, which has already been attached to the GREEN GLASS material and displays the Gathering objects...1 found. Select objects to attach GREEN GLASS to: message. At the Select objects: prompt, select the plate on the table and press Enter to return to the dialog box.

6. Click OK to return to your drawing.

7. Save your drawing. Keep it open if you are continuing to the next Step-by-Step exercise.

Using Backgrounds

Release 14 adds some sophisticated features for adding backgrounds to your rendering. For example, you can place a picture of the sky in the background. You can also add landscape features such as trees and bushes. This section covers the basics of backgrounds.

You have a choice of four types of backgrounds:

✦ **Solid** places a solid color in the background. You might use a solid black for a night scene.

✦ **Gradient** creates a background of up to three colors in a graded blend.

✦ **Image** places an image in the background (for example, an image of the sky).

✦ **Merge** lets you combine your rendering with the image you currently have on your screen.

To create a background, choose Background from the Render toolbar to open the Background dialog box, shown in Figure 25-22.

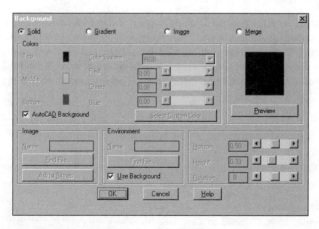

Figure 25-22: The Background dialog box.

If you choose Solid, you can use the current AutoCAD background (usually white or black) or define a color using the same color controls you use for lights and materials and explained earlier in this chapter.

If you choose Gradient, you set separate top, middle, and bottom colors. Then use the Horizon setting to determine the center of the gradient. The height determines, in percentage form, where the second color starts. For example, 33 percent would create three equal levels of color. If you want only two colors, set the height to zero. Use Rotation to rotate the gradient.

If you choose Image, use the Image section to specify a file. If you did a full installation of Release 14 (or a custom installation including textures), you have a number of *.tga* files to choose from in the *textures* subfolder of AutoCAD. Of course, you can use your own files. You can use the following file types:

✦ BMP	✦ PCX
✦ GIF	✦ TGA
✦ JPG	✦ TIF

Merge uses the current AutoCAD background (usually solid white or black) as the background for the rendering. It doesn't require any settings.

You can choose an additional file in the Environment section (at the bottom of the dialog box) to create reflection and refection effects. You can use the same types of files as for images. AutoCAD maps the image onto a sphere surrounding the scene.

Foggy landscapes

Also new for Release 14 are the landscape commands, letting you create and edit landscapes. Release 14 comes with a small library of trees, bushes, people, and a DO NOT ENTER road sign. Choose Landscape New from the Render toolbar, choose an item, and preview it. When you find one that you like, set the geometry. Single Face results in quicker rendering than crossing faces but is less realistic. Choose View Aligned if you want the object to always face the viewer, like a tree. You might uncheck this for the road sign – you don't want the sign to face the viewer from both directions. Set the height (usually in inches) and click Position to place it in your drawing.

Note: When you place the landscape object, it appears as a triangle or a rectangle. You don't see the object until you render the view.

Choose Landscape Edit to edit the characteristics of an existing landscape object. Choose Landscape Library to edit, delete, and add landscape objects.

Another new feature is fog. Choose Fog from the Render toolbar to open the Fog/Depth Cue dialog box. Fog is used to give a sense of distance, because objects in the distance are not as clear as those close up. Choose Enable Fog to turn fog on. You set the color, near and far distances (where the fog starts and ends), and near and far percentages of fog (how much fog there should be at the near and far distances).

This exercise adds a background to your drawing.

Step-by-Step: Adding a Background

1. If you have *ab25-7.dwg* open, use it. Otherwise, open it from your *AutoCAD Bible* folder if you did the previous exercise or from the *Results* folder of the CD-ROM.

2. Save it as *ab25-8.dwg* in your *AutoCAD Bible* folder.

3. Choose Background from the Render toolbar.

4. Choose Image at the top of the Background dialog box.

5. In the Image section, choose Find File.

6. If you did a full AutoCAD installation, open the *Textures* subfolder and choose *sky.tga.* (Make sure the Files of type drop-down list box says **.tga*.) If not, find *sky.gif* on the CD-ROM, and copy it to AutoCAD's *support* subfolder. Then start at Step 3, and choose *sky.gif* in this step. Click Open.

7. Click Preview. AutoCAD displays the file.

8. Click OK. You don't see the result until you render the drawing.

9. Save your drawing. If you are continuing to the next Step-by-Step exercise, keep the drawing open.

Doing the Final Render

You are finally ready to render. Preparing to render can be a long process. If you wish, you can choose Preferences from the Render toolbar first to open the Rendering Preferences dialog box. This dialog box is an exact copy of the Render dialog box and lets you preset the rendering settings. However, you can also make all these settings in the Render dialog box.

To render, choose Render from the Render toolbar. This opens the Render dialog box, shown in Figure 25-23.

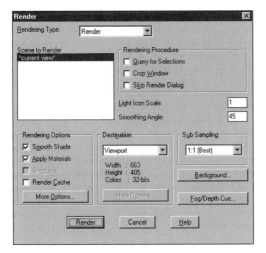

Figure 25-23: The Render dialog box.

This dialog box has the following components:

✦ In the Rendering Type drop-down list, choose the type of rendering you want.

✦ In the Scene to Render box, choose a scene.

✦ In the Rendering Procedure section, check one of the options if you wish. Query for Selections means that AutoCAD asks you to select objects. Use this to test a rendering on one or more objects. Choose Crop Window to choose a window to render. Choose Skip Render Dialog to render immediately without even opening the dialog box (the next time).

✦ Set the Light Icon Scale. Use the drawing scale factor for this.

✦ Set the Smoothing Angle. The smoothing angle determines the angle at which AutoCAD assumes an edge as opposed to a smooth curve. The default is 45 degrees. A lower angle would result in more edges.

✦ In the Rendering Options section, check Smooth Shade to smooth out a multiedged object. AutoCAD blends colors across adjacent faces.

✦ Check Apply Materials to use the materials you imported and attached.

✦ Check Shadows to generate shadows. You can only create shadows with the Photo Real and Photo Raytrace rendering types. Remember that using shadows greatly increases rendering time.

✦ Check Render Cache to save rendering information in a file. AutoCAD can reuse this information for subsequent renderings, saving time.

✦ Click More Options to open a dialog box that varies with the type of rendering. Usually, you can use the defaults, but you can click Help to get an explanation of each item.

✦ In the Destination section, choose where you want the rendering to appear. The default is viewport. If you have one viewport, the rendering covers the entire drawing area. If you are using several viewports, the rendering appears in the active viewport. You can also render to the Render Window. The render window is a regular Microsoft Windows window that lets you copy the rendering to the Clipboard or save the rendering as a bitmap (*.bmp*) file. Finally, you can save the rendering directly to a file.

✦ Use the Sub Sampling drop-down box to set the sampling of pixels that AutoCAD renders. The default is 1:1, which means all the pixels are rendered. You can speed up the rendering by choosing a lower ratio.

✦ The Render dialog box has buttons to take you to the Background and Fog/Depth Cue dialog boxes if you decide at the last minute that you want to use these features.

When you have finished the settings, click Render to render the drawing.

Step-by-Step: Creating the Final Rendering

On the CD-ROM

1. If you have *ab25-8.dwg* open, use it. Otherwise, open it from your *AutoCAD Bible* folder if you did the previous exercise or from the *Results* folder of the CD-ROM.

2. Save it as *ab25-9.dwg* in your *AutoCAD Bible* folder.

3. Choose Render from the Render toolbar.

4. Set the rendering type to Photo Real.

5. The scene to render should be set to MORNING. Shadows should be checked.

6. Choose Lights from the Render toolbar. In the Lights box, choose P1 and click Modify. Change the Intensity to 200 and click OK twice to return to your drawing. This is the type of adjustment you often make when doing the final rendering.

7. Click Render. Wait until AutoCAD finishes the rendering. Look at those shadows! Look at the transparent green bowl with the orange in it. Note the sky image outside the window. Okay, so the pink marble is a bit gaudy.

8. The rendering should look like Figure 25-24, only a lot better because you see it in color on your screen. Save your drawing

Remember that rendering is a trial-and-error process. Don't expect to get it right the first time. You can probably see several areas for improvement. At this point, you would go back and tweak the lights, materials, and so on until you were satisfied.

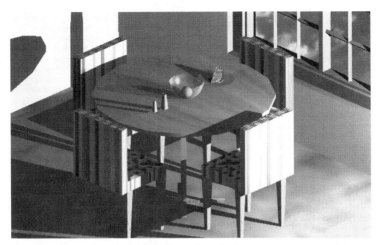

Figure 25-24: The final rendering with shadows, transparent objects, and a background.

Credit: Thanks to Autodesk for the *sky.gif* file. This material has been reprinted with permission from and under the copyright of Autodesk, Inc.

Statistics

Choose Statistics on the Render toolbar to open a window that lists statistics relating to your rendering. You can save these to a file. This information is very helpful if you can't remember which rendering type you used or if you want to compare the time it takes to render a scene using different options. Figure 25-25 shows an example.

Figure 25-25: A statistics listing of a rendering.

Saving rendered images

You can save your rendered images and redisplay them at another time. You can also use saved rendered images in other applications and print them from those applications.

After rendering to a viewport, choose Tools⇨Display Image⇨Save. In the Save Image dialog box, choose the file type — *.bmp*, *.tga*, or *.tif*.

If you wish, you can change the size and placement (offset) of the image or accept the defaults. Click OK. AutoCAD opens the Image File dialog box so you can specify a file name. Click OK.

After rendering to a Render Window, choose File⇨Save from that window's menu and enter a filename. Click OK. AutoCAD saves the image as a *.bmp* (bitmap) file.

To redisplay a rendered image, choose Tools⇨Display Image⇨View. Choose the file and click Open in the Replay dialog box. You have the opportunity to crop the image or you can accept the original size. AutoCAD displays the image. Do a regen to return to your regular drawing display.

Cross-Reference

You can import these saved rendered images back into your drawing. Figure 25-26 shows three floating viewports. One of the views shows the rendered image. See Chapter 27 for detailed instructions on importing images.

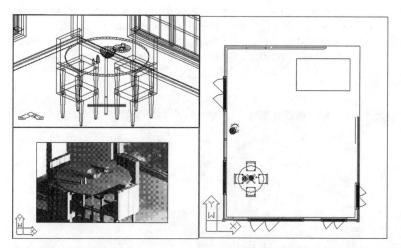

Figure 25-26: You can include your rendered images in your drawings.

Unloading Render

The procedure for unloading Render has changed, and the RENDERUNLOAD command no longer exists. To unload Render, follow these steps:

1. Type **arx** ↵.

2. At the `?/Load/Unload/Commands/Options:` prompt, type **u** ↵ to use the Unload option.

3. At the `Unload ARX file:` prompt, type **render** ↵.

4. AutoCAD informs you that Render was unloaded.

This frees up memory for other tasks.

Summary

In this chapter I covered a great deal of material related to rendering, including creating lights, creating scenes, importing and creating materials, attaching materials, using backgrounds, and the actual rendering process itself.

This chapter ends Part IV, Drawing in Three Dimensions. Part V, Organizing and Managing Drawings, explains how to manage drawings, work with other applications and file types, and use AutoCAD on the Internet.

✦   ✦   ✦

Organizing and Managing Drawings

This part is all about how to manage drawings.

In Chapter 26, I discuss how to keep control of your drawings by setting standards, controlling access on a network, working with prior AutoCAD releases, and other techniques. Chapter 27 explains how to interface with other applications and file formats. Finally, Chapter 28 explains how to get your drawings onto the Internet.

Keeping Control of Your Drawings

✦ ✦ ✦ ✦

In This Chapter

Setting standards for drawings

Keeping track of your drawings

Using AutoCAD on a network

Auditing and recovering damaged drawings

Working with prior AutoCAD releases

✦ ✦ ✦ ✦

Setting Standards for Drawings

One person rarely has complete control over a drawing. You may xref in other drawings, or others may xref in your drawings. Several people may work on one drawing. You may send a drawing to a client who may work on it as well. More and more, working in AutoCAD is becoming a collaborative effort — and it can get out of control.

One way to get in control is to set standards for drawings — and issue those standards so that everyone involved has access to them. If you don't have agreed-upon standards, you not only waste time changing layers, text styles, and so on, but your drawings get very complicated. You should set standards for the following:

- ✦ Drawing names
- ✦ Blocks, including names, layers, and insertion points
- ✦ Layers, including uses, names, colors, and linetypes
- ✦ Text styles, including uses, names, and properties
- ✦ Dimension styles and tolerances, if any
- ✦ Multiline styles
- ✦ Units settings
- ✦ Limits settings
- ✦ Standardized viewport configurations
- ✦ Standardized drawing sizes

In some cases, your standards are set by outside conventions. For example, the American Institute of Architects (AIA) and the Construction Standards Institute (CSI) publish layering standards for members.

You need to consider who may use your drawings. For example, if your clients do not have Windows 95 or NT, and they access your drawings, you may have to restrict yourself to eight-character filenames. If you use coded names, such as *97GR134.dwg*, you may want to keep a list of the drawing names with a description of the drawing next to it.

Keeping Track of Your Drawings

Some offices keep track of thousands of drawings. You must not only track your drawings but also make sure you don't lose them!

Archiving drawings

You should use AutoCAD's Autosave feature to save a backup of the drawing to the hard drive every 15 to 20 minutes. The default is a ridiculous 120 minutes. Choose Tools⇨Preferences⇨General tab and change the Automatic Save setting. Click OK.

Backing up to the hard drive doesn't provide sufficient security. Hard drives can fail. Every time you exit AutoCAD, you should back up every drawing you worked on to some type of external storage medium. Backing up drawings for storage is called *archiving*.

**On the
CD-ROM**

On the CD-ROM, I include an AutoLISP program, *savea.lsp,* that backs up to the *a:* drive without leaving your drawing. This lets you back up while working on a drawing. See the *Software\Chap01\Savea* folder of the CD-ROM.

Some drawings are too large to fit on a diskette, and the number of diskettes you need to store all your drawings may be too great for easy storage. You will probably want to invest in one of the many types of removable backup systems. These come in four main types:

- ✦ Tape drives — internal or external — are cheap and good for entire hard drive backups.

- ✦ Disk cartridge drives offer the convenience of a diskette but with more capacity.

- ✦ Read/write CD-ROM drives let you write to a CD-ROM as you would to a diskette.

- ✦ Optical drives have the longest life (at least 30 years) and resist accidental erasure.

If your drawings are *really* important to you, back them up twice and store one backup set off-site. That way, if your office burns down, you haven't lost everything. There are remote backup services that provide this type of archiving for you, and you can access your files via modem or the Internet.

The secret to backing up is to create a schedule and then stick to it. For example, you may do a complete hard drive backup once a week, and drawing backups at the end of each day. Each situation is different, but take the time to think about your needs, create the system, and let everybody know about it. Then do it.

Finding drawings

Let's say your client calls and says, "I want to see the apartment building on Fourth Street that we did two years ago." How do you find the drawing, especially if you were working on a DOS system two years ago and the drawing names were short and inexplicable?

One low-tech way is to keep a book of $8\frac{1}{2} \times 11$ plots. Using Release 14's new Batch Plot Utility, you can plot out a week's drawings overnight and put them in a book. Amazingly, it doesn't take that long to leaf through even a few hundred pages. (You usually have *some* idea of when you did the drawing.)

Tip

Place the drawing name and date written in large text on a separate layer in the drawing. Freeze the layer for regular plots and thaw it for your batch plots. Then, even reduced, you'll know the drawing name when you look at the drawing in the book. Or, use the Batch Plot Utility's plot stamping feature.

There are a number of third-party drawing management programs available. Some of these let you view and manage drawings created in other CAD programs as well. Some also manage workflow by letting you route drawings to team members. A few of these are:

- ✦ AutoManager Workflow (404-634-3302)
- ✦ Aimaview (www.aimasoft.com)
- ✦ CADEXNET (415-593-3477)
- ✦ DDS Document Database Systems (504-297-9321)
- ✦ Slick! ForWindows (www.slickwin.com)
- ✦ Autodesk's own WorkCenter and WorkCenter for the Web (415-507-5000)

Release 14

Before backing up drawings, purge any unused layers, blocks, text styles, and so on. Release 14's PURGE command has a great new option that lets you purge them without having to approve each one individually. At the `Verify each name to be purged? <Y>` prompt, type **n** ↵, and AutoCAD purges without further input from you.

Album is freeware that displays small windows of all the drawings in a folder.
Figure 26-1 shows a sample screen. You can't print out the display but you can
either drag and drop to insert the file into AutoCAD or double-click to open
AutoCAD with the selected file. Album can also be used as a simple block manager.
Look in *\Software\Chap26\Album*.

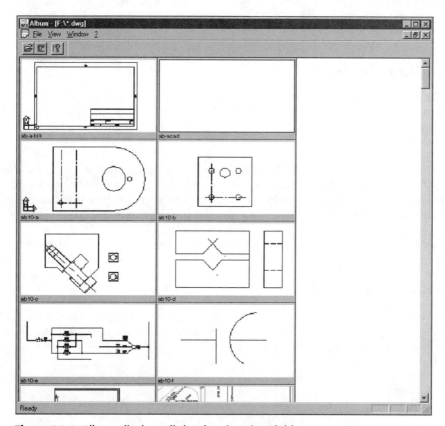

Figure 26-1: Album displays all the drawings in a folder.

Finding drawings from within AutoCAD

If you know a drawing is on the hard drive, you can use the Browse or Search
functions. Click Open on the Standard toolbar. In the Select File dialog box, find the
folder you want. Choose Find File. The Browse tab of the Browse/Search dialog box
shows you images of all the drawings in the folder, similar to the display created
with Album.

Using AutoCAD on a Network

Although an in-depth analysis of networks is beyond the scope of this book, a few pointers may be helpful.

There are two types of networks — client/server and peer-to-peer.

Client/server networks use a *server* — a powerful computer that stores the applications and data files for all users. Users work on regular desktop computers that act as *clients* — they have access to the applications and data available from the server.

Peer-to-peer networks simply connect computers of equal status. You can still designate one computer to store necessary shared files such as those in the *Support* folder. This makes it easier to update and control the files that are used by everyone.

Release 14 no longer contains a file-locking mechanism to control access to drawings. Instead, the Windows operating system handles file locking.

Networks have a *system administrator* who is responsible for the following:

✦ Determining where the *Support*, *Sample*, and other shared folders (such as block libraries and custom fonts) are located

✦ Controlling drawing access

✦ Managing multiple configurations

✦ Maintaining the backup system

When you are on a network, it often does not pay to buy a *seat* (an instance) of AutoCAD for every computer. You may not have someone working on AutoCAD on every computer all day. Network, or site, licensing offers more flexibility, and lets a certain number of people open AutoCAD, regardless of which machine they are using.

Release 14 introduces a new system for network licensing, called Autodesk License Manager.

Autodesk lists these advantages:

✦ Any user can open AutoCAD until the total number of seats of the license are reached, and individual users can open multiple sessions of AutoCAD on their computer.

✦ You can add additional seats by entering a new authorization code.

✦ No hardware locks are required for installation.

✦ There is more flexibility for different configurations and installation options.

Release 14 also includes improvements in its handling of shared printing on networks. You can configure Release 14 to plot directly to the network print queue with a simpler print setup. Also, support for the system print spooler is available even with nonsystem ADI drivers.

Handling Errors and Crashes

Release 14 is probably the most stable release of AutoCAD ever. In addition, Windows 95 and especially Windows NT are more stable than Windows 3.1. However, nothing can eliminate the occasional crash.

Managing the Windows swap file

The most common cause of crashes is probably lack of computer memory. Note that Windows 95 and NT use a variable-size swap file that uses your hard drive's free space when there is not enough memory. Therefore, it is important to leave enough free space on your hard drive to let the swap file wax and wane as necessary.

If you have a partitioned hard drive or more than one hard drive, you can gain some advantage by moving the swap file to a drive that is faster or has more room. Here's how to move the swap file in Windows 95:

1. Before you start, close all applications.

2. Click the Start button.

3. Choose Settings.

4. Click Control Panel.

5. Double-click the System icon to open the System Properties dialog box.

6. Choose the Performance tab.

7. Click Virtual Memory to open the Virtual Memory dialog box, shown in Figure 26-2. This window comes with a warning that changing the settings should be done only by advanced users. The default selection is to let Windows manage your virtual memory settings.

8. Choose `Let me specify my own virtual memory settings`. The current settings are grayed out and you can see which hard disk contains the swap file and how much free space it has. (You can also disable virtual memory — not recommended!)

9. Click the Hard disk drop-down list. A list of your hard drives drops down, including the free space on each.

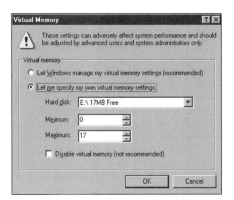

Figure 26-2: The Virtual Memory dialog box.

10. Select a new drive, preferably one that is faster, or has more free space. Click OK. A warning message appears, asking if you are sure you want to do this.

11. If you're sure, click OK.

12. Click OK to close the System Performance window and click the Close box to close the Control Panel.

Taking care of temporary files

When AutoCAD is loaded it opens one or more temporary files as part of its normal functioning. There are two points to note regarding these files:

✦ You need to leave room on your hard drive for these files — 50 MB is a good starting point.

✦ Never erase current temporary files if you are on a network because someone else might be using them.

Never erase these files (they have an extension of *.ac$*) while AutoCAD is open.

However, if AutoCAD or your entire computer crashes, you will probably be left with one or more *.ac$* files. These should be erased. Figure 26-3 shows some temporary AutoCAD files (as well as others), displayed in Windows Explorer.

A good guideline for erasing *ac$* files is to only erase those from yesterday or earlier. Leave today's alone.

If you don't see the date and time of the files in Explorer, choose View⇨Details.

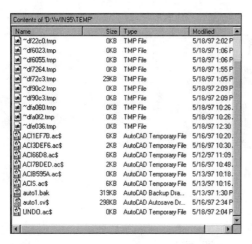

Figure 26-3: AutoCAD and other temporary files.

You can also specify where AutoCAD places these temporary files. You might want to place them on a hard drive with more room. If you are on a network, you might want to place them on your local drive so there is less traffic back and forth on the network. If you don't specify the temporary file location, AutoCAD places temporary files in the Windows 95 temporary folder (probably *c:\win95\temp*). Here's how to change the location:

1. In AutoCAD, choose Tools⇨Preferences. The Files tab should be on top.

2. Click the plus sign next to Temporary Drawing File Location to open the current location, as shown in Figure 26-4.

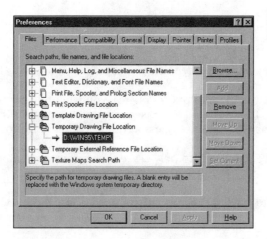

Figure 26-4: The Files tab of the Preferences dialog box.

3. Click the current location and click Browse.

4. In the Browse for Folder list, find and choose the desired folder and click OK.

5. Click OK to close the Preferences dialog box.

Opening new instances of AutoCAD

Remember that AutoCAD can still open only one drawing at a time. If you need to open more than one drawing, you need to open more than one instance of AutoCAD. This takes up a lot of memory. Save your current drawing *before* opening another AutoCAD session.

Repairing corrupted drawing files

The most common cause for a corrupted drawing file is an AutoCAD crash, but power surges and system crashes can also be causes. If AutoCAD detects an error in a file during loading, it attempts to fix the problem automatically. In many cases, it is successful.

When it is not, you can try AutoCAD's AUDIT or RECOVER commands. These commands search the database for errors and try to fix them. If they cannot fix an error, they simply move on, letting you recover at least part of the file.

If you have a drawing open and get an error message that AutoCAD can't read the file or part of it, follow these steps:

1. Choose File⇨Drawing Utilities⇨Audit.

2. At the `Fix any errors detected? <N>` prompt, type **y** ↵. This tells AutoCAD to fix any errors it finds.

3. Watch the screen as it displays messages for errors.

Use RECOVER when you can't even load the drawing. Follow these steps:

1. Open a new drawing.

2. Choose File⇨Drawing Utilities⇨Recover.

3. In the Recover Drawing File dialog box, choose the corrupted drawing file and click Open. AutoCAD begins recovery and displays the results in the text window.

Using backup drawings

If you can't repair a drawing, hopefully you have a backup copy you can use. If not, AutoCAD automatically creates backup drawings that have the same name as your drawings but a *.bak* extension. You can change the extension to *.dwg* and open it. You may also find one of the *.ac$* drawings. You can also try changing the extension of this file to *.dwg*. The temporary files are less likely to be useful, however.

If you want to troubleshoot a persistent crash, try turning on the log file. Choose Tools⇨Preferences and choose the General tab. Check `Maintain a log file`. This log file lists all your activity and can be used to try to determine what actions cause a crash. You can also customize the log file's location using the Files tab of the Preferences dialog box.

Taking care of your hard disk after a crash

After your hard disk crashes, you should run ScanDisk. Choose Start⇨Programs⇨Accessories⇨ScanDisk. This deletes lost chains and clusters, which are orphaned bits of data that are not in a file.

It's also a good idea to defragment your hard drive regularly. Files become *fragmented,* meaning that they are stored in noncontiguous locations on your hard drive. This slows down disk access. Choose Start⇨Programs⇨Accessories⇨Disk Defragmenter.

Managing Drawings in Prior Releases

Earlier releases of AutoCAD cannot read Release 14 drawings. Release 14 reads Release 12 and Release 13 drawings automatically. (Some of the drawings contributed for this book were done in Release 12 or Release 13 and opened in Release 14.)

However, you can easily save your Release 14 drawings in Release 12 or 13 format, as well as in AutoCAD LT 2 and AutoCAD LT 95 formats. Just choose File⇨Save As and choose the file type in the Save as type drop-down list. Then AutoCAD Release 12 and 13 users can open your drawings.

A nice feature of Release 14 is that objects specific to Release 14, such as lightweight polylines and hatches, make the round trip intact. When you save to Release 12 or 13 format, the lightweight polylines are converted to regular polylines. When you open those drawings in Release 14, they are automatically converted to lightweight polylines again.

Summary

In this chapter I covered various methods for managing drawings, both in your regular routine and when something goes wrong. I also explained how AutoCAD is used on a network. Finally I gave some pointers for working with prior releases of AutoCAD.

In the next chapter, I cover how to use AutoCAD with other applications.

✦   ✦   ✦

Working with Other Applications

✦ ✦ ✦ ✦

In This Chapter

Importing and exporting other file formats

Working with raster images

Pasting, linking, and embedding objects

✦ ✦ ✦ ✦

Coordinating AutoCAD and Other Data

AutoCAD is not a world unto itself. Many times you need to work with files or data from other applications. Here are some possibilities:

✦ Working for a client who uses another CAD program

✦ Placing a logo into your title block

✦ Inserting an AutoCAD drawing into a report

✦ Inserting a spreadsheet into your AutoCAD drawing

✦ Using a satellite photo as a basis to create a map

There are several ways of working with other applications:

✦ You can import another file format so that the entire file is brought into AutoCAD.

✦ You can export to another file format so that the entire drawing can be imported into another application.

✦ You can import a *raster* image without changing any file format. A raster image is made up of dots, called *pixels*, as opposed to vectors. AutoCAD is a vector program.

✦ You can import, or export to, a DXF file, which is a way of interchanging drawings between AutoCAD and other CAD programs.

As you can imagine, the possibilities are endless. This chapter explains how to work with other applications, including Release 14's improved support for raster images.

Importing and Exporting Other File Formats

AutoCAD can export to several other file formats. This means that you save the file in another format. You can also import several formats. This section explains how to do both.

Exporting to other file formats

Table 27-1 shows the file formats AutoCAD can create. Except as noted, you are prompted to select objects to export.

Table 27-1 Export File Formats	
Format	**Description**
WMF	(Windows Metafile Format); a Windows vector format
ACIS	A solid modeling file format stored as *.sat* files, in text (ASCII) form
STL	Exports a single solid only in a format usable with stereo-lithography apparatus.
BMP	(Windows bitmap); a raster format
EPS	(Encapsulated PostScript); a format used by certain printers to create high-quality text and images. Exports all objects.
DXX Extract	A text file containing only block attributes. A variation of DXF format that is used to extract attributes.
3DS	The format used by Autodesk's 3D Studio
DXF	(Drawing Interchange Format); a text format for CAD drawings that most CAD programs accept. There is also a *DXB* format, which is a binary file (not text) and is used less often. You can choose from Release 14, 13, and 12 DXF file formats. Exports the entire drawing.
DWF	(Drawing Web Format); a format for placing a drawing on a Web site

Cross-Reference

The DWF file format is covered in the next chapter.

Figure 27-1 shows the part of a DXF file that defines a line. Not only are all objects defined, but all layers, linetypes, and other settings are defined as well. Between the actual drawing data, AutoCAD places codes that specify what the data refers to. Since most CAD programs accept this format, you can export to DXF and send the file to someone else who can import it into another CAD program.

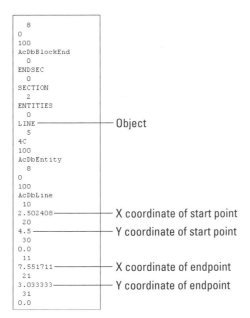

Figure 27-1: The DXF file format is accepted by most CAD programs.

To export a drawing to another format, follow these steps:

1. Choose File⇨Export to open the Export Data dialog box, shown in Figure 27-2.

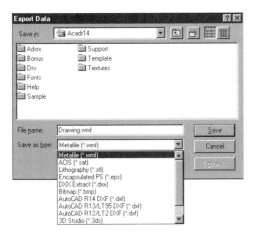

Figure 27-2: The Export Data dialog box.

2. Choose the file format you want in the Save as type drop-down list.

3. Find the desired folder using the Save in drop-down list and the Folder box.

4. If the Options button is available, click it to access options for the type of file you are exporting. These options are different for each type of file. Specify the desired options and click OK.

5. Click Save.

Step-by-Step: Exporting a WMF File

On the CD-ROM

1. Open *ab27-a.dwg* from the CD-ROM.

2. Save it as *ab27-1.dwg* in your *AutoCAD Bible* folder.

3. Choose File➪Export. The Save as type drop-down list should say `Metafile` (`*.wmf`). The filename automatically reads *ab27-1.wmf*.

4. If necessary, locate your *AutoCAD Bible* folder. Choose Save.

5. At the `Select objects:` prompt, make a window around the red rectangle to include all three objects. End object selection to end the command.

6. Save your drawing.

You have created a WMF file.

Importing other file formats

For most file formats, choose Insert from the menu and then the file type you want to import. Find the file in the dialog box and click Open. AutoCAD then prompts you for an insertion point, X and Y scale factors, and a rotation angle, just like block insertion.

Each of the Import dialog boxes are slightly different depending on the type of file you are importing. Most have an Options button that you can use to customize how AutoCAD imports the file.

AutoCAD does not include the DXF format on the Insert menu.

Release 14

To import drawing settings stored in a DXF file, you should import DXF files into a new drawing so that there is no conflict with current settings. Even if you want to insert a DXF file into an existing drawing, you should first import the DXF file into a new drawing, save the drawing, then insert the new drawing into the existing drawing.

To import a DXF file, follow these steps:

1. Start a new drawing using the Start from Scratch option in the Create New Drawing dialog box.

2. Choose Open from the Standard toolbar.

3. In the Select File dialog box, choose DXF from the File of type drop-down list box.

4. Locate and choose the DXF file.

5. Click Open. AutoCAD converts the DXF file to a drawing file.

In the following Step-by-Step, you import a WMF file.

Step-by-Step: Importing a .WMF File

1. Open a new drawing using the *acad.dwt* template.

2. Save it as *ab27-2.dwg* in your *AutoCAD Bible* folder.

3. Choose Insert⇨Windows Metafile.

On the CD-ROM

4. If you did the last Step-by-Step exercise, locate your *AutoCAD Bible* folder in the Import WMF dialog box. Choose *ab27-1.wmf.* If you didn't do the last exercise, find *ab27-1.wmf* in the *Results* folder of the CD-ROM. Choose Options, check Wire Frame (No Fill), and click OK. Click Open.

5. At the `Insertion point:` prompt, pick any point near the top of your screen. Notice that the insertion point is at the top-left corner of the image.

6. Press Enter to accept the defaults for X and Y scales and rotation angle. Notice that you've lost the text font and the solid fill in the logo. The red rectangle came in fine. Also, AutoCAD has added a rectangle around the extents of the image where the extents of the screen were when the WMF was created.

7. Pick the image. Notice that AutoCAD selects everything with one grip at the insertion point. Choose Explode from the Modify toolbar.

8. Choose List from Tools⇨Inquiry and pick any part of the logo. Press Enter. Notice from the listing that AutoCAD has converted everything to polylines. Repeat the LIST command with the text. It has been converted to a TEXT object. Because AutoCAD converts WMF files to AutoCAD objects, you can edit them, but they may require a good deal of cleanup to attain a pleasing result.

9. Choose Format⇨Text Style. Choose New and type **book** in the Style Name text box. Click OK. From the Font Name drop-down list, choose Book Antiqua. From the Font Style drop-down list, choose Bold Italic. Choose Apply, then click Close. (If you don't have Book Antiqua, choose another font.)

10. Choose Insert⇨Windows Metafile. Choose *ab27-1.wmf.* Click Options to open the Import Options (WMF In) dialog box, as shown in Figure 27-3. This time check Wide Lines, uncheck Wire Frame, and click OK. In the Import WMF dialog box, choose Open to import the file. Choose a different location in your drawing. Notice that this time, the entire outer rectangle is filled in.

Figure 27-3: The Import Options (WMF In) dialog box.

11. Explode the rectangle. (You may have to pick it at its edge.) Erase the rectangle and the line at the right that remains. Now you have an image that is very close to the original. The text comes in with the Book Antiqua font (or the font you used — the same font as the original), although the spacing is not exact. Also, the logo now has its solid fill.

12. Save your drawing. It should look like Figure 27-4.

Figure 27-4: Your drawing with an imported WMF file using different text styles and WMF options.

Later in this chapter I show how you can create a WMF file from almost any image by copying it to the Clipboard. Since AutoCAD converts these files to AutoCAD objects, you have almost limitless possibilities when importing images into AutoCAD.

Working with Raster Images

While Release 13 introduced support for raster (bitmap) images, Release 14 has gone further to make it possible to create combination raster/vector drawings. You can now easily import scanned images and digital photographs into your drawings. Although raster images are generally much larger files than vector drawings, Release 14 lets you quickly zoom and pan throughout your drawing. There is greater support for plotting these raster images as well. Table 27-2 shows the raster formats that Release 14 supports.

Table 27-2		
Raster Formats Supported by AutoCAD 14		
File Type	*File Extension*	*Comments*
BMP	.bmp, .dib, .rle	Windows bitmap
CALS-I	.gp4, .mil, .rst, .cg4, .cal	Mil-R-Raster I
GIF	.gif	CompuServe Graphics Exchange Format
JFIF	.jpg	JPEG
FLIC	.flc, .fli	Animator FLIC
PCX	.pcx	PaintBrush
PICT	.pct	Macintosh picture
PNG	.png	
TARGA	.tga	
TIF/LZW	.tif	Tagged Image File Format

Images may be two-tones (bitonal), 8-bit gray scale, 8-bit color, or 24-bit color.

Inserting images

To insert an image, choose Insert⇨Raster Image to open the Image dialog box, shown in Figure 27-5.

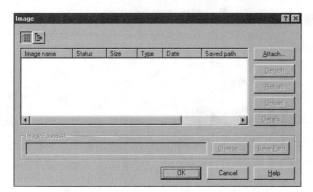

Figure 27-5: The Image dialog box.

If you are having a sense of déjà vu, it's because this dialog box looks just like the External Reference dialog box. This new Image Manager lets you control raster images in the same way you control external references. The Image Manager offers you both control and flexibility.

Choose Attach in the Image dialog box to open the Attach Image File dialog box shown in Figure 27-6. Locate and choose the file that you want to attach and click Open.

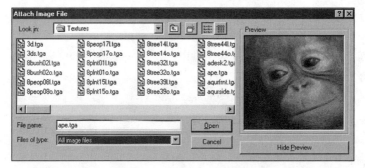

Figure 27-6: The Attach Image File dialog box.

AutoCAD now opens the Attach Image dialog box, shown in Figure 27-7, which lets you specify how to insert the image.

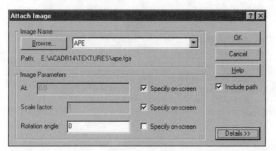

Figure 27-7: The Attach Image dialog box.

You can specify the insertion point, scale, and rotation in the dialog box or on screen.

Note The insertion point is at the bottom-left corner of the image.

Check Include path if you don't plan to move the image file's location and if the file is not in AutoCAD's *support* file or *project* file search path. The support and project search paths can be customized by choosing Tools⇨Preferences and using the Files tab.

Choose Details to open the bottom of the dialog box, shown in Figure 27-8.

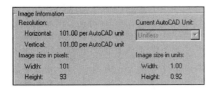

Figure 27-8: The Details section of the Attach Image dialog box.

Here AutoCAD lists the resolution (number of pixels) per drawing unit and the size in pixels, as well as the size in drawing units. You can use the Current AutoCAD Unit drop-down list to specify which unit AutoCAD should use when calculating the scale as you insert the drawing. This function is only available when resolution information is included with the image.

Note Raster images don't scale very well. If you enlarge them too much, the dots get too far apart and the image looks grainy.

Click OK to insert the image.

Managing images

Just as you can manage external references from the External Reference dialog box, you can manage your images from the Image dialog box. You can use the List view and Tree view buttons at the top of the dialog box to view your images in a *flat* list or a hierarchical (tree) format. Here are the other options:

✦ **Detach** erases the image from your drawing and deletes all reference to it in the drawing database.

✦ **Reload** redisplays an image after you have unloaded it.

✦ **Unload** removes the display of the image but retains the reference to it. Later, you can reload the image to redisplay it.

✦ **Details** provides you with a preview, as well as information about the image, its path, and its size.

✦ The **Image Found At** box shows you the location of the image. If you didn't save a path when attaching the image, you can do so by clicking Save Path. You can also find an image whose Status shows Not Found by choosing Browse. This would happen if you moved the image after attaching it.

You can attach rendered images that you have saved as TIF, TGA, or BMP files. A great way to do this is to create a floating viewport in paper space for the rendered image, letting your clients see not only the regular drawing but the rendered result on one sheet of paper. Figure 25-26 in Chapter 25 was created this way.

Clipping images

A powerful new feature of Release 14 lets you clip images just as you clip external references. Because images increase file size so dramatically, they can slow down your drawing. You may also simply find it distracting to see parts of an image that you don't need for your work. For example, if you attach an aerial photograph of a city block, but want only one house, it is a great advantage to be able to clip around the house and not display the rest of the image.

To clip an image, follow these steps:

1. Attach an image.

2. Choose Modify⇨Object⇨Image Clip.

3. At the Select image to clip: prompt, select the image.

4. At the prompt, press Enter to accept the default of creating a new clipping boundary.

5. At the Polygonal/<Rectangular>: prompt, press Enter to create a rectangular clip or type **p** to create a multisided boundary.

6a. For a rectangular boundary, pick a first point and the opposite corner to create the boundary.

6b. For a polygonal boundary, use the Close/Undo/<Next point>: prompt to pick points until you have completed the boundary. You can use the Undo option to undo the last pick or Close to close the final boundary. AutoCAD creates a rubber-band boundary as you pick points so you can see the result. Press Enter when you are done.

At the ON/OFF/Delete/<New boundary>: prompt, you can also use the following options:

✦ Choose ON to turn on a boundary that you previously turned off.

✦ Choose OFF to turn off a boundary and redisplay the entire image.

✦ Choose Delete to delete the clipping boundary.

Note

Images are 2D objects. The clipping boundary must be parallel to the plane of the image.

Controlling image display

Release 14

You can now control several aspects of image display using several new commands detailed in this section.

Image Display

Choose Modify➪Object➪Image➪Adjust to start the IMAGEDISPLAY command and open the Image Adjust dialog box, shown in Figure 27-9.

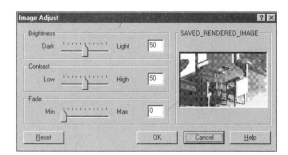

Figure 27-9: The Image Adjust dialog box.

This dialog box lets you dynamically change the brightness, contrast, and fade of the image, using the slider bars or text boxes. You immediately see the results in the preview box. Choose Reset to return the image to its original status.

Tip

If you know the settings you want by number, you can type **-imagedisplay** on the command line, which lets you select more than one image at a time. You then need to specify the brightness, contrast, and fade settings on the command line. This would be useful if you wanted to adjust a number of images at one time.

Image Quality

Choose Modify➪Object➪Image➪Quality to start the IMAGEQUALITY command. AutoCAD displays the High/Draft <Draft>: prompt. Choose either High or Draft. This command affects the display of all the images in a drawing. Use it when a high-quality image slows down performance. A regen is not necessary after you change this setting. Plotting is always done at high quality.

Image Transparency

If the image format you are using supports transparent pixels, you can use the new TRANSPARENCY command to create a transparent background for your image. This works for bitonal or gray-scale images. By default, transparency is off.

To turn transparency on, choose Modify⇨Object⇨Image⇨Transparency and select the image(s) you want to change. At the `ON/OFF <OFF>:` prompt, type **on** ↵ and do a regen. Other objects in your drawing will now be visible through the background of your image.

Image Frame

The new IMAGEFRAME command turns off the frame that surrounds all images in a drawing. Choose Modify⇨Object⇨Image⇨Frame. Turning off the frame often improves the way the image looks. However, you select an image by clicking its frame. Therefore, an Off setting means you cannot select the image!

Tip

Don't turn the frame off until you have finished editing the image.

Step-by-Step: Working with Raster Images

On the
CD-ROM

1. Open *ab27-b.dwg* from the CD-ROM.

2. Save it as *ab27-3.dwg* in your *AutoCAD Bible* folder.

3. Choose Top View from the Viewpoint flyout of the Standard toolbar.

4. Choose Insert⇨Raster Image. In the Image dialog box, choose Attach.

On the
CD-ROM

5. In the Attach Image File dialog box, choose *ab27-b.tif* from the CD-ROM. Click Open. Choose Details. Notice that the image is 1 × .61 units. Compared to the house, it is tiny.

6. In the Attach Image dialog box, uncheck Specify on-screen for the Scale factor and change the scale factor to 5. Click OK.

7. At the `Insertion point <0,0>:` prompt, pick any point on the left side of the screen. The image is still tiny, but that's okay. Choose Zoom Window from the Zoom flyout of the Standard toolbar to zoom closely into the image.

8. Choose Modify⇨Object⇨Image⇨Adjust. At the `Select image to adjust:` prompt, select the image by picking its frame. In the Image Adjust dialog box, change the Contrast to 60 and the Brightness to 40. Choose OK.

9. Choose Modify⇨Object⇨Image Clip. At the `Select image to clip:` prompt, select the image again, which is shown in Figure 27-10. Follow the prompts:

```
ON/OFF/Delete/<New boundary>: ↵
Polygonal/<Rectangular>: ↵
First point: Pick ① in Figure 27-10.
Select second corner: Pick ②.
```

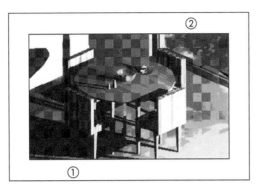

Figure 27-10: Clipping the raster image.

10. Use Zoom Realtime to zoom out so you have room to insert another image. Choose Insert⇨Raster Image and attach *ab27-b1.bmp* (located on the CD-ROM) with a scale factor of 2. Insert it below the first image.

11. Double-click TILE on the Status bar to enter paper space, which has three floating viewports. Double-click PAPER to enter model space. Click the bottom left viewport. Choose Top View from the Viewpoints flyout. You should now see the images as a small dot to the left of the house. Use Zoom Window to zoom into the rendered table. Your drawing should now look like Figure 27-11.

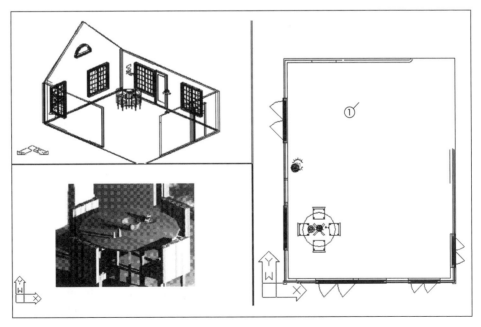

Figure 27-11: The drawing with a rendered view in one viewport.

12. Click the right viewport. If necessary, pan the house to the right until you can see the two images you attached. Move the Cottonmill Houses image to ① in Figure 27-11. Scale it, using a scale factor of 100. Move it until it fits nicely in the upper right corner of the floor plan. Pan again to center the house in the viewport.

13. Choose Modify⇨Object⇨Image⇨Frame. Type **off** ↵. AutoCAD removes the frames from the two images.

14. Save your drawing.

The DRAWORDER command changes the display order of objects, including raster and OLE objects. This command is very helpful when working with raster and OLE objects, where you may or may not want to hide the other objects in your drawing. You can move an object to the top or bottom or change its order in relation to another object — above or below it.

To change an object's display order, choose Tools⇨Display Order and choose one of the submenu options. AutoCAD then prompts you to select objects.

Pasting, Linking, and Embedding Objects

In Chapter 18, I explain how to use the Windows Clipboard to copy and move material from one drawing to another.

There are three ways your can insert data (text or images) created with other applications into an AutoCAD drawing:

✦ *Embed* the object to retain the ability to return to the source application to edit the object. When you double-click the object, the source application opens so that you can edit the object.

✦ *Paste* the object when you don't need any connection with the source application — perhaps you want to be able to edit it using AutoCAD or you just want to display it.

✦ *Link* the object when you want to retain a permanent link to the source file so that when the source file is changed the change is updated in your AutoCAD file.

In this chapter, I explain how to use the Clipboard to move material from one application to another, taking advantage of the special options for pasting, linking, and embedding data. Linking and embedding are often referred to as *OLE* — Object Linking and Embedding. You can also use drag-and-drop between applications.

The instructions in this section assume that the source application — the application that contains the data you want to insert — is also a Windows 95 or Windows NT application.

Embedding objects into AutoCAD

There are three ways to embed data from other applications. Each method has its advantages and disadvantages.

Here's the first way:

1. From AutoCAD, choose Insert⇨OLE Object to open the Insert Object dialog box, shown in Figure 27-12. This starts the INSERTOBJ command.

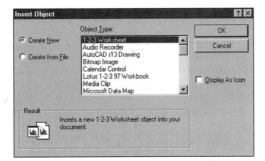

Figure 27-12: The Insert Object dialog box.

2. If you want to create a new file in the other application, choose Create New. Choose the application you want to use from the Object Type list. The other application opens, so you can create the new data.

3. When you are done, choose File⇨Update from the other application's menu. Click the Close button at the top right corner of the application to close it and return to AutoCAD. The new file has been inserted.

4. If you want to choose an existing file, choose Create From File. Click Browse to find the file. Click Insert. You return to the Insert Object file where you can choose Link to link the data (described in the next section of this chapter). Choose OK. AutoCAD places the file at the top left corner of your screen with handles that you can use to move and/or resize the object.

Here's the second way:

1. Open the source application, select the data, and copy it to the Clipboard. (Click Copy on the Standard toolbar or choose Edit⇨Copy.) Leave the source application open.

2. If AutoCAD is open, switch to it by choosing its button on the Taskbar. Otherwise, open it.

3. In your drawing choose Edit⇨Paste Special.

4. In the Paste Special dialog box, choose the first option, which lets you embed the object as an object of the source application. Click OK.

5. You can now close the other application.

The third way of inserting data is to use drag-and-drop:

1. If AutoCAD is not open, open it. Open the drawing where you want to embed the data.

2. Open the source application and select the data.

3. Press Ctrl and click the selected data again, holding down the mouse button.

4. Drag the data to the AutoCAD button on the Windows 95 Taskbar and continue to hold down the mouse button until the AutoCAD screen comes up.

5. Drag the data to the desired location in your drawing.

Note

This drag-and-drop technique doesn't work with all applications. It works with most word processors and spreadsheets, but not with most graphical applications. Also, you can't drag AutoCAD objects into another application.

Cross-Reference

In Chapter 18, I explain how to drag entire files into AutoCAD using drag-and-drop.

Using INSERTOBJ gives you the option of creating a new file on the spot in the other application. You don't have to keep the other application open when you return to AutoCAD. Note that you cannot create a link if you are creating a new file.

Using the Clipboard lets you insert part of a file — for example, part of a spreadsheet, which can be a great advantage. You need to keep the other application open until you paste the object into AutoCAD.

OLE objects have a few limitations in AutoCAD:

✦ If they are contained in a block or an external reference, they may not be displayed or plotted.

✦ Release 14 supports printing of embedded OLE objects with ADI (Autodesk Device Interface) drivers — the files that communicate between AutoCAD and your plotter or printer. In certain cases, OLE objects can be printed out only on Windows system printers. You can configure your plotter to be the system printer.

Note

The capability to print OLE objects using ADI drivers is included only in a Full installation or a Custom installation when you choose the OLE/ADI printing feature.

✦ If the embedded objects are raster images, you cannot print them with ADI drivers. Use the Windows system printer. You can also try embedding the object as a metafile (WMF) format.

Tip

If you try to use HIDE on a 3D model that contains OLE objects, the OLE objects disappear! The solution is to insert them in paper space. You can then hide the 3D model in one floating viewport and display the OLE object in another.

Using Paste Special

When you copy data to the Clipboard, it is stored in several formats, depending on the type of data. You can then choose which format you want to use when you paste it into your drawing, using the PASTESPEC command. Choosing the right format can make a big difference, allowing you to edit the data in your drawing as you wish.

Pasting data into AutoCAD

To paste data using PASTESPEC, open the source application, select the data, and copy it to the Clipboard. (Click Copy on the Standard toolbar or choose Edit⇨Copy.) Leave the source application open.

If AutoCAD is open, choose its button on the Taskbar. If not, open it.

In your drawing, choose Edit⇨Paste Special. This opens the Paste Special dialog box, shown in Figure 27-13. In this figure, you see the options available when you paste in a range of cells from a spreadsheet.

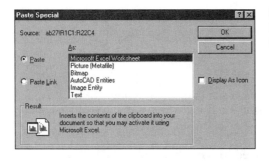

Figure 27-13: The Paste Special dialog box after copying spreadsheet data to the Clipboard.

The choices you see in the As box of the Paste Special dialog box depend on the type of data you copied. In most cases, you can paste as an object of the source application, as a picture (metafile), as a bitmap, and as text. Table 27-3 describes the characteristics of the six choices shown in Figure 27-13.

Table 27-3	
Paste Special Data Types	

Data Type	Characteristics
Object of source application	AutoCAD places the object at the top left corner of your drawing. You cannot explode the object, but you can select it and then resize it or move it using its handles. This is an embedded object — if you double-click it, the source application opens, letting you edit the object using the source application's tools.
Picture (Metafile)	AutoCAD places the object at the top left corner of your drawing. You cannot explode the object, but you can select it and then resize it or move it using its handles. You cannot edit the object using the source application (or using AutoCAD). It maintains good quality when scaled up.
Bitmap	AutoCAD places the object at the top left corner of your drawing. You cannot explode the object, but you can select it and then resize it or move it using its handles. You cannot edit the object using the source application (or using AutoCAD).
AutoCAD Entities	AutoCAD prompts for an insertion point, scale factor, and rotation angle. You can explode the object into AutoCAD objects. (Objects were once called entities in AutoCAD.) Text objects maintain their original font and formatting.
Image Entity	AutoCAD prompts for an insertion point, scale factor, and rotation angle. The object is inserted as a 1 × 1 unit square — approximately. It is a kind of bitmap. You can explode it, but then you lose the image!
Text	AutoCAD places the object at the top left corner of your drawing. You can explode it, but the text then loses the original formatting and font.

The best choice depends on the type of data you are pasting. For a spreadsheet, the Picture, Bitmap, and Image Entity choices are not useful, but they would be quite appropriate if you were pasting in an image.

Tip

Some pasted objects can be converted to other types of objects. Try right-clicking anywhere on the object that was pasted. If you get a menu, choose Convert Picture Object to open the Convert dialog box, shown in Figure 27-14. Sometimes there are no choices available other than the current image type. Figure 27-14 shows how you can choose to convert a Picture object to a Paintbrush Picture.

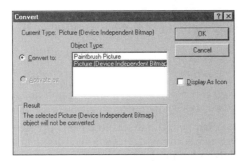

Figure 27-14: Sometimes you can convert one object type into another with the Convert dialog box.

Pasting AutoCAD objects into another application

You can also copy AutoCAD objects to the Clipboard and paste them into another application, such as a word processing document, a spreadsheet, or a presentation program. Figure 27-15 shows a PowerPoint presentation that includes a model from an AutoCAD drawing. To paste AutoCAD objects into another application, select the objects you want to copy. Click Copy on the Standard toolbar. Load the other application (in this case PowerPoint), create a document or file (in this case a slide), and click Paste from the application's Standard toolbar.

You can hide a 3D view and copy and paste the view into another application. However, you cannot copy and paste a rendered view. To bring a rendered view into another application, save it as an image and import it. Saving rendered images is covered in Chapter 25.

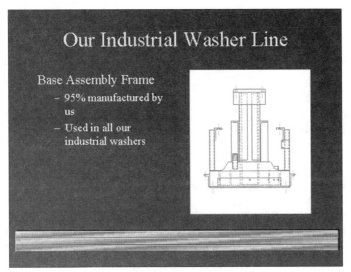

Figure 27-15: Placing part of an AutoCAD drawing on a PowerPoint slide.

Tip

You can freeze any layers that you don't want to include, such as dimension and text layers.

Linking data

You can insert data from a spreadsheet or text document and maintain a link to the original file, so that if the original file changes, the inserted data is updated as well. You could use this feature to place a schedule of doors and windows in an architectural drawing or a bill of materials in a mechanical drawing, for example. There are two ways to link data.

You can link data using INSERTOBJ as described earlier in this chapter. You can also use the Clipboard, using these steps:

1. Open the source application, select the data, and copy it to the Clipboard. (Click Copy on the Standard toolbar or choose Edit➪Copy.)

2. If AutoCAD is open, choose its button on the Taskbar. If not, open it.

3. In your drawing, choose Edit➪Paste Special.

4. In the Paste Special dialog box, choose Paste Link, as shown in Figure 27-16. Click OK.

Note

When you create a link, you don't have all the format options you do when you simply paste. You can only create a link in the source application's format.

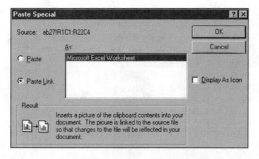

Figure 27-16: Creating a link using the Paste Special dialog box.

When you open an AutoCAD drawing containing a link, AutoCAD displays a message asking if you want to update the links. In this way, you can update the links whenever you open the drawing. You can manage links using the Links dialog box, shown in Figure 27-17.

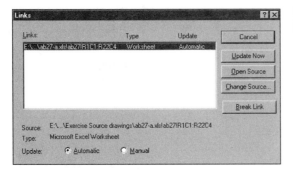

Figure 27-17: Use the Links dialog box to manage your links.

The Links dialog box (choose Edit⇨OLE Links) lets you manually update the links at any time by choosing Update Now. You may wish to do this if you know that someone has changed the source of the link during your drawing session. You can also break the link, open the source, or change the source in this dialog box.

In order to do the next exercise, you need a spreadsheet application. I use Microsoft Excel in this exercise, but you can use Lotus 1-2-3 or Quattro Pro as well.

Note

Remember that if you give a drawing to someone else, you also need to include any attached images or embedded objects. If the person does not have the source application for an embedded object, you can paste it in as an image.

Step-by-Step: Pasting, Linking, and Embedding Objects

On the CD-ROM

1. Open *ab27-c.dwg* from the CD-ROM.

2. Save it as *ab27-4.dwg* in your *AutoCAD Bible* folder.

3. Choose Insert⇨OLE Object. Choose Create New and choose your worksheet from the list. Click OK. Your worksheet program opens.

4. Create the worksheet shown in Figure 27-18. Adjust the width of the columns to fit the data.

	A	B	C	D
1	Tag	Part No.	Description	
2	11	9076-052-002	Collar-Shaft	
3	17	9029-072-001	Bracket-Tube Assembly	
4	19	9081-114-001	Channel-Motor Mtg. Rod	
5				

Worksheet in ab27-4.dwg

Figure 27-18: Creating a worksheet to insert into an AutoCAD drawing.

5. In the spreadsheet application, choose File⇨Update, then File⇨Exit. The worksheet appears in the AutoCAD drawing, as shown in Figure 27-19.

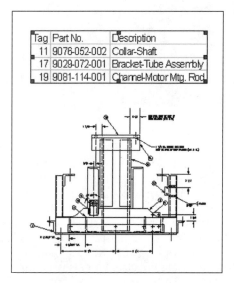

Figure 27-19: The spreadsheet as it appears when inserted into the drawing.

6. Place the cursor in the spreadsheet object and drag it down so it is just above the model in the drawing. Press Esc to remove the handles.

On the
CD-ROM

7. Open *ab27-c.xls* from the CD-ROM. (If you don't have Excel, open this file from your spreadsheet application.) Select the last three columns, as shown in Figure 27-20. Choose Edit⇨Copy.

	A	B	C	D	E	F	G	H
1	Qty.	Tag	Part No.	Description	Dwg. Size	Pur/Made	Units	
2	2	19	9081-114-001	CHANNEL-MOTOR MTG ROD	B	P	EACH	
3	2	17	9029-072-001	BRACKET-TUBE ASSY	D	M	EACH	
4	2	11	9076-052-002	COLLAR-SHAFT	B	M	EACH	
5								

Figure 27-20: Selecting part of a file to insert into AutoCAD.

8. Leave your spreadsheet open and click the AutoCAD button on the Windows Taskbar. Choose Edit⇨Paste Special. While you would probably insert this as an Excel Worksheet (or object from your spreadsheet application), to try another method, choose AutoCAD Entities and click OK. Pick an insertion point near the top right corner of the existing OLE object and accept the defaults for scale and rotation angle.

9. Type **xplode** ↵ and select the new object. At the `All/Color/LAyer/LType/ Inherit from parent block/<Explode>:` prompt, type **la** ↵. At the `XPlode onto what layer? <TITLE>:` prompt, type **notes** ↵. (If you don't do this, the object disappears when you explode it — this solves the problem. This can sometimes happen when you mix objects from different environments.)

10. Choose List from the Inquiry flyout on the Standard toolbar and select any of the new text objects. A sample is shown in Figure 27-21. Notice that AutoCAD has created a new text style that closely matches the original text in the spreadsheet.

```
Command: _list
Select objects: 1 found

Select objects:
                        TEXT        Layer: NOTES
                                    Space: Model space
                        Handle = AFFE
             Style = WMF-ARIAL0
             Typeface = Arial
             start point, X=105 19/32   Y= 57 61/64  Z=        0
          height     1 3/32
          text Dwg. Size
       rotation angle   0.00
             width scale factor   0.750000
       obliquing angle   0.00
     generation normal
```

Figure 27-21: A listing of one of the new text objects.

11. Return to your spreadsheet and choose Edit⇨Copy again. (AutoCAD only lets you paste once with all the options.) Return to AutoCAD and choose Edit⇨Paste Special. Choose Paste Link. Now you can only paste in your spreadsheet's format. Click OK. AutoCAD inserts the spreadsheet at the top left of your screen.

12. Return to your spreadsheet and change the cell F2 (which now says *P*) to *M*. Go back to AutoCAD and watch the *P* change to an *M*. Any changes made to the spreadsheet are updated in your AutoCAD drawing.

13. Save your drawing.

On the CD-ROM The CD-ROM contains a hidden word game, Hidden, that you can play from within AutoCAD (if your boss lets you). Look in *\Software\Chap27\Hidden.*

Summary

In this chapter you learned how to import and export other file formats, including both vector and bitmap (raster) formats. You also learned how to work with DXF files.

I explained the new raster image features of Release 14. Finally, I covered pasting, linking, and embedding objects into AutoCAD.

The next chapter discusses how to integrate AutoCAD with the Internet.

✦   ✦   ✦

Getting on the Internet

AutoCAD and the Internet

Release 14 offers many ways to integrate your drawings with the Internet. You can fax and e-mail AutoCAD drawings, publish them on a Web site, and launch your Web browser from within AutoCAD. When you launch your Web browser, you can access a Web site (perhaps your company's intranet), find blocks or other data, and drag them into your drawing. This chapter covers this new way to work with AutoCAD.

Faxing and E-mailing Drawings

Release 14 now lets you get your AutoCAD drawings to others on your team or your clients instantly — by either faxing or e-mailing them. Fax a drawing if the recipient doesn't have AutoCAD or wants to quickly see the drawing on paper. Use e-mail if the recipient has AutoCAD and may need to edit the drawings.

Faxing a drawing from within AutoCAD

You may have fax software installed that you use to fax files from your computer. Here I give instructions using Windows 95's Exchange program. The first time you open Exchange, you need to set it up. Once that is done, you can easily fax drawings from within AutoCAD, as long as your computer has a fax/modem card.

To fax a drawing, follow these steps:

1. Open the drawing you want to fax.

2. Choose File⇨Send to open Microsoft Exchange. Exchange displays the Choose Profile dialog box, shown in Figure 28-1. The listing depends on your setup. Choose the profile you want and click OK.

Figure 28-1: Choosing a profile in Microsoft Exchange.

3. Exchange opens the New Message dialog box, shown in Figure 28-2. Your drawing is shown in the message box. Type a name in the To box or click the To button to open the Address Book, shown in Figure 28-3. (If you type a new name in the To box, Exchange opens the Address Book so you can specify a phone number.)

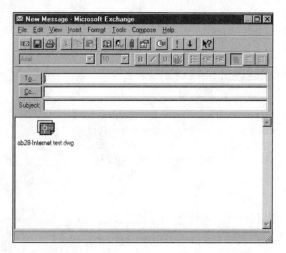

Figure 28-2: The New Message dialog box in Microsoft Exchange.

4. Choose the desired recipient in the Address Book and click To. Click Cc if you want to send copies. Click OK. (You can choose File⇨Send Options to configure a cover page and set other fax properties.)

5. Click Send on the Standard toolbar to send the fax. AutoCAD opens the Print/Plot Configuration dialog box so you can set your plotting parameters. Because a fax is actually a printout of your drawing, you need to specify how you want the printout to appear. When you are done, choose OK.

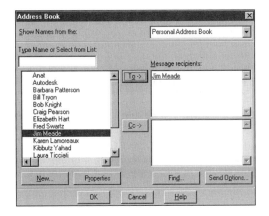

Figure 28-3: The Address Book in Microsoft Exchange.

Tip

Use the Scaled to Fit option so your drawing fits on the recipient's $8^1/2 \times 11$ sheet of fax paper.

6. AutoCAD plots the drawing. Exchange opens the Microsoft Fax Status dialog box (shown in Figure 28-4), prepares the fax format, dials the recipient's number, and faxes the drawing.

Note

Although it may seem extraneous, AutoCAD also prints/plots your drawing.

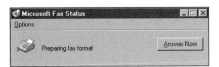

Figure 28-4: The Microsoft Fax Status dialog box.

E-mailing a drawing

You can e-mail a drawing from Microsoft Exchange, too, but most people use their own e-mail program. Internet Service Providers (ISPs), whether local or national, such as America Online or CompuServe, all offer e-mail services.

In most cases, when you e-mail a drawing, you write an e-mail message and include the drawing file as an attachment. However, all data traveling via the Internet must be in plain text (ASCII) format. When you see a Web page full of graphics, it has been converted from a binary (coded) format, to a text format, and back to binary format.

Most e-mail services automatically encode and decode attachments. You may have to choose an option in your application to enable this feature when sending the drawing as an attachment. This means that the application translates your drawing to an ASCII format when sending it and back to binary format when receiving it.

Use your standard procedure for sending e-mail and including attachments, as applicable to your e-mail software.

Publishing Drawings on the World Wide Web

Release 14 now includes Autodesk's Drawing Web File Publishing program. This feature lets you save drawings as DWF (Drawing Web Format) files. You can place a DWF drawing on a Web site so others can view the drawing. They can zoom, pan, and print the drawing. You can place links in your drawing so that viewers can jump to supporting data, to other DWF drawings, or to other Web sites.

Understanding DWF files

Most graphics that you view on the Web are bitmaps, often in GIF or JPEG format. This is not very useful for technical drawings because you want viewers to be able to zoom in to see the details. Zooming in on a bitmap format just displays dots.

The DWF format has several advantages:

✦ It is a vector format. Viewers can zoom in closely and see the details clearly.

✦ DWF files are 2D representations, similar to a plot. The actual objects are not available to the viewer. They cannot edit the drawing or access object information such as layers, object coordinates, and so on. This maintains security for the creator of the drawing.

✦ DWF files are compressed while being transmitted to reduce the time it takes to download and view them.

✦ DWF files support URL links to other drawings, data, or files, so you can provide the viewer with supporting schedules, and so on.

Creating DWF files

Once you have created the drawing you want to publish on the Web, creating the DWF file involves two basics steps:

1. Create the links.
2. Export the drawing in DWF format.

URL links

You link your drawing with other data by associating an object or area with a *URL* (Universal Resource Locator or, according to some, Uniform Resource Locator). A URL is an address — it tells your Web browser where to go.

Tip

To work with URL links, open the Internet Utilities toolbar, shown in Figure 28-5. Right-click any toolbar and choose *inet* from the Menu Group drop-down list. Check Internet Utilities and close the Toolbars dialog box.

Note

If inet is not listed, return to the command line and type **menuload** ↵. Choose Browse in the Menu Customization dialog box and locate *inet.mnc* (probably in *AutoCADR14\support*). Choose it and click Open. Then click Load to load the menu. Click Close to close the dialog box. You can now choose inet from the Menu Group drop-down list in the Toolbars dialog box, as described in the previous paragraph.

Figure 28-5: The Internet Utilities toolbar.

To create a URL link, follow these steps:

 1. Choose Attach URL from the Internet Utilities toolbar.

 2. At the URL by (Area/<Objects>): prompt, press Enter to attach by object (the default). Type **a** ↵ to attach by area.

 3a. If you are attaching by object, AutoCAD prompts you to select objects. Press Enter when you have completed object selection.

 3b. If you are attaching by area, AutoCAD prompts you for two corners. Pick the corners and AutoCAD creates the area.

 4. At the Enter URL: prompt, type in the URL.

Note

A full URL generally has the form: *http://www.idgbooks.com*. However, your browser may not require the *http://* part — in that case you can leave it out. There may be additional sections to the address that represent various pages on the same Web site. Also, if the entire viewing will be within one Web site, as on an intranet, you may enter only the name of the Web page.

Tip

You can even create URLs to your own computer or local network by referring to a file rather than an Internet location. However, the file must be in a format viewable by your Internet browser, such as HTML, text, or certain graphic file types.

Caution

When you attach a URL by area, AutoCAD places a rectangle on a special layer, URLLAYER. Do not freeze, lock, or change the visibility of this layer. Don't erase or modify the rectangle in any way. You also should not attach a URL to one of these rectangles. You can turn off URLLAYER if the rectangles interfere with your work but be sure to turn the layer back on before exporting the drawing to DWF format.

The other URL management commands are as follows:

✦ Choose Detach URL to detach a URL from objects or areas. If you have already created the DWF file, be sure to save the drawing and then re-export it as a DWF file.

✦ Choose List URLs to get a list of URLs for selected objects.

✦ Choose Select URLs to select all objects attached to URLs.

Before creating the DWF format, save the drawing so that the URLs are saved in the drawing database.

The DWF format supports the HIDE command. If you do a HIDE before exporting to DWF, the DWF display will be the same as after the HIDE command.

TrueType fonts are not well supported in the DWF format — the resulting files are very large. You may want to use the simpler *.shx* fonts. Also, DWF currently does not support paper space — it only displays the model space drawing.

DWF format

To create a DWF file, follow these steps:

1. Choose File⇨Export.

2. Choose DWF from the Save as type drop-down list.

3. Once you choose the file type, choose Options to specify low, medium, or high precision (the default is medium). You can also turn compression off.

4. Name the file in the File name text box. By default, AutoCAD assigns the same name as the current drawing but with the *.dwf* extension.

5. Choose Save.

Posting the DWF file on the Web

The actual procedure for posting the DWF file on the Web involves creating HTML code. HTML is the code used to create Web pages; its details are beyond the scope of this book. However, the last button on the Internet Utilities toolbar, Internet Help, offers a topic on *Adding DWF Files to a Web Page*, which provides some sample HTML code and instructions on how to customize it for your needs. Included are special HTML tags to allow both Netscape Navigator and Microsoft Internet Explorer users to view the DWF files.

You can also place actual DWG drawings on your Web site. If they are placed in the same folder as the DWF file, viewers can access the actual drawings, as explained later in this chapter.

 To post a drawing to a Web site, choose Save to URL from the Internet Utilities toolbar. AutoCAD opens the Save DWG to URL dialog box, shown in Figure 28-6.

Figure 28-6: The Save DWG to URL dialog box.

Type the URL in the Save DWG to Internet text box, then choose Save. You must enter a URL in the following format (http and file schemes are not supported):

```
ftp://servername/pathname/filename.dwg
```

The first part, `ftp://`, is already entered for you. FTP (File Transfer Protocol) is a means for transferring files across the Internet.

Choose Options to set passwords if you need them (for example, if you are using an intranet that requires passwords for security reasons). You can also provide proxy server information. Proxy servers are used by intranets to provide a barrier between the company's own intranet and the Internet. Your network system administrator should be able to provide you with this information, if needed.

Note

Your Internet server must be able to recognize the DWF file type. To register the DWF file type, your Web site administrator (sometimes called the Webmaster) or Internet Service Provider must add the MIME type "drawing/x-dwf" to your Internet server so that it is registered with your Internet server software.

Viewing the drawing

The final step is to view the drawing. In order to view a DWF drawing, you need a special program called WHIP! Release 2, created by Autodesk. This program is free, but not included with AutoCAD. You can download WHIP! from Autodesk's Web site at `www.autodesk.com`. (The full address is `http://www.autodesk.com/products/autocad/whip/whip.htm`.) WHIP! lets you pan and zoom in a DWF file, print, and use any embedded links.

Note

Release 14 requires Release 2 of WHIP!

There are two flavors of WHIP!:

✦ If you use the Netscape Navigator browser, use the WHIP! Plug-in.

✦ If you use the Microsoft Internet Explorer browser, use the WHIP! Control for ActiveX.

Once WHIP! is installed, you can automatically view DWF files. When you go to any page with a DWF drawing, it regenerates before your eyes. Figure 28-7 shows a DWF drawing on a Web site.

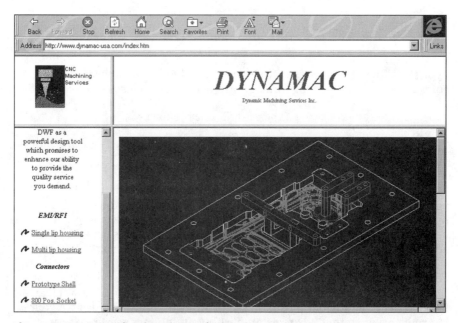

Figure 28-7: A DWF drawing on a Web site.

Credit: Thanks to Kelly D. Grills of Dynamac Corporation, Wood Dale, Illinois, for this image.

WHIP!'s functions are accessed by right-clicking anywhere in the DWF image to open the menu shown in Figure 28-8.

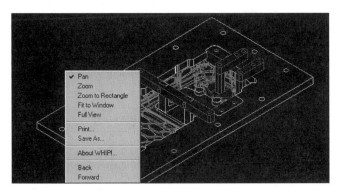

Figure 28-8: Using the WHIP! menu to zoom and pan in a DWF file.

Although the terms are somewhat different than those you are used to, you'll quickly get the hang of zooming and panning in a DWF drawing.

✦ *Pan* works just like real-time pan. Just click and drag in the direction you want the image to go.

✦ *Zoom* works just like real-time zoom. Drag up to zoom in and drag down to zoom out.

✦ *Zoom to Rectangle* is like ZOOM Window, but you have to hold down the mouse button and drag the window instead of just clicking the two corners.

✦ *Fit to Window* is like ZOOM Extents. It restores the view to its original view.

✦ *Full View* is like ZOOM All. This item is not always available.

Besides zooming and panning, you can also print the currently displayed view to your system printer. Just choose Print from the menu.

You can even copy the DWF file to your hard drive in one of two raster formats. Follow these steps:

1. Choose Save As to copy the DWF file to your hard drive.

2. In the Save WMF File As dialog box, choose a name and folder.

3. In the Save as type drop-down list, choose WMF or BMP (to save the image as a bitmap).

4. Click Save.

If the DWF file has URLs attached, the menu includes Highlight URLs. If you turn this on, you see rectangles that show where the URLs are. You'll probably want to click the item again to turn off the rectangles, since they are distracting.

When your cursor passes over a URL area, the cursor changes to a pointing hand, as shown in Figure 28-9. You're probably familiar with this cursor from surfing the Web because it is universally used to indicate a link. At the bottom left corner of the screen, the URL is displayed. Always check this URL, because the areas of the screen covered by a URL may overlap, especially if the objects attached to URLs are close.

To go to the URL, click. WHIP! transfers you to the new location.

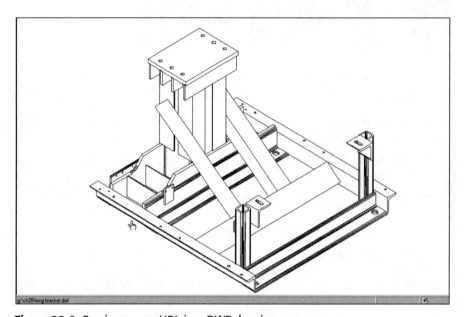

Figure 28-9: Passing over a URL in a DWF drawing.

The menu also has Back and Forward items that act like the Back and Forward buttons of your browser. For example, after clicking on a URL and seeing the new image, click Back to return to the original DWF drawing.

Getting drawings from the Web

As you can see, the DWF format offers great potential for displaying drawings. However, the Internet Utilities toolbar also lets you access actual drawings from the Internet. If you include the actual drawing (DWG format) on a Web site with the DWF file, viewers can download the drawing.

 To open an AutoCAD drawing from the Web, an intranet, or a network, choose Open from URL from the Internet Utilities toolbar. AutoCAD downloads the drawing (if it's on the Web).

To insert an AutoCAD drawing into your current drawing, choose Insert from URL from the Internet Utilities toolbar.

You can even use drag-and-drop to open or insert AutoCAD drawings from the Internet. Follow these steps:

1. View the DWF file.

2. If you wish, configure the browser and AutoCAD windows so both are visible.

3. Press and hold both Ctrl and Shift to open a drawing. Hold just Ctrl to insert a drawing.

4. Click the DWF image and drag the DWF image from your browser into AutoCAD. If the AutoCAD window is not visible, drag the image onto the AutoCAD button on the taskbar, wait for AutoCAD to open (keep the mouse button down!), and then continue to drag into AutoCAD.

5. First release the mouse button, then Ctrl and Shift (or just Ctrl if you are inserting a drawing).

Note

For drag-and-drop to work, the DWG file used to create the DWF file must exist in the same directory as the DWF file at the time you drag-and-drop.

Imagine the possibilities — accessing drawings, blocks, and so on from the Internet in the same way you currently access them on your hard drive or network! Sharing drawings around the world is now available by simply dragging and dropping.

On the CD-ROM

The CD-ROM includes a program that exports 3D drawings to VRML format, which creates virtual reality models for the world wide web. You need an appropriate add-on to view these files in your browser, such as Live 3D. Look in *\Software\Chap28\VRML*.

Launching Your Web Browser

 AutoCAD can launch your Web browser for you. Just click Launch Browser on the Standard toolbar. AutoCAD finds your connection settings and opens the dialog box you use to connect to the Internet.

 Choose Configure Internet Host from the Internet Utilities toolbar to add passwords and specify a proxy server, if necessary.

You can do the first eight steps of the Step-by-Step exercise that follows with no additional software. In order to complete it, you need an Internet browser (either Netscape Navigator or Microsoft Internet Explorer) and the WHIP! edition for that browser. You can download the WHIP! at no charge from Autodesk's Web site at http://www.autodesk.com. Click Products and do a search for *whip*.

You can download Netscape Navigator from Netscape (http://www.netscape.com) and Microsoft Internet Explorer from Microsoft (http://www.microsoft.com).

In the Step-by-Step exercise that follows, I use a little-known feature of Internet browsers — they can browse your hard drive as well as the Internet. This lets you complete the exercise even if you don't have an Internet connection available, using just the files on the *AutoCAD 14 Bible* CD-ROM, your Internet browser, and WHIP!

Step-by-Step: Creating and Viewing DWF Drawings

On the CD-ROM

1. Open *ab28-a.dwg* from the CD-ROM.

2. Save it as *ab28-1.dwg* in your *AutoCAD Bible* folder. This is a 3D drawing of a base assembly frame for an industrial washer, shown in Figure 28-10.

On the CD-ROM

3. Copy *ab28-a.txt* and *ab28-b.dwf* from the CD-ROM to your *AutoCAD Bible* folder. (You can use Windows Explorer to drag them.)

4. Right-click any toolbar to open the Toolbar dialog box. From the Menu Group drop-down list choose inet. Check Internet Utilities and close the dialog box.

Note: If inet is not there, choose Toolbars⇨Customize Menus. In the Menu Customization dialog box, click Browse. From the Select Menu File dialog box, choose *inet.mnc* (probably in *\AcadR14\support*) and click Open. Click Load, then click Close. Now do Step 4.

5. Choose Attach URL from the Internet Utilities toolbar. Follow the prompts:

```
URL by (Area/<Objects>): ↵
Select objects: Pick ① in Figure 28-10.
Select objects: Pick ②.
Select objects: ↵
Enter URL: c:\AutoCAD Bible\ab28-a.txt ↵
```

(Substitute the actual location of your *AutoCAD Bible* folder if necessary.)

6. Press Enter to repeat the ATTACHURL command. This time attach ③ and ④ in Figure 28-10 to **c:\AutoCAD Bible\ab28-b.dwf**. (Don't forget to type **dwf** instead of **dwg**.)

(Substitute the actual location of your *AutoCAD Bible* folder if necessary.)

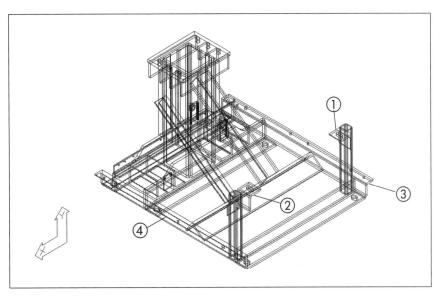

Figure 28-10: The base assembly frame.

Credit: Thanks to Robert Mack of The Dexter Company, Fairfield, Iowa, for this drawing.

7. Save the drawing. Type **hide** ↵.

8. Choose File⇨Export and choose Drawing Web Format (.dwf) from the bottom of the Save as type drop-down list. Set the folder for your *AutoCAD Bible* folder. Leave the name as is — it should be *ab28-1.dwf*. Click Save and wait while AutoCAD generates the DWF file.

9. Start your Internet Browser without connecting to the Internet. (This procedure may vary depending on your system. On mine, I start the browser from the Start⇨Programs menu and click Cancel when prompted to connect.) You may also have to cancel your connection to your default start-up page. In the place where you usually type Web site addresses, type **c:\Autocad Bible\ab28-1.dwf** (or as appropriate for your system). You should see the DWF file you just created, as shown in Figure 28-11. Notice that when you point to any of the objects with URLs attached, you see the URL at the bottom left corner of the image.

10. Click ① in Figure 28-11. You see the text shown in Figure 28-12. This comes from an Excel spreadsheet saved in text format. (Browsers can display text and graphics only.) Click the Back button on your browser to return to the original DWF file.

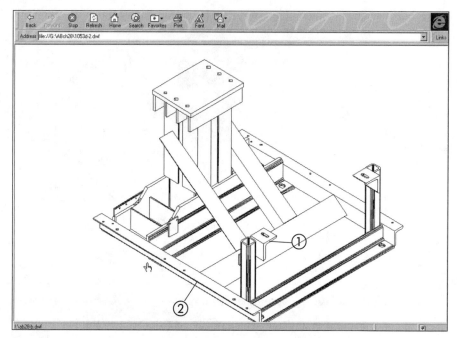

Figure 28-11: The DWF file as seen in Microsoft Internet Explorer.

11. Right-click in the drawing to open the WHIP! menu. Choose Zoom. Drag the cursor up to zoom in. Choose Pan from the menu and pan to the left. Choose Zoom to Rectangle and drag a small window to zoom in very close. Choose Fit to Window to return to the original view. (If you wish, choose Print to print the drawing to the system printer.)

12. Click ② in Figure 28-11. You see the horizontal angle.

13. Close your browser. Save your drawing.

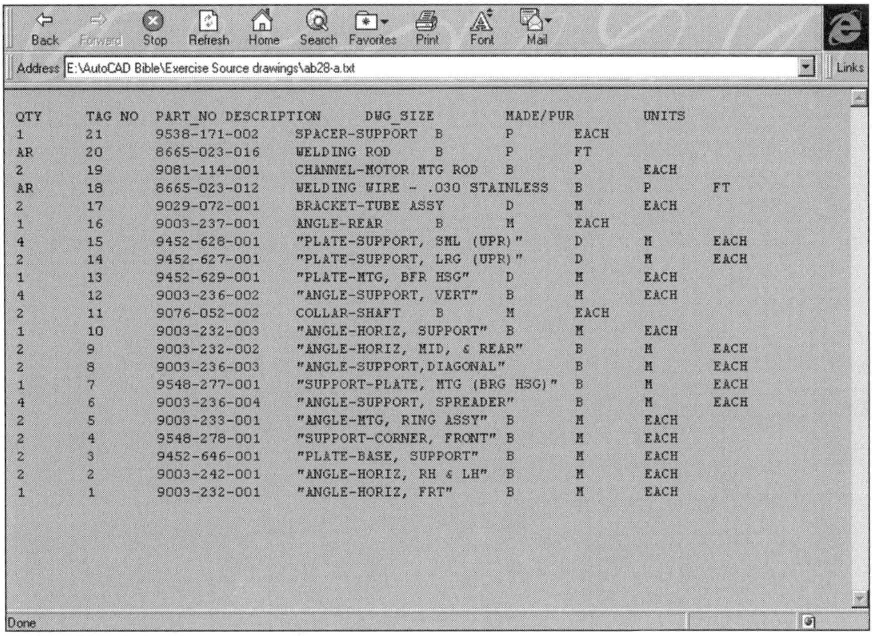

QTY	TAG NO	PART_NO	DESCRIPTION	DWG_SIZE	MADE/PUR	UNITS
1	21	9538-171-002	SPACER-SUPPORT	B	P	EACH
AR	20	8665-023-016	WELDING ROD	B	P	FT
2	19	9081-114-001	CHANNEL-MOTOR MTG ROD	B	P	EACH
AR	18	8665-023-012	WELDING WIRE - .030 STAINLESS	B	P	FT
2	17	9029-072-001	BRACKET-TUBE ASSY	D	M	EACH
1	16	9003-237-001	ANGLE-REAR	B	M	EACH
4	15	9452-628-001	"PLATE-SUPPORT, SML (UPR)"	D	M	EACH
2	14	9452-627-001	"PLATE-SUPPORT, LRG (UPR)"	D	M	EACH
1	13	9452-629-001	"PLATE-MTG, BFR HSG"	D	M	EACH
4	12	9003-236-002	"ANGLE-SUPPORT, VERT"	B	M	EACH
2	11	9076-052-002	COLLAR-SHAFT	B	M	EACH
1	10	9003-232-003	"ANGLE-HORIZ, SUPPORT"	B	M	EACH
2	9	9003-232-002	"ANGLE-HORIZ, MID, & REAR"	B	M	EACH
2	8	9003-236-003	"ANGLE-SUPPORT,DIAGONAL"	B	M	EACH
1	7	9548-277-001	"SUPPORT-PLATE, MTG (BRG HSG)"	B	M	EACH
4	6	9003-236-004	"ANGLE-SUPPORT, SPREADER"	B	M	EACH
2	5	9003-233-001	"ANGLE-MTG, RING ASSY"	B	M	EACH
2	4	9548-278-001	"SUPPORT-CORNER, FRONT"	B	M	EACH
2	3	9452-646-001	"PLATE-BASE, SUPPORT"	B	M	EACH
2	2	9003-242-001	"ANGLE-HORIZ, RH & LH"	B	M	EACH
1	1	9003-232-001	"ANGLE-HORIZ, FRT"	B	M	EACH

Figure 28-12: The text database for the drawing.

Summary

In this chapter you learned how to work with AutoCAD and the Internet. Besides faxing and e-mailing drawings, you can publish them on a Web site in the DWF format. You can create URL links in your DWF drawings so that viewers can jump to data or other drawings. You can even download drawings from the Internet by dragging them into AutoCAD.

This chapter ends Part V, Organizing and Managing Drawings. Part VI, Customizing AutoCAD, shows you the inner workings of AutoCAD so you can make adjustments to best suit your needs. Chapter 29 explains how to create customized command shortcuts and toolbars.

✦ ✦ ✦

Customizing AutoCAD

In this part you learn how to make AutoCAD work *your* way. Customizing AutoCAD can speed up your work, make it easier, create standards for all drawings where you work, and automate often-used or repetitive tasks. You can customize the process of issuing commands (Chapter 29), create macros and slide shows with script files (Chapter 30), create your own linetypes and hatch patterns (Chapter 31), create your own fonts and other shapes (Chapter 32), and customize AutoCAD's menus (Chapter 33).

Customizing Commands and Toolbars

◆ ◆ ◆ ◆

In This Chapter

Understanding customizing basics

Creating keyboard shortcuts for commands

Customizing the toolbars

◆ ◆ ◆ ◆

Customizing Basics

Before you start customizing, there are some basics that you need to know that apply to almost all AutoCAD customization. Once you understand these basics, the process becomes much easier.

Working with customizable files

The ability to customize AutoCAD is based on its famous *open architecture,* which means that most of AutoCAD's support files are text files that you can edit yourself. Table 29-1 lists the most important of these files and their functions.

Table 29-1 Customizable Files	
Filename	**Function**
*.cus	Custom dictionary files. You can add words to a custom dictionary for use with the SPELL command.
acad.pgp	AutoCAD's program parameters file. This file is generally used to create keyboard shortcuts (called aliases) for commands.

(continued)

Table 29-1 (*continued*)

Filename	Function
acad.mnu	AutoCAD's template menu file. You can also create your own menu template files.
acad.mnd	A file of menu macros.
acad.mnl	AutoLISP routines used by AutoCAD's main menu. If you create your own menus, you can have an *.mnl* file with the same name as your menu for AutoLISP routines.
acad.mns	AutoCAD's menu source file generated from the template *.mnu* file. You can also create your own menu source files from custom template files.
acad.hlp	AutoCAD help files.
acad.cfg	AutoCAD configuration file for storing digitizer and plotter selections. Usually, you use the Preferences dialog box to make these selections rather than manually editing this file. Keep in mind, however, that it is a text file that you can customize.
acad.dcl	AutoCAD's Dialog Control Language (DCL) file. This file describes the AutoCAD standard dialog boxes. You can create your own DCL files to create dialog boxes for your AutoLISP routines.
acad.lin	AutoCAD's linetype definition file. You can also create your own linetype definition (**.lin*) files or add your own definitions to *acad.lin.*
acad.lsp	AutoCAD's AutoLISP file. You can edit or add to this file to create and automatically load AutoLISP routines, or create your own AutoLISP files.
acad.mln	AutoCAD's multiline library file.
acad.pat	AutoCAD's hatch pattern file. You can also create your own.
acad.pcp	AutoCAD partial plot configuration parameters file that can be used with either R13 or R12. You can also create your own. A PCP file contains the configuration for a specific plotter. You can use these files with the Batch Plotting Utility.
acad.pc2	AutoCAD complete plot configuration parameters file. You can also create your own. A PC2 file contains all configuration settings for a specific plotter. You can use these files with the Batch Plotting Utility.
fontmap.ps	The AutoCAD PostScript Font Map file. This file is used by PSIN and lists fonts available in AutoCAD.
acad.fmp	AutoCAD Font mapping file. AutoCAD uses this to substitute fonts when the original fonts in a drawing are not available on your system.
acad.psf	The AutoCAD PostScript Support file. It is used for the PSOUT and PSFILL commands.
acad.slb	The AutoCAD slide library file used for hatch pattern examples in menus. You can use this file or create your own slide libraries.

Filename	Function
*.scr	A script file that you create and name. Script files are macros of commands and options that run automatically.
*.shp	A shape file that you create and name. Shape files usually hold fonts but can hold other shapes as well. A shape file is then compiled into a file with a .shx extension for more efficient use.
acad.rx	A list of ARX applications that load automatically.
mtextmap.ini	Font mapping for the appearance of text in the MTEXT editor.
acad.unt	A file that defines every conceivable type of unit.
*.rpf	Fill patterns for raster fills.

Figure 29-1 shows a portion of the *acad.pgp* file that lists command shortcuts, or aliases.

```
;  Sample aliases for AutoCAD commands
;  These examples include most frequently used commands.

3A,        *3DARRAY
3F,        *3DFACE
3P,        *3DPOLY
A,         *ARC
AA,        *AREA
AL,        *ALIGN
AP,        *APPLOAD
AR,        *ARRAY
AAD,       *ASEADMIN
AEX,       *ASEEXPORT
ALI,       *ASELINKS
ASQ,       *ASESQLED
ARO,       *ASEROWS
ASE,       *ASESELECT
AT,        *DDATTDEF
-AT,       *ATTDEF
ATE,       *DDATTE
-ATE,      *ATTEDIT
B,         *BMAKE
-B,        *BLOCK
BH,        *BHATCH
BO,        *BOUNDARY
-BO,       *-BOUNDARY
BR,        *BREAK
C,         *CIRCLE
CH,        *DDCHPROP
-CH,       *CHANGE
CHA,       *CHAMFER
COL,       *DDCOLOR
CO,        *COPY
D,         *DDIM
DAL,       *DIMALIGNED
```

Figure 29-1: *Acad.pgp*, one of AutoCAD's customizable files.

Editing customizable files

In order to customize AutoCAD you have to edit the appropriate customizable file. These files are in text only (ASCII) format. To edit them, you need a text editor, which is like a word processor but does not place any codes in the file. For most files, you can use Notepad, which comes with Windows 95. However, the menu files are too long for Notepad to handle. You can use WordPad, which also comes with

Windows 95. However, be careful to use the Save as type drop-down box in the Save As dialog box to save the document as a Text Only document. All major word processors let you save documents as Text Only documents — just remember not to click that Save button until you have specified the right file format.

Backing up customizable files

Before editing any pre-existing AutoCAD files, back them up. Some of these files, especially the menu files, are critical to AutoCAD's functioning. You should back up in two stages:

✦ Back up the original file as it came out of the box. Keep a diskette with all the customizable files that you might ever edit in their original form.

✦ Once you edit the file, back it up before each editing session. That way you always have your most recent version of the file. If you make a mistake, it's easy to copy that file on top of the one with the mistake and put everything back to normal.

In some cases it is safer to create your own files rather than edit AutoCAD's original file. For example, when customizing AutoCAD's menus, you can copy *acad.mnu* to a file named *mymenu.mnu*, edit it, and then load your new menu instead of AutoCAD's standard menu.

This means you should have two diskettes, one with the original customizable files, and one with your most recent versions of them. At the very least, these diskettes should contain the following files:

✦ *acad.lin*

✦ *acad.lsp*

✦ *acad.mln*

✦ *acad.mnl*

✦ *acad.mns*

✦ *acad.mnu*

✦ *acad.pat*

✦ *acad.pgp*

You will use these diskettes not only when you make a mistake, but also whenever you need to reinstall AutoCAD whether due to hard disk failure, a virus on your system, the replacement of your old computer with a new one, and so on. Also, when you upgrade AutoCAD to the next release, you can continue to work with your familiar, customized files (usually).

Using the command-line form of commands

For many customization tasks, you need to work with commands. When you create a script file, which is a series of commands, or when you edit the menu file, you need to type out the commands you want to execute. In these cases, AutoCAD's customizable files can only contain the command-line form of the commands. There is no way to enter values in a dialog box from within a script or menu file. As a result, you need to learn a whole new way of working in AutoCAD — the old-fashioned way — by typing commands on the command line.

Tip

If you're not sure of the command name but know the menu or toolbar item, execute the command on the menu or toolbar and then press Esc. AutoCAD displays the command name on the command line.

A number of commands have a non-dialog-box version. Several commands can also be run in their command-line version by placing a hyphen (-) before the command name. For some commands that have no command-line equivalent, you can use system variables to create the same effect. Table 29-2 lists these commands.

Table 29-2	
Command-Line Forms of Commands	
Command	*Command-Line Form*
BHATCH	-BHATCH
BOUNDARY	-BOUNDARY
GROUP	-GROUP
HATCHEDIT	-HATCHEDIT
MTEXT	-MTEXT
TOOLBAR	-TOOLBAR
DDATTDEF	ATTDEF
DDATTE	ATTEDIT
DDATTEXT	ATTEXT
DDCHPROP	CHANGE or CHPROP
DDCOLOR	COLOR
DDGRIPS	GRIPBLOCK, GRIPCOLOR, GRIPHOT, GRIPS, GRIPSIZE
DDMODIFY	CHANGE or CHPROP, LAYER, COLOR, LINETYPE, LTSCALE, CELTYPE, CELTSCALE

(continued)

Command	Command-Line Form
DDOSNAP	OSNAP
DDPTYPE	PDMODE, PDSTYLE
DDRENAME	RENAME
DDRMODES	ORTHO, FILL, QTEXT, BLIPMODE, HIGHLIGHT, GROUP, PICKSTYLE, SNAP, GRID, ISOPLANE
DDSELECT	PICKADD, PICKAUTO, PICKBOX, PICKDRAG, PICKFIRST, SOTRENTS, TREEDEPTH
DDSTYLE	STYLE
DDUCS, DDUCSP	UCS
DDUNITS	UNITS
DDVIEW	VIEW
DDVPOINT	VPOINT

Table 29-2 (continued)

In addition, you can use the dimension variables to format dimensions in place of using the DDIM command, which opens the Dimension Styles dialog box.

Tip

If you can't find a command, look for a system variable that can accomplish the task.

The following commands can be used as is on the command line if the CMDDIA system variable is set to zero:

✦ PLOT

✦ ASEADMIN

✦ ASEEXPORT

✦ ASELINKS

✦ ASEROWS

✦ ASESELECT

✦ ASESQLED

By setting the FILEDIA system variable to zero, you can use all commands that request files — such as SAVEAS — on the command line.

Documenting your files

It is standard practice to place comments in customized files to explain how you have customized them. While it may seem obvious at the time, if you go back later to a file, you may not understand what it is you were trying to accomplish. Also, other people may need some explanation.

You can place comments in customizable files by placing a semi-colon (;) before any line of text. AutoCAD ignores these lines. In menus only, you create comments by placing a / or // before any line of text.

Now that you know the basics of customizing AutoCAD files, let's move on to creating keyboard shortcuts and customizing toolbars.

Creating Keyboard Shortcuts for Commands

You can use the *acad.pgp* file for two purposes:

✦ To create shortcuts to Windows programs

✦ To create keyboard shortcuts for AutoCAD commands

Note

You can also use *acad.pgp* to create shortcuts to DOS commands.

Creating shortcuts to Windows programs

The *acad.pgp* file includes the following three shortcuts to Windows programs:

```
EXPLORER,   START EXPLORER, 1,,
NOTEPAD,    START NOTEPAD,  1,*File to edit: ,
PBRUSH,     START PBRUSH,   1,,
```

The first column is the command name you type at the AutoCAD command line. The second column is the command you want Windows to execute. The 1 tells AutoCAD to start the application but not to wait until you have finished using it. This lets you return to AutoCAD at any time. After the 1, you can finish with two commas. However, notice that the Notepad entry has *File to edit: before the last comma. This is a prompt that you see on the AutoCAD command line. Type the name of the file to edit, and Windows opens it in Notepad. (You need to type in the complete path of the file.)

Creating keyboard shortcuts to commands

Most of the *acad.pgp* file contains aliases, or keyboard shortcuts, for common AutoCAD commands. You can change these or add your own. Once you get used to them, it's generally faster to type shortcuts at the command line than to click the toolbar button or menu item. You cannot include a command option in the *acad.pgp* file. To do that, you need to create a menu item, toolbar button, or AutoLISP routine.

The format for creating an alias is as follows:

```
Shortcut,*Full command name
```

Refer back to Figure 29-1 for some examples of shortcuts. Note that the space between the columns is not necessary — it simply improves readability.

You can use aliases transparently if the command itself can be used transparently. Aliases cannot be used in script files or menus.

Using the Alias Editor

AutoCAD includes an Alias Editor that lets you edit aliases in a dialog box. This editor comes with the Bonus Pack. If you did a Full installation (or a Custom installation that included the Bonus Pack), you will find it in your *Acadr14\bonus\cadtools* folder. You can run the Alias Editor in two ways:

✦ From within AutoCAD, type **aliasedit** ↵.

✦ If AutoCAD is not open, double-click *alias.exe* in the *Acadr14\bonus\cadtools* folder or choose Start⇨Run, locate the file, and click OK.

If you open the Alias Editor from within AutoCAD, or from outside AutoCAD but while AutoCAD is running, the Alias Editor automatically loads all the current aliases from the *acad.pgp* file in alphabetical order, as shown in Figure 29-2.

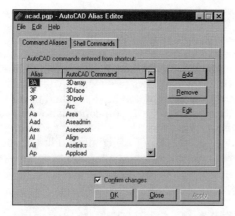

Figure 29-2: The Alias Editor.

Using the Alias Editor is very intuitive, although there is a small help file. Choose the Command Aliases tab to work on command aliases and choose the Shell Commands tab to work on Windows (or DOS) command aliases. Choose Add to add a new command, Remove to delete one, and Edit to edit one.

In this Step-by-Step exercise, you use the text editor method of customizing the *acad.pgp* file. Not all users may have the Alias Editor installed and using a text editor is a good introduction to other customization tasks.

Step-by-Step: Customizing the *acad.pgp* File

Caution

If you are working on someone else's computer do not do this exercise without that person's permission. It is not good computer etiquette to modify other people's AutoCAD files without asking first.

1. Start AutoCAD.

2. Place a blank diskette in your diskette drive. Type **explorer** ↵. After opening a preliminary window, AutoCAD opens Windows Explorer, using the *acad.pgp* shortcut.

3. Find your *Acadr14* folder and open it (click the plus sign next to it). Click the *Support* folder. Find *acad.pgp*, click it, and drag it to the drive (in the All Folders window) that contains your diskette. Windows copies *acad.pgp* to the diskette. If you haven't already backed up your other customizable files, copy *acad.lin*, *acad.lsp, acad.mln, acad.mnl, acad.mnu,* and *acad.pat* to the diskette as well. Remove the diskette and label it *AutoCAD customizable files — original form*.

4. While Explorer is open, double-click *acad.pgp*. Windows opens it in Notepad. (If Windows opens the Open With dialog box, choose Notepad from the list. Make sure that the Always use this program to open this file option is checked and click OK. From now on, Windows will automatically open your *acad.pgp* file with Notepad.)

5. Scroll down until you see the three Windows commands, as shown in Figure 29-3. Place the cursor at the end of the PBRUSH line and press Enter.

```
; Examples of external commands for Windows
; See also the STARTAPP AutoLISP function for an alternative method.

EXPLORER,   START EXPLORER, 1,,
NOTEPAD,    START NOTEPAD,  1,*File to edit: ,
PBRUSH,     START PBRUSH,   1,,
```

Figure 29-3: The Windows commands in the *acad.pgp* file.

6. Type the following and press Enter. (The uppercase and spaces are not necessary but match the format of the rest of the file.)

```
WORDPAD,    START WORDPAD,  1,,
```

7. Scroll down to the next section of *acad.pgp.* Read AutoCAD's guidelines for creating new aliases.

8. Scroll down until you see the following two lines:

```
CH,          *DDCHPROP
-CH,         *CHANGE
```

The alias for the CHANGE command follows the guideline of using a hyphen to distinguish command-line versions of commands. Suppose you have trouble finding that hyphen quickly (you end up typing =ch instead). You want to change the alias to cg (with no hyphen).

9. To be extra careful, add a new alias rather than changing the current alias (which someone may be in the habit of using). Place the cursor after the word *CHANGE and press Enter. Type the following and press Enter. (Don't worry about the spaces — I've matched the spacing of the *acad.pgp* file.)

```
CG,          *CHANGE
```

10. Choose File⇨Save. This section of *acad.pgp* that you worked on should look like Figure 29-4.

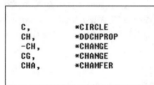

Figure 29-4: A section of the edited *acad.pgp* file.

11. Close Notepad. Generally, AutoCAD only reads *acad.pgp* when loading a new or existing drawing. However, you can use the REINIT command to reload the file at any time. Type **reinit** ↵. AutoCAD opens the Re-initialization dialog box, shown in Figure 29-5.

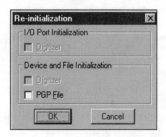

Figure 29-5: The Re-initialization dialog box.

12. Check PGP File and click OK. In your drawing, draw any line.

13. Type **cg** ↵. AutoCAD starts the CHANGE command. Select the line, press Enter to end selection, and pick a new endpoint location. AutoCAD changes the endpoint of the line.

14. Do not save your drawing.

You can print out *acad.pgp* and tape it up on the wall where you work. The Alias Editor lets you export the file in a text format and can also print it.

The Alias Editor automatically reloads *acad.pgp* for you after you finish editing, so you don't need to use REINIT.

The edited *acad.pgp* is on the CD-ROM in the *Results* folder.

You cannot use control or function keys in command aliases in the *.pgp* file.

Customizing Toolbars

In the Windows 95 environment, you find yourself using toolbar buttons for many of your tasks. Nevertheless, how many times have you found yourself typing a command because you couldn't find it quickly on a toolbar, or because it was on a flyout that was too annoying to deal with? Think how often you start a command with a toolbar button, only to have to return to the keyboard to type in a simple option.

You can customize AutoCAD's toolbars to make your work easier and faster. You can create new toolbars from scratch, or edit the existing ones. You can even create your own toolbar buttons. When you create a toolbar button, you can attach any sequence of commands to it — a complex macro or even an AutoLISP expression.

Using the Toolbars dialog box

The Toolbars dialog box, shown in Figure 29-6, has been restructured to make it easier to manage toolbars.

Simply check the toolbar you want to see. This list includes flyouts. It is therefore very easy to turn a flyout into a toolbar if you want. Just click the flyout — for example, Viewpoints or Zoom — and it appears as a regular toolbar.

You also use this dialog box to create new toolbars, delete toolbars, and customize existing toolbars. If you create your own menus, they can have toolbars as well. You can then choose toolbars from your menus using the Menu Group drop-down list.

Figure 29-6: The Toolbars dialog box.

Creating a new toolbar

To create a new toolbar, choose New in the Toolbars dialog box. In the New Toolbar dialog box, shown in Figure 29-7, name your toolbar (and the Menu Group if you have created one), then click OK. Your toolbar now appears in the Toolbars list of the Toolbars dialog box, and there is a small, new toolbar on the screen, as shown in Figure 29-8.

Figure 29-7: The New Toolbar dialog box.

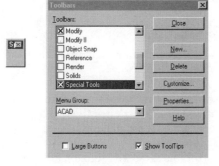

Figure 29-8: The new toolbar shown in the Toolbar list and on the screen.

The new toolbar is just a baby, but as you add buttons to it, it grows automatically.

Tip

An important part of managing toolbars is finding a place to dock them so they don't take up valuable real estate on the screen. You can make several small toolbars and fit them in the blank spaces next to existing toolbars.

Removing buttons

If you have opened a toolbar by checking a toolbar or flyout from the Toolbars dialog box, you may wish to customize it by removing buttons that you rarely use. To remove buttons from a toolbar, follow these steps:

1. Open the Toolbars dialog box if it is not already open.

2. Choose Customize to open the Customize Toolbars dialog box, shown in Figure 29-9. If necessary, move it out of the way so you can access the toolbar that needs a button removed.

3. Drag the unwanted button off the toolbar and onto the screen area and release the mouse button.

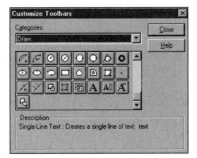

Figure 29-9: The Customize Toolbars dialog box.

Note

It's easy to forget that you need to have the Customize Toolbars dialog box open to remove buttons, because there's no direct connection between dragging buttons off the toolbar and the dialog box — but you can't drag buttons off a toolbar unless the dialog box is open. It's also easy to drag a button off of the Customize Toolbars dialog box — if you do, you create a new toolbar inadvertently.

Adding buttons

If you have created a new toolbar, you need to add buttons to it. There are several ways to do this:

✦ **Add a button from the Customize Toolbars dialog box.** Open the Customize Toolbars dialog box and choose a category. AutoCAD provides a number of preset buttons in each category (including many of the flyout buttons from Release 13). Click a button to see its description at the bottom of the dialog box. When you have found the button you want, drag it to your new toolbar.

✦ **Move a button from another toolbar.** With the Customize Toolbars dialog box open, drag a button from one open toolbar to your new toolbar. This moves the button, deleting it from the original toolbar.

✦ **Copy a button from another toolbar.** If you want to leave the original toolbar intact, use the same technique as for moving a button, but hold down the Ctrl key as you drag a button from one open toolbar to your new toolbar. This copies the button.

Creating your own button definition

You can also create your own button definition from scratch. Follow these steps:

1. With the Customize Toolbars dialog box open, choose Custom from the Categories list. You see two blank buttons, a regular toolbar button, and a flyout button that has a little black triangle on it.

2. Drag the button you want onto your toolbar.

3. Right-click the blank button to open the Button Properties dialog box, shown in Figure 29-10.

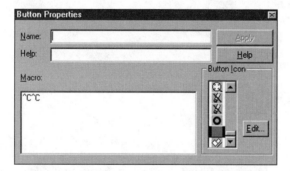

Figure 29-10: The Button Properties dialog box.

4. Type a name for the button. This name will appear as a ToolTip, so don't make it too long.

5. Type a help description in the Help text box. This text will appear on the status line to further explain the function of the button.

6. Write the macro. AutoCAD places ^C^C there for you. This cancels any other command that may be active when you use the button. You can place any valid command string as it would be typed on the command line or even an AutoLISP expression.

Cross-Reference

You should use menu syntax for the macro. I explain the details of creating command strings in Chapter 32.

7. Choose a button icon from the Button Icon list, or choose Edit to create your own button, as explained in the next section.

8. Click Apply and click the Close button of the Button Properties dialog box to close it. Close any other open dialog boxes.

AutoCAD updates the menus, showing its progress on the status bar.

Using the Button Editor

The Button Editor, shown in Figure 29-11, lets you make your own button icons. You can choose one of the provided buttons and edit it — which I recommend — or start from scratch if you are the artistic type.

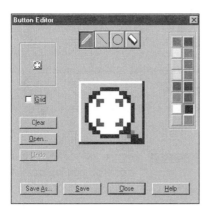

Figure 29-11: The Button Editor.

The center of the editing area shows an enlarged view of the button. You see the button's actual size at the top left of the dialog box. Check Grid to show a grid of pixels — this is just for your reference. Choose a color from the color palette and then choose one of the four tools at the top of the dialog box:

✦ The Pencil tool draws any shape. To draw, drag it across the editing area.

✦ Click and drag the Line tool to draw a straight line.

✦ The Circle tool draws circles. You click the center and drag out to the circumference to indicate the radius.

✦ The Erase tool erases. You can click to erase pixel by pixel or drag to erase a series of pixels.

Here are the other features of the Button Editor:

✦ Choose Clear to clear the editing area and start from scratch.

✦ Choose Open to open an existing button for editing. Button icons are stored as *.bmp* files.

✦ Choose Undo to undo your last action.

✦ Choose Save to save the button icon as a *.bmp* file.

✦ Choose Close to close the Button Editor.

Creating flyouts

You can also create your own flyouts, or you can use one of the custom flyouts. To use a custom flyout, open the Configure Toolbars dialog box and choose Custom Flyouts. If these look familiar, that's because they are the Release 13 flyouts that disappeared in Release 14. You can simply drag one of these to a toolbar.

To create your own flyout, follow these steps:

1. Open the Configure Toolbars dialog box.

2. Choose Custom from the Categories drop-down list and choose the blank flyout button (the one with the small black triangle).

3. Right-click the new flyout button to open the Flyout Properties dialog box, shown in Figure 29-12.

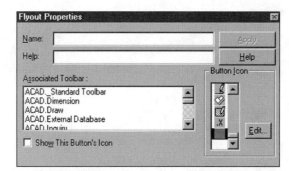

Figure 29-12: The Flyout Properties dialog box.

4. As with the Button Properties dialog box described earlier, type a name and help description.

5. Instead of choosing a macro as you do for a regular button, choose a toolbar. This toolbar will be the flyout from the flyout button you just added. AutoCAD provides a number of predefined flyouts, but any toolbars that you have created are also listed and you can therefore choose a custom toolbar for your flyout.

6. Choose a button for the flyout button. You can edit it using the Button Editor if you want.

7. If you want the button you chose to always show, check Show This Button's Icon. Otherwise, the last used button in the flyout will show.

8. Choose Apply and close the dialog boxes.

The following Step-by-Step exercise changes your menu files. After the exercise, I explain how to undo the changes if you wish.

Step-by-Step: Customizing Toolbars

Caution

If you are working on someone else's computer, do not do this exercise without that person's permission. It is not good computer etiquette to modify other people's AutoCAD files without asking first.

1. Open Windows Explorer and copy *acad.mnu, acad.mnc,* and *acad.mns* from the *Acadr14\support* folder to a diskette. Label and date the diskette.

2. Start a new drawing using the *acad.dwt* template. Save it as *ab29-1.dwg* in your *AutoCAD Bible* folder.

3. Right-click any toolbar to open the Toolbars dialog box. From the Toolbars list, scroll down to find the Zoom toolbar and check it. When it appears, drag it away from the Toolbars dialog box.

4. Choose Customize to open the Customize Toolbars dialog box. You can now drag buttons off the Zoom toolbar.

5. Drag the Zoom Center and Zoom All buttons off the toolbar (or choose the two buttons that you use least and drag them off). There is a small space between the last (Zoom Extents) button and the rest of the buttons. Drag the Zoom Extents button to the left slightly to eliminate the space.

6. Drag the toolbar to the space at the right of the Standard toolbar and dock it there.

7. Close the Customize Toolbars dialog box and choose New in the Toolbars dialog box. In the New Toolbar dialog box, type **Special** in the Name text box and click OK. A small toolbar appears on your screen.

8. Click Customize. From the Categories list, choose Draw. Find the Donut button and drag it to your new toolbar. Choose the Modify category and find the Align button (it's the sixth button in the second row). Drag it to your new toolbar. Also drag the Edit Polyline (first button, last row) to the toolbar. Choose the Render category and drag the Hide button (first button, first row) to the toolbar.

9. Choose the Custom category and drag the blank toolbar button (without the triangle) to the new toolbar. Right-click the blank button to open the Button Properties dialog box.

10. Complete the dialog box as shown in Figure 29-13. Type the macro as follows after the ^C^C, which is already there, being careful to include the spaces as well:

```
pedit \w .1 x
```

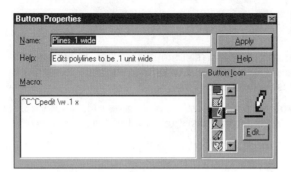

Figure 29-13: The completed Button Properties dialog box.

11. Choose the Polyline Edit button from the Button Icon list (it's about 1/4 of the way down), as shown in Figure 29-13. Choose Edit to open the Button Editor.

12. You want to change the button so it looks like a zero width polyline is being changed to a wider polyline, since that's what the macro does. Click the red color. Choose the pencil tool (by default, it is already chosen). Click Grid to help you work. Click the point of the pencil tool in each box, using Figure 29-14 as a guide (Figure 29-14 shows the button in black and white). When you're done, choose Save, then Close.

If you make a mistake, it's easy to correct. If you place a red pixel over an existing black pixel, choose black and redraw the black pixel. If you place a red pixel in a wrong spot, choose the Erase tool and click the pixel.

13. In the Button Properties dialog box, click Apply. The new button appears in your toolbar. Click the Close button to close the Button Properties dialog box, and close the other two dialog boxes as well. AutoCAD saves the changes to your menu source file (.mns).

14. Drag the new toolbar under the first Zoom toolbar you created.

15. Choose Polyline from the Draw toolbar and draw any series of polyline segments. Choose the Plines .1 wide button from the new toolbar. At the Select polyline: prompt, pick the polyline. AutoCAD changes its width to .1. (If it doesn't work, check the macro. Right-click the Plines .1 wide button to open the Button Properties dialog box for that button.)

16. Save your drawing.

If you later customize the ACAD menu by editing *acad.mnu*, your toolbar modifications will be erased! In Chapter 33, where I discuss customizing AutoCAD's menus, I explain how to avoid this problem.

Figure 29-14: The new toolbars.

New toolbars

Undoing toolbar changes

In order to undo your toolbar changes, you need to reload the template menu, *acad.mnu*. This overwrites the compiled and source menu files that include your toolbar changes. Follow these steps:

Be sure to have a backup of your *acad.mnu, acad.mnc,* and *acad.mns* files from the *Acadr14\support* folder.

1. Choose Tools⇨Customize Menus. The Menu Groups tab should be on top. In the Menu Groups box, ACAD should be highlighted, as shown here.

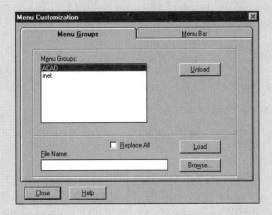

2. In the bottom section of the dialog box, check Replace All so that AutoCAD loads all your menu files on the menu bar. In the File Name box, type **acad.mnu** and click Load. When you load the *acad.mnu* file, AutoCAD warns you that you will lose any toolbar customization changes you have made, as shown in the following figure. Click Yes since you want to overwrite all your toolbar customization changes.

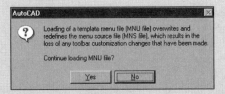

3. AutoCAD loads the menu and displays the Menu loaded successfully. MENUGROUP: ACAD message. Click Close. Your toolbars disappear.

I cover the topic of menu files in more detail in Chapter 32.

Here's how the pedit macro works:

```
pedit \w .1 x
```

1. `pedit` issues the PEDIT command. The space after `pedit` is equivalent to pressing Enter after you have typed the command on the command line. PEDIT then displays the `Select polyline:` prompt.

2. The backslash (\) is a special character that pauses the macro for your input. When you select the polyline, the macro continues, displaying the `Close/Join/Width/Edit vertex/Fit/Spline/Decurve/Ltype gen/ Undo/eXit <X>:` prompt.

3. The `w` then chooses the Width option. The space following it is like pressing Enter. PEDIT then displays the `Enter new width for all segments:` prompt.

4. The macro then specifies .1. The space after it is like pressing Enter again. PEDIT then issues the `Close/Join/Width/Edit vertex/Fit/Spline/ Decurve/Ltype gen/Undo/eXit <X>:` prompt.

5. The macro then chooses the `X` option, which ends the command.

Summary

In this chapter you started to customize AutoCAD by creating command shortcuts in the *acad.pgp* file. You also learned how to create your own toolbars that can contain any command sequence you need.

In the next chapter you learn how to create macros with script files.

✦   ✦   ✦

Creating Macros and Slide Shows with Script Files

Creating Macros with Script Files

Script files are like macros that you create in your word processor or spreadsheet. They execute a series of commands automatically. You can use script files to automate plotting, set up a drawing, clean up a drawing, create a slide show, or do any repetitive task.

Script files have the following characteristics:

+ They must use the *.scr* filename extension.

+ They are text-only (ASCII) files.

+ They must use command line syntax only.

Note   One of the most common uses for script files before Release 14 was to automate plotting. Release 14 now includes the Batch Plot Utility, which can do many multiple plotting tasks for you.

Creating the script file

You create the script file using a text editor such as Notepad. Type each command on its own line. You can use either a space or a return (press Enter) at the end of a line to represent pressing Enter. If you need two returns one after another at the end of a line, use a blank line for the second return. Every space is meaningful — getting those spaces right is probably the hardest part of creating a script file.

Tip   Here are some tips to help you create successful script files with the least aggravation:

✦ Go through the steps once using the command line only before creating the script file.

✦ Set the system variable CMDDIA to zero (off) before experimenting with the commands you will use in the script file. This lets you practice the keystrokes without opening dialog boxes.

✦ Set CMDDIA to zero at the beginning of the script file itself and to 1 at the end.

✦ If you will use any dialog boxes that ask for files, do the same with FILEDIA as for CMDDIA.

✦ Place comments in your script file to explain what you are doing. A comment is any line that starts with a semicolon.

✦ Keep Notepad open as you work. When you have completed a set of keystrokes that you want, open the AutoCAD Text Window (press F2), select the command string you want, right-click, choose Copy, switch back to Notepad, and paste. Then cut out all the prompts, leaving only the keyboard entry. You will probably have to readjust the spaces between the words.

Remember, you can open Notepad from within AutoCAD by typing **Notepad** at the command line. At the `File to open:` prompt, press Enter to open a new file. The *acad.pgp* file includes this Windows command by default.

Another option is to simply write down what you type at the command line. As you write, use an underscore to represent each space. It's very hard to remember that you left three spaces between two words unless you see three underscores. Of course, when you create the script file, you must use spaces, not underscores.

Once you have completed the script file, save it with any name that is meaningful to you and an extension of *.scr*. Then close Notepad before running the script.

Here's an example of a script file that draws a series of circles:

```
circle 2,2 1.5
circle 6,2 1.5
circle 10,2 1.5
circle 14,2 1.5
```

This script file starts the CIRCLE command, specifies a center point, and specifies a radius four times. The results are shown in Figure 30-1.

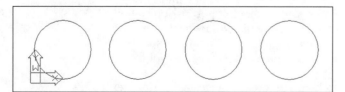

Figure 30-1: This drawing was created by running a script file.

Running script files

You can run a script file from within a drawing. Use this technique when you want the script to apply only to that drawing. You can also run a script file when loading AutoCAD. You would do this when you want the script file to apply to more than one drawing. For example, you could use script files in the following situations:

✦ You want to use a script file to set up all drawings you open. Although the script file applies to only one drawing at a time, over time it is used on many drawings.

✦ You want to use a script file to clean up a list of drawings in one batch — such as thawing all layers on all the drawings in a folder.

Running a script file from within a drawing

To run a script from within a drawing, follow these steps:

1. Choose Tools⇨Run Script. This opens the Select Script File dialog box, shown in Figure 30-2.

Figure 30-2: The Select Script File dialog box.

2. Choose the script file you want.

3. Click Open. AutoCAD runs the script file.

Running a script when loading AutoCAD

Run a script when loading AutoCAD by changing the target expression that Windows uses to open AutoCAD. The easiest way to do this is to create a shortcut to AutoCAD on your desktop and modify the target there.

Cross-
Reference

I explain how to create a shortcut on the desktop in Chapter 1.

Right-click the AutoCAD shortcut and choose Properties. Click the Shortcut tab, shown in Figure 30-3.

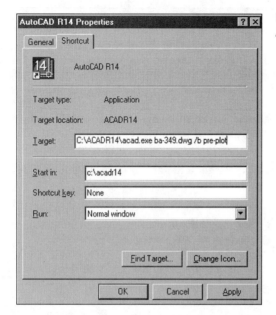

Figure 30-3: The Shortcut tab of the AutoCAD R14 Properties dialog box.

The Target text box displays the command expression that Windows uses to open AutoCAD. Don't make any change to the current expression — you just add to it. The format for starting a script file is:

```
drive:\path\acad.exe existing_drawing /b script_file
```

For example, if your current target reads *C:\ACADR14\acad.exe* and you want to open a drawing named *ba-349.dwg* and run a script file named *pre-plot.scr*, your target should read:

```
C:\ACADR14\acad.exe ba-349.dwg /b pre-plot
```

You don't need to add the *.scr* extension after the script file name. Long filenames that contain spaces must be enclosed in quotation marks — both in the target and in the script file itself. For example:

```
c:\ACADR14\acad.exe  c:\aec\drc\Dobbs Ferry Apartments.dwg  /b
c:\aec\drc\cleanup
```

If either the drawing or the script file are not in AutoCAD's support path, include the entire path.

If you want to start a new drawing, you need to specify a template. In the above format, replace the AutoCAD drawing filename with:

```
/t template_name
```

When you have finished typing your additions in the Target text box, click OK. Now, when you start AutoCAD, the drawing or template opens, and the script starts.

Once you have started a script file, you can open other drawings. In this way you can run a script file on as many drawings as you want. Figure 30-4 shows a script file, *multi-cleanup.scr,* which is used when loading AutoCAD. The target is set so that AutoCAD opens *Apt 1A.dwg.*

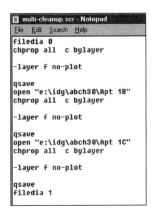

Figure 30-4: A script file that cleans up three drawings.

Here's how it works:

1. In *Apt 1A.dwg,* the script file sets the FILEDIA system variable to 0 so it can open other drawings without opening a dialog box.

2. The CHPROP command selects all objects and sets their color to BYLAYER.

3. The LAYER command is used with a hyphen so it doesn't open a dialog box. It then freezes the no-plot layer.

4. The script file saves the drawing and opens the next drawing.

5. This process is repeated until the last drawing is edited and saved.

6. FILEDIA is set back to 1.

Tip It's nice to leave the last drawing open so that when you return to see the results you can see that the last drawing has been properly edited. You then feel pretty sure that all the previous drawings were similarly edited.

Notice the quotation marks around the filenames in the script file. These are necessary because the drawing filenames include spaces.

In this Step-by-Step exercise, you create and use a script file similar to the multi-cleanup script file used in the previous example, but for only one drawing.

Ddscript writes a script file to run on multiple drawings and runs it. Look in
*Software**Chap30**Ddscript*.

Step-by-Step: Creating and Using a Script File

1. Open *ab30-a.dwg* from the CD-ROM.

2. Save it as *ab30-1.dwg* in your *AutoCAD Bible* folder.

3. Type **notepad** ↵. At the File to open: prompt, press Enter to open a new file.

4. Type the following, replacing the underscores with spaces. Note that there are two spaces between all and c in the first line. Press Enter after the last line.

   ```
   Chprop_all__c_bylayer

   -layer_f_no-plot

   filedia_0
   save

   filedia_1
   ```

5. Save the file as *cleanup.scr* in your *AutoCAD Bible* folder. Close Notepad.

6. The script file changes the color property of all objects to Bylayer and freezes the no-plot layer. Notice that the drawing has some text that has been set to a blue color (maybe to make it more easily readable). The title block is on the no-plot layer. Choose Tools⇨Run Script.

7. In the Select Script File dialog box, find *cleanup.scr* in your *AutoCAD Bible* folder and click Open. AutoCAD runs the script, changing the text's color to Bylayer (green) and freezing the no-plot layer. It also saves the drawing.

   If the script file doesn't work, press F2 to open the Text Window and see where it got hung up. That will help you see where to correct the script file. Reopen it (choose Start⇨Documents and choose *cleanup.scr*) and make the correction. Save it, close it, and try again.

8. Save your drawing.

Taking script files to the max

What if you want to perform that multi-cleanup script file on 200 drawings? Typing in all those filenames would take so long you would wonder if you were saving any time.

There is a way. First, you need to find a text editor or word processor that can create *vertical blocks* of text. This means that you can select columns of text rather than lines of text. You can do this in Microsoft Word by holding down Alt and dragging down the text. Then, you need to format the script file so that the entire set of commands is in one row, as in the figure shown here. In Microsoft Word you can use Page Setup to set the paper to landscape and make it as wide as you need, so that the text doesn't wrap. (Of course, you type the script once, then copy the line and paste it as many times as you need.)

You do this so that all the filenames will be in one column. Here you see the path but no filename at the end of each line. The filename will be inserted before the quotation mark at the end of each line.

```
filedia 0
chprop all c bylayer -layer f no-plot qsave open "e:\aec\drc\ "
chprop all c bylayer -layer f no-plot qsave open "e:\aec\drc\ "
chprop all c bylayer -layer f no-plot qsave
filedia 1
```

Now, open a DOS window. (Choose Start➪Programs➪MS DOS Prompt.) Use the DOS cd command to navigate to the folder where all your drawings are. (They should all be in one folder.) Type **dir *.dwg /b >dwglst.txt** and press Enter. This creates a listing of all the files in that folder and places it in a text file named *dwglst.txt*. The /b parameter creates a file that contains only the names of the drawings.

Open the file in your text editor or word processor that can create vertical blocks. Create a vertical block over the drawing names and copy it to the Clipboard.

Return to your script file, place the cursor at the top left of the vertical block, and paste. You should get all the drawing names inserted in the right place, as shown here with two drawings. If you're in a word processor, don't forget to save it as a Text Only document.

```
filedia 0
chprop all c bylayer -layer f no-plot qsave open "e:\aec\drc\Apt 1B"
chprop all c bylayer -layer f no-plot qsave open "e:\aec\drc\Apt 1C"
chprop all c bylayer -layer f no-plot qsave
filedia 1
```

Used in this way, script files can be an extremely powerful tool for editing large numbers of drawings in one batch.

Creating Slide Shows

One common use for script files is to create a slide show. AutoCAD lets you save a view of a drawing as a slide. You can then create a slide library from the slides and show the slides one after another automatically.

Tip

You can save any drawing as a *.tif*, *.bmp*, or *.wmf* file and import it into a presentation program that creates slide shows, such as Microsoft PowerPoint, Lotus Freelance Graphics, or Corel Presentations. You can add text, special effects, and so on to create a professional slide show.

Creating slides

A slide is like capturing the screen of your drawing. AutoCAD makes a raster image from the current viewport in model space, or from all viewports in paper space. You can also create a slide of a wireframe, hidden, or shaded display. Unfortunately, you cannot make slides of rendered images.

To create a slide, follow these steps:

1. Display the view of the drawing that you want to save as a slide.

2. Type **mslide** ↵.

3. In the Create Slide File dialog box, choose a location and name for the slide. Its extension will be *.sld*.

4. Choose Save.

Viewing slides

To view a slide, follow these steps:

1. Type **vslide** ↵.

2. In the Select Slide File dialog box, choose the slide you want to view.

3. Choose Open. AutoCAD displays the slide.

Note

Do a Redraw to return to your drawing. You cannot draw in or edit a slide.

Step-by-Step: Creating and Viewing Slides

On the
CD-ROM

1. Open *ab30-b.dwg* from the CD-ROM.

2. Save it as *ab30-2.dwg* in your *AutoCAD Bible* folder.

3. Type **mslide** ↵. In the Create Slide File dialog box, click the Save in drop-down box and select your *AutoCAD Bible* folder. In the File name text box, change the name from its default of *ab30-2.sld* to *ab30-2a.sld.* Click Save.

4. Type **hide** ↵. AutoCAD hides the drawing.

5. Issue the MSLIDE command again. This time save the slide as *ab30-2b.sld.*

6. Change the SHADEDGE system variable to 1. Type **shade** ↵.

7. Issue the MSLIDE command again and save the slide as *ab30-2c.sld.*

8. Do a regen to return to wireframe display. Type **vslide** ↵. In the Select Slide File dialog box, choose the first slide, *ab30-2a.sld.* Click Open. AutoCAD displays the slide.

9. Repeat the VSLIDE command and display *ab30-2b.sld.* Do the same with *ab30-2c.sld.* Notice that the slide of the shaded model takes much longer to display and its quality is not as good as the original shaded model.

10. Click Redraw on the Standard toolbar. You return to your last display, the shaded model.

11. Save your drawing.

Using scripts to create slide shows

You can create a script file that displays slides one after another, resulting in a slide show. AutoCAD provides two special script file commands for this purpose:

✦ DELAY *nnnn* pauses the script for the number of milliseconds you specify. For example, DELAY 3000 pauses the script for three seconds.

✦ RSCRIPT repeats the script from the beginning. Use this command to create a continuously running script. To stop the script (whether repeating or not), press Esc.

✦ RESUME restarts a script file after you have stopped it by pressing Esc.

The VSLIDE command, which displays a slide, can also be used to preload the next slide into memory. You use this command to preload a slide while viewers are looking at the previous slide. This reduces the waiting time between slides. To use this feature, put an asterisk (*) before the filename in the VSLIDE command. The next VSLIDE command detects that a slide has been preloaded and displays it without asking for the slide name. Here's how it works:

```
vslide ab30-2a
vslide *ab30-2b
delay 3000
vslide
vslide *ab30-2c
delay 3000
vslide
rscript
```

This script file does the following:

1. It displays *ab30-2a.sld*.

2. It preloads *ab30-2b.sld*.

3. It waits three seconds, displaying *ab30-2a.sld*.

4. It displays *ab30-2b.sld*.

5. It preloads *ab30-2c.sld*.

6. It waits three seconds, displaying *ab30-2b.sld*.

7. It displays *ab30-2c.sld*.

8. It repeats the script from the beginning.

Try creating this slide show script in the following Step-by-Step exercise.

Step-by-Step: Creating a Slide Show

1. Open Notepad and type the following script:

```
vslide ab30-2a
vslide *ab30-2b
delay 3000
vslide
vslide *ab30-2c
delay 3000
vslide
rscript
```

2. Remember to add a blank line after the last line. Save it as *ab30-2.scr* in your *AutoCAD Bible* folder. Close Notepad.

3. So that AutoCAD can find the slide files, place your *AutoCAD Bible* folder in AutoCAD's support file search path. Choose Tools⇨Preferences⇨Files tab. Click Support File Search Path and choose Add. Choose Browse and find your

AutoCAD Bible folder. Click OK twice. You may see a message that AutoCAD may need to be started again for the changes to go into effect. Try running the script without restarting AutoCAD. If it doesn't work, restart AutoCAD.

4. In any AutoCAD drawing, choose Tools⇨Run Script. Locate *ab30-2.scr* in your *AutoCAD Bible* folder and choose Open. AutoCAD runs the slide show. Notice that the last slide still takes a while to display.

5. Let the slide show run through twice. The last slide displays a little more quickly the second time. Press Esc to stop the slide show.

6. Do not save your drawing.

Tip

When running a slide show, you might want to maximize the screen area by reducing menu and command line space. You can unload your menu, thus quickly dismissing toolbars from the screen. Use Preferences⇨Display to reduce the number of lines of text to show on the command line to 1. Remember, when you unload the menu, you have no menus available. You can reload the menu — instructions for unloading and loading menus are in Chapter 33.

Creating Slide Libraries

You can organize your slides into slide libraries. Slide libraries have an extension of *.slb.* One reason for creating slide libraries is to create image tiles when you are customizing your menu. To see an example of an image tile menu, choose Modify⇨Object⇨Multilines or Draw⇨Surfaces⇨3D Surfaces. These image tiles are created with slides organized into libraries.

To view slides in a library, use the following format:

```
library (slidename)
```

Let's say you placed the three slides used in the last Step-by-Step exercise in a slide library called *3dmodel.slb.* You would then use the following command in the script file to preload the second slide (the second line of the script file):

```
vslide *3dmodel (ab30-2b)
```

To create a slide library, you need to use the DOS prompt. (One day, there may be a dialog box for this!) AutoCAD provides the SLIDELIB utility in its *acadr14\support* folder to create slide libraries.

Note

To get to the DOS prompt, choose Start⇨Programs⇨MS-DOS Prompt.

Follow these steps to create a slide library:

1. Create a text file (you can use Notepad) containing the names of the slide files. Include the paths of the slide files if they are not in AutoCAD's support file search path. Place each slide filename on a new line.

Tip

SLIDELIB can read a listing created using DOS's `dir` command with the `/b` parameter, which creates a simple listing of just the file names. Therefore, you can place all the slide files in a folder and redirect the `dir` listing to a file. For example, you can create a list named *ab30sld.lst* by typing the following at the DOS prompt:

```
dir *.sld /b >ab30sld.lst
```

This creates the list in the same folder as the slide files.

2. Assuming you are still in the same folder where you created the slide file list and you want to create a library called *ab30sld.slb* in the same folder, type the following at the DOS prompt:

```
c:\acadr14\support\slidelib ab30sld < ab30sld.lst
```

Note

SLIDELIB cannot accept filenames with spaces but it can handle long filenames, provided you use a character such as an underscore where you might normally have a blank space.

Summary

You can create script files to automate repetitive commands. Script files are text-only files that contain commands, options, and values in command-line format. You can run script files from within a drawing or when loading AutoCAD.

You can create a slide, which is a raster image, from the display in your viewport. You can then create a script file that displays several slides one after another, resulting in a slide show. You can organize your slides into slide libraries.

In the next chapter you learn how to create your own linetypes and hatch patterns.

✦   ✦   ✦

Creating Your Own Linetypes and Hatch Patterns

◆　◆　◆　◆

In This Chapter

Creating linetypes

Creating hatch
patterns

◆　◆　◆　◆

Creating Linetypes

As you know, AutoCAD comes with a large number of
linetypes. However, sometimes these may not serve your
particular needs. You can therefore create your own linetypes
and use them in your drawings in the same way you use the
linetypes that AutoCAD provides. Linetypes are useful
whenever you don't want a continuous linetype. They apply
not only to lines, but also to polylines, arcs, ellipses,
wireframes, and solids — in fact, to most AutoCAD objects.

There are two types of linetypes: simple and complex. Simple
linetypes consist of dashes and dots only. Complex linetypes
also usually have dashes and/or dots but also contain text
and/or shapes.

The default linetype file is *acad.lin.* You can add your own
linetype definitions to this file or create your own linetype
files. Linetype files are text files and must have an extension
of *.lin.* Of course, be sure to make a copy of *acad.lin* before
you edit it.

Creating simple linetypes

The syntax for creating simple linetypes is quite easy. Each
linetype is defined using two lines of text. The first line
contains the linetype name and an optional description,
formatted as follows:

```
*linetype name[, description]
```

Here are the points to note:

✦ Always start the definition with an asterisk.

✦ The description is limited to 47 characters.

✦ If you include a description, precede it with a comma.

The Linetype tab of the Layer & Linetype Properties dialog box now contains an Appearance column that graphically displays each linetype. Previously, it was common to use the description section of the linetype definition to show a text approximation of the linetype, such as —..—.. for a linetype containing two dashes, then two dots. This is no longer necessary. You could instead include a description explaining the use of the linetype, such as Future location of hedges.

The second line of the linetype syntax is its definition. With simple linetypes you are limited to dashes, dots, and spaces, measured in units and shown as follows:

✦ A dash is indicated by a positive number.

✦ A dot is indicated by a zero.

✦ A space is indicated by a negative number.

✦ Each item is separated by a comma, there are no spaces, and the maximum line length is 80 characters.

✦ Each line must start with the letter A.

The following definition creates a line with two dashes of .25 units, each followed by two dots, all separated by spaces of .1 unit.

```
*seeingdouble, Future hedge line
A,.25,-.1,.25,-.1,0,-.1,0,-.1
```

The result is shown in Figure 31-1.

Figure 31-1: The seeingdouble linetype.

If you feel quite confident, you can even create linetypes on the fly, using the command-line form of the LINETYPE command. Type **-linetype** ↵ and use the Create option. If you make a mistake, you still have to open the linetype file in a text editor to make corrections.

Tip   You'll get best results if you start a linetype definition with the dash if it will include both dashes and dots as part of the definition.

Step-by-Step: Creating a Simple Linetype

1. Open a drawing based on the *acad.dwt* template.

2. Save your drawing as *ab31-1.dwg* in your *AutoCAD Bible* folder.

3. Type **Notepad** and press Enter at the `File to edit:` prompt to open a new file in Notepad.

4. Type the following:

```
*3dotsandadash, temporary fencing
A,.5,-.25,0,-.1,0,-.1,0,-.25
```

5. Press Enter after the last line. Save the drawing as *ab31-1.lin* in your *AutoCAD Bible* folder and close Notepad.

6. In your drawing, choose Layers on the Object Properties toolbar, then choose New. Name the new layer `tfence`. Set its color to red.

7. Click Continuous in the Linetype column to open the Select Linetype dialog box. Choose Load.

8. In the Load or Reload Linetypes dialog box, choose File. In the Select Linetype File dialog box, find *ab31-1.lin* in your *AutoCAD Bible* folder, choose it, and click Open.

9. Back in the Load or Reload Linetypes dialog box, choose 3dotsandadash and click OK.

10. Again, in the Select Linetype dialog box, choose 3dotsandadash and click OK. The layer `tfence` now shows the correct linetype. Click Current, then OK.

11. Start the LINE command and turn on ORTHO. Draw any line to see the linetype. Save your drawing. The linetype should look like Figure 31-2.

— ·· — ·· — — ·· — ·· — · — — ·· — ·· — ·· — —

Figure 31-2: The 3dotsandadash linetype.

Creating complex linetypes

A complex linetype includes either shapes or text in the linetype definition. Figure 31-3 shows an example of each.

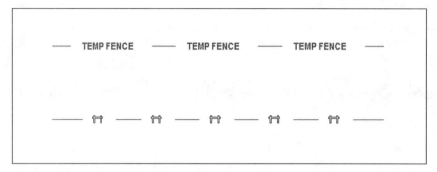

Figure 31-3: Complex linetypes include shapes or text.

Complex linetype definitions are similar to those for simple linetypes, except that they add a definition for a shape or text.

Shapes are covered in the next chapter — for now you only need to know that they are contained in files with the extension *.shx*.

The first line of the linetype definition is the same as for simple linetypes. The second line of the definition can contain all the same features as those for simple linetype. However, you add the special shape or text definition in square brackets:

✦ Syntax for shapes: `[shapename,shxfilename,details]`

✦ Syntax for text: `[ text string ,textstyle,details]`

Details refers to an optional series of rotation, scale, and offset specifications that you can add to the definition. These specifications are described in Table 31-1.

The following complex linetype definition uses a shape and has no details:

```
*TEMPFENCE, FENCE SHAPE AND DASH
A,.5,-.25,[FENCE, C:\AUTOCAD BIBLE\FENCE.SHX ],-.5
```

Note that the specification for the shape is simply part of the rest of the definition that includes a dash, and spaces before and after the shape. The shape is enclosed in both commas and square brackets. The first part of the shape definition is the name of the shape (which is defined in the shape's definition file), and the second part is the name of the shape file. Because in this case the shape file is not in AutoCAD's support file search path, the entire path needs to be specified. Don't forget to use quotation marks around the shape filename if the folder name or filename contains embedded spaces.

Tip   Note that the space after the shape (created with the –.5 code) is larger than the space before it (created with the –.25). You need to make allowance for the space that the shape takes up. This is largely a matter of trial and error, but if you know the shape definition well, you can make a good estimate. When you go back and change the linetype definition (because your first trial was an error), don't forget to reload the linetype (by using the Load option).

The following complex linetype definition uses text and has no details:

```
*TFENCE, DASH & TEXT
A,.5,-.25,[ TEMP FENCE ,FENCE],-1.5
```

Again, the specification for the text is placed within a linetype definition that includes a dash and spaces. The first part of the text definition is the text string, which is always in quotation marks. The second part of the definition is the text style. Again, the space after the text is larger than the space before, to leave room for the text.

Note

You must define this text style in the drawing before you load the linetype.

Table 31-1 lists the details that you can add to both the shape and text portion of complex linetype definitions.

Table 31-1 Optional Details for Shape and Text in Complex Linetype Definitions		
Detail	*Syntax*	*Description*
Relative rotation	R=##	Rotates the shape or text relative to the angle of the line you draw. This number is in degrees unless you put a g (for grads) or r (for radians) after it.
Absolute rotation	A=##	Rotates the shape or text based on the World Coordinate System, regardless of the angle of the line. Because the default is a relative rotation of zero, you can use absolute rotation to keep text facing upright, no matter what the direction of the line. This number is in degrees unless you put a g (for grads) or r (for radians) after it.
Scale	S=##	Scales the text or shape. This scale is multiplied by any scale contained in a shape definition or height in a text style. If you use a text style with a height of zero, this scale number defines the text's height.
X offset	X=##	A positive number moves the shape or text toward the endpoint of the line. A negative number moves the shape or text toward the start point of the line. You can use an X offset to place a shape or text along a continuous linetype. You can also use an X offset to adjust the spacing of a shape or text between dashes, instead of changing the spaces before or after the dashes.
Y offset	Y=##	Moves the shape or text perpendicular to the direction of the line. A positive number moves the shape or text up if the line is drawn from left to right. Use a Y offset to center text and shapes along a linetype.

Here is a definition that includes a shape with a scale and a Y offset:

```
*TEMPFENCE, FENCE SHAPE AND DASH
A,.5,-.25,[FENCE, C:\AUTOCAD BIBLE\FENCE.SHX ,S=.025,Y=-.07],
-.5
```

This shape definition scales the shape to .025 of its original size. This results in the linetype shown in Figure 31-4. Of course, in order to scale the shape, you need to know its original size. You can use the SHAPE command to insert a shape and get an idea of what it looks like. In this case, the shape's original definition is much too large for a linetype and needs to be scaled down.

The shape definition also moves the shape in the minus Y direction by .07 units. This nicely centers the shape within the linetype.

Figure 31-4: The TEMPFENCE linetype.

When you create drawings using shapes or custom fonts, as in the case of complex linetypes, you need to include the shape files or font files when you distribute the drawings to others.

By including more involved shapes in a complex linetype and not much else, you can create a linetype that is, for all practical purposes, a series of shapes displayed one after the other. You can create some interesting effects in this way.

AutoCAD comes with several complex linetypes that are at the end of the \support\acad.lin linetype definition file. Look at their definitions and try them out to get ideas for your own complex linetypes.

Step-by-Step: Creating a Complex Linetype

1. Open *ab31-a.dwg* from the CD-ROM.

2. Save it as *ab31-2.dwg* in your *AutoCAD Bible* folder. This is a simple plan for a trailer park.

3. Choose Format⇨Text Style. Click New and type **TVCABLE** for the Style name. Click OK. In the Font name drop-down list, choose Arial Narrow. Click Apply, then Close.

4. Type **notepad** ↵ and press Enter at the `File to edit:` prompt. AutoCAD opens Notepad. Type the following:

```
*TV, Buried television cable
A,.5,-.5,["TV",TVCABLE,S=.3,X=-.1,Y=-.15],-.75
```

5. Choose File⇨Save and save it in your *AutoCAD Bible* folder as *ab31-2.lin.*

6. Choose Layers from the Object Properties toolbar. Choose Buried_cable and click its Continuous linetype in the Linetype column. In the Select Linetype dialog box, choose Load. Click File. Find *ab31-2.lin* in your *AutoCAD Bible* folder, choose it, and click Open.

7. In the Load or Reload Linetypes dialog box, choose Tv and click OK. Do the same in the Select Linetypes dialog box. Click Current.

8. Click the Linetype tab, and then Details to display the Details section. Change the Global scale factor to 192. Click OK.

9. Draw some lines and polylines. You should zoom in to see the linetype more clearly. Figure 31-5 shows the resulting linetype.

10. Save your drawing.

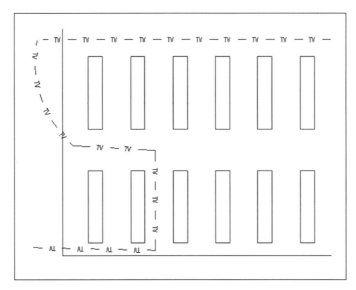

Figure 31-5: The TV linetype.

Creating Hatch Patterns

Hatch patterns are sets of parallel line patterns that are used to fill in an enclosed area. Although the part of the hatch pattern definition that defines each line has some similarities to a linetype definition, for hatch patterns you also need to specify the angle and spacing of the lines. You cannot include text or shapes in hatch patterns.

Hatch patterns are stored in files with an extension of *.pat*. AutoCAD includes a large number of hatch patterns in *acad.pat*. You can add to or edit this file or create your own *.pat* file. As always, don't forget to make a copy of *acad.pat* before you edit it.

Note

If you are not adding patterns to *acad.pat*, you can only put one hatch pattern in a custom *.pat* file. The filename and pattern name must be the same.

You can insert comments in your *.pat* file after a semicolon.

Here is the syntax for hatch patterns:

```
pattern-name [, description]
angle, x-origin,y-origin, delta-x,delta-y [, dash1, dash2,
...]
```

Note

You must press Enter after the end of the last line of the hatch definition.

Here are some general points for hatch pattern definitions:

✦ The pattern name cannot have spaces.

✦ The description is optional.

✦ Add the dash specifications only for noncontinuous lines.

✦ You can have more than one definition line (the second line in the above syntax), creating sets of hatch definitions that combine to create the hatch pattern.

✦ Each definition line can be a maximum of 80 characters.

✦ You can include a maximum of six dash specifications (which include spaces and dots).

✦ You can add spaces in the definition lines for readability.

Table 31-2 describes the features of a hatch pattern definition.

	Table 31-2 **Hatch Pattern Definitions**	
Specification	**Explanation**	
Angle	Defines the angle of the lines in the hatch pattern. If you also specify an angle in the Boundary Hatch dialog box, the two angles are added. For example, if a hatch pattern defines lines at 105 degrees and you specify a hatch angle of 30 degrees, you end up with lines running at 135 degrees.	
X-origin	Specifies the X coordinate of the base point of the hatch pattern. Although your hatch probably won't go through 0,0, AutoCAD uses this point to line up sets of lines in hatch patterns as well as to align hatch patterns in different areas. Since all hatch patterns are calculated from the base point, they are always aligned, no matter where they actually appear in the drawing.	
Y-origin	Specifies the Y coordinate of the base point of the hatch pattern.	
Delta-x	Specifies the offset of successive lines. This only applies to dashed lines and is measured along the direction of the lines. Specifying a delta-x staggers each successive line by the amount you specify so that the dashes do not line up.	
Delta-y	Specifies the distance between lines, measured perpendicular to the direction of the lines. This applies to both continuous and dashed lines.	
Dash	Defines a noncontinuous line using the same system as linetype definitions: positive for a dash, negative for a space, and zero for a dot.	

The following hatch pattern, shown in Figure 31-6, is the simplest form of hatch pattern. Although you could specify this simple hatch pattern in the Boundary Hatch dialog box by specifying a user-defined hatch with an angle and spacing, it shows the syntax clearly. The lines are at an angle of 105 degrees, the hatch pattern starts at 0,0, and the spacing between the lines is .5 units. The lines are continuous.

```
*ftrailer, proposed future trailers
105, 0,0, 0,0.5
```

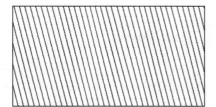

Figure 31-6: The ftrailer hatch pattern
with continuous lines.

Adding one level of complexity, you can make the lines in the hatch pattern
noncontinuous, as follows:

```
*ftrailer, proposed future trailers
105, 0,0, 0,0.5, .5,-.25,0,-.1,0,-.25
```

Note that this definition uses the maximum of six dash specifications (the dash,
space, dot, space, dot, and space).

A close-up of this hatch pattern is shown in Figure 31-7.

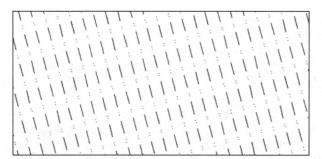

Figure 31-7: The ftrailer hatch pattern with a dash and two dots.

If you add a delta-x of .25, the lines in the pattern are staggered by .25 units, along
the direction of the lines, as shown in this code and in Figure 31-8:

```
*ftrailer, proposed future trailers
105, 0,0, 0.25,0.5, .5,-.25,0,-.1,0,-.25
```

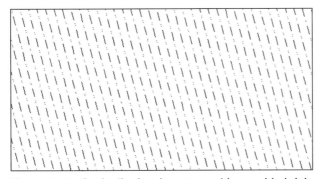

Figure 31-8: The ftrailer hatch pattern with an added delta-x.

You might wonder why the pattern staggers downward when you added a positive x-delta. The answer is that the direction of the lines (in this case, 105 degrees) becomes the X axis for this calculation. Figure 31-9 shows a zoomed-in display of the hatch pattern around 0,0, which is the base point. The hatch pattern is being generated up and to the left. The first line starts at 0,0, and the second line starts to the left by .5 units (the y-delta) and up by .25 units (the x-delta), as shown by the dimensions.

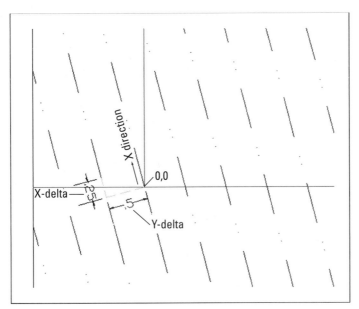

Figure 31-9: Calculating how the x-delta and y-delta affect a hatch pattern.

Finally, you can add additional definition lines. One of the definition lines should start at 0,0, but the others may start anywhere. Here is the definition for the pattern in Figure 31-10. It actually creates the shape of the trailers. Although you see the rectangular shape, the hatch pattern is created from four separate lines, two at 0 degrees and two at 90 degrees. Note that the two 0-degree lines are the same except that they start at different base points. The same is true for the two 90-degree lines.

```
*trail, whole trailers-proposed
0, 0,0, 0,2, .5,-1
90, 0,0, 0,1.5, .5,-.25,0,-.25,.5,-.5
90, .5,0, 0,1.5, .5,-.25,0,-.25,.5,-.5
0, 0,1.5, 0,2, .5,-1
```

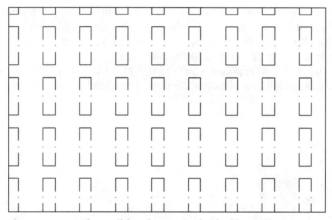

Figure 31-10: The trail hatch pattern looks like trailers.

Step-by-Step: Creating and Using a Hatch Pattern

1. Open a drawing based on the *acad.dwt* template.

2. Save it as *ab31-3.dwg* in your *AutoCAD Bible* folder.

3. Type **notepad** ↵ and press Enter at the `File to edit:` prompt.

4. Type the following:

```
*lightning, interwoven lightning
90, 0,0, 0,.5, .5,-.25
0, -.25,.5, 0,.75, .25,-.25
90, -.25,.5, 0,.5, .5,-.25
```

5. Press Enter after the last line. Save the file as *lightning.pat* in your *AutoCAD Bible* folder.

6. If you haven't already done so, you need to add your *AutoCAD Bible* folder to AutoCAD's support file search path. Choose Tools⇨Preferences⇨Files tab. Click the plus sign to the left of Support File Search Path. Choose Add. Choose Browse. Find your *AutoCAD Bible* folder and click OK. Click Apply and click OK. AutoCAD displays a message that you may have to restart AutoCAD, but that is not usually necessary in this case.

7. Choose Rectangle from the Draw toolbar. At the first prompt, type **0,0** ↵. At the `Other corner:` prompt, type **@10,6** ↵.

8. Choose Hatch from the Draw toolbar. In the drop-down list in the Pattern Type section of the Boundary Hatch dialog box, choose Custom.

9. Under Pattern Properties, click in the Custom Pattern text box and type **lightning** ↵.

10. Choose Select Objects and pick the rectangle in your drawing. Press Enter. Choose Apply. AutoCAD fills the rectangle with the lightning hatch, as shown in Figure 31-11.

11. Save your drawing.

Figure 31-11: The lightning hatch pattern.

Tip

Check out AutoCAD's *acad.pat* file for some ideas on how to create your own hatch pattern definitions.

Summary

In this chapter you learned how to create your own linetypes and hatch patterns. You can create simple linetypes containing only dashes, dots, and spaces, or you can create complex linetypes that include shapes and text.

You can create your own hatch patterns that are made up of a set of parallel lines.

In the next chapter you learn how to create shapes and fonts.

✦   ✦   ✦

Creating Shapes and Fonts

Creating Shapes

Shapes are similar to blocks. You create them, store them, and insert them. There are several differences, however:

✦ Shapes are much harder to create.

✦ Shapes are compiled into a format that conserves storage space, memory, and regeneration time.

✦ You can use shapes to create fonts.

✦ Font and shape files are support files — if you distribute a drawing, be sure to include any font or shape files that the drawing uses.

You would use shapes for simple forms that you need to insert many times quickly. Examples are shapes inserted into complex linetypes and font characters.

Understanding shape files

Shape files are used for both shapes and fonts. You create them with a text editor and save them with the extension *.shp*. You then use the COMPILE command (by typing it on the command line), which opens the Select Shape or Font File dialog box, shown in Figure 32-1.

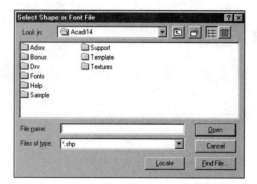

Figure 32-1: The Select Shape File dialog box.

Choose the *.shp* file and click Open. AutoCAD automatically compiles the file into a new file with the same name but an extension of *.shx* and displays a message on the command line that compilation has been successful.

Note

You can also compile Type 1 PostScript fonts with an extension of *.pfb*. These fonts can be used uncompiled, but load more quickly when they are compiled.

Using shape files

Once you have a compiled shape file, you must load it before you can place it in a drawing, using the LOAD command. AutoCAD opens the Select Shape File dialog box. Choose the *.shx* file and click Open.

Note

Font files do not have to be loaded.

To insert a shape, use the SHAPE command as follows:

✦ Shape name (or ?): Type the name of the shape or type ? ↵ to get a list of loaded shapes.

✦ Starting point: Pick a point on the screen. AutoCAD drags the shape as you move the cursor.

✦ Height <1.0000>: This functions like a scale factor. For example, type .5 ↵ to insert the shape at one-half its original size.

✦ Rotation angle <0>: Type a rotation angle.

Creating shape files

Shape files and font files are essentially the same. In this section I explain how to create shapes. At the end of the chapter I explain the few distinctions you need to make to create a font file.

As with all customizable files, use a text editor to create shape files. You can edit the *.shp* files that come with AutoCAD. You can find the *.shp* files on the AutoCAD CD-ROM in the *\acad\bonus\fonts* folder. This includes all the fonts as well as several shape files. Be sure to back up these files before editing them, although editing them does not affect the *.shx* files that AutoCAD actually uses.

You can add comments following a semicolon.

A shape definition has the following syntax:

```
*shapenumber,#ofspecs,shapename
spec1,spec2,...,0
```

The definition must start with an asterisk. Each line can not contain more than 128 characters.

Table 32-1 explains the parts of this shape definition.

Table 32-1	
The Parts of a Shape Definition	
Item	*Explanation*
shapenumber	You can use any number between 1 and 255. Each shape in a file must have a unique number.
#ofspecs	This is the number of specifications in the second line of the definition, including the mandatory zero at the end.
shapename	You must use uppercase for the shape name. This is the name you use with the SHAPE command.
spec1...	This is a code that defines the actual shape. Each specification code defines a part of the shape, for example, a line segment or an arc. Together, all the specifications draw the shape.
0	The definition must end with a zero.

Length and direction codes

There are two sets of codes that you can use to define a shape. The first set, the length and direction codes, only let you draw straight line segments. You use this system to create specifications in the three-character hexadecimal format.

The first character is zero, which tells AutoCAD that the next two characters are hexadecimal values.

The second character is a length in units. The maximum is 15 units. The number values can range from 0 to 9. For values from 10 to 15, use A to F. However, the length is measured along the nearest X or Y distance. Therefore, diagonal lengths are not true lengths.

The third character is a direction code. Figure 32-2 shows how this code works. Use the code that represents the desired direction of the line from the start point.

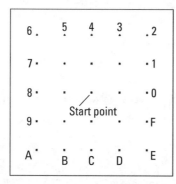

Figure 32-2: The direction codes.

Here is the code for the shape shown in Figure 32-3:

```
*2,4,PENNANT
044,02F,029,0
```

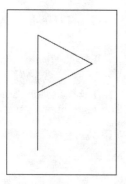

Figure 32-3: The PENNANT shape.

Here's how this shape works:

✦ 2 is the shape's unique number.

✦ 4 is the number of bytes (specifications) on the second line of the definition.

✦ PENNANT is the name of the shape.

✦ 044 draws the pole, a line that is four units in the vertical direction.

✦ 02F draws the top line of the pennant, a line that is approximately two units in the F direction. (See note below.)

✦ 029 draws the bottom line of the pennant, a line that is approximately two units in the 9 direction. (See note below.)

Note

Although the length of the two diagonal lines was specified as 2, they are actually about 2.22 units long because the line endpoints snapped to the nearest grid imaginary point.

Supplemental codes

The length and direction codes have a number of limitations:

✦ You can only draw in 16 directions.

✦ The maximum length of a line is 15 units.

✦ You can only draw straight line segments.

✦ The shape has to be continuous — you cannot lift the "pen" up and start in a new place.

The supplemental codes offer additional flexibility (and complexity) to your shapes.

Table 32-2 lists these codes, which can be in either hexadecimal or decimal format.

Table 32-2 Supplemental Shape Codes		
Hexadecimal Code	**Decimal Code**	**Explanation**
000	0	Specifies the end of the shape definition.
001	1	Starts draw mode (puts the "pen" down).
002	2	Ends draw mode (puts the "pen" up) so you can move to a new location.
003	3	Divides the vector lengths by the specification that follows, for example, 3,5 to divide the lengths by five. This scales down the shape. You should reverse this at the end of the shape by using the 4 code.
004	4	Multiplies the vector lengths by the specification that follows, for example, 4,2 to multiply the lengths by two. This scales up the shape. You should reverse this at the end of the shape by using the 3 code.
005	5	Saves the current position so you can return to it later in the shape definition. You must use (restore) every position you save (a maximum of four).

(continued)

Table 32-2 (*continued*)

Hexadecimal Code	Decimal Code	Explanation
006	6	Restores the last saved position.
007	7	Draws another shape defined within the same shape file, whose number follows. For example, use 7,230 to draw shape 230. When the other shape is complete, AutoCAD returns to the current shape definition.
008	8	Draws a line specified by X and Y displacements that follow the code. For example, 8,(8,-12) draws a line whose endpoint is 8 units to the right and 12 units down from the current coordinate. (You can add parentheses to your shape codes for readability.)
009	9	Draws multiple X,Y displacements. You end this code with a displacement of 0,0. For example, 9,(8,-12),(1,0),(0,12), (-8,0),(0,0) draws four X,Y displacements. (You can add parentheses to your shape codes for readability.)
00A	10	Draws an *octant* arc specified by its radius, and a second code in the syntax (-)0SC where the minus optionally indicates a clockwise arc, the zero is mandatory, S specifies the starting octant, and C specifies the number of octants that the arc covers. An octant is an eighth of a circle. Figure 32-4 shows the octant codes you must use for the starting octant. For example, 10,(2,014) indicates an arc with a radius of 2 that is drawn counterclockwise from octant 1 and covers 4 octants (ending at octant 5). This is a semicircle.
00B	11	Draws a fractional arc not limited by octants specified by the five following codes in the syntax: start_offset, end_offset,high_radius,radius,(-)0SC. The start offset specifies how far past an octant the arc begins and is calculated as follows: starting degrees – degrees of the last octant passed) * 256/45. The end offset specifies how far past an octant the arc ends and is calculated as follows: (ending degrees – degrees of the last octant passed) * 256/45. For both the start and the end of the arc, the last octant passed is specified in degrees, not the numbers in Figure 32-4, and is always a multiple of 45. The high radius is zero unless the radius is more than 255. If your radius is larger, the high radius is the maximum number of 256 multiples in the value of the radius (for example, 2 if your radius is 600). The difference (the radius minus 256 times the high radius value – 88 if your radius is 600) is placed in the radius specification. The radius is just the radius of the arc. The (-)0SC part of the code is the same as for code 10 except that you use the octant the arc starts in for the starting octant and then calculate the number of octants the arc covers.

Hexadecimal Code	Decimal Code	Explanation
00C	12	Draws an arc using a system of X,Y displacement and bulge specified in the following three codes using the syntax X-displacement, Y-displacement, bulge. These three codes can range from −127 to +127. The X and Y displacements just specify the endpoint of the arc. The bulge equals (2 * H/D) *127) where D is the chord length (the distance from the start point to the endpoint) and H is the height measured from the midpoint of the chord to the circumference of the arc. The bulge should be negative if the arc is drawn clockwise.
00D	13	Draws multiple arcs using the X,Y displacement and bulge system. End the arcs with (0,0). You can use zero for a bulge to place a line segment in the midst of several arcs.
00E	14	This code is used only for text fonts that can be used in the vertical orientation (each letter is drawn under the previous letter). When the vertical orientation is chosen, the specifications after this code are used. Use this code to move the starting and ending point of letters to a point appropriate for vertical orientation, that is, on top of and below the letter. See the section "Creating Font Files" later in this chapter for more information.

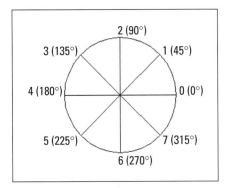

Figure 32-4: The codes for octant arcs.

All these codes can seem pretty overwhelming. The most common use for shapes is for fonts. Here are a few examples:

```
*3,22,ALEF
010,07E,010,2,8,(−6,5),1,8,(−2,−4),01C,2,8,(5,2),1,8,(2,4)
,014,0
```

This is a squared-off alef, the first letter of the Hebrew alphabet, shown in Figure 32-5. Displaying non-romanic fonts is a common use for shapes.

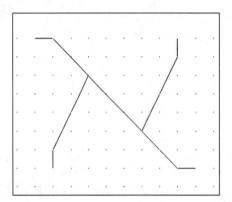

Figure 32-5: A squared-off alef.

It is almost essential to plan in advance by drawing the shape in a drawing on a grid set to 1-unit spacing. You can only use integers in your shape codes, so you must often scale the shape up so the smallest line segment is one unit.

Here's how the code for the alef works:

✦ The shape starts at the top left. The code 010 is a hexadecimal length and direction code and specifies a line with a length of one unit and a direction of 0 degrees.

✦ The second code, 07E, is also a hexadecimal length and direction code. It specifies a line with a length of 7 units in the E direction (315 degrees). The line is not actually 7 units long, but its X (and in this case Y) distance is 7.

✦ The third code, 010, is the same as the first code and ends the first set of line segments.

✦ The fourth code, 2, lifts up the pen so you can move to the start of the next line.

✦ The fifth code, 8, indicates that the following two codes will be an X,Y displacement.

✦ The sixth and seventh codes, (-6,5), are placed in parentheses for readability. They move the pen (while it is up) –6 in the X direction and +5 in the Y direction from the end of the last line to the start of the next line. (Count the grid dots to find it.)

✦ The eighth code, 1, puts the pen down so you can draw.

✦ The ninth code, 8, is the same as the fifth code.

✦ The 10th and 11th codes, (-2,-4), draw the first segment of the second line so that the endpoint is –2 units in the X direction and –4 units in the Y direction from the start point.

✦ The 12th code, 01C, is a hexadecimal code and finishes the second line with a 1-unit line segment in the C direction (270 degrees).

✦ The 13th code, 2, lifts up the pen again.

✦ The 14th code, 8, is the same as the fifth code.

✦ The 15th and 16th codes, (5,2), move the pen (which is up) +5 in the X direction and +2 in the Y direction.

✦ The 17th code, 1, puts the pen down again.

✦ The 18th code, 8, is the same as the fifth code.

✦ The 19th and 20th codes, (2,4), draw a line whose endpoint is 2 units in the X direction and 4 units in the Y direction from its start point.

✦ The 21st code is a hexadecimal length and vector code and draws a 1-unit line in the 4 (90-degree) direction.

✦ The 22nd code ends the shape definition.

Here's another example, in this case a script alef, shown in Figure 32-6:

```
*4,10,S-ALEF
06C,2,8,(6,5),1,10,(3,016),0
```

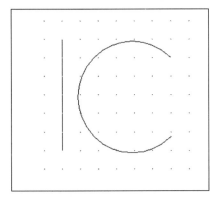

Figure 32-6: A script alef.

Here's the explanation of the code for the script alef:

✦ The first code, 06C, creates the line on the left, starting at the top and six units long.

♦ The second code, 2, lifts up the pen.

♦ The third code, 8, specifies an X, Y displacement, in this case with the pen up.

♦ The fourth and fifth codes, (6,5), move the pen 6 units to the right and 5 units up, to the start of the arc.

♦ The sixth code, 10, introduces an octant arc.

♦ The seventh and eighth codes, (3,016), specify an arc with a radius of 3 that starts at octant 1 and covers 6 octants (to octant 7). (See Figure 32-4 to review the octant codes.)

♦ The last code, 0, ends the definition.

Step-by-Step: Creating a Shape

On the CD-ROM

1. Open *ab32-a.dwg* from the CD-ROM.

2. Save it as *ab32-1.dwg* in your *AutoCAD Bible* folder. This shows an uppercase P, with dashed lines to indicate space before and after the letter, as shown in Figure 32-7.

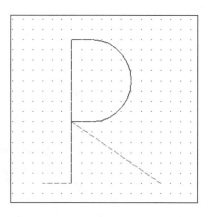

Figure 32-7: An uppercase P.

3. Type **notepad** ↵ on the command line and press Enter at the `File to edit:` prompt to open a new file.

4. Type the following in Notepad:

```
*80,15,UCP
2,030,1,0E4,020,12,(0,-8,127),028,2,8,(9,-6),0
```

5. Press Enter at the end of the last line. Choose File⇨Save in Notepad and save the file in your *AutoCAD Bible* folder as *ab32-1.shp.* Close Notepad.

6. In AutoCAD, type **compile** ↵. Double-click *ab32-1.shp.* AutoCAD compiles the *.shp* file.

7. Type **load** ↵ and choose *ab32-1.shx*. Click Open. Type **shape** ↵. To insert the shape, follow the prompts:

```
Shape name (or ?): ucp ↵
Starting point: Pick any point.
Height <1.0000>: ↵
Rotation angle <0>: ↵
```

8. Save your drawing. It should look like Figure 32-8.

Figure 32-8: The picture and shape of the letter P.

Editing shape files

You don't often get a shape right the first time. You don't see the result until after you have compiled, loaded, and inserted the shape. Editing shape files involves the following steps:

1. Erase all copies of the shape.

2. Purge the *.shx* file using the SH option of the PURGE command. (You may sometimes need to purge more than once.) If you forget this step, when you try to insert the corrected shape, AutoCAD uses the old definition!

3. Edit the *.shp* file. Don't forget to change the #of specs value in the first line if necessary. Save the file.

4. Recompile the *.shp* file.

5. Reload the *.shx* file.

6. Reinsert the shape using the SHAPE command.

Creating Font Files

Release 14 provides additional support for TrueType fonts. There are so many fonts available now that the need to create your own is certainly less than with earlier versions. However, you might want to add special symbols to some existing fonts, especially if you often use these symbols within text.

Font files use the same codes to define the characters as shape files. They have the following unique characteristics:

✦ The `shapenumber` part of the definition must correspond to the ASCII code value for the character you are defining. Appendix A of the AutoCAD *Customization Guide* (choose Help⇨AutoCAD Help Topics⇨Contents⇨ Customization Guide⇨Appendix A) contains all the ASCII codes in octal, hexadecimal, and decimal formats. Fonts generally use either hexadecimal or decimal format.

✦ The `shapename` part of the definition is lowercase and is usually used to label the character — for example, `ucp` for uppercase p and `lcr` for lowercase r.

✦ The file must include a special shape number 0 that defines the entire font, using the following syntax:

```
*0,4,font-name
above,below,modes,0
```

The `above` value specifies how far above the baseline uppercase letters extend. The `below` value specifies how far below the baseline lowercase letters such as p or q extend. Together these two values define the size of the characters. AutoCAD uses these values to scale letters when you define a text height for the font. Modes should be 0 for a horizontal font and 2 for a font that supports both horizontal and vertical orientations.

✦ You must define the line feed (LF), which drops down one line without drawing so that lines of text can be placed beneath each other. The line feed is ASCII code 10.

✦ You need to create a start point and endpoint with the pen up to create spacing between letters. See the previous Step-by-Step exercise for an example.

For example, a header for a font named *arch* with capital letters 21 units high and lowercase letters that extend 7 units below the line could be:

```
*0,4,arch
21,7,0,0
```

As mentioned earlier, look at the fonts that come with AutoCAD as a guideline. There are a number of conventions that you can discover by using an existing font as a basis. The *txt.shp* file, which defines the `txt` font, is a good starter because it is fairly simple (no arcs). Remember to look on the AutoCAD CD-ROM in the *acad**bonus**fonts* folder.

Big fonts and Unicode fonts

The Japanese and Chinese written languages use fonts with thousands of characters because each character represents a word. AutoCAD uses big fonts to support these languages. It is beyond the scope of this book to go into detail about how to create these fonts, but a short explanation is useful. Big font files use special codes to allow for the larger number of shapes. Big fonts allow up to 65,535 shape numbers.

Unicode fonts support the ISO10646 standard, which uses 16-bit encoding to support many languages in one font file. If you open one of the *.shp* files, you will see characters for all the letters that may have accents in French, Spanish, and so on. All the fonts in AutoCAD are now compliant with this standard.

The advantage of Unicode fonts is that characters that you type appear the same in all systems and countries. This is important if you exchange drawings with clients or colleagues in other countries. Unicode fonts use a special header that includes two extra codes.

Unicode special characters can be inserted by typing **\u+** and the hexadecimal Unicode value in the font file. (For this reason, Unicode font files use hexadecimal shape numbers.) For example, the hexadecimal code for the plus/minus sign is 00B1. If you type **\u+00b1** and press Enter (using DTEXT in this example), you get the plus/minus sign. (It works with multi-line text, too.)

If you don't need the additional capabilities of big fonts or Unicode fonts, you can create fonts without them.

As with all shapes, you probably want to draw all the characters in AutoCAD on a grid with a spacing of 1. Decide on the height of the letters and be consistent.

Summary

In this chapter you learned how to create shape files. Shape files are used like blocks when you need to insert a shape many times using as little memory as possible. Two common examples are shapes in complex linetypes and fonts. Fonts are created using shape files with a few special codes that define both the font as a whole and each character.

✦　　✦　　✦

Customizing Menus

Creating Your Own Menus

You probably use AutoCAD's menus all the time. (If you don't, you can skip this chapter.) AutoCAD's menus are designed to be useful for most people, but the whole point of customization is that everyone has different needs. You can draw a lot easier and faster by customizing the menus for your needs.

Not only can you add commands to a menu, but you can also add menu items consisting of a series of commands that run just like a macro. You can even add AutoLISP routines to your menus. You can edit the menu that comes with AutoCAD or create your own menu. You may want to create specialized menus that are used only for one drawing — for example, a menu to help clients view a drawing. The only limit is your imagination — and the time you can devote to customization.

Working with Menu Files

Menu files were once simple. Now, under Windows 95 or Windows NT, menu files are a complex subject indeed. However, you need to understand the menu files and how they interact with each other before starting to change them.

Caution

Don't even think about customizing a menu until you have backed up at least *acad.mnu*. Better yet, back up all the menu files (see Table 33-1 for a listing of menu files).

Understanding the menu files

Table 33-1 lists all the menu file types and their functions.

	Table 33-1	
	Menu Files and Functions	
File	**Function**	
.mnu	This is the template menu file. AutoCAD comes with *acad.mnu.* This is an ASCII file that you can edit. When AutoCAD senses changes in this menu, it automatically creates a new *.mns* and *.mnc* file. This is the file that you edit when you customize the menu.	
.mns	This is the source menu file generated by AutoCAD based on the *.mnu* file. It is also an ASCII file. When you customize your toolbars as described in Chapter 29, AutoCAD places the changes in this file.	
.mnc	This is the compiled, binary file that AutoCAD actually uses when you choose an item on a menu. AutoCAD compiles menu files for faster access. When AutoCAD senses changes in the *.mnu* or *.mns* menu files, it recompiles, creating a new *.mnc* file.	
.mnr	This is a binary file that contains bitmaps used by the menu, such as slides for image tiles.	
.mnl	This is an ASCII file that contains AutoLISP routines used by the menu. When AutoCAD loads a menu file, it automatically loads this file if it has the same filename. AutoCAD contains a number of commands that are actually AutoLISP routines — these are found in *acad.mnl.*	

These file types constitute a family of menu files. For example, AutoCAD comes with *acad.mnu, acad.mns, acad.mnc, acad.mnr,* and *acad.mnl.* If you create your own menu, you create a file called, let's say, *custom.mnu.* From that AutoCAD creates *custom.mns* and *custom.mnr* as a minimum. You can also place AutoLISP routines in a file called *custom.mnl,* which will be automatically loaded whenever *custom.mnc* is loaded. If your menu has bitmaps, AutoCAD also creates *custom.mnr.* You can place your custom menus in any support file search path.

Note

Remember that you can add to the support file search path by choosing Tools⇨Preferences⇨Files tab, choosing Support file search path, and clicking Add.

Loading and unloading menu files

AutoCAD supports two types of menus — complete and partial. A partial menu may have only one or two pull-down menus (or toolbars). You can then load this partial menu into your regular base menu. If your menu customization consists of simply adding a few menu items, you can simply create a partial menu and add it to your current menu.

However, you may also wish to have alternate complete menus. Perhaps two different people work on one computer and have different menu needs. Or you may find it useful to have one menu for architectural drawings, another for mechanical drawings, and a third for electrical schematics.

Loading a complete menu

To load a complete menu, use the MENU command at the command line. AutoCAD opens the Select Menu File dialog box, shown in Figure 33-1.

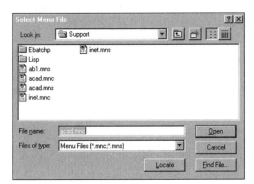

Figure 33-1: The Select Menu File dialog box.

AutoCAD assumes that you want to load either an *.mnc* or *.mns* menu file. However, you can use the Files of type drop-down list to choose an *.mnu* template file. You do this when you are customizing a menu and want to recompile all the menu files that arise from the *.mnu* file. If you are simply loading a different menu to use, you should load either the *.mnc* or *.mns* file. Select the file and click Open to load the menu.

When you load AutoCAD, the last menu you used, which is stored in the system registry, is loaded. For Release 14, AutoCAD does not reload menus between drawings. If you want to use a new menu while in AutoCAD, you must load it.

When you load an *.mnu* file, AutoCAD warns you that loading the file will overwrite any changes you have made to your toolbars. Here's how you save the changes you have made to your toolbars while you are customizing a menu:

1. Make the changes to the toolbars.

2. Open the *.mns* file of the menu you are using. You can use Wordpad to do this.

3. Select the entire toolbar section. It starts with ✳✳✳TOOLBARS. Copy it to the Clipboard.

4. Close the *.mns* file.

5. Open the *.mnu* file of the same menu. (It has the same filename.)

6. Select the entire toolbar section.

7. Choose Paste from the Standard toolbar. Wordpad (or your text editor) replaces the entire toolbar section with the new one from the *.mns* file.

8. Save the *.mnu* file and close it.

Now your customized toolbars are incorporated into your template *.mnu* menu file. You can customize this file as much as you like and ignore any messages about overwriting your toolbar changes.

Of course, if you make a mistake, you have backed up your *.mnu, .mns,* and *.mnc* menu files, so you can simply copy them back over the ones on your hard disk.

Loading or unloading a partial menu

To load a partial menu, choose Tools➪Customize Menus to start the MENULOAD command. AutoCAD opens the Menu Customization dialog box, shown in Figure 33-2.

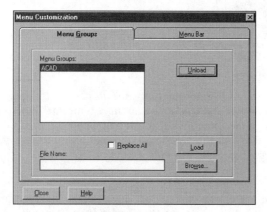

Figure 33-2: The Menu Customization dialog box.

Use the Menu Groups tab to load and unload partial menus. Every menu, both complete and partial, has a menu group name. The menu group name of the menu that AutoCAD comes with is ACAD. When you create your own menus, you give them a menu group name, often (but not necessarily) the name of the file. For example, the files for the ACAD menu group are *acad.mnu, .mns, .mnc,* and so on.

To unload a loaded partial menu, choose the menu you want and click Unload. To load a partial menu, type the name of the file in the File Name text box or choose Browse to locate the file. Then click Load. AutoCAD immediately loads the menu. If you modify a menu, you must unload it first and then reload it.

Use the Menu Bar tab, shown in Figure 33-3, to display, hide, or reorder pull-down menus. First choose the menu group you want in the Menu Group drop-down list. The Menus box on the left lists all the available pull-down menus. The Menu Bar list on the right displays the current order of the menu bar, from left to right.

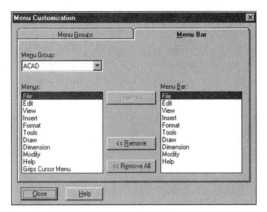

Figure 33-3: The Menu Bar tab of the Menu Customization dialog box.

To remove a pull-down menu, choose it from the Menu Bar list and click Remove. Click Remove All to remove all the pull-down menus.

To insert a pull-down menu, follow these steps:

1. Choose the menu from the Menu Bar list that will be to the left of the menu you are inserting. For example, to insert the Modify menu to the left of the Dimension menu, choose Dimension.

2. Then choose the menu that you want to insert, for example, the Modify menu.

3. Click Insert.

Tip

You can move menus by first removing them and then reinserting them in a new location.

Choose Close when you have finished using the dialog box.

Customizing a Menu

Menu files are long and complex. However, you often do not need to deal with every part of the menu file. And even simple changes can be very useful. Start simple and take it from there.

There are eight different kinds of menus:

✦ Button menus control the buttons on your mouse or puck.

✦ Pop menus are the pull-down menus at the top of your screen.

✦ Toolbar menus create toolbars.

✦ Image menus create dialog boxes with images, such as the one you see when you choose View⇨Tiled Viewports⇨Layout.

✦ The screen menu is AutoCAD's original menu that used to appear at the right side of your screen. By default, it is not displayed, but it still exists in the menu file and you can display it by choosing Tools⇨Preferences and clicking the Display tab.

✦ Tablet menus control the menu that can be overlaid on a digitizing tablet.

✦ Helpstrings create the short descriptions of each command that appears on the status bar when you place the mouse cursor over a toolbar or a menu item.

✦ Accelerators are keyboard shortcuts. An example is Ctrl+C for the COPYCLIP command.

The AutoCAD menu file *acad.mnu* contains sections for all these types of menus. Each section starts with three asterisks — for example, ***TOOLBARS. Most sections also have subsections that start with two asterisks. You do not need to customize all the types of menus. You may wish to customize only the pull-down menus. If you use a digitizer, you will want to customize the tablet menus. You can customize any menu that you wish.

Looking at *acad.mnu*

The best way to start customizing a menu is to look at AutoCAD's *acad.mnu* file and use it as a guide. Each type of menu has its own unique features, but certain features apply to most, if not all, menu types.

Note

When you create a new, complete menu file based on *acad.mnu*, don't forget that AutoCAD uses the AutoLISP routines in *acad.mnl* for many commands. You should therefore make a copy of *acad.mnl* with the same name as your new menu. For example, if you created a menu called *mech.mnu* from *acad.mnu,* make a copy of *acad.mnl* and name the copy *mech.mnl*.

Here you see the beginning of the pull-down Format menu:

```
***POP5
**FORMAT
ID_MnFormat    [F&ormat]
ID_Layer       [&Layer...] _layer
ID_Ddcolor     [&Color...] _ddcolor
ID_Linetype    [Li&netype...] _linetype
               [--]
ID_Style       [Text &Style...] _style
ID_Ddim        [&Dimension Style...]^C^C_ddim
ID_Ddptype     [&Point Style...] _ddptype
ID_Mlstyle     [&Multiline Style...]^C^C_mlstyle
```

```
                 [--]
ID_Ddunits    [&Units...] _ddunits
ID_Thickness  [&Thickness] _thickness
ID_Limits     [Dr&awing Limits] _limits
                 [--]
ID_Ddrename   [&Rename...]^C^C_ddrename
```

Notice that each menu item has three parts:

✦ The first part is a name tag. Each name tag must be unique. The most common use for the name tag is to link pull-down menu items and toolbar buttons to their status line help. You can also use the name tag to link a keyboard shortcut to a menu item. Name tags are only used in Pop (pull-down) and Toolbar sections of the menu. They must not be more than 12 characters and cannot have spaces — or they are ignored.

✦ The second part, in square brackets, is the label. This is what you actually see on the menu. Notice the ellipses (. . .) after menu items that open dialog boxes. The Buttons, Aux, and Tablet menus do not display any label, but you can use the label for your own notes.

✦ The third part is the actual command, called a menu macro. This can be a simple command, any group of commands, or an AutoLISP expression. Note the following conventions:

  ✦ Transparent commands start with an apostrophe (').

  ✦ All other commands start with ^C^C, which is equivalent to pressing Esc twice. This cancels any other command that may be active. One Esc is generally enough, but sometimes two are necessary.

  ✦ The underscore is used before each command. This tells AutoCAD to translate the command into whatever language version of AutoCAD is being used. Your menus would automatically be translated into French in France!

Figure 33-4 shows the Format menu. Compare it to the text of the menu file.

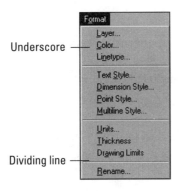

Underscore

Dividing line

Figure 33-4: The Format menu displays the labels shown in the menu file and underscores immediately following each ampersand. You also see the three lines that divide up the menu.

Writing menu macros

The menu macro is the heart of the menu. There are a number of special characters and conventions that you need to know to write menu macros. Table 33-2 lists the most common ones.

Table 33-2
Special Characters for Menu Macros

Character	Description
;	Equivalent to pressing Enter. The end of a line in a menu macro is also equivalent to pressing Enter. Use the semicolon when you need two returns at the end of a line. Some commands, such as DTEXT and TEXT, also require a return to complete.
Space	Equivalent to pressing Enter. Use between the command and its options. Note that you can use a space even on the command line for many commands.
\	Pauses for user input, such as picking a point or typing a value.
+	Used at the end of a line that won't fit on one line. Indicates that the macro continues on the next line.

Note

Because the backslash pauses for user input, you cannot use it to specify a path, as in *c:\acadr14\support*. Use the regular slash (/) instead.

Here is one line from AutoCAD's Draw pull-down menu that uses the backslash and the space:

```
ID_ArcStCeAn    [S&tart, Center, Angle]^C^C_arc \_c \_a
```

Here's how this command works:

^C^C	Cancels any previous command.
_arc	Starts the ARC command, allowing translation to another language version of AutoCAD.
Space	Equivalent to pressing Enter after typing **arc** on the command line.
\	AutoCAD displays the Center/<Start point>: prompt. The backslash lets you specify a start point.
_c	Chooses the Center option, allowing translation to another language.
Space	Equivalent to pressing Enter after typing **c** on the command line (for the Center option).

\	AutoCAD displays the Center: prompt. The backslash lets you specify a center point.
_a	Chooses the Angle option. Because this is at the end of the command, you don't need to specify a pause. The user specifies an angle and presses Enter, ending the command. AutoCAD draws the arc.

The backslash allows for only one input, except when used with the SELECT command. Therefore, you can use the SELECT command in menu macros to collect a selection set and use another command with the Previous option to act on the entire selection set. For example:

```
ID_MoveRight [Move .1 Right]select \move previous ;.1,0 ;
```

This macro starts the SELECT command and lets you select as many objects as you want. You end object selection by pressing Enter. Then the macro automatically moves those objects to the right by .1 unit.

Here are a few more examples of macros from earlier chapters.

You could place this macro on a pull-down menu to make a selected polyline .1 unit wide:

```
pedit \w .1 x
```

You would use the following macro to automatically draw four circles with the specified centers and radius. It uses a plus at the end because the macro is too long to fit on one line.

```
circle 2,2 1.5 circle 6,2 1.5 circle 10,2 1.5 circle +
14,2 1.5
```

You could use this macro to clean up a drawing. It uses CHPROP to select all the objects in a drawing, and the Color option to change their color to BYLAYER. Then it uses the LAYER command to freeze the no-plot layer and saves the drawing.

```
chprop all  c bylayer  -layer f no-plot  qsave
```

Notice that using the All selection option also allows you to select more than one object in a menu macro.

Swapping menus

Here is AutoCAD's Buttons2 menu. The Aux2 menu is exactly the same.

```
***BUTTONS2
// Shift + button
$P0=SNAP $p0=*
```

This menu introduces some new special characters that are used in AutoCAD's menus. Sometimes you want a menu item to switch to another menu item. This is called menu swapping. Since you cannot customize the pick button, the first button listed is the second button. In this case, pressing Shift and the second button (the right button on a two-button mouse) opens the Object Snap menu (as you probably know). The Object Snap menu, however, is elsewhere in the menu. In fact, it is contained in the POP0 pull-down menu. This menu item therefore switches you to the POP0 pull-down menu and displays that menu.

The special syntax is as follows:

```
$section=menugroup.menuname $section=*
```

If the menu group is the same as that of the menu where you are placing the macro, you can leave it out. The different sections or menu types have their own special abbreviations for menu swapping, shown in Table 33-3.

Table 33-3
Menu Section Abbreviations for Menu Swapping

Abbreviation	Menu Section
A1-A4	The AUX menus 1 through 4
B1-B4	The BUTTONS menus 1 through 4
P0-P16	The POP (pull-down) menus 1 through 16 (17 is used for the Grips cursor menu)
I	The IMAGE menu
S	The SCREEN menu
T1-T4	The TABLET menus 1 through 4

Here's another example from the Draw pull-down menu. The first line is the Surfaces item on the Draw menu. The next three items are items on the Surfaces submenu. The last item swaps to and displays the subsection of the IMAGE section called image_3dobjects.

```
ID_MnSurface  [->Sur&faces]
ID_Solid      [&2D Solid]^C^C_solid
ID_3dface     [3D &Face]^C^C_3dface
ID_3dsurface  [&3D Surfaces...] $I=ACAD.image_3dobjects
$I=ACAD.*
```

In the section "Image tile menus" later in this chapter, I show the image tile portion of the menu that this 3D Surfaces menu item displays.

In other words, when you choose Draw⇨Surfaces⇨3D Objects, you get a dialog box displaying all the 3D surface objects you can draw.

Tip

You could use this technique to create a menu that swaps to an image menu that inserts commonly used blocks.

Working on menu sections

Table 33-4 lists the sections in *acad.mnu*. There may be several sections for a type of menu; for example, there are a number of button menu sections.

You can add sections. For example, users can, and often do, add a pull-down menu. However, for pull-down menus you are constrained by the space available across the top of the screen.

Table 33-4 *Acad.mnu* Sections	
Section	**Function**
***BUTTONS1	This menu defines what happens when you press a button on a digitizing puck or other input device (but not the system mouse). The first button (pick) cannot be customized and one button is usually reserved for the Return (Enter) button, so you generally only customize this button menu if you have three or more buttons on your pointing device.
***BUTTONS2	This menu defines what happens when you hold down Shift and press a button on a digitizing puck or other input device (but not the system mouse).
***BUTTONS3	This menu defines what happens when you hold down Control and press a button on a digitizing puck or other input device (but not the system mouse).
***BUTTONS4	This menu defines what happens when you hold down both Control and Shift and press a button on a digitizing puck or other input device (but not the system mouse).
***AUX1	This is an auxiliary button menu that defines what happens when you press a button on your system mouse. The first button (pick) cannot be customized and one button is usually reserved for the Return (Enter) button, so you generally only customize a button menu if you have three or more buttons on your pointing device.
***AUX2	This is an auxiliary button menu that defines what happens when you hold down Shift and press a button on your system mouse.

(continued)

Table 33-4 (*continued*)

Section	Function
***AUX3	This is an auxiliary button menu that defines what happens when you hold down Ctrl and press a button on your system mouse.
***AUX4	This is an auxiliary button menu that defines what happens when you hold down Ctrl and Shift and press a button on your system mouse.
***POP0	This is the first pull-down menu. Although you can display it on the menu, it is meant to be used for the cursor menu and usually displays the object snaps.
***POP1	This is the second pull-down menu. It usually displays the File menu commands.
***POP2	This is the third pull-down menu. It usually displays the Edit menu commands.
***POP3	This is the fourth pull-down menu. In *acad.mnu* it displays the View menu commands.
***POP4	This is the fifth pull-down menu. In *acad.mnu* it displays the Insert menu commands.
***POP5	This is the sixth pull-down menu. In *acad.mnu* it displays the Format menu commands.
***POP6	This is the seventh pull-down menu. In *acad.mnu* it displays the Tools menu commands.
***POP7	This is the eighth pull-down menu. In *acad.mnu* it displays the Draw menu commands.
***POP8	This is the ninth pull-down menu. In *acad.mnu* it displays the Dimension menu commands.
***POP9	This is the tenth pull-down menu. In *acad.mnu* it displays the Modify menu commands.
***POP10	This is the eleventh pull-down menu. In *acad.mnu* it displays the Help menu commands.
***POP17	This is the twelfth pull-down menu. In *acad.mnu* it displays the Grips menu commands that appear at the cursor when there is a hot grip and you right-click.
***TOOLBARS	This section defines all the toolbars. You can add as many as you like. You can define toolbars using *acad.mnu* or your own menu, but it is easier to do so in AutoCAD, as described in Chapter 29.
***IMAGE	This section defines image tiles that occasionally appear in dialog boxes.
***SCREEN	This section creates the screen menu.

Section	Function
***TABLET1	The Tablet menu is divided into four parts. Each part represents a section of the menu area on your digitizing tablet. The parts are divided into small squares, each of which can contain a menu item. This first part is left blank for you to configure. Figure 33-5 shows AutoCAD's tablet and its four parts.
***TABLET2	This is the second part of the Tablet menu.
***TABLET3	This is the third part of the Tablet menu.
***TABLET4	This is the fourth part of the Tablet menu.
***HELPSTRINGS	This section creates status line descriptions of menu and toolbar items that appear when you highlight a menu item or place your cursor over a toolbar button.
***ACCELERATORS	The Accelerators section lets you create keyboard shortcuts. These include several standard Windows shortcuts, which you should not change, such as Ctrl+C, Ctrl+V, and Ctrl+X.

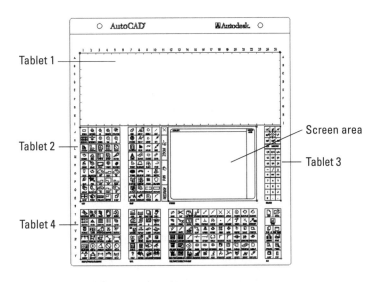

Figure 33-5:
AutoCAD's standard digitizer tablet menu and its four parts, which correspond to four sections in the menu file.

You don't need to have all of these sections in your menu. After backing up your menu files, you can delete the button sections (if you only use a system mouse), the screen menu, and the tablet menus (if you don't have a digitizing tablet).

The Buttons menu

The first item on the Buttons menu, BUTTONS1, is the second button, because you cannot customize the pick button. You can add as many menu items as your input device has buttons. Here is AutoCAD's BUTTONS1 menu. The AUX1 menu is identical.

```
***BUTTONS1
// Simple + button
// if a grip is hot bring up the Grips Cursor Menu (POP 17),
else send a carriage return
$M=$(if,$(eq,$(substr,$(getvar,cmdnames),1,5),GRIP_),$P0=ACAD.
GRIPS $P0=*);
$P0=SNAP $p0=*
^C^C
^B
^O
^G
^D
^E
^T
```

The first part of the menu includes an expression in a programming language called DIESEL, which is beyond the scope of this book. However, the comment explains the purpose of the code. The second button usually functions as a return (the semicolon at the end of the line represents the return). The Grips cursor menu only appears if you have a hot grip in your drawing.

The third button, if you have one, displays the Object Snap menu. You can change this to whatever you want.

The fourth button, ^C^C, is equivalent to pressing Esc twice.

The fifth button, ^B, is equivalent to pressing Ctrl+B, which turns Snap on and off.

The sixth button, ^O, is equivalent to pressing Ctrl+O, which turns Ortho on and off.

The seventh button, ^G, is equivalent to pressing Ctrl+G, which turns the grid on and off.

The eighth button, ^D, is equivalent to pressing Ctrl+D, which toggles the coordinate display mode.

The ninth button, ^E, is equivalent to pressing Ctrl+E, which switches to the next isometric plane.

The tenth button, ^T, is equivalent to pressing Ctrl+T, which turns the tablet on and off.

If you have a number of buttons on your pointing device, you can leave these macros as is or change them to suit your needs.

This Step-by-Step exercise shows you how you can customize even a two-button device. Because you may be working on someone else's computer, the exercise undoes the customization at the end.

Step-by-Step: Customizing the Buttons Menu

1. Copy *acad.mnu, acad.mns, acad.mnc, acad.mnr,* and *acad.mnl* to a floppy diskette.

Do not continue until you have completed step 1. If you are working on someone else's computer, ask permission before doing this exercise.

2. To make a duplicate of *acad.mnu,* right-click *acad.mnu* in Windows Explorer and choose Copy from the shortcut menu. Right-click again and choose Paste. Windows places a copy of *acad.mnu,* called *Copy of acad.mnu* in the same folder as *acad.mnu.*

3. Click the copied menu and rename it *ab1.mnu* (that's the number one, not the letter "L"). Press Enter.

4. Do the same with *acad.mnl,* making a copy and renaming the copy *ab1.mnl.*

5. Open Wordpad. (Choose Start⇨Run. Type **Wordpad** and click Run.) Open *ab1.mnu.* Remember to change the Files of type drop-down list in the Open dialog box to All documents (*.*) so you can find the file.

6. Press PageDown until you see `***MENUGROUP=ACAD`. Change `ACAD` to `AB1`.

7. If you use a digitizing tablet or other non-system input device, scroll down to the `***BUTTONS3` and `***BUTTONS4` sections. If you use a system mouse, scroll down to the `***AUX3` and `***AUX4` sections. Change the current macros, if any, so they read as follows:

```
***BUTTONS3
// Control + button
^B
***BUTTONS4
// Control + shift + button
^F

***AUX3
// Control + button
^B
***AUX4
// Control + shift + button
^F
```

This lets you turn Snap on and off using Ctrl + the right button on your pointing device, and let's you turn OSNAP on and off using Ctrl + Shift + the right button.

8. Save the file and close Wordpad.

9. Start AutoCAD if it is not already open. Open a new drawing using the *acad.mnu* template.

10. Type **menu** ↵. In the Select Menu File dialog box, choose Menu Template (*.mnu) from the Files of type drop-down list. Choose *ab1.mnu* and click Open. AutoCAD warns you that this will overwrite any toolbar changes you have made. Since you haven't made any toolbar changes to the new menu, click Yes. (You will have the same toolbars you had in *acad.mnu*.) AutoCAD responds with the `Menu loaded successfully. MENUGROUP: AB1` message on the command line.

11. Hold Ctrl and click the right button. The SNAP button on the status bar darkens. Move your cursor around to verify that Snap is on.

12. Hold Ctrl + Shift and click the right button. The Osnap settings dialog box opens because there are no current running object snaps. Choose Endpoint and click OK. OSNAP turns on.

13. Hold Ctrl + Shift and click the right button again. OSNAP turns off.

14. To return to your original menu, type **menu** ↵. Choose *acad.mnc* and click Open. AutoCAD loads *acad.mnc*.

15. Again try using Ctrl + the right button and Ctrl + Shift + the right button. It no longer works as before.

16. Do not save your drawing.

The Pop menus

The Pop menus control the pull-down and cursor menus. The cursor menus — AutoCAD comes with only two — appear at the cursor: the Snap menu, which is set to appear when you press Shift and the right mouse button, and the Grips menu, which appears when there is a hot grip and you right-click. The cursor menus are accessed from the Buttons menu by swapping, as described in the previous section.

The use of the ampersand (&) in the menu label is unique to the pull-down menus. This places an underscore under the following letter to let you choose the menu item using the keyboard instead of the mouse. You also see [--] in several places. This adds a dividing line in a pull-down menu and is used only to organize the menu into logical sections.

Here is the beginning of AutoCAD's POP0 menu:

```
***POP0
**SNAP
// Shift-right-click
               [&Object Snap Cursor Menu]
ID_Tracking   [Trac&king]_tracking
```

```
ID_From       [&From]_from
ID_MnPointFi [->Point Fi&lters]
ID_PointFilx   [.X].X
ID_PointFily   [.Y].Y
ID_PointFilz   [.Z].Z
              [--]
ID_PointFixy   [.XY].XY
ID_PointFixz   [.XZ].XZ
ID_PointFiyz   [<-.YZ].YZ
              [--]
ID_OsnapEndp [&Endpoint]_endp
ID_OsnapMidp [&Midpoint]_mid
ID_OsnapInte [&Intersection]_int
ID_OsnapAppa [&Apparent Intersect]_appint
              [--]
ID_OsnapCent [&Center]_cen
ID_OsnapQuad [&Quadrant]_qua
ID_OsnapTang [&Tangent]_tan
              [--]
ID_OsnapPerp [&Perpendicular]_per
ID_OsnapNode [No&de]_nod
ID_OsnapInse [In&sert]_ins
ID_OsnapNear [Nea&rest]_nea
ID_OsnapNone [&None]_non
              [--]
ID_Osnap      [&Osnap Settings...] _osnap
```

Notice that, unlike a regular pull-down menu, the title — Snap — doesn't appear at the top of the cursor menu. Figure 33-6 shows how this appears in AutoCAD.

Figure 33-6: The Snap cursor menu accessed by Shift + right click. Compare it to the menu code and look for the dividing lines and the underscored letters.

The Pop menus can have submenus. Use the following codes to start and end submenus:

->	Starts a submenu
<-	Ends a submenu
< <	Ends a submenu and a regular menu. Use this only when the last item on a menu has a submenu.

Here is an example from the end of the Draw menu. Notice that both the Surfaces and Solids items have submenus. At the end of the Solids submenu, the Setup item has a second-level submenu. Therefore, the Profile menu item is preceded by <-<-.

```
ID_MnSurface  [->Sur&faces]
ID_Solid      [&2D Solid]^C^C_solid
ID_3dface     [3D &Face]^C^C_3dface
ID_3dsurface  [&3D Surfaces...]$I=ACAD.image_3dobjects
$I=ACAD.*
              [--]
ID_Edge       [&Edge]^C^C_edge
ID_3dmesh     [3D &Mesh]^C^C_3dmesh
              [--]
ID_Revsurf    [Revolved &Surface]^C^C_revsurf
ID_Tabsurf    [&Tabulated Surface]^C^C_tabsurf
ID_Rulesurf   [&Ruled Surface]^C^C_rulesurf
ID_Edgesurf   [<-E&dge Surface]^C^C_edgesurf
ID_MnSolids   [->Sol&ids]
ID_Box        [&Box]^C^C_box
ID_Sphere     [&Sphere]^C^C_sphere
ID_Cylinder   [&Cylinder]^C^C_cylinder
ID_Cone       [C&one]^C^C_cone
ID_Wedge      [&Wedge]^C^C_wedge
ID_Torus      [&Torus]^C^C_torus
              [--]
ID_Extrude    [E&xtrude]^C^C_extrude
ID_Revolve    [&Revolve]^C^C_revolve
              [--]
ID_Slice      [S&lice]^C^C_slice
ID_Section    [S&ection]^C^C_section
ID_Interfere  [&Interference]^C^C_interfere
              [--]
ID_MnSetup    [->Set&up]
ID_Soldraw    [&Drawing]^C^C_soldraw
ID_Solview    [&View]^C^C_solview
ID_Solprof    [<-<-&Profile]^C^C_solprof
```

Figure 33-7 shows how this code looks on the AutoCAD Draw menu.

Tip

The titles of pull-down Pop menus appear as the menu title. Keep these fairly short to keep the menu titles from running into each other. Don't place spaces in menu title names — it becomes hard to distinguish where one menu ends and the next one starts.

Figure 33-7: The Draw menu with the Solids and Setup submenus.

Step-by-Step: Creating a Pull-Down Partial Menu

Caution

1. If you haven't already done so, copy *acad.mnu, acad.mns, acad.mnc, acad.mnr,* and *acad.mnl* to a floppy diskette.

Do not continue until you have completed step 1. If you are working on someone else's computer, ask permission before doing this exercise.

2. Open Notepad. (Choose Start⇨Run. Type **Notepad** and click OK.)

3. To create the menu group name, the pull-down menu, and the menu name (which will appear on the menu bar), type the following:

```
***MENUGROUP=AB2
***POP1
[&AB2]
```

4. To create the first menu item with a submenu, type the following:

```
ID_SpecEdits [->&Special Edits]
ID_MoveRight [&Move .1 Right]_select \_move _previous ;.1,0 ;
ID_Plinewdth [<-&PEDIT .1]_pedit \_w .1 _x
```

5. To create the next few menu items, ending with a dividing line, type the following. The ALIGN command is there because it is at the bottom of a submenu currently — you can place it here to make it more accessible.

```
ID_4circles   [&4 circles]_circle 2,2 1.5 _circle 6,2 + 1.5
_circle 10,2 1.5 _circle 14,2 1.5
ID_Cleanup    [&Clean up]_chprop _all  _c _bylayer
-layer _f no-plot  _qsave
ID_Align      [&Align]^C^C_align
[--]
```

6. To create the last menu item, type the following. This item turns the FILEDIA system variable on and off, as explained in the sidebar "Creating toggles on pull-down menus."

```
ID_Filedia  [$(if,$(and,$(getvar,filedia),1),!.)&File Dialogs
On]+
$M=$(if,$(and,$(getvar,filedia),1),^C^C_filedia 0,^C^C_filedia
1)
```

7. End the menu file with a return. Save the file as *ab2.mnu* in the *acadr14/support* folder or any other folder that you have placed in the support file search path. Close Notepad.

8. Open *ab33-a.dwg* from the CD-ROM. Save it as *ab33-1.dwg* in your *AutoCAD Bible* folder.

9. Choose Tools⇨Customize Menus. In the Menu Groups tab of the Menu Customization dialog box, choose Browse. Select Menu Template (*.mnu) from the Files of type drop-down list. Find and choose *ab2.mnu* and click Open. Click Load. Click Yes to the AutoCAD message that warns you about overwriting toolbar changes (this little menu doesn't have any toolbars).

10. Choose the Menu Bar tab. In the Menu Bar list, choose Help so that your menu will be inserted just before the Help menu. Choose Insert. AutoCAD inserts the menu. Choose Close. The menu should look like Figure 33-8. Notice the submenu and the dividing line. Also notice the checkmark before the File Dialogs On item.

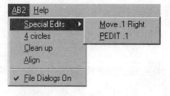

Figure 33-8: The AB2 menu, including the submenu.

11. To try out the menu, choose AB2⇨Special Edits⇨Move .1 Right. At the Select objects: prompt, pick the vertical red line and press Enter to end object selection. The menu macro moves the two lines .1 unit to the right.

12. Choose AB2⇨Special Edits⇨PEDIT .1. At the Select objects: prompt, choose the green polyline. AutoCAD makes it .1 unit wide.

13. Choose AB2⇨File Dialogs On. Notice that AutoCAD issues the FILEDIA system variable and changes its value to zero. Choose AB2 again and notice that the checkmark is gone. Choose File Dialogs On again to turn FILEDIA back on.

14. Choose AB2⇨Cleanup. AutoCAD changes the color of all the objects to BYLAYER and freezes the no-plot layer.

15. Choose Tools⇨Customize Menus and unload AB2.

16. Save your drawing.

Note

If you made a mistake and some of the items don't work properly, re-edit *ab2.mnu*. Then choose Tools⇨Menu Customization, unload AB2, reload it, and insert it again.

Creating toggles on pull-down menus

By examining *acad.mnu*, you can accomplish some interesting things with your menus, even if you don't understand the code. You may have noticed that when the UCS icon is displayed, the View⇨Display⇨UCS Icon⇨On menu item shows a checkmark. If you choose this item again, not only does the UCS icon disappear, but the checkmark does too. This is called a toggle and is created using DIESEL programming language, a language that lets you customize the command line and works only with text strings. However, you can use it for your own menus, even if you don't know any DIESEL — by simply examining the code and making a few educated guesses. Here is the code:

```
ID_UcsiconOn [$(if,$(and,$(getvar,ucsicon),1),!.)&On]+
$M=$(if,$(and,$(getvar,ucsicon),1),^C^C_ucsicon + _off,^C^C_ucsicon
_on)
```

First, you see the `ucsicon` system variable mentioned in the expression (`getvar`, `ucsicon`). Then you see the expression &On. By now you know that this is the menu label. Finally, you see the two commands at the end that issue the UCSICON system variable and turn it off and on.

Perhaps you could use a similar example in your own menu. For example, when customizing AutoCAD, you often have to turn the FILEDIA system variable on and off. Perhaps you always forget if it is FILEDIA or DIAFILE and then have to look it up, so you'd like to put it on your menu. Here's what you would do:

```
ID_Filedia    [$(if,$(and,$(getvar,filedia),1),!.)+
&File Dialogs On/Off]$M=$(if,$(and,$(getvar,filedia),1),+
^C^C_filedia 0,^C^C_filedia 1)
```

All you've done is substitute `filedia` for `ucsicon` in two places, &File Dialogs On/Off for &On, and the new commands at the end (you use zero and 1 for `filedia` instead of off and on). It's okay if you don't understand the code; the point is that it works!

Replacing your partial menus

When you are customizing a partial menu, the process of unloading, loading, and inserting a partial menu can get pretty tedious. Here's a routine that you can put on your partial menu. You can't use it the first time (because the partial menu isn't on your menu bar yet), but after that you can use it to quickly replace your old partial menu with the new one. This routine turns off the FILEDIA system variable so you can load and unload the partial menu on the command line, then it unloads and loads the menu. It then uses a simple AutoLISP expression to place the menu where you want it.

```
ID_MenuLoad  [&Reload ab2 menu]_filedia 0 +
_menuunload ab2 menuload ab2.mnu (menucmd +
P10=+ab2.pop1 ) _filedia 1
```

The first part is the name tag, which can be anything you want. The second part is the label that you see on the menu. It can also be anything you want. Then comes the menu macro. Here I have used the menu group name ab2 and the menu file name *ab2.mnu*. Replace these with your menu group and menu file names. The AutoLISP expression syntax is:

```
(menucmd  Pn=+menugroup.section )
```

where *n* is the number of the Pop menu to the right of where you want to insert your partial menu (P10 is usually the Help file), *menugroup* is the menugroup name, and *section* is the section name (usually Pop1 if your partial menu has one pull-down menu).

If your partial menu has more than one pull-down menu, you must place each Pop section using the same syntax.

Customizing the toolbars from the menu file

Although it is much easier to customize toolbars directly, as explained in Chapter 29, you can also customize them from the menu file. Here is a section of the Standard toolbar code from *acad.mnu:*

```
**TB_STANDARD
ID_TbStandar [_Toolbar( _Standard Toolbar , _Top, _Show, 0, 0,
1)]
ID_New        [_Button( New , ICON_16_NEW,
ICON_24_NEW)]^C^C_new
ID_Open       [_Button( Open , ICON_16_OPEN,
ICON_24_OPEN)]^C^C_open
ID_Save       [_Button( Save , ICON_16_SAVE,
ICON_24_SAVE)]^C^C_qsave
                [--]
ID_Print      [_Button( Print , ICON_16_PRINT,
ICON_24_PRINT)]^C^C_plot
```

```
ID_Preview    [_Button( Print Preview , ICON_16_PREVIEW,
ICON_24_PREVIEW)]^C^C_preview
ID_Spell      [_Button( Spelling , ICON_16_SPELL,
ICON_24_SPELL)]^C^C_spell
              [--]
ID_Cutclip    [_Button( Cut to Clipboard , ICON_16_CUT,
ICON_24_CUT)] _cutclip
ID_Copyclip   [_Button( Copy to Clipboard , ICON_16_COPY,
ICON_24_COPY)] _copyclip
ID_Pasteclip [_Button( Paste from Clipboard , ICON_16_PASTE,
ICON_24_PASTE)] _pasteclip
ID_Matchprop [_Button( Match Properties , ICON_16_MATCH,
ICON_24_MATCH)]_matchprop
              [--]
ID_U          [_Button( Undo , ICON_16_UNDO, ICON_24_UNDO)]_u
ID_Redo       [_Button( Redo , ICON_16_REDO,
ICON_24_REDO)]^C^C_redo
              [--]
ID_Browser    [_Button( Launch Browser , ICON_16_URL,
ICON_24_URL)]^C^C_browser;;
              [--]
ID_TbOsnap    [_Flyout( Object Snap , ICON_16_OSNAP,
ICON_24_OSNAP, _OtherIcon, ACAD.TB_OBJECT_SNAP)]
ID_TbUcs      [_Flyout( UCS , ICON_16_UCS, ICON_24_UCS,
_OtherIcon, ACAD.TB_UCS)]
ID_TbInquiry [_Flyout( Inquiry , ICON_16_LIST, ICON_24_LIST,
_OtherIcon, ACAD.TB_INQUIRY)]
```

The first line below the heading defines the entire toolbar. The codes refer to the toolbars display status (show/hide), shape, whether it is floating or docked, and so on. Since you routinely change these directly in AutoCAD, they are not crucial.

Note

Remember that AutoCAD saves toolbar changes that you make directly in AutoCAD in the *.mns* file.

The next several lines define buttons. The first section of each line is the name tag. In brackets, you specify the actual bitmap that creates the button. Then specify the macro.

Notice that the last three items create flyouts. The OtherIcon code means that whichever button is used last remains on top. You can specify OwnIcon to keep the icon specified here, where the flyout is defined, always on top. The last part refers to the toolbar section that creates the flyout. There are no macros here because they are in the referenced toolbar section.

Because Windows lets you display toolbar buttons in both large and small formats, each button actually has two bitmaps.

Tip

You can copy the ***TOOLBARS section of the *.mns* menu file and paste it into the *.mnu* file. That way you save any toolbar modifications you made in AutoCAD.

Image tile menus

Image tile menus are created with slides. The image tile displays the contents of the slides.

The first line after the section or subsection heading appears at the top of the image tile menu (there is an example following Table 33-3 earlier in the chapter).

Image tile menus have both a list box and an image tile for each item. The menu labels use a special format that provides the slide library name, the slide, and a label for the list box. You have the following options:

✦ [slidename] puts the slide name in the list box and displays the slide in the image tile.

✦ [slidelibrary(slidename)] does the same as the first option, but specifies the slide library that contains the slide.

✦ [slidename,labeltext] puts the label text in the list box and displays the slide in the image tile.

✦ [slidelibrary(slidename,labeltext)] does the same as the third option but specifies the slide library that contains the slide.

Slide and slide libraries were discussed in Chapter 30.

Note

Image tile menus cannot contain name tags.

Here's the image_3Dobjects subsection of the IMAGE section of *acad.mnu*:

```
***IMAGE
**image_3DObjects
[3D Objects]
[acad(Box3d,Box3d)]^C^Cai_box
[acad(Pyramid,Pyramid)]^C^Cai_pyramid
[acad(Wedge,Wedge)]^C^Cai_wedge
[acad(Dome,Dome)]^C^Cai_dome
[acad(Sphere,Sphere)]^C^Cai_sphere
[acad(Cone,Cone)]^C^Cai_cone
[acad(Torus,Torus)]^C^Cai_torus
[acad(Dish,Dish)]^C^Cai_dish
[acad(Mesh,Mesh)]^C^Cai_mesh
```

Figure 33-9 shows the resulting dialog box.

As explained in the earlier section on Menu Swapping, you display an image tile menu from another menu. For example, to display the 3D Objects menu, AutoCAD uses the following code in the Draw pull-down menu:

```
ID_3dsurface    [&3D Surfaces...]$I=ACAD.image_3dobjects
$I=ACAD.*
```

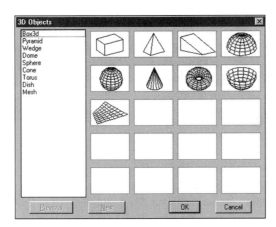

Figure 33-9: The 3D Objects dialog box is created by a subsection of the IMAGE menu.

This swaps to the 3D Objects image tile menu and displays it.

AutoCAD automatically creates the dialog box. If there are more than 20 items, AutoCAD creates Previous and Next boxes as well.

To create your own image tile menus, you need to create the slides. So that they fit into the image tiles properly, you should create a floating viewport 3 units wide by 2 units high, center the drawing so it takes up most of the viewport, and create the slide.

Step-by-Step: Creating an Image Tile Menu

1. If you haven't already done so, copy *acad.mnu, acad.mns, acad.mnc, acad.mnr,* and *acad.mnl* to a floppy diskette.

Caution

Do not continue until you have completed step 1. If you are working on someone else's computer, ask permission before doing this exercise.

On the CD-ROM

2. Use Notepad to open *ab3.mnu* from the CD-ROM. This includes the AB2 menu from the previous Step-by-Step exercise, an Image menu, and a new item in the POP1 menu that calls the image menu, as shown in Figure 33-10. Note that the macros in the image menu simply use the INSERT command to insert the files. Read over *ab3.mnu* so that you understand how the new image tile feature is created. Close *ab3.mnu*.

```
***MENUGROUP=AB3
***POP1
[AB&3]
ID_SpecEdits  [->&Special Edits]
ID_MoveRight  [&Move .1 Right]_select \_move _previous ;.1,0 ;
ID_Plinewdth  [<-&PEDIT .1]_pedit \_w .1 _x
ID_4circles   [&4 circles]_circle 2,2 1.5 _circle 6,2 1.5 _circle 10,2 1.5 _circle 14,2 1.5
ID_Cleanup    [&Clean up]_chprop _all  _c _bylayer  -layer _f no-plot  _qsave
ID_Align      [&Align]^C^C_align
[--]
ID_Filedia    [$(if,$(and,$(getvar,filedia),1),!.)&File Dialogs On/Off]+
$M=$(if,$(and,$(getvar,filedia),1),^C^C_filedia 0,^C^C_filedia 1)
[--]
ID_AEC_sym    [Architectural &Elect Symbols]$I=AB3.AEC_sym +
$I=AB3.*

***IMAGE
**AEC_sym
[Architectural Electrical Symbols]
[ab33-b01,Duplex Receptacle Outlet]^C^C_insert ab33-b01;\  ;
[ab33-b02,Dryer Outlet]^C^C_insert ab33-b02;\  ;
[ab33-b03,Surface Mounted Light]^C^C_insert ab33-b03;\  ;
[ab33-b04,Recessed Light]^C^C_insert ab33-b04;\  ;
[ab33-b05,Wall Washer Light]^C^C_insert ab33-b05;\  ;
[ab33-b06,Recessed Eye Ball Light]^C^C_insert ab33-b06;\  ;
[ab33-b07,Pendant Light]^C^C_insert ab33-b07;\  ;
[ab33-b08,Wall Mounted Light]^C^C_insert ab33-b08;\  ;
[ab33-b09,Sconce]^C^C_insert ab33-b09;\  ;
[ab33-b10,Flood Lights]^C^C_insert ab33-b10;\  ;
[ab33-b11,Thermostat]^C^C_insert ab33-b11;\  ;
[ab33-b12,Single Pole Switch]^C^C_insert ab33-b12;\  ;
[ab33-b13,Three-Way Switch]^C^C_insert ab33-b13;\  ;
[ab33-b14,Master Switch]^C^C_insert ab33-b14;\  ;
[ab33-b15,Exhaust Fan]^C^C_insert ab33-b15;\  ;
[ab33-b16,Smoke Detector]^C^C_insert ab33-b16;\  ;
[ab33-b17,Whole House Fan]^C^C_insert ab33-b17;\  ;
```

Figure 33-10: The AB3 menu. The Image menu label format is [slidename,labeltext].

On the CD-ROM

3. In order for this exercise to work, you need to copy *ab3.mnu* and all the slides and drawings used in *ab3.mnu* from the CD-ROM to a folder in AutoCAD's support file search path. You can copy them to \acadr14\support, but since there are so many files (the menu file plus 17 drawings and 17 slides), it is probably better to create a new folder and add the folder to AutoCAD's support file search path. You can copy them to your *AutoCAD Bible* folder and add that folder to AutoCAD's support file search path. Then copy *ab3.mnu*, *ab33-b01.dwg* through *ab33-b17.dwg*, and *ab33-b01.sld* through *ab33-b17.sld* to that folder.

Note

Remember that you can add any folder to the support file search path by choosing Tools⇨Preferences⇨Files, expanding Support File Search Path, and choosing Add.

On the CD-ROM

4. Open *ab33-b.dwg* from the CD-ROM. This drawing just shows a rectangle 40 feet long by 30 feet wide, which could represent any building.

5. Save it as *ab33-2.dwg* in your *AutoCAD Bible* folder.

6. Choose Tools⇨Customize Menus. In the File name text box, type **ab3.mnu** and click Load. As long as the menu file is in AutoCAD's support file search path, AutoCAD will find the menu. Click Yes in the message dialog box that warns you about overwriting toolbar changes.

7. Choose the Menu Bar tab. AB3 should be listed as the Menu Group. Choose Help and click Insert. AutoCAD inserts AB3 before the Help menu. Click Close.

8. Click the AB3 menu. It now has a new item, Architectural Elect Symbols. Choose this item. The Architectural Electrical Symbols dialog box opens, created by the Image Tile section, as shown in Figure 33-11.

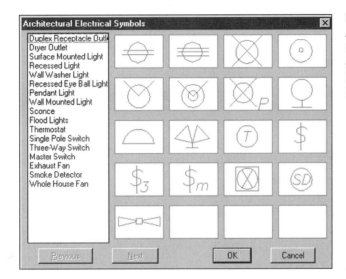

Figure 33-11: The Architectural Electrical Symbols dialog box is created by the AB3 menu's Image Tile section.

9. Look at the List box on the left and compare it to the `**AEC_sym` subsection shown in Figure 33-10. You can see that all the labels in the list box were created using the `labeltext` part of the slide definition. The image tiles are created by the slides.

10. Choose any image tile. The corresponding item in the list is also selected. Click OK. At the `Insertion point:` prompt, pick any point in the rectangle. The macro of the image tile section inserts the drawing.

11. Choose any item from the list. The corresponding image tile is also selected. Click OK. Pick any point to insert the drawing. You can continue to insert as many symbols as you wish.

12. Choose Tools⇨Customize Menus and unload AB3. Save your drawing.

Tablet menus

Tablet menus are fairly straightforward. You can print out AutoCAD's standard tablet drawing, *acadr14\sample\tablet14.dwg*, and compare it to the TABLET section of *acad.mnu*. The entire first section is left blank for you to configure. This menu section is preset to contain 9 rows and 25 columns. If you configure this menu area (using the TABLET command) to contain 9 rows and 25 columns, you can place your own macro in each of these boxes.

Here is the beginning of the TABLET1 section from *acad.mnu:*

```
***TABLET1
**TABLET1STD
[A-1]\
[A-2]\
[A-3]\
[A-4]\
[A-5]\
[A-6]\
[A-7]\
[A-8]\
[A-9]\
[A-10]\
```

This section continues through [I-25].

The TABLET2 sections starts this way:

```
//          TABLET2 menu.
//          Rows: J to R (9)
//          Columns: 11
//
***TABLET2
**TABLET2STD
// Row J View
^C^C_regen
 _zoom _e
 _zoom _a
 _zoom _w
 _zoom _p
[Draw]\
^C^C_box
^C^C_mtext
^C^C_circle
^C^C_line
^C^C
```

As you can see, the menu includes instructions to help you configure the tablet. When you configure the tablet, you need to specify the number of rows and columns so the menu tells you here that the Tablet2 section has 9 rows and 11 columns.

The syntax of the Tablet menu is very simple; you don't need name tags or labels, just the menu macro itself.

Note

If you customize the Tablet menu, don't forget to also open *tablet14.dwg* provided by AutoCAD in the *acadr14\sample* folder, make the corresponding changes, and print it out to overlay on your digitizer, so that the drawing you place on your tablet reflects the menu properly.

Working with the screen menu

I don't spend much time on the screen menu here because it is not used very much any more. If you are interested in customizing it, read the comments at the beginning of the ***SCREEN section of *acad.mnu*.

Tip

The screen section is very long. If you don't use the screen menu, you can delete it from *acad.mnu* or the menu file you are using. Don't forget to back up *acad.mnu* first.

Creating status line help messages

The ***HELPSTRINGS section of a menu file creates help messages on the status line for pull-down and toolbar menu items. This section uses the name tag of the menu item. Here is part of the HELPSTRINGS section of *acad.mnu*. Here, the help messages are listed in alphabetical order by name tag, but you can add your own in any order you want.

```
***HELPSTRINGS
ID_3darray     [Creates a three-dimensional array:   3darray]
ID_3dface      [Creates a three-dimensional face:   3dface]
ID_3dmesh      [Creates a free-form polygon mesh:   3dmesh]
ID_3dpoly      [Creates a polyline of straight line segments in
three-dimensional space:   3dpoly]
ID_3dsin       [Imports a 3D Studio file:   3dsin]
```

In *acad.mnu*, the help string gives the actual text that appears on the status line followed by a colon, two spaces, and the name of the command. You can follow this convention for the sake of consistency — however, some of your macros may use more than one command, so it is not always appropriate. The space between the name tag and the help string is for readability only.

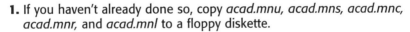

Step-by-Step: Creating Help Strings

Caution

1. If you haven't already done so, copy *acad.mnu, acad.mns, acad.mnc, acad.mnr,* and *acad.mnl* to a floppy diskette.

   Do not continue until you have completed step 1. If you are working on someone else's computer, ask permission before doing this exercise.

On the CD-ROM

2. Use Notepad to open *ab3.mnu* from the CD-ROM. If you did the last Step-by-Step exercise and copied it to your hard disk, open it from there.

3. Add the following lines to the end of the file. The name tags come from the first section of *ab3.mnu* but don't include the first item, which only opens a submenu.

```
***HELPSTRINGS
ID_MoveRight [Moves selected objects .1 unit to the right]
```

```
ID_Plinewdth [Makes the width of one polyline .1]
ID_4circles  [Draws 4 circles in one row with radius 1.5]
ID_Cleanup   [Changes color of all objects to BYLAYER,
freezes no-plot layer, and saves]
ID_Align     [Moves and rotates objects to align with other
objects: align]
ID_Filedia   [Turns FILEDIA system variable on and off]
ID_AEC_sym   [Inserts AEC electrical symbols using a dialog
box]
```

4. If you did the previous Step-by-Step exercise, save the file as *ab4.mnu* in the same location as *ab3.mnu*. If you opened *ab3.mnu* from the CD-ROM, save it as *ab4.mnu* in *acadr14**support* or another folder in AutoCAD's support file search path. Note that the file is still Menu Group AB3. Close Notepad.

5. Start AutoCAD with any drawing. Choose Tools➪Menu Customization. In the File name text box, type **ab4.mnu** and click Load. Choose Yes at the message warning you about overwriting toolbar changes. AutoCAD loads the menu file.

6. Choose the Menu Bar tab. Click Help on the Menu Bar list and click Insert. AutoCAD inserts the partial menu to the left of the Help menu. Click Close.

7. Open the AB3 menu and place the cursor over the items, including the submenu. The help strings appear on the status bar.

8. Unload AB3. Do not save your drawing.

Creating keyboard shortcuts

The ***ACCELERATORS section creates keyboard shortcuts. Here is the Accelerators section of *acad.mnu:*

```
***ACCELERATORS
// Toggle PICKADD
[CONTROL+ K ]$M=$(if,$(and,$(getvar,pickadd),1), _pickadd
0, _pickadd 1)
// Toggle Orthomode
[CONTROL+ L ]^O
// Next Viewport
[CONTROL+ R ]^V
// ID_Spell       [ \ F7\ ]
// ID_PanRealti   [ \ F11\ ]
// ID_ZoomRealt   [ \ F12\ ]
ID_Copyclip    [CONTROL+ C ]
ID_New         [CONTROL+ N ]
ID_Open        [CONTROL+ O ]
ID_Print       [CONTROL+ P ]
ID_Save        [CONTROL+ S ]
ID_Pasteclip   [CONTROL+ V ]
ID_Cutclip     [CONTROL+ X ]
ID_Redo        [CONTROL+ Y ]
ID_U           [CONTROL+ Z ]
```

You can create keyboard shortcuts in two ways:

✦ You can use a name tag, such as ID_Spell, followed by a label in brackets containing the keyboard shortcut. When you execute the shortcut, AutoCAD looks for the name tag in the rest of the menu file and executes the command attached to that name tag.

✦ You can start with the label containing the shortcut, such as [CONTROL+"L"], and follow it with the menu macro you want the shortcut to execute. Use this method to create shortcuts for macros that do not exist elsewhere in the menu.

Table 33-5 lists the expressions you need to use for all the keys you can use to create shortcuts.

Table 33-5	
Expressions for Keys in the Accelerators Section of the Menu File	
Key	**Expression**
F1-F12	"F1", "F2", and so on, excluding F10, which is reserved by Windows
Insert	"INSERT"
Delete	"DELETE"
Arrow keys	"UP", "DOWN", "LEFT", "RIGHT" — must be used with Ctrl key.
Numeric keypad	"NUMPAD0", "NUMPAD1", and so on through "NUMPAD9"

In general, you should not reassign the commonly used Windows shortcuts, such as Ctrl+C, Ctrl+V, and so on.

Have you ever worked in another Windows program, then started AutoCAD, and by habit tried to select an object and press Del to erase it? In this Step-by-Step exercise, you create this and two other keyboard shortcuts.

Step-by-Step: Creating Keyboard Shortcuts

1. If you haven't already done so, copy *acad.mnu, acad.mns, acad.mnc, acad.mnr,* and *acad.mnl* to a floppy diskette.

Do not continue until you have completed step 1. If you are working on someone else's computer, ask permission before doing this exercise.

2. Use Notepad to open *ab4.mnu* from the CD-ROM. If you did the last Step-by-Step exercise and copied it to your hard disk, open it from there.

3. Type the following at the end of the file, then press Enter:

```
***ACCELERATORS
["delete"]          _erase
[CONTROL "up"]      ^C^C_snap 1
[CONTROL "down"]    ^C^C_snap .25
```

4. If you did the previous Step-by-Step exercise, save the file as *ab5.mnu* in the same location as *ab4.mnu*. If you opened *ab4.mnu* from the CD-ROM, save it as *ab5.mnu* in *\acadr14\support* or another folder in AutoCAD's support file search path. Note that the file is still Menu Group AB3. Close Notepad.

5. Start AutoCAD with any drawing. Choose Tools⇨Customize Menus. In the File name text box, type **ab5.mnu** and click Load. Choose Yes at the message warning you about overwriting toolbar changes. AutoCAD loads the menu file.

6. Choose the Menu Bar tab. Click Help on the Menu Bar list and click Insert. AutoCAD inserts the partial menu to the left of the Help menu. Click Close.

7. Press Ctrl+Up (the up arrow on the numeric pad). AutoCAD sets the snap to 1. Press Ctrl+Down. AutoCAD sets the snap to .25.

8. Draw a few objects. Select them. Press Del. AutoCAD erases them.

9. Unload the AB3 menu group. Don't save your drawing.

Note

AutoCAD's regular *acad.mnu* has an Edit⇨Clear item that erases objects. To the right it says Del. This means to say that you can press Del to erase items but it only works if you press Del *before* selecting the objects. You can't select the objects and then press Del as you do with other Windows programs. The Delete shortcut you just created lets you select objects first.

Summary

In this chapter you learned how to customize the menu to suit your situation and speed up your everyday work. Menu customization is a very powerful tool. When you start customizing your menus, you will suddenly find yourself thinking of new ways to use this tool. The result will be a major improvement in the way AutoCAD serves your needs.

This chapter ends Part VI on Customizing AutoCAD. Part VII challenges you to go further in your customization of AutoCAD by starting to program with AutoLISP.

✦   ✦   ✦

AutoLISP

Part VII invites you to go the distance and start programming AutoCAD with AutoLISP. AutoLISP is a powerful programming language that lets you create your own commands and create routines tailored to your needs. While these two chapters only cover a small portion of the available material on AutoLISP, they should get you started creating simple, useful AutoLISP programs.

Learning AutoLISP Basics

Understanding AutoLISP

AutoLISP is a programming language that can enhance productivity markedly by automating often-used or repetitive tasks. AutoLISP allows a glimpse into the inner workings of AutoCAD and can serve as an excellent stepping stone to learning more advanced automation methods such as ObjectARX.

AutoLISP expressions can be entered live on the command line in response to prompts, or can be saved to a file to be loaded and used when needed. AutoLISP offers wide and varied possibilities for shortcuts — best of all, AutoLISP can be customized to any level of complexity.

AutoLISP intimidates many users of AutoCAD, but this is unwarranted. The many benefits of AutoLISP well justify the initial time you invest to learn this rich and full-featured language.

Using Existing AutoLISP Routines

The number of AutoLISP routines available to the user is tremendous. Every office with more than a trivial number of AutoCAD workstations has probably created at least one AutoLISP routine to expedite some common task.

Many of the commands you already use in AutoCAD are in AutoLISP routines, for example, 3DARRAY, BMAKE, DDATTDEF, DDCHPROP, DDMODIFY, DDSELECT, DDUCSP, DDUNITS, DDVIEW, MVSETUP, AI_BOX, DDINSERT, and others. Users of AutoLISP often get examples of how to handle complex problems by reviewing these applications.

LISP stands for *LISt Processing*, and as will be seen in this and the next chapter, the understanding of lists is crucial to using AutoLISP.

Loading AutoLISP routines

You can load AutoLISP routines in a variety of ways. One method is on the command line. To load 3DARRAY from the command line, type **(load "3darray")** ↵. The parentheses are required, and indicate that you are entering an AutoLISP expression. The quotation marks are required by AutoLISP because you are specifying a filename. AutoCAD responds with 3DARRAY loaded.

When you enter the command to load 3DARRAY, AutoCAD searches all support paths for a file called *3darray.lsp*. At installation time, AutoCAD automatically configures the support file search path to include the path of *\AutoCAD\support*.

Note

All AutoLISP files must have the extension of *.lsp*.

To specify the full path to the routine type, you would enter:

```
(load  c:/AutoCAD/support/3darray )↵
```

or

```
(load  c:\\AutoCAD\\support\\3darray )↵
```

The backslash (\) has special meaning in AutoLISP, and you therefore need to use two of them or a regular slash (/) when specifying a path. The backslash character tells AutoLISP to interpret the following character literally. To use a double-quote in an AutoLISP expression, for example, precede it by a backslash.

You can also load AutoLISP routines with the APPLOAD command by choosing Tools⇨Load Application or typing **appload** at the command line. AutoCAD opens the Load AutoLISP, ADS, and ARX Files dialog box, shown in Figure 34-1.

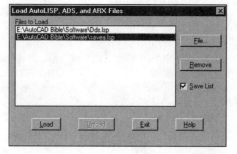

Figure 34-1: The Load AutoLISP, ADS, and ARX Files dialog box.

Use this dialog box to load ADS, ARX, and AutoLISP applications. If you check Save List, AutoCAD displays the list of applications in the dialog box whenever you open it.

Click File to choose ADS (.exe), ARX (.arx), or AutoLISP (.lsp) files. AutoCAD lists the files in the dialog box. Choose one and click Load to load the application.

AutoCAD also comes with two .lsp files that you can use for your AutoLISP routines. One, acad.lsp, is initially empty. The other, acadr14.lsp, comes with some routines that AutoCAD needs to load. You can place routines in either of these files. Routines in both of these files are automatically loaded when you open a drawing, so you don't need to load them individually — they are ready for you to use.

Using AutoLISP routines

The nature of an AutoLISP routine allows you complete control of its interaction with the user and what it does once loaded.

Most AutoLISP routines define a command name, which you then type at the command line to run the routine. Some routines include a dialog box to help you choose options and specifications.

In this Step-by-Step exercise, you load and use a simple AutoLISP routine.

Step-by-Step: Loading and Using an AutoLISP Routine

On the
CD-ROM

1. Use Windows Explorer to copy *circle3.lsp* from the CD-ROM to your \AcadR14\support\ folder or to a folder you have created for AutoLISP files and added to the support file search path.

2. Open a new drawing using the Start from Scratch option.

3. To load the circle3 AutoLISP routine, type **(load "circle3")** ↵. AutoCAD responds with C:CIRCLE3. AutoLISP treats all characters as uppercase, so circle3 is the same as CIRCLE3.

4. Now that circle3 has been loaded, at the command prompt, type **CIRCLE3** ↵.

5. At the Please click a point: prompt, pick any point on screen. You see a 3-unit radius circle with its center at the point you picked, as shown in Figure 34-2.

6. Save your drawing in your *AutoCAD Bible* folder as *ab34-1.dwg*.

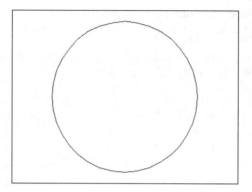

Figure 34-2: The circle drawn using the circle3 AutoLISP routine.

Looking at an AutoLISP routine

To examine the contents of the *circle3.lsp* file, open it in any text editor. (Notepad is probably best, as many word processing applications insert formatting codes into the file.) To run Notepad, click Start⇨Run, type **notepad**, and click OK. Figure 34-3 shows the circle3 routine in Notepad.

```
circle3.lsp - Notepad
File  Edit  Search  Help
(defun c:circle3 (/ pt) ;Creates a circle of radius 3
  (princ "Please click a point: ")
  (setq pt (getpoint))
  (command "_circle" pt "3")
)
```

Figure 34-3: The circle3 AutoLISP routine.

This figure illustrates a number of characteristics of AutoLISP routines:

✦ As in many other programming languages, indentation is used in AutoLISP for clarity when reading, and has no effect on the operation of the routine.

✦ The returns at the end of each line are also for clarity. All five lines could be placed on a single line with no effect on program execution — the program would work exactly the same way.

✦ All AutoLISP statements are placed in parentheses. Therefore, whenever you open a parenthesis you must close it. There are always the same number of left and right parentheses in an AutoLISP routine. The physical location of a right parenthesis is not relevant — it can be placed on a new line or several spaces away from the left parenthesis (in both cases the pair is interpreted the same way).

✦ AutoLISP is interpreted from the innermost parenthesis pair first. On line three of Figure 34-3, for instance, (getpoint) is done first, and then the result is used for the (setq pt (getpoint)) expression. This is analogous to mathematics, as in the expression $(3 + (5 \times 4))$, where 5×4 is computed first and the result is added to 3.

✦ At the end of the first line is a comment, ;Creates a circle of radius 3. Any text preceded by a semicolon is ignored by the program. Use this technique to place explanations in your routines to help you and others understand what the routine is doing.

The following explains the routine in Figure 34-3 line by line:

1. Line one begins with an open parenthesis that is balanced with the one on line five. This pair of parentheses delineates the body of the function. The line begins with defun, which means *DEFine FUNction,* and the function is called c:circle3. You could use just circle3, but you would have to type **(circle3)** at the command line to use the routine. When you prefix the function with c:, you can use it in AutoCAD by just entering **circle3** at the command line. The last item on Line 1 is (/ pt). The pt after the slash means that pt is a *local variable*. A variable stores a value for later use in the routine. A local variable is used only in its own routine and is not retained for use in other routines. If you replaced (/ pt) with simply ( ) the pt variable would be available to other AutoLISP routines as well.

2. Line two is the simplest line in this routine — it simply prints the statement Please click a point: at the command line. Anything in the quotes after princ will be printed on the AutoCAD command line. In this case the statement is used as a prompt to tell the user to pick a point.

3. Line three is typical of AutoLISP routines where nested parentheses can drive the reader crazy. It's easier if you remember to simply read from the innermost parenthesis pair outward. So reading from the innermost parenthesis pair, you have first (getpoint). This means to simply get a point. In response to this, any of the AutoCAD input methods will work — clicking on the screen, typing coordinates for a point, or using object snaps. Reading outward you have (setq pt (getpoint)). The statement setq means that the variable pt is set to whatever comes back from getpoint. So if the coordinates 2,2,2 are entered by typing or picking on the screen, then the variable pt is 2,2,2.

4. Line four reads (command _circle pt 3). The command function in AutoLISP is one of the easier functions to understand. It simply executes whatever command is specified in the quotes that follow, using all subsequent arguments. When the CIRCLE command is invoked in AutoCAD, it asks for the center point first and then the radius. So line four starts the CIRCLE command, uses for the center point whatever is assigned to pt, and sets the radius to 3 units.

Note

An underscore precedes the CIRCLE command, so that it can be translated into other language versions of AutoCAD.

Creating Your Own AutoLISP Expressions

AutoLISP is very easy to develop because changes to the AutoLISP code can be tested immediately. In the case of compiled languages, a great many extra steps are required for development — every time a code change is made, the code must be recompiled and relinked to see the changes in AutoCAD. This is the case with the AutoCAD Development System (ADS) and ObjectARX.

Understanding AutoLISP syntax

In AutoLISP an operator always comes first, followed by a number of operands. An operator can be thought of as a function that *does* something, and the operands are what the function operates *on*.

Working with numbers and text

Table 34-1 lists the basic arithmetic functions. You can use these functions on anything that has a value. For example, if you create a variable with a value of 2, you can use that variable with the arithmetic functions.

Table 34-1
Basic Arithmetic Functions

Function	Description
+	Addition
-	Subtraction
*	Multiplicaton
/	Division
SQRT	Square root

Table 34-1 lists only a few fundamental arithmetic operators (or functions). There are a great number of operators available to the AutoLISP programmer, which you can find in the AutoCAD *Customization Guide.*

Some fundamental arithmetic operations can provide a feel for the fundamentals. If you type:

```
(+ 2 3)↵
```

AutoLISP responds with 5. This syntax of having the operator (the plus sign) come before the operands (2 and 3) is very different from that of many languages, but is important to understand if a working knowledge of AutoLISP is to be gained.

To nest expressions, simply add another set of parentheses to enclose the nested expression. For example, to (* 5 (+ 2 3)) AutoCAD responds with 25.

The nested expression is evaluated from the innermost parenthesis pair out, first two and three are added, then that sum is multiplied by five. This is the bread and butter of AutoLISP.

Working with floating-point numbers is as easy as integers. If you type:

```
(/ 7.3 5.84)↵
```

AutoLISP responds with 1.25.

Working with text is as easy as numbers, but operations such as addition, subtraction, multiplication, and division have no meaning when operating on text. In AutoLISP, a *string* is simply some text. Table 34-2 lists some common string functions.

	Table 34-2 **Basic String Functions**	
Function	*Description*	
STRCAT	Appends one string to another	
SUBSTR	Returns (provides you with) a substring (a portion) of a string. The first argument is the string, the second is an integer that specifies the position of the first character you want, and the third (optional) is the number of characters you want	
STRLEN	Returns the number of characters including spaces in the string	

Here are two examples:

```
(strcat  Today is   a good day   . )
 Today is a good day.
(substr  Today is a good day.  12 4)
 good
```

STRCAT stands for *STRing conCATenate* and appends one string with another. Any number of strings can come after the STRCAT function (There are three strings enclosed in quotes in the STRCAT example).

SUBSTR stands for *SUBSTRing* and in this example returns the four characters starting at position 12 as shown in the example.

Caution

AutoLISP counts the position of the characters starting from zero, not 1. Therefore, the T of Today is at position zero, and the g of good is at position 12.

Table 34-3 offers you a few more functions that work with numbers and strings.

Table 34-3
AutoLISP Functions for Numbers and Strings

Function	Description
ABS	Returns the absolute value of the argument. (abs -76) returns 76.
ASCII	Returns the ASCII code of a character. (ascii B) returns 66.
CHR	Returns the text string for an ASCII code. (chr 66) returns B .
ATOI	Converts a string to an integer. (atoi 2.7) returns 2.
ATOF	Converts a string to a real number. (atof 7.6) returns 7.6.
ITOA	Converts an integer to a text string. (itoa 76) returns 76 .
RTOS	Converts a real number to a text string. You can add a mode (1=scientific, 2=decimal, 3=engineering, 4=architectural, 5=fractional) and a precision. Otherwise, RTOS uses the current settings. (rtos 87.3 2 2) returns 87.30.
=	Equal to. Returns T for true if all arguments are numerically equal. (= 3 3.0) returns T. If the arguments are not equal, it returns nil.
/=	Not equal to. Returns T if all arguments are not numerically equal. (/= 5 6) returns T. If they are equal, it returns nil.
<	Less than. Returns T if each argument is numerically less than the next argument. Otherwise returns nil.
>	Greater than. Returns T if each argument is numerically greater than the next argument. Otherwise returns nil.
>=	Greater than or equal to. Returns T if each argument is numerically greater than or equal to the next argument. Otherwise returns nil.
<=	Less than or equal to. Returns T if each argument is numerically less than or equal to the next argument. Otherwise returns nil.

Using AutoLISP on the Command Line

AutoLISP can be used on the fly in AutoCAD because it is *interpreted*. By typing an expression on the command line, you get the result immediately. An interpreted language is one in which a single source statement is translated to machine language, executed, and then each subsequent source statement is operated on in the same way. This allows interactive entry of AutoLISP code into AutoCAD.

The output of an AutoLISP expression can be used in response to AutoCAD prompts as well. For example, you can type (+1 7) at the Diameter/<Radius>: prompt of the CIRCLE command for a circle with a radius of eight units.

This ability to place AutoLISP expressions into AutoCAD commands is a very powerful tool.

Release 14 lets you edit the command line, which is very useful when experimenting with AutoLISP expressions. You can use the left and right arrow keys, as well as the Del and Backspace keys. You can also open the Text Window (press F2), select any previous line, right-click, and choose Paste to CmdLine. This copies the line to the current command line where you can press Enter to execute it or edit it first.

If you leave out a closing parenthesis, AutoCAD returns 1> when you press Enter. This tells you that there remains one open parenthesis to be closed. If two open parentheses remained to be closed AutoCAD would respond with 2>. Just type the correct number of closing parentheses at the command line and AutoCAD accepts the expression.

Step-by-Step: Working with Numbers and Text on the Command Line

1. Open a new drawing using the Start from Scratch option.

2. Type **circle** ↵. Follow the prompts:

   ```
   3P/2P/TTR/<Center point>: Pick any point.
   Diameter/<Radius>: (- 5 3)↵
   ```

   AutoCAD draws a circle with a radius of 2.

3. Type **(strcat "This is an example of " "regular text.")** ↵. Don't forget the space between of and the quotation mark. When the two phrases are put together, this creates the space between of and regular. AutoCAD returns
   ```
   This is an example of regular text.
   ```

4. Press the up arrow and press Enter. AutoCAD repeats the last line. Use the left arrow to move to the right of the last r in regular and use Backspace to delete the word regular. Type **italic** ↵. AutoCAD returns the new string concatenation.

5. Save the drawing in your *AutoCAD Bible* folder as *ab34-2.dwg*.

When you create AutoLISP expressions on the command line, they are not saved with the drawing. They have the same status as any input you type at the command line.

Creating AutoLISP Files

If you want to use your AutoLISP expressions more than a couple of times, you should save them in a file. As with all AutoCAD customization, use a text editor that saves the file in text only (ASCII) format. Notepad is ideal for most AutoLISP routines.

Once you have created the routine, save it with an extension of *.lsp*.

Tip

A common practice is to consolidate all AutoLISP routines in one folder for ease of use. To do this, create a folder in the AutoCAD folder called *LISP*. Then choose Tools⇨Preferences. On the Files tab, expand the Support File Search Path and click Add. Add the path *\Acadr14\LISP* by typing it directly in the edit box or clicking Browse.

A dialog box appears that says the changes may not go into effect until AutoCAD is restarted. If this proves to be the case (you try to load an AutoLISP file and AutoCAD can't find it), close and restart AutoCAD to be sure the changes take effect.

Acadr14.lsp loads all the routines mentioned earlier (such as 3DARRAY, BMAKE, and so on) that you use as regular AutoCAD commands. It also loads a few additional routines that you may or may not ever need. You can also add your routines to this file.

Caution

Because *acadr14.lsp* is loaded before AutoCAD is ready to accept commands, do *not* add any commands to *acadr14.lsp* that execute anything — only function definitions (defun routines) should be added to *acadr14.lsp*. This applies to the *acad.lsp* file as well. Any operations that are executed in either of these files will not work because the drawing database is not yet available when these files are loaded.

The *acad.lsp* file is loaded after the *acadr14.lsp* file; and other than this the two files serve the same purpose — they are automatically loaded each time a new drawing session is started (either AutoCAD is started or a new drawing is started). The *acad.lsp* file is available to keep your own customizations separate from those that are included with AutoCAD in the *acadr14.lsp* file.

Creating Variables

A very useful item in most programming languages is the variable. A *variable* is a symbolic name that can be operated on in a given program. An important part of using variables is being able to assign values to them.

Here's an example:

```
(setq radius 3)
3
```

This sets the value of 3 to a variable named radius.

If you want to use this variable on the command line, precede it with an exclamation point (!). For example,

```
!radius
3
```

The exclamation point before a variable evaluates the value stored in the variable and returns it to the command line.

Assigning strings to a variable is as easy as assigning numerals to a variable:

```
(setq name  Robin )
 Robin
```

You can also nest AutoLISP expressions — place one inside the other.

```
(setq radius (+ 2 1))
3
!radius
3
```

As can be seen in this example, AutoLISP must be read from the innermost parenthesis set outward. AutoLISP evaluated (+ 2 1) first, and then assigned the result to the variable radius.

By default, AutoCAD reloads AutoLISP when you open a new drawing. In the Compatibility tab of the Preferences dialog box (Tools⇨Preferences), you can choose to retain variables from drawing to drawing by unchecking Reload AutoLISP between drawings.

Step-by-Step: Using Variables on the Command Line

1. Open a drawing using the Start from Scratch option.

2. Type **(setq radius (+ 2 1))** ↵. AutoLISP returns 3.

3. Start the CIRCLE command. Pick any center point. At the Diameter/<Radius>: prompt, type **!radius** ↵. AutoCAD draws a circle with a radius of 3 units.

4. Type **(setq color "green")** ↵. AutoLISP returns green .

5. Type **color** ↵. At the New object color <BYLAYER>: prompt, type **!color** ↵.

6. Draw a new circle. The circle is green because the current color is now green.

7. Save your drawing in your *AutoCAD Bible* folder as *ab34-3.dwg*.

   In response to the prompt for the new object color in step 5, !color evaluated to "green", and the current object color was set to green as well.

Working with AutoCAD Commands

Accessing AutoCAD commands from within AutoLISP is a powerful tool for automating commonly used functions. By combining the access to commands from AutoLISP with variables as described in the previous section, you gain a great deal of flexibility.

Accessing AutoCAD commands

Earlier in this chapter when you looked at an AutoLISP routine (see Figure 34-3), you saw an example of the COMMAND function. You use the COMMAND function in AutoLISP to execute AutoCAD commands. This function treats all subsequent operands as if they were typed at the command line interactively. When programming COMMAND functions in AutoLISP, exactly duplicate what you would do at the command line. For example, to draw a line, you follow the steps shown in the following table. The second column shows how you would accomplish the same action in an AutoLISP routine.

Enter **line** at the command line	`line` (or `_line`).
Press Enter	Use a space to represent pressing Enter after issuing a command.
Specify the start point for the line	You can use a variable, actual coordinates, or pause for user input.
Specify the endpoint	You can use a variable, actual coordinates, or pause for user input.
Press Enter to end the LINE command	Use an empty set of two quotation marks to represent pressing Enter within a command or to end a command.

For example, if you are using the variables `startpt` and `endpt` for the start point and endpoint of a line, here's how you would access the LINE command in an AutoLISP expression:

```
(command _line startpt endpt )
```

Creating functions and commands

The use of functions always begins with the operator DEFUN. You can define three principal types of functions:

1. The type you have been using thus far precedes the command name defined by DEFUN with c:, which lets you use the function by name at the AutoCAD command line. The function becomes usable like any other AutoCAD command.

2. You can also create a function definition without preceding the name with c:. This type is most valuable when it is called by other AutoLISP operations. If you need to execute it at the command line, you must enclose the function name in parentheses.

3. The third type is s::STARTUP. By defining a function (usually in *acadr14.lsp* or *acad.lsp*) with the name s::STARTUP, every AutoLISP function in the routine automatically executes when you start a new drawing or first start AutoCAD.

Using s::STARTUP is a great tool for enhancing productivity. In this way, you can automate whatever general setup operations you normally do at the beginning of a drawing session.

Here's an AutoLISP routine that uses both DEFUN and COMMAND:

```
(defun c:redline (/ startpt endpt)
  (terpri) (setq startpt (getpoint  Select the redline start
      point: ))
  (terpri) (setq endpt (getpoint  Select the redline end
      point ))
  (command _line  startpt endpt   )
  (command _chprop  _last    _color  red    )
)
```

Here's an explanation of the above routine:

✦ The first line of this routine defines a function called `redline`. Because `redline` is preceded by c:, you can type **redline** at the command line. As you may remember from the discussion of the *circle3* routine, the expression `(/ startpt endpt)` means that redline has two local variables that are available only to this routine. These variables are used in the next two lines.

✦ The new instruction, `terpri`, on the second line, tells AutoCAD to print a blank line at the command line. You can use this to improve readability of the prompts. Otherwise, two or more prompts run together on one line.

✦ Reading the second line from the innermost parenthesis pair outward, AutoCAD obtains the redline's start point from the user with the prompt `Select the redline start point` and sets the variable `startpt` equal to that start point's value. Similarly, the third line obtains the redline's endpoint and sets the variable `endpt` to that value.

✦ Line four uses the AutoLISP COMMAND function. It issues the LINE command, specifies the start and endpoints, and uses a set of empty quotation marks to replicate pressing Enter to end the LINE command.

✦ Line five analogously uses the same syntax for the CHPROP command. It issues the CHPROP command, selects the line you just used by using the Last selection option, ends object selection by using the empty set of quotation marks, specifies the Color option, and sets the color to red. Another empty set of quotation marks ends the command.

✦ Line six ends the `redline` routine with a closing parenthesis.

To use this routine, you would use the following steps:

1. Open Notepad and type in the routine.

2. Save the routine as *redline.lsp* and place it in AutoCAD's *support* folder or any other folder you may have created for AutoLISP routines and added to AutoCAD's support file search path as described earlier in this chapter.

3. Close Notepad.

4. At the command line, type **(load "redline")** ↵. AutoLISP returns C:REDLINE.

5. At the command prompt, type **redline** ↵.

6. In response to the prompts for the start point and endpoint of the redline, choose any two points on screen. AutoCAD draws a red line between the two points selected.

On the CD-ROM

The file *redline.lsp* is on your *AutoCAD Bible* CD-ROM.

Here is another example of an AutoLISP routine that creates an S::STARTUP function. It uses several of the features I have been discussing in this chapter.

```
(defun s::startup ()
  (command _rectang _width  0.1   0,0   10,10 )
  (command _text  8,1   0.2   0   name )
  (command _text  8,0.7  0.2   0   date )
  (command _text  8, 0.4  0.2   0   revision )
  (command _zoom  _extents )
)
```

This routine creates a simple title block and border each time you open a new drawing, as shown in Figure 34-4. If AutoCAD is closed and restarted, AutoCAD again generates the title block and border for you.

Figure 34-4: The result of the S::STARTUP routine.

In order to use this routine — or one of your own — add this to the end of either *acad.lsp* or *acadr14.lsp*.

Caution

Before using the s::startup function, be sure an s::startup function does not already exist in the *acad.lsp* or *acadr14.lsp* file. In Notepad, choose Search⇨Find and type **s::startup** in the Find what text box. Click Find Next. If an s::startup routine already exists, then add the body of this s::startup (minus the first line, which already exists) to the end of the existing s::startup routine and save the file.

Creating functions with arguments

You can create functions that accept arguments. An *argument* is a value that must be supplied with the function. The function then uses the value of that argument in its operation.

Earlier in this chapter I explained that local variables are placed in parentheses after a slash. Arguments go in the same parentheses but before the slash. If there are no local variables, you don't need the slash. Here is an example of a function with one argument:

```
(defun chg2red (selected_object)
...
)
```

To actually use this routine in AutoCAD or another AutoLISP routine, use the format (ch2red selected_object). The argument is sent to the *chg2red* routine by adding the argument after the function name, all enclosed in parentheses.

Whenever you use the *chg2red* function within a routine, you must follow it by its argument. You can obtain the argument by using a variable whose value you have set in the routine, by obtaining a value through user input, or by typing in a specific value when you use the function.

The following Step-by-Step exercise creates a function that is called from within the routine.

Step-by-Step: Using AutoLISP Functions and Commands

1. Start a new drawing using the Start from Scratch option.

On the CD-ROM

2. Use Windows Explorer to copy *ab34-a.lsp* from the CD-ROM to AutoCAD's *support* folder or any folder you have created for AutoLISP routines and added to AutoCAD's support file search path as described earlier in this chapter. This file is shown in Figure 34-5.

```
(defun chg2red (selected_object)
        (command "_chprop" selected_object "" "_color" "red" "")
)
(defun c:chgcolor (/ selected)
        (terpri)
        (setq selected (entsel "Select an object to change to red:"))
        (chg2red selected)
```

Figure 34-5: An AutoLISP routine to change an object's color to red.

3. Load the routine by typing **(load "ab34-a.lsp")** ↵.

4. Draw any object.

5. At the command line, type **chgcolor** ↵.

6. At the `Select an object to change to red:` prompt, select the object you drew in step 4. Watch it change color to red.

7. Do not save your drawing.

Here's how the routine works:

✦ This routine defines a function, `chg2red`, which is not preceded by `c:`. It has one argument, `selected_object`.

✦ What AutoLISP actually ran when you typed **chgcolor** in step 5 is the function `c:chgcolor`. In the last AutoLISP statement in that function — (`chg2red selected`) — the variable `selected` derives from the previous step as a result of the operation `entsel` (*ENTity SELect*).

✦ The variable `selected` is the argument passed to the function `chg2red`. The function `chg2red` now knows what object to operate on.

✦ `Chg2red` then uses the CHPROP command to change the object's color to red.

Note

To actually call this function at the command line, you would need to type **(ch2red arg)**, where *arg* is an argument (in this case it must be an entity name). Entity names are discussed in the next chapter.

Working with system variables

AutoCAD has a wide variety of system variables to control the drawing environment. Thankfully, the creators of AutoLISP enabled the AutoLISP programmer to automate setting and retrieving AutoCAD system variables.

Note

Don't get the terms *variable* and *system variable* confused. A variable is a value that is stored for use in a routine. A system variable is an AutoCAD setting that changes how AutoCAD works.

To set or retrieve AutoCAD system variables, you use two operators, SETVAR and GETVAR, which can be used on any of the AutoCAD system variables. Here's how they work:

✦ SETVAR stands for *SET VARiable*. You use SETVAR to change a system variable. Place the system variable in quotes, followed by the new value, as in (setvar cmdecho 0).

✦ GETVAR stands for *GET VARiable*. It lets you obtain the value of any system variable. Once you have the value, you can set it to a variable. This is often done so that you can return a system variable to its previous value if you have changed it during a routine. Place the system variable in quotes after using GETVAR, as in (getvar cmdecho).

While you can use SETVAR and GETVAR on any system variable, here are three system variables that are often changed in an AutoLISP routine:

✦ In all the AutoLISP routines created thus far, AutoCAD's command responses could be seen scrolling off the command-line window. The CMDECHO system variable determines whether you see prompts and input during the functioning of AutoLISP's COMMAND function. By default, echoing is on (set to 1). If you set it to zero, you do not see prompts and input, and the functioning of the AutoLISP routine looks cleaner and runs slightly faster.

✦ The FILEDIA system variable turns on and off the display of dialog boxes that let you choose files. Turning off this system variable lets you work with files on the command line in AutoLISP routines.

✦ The CMDDIA system variable turns on and off dialog boxes for the various commands that normally display a dialog for its command set. ASE commands and PLOT are examples of dialogs that would be affected. Turning off this system variable lets you use the PLOT command, for example, in an AutoLISP routine.

Step-by-Step: Using AutoLISP to Work with System Variables

On the CD-ROM

1. If you did the previous exercise and copied *ab34-a.lsp* to AutoCAD's *\support* folder (or another folder you created for AutoLISP routines and added to AutoCAD's support file search path), open it from that folder. If you did not do the previous exercise, copy *ab34-a.lsp* from the CD-ROM to AutoCAD's *\support* folder or another folder you created for AutoLISP routines and added to AutoCAD's support file search path.

2. Open *ab34-a.lsp* from its new location in Notepad. Edit it to read as follows:

```
(defun chg2red (selected_object)
  (command "_chprop" selected_object "" "_color" "red" "")
  )
(defun c:chgcolor (/ selected old_cmdecho)
  (setq old_cmdecho (getvar "cmdecho"))
  (setvar "cmdecho" 0)
  (terpri)
  (setq selected (entsel "Select an object to change to
red:"))
  (chg2red selected)
  (setvar "cmdecho" old_cmdecho)
  )
```

3. Save the file as *ab34-1.lsp* in the same location and close Notepad.

4. Load the routine by typing **(load "ab34-1.lsp")** ↵.

5. Draw any object.

6. At the command line, type **chgcolor** ↵.

7. At the `Select an object to change to red:` prompt, select the object you drew in step 4. You no longer see the prompts scrolling by. The object you select turns red, and AutoCAD immediately displays the command prompt.

8. Do not save your drawing.

Here's how this routine works. This discussion assumes you have already read the discussion of the previous routine, which was very similar.

✦ First, you added a new variable, `old_cmdecho`, to the `chgcolor` function.

✦ In the following line, you set this variable to the current value of the CMDECHO system variable. You obtain this current value using GETVAR.

✦ You then use SETVAR to set the AutoCAD system variable CMDECHO to zero.

✦ You may need to see the commands echoed for debugging purposes, so it would prove best to set CMDECHO to the value it was set to before running the routine. Therefore, in the last line you use SETVAR again to reset CMDECHO to the variable `old_echo`, which stored the original value of CMDECHO.

✦ As a result of these changes, the CHGCOLOR program always sets the CMDECHO system variable back to the value it had before being run.

On the CD-ROM The CD-ROM includes two AutoLISP checkers and editors, Lisplink and Lck. Look in the *Software\Chap34\Lisplink* and *Lck* folders. To use Lisplink on your hard drive, remove the Read-only attribute as explained in Appendix E. There is also a bonus routine that comes with AutoCAD, PQCHECK, that checks for missing parentheses and closing quotes.

Summary

In this chapter, I discussed the fundamentals of AutoLISP. You learned how to use AutoLISP on the command line and how to create *.lsp* files and load them. The chapter explained how to work with numbers and text, how to create variables, and how to work with AutoCAD commands and system variables, introducing you to the power available at your fingertips as an AutoLISP programmer.

In the next chapter you examine how you can modify AutoCAD objects (or entities as they are often still called in AutoLISP) with AutoLISP, and how to work with the fundamental units of AutoLISP known as lists.

✦　　✦　　✦

Exploring AutoLISP Further

Working with Lists

Lists are the primary structures you work with while programming in AutoLISP. As you work with this chapter you will begin to understand the use of lists to modify objects (also called entities) in the AutoCAD database, and in a variety of other contexts with AutoLISP. AutoCAD represents all object data in a list that contains many smaller lists, but the lists are amazingly simple to use and manipulate.

Using lists for coordinates

A list is always enclosed in parentheses with spaces between the elements of the list. One common use for lists is for coordinates. For example,

```
(1.0 3.5 2.0)
```

is a list that represents the X,Y,Z coordinate 1.0,3.5,2.0. You often need to extract one or more of the elements in a list. Table 35-1 shows the common list extraction functions using the example list (1.0 3.5 2.0).

		Table 35-1	
	Basic List Extraction Functions		
Function	*Pronunciation*	*Example Output*	*Description*
CAR	"car"	1.0	Returns the first element in a list
CDR	"could-er"	(3.5 2.0)	Removes the first element from a list
CADR	"cad-er"	3.5	Returns the second element in a list
CADDR	"ca-did-der"	2.0	Returns the third element in a list

For more flexibility, you can use the NTH function. Use the NTH function to access any element in a list by passing two arguments that specify the number of the element (items are numbered starting from zero) and the list that you want.

The name of the list is usually a variable set with setq. For example,

```
(setq corner (list 1.0 3.5 2.0))
```

(nth 0 corner) returns 1.0 because 1.0 is the first item in the list corner.

The LIST function creates a list. If all the items in a list are constant values (not variables), you can use the QUOTE function to create a list. You can use a single quote (the same as an apostrophe on the keyboard) as a shortcut for the QUOTE function. The following two functions are equivalent:

```
(setq corner (list 1.0 3.5 2.0))
(setq corner  (1.0 3.5 2.0))
```

There are many more AutoLISP list extraction functions, detailed in the AutoCAD *Customization Guide*. You can go a long way by remembering the functions listed here.

Creating dotted pairs

A dotted pair is a special type of list that contains only two elements. Some AutoLISP functions do not accept dotted pairs as an argument, but they are used for representing AutoCAD database objects. To construct a dotted pair, use the CONS function. For example,

```
(cons 2.1 4.5)
```

returns (2.1 . 4.5). This list type is known as a *dotted pair,* because it contains exactly two elements, and the elements are separated by a period or dot.

Step-by-Step: Working with Lists

1. Open a drawing using the Start from Scratch option.

2. Type **(setq endpt '(3.5 2.0 1.4))** ↵. AutoLISP returns (3.5 2.0 1.4).

3. Type **(car endpt)** ↵. AutoLISP returns 3.5.

4. Type **(cadr endpt)** ↵. AutoLISP returns 2.0.

5. Type **(cdr endpt)** ↵. AutoLISP returns (2.0 1.4).

6. Type **(nth 1 endpt)** ↵. AutoLISP returns 2.0.

7. Do not save your drawing.

Setting Conditions

Often you want to execute a procedure based on a certain condition. One way of doing this is with the IF statement, which does one thing if a statement is true and another thing if it is false. In other words, the operation is conditioned on the truth of a certain statement.

Looping is an important part of programming. Frequently you want to execute a procedure over and over until the routine has finished operating on all the objects or items you want. Looping sets up the condition that determines when the operation starts, on how many and which objects it operates, and when it ends.

Conditional structures

Conditional structures allow program flow to be determined based on the outcome of a given decision. These decisions will result in the return of either true or false. For instance, for the statement

    (< 3 5)

AutoLISP returns T for true. Here we have determined that 3 is less than 5. For the statement

    (> 3 5)

AutoLISP returns F for false. Here we have determined that 3 is not greater than 5. For the statement

    (= 3 5)

AutoLISP returns F. Here we have determined that 3 is not equal to 5. Because these statements return either T or F, you can use the IF statement. The general syntax of the IF statement is (if conditional-test if-true if-false).

Say you want to find circles whose radius is less than .25. Here's a sample IF statement. In this example, *radius* is a variable that has been previously set.

```
(if (< radius .25)
   (princ  The radius is less than .25 )
   (princ  The radius is not less than .25 )
   )
```

The conditional test is (< radius .25). The if-true statement is (princ The radius is less than .25). The if-false statement is (princ The radius is not less than .25). This IF statement is equivalent to saying, "If the radius is less than .25, print 'The radius is less than .25' but if not, print 'The radius is not less than .25.'"

You can leave out the if-false statement. Then AutoLISP executes the if-true statement if the conditional statement is true and does nothing if it is false and continues to the rest of the program.

In this Step-by-Step exercise, you see both types of IF statements.

Step-by-Step: Using the IF Statement

1. Open a new file in Notepad and type the following:

```
(defun c:compare2three ( / entered_num)
   (princ  Enter a number: )
   (setq entered_num (getint))
   (terpri)
   (if (< entered_num 3)
      (princ  The entered number is less than 3 )
      (if (= entered_num 3)
      (princ  The entered number is equal to 3 )
      (princ  The entered number is greater than 3 )
      )
   )
   (princ)
)
```

The GETINT function gets an integer from the user and is covered later in this chapter. Using (princ) at the end of a routine is also covered later in this chapter.

2. Save the file as *ab35-1.lsp* in a folder that is in the support file search path, or in *acadr14\support\,* and close Notepad.

3. Open AutoCAD with any drawing. Type **(load "ab35-1")** ↲.

4. To try out the IF statement, type **compare2three** ↲. At the Enter a number: prompt, type **5** ↲. AutoCAD displays: The entered number is greater than 3.

5. Repeat the COMPARE2THREE command. At the Enter a number: **prompt,** type **3** ↲. AutoCAD displays: The entered number is equal to 3.

6. Repeat the COMPARE2THREE command. At the Enter a number: **command,** type **2** ↲. AutoCAD displays: The entered number is less than 3.

7. Do not save your drawing.

Loop structures

Looping provides the ability to execute a step or a number of steps a given number of times based on an evaluation you make in your application. One way to do this is with the WHILE function.

The format of the WHILE function is (while conditional-test if-true).

A common method of setting up the condition is to include a *counter* in the while statement. A counter counts how many times an operation is executed. You can then end the operation when the counter reaches a certain number. To create a counter, set a variable (perhaps named counter) to the number at which you want to start. Then write the code for one pass through the operation. Then set the counter to the next higher number using an expression like the following:

```
(setq counter (+ 1 counter))
```

The routine then loops back over the operation until the counter reaches the value you set.

Here's a simple example:

```
(defun c:process (/ counter)
  (setq counter 1)
  (while (< counter 6)
    (princ  Processing number  )
    (princ counter)
    (terpri)
    (setq counter (+ 1 counter))
  )
)
```

In this example, the `process` function starts by setting the variable `counter` to 1. Then you start the WHILE statement and specify that `counter` must be less than 6. Within the WHILE statement, you print the text string `Processing number` and then the value of the `counter` variable. You use `(terpri)` so that each text string starts on a new line. Then you set the counter to the next higher number. Each time through the WHILE loop, the value of counter is incremented by 1. Without the increment statement, line 3 would always evaluate to true and the WHILE loop would never exit because the counter would always be 1.

If you accidentally program an infinite loop like this, you can stop the execution of your AutoLISP routine by pressing Esc.

In the above example, the WHILE loop continues as long as `counter` is less than 6. When `counter` reaches 6, the routine stops. The WHILE statement returns the last value of the routine, so AutoCAD prints 6 on the last line. Figure 35-1 shows the result.

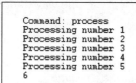

```
Command: process
Processing number 1
Processing number 2
Processing number 3
Processing number 4
Processing number 5
6
```

Figure 35-1: The result of the `process` function.

When using WHILE, you may want to combine several operations under the condition. However, the WHILE function only allows one argument to specify what to do if the conditional test evaluates to true. To execute more than one statement, use the PROGN function, which tells AutoLISP to treat everything enclosed in the PROGN construct as if it were one statement.

In the next Step-by-Step exercise, you practice using WHILE, PROGN, and a counter.

If you make a mistake while typing an AutoLISP routine in a *.lsp* file, you usually get an error message when you try to load it. Often you have to go back and re-edit the file a number of times. You can save a few steps by keeping the LISP routine open in the text editor after you save your edits to it. Click the AutoCAD button on the status bar to switch to AutoCAD and try loading and using the routine. If it doesn't work, just click the status bar button for the text editor with the AutoLISP file to return to it.

Step-by-Step: Looping with WHILE and a Counter

1. Open Notepad and type the following:

```
(defun c:print0to10 ( / counter)
(setq counter 0)
(terpri)
     (while (< counter 11)
          (progn
               (princ  The Counter value is:  )
               (princ counter)
               (terpri)
               (setq counter (+ counter 1))
          )
        )
 )
```

2. Save it as *ab35-2.lsp* in *\acadr14\support* or any folder in the support file search path. Minimize the window by clicking the Minimize button.

3. Start AutoCAD with any drawing. Load *ab35-2.lsp.*

4. Type **print0to10** ↵. Figure 35-2 shows the result.

```
Command: print0to10

The Counter value is: 0
The Counter value is: 1
The Counter value is: 2
The Counter value is: 3
The Counter value is: 4
The Counter value is: 5
The Counter value is: 6
The Counter value is: 7
The Counter value is: 8
The Counter value is: 9
The Counter value is: 10
11
```

Figure 35-2: The result of the `print0to10` function.

5. Do not save your drawing.

Managing Drawing Objects

The real power of AutoLISP is in manipulating drawing objects. This section reveals how many of the AutoLISP routines perform their magic.

Getting information about an object

Every object in the AutoCAD database has an entity name. This name allows you to reference that object anywhere in your AutoLISP application. To see an example of an entity name, type the following after starting a new drawing:

```
(command _line  3,3  5,5   )
(entlast)
```

AutoLISP responds with <Entity name: 2ed0520>.

The numbers will probably differ on your system, but using the information returned from ENTLAST allows you to programmatically get or set a variety of options on any given database object by referencing its entity name.

The ENTGET (*ENTity GET*) function is the key to making modifications to the drawing database. The ENTGET function takes an entity name as its one and only argument. After drawing the line in the steps above, type:

```
(setq myline (entget (entlast)))
```

AutoLISP responds with:

```
((-1 . <Entity name: 2ed0520>) (0 .  LINE ) (5 .  4C ) (100 .
 AcDbEntity ) (67 . 0)
(8 .  0 ) (100 .  AcDbLine ) (10 3.0 3.0 0.0) (11 5.0 5.0
0.0) (210 0.0 0.0 1.0))
```

This is a representation of how the line is stored in the AutoCAD drawing database. AutoLISP returned one large list that contains 10 smaller lists. Each of the smaller lists is referred to as a group indexed by the first element. The entity name is in group -1.

The most often used groups are listed in Table 35-2.

Table 35-2
Commonly Used AutoCAD Object Group Codes

Group code	Description
-1	Entity name
0	Entity
1	Text value
8	Layer
10	Start point (or center)

Group code	Description
11	Endpoint (or alignment point)
38	Elevation
39	Thickness
40	Radius (or height of text)
62	Color
67	Paper space flag

Not all these group codes are present in the line you drew. For instance, group 62 (color) is absent in the list returned by AutoLISP. Every time you draw a line, you do not explicitly set its color. As a result, it defaults to the current color. In the same way, AutoLISP does not explicitly set every attribute of every group. In this case, the color is ByLayer and the current layer is 0. AutoLISP returned (8 . 0) in the list above to signify the line is on layer 0.

There are many other group codes than the ones listed in Table 35-2, and they can be found in the AutoCAD *Customization Guide*. In many cases, one group code can have different meanings depending on the entity in which it appears. For example, in the list representing the line you drew, group 10 is represented by (10 3.0 3.0 0.0), which means the start point of the line is at X=3.0, Y=3.0, Z=0.0. If group 0 were a circle instead, then the coordinates of group 10 would specify the center point of the circle.

To manipulate a given attribute of an object, two important functions are ASSOC and SUBST;

✦ ASSOC returns a list that finds the entry associated with an item in a list. It takes two arguments, the item in the list and the list itself. For example, if you specify the group code (such as 10) as the first argument, it returns the code's value (which would be the start point of a line). If a list named myobject contains three groups, as in ((0 . group 0) (1 1.0 2.0) (3 4.2 1.5 6.75)), then (assoc 1 myobject) would return (1 1.0 2.0).

✦ SUBST substitutes one value for another in a list. The SUBST function takes three arguments. To make the substitution, the first argument specifies what to substitute with, the second argument specifies what to substitute for, and the third argument specifies on what list to perform this operation.

To manipulate the start point of your line, first get the start point:

```
(setq startpt (assoc 10 myline))
```

AutoLISP responds: (10 3.0 3.0 0.0).

To modify the start point of your line, use:

```
(setq new_startpt  (10 6.5 1.0 0.0))
(setq myline (subst new_startpt startpt myline))
```

AutoLISP responds:

```
((-1 . <Entity name: 2ed0520>) (0 .  LINE ) (5 .  4C )
(100 .  AcDbEntity ) (67 . 0) (8 .  0 ) (100 .  AcDbLine )
(10 6.5 1.0 0.0)
(11 5.0 5.0 0.0) (210 0.0 0.0 1.0))
```

In this case, the new_startpt is substituted for the existing startpt in the object myline. No changes to the line are yet apparent. To commit the change, you need the ENTMOD function.

Modifying objects

The key to modifying objects is the ENTMOD (*ENTity MODify*) function. The list returned by AutoLISP can be modified and then passed to ENTMOD as an argument to update the AutoCAD database. Continuing with the example, if you enter:

```
(entmod myline)
```

AutoLISP responds:

```
((-1 . <Entity name: 2ed0520>) (0 .  LINE ) (5 .  4C )
(100 .  AcDbEntity ) (67 . 0) (8 .  0 ) (100 .  AcDbLine )
(10 6.5 1.0 0.0)
(11 5.0 5.0 0.0) (210 0.0 0.0 1.0))
```

The AutoCAD database is changed as well, and the start point of your line is now at X=6.5, Y=1.0, Z=0.0.

Creating selection sets

A selection set is created with the SSGET (*Selection Set GET*) function. This prompts the user with the familiar Select object: prompt. The commonly used selection set functions are shown in Table 35-3.

You can use a maximum of 256 selection sets at any given time. To release a selection set back to AutoLISP so it can be used again, set the selection set to nil — for example, (setq ss nil).

<table>
<tr><td colspan="2" align="center">Table 35-3
Common AutoCAD Selection Set Functions</td></tr>
</table>

Function	Description
SSGET	Obtains a selection set from the user.
SSLENGTH	Returns the number of objects in a selection set. It takes one argument, the selection set.
SSNAME	Returns the entity name of a given object in a selection set. It takes two arguments: the selection set and the number of the object in the selection set.

As an example, you could enter the following in a new drawing:

```
(command _circle  3,3  2 )
(command _circle  4,4  3 )
(command _line  7,2  6,6  3,4  5,5  )
(setq mysset (ssget))
Select objects: all ↵
5 found
Select objects: ↵
<Selection set 1>
```

Now mysset is set to the selection set specified by all, which includes the three lines and the two circles. To see what you have in your selection set, enter:

```
(sslength mysset)
5
```

You now know that you have five objects in your selection set. The first object is number 0, and the fifth object is number 4. To see what the first object is:

```
(ssname mysset 0)
<Entity name: 3fe0550>
```

To get the database data on the object, enter:

```
(entget (ssname mysset 0))
```

AutoCAD responds:

```
((-1 . <Entity name: 3fe0550>) (0 .  LINE ) (5 .  2A ) (100 .
 AcDbEntity ) (67 . 0)
(8 .  0 ) (100 .  AcDbLine ) (10 3.0 4.0 0.0) (11 5.0 5.0
0.0) (210 0.0 0.0 1.0))
```

By stepping through each of the entity names returned by SSNAME from 0 to 4, you can manipulate each of the objects in the selection set.

Using AutoLISP to match properties

This routine modifies the layer of objects to match the layer of one other object. This powerful routine was a mainstay of many AutoCAD users before the advent of the MATCHPROP command now available as an AutoCAD R14 standard. The general method used here for matching layers can be used to change any properties you wish on any AutoCAD object.

Notice the new function ENTSEL on Line 4. This is a type of shorthand for SSGET. Use it when you wish to limit the user to selecting a single object. ENTSEL returns an entity name and the coordinates of your pick point in a dotted-pair list. Therefore, you can use CAR before ENTSEL to get the entity name for ENTGET.

```
(defun c:matchlayer ( / src_object mysset counter cur_ent ent_layer)
    (terpri)
    (princ  *** Select Source object to match *** )
    (setq src_object (car (entsel)))
    (setq src_layer (assoc 8 (entget src_object)))
    (princ  *** Select Destination objects to match layer *** )
    (setq mysset (ssget))
    (setq counter 0)
    (while (< counter (sslength mysset))
        (progn
          (setq cur_ent (entget (ssname mysset counter)))
          (setq ent_layer (assoc 8 cur_ent))
          (entmod (subst src_layer ent_layer cur_ent))
          (setq counter (+ counter 1))
          )
      )
  (princ)
  )
```

This routine first gets the name of the selected object with `(car (entsel))`. It determines its layer by using ENTGET on the object name and using ASSOC with the 8 group code. Then it gets a selection set of the Destination objects. It creates a loop that cycles through these objects, gets their layers (the `ent_layer` variable), and uses ENTMOD and SUBST to change the object's current layer to the source object's layer.

On the CD-ROM   Quicklsp is a reference chart of AutoLISP functions that you might find helpful. Look in \Software\Chap35\Quicklsp.

In this Step-by-Step exercise, you create a list of the type of each object in your drawing.

The last function, PRINC, ensures that no extraneous evaluation return values are echoed on the command line. If you remove this function, AutoCAD evaluates the last counter value and echoes it to the command line (this will equal the total number of objects you selected). Using the PRINC function in this way is called *exiting cleanly* or *quietly*.

Step-by-Step: Listing Drawing Objects

1. Type the following in Notepad and save it as *ab35-3.lsp* in your *\acadr14\support* folder or any folder in the support file search path.

```
(defun c:listsset ( / mysset counter)
  (setq mysset (ssget))
  (setq counter 0)
    (while (< counter (sslength mysset))
      (progn
      (terpri)
      (princ (cdr (assoc 0 (entget (ssname mysset
counter)))))))
      (setq counter (+ counter 1))
    )
  )
 (princ)
)
```

2. Open AutoCAD with any drawing and load *ab35-3.lsp.*

3. Draw any number of objects on screen — at least two different types of objects.

4. Type **listsset** ↵. AutoCAD prompts you to select objects (because of the SSGET function).

5. Select all the objects in your drawing. The routine prints the type of each object you selected. Figure 35-3 shows the result. Of course, your result will be different since you probably drew different types of objects.

```
Command: listsset

Select objects: all
5 found

Select objects:

LWPOLYLINE
CIRCLE
TEXT
LINE
LINE
```

Figure 35-3: One possible result of the listsset routine.

Tip

If line 7 of the routine is hard to understand, remember to work from the inside set of parentheses out. The counter variable is used to specify the number of the object in the selection set. Also remember that CDR removes the first item in a list, in this case leaving only the last item, the object.

Getting Input from the User

The course of your AutoLISP routines may often depend on user input. To satisfy this need, AutoCAD has a family of functions prefaced with the word "GET." You have seen GETVAR for obtaining system variable information. Table 35-4 shows some other useful GET functions.

Table 35-4
Basic User Input Functions

Function	Description
GETDIST	Returns the distance between two points.
GETINT	Returns an integer.
GETREAL	Returns a real number (which can be a non-integer, negative, and so on).
GETSTRING	Returns a text string.

Within the COMMAND function, you can use the PAUSE function to pause the operation of the routine and allow user input such as picking a point or typing a value. For example, the expression (command circle pause 3) pauses to let the user specify a center point and then creates a circle with a radius of 3.

Step-by-Step: Getting User Input

1. Enter the following routine in Notepad and save it as *ab35-4.lsp* in *acadr14\support* or a folder that you have added to the support file search path.

```
(defun c:chgmytext ( / src_object new_ht new_str)
 (terpri)
 (setq src_object (entget (car (entsel))))
 (princ  What is the new height for the text?  )
 (setq new_ht (getreal))
 (princ  What is the new text value?  )
 (setq new_str (getstring))
   (setq src_object (subst (cons 40 new_ht) (assoc 40
src_object)src_object))
   (setq src_object (subst (cons 1 new_str) (assoc 1
src_object)src_object))
   (entmod src_object)
(princ)
)
```

2. Start AutoCAD with any program and load *ab35-4.lsp.*

3. Create some text using either the DTEXT or the TEXT command and run `chgmytext` on it. AutoCAD changes the text object's height and content to the values you input in response to the prompts.

4. Do not save your drawing.

Putting on the Finishing Touches

The AutoLISP applications thus far do not include much in the way of error handling. You have seen the PRINC function used in a couple of routines to exit quietly and not return AutoLISP evaluations to the command line. You can extend this type of cleanliness even further.

A new function EQUAL, is used on line 4 of the final routine in the next Step-by-Step exercise. EQUAL is different than = in that EQUAL returns true only if two expressions are equal (each of the two objects tested for equality are evaluated before checking if they are equal). A simple rule of thumb is to use EQUAL for list comparisons, and = for numeric comparisons.

Now if you select an object that is not a text object, the program jumps to line 14 and prints the error message: You must select a text object.

This type of error handling is crucial to making your AutoLISP programs look fit and finished, and contributes to a more professional look for your applications.

Another way to finish off your routine is to add a comment at the beginning that states the purpose and function of the routine. This helps others understand what the routine does and can help you as well when you look at the routine again a few months later! Comments are prefaced with a semicolon.

Step-by-Step: Putting on the Finishing Touches

1. Load the application completed in the last Step-by-Step exercise. If you didn't do the last exercise, enter it from that exercise in Notepad and save it as *ab35-4.lsp* in *\acadr14\support* or a folder that you have added to the support file search path. Then load it in any drawing.

2. Now run `chgmytext` and choose an object that is not a text object (such as a circle) in response to the Select object: prompt. Answer the prompts for new height and new text value.

If you have done this to a circle, you see its radius change to match the value you specified to be the new text height. This is definitely not what you intended when writing this program.

3. Modify the program so it reads this way and save it as *ab35-5.lsp*:

```
;modifies text height and content (value)
(defun c:chgmytext (/ src_object new_ht new_str)
  (terpri)
  (setq src_object (entget (car (entsel))))
  (if (equal (assoc 0 src_object) (0 .  TEXT ))
  (progn
    (princ  What is the new height for the text?  )
    (setq new_ht (getreal))
    (princ  What is the new text value?  )
    (setq new_str (getstring))
    (setq src_object (subst (cons 40 new_ht) (assoc 40
src_object) src_object))
    (setq src_object (subst (cons 1 new_str) (assoc 1
    src_object) src_object))
    (entmod src_object)
    )
    (princ  You must select a text object. )
  )
  (princ)
)
```

4. Load *ab35-5.lsp.* Start chgmytext and try out the routine again with a circle or other non-text object.

5. Do not save your drawing.

Moving on to Advanced Programming

This chapter and the previous chapter have reviewed the fundamentals of AutoLISP, and you have seen the power AutoLISP provides for automating your work.

There are several other customization tools available to the AutoCAD programmer, including ObjectARX, ADS, and VBA.

ADS

The AutoCAD Development System (ADS) was introduced as a method of allowing C and C++ programmers to write applications for AutoCAD.

Because ADS is written in C or C++, the development time is generally much longer than that of AutoLISP.

ADS applications communicate with AutoCAD through AutoLISP, so equivalent operations in both languages execute at close to the same speed. ADS excels, however, when your application needs to communicate with the operating system, or execute complex calculations. These operations are done outside of AutoCAD's knowledge, and only the results are communicated back to AutoCAD.

If you do a full AutoCAD R14 installation, an *adsrx* subfolder is created under *acadr14*. This subfolder contains samples of ADS applications (it is called ADSRX because it is actually a type of hybrid of ObjectARX and ADS). Be aware that creating ADS applications requires that you obtain and use a C++ compiler.

ObjectARX

ObjectARX applications share the same memory space as AutoCAD and prove to be many times faster than ADS. ObjectARX is based on C++ and allows full *object-oriented* interfacing with AutoCAD. An object-oriented interface allows the programmer to create an object in memory (such as an arc), modify its attributes, and then modify the AutoCAD database.

You can create custom objects that inherit properties from AutoCAD objects; that is, your object can assume all the properties of a given object already in AutoCAD and you can add to it. For example, you can inherit from a line so your custom object has everything the line does, then you can add width to it if you wish. A wide variety of tools unavailable to ADS and AutoLISP programmers are also available with ObjectARX, including *reactors*. Reactors allow your application to be notified when a change occurs anywhere in AutoCAD (for example, if a line is erased or modified, your application is notified).

ObjectARX, like ADS, involves much greater development time than AutoLISP. ObjectARX also requires a C++ compiler to compile and link applications for use with AutoCAD.

ObjectARX can be obtained from CompuServe by visiting the AutoCAD forum (GO ACAD), or at Autodesk's Web site (www.autodesk.com).

ActiveX automation and Visual Basic

ActiveX is a set of specifications that define how different applications communicate. It is the child of Microsoft OLE Automation. The ActiveX interface is a part of VBA (Visual Basic for Applications) and is only available as a preview in the current release of AutoCAD R14.

To write a VBA routine, you need to know VB (Visual Basic), which is easier to learn than C or C++. The execution time is slower than ObjectARX, but much faster than either ADS or AutoLISP. However, while the full power of ObjectARX is not currently available in VBA, it offers many more capabilities than AutoLISP or ADS.

A preview edition of VBA is included on the R14 CD-ROM. It has its own *setup.exe* for installation in the *vbainst* folder. By the time you receive this book, the full VBA version for AutoCAD should be available.

Summary

In this chapter you learned how to extend AutoLISP's power by using lists, looping, and managing drawing objects. Using these techniques, along with user input, you can automate the modification of objects in your drawing to suit your needs.

You should always finish off your AutoLISP routines by adding some error handling, making sure the routine exits quietly, and adding helpful comments about the routine's function.

This chapter ended with a brief overview of the other possibilities available to the serious programmer.

A Final Word

AutoCAD offers almost unlimited potential for the design and drawing of real-world objects. I hope this book has helped you understand the world of AutoCAD and made it easier for you to create the profssional drawings you need. I would be happy to hear your comments and suggestions at ellenfinkl@compuserve.com. Good luck and enjoy!

✦   ✦   ✦

Appendixes

Installing and Configuring AutoCAD

♦ ♦ ♦ ♦

In This Appendix

Installing AutoCAD

Creating multiple and customized configurations

Configuring AutoCAD with the Preferences dialog box

♦ ♦ ♦ ♦

Installing AutoCAD

Installing AutoCAD, once something to avoid as long as possible, is now a breeze. AutoCAD Release 14 is available only on CD-ROM. For all practical purposes, all you do is put the CD-ROM in your CD-ROM drive and follow the instructions. As with all software that comes with an installation program, you should close all other applications before starting. Setup presents you with a series of windows. Provide the information requested and click Next to move on to the next window.

AutoCAD requires Windows 95, Windows NT 3.51, or Windows NT 4.0 and 16MB of RAM (memory).

I have not covered information that is unique to installing AutoCAD on a network. For that information, please refer to Chapter 3 of the AutoCAD *Installation Guide*.

Caution
You must install Release 14 in a new folder, not on top of an existing prior release.

To install AutoCAD R14, follow these steps:

1. Place the CD-ROM in your CD-ROM drive and close the drive door. In most cases, AutoRun starts the installation for you. If you have turned off AutoRun, choose Start⇨Run. In the text box, type **d:\setup** ↵ where d is your CD-ROM drive.

Note If you are using Windows NT 3.51, in Program Manager choose File⇨Run and type **d:\setup** ↵ where d is your CD-ROM drive.

2. Type the serial number and CD key from the CD case or jacket.

3. Type your name, organization, and AutoCAD dealer and phone number.

4. Confirm the information in item 3.

5. Setup asks you to choose a drive and folder. The default is c:\Program files\ACADR14. Feel free to change this to any folder you want — for example, c:\ACADR14. Setup creates the folder if necessary.

6. Select the type of installation you want. Setup tells you the space required for each type:

   ✦ Typical — 82MB

   ✦ Full — 112MB

   ✦ Compact — 46MB

   ✦ Custom Varies — up to 112MB

   A typical installation installs the most commonly used tools. However, it doesn't install the bonus routines and applications or the textures (used for rendering). A compact installation would be ideal for a laptop or a situation in which you have limited hard drive space. A custom installation lets you individually choose the items you want to install. When you choose a custom installation, you have the following choices:

   ✦ Program files: executables, menus, toolbars, help, templates, TrueType fonts, and additional support files

   ✦ Fonts

   ✦ Samples

   ✦ Learning tools

   ✦ Bonus routines and applications

   ✦ Dictionaries

   ✦ External database

   ✦ ADSRx

   ✦ Batch Plotting

   ✦ Texture maps

   ✦ Internet

   ✦ OLE/ADI Plot

Of course, you want the program files, since you can't use AutoCAD without them. You might be able to do without the samples, learning tools, and bonus routines and applications, however. You can go back later and add items if you decide you need an item you didn't initially install.

7. Once you have chosen the type of installation, AutoCAD checks that you have enough space on your hard drive.

8. AutoCAD tells you where it will add the program icons. You can change this later in Windows if you wish.

9. Setup displays the installation options that you've chosen and asks you to confirm them. Once you do, it starts copying files. This takes a few minutes. You can take a break or read the advertising that appears during the process.

10. Setup asks if you want to read the Readme file. You should usually check Yes even though chances are that most of the stuff doesn't affect you. Every once in a while, you find something crucial — after all, that's why it's there. You can find it later in *\acadr14\help\readme.hlp*.

11. Click Finish. AutoCAD opens the Readme file if you asked for it. You're done!

You can now choose Start➪Programs➪AutoCAD R14 to start AutoCAD. If you chose the default location for the program files, a submenu opens, which includes some or all of the following items:

✦ **AutoCAD R14:** starts AutoCAD

✦ **AutoCAD Readme:** opens the Readme file

✦ **Batch Plot Utility:** lets you plot a list of drawings

✦ **External Database Configuration:** configures external databases so you can access them

✦ **Online Help:** starts Help

✦ **Quick Tour:** starts the multimedia Quick Tour, which has a section on what's new for Release 14, and a quick tour that shows you how to accomplish several basic tasks in AutoCAD

✦ **Uninstall AutoCAD R14.0:** uninstalls AutoCAD

✦ **What's New:** starts the multimedia Quick Tour, which focuses on the new features of Release 14

Authorizing AutoCAD

As with earlier versions, you still need to call or e-mail Autodesk to obtain an Authorization Code, except that now you have only seven days to do it. When you first open AutoCAD, the dialog box shown in Figure A-1 opens.

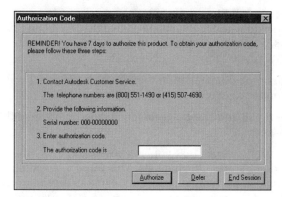

Figure A-1: The Authorization Code dialog box.

Call one of the phone numbers listed. (You can also send a request to authcodes@autodesk.com or submit a request on the web site at http://www.autodesk.com.) Your serial number is conveniently listed right on the dialog box. When you get the authorization code, enter it in the text box and click Authorize. AutoCAD is now ready to use. By default, your system uses the current system pointing device and the current system printing device. You can further configure AutoCAD by choosing Tools⇨Preferences and using the Preferences dialog box. This dialog box is covered in more detail later in this appendix.

The bonus routines

If you choose a full installation, you get a set of bonus routines, which are AutoLISP programs that add several useful commands to AutoCAD. You can also install them by choosing the Bonus and Batch Plotting options in a custom installation (they need to go together for all the bonus routines to work). Autodesk has included these routines in response to customers' requests. They are the first step to possible implementation as a command in AutoCAD. They are not supported or thoroughly tested by Autodesk. If you like or use any of these bonus routines, let Autodesk know by sending feedback through your dealer or to the Autodesk Web site.

AutoCAD installs the bonus routines in a subfolder of *acadr14* called *bonus*. This subfolder has three subfolders (most of the files are in a subfolder called *Cadtools*). The bonus routines come with a set of three toolbars and a special menu. If they are not automatically installed, you can install them by choosing Tools⇨Customize Menus and installing the *ac_bonus.mnc* file.

Cross-Reference

Full instructions for installing menus are in Chapter 33.

Figure A-2 shows the three toolbars that come with the bonus routines.

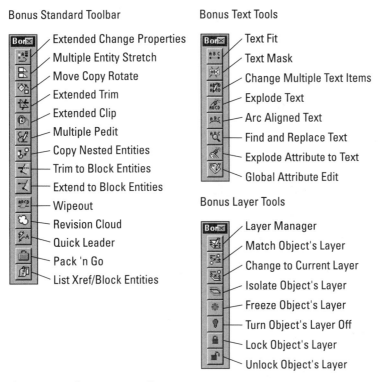

Bonus Standard Toolbar

- Extended Change Properties
- Multiple Entity Stretch
- Move Copy Rotate
- Extended Trim
- Extended Clip
- Multiple Pedit
- Copy Nested Entities
- Trim to Block Entities
- Extend to Block Entities
- Wipeout
- Revision Cloud
- Quick Leader
- Pack 'n Go
- List Xref/Block Entities

Bonus Text Tools

- Text Fit
- Text Mask
- Change Multiple Text Items
- Explode Text
- Arc Aligned Text
- Find and Replace Text
- Explode Attribute to Text
- Global Attribute Edit

Bonus Layer Tools

- Layer Manager
- Match Object's Layer
- Change to Current Layer
- Isolate Object's Layer
- Freeze Object's Layer
- Turn Object's Layer Off
- Lock Object's Layer
- Unlock Object's Layer

Figure A-2: The Bonus toolbars.

The following routines are found only on the Bonus pull-down menu.

✦ Turn all layers on

✦ Thaw all layers

✦ Extended Explode (XPLODE)

✦ Attach Leader to Annotation

✦ Detach Leaders from Annotation

✦ Global Attach Leader to Annotation

✦ Get Selection Set (creates a selection set with the specified layer and/or type of object)

✦ Pline Converter to lightweight polylines

✦ Command Alias Editor

✦ System Variable Editor

♦ Xdata Attachment — attaches extended data to objects

♦ List Entity Xdata

♦ Dimstyle Export

♦ Dimstyle Import

There is also an additional group of bonus tools that you must enter on the command line. These are explained in Table A-1.

Table A-1
Command Line Bonus Tools

Bonus Tool	Description
ASCPOINT	Imports coordinates from a text (ASCII) file and creates line segments, a polyline, a 3D polyline, and multiple copies of a selected set of objects, or points, based on the coordinates.
BLK_LST.LSP	This AutoLISP file contains four routines. Use BLKTBL to list all block definitions in a drawing. Use BLKLST to list any block you select. Use CATTL to list all the attributes of a block you select. Use ATTLST to list all attributes in an inserted block. Constant attributes are listed from the block definition, and variable ones are listed from the inserted block.
BLOCK	Lists the objects in a block.
COUNT	Creates a chart of all the insertions of each block.
CROSSREF	Lists blocks containing the layer, linetype, style, dimstyle, mlinestyle, or block you specify.
DBTRANS	Helps you translate text from Release 11 or earlier drawings to Release 14. Load it with APPLOAD or ARX.
DOSLIB	A DOS library of DOS functions you can use in AutoLISP. For example, you can rename a folder (directory) or move a file. The full listing is in *acadr14\bonus\cadtools\doslib14.doc* (a Microsoft Word document).
JULIAN	Contains several routines to convert between AutoCAD and Julian date / calendar dates.
PQCHECK	Checks AutoLISP programs for missing parentheses and closing quotes.
SSX	Creates a selection set with filter options. You can select the objects with those that match layer, color, linetype, thickness, and so on.

The Bonus menu has a Help item that contains help for all the bonus items.

Configuring AutoCAD

In Release 14, you configure AutoCAD using the Preferences dialog box. This dialog box contains all the settings previously available with the CONFIG command. Choose Apply to configure a setting and keep the dialog box open. Choose OK to configure a setting and close the dialog box.

A quick way to get to the Preferences dialog box is to right-click while your pointer is in the command line area or text window. From the shortcut menu that appears, choose Preferences.

The Files tab

Figure A-3 shows the Files tab, which lets you configure search paths as well as specify file names and locations. You will probably most often use the Support File Search Path, which contains a listing of the folders that AutoCAD uses to search for menus, fonts, blocks, linetypes, and hatch patterns. Rather than add your customized menus, hatches, and so on to the *acadr14\support* folder, you can create a folder especially for these files and add the folder to the support file search path.

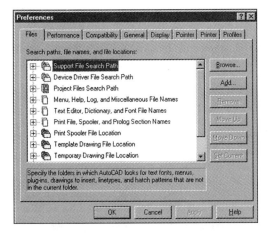

Figure A-3: The Files tab of the Preferences dialog box.

As you click on an item in the main listing of the dialog box, AutoCAD displays an explanation at the bottom. To edit the item, click the plus to the left of the item. This works like Windows Explorer. You can then click on a sub-item and remove it or click Add to add a sub-item. Click Browse to find a folder or file. When you're done, click OK.

The Performance tab

Figure A-4 shows the Performance tab of the Preferences dialog box. All the settings on this tab affect performance — for example, the speed of regeneration, save time, and so on.

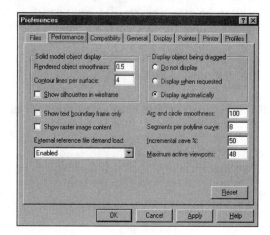

Figure A-4: The Performance tab.

In the top left section, you can set Rendered object smoothness, which is equivalent to setting the FACETRES system variable. The contour lines setting is the same as the ISOLINES system variable. Showing silhouettes is equivalent to setting DISPSILH to 1.

At the top right, you specify how you want dragged objects to display. By default, you see the object as it is being dragged. You can disable this display or display it only when you type **drag** ↵ after selecting the object. You can also control drag display with the DRAGMODE system variable.

At the bottom left, you can show text in a frame, which is the same as turning QTEXT on. Release 14 now lets you toggle the display of raster images — equivalent to setting the RTDISPLAY setting variable. This setting affects the display of raster images only during realtime zoom and pan — displaying raster images in realtime mode can slow down your zooming and panning.

In Release 14 you can also turn on and off demand loading of external references, which you can also do with the XLOADCTL system variable. Demand loading loads only the part of the xref necessary for regenerating the display and therefore speeds up display. You can also set demand loading to Enabled with copy, which loads a copy of the xref, letting other users on a network use the xref simultaneously.

At the bottom right, you set arc and circle smoothness (equivalent to the VIEWRES). You can also use the SPLINESEGS system variable.

Setting the incremental save percent lets you control when AutoCAD saves the entire drawing as opposed to just your changes — an incremental save. The default is 50 percent, which avoids too many long full saves.

You can set the maximum number of active viewports. Inactive viewports are not regenerated so you can speed up display by lowering this number.

Use the Reset button to return all settings to their default values.

You can read details on each option by using the Help icon in the upper right corner of the dialog. Click on the ?, move the ? pointer over the item you need information about, and click.

The Compatibility tab

Figure A-5 shows the Compatibility tab of the Preferences dialog box. This box lets you set certain features that control how AutoCAD works with other applications.

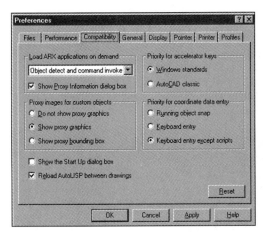

Figure A-5: The Compatibility tab.

At the top left, you can set how AutoCAD works with ARX applications and the objects they create. ObjectARX is a programming language for creating applications that work with AutoCAD. For example, the RENDER command is an ARX application.

At the middle left, you can choose whether objects created with other applications are displayed.

At the top right, you choose whether keyboard shortcuts, also called accelerator keys, follow Windows standards or prior release AutoCAD usage. For example, Ctrl+C issues the COPYCLIP command if you choose Windows standards but is equivalent to cancel (or pressing Esc) if you choose AutoCAD classic (sounds like a soft drink).

At the middle right, you specify which gets priority — running object snaps or keyboard entry. Because of the new OSNAP button, you will be using running objects snaps more often than before. By default, keyboard entry gets priority except in scripts. This lets you use running object snaps when picking points on the screen but overrides them when you want to type in coordinates.

At the bottom, you can get rid of that annoying Start Up dialog box. Later in this appendix I tell you how you can automatically start AutoCAD the way you want.

You can also determine whether AutoLISP variables are reloaded each time you start a new drawing or whether they persist from drawing to drawing.

Choose Reset to return all settings to their default values.

The General tab

This tab lets you set some miscellaneous, but important, features, as shown in Figure A-6.

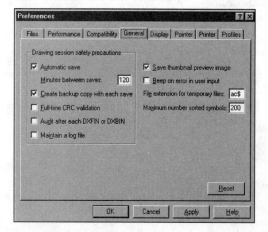

Figure A-6: The General tab.

You should definitely change the time between automatic saves to 20 minutes maximum. By default, AutoCAD creates back-up drawings whenever you save a drawing. Back-up drawings have the same name as your drawing with an extension of *.bak*. Although you probably spend some time erasing these back-up drawings, they can be very useful if a drawing becomes corrupted. You can just change the extension to *.dwg* and use it.

Check Full-time CRC validation if data that you import is getting corrupted and you suspect a hardware problem. A cyclic redundancy check performs a validation during the importing process and can help you troubleshoot this problem.

Choose Audit after each DXFIN or DXBIN if you are having problems when you import DXF or DXB files. The AUDIT command finds and fixes errors in drawings.

A log file keeps a record of the contents in the text window. Each time you work in AutoCAD, the new material is added to the end of the existing log file, so you should periodically edit or delete material from the log file. Choose Maintain a log file to start keeping a log file.

By default, AutoCAD saves a thumbnail preview of each drawing so that you can see it in the Preview window when you open a drawing using the Select File dialog box. You can turn this off, which makes the drawing size smaller.

Check Beep on error in user input if you want to hear a beep whenever you make a mistake.

AutoCAD, like all programs, creates temporary files while you are working. By default, the extension for these files is *ac$*. You can change this extension in the File extension for temporary files text box.

When you list objects, AutoCAD sorts them in alphabetical order up to the maximum number of sorted symbols listed on the General tab (200 by default). If the number of objects exceeds the number in this text box, they are listed in the order they were created.

The Reset button returns all settings to their defaults.

The Display tab

The Display tab contains settings relating to the drawing and text windows. It is shown in Figure A-7.

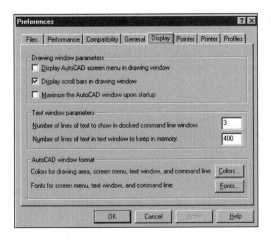

Figure A-7: The Display tab.

The top section turns on and off AutoCAD's screen menu and scroll bars and specifies whether AutoCAD takes up the entire screen when it opens.

The middle section configures the text window. You can set the number of lines that appear in the command line window and the number of text lines that AutoCAD keeps in memory — from 25 to 2,048.

The bottom section determines the colors for the drawing area, screen menu, text window, and the command line. To change the colors, choose Colors to open the AutoCAD Window Colors dialog box, shown in Figure A-8. Notice that there is no Reset option here!

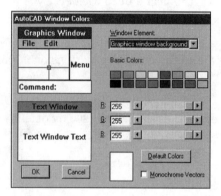

Figure A-8: The AutoCAD Window Colors dialog box.

To use this dialog box, choose one of the elements in the Window Element drop-down list box. Then choose a color, either from the color swatches or by using the Red, Green, Blue slider bars. You see the result in the images at the left. One of the most important settings is the Graphics window background. By default, it is black. You can change it to white to make it more consistent with other Windows programs. Click OK when you have finished setting the colors.

You can also change the fonts used for the screen menu, text window, and the command line. Choose Fonts to open the Graphics Window Font dialog box, shown in Figure A-9.

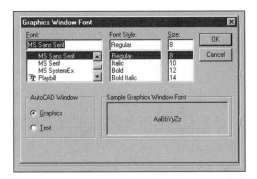

Figure A-9: The Graphics Window Font dialog box.

In this dialog box, choose Graphics to set the font for the graphics window (the screen menu) and Text to switch to the Text Window Font dialog box so you can set the font for the text window and the command line. In both cases, you can set the font, font style (bold, italic, and so on), and the size.

The Pointer tab

The Pointer tab finally looks like the familiar digitizer configuration you are used to and is shown in Figure A-10. Here you choose your pointing device. Choose Set Current to either switch between configured pointing devices or to configure a new device. If the device you choose is not configured, AutoCAD opens the text window and offers you all the suboptions available. Follow the prompts to specify all the features of your device.

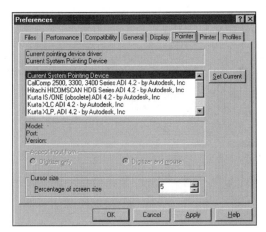

Figure A-10: The Pointer tab.

If you have both a digitizer and a mouse, you can choose Digitizer only to tell AutoCAD to ignore any mouse input (you might use the mouse only for other applications). Choose Digitizer and mouse to let AutoCAD accept input from both.

In Release 14, the cursor size covers only 5 percent of the screen by default. You can return to the familiar full-screen cursor and crosshairs by changing the value to 100 percent, or choose another percentage that works for you.

The Printer tab

The Printer tab, shown in Figure A-11, lets you specify a printer and/or a plotter. You can specify as many as you need.

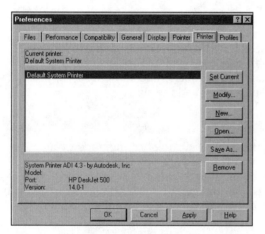

Figure A-11: The Printer tab.

To add a new printer or plotter, choose New to open the Add a Printer dialog box, shown in Figure A-12.

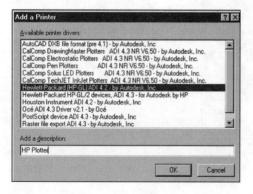

Figure A-12: The Add a Printer dialog box.

Choose a printer driver, add a meaningful description at the bottom, and click OK. AutoCAD opens the text window and continues to prompt you for the information it needs, including the model number, the port that the devices are connected to, and the default plotting parameters.

Choose Set Current in the Printer tab to choose between configured printers and plotters. You can also modify the settings for a device, add a new device, or remove one. You can also open a printer configuration (*.pc2*) file. You can use a *.pc2* file when plotting or with the Batch Plot Utility. Choose Save As to save your configuration information as a *.pc2* file.

Many printer and plotter selections can now print raster images embedded in a drawing. If this is not supported for a particular selection, you see NR in the description for the printer driver.

The Profiles tab

The Profiles tab, shown in Figure A-13, lets you create user profiles. A profile is a set of preferences as set in the Preferences dialog box. You may share your system with someone else, and each of you may wish to store a different set of preferences. Or you might want a different set of preferences for different projects. You then name your profile and make it current when you open AutoCAD.

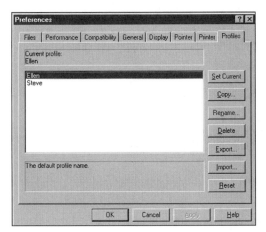

Figure A-13: The Profiles tab with two profiles.

Whatever settings you create with the Preferences dialog box are automatically part of the default profile, which starts out with the exciting name of Unnamed Profile. Here's how you create a new profile:

1. It's usually easier to copy the current profile and work from there. Choose Copy to open the Copy Profile dialog box, shown in Figure A-14. Type in a profile name and description and click OK.

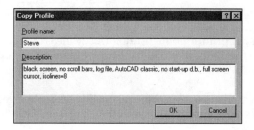

Figure A-14: The Copy Profile dialog box.

2. Go through the other tabs and make the changes you want. In the example, the description is used to summarize the changes from the default profile — black screen, no scroll bars, creation of a log file, use of AutoCAD classic keyboard shortcuts, no start-up dialog box, full-screen cursor, and isolines (contour lines) set at 8.

3. Choose Export to open the Export Profile dialog box, shown in Figure A-15. Choose a name and location. The extension is *.arg*. Click Save.

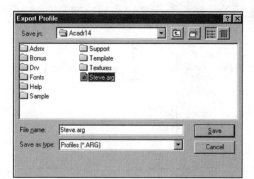

Figure A-15: The Export Profile dialog box.

Note If you are editing an existing profile, choose the profile you are editing and click Save. AutoCAD asks you to verify that you want to replace the existing file. Choose Yes.

4. To use the profile, choose it on the Profiles tab of the Preferences dialog box and click Set Current. Click OK to return to your drawing. You see the results immediately, as shown in Figure A-16. Of course, some of the settings are not visible but make themselves evident in other ways, such as the AutoCAD classic keyboard shortcuts, the lack of the start-up dialog box, and the creation of a log file.

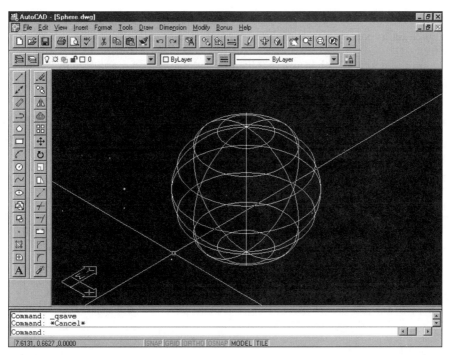

Figure A-16: An example of a profile that sets the screen to black, does not display scroll bars, uses a full-screen cursor, and sets isolines to 8.

The other Profile tab options let you edit a profile name or description, delete a profile, import a profile, and reset a profile to the original defaults.

Tip

You can also specify a profile using a command line switch, as explained in the next section.

Starting AutoCAD your way

When you click on the AutoCAD icon to open AutoCAD, Windows notwithstanding, you execute a statement similar to the one you probably once typed at the DOS prompt. This is called a *command line* statement. By default, it looks something like this:

```
C:\ACADR14\acad.exe
```

Your command line statement depends on where you installed AutoCAD.

Command line switches

You can add parameters, called *switches*, to this command line and control what AutoCAD does when you launch it. Always add a space between the *acad.exe* command and a switch. Table A-2 lists the available command line switches and their functions.

<table>
<tr>
<td colspan="3" align="center">Table A-2
Command line switches</td>
</tr>
<tr>
<td>*Switch*</td>
<td>*Example*</td>
<td>*Function*</td>
</tr>
<tr>
<td>/c</td>
<td>/c c:\steve\steve.cfg</td>
<td>Specifies the location and, optionally, the filename of the hardware configuration file you want to use. Configuration files are discussed in the next section.</td>
</tr>
<tr>
<td>/s</td>
<td>/s c:\steve</td>
<td>Specifies support folders for fonts, menus, AutoLISP files, linetypes, and hatch patterns. Use this when you want to use support files that are not in AutoCAD's support file search path.</td>
</tr>
<tr>
<td>/d</td>
<td>/d c:\drivers</td>
<td>Specifies the location for ADI (AutoCAD Device Interface) drivers. Use this if you have created or bought ADI device drivers or if you keep your drivers in a separate folder.</td>
</tr>
<tr>
<td>/b</td>
<td>Union Hill Apts
/b setup</td>
<td>Opens a drawing (here named "Union Hill Apts") and runs a script (here named setup). Omit the drawing to run the script with a new drawing.</td>
</tr>
<tr>
<td>/t</td>
<td>/t a-tb</td>
<td>Opens a new drawing based on a template file (here named *a-tb*).</td>
</tr>
<tr>
<td>/nologo</td>
<td></td>
<td>Starts AutoCAD without displaying the AutoCAD logo.</td>
</tr>
<tr>
<td>/v</td>
<td>Union Hill Apts
/v front</td>
<td>Opens a drawing and immediately displays the specified view.</td>
</tr>
<tr>
<td>/r</td>
<td>/r</td>
<td>Resets AutoCAD to the default configuration including the default system printer and system pointing device.</td>
</tr>
<tr>
<td>/p</td>
<td>/p steve</td>
<td>Specifies an existing profile (here named steve) to use when starting AutoCAD. This profile is used only for the current session. You can also change profiles using the Profile tab of the Preferences dialog box.</td>
</tr>
</table>

You can combine switches. For example, the following command line statement opens the drawing "Union Hill Apts" in the front view and runs the setup script:

```
c:\acadr14\acad.exe  Union Hill Apts  /v front /b setup
```

Caution

If you have been using command line switches with previous releases, you may need to change their syntax if you are now using long filenames and/or folder names.

Changing command line switches

The easiest way to change your command line switch is to create a shortcut to AutoCAD on your desktop. To do this, use Explorer to find *acad.exe* (usually in \acadr14). Right-click it and choose Create Shortcut from the menu. Windows creates a shortcut named *Shortcut to acad.exe*. Drag this to your desktop and rename it — usually AutoCAD R14 or just AutoCAD is fine.

Now follow these steps:

1. Right-click the shortcut on your desktop.
2. Choose Properties.
3. Choose the Shortcut tab.
4. In the Target text box, add your switches to the end of the current command line statement.
5. Choose OK.

If you don't like the AutoCAD Start Up dialog box, and you usually start new drawings based on one template, and are impatient to get started drawing as soon as possible, try a command line like this:

```
c:\acadr14\acad.exe /nologo /t  My template
```

Then uncheck Show the Start Up dialog box item in the Compatibility tab of the Preferences dialog box. The Start Up dialog box itself also has a box you can uncheck.

If you have customized *acad.dwt,* use that template in your command line statement.

Understanding configuration files

Every time you open AutoCAD, a configuration file (*acad14.cfg* by default) is created, which is an ASCII file containing mostly hardware configuration information such as the platform, the number of configured plotters, the configured digitizers and their ports, the plot drivers, pen color assignments, and so on. Figure A-17 shows the beginning of the default file.

Figure A-17: The beginning of the *acad14.cfg* file.

If you use multiple plotters, display drivers, and other equipment, you may want to create more than one configuration file to make it easy to switch from one configuration to another.

You should not edit the configuration file but rather let AutoCAD create it for you. The problem is that AutoCAD assumes one configuration file and overwrites the previous one whenever you make changes that affect the file, such as adding a plotter or pointing device.

Remember that you can use the /c command line switch to specify a configuration file. To create a new file, follow these steps:

1. Use Windows Explorer to back up your current configuration file under a new name such as *acad14-orig.cfg*.

2. Open AutoCAD and make the hardware configuration changes you want using the Preferences dialog box.

3. Close AutoCAD.

4. In Explorer, find the new *acad14.cfg* that AutoCAD created. Change its name, using something meaningful such as *LaserPrinter.cfg*

5. If you want to keep the original *acad14.cfg*, change its name back to *acad14.cfg*.

You now have two configuration files. (You can create more if you want.) To use them, you can change the command line switch as needed, but there's an easier way.

Creating multiple configurations

This appendix has discussed three separate ways to create session configurations:

✦ Profiles

✦ Configuration files

✦ Command line switches

You can use command line switches to specify a profile and a configuration file, as well as to configure AutoCAD in other ways, such as opening a drawing with a certain template or running a script file when you open a drawing.

If you regularly use these features, you should create multiple configurations to make it easy to open AutoCAD the way you want. To do this:

✦ Create the profiles and configuration files you need.

✦ Make as many desktop shortcuts as you need, as described in the earlier section Changing command line switches.

✦ Change the command line switches to specify the profiles and configuration files you want and add any other command line switches you need.

For example, here are command lines for two separate AutoCAD desktop shortcuts:

```
E:\ACADR14\acad.exe /t acad /nologo
E:\ACADR14\acad.exe /p steve /c steve.cfg /t arch
```

The first command line statement opens drawings using the *acad.dwt* template and doesn't display the logo. It also uses the default profile and configuration file.

The second command line statement opens drawings using the *arch.dwt* template and displays the logo. It also uses the steve profile and the steve configuration file.

You could also have each configuration run different script files.

This technique takes some time to set up but once done saves time and reduces errors each time you open AutoCAD.

Release 14 Menus and Toolbars

Many of the menus have changed significantly for Release 14, and it can sometimes be difficult to find the commands you are looking for. A few commands are no longer on any menu and must be typed on the command line.

The toolbars have also changed considerably. Most of the flyouts are gone (by popular request). The flyouts that remain can also be displayed as stand-alone toolbars.

This appendix displays all the menus and toolbars so you can find commands at a glance.

Release 14 Menus

The File menu

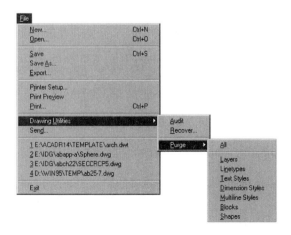

The Edit menu

The View Menu

The View menu with Zoom submenu

The View menu with Pan submenu

The View menu with Tiled Viewports submenu

The View menu with Floating Viewports submenu

The View menu with 3D Viewpoint submenu

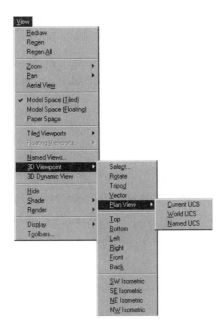

The View menu with Shade submenu

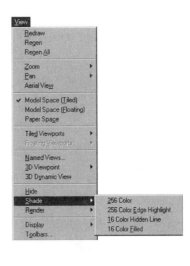

The View menu with
Render submenu

The View menu with Display submenus

The UCS Icon submenu

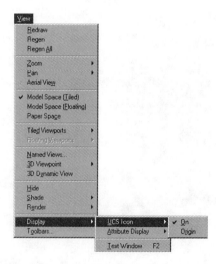

The Attribute Display submenu

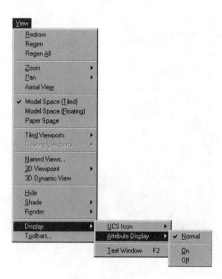

The Insert menu

The Format menu

The Tools menu

The Tools menu with Display Order submenu

The Tools menu with Inquiry submenu

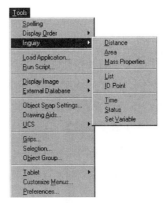

The Tools menu with Display Image submenu

The Tools menu with External Database submenu

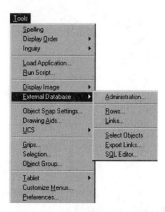

The Tools menu with UCS submenu

The Tools menu with Tablet submenu

The Draw menu

The Draw menu with Arc submenu

The Draw menu with Circle submenu

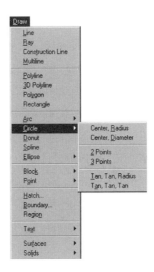

The Draw menu with Ellipse submenu

The Draw menu with Block submenu

The Draw menu with Point submenu

The Draw menu with Text submenu

The Draw menu with Surfaces submenu

The Draw menu with Solids submenu

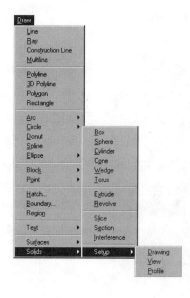

The Dimension menu

The Modify menu

The Object submenu with External Reference submenu

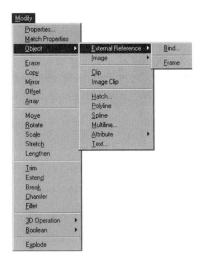

The Object submenu with Image submenu

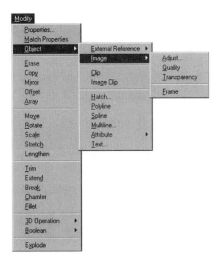

The Object submenu with Attribute submenu

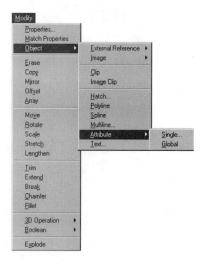

The Modify menu with 3D Operation submenu

The Modify menu with Boolean submenu

The Help menu

Release 14 Toolbars

The Standard toolbar

New
Save
Print Preview
Cut to Clipboard
Paste from Clipboard
Undo
Launch Browser
UCS flyout
Redraw All
Viewpoint flyout
Zoom Realtime
Zoom Previous

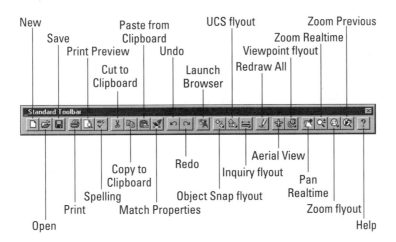

Open
Print
Spelling
Copy to Clipboard
Match Properties
Redo
Object Snap flyout
Inquiry flyout
Aerial View
Pan Realtime
Zoom flyout
Help

The Object Snap flyout/toolbar

Tracking
Snap to Endpoint
Snap to Intersection
Snap to Center
Snap to Tangent
Snap to Insert
Snap to Nearest
Snap to None

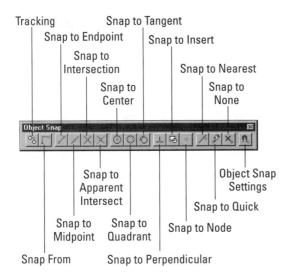

Snap From
Snap to Midpoint
Snap to Apparent Intersect
Snap to Quadrant
Snap to Perpendicular
Snap to Node
Snap to Quick
Object Snap Settings

The UCS flyout/toolbar

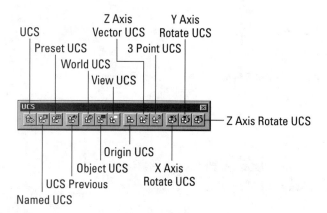

The Inquiry flyout/toolbar

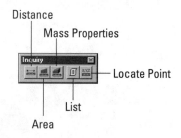

The Zoom flyout/toolbar

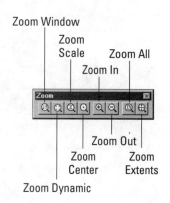

The Viewpoint flyout/toolbar

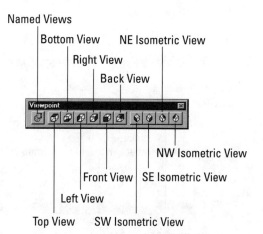

The Object Properties toolbar

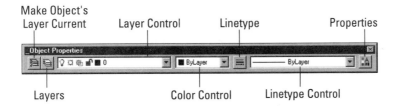

The Draw toolbar

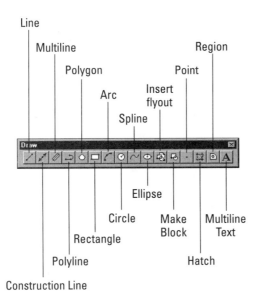

The Insert flyout/toolbar

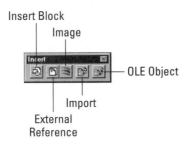

The Modify toolbar

Erase
Mirror
Array
Rotate
Stretch
Break
Fillet
Trim

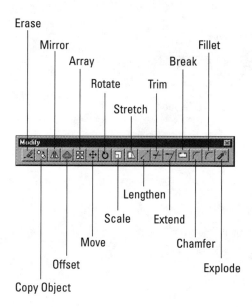

Lengthen
Scale
Extend
Move
Chamfer
Offset
Explode
Copy Object

The Dimension toolbar

Linear Dimension
Ordinate Dimension
Diameter Dimension
Leader
Baseline Dimension
Center Mark
Dimension Text Edit
Dimension Update

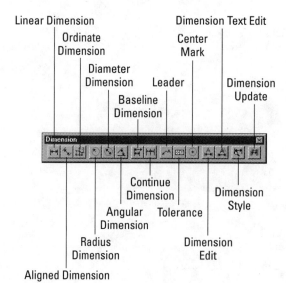

Continue Dimension
Angular Dimension
Tolerance
Dimension Style
Radius Dimension
Dimension Edit
Aligned Dimension

The External Database toolbar

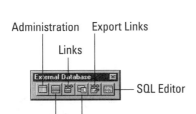

The Modify II toolbar

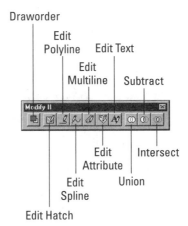

The Reference toolbar

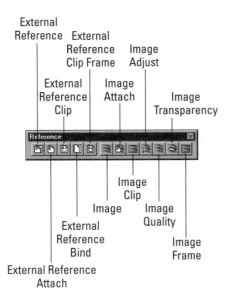

The Render toolbar

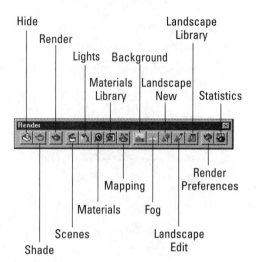

The Solids toolbar

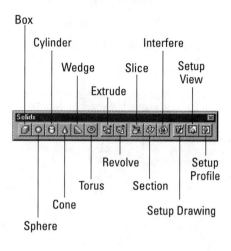

The Surfaces toolbar

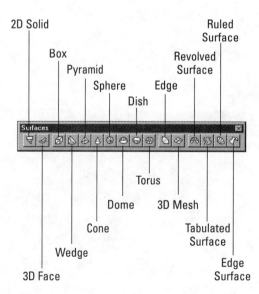

The Internet Utilities toolbar

In order to display this toolbar, the `inet` menu group must be loaded. Choose Tools⇨Customize Menus to load it. If it is not listed, choose Browse to locate it. There is no menu for Internet Utilities, just a toolbar. Once it is loaded, choose the `inet` menu group in the Toolbars dialog box.

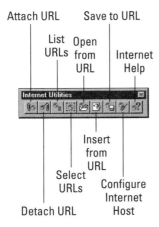

Cross-Reference

The Bonus menu and toolbar are covered in Appendix A.

Command and System Variables Changes

◆   ◆   ◆   ◆

In This Appendix

New commands

Discontinued and
changed commands

New system
variables

Discontinued and
changed system
variables

Command line
system variables

◆   ◆   ◆   ◆

Learning the Ropes in Release 14

When you upgrade to a new release of AutoCAD, one way
to quickly identify what's new is to look at a list of new
commands. Also, you need to know which commands have
been discontinued or significantly changed — you may have
to redo some script files and customized menus, or simply
find new ways of accomplishing old tasks. This appendix
provides this information for you.

All system variables used to be command line affairs, but now
most are set in dialog boxes. When a system variable is set in
a dialog box, you hardly need to know about it (unless you
are customizing AutoCAD). However, because some system
variables still need to be typed on the command line, it's
useful to know about them. Others can be set in a dialog box
but are easier to use on the command line, perhaps because
they are used so often. This chapter lists these system
variables. I also list new and changed system variables.

AutoCAD's Help contains a Command Reference that includes
every command and system variable. The Readme file
(choose Start on the Windows taskbar⇨Programs⇨AutoCAD
R14⇨AutoCAD Readme) also has information on command
and system variable changes that didn't make it into the in-
program documentation.

Commands

Table C-1 lists the commands that are new to Release 14.

Table C-1 New Commands	
Command	**Description**
BACKGROUND	Adds a background to a rendered scene.
BMAKE	Defines a block.
BROWSER	Launches your default Web browser.
CONVERT	Converts 2D polylines to lightweight polylines and hatches to Release 14 hatches.
DRAWORDER	Changes the display order of images and objects (which object appears on top).
DWFOUT	Exports a Drawing Web Format file.
FOG	Creates a fog or depth cue that determines the clarity of objects in a rendered scene.
IMAGE	Inserts images into a drawing.
IMAGEADJUST	Sets brightness, contrast, and fade of an image.
IMAGEATTACH	Attaches an image to a drawing.
IMAGECLIP	Creates a clipping boundary for an image.
IMAGEFRAME	Displays or hides an image's frame.
IMAGEQUALITY	Displays an image in high or draft quality.
LSEDIT	Lets you edit a landscape object.
LSLIB	Maintains a library of landscape objects.
LSNEW	Inserts a new landscape object.
MATCHPROP	Copies properties from one object to other objects.
SETUV	Projects (maps) an image onto an object.
SHOWMAT	Lists the material and method of attachment (by object, color, or layer) for an object.
TRANSPARENCY	Lets the background of some images be transparent or opaque.
XCLIP	Defines an external reference or block clipping boundary and sets the clipping planes.

Table C-2 shows the commands that have been discontinued, along with any available alternatives.

Table C-2 Discontinued Commands	
Command	*Alternative*
DDEMODES	Use the Object Properties toolbar, the LTSCALE, STYLE, and ELEV commands, as well as the THICKNESS system variable.
END	Use QUIT.
FILES	Manage files using Windows instead of AutoCAD.
FILMROLL	
GIFIN	Use IMAGE.
LOGIN	
MAKEPREVIEW	You can no longer create preview images for Release 12 drawings.
PCXIN	Use IMAGE.
RCONFIG	AutoCAD automatically configures rendering for Windows.
RENDERUNLOAD	Use ARX with the Unload option.
TIFFIN	Use IMAGE.
TYPE	Use Notepad or a word processor to open a file.
UNLOCK	AutoCAD no longer locks files with its own locking system.
VLCONV	This command is no longer applicable because AutoVision's features have been included in Release 14.
XREFCLIP	Use XCLIP.

The commands in Table C-3 have changes that may affect script or AutoLISP files that use these commands.

<table>
<tr><td colspan="2" align="center">Table C-3
Changed Commands</td></tr>
<tr><td>*Command*</td><td>*Changes*</td></tr>
<tr><td>ACADPREFIX</td><td>The path no longer ends with a double backslash.</td></tr>
<tr><td>ALIGN</td><td>When you specify two destination points, it now includes an option letting you scale the object to the alignment points.</td></tr>
<tr><td>ATTEDIT</td><td>In prior releases, this command continued immediately after you used one selection method. Now you use standard selection methods.</td></tr>
<tr><td>BHATCH</td><td>Automatically uses the command line when used in a script or AutoLISP routine.</td></tr>
<tr><td>CONFIG</td><td>Opens the Preferences dialog box.</td></tr>
<tr><td>DXFIN</td><td>You may use this only in a new drawing. Instead, you can use the OPEN command.</td></tr>
<tr><td>LAYER</td><td>Now displays the Layer & Linetype Properties dialog box. Use -layer to use it on the command line.</td></tr>
<tr><td>MTEXT</td><td>Automatically uses the command line when used in a script or AutoLISP routine.</td></tr>
<tr><td>NEW</td><td>Now prompts for a template. You cannot assign a name to a new drawing.</td></tr>
<tr><td>PURGE</td><td>Now lets you purge all items without verifying each purged item.</td></tr>
<tr><td>SAVEAS</td><td>You must specify the file format before specifying the file name.</td></tr>
</table>

System Variables

Table C-4 lists new system variables.

<table>
<tr><td colspan="2" align="center">Table C-4
New System Variables</td></tr>
<tr><td>*System Variable*</td><td>*Description*</td></tr>
<tr><td>ACISOUTVER</td><td>Sets the ACIS version of SAT files created when you use the ACISOUT command. The only possible value is 16 (for ACIS version 1.6). Future releases of AutoCAD are expected to support other versions.</td></tr>
</table>

System Variable	Description
APBOX	Turns the AutoSnap aperture box (at the crosshairs when you snap to an object) on or off. By default (1) the aperture box is displayed. Set to 0 if you don't want to display it.
AUTOSNAP	Controls the AutoSnap marker, tip, and magnet. A value of 0 turns them all off, 1 turns on the marker, 2 turns on the tip, and 4 turns on the magnet. The value of this system variable is the sum of these values. By default it is 7 (1+2+4), which means that all three are turned on.
CURSORSIZE	Sets the size of the crosshairs as a percentage of the screen. By default it is set to 5 (5% of the screen).
DEMANDLOAD	Determines how AutoCAD loads a third-party application (such as an ARX application) if a drawing contains custom objects (not AutoCAD objects) created in that application. A value of 0 turns off demand loading, 1 loads the source application when you open a drawing containing custom objects but not when you use one of the application's commands, 2 loads the source application when you use one of the application's commands but not when you open such a drawing, and 3 (the default) loads the source application when you either open such a drawing or when you use one of the application's commands.
DIMADEC	Determines the number of decimal places for dimension text of angular dimensions. By default this is set to -1, which uses the DIMDEC system variable's value. To create angular dimensions with different precision than linear dimensions, set this to a value of 0 to 8 to specify the number of decimal places.
FACETRATIO	Controls the density of the mesh used to create facets in cylindrical and conic 3D solid objects. The default, 0, creates a normal mesh. Set FACETRATIO to 1 to increase the density of the mesh. This should improve the quality when you render or shade cylindrical or conic 3D solids.
HIDEPRECISION	Controls the precision of calculations for hides and shades. The default, 0, uses single precision. Set it to 1 to specify double precision to calculate the hide. A setting of 1 requires more memory than a setting of 0.
INDEXCTL	Determines whether layer and spatial indexes are created and saved, which can be used when attaching external references. By default (0), no indexes are created. Set to 1 for a layer index, set to 2 for a spatial index, and set to 3 for both indexes.
INETLOCATION	Stores the Internet location used by the new BROWSER command. Set by default to "www.autodesk.com/acaduser".
LASTPROMPT	Stores the last text string that appears on the command line, including user input.

System Variable	Description
LISPINIT	Sets whether AutoLISP functions and variables are preserved from drawing to drawing or whether they are valid in the current drawing only. Set to 0 to preserve them from drawing to drawing, or to 1 (the default) so they are kept only in the current drawing.
LOGFILEMODE	Determines if the contents of the text window are saved in a log file. By default (0), no log file is created. Set to 1 to maintain a log file.
LOGFILENAME	Sets the path and name for the log file. By default the log file goes to the current working directory.
MEASUREINIT	Sets the type of measurement used, English (setting of 0) or Metric (setting of 1), when you open an existing drawing. It affects which hatch pattern and linetype file AutoCAD uses. Set it to 0 to use the files based on the ANSI standard and to 1 to use the files based on the ISO standards. The default varies according to your country.
MEASUREMENT	Sets drawing units as English or metric. (You usually set this with the Start-up dialog box.) Controls which hatch pattern and linetype file AutoCAD uses. Set to 0 (the default) to use English measurement — AutoCAD uses ANSI hatch and linetype files. Set to 1 to use metric measurement — AutoCAD uses ISO hatch and linetype files.
OLEHIDE	Determines whether OLE objects are visible on screen and printed/plotted. By default (value = 0), they are visible. 1 makes them visible in paper space only, 2 makes them visible in model space only, and 3 suppresses their visibility.
OSNAPCOORD	Determines whether coordinates entered using the keyboard override running object snaps. Set to 0 to have running object snaps override keyboard entry of coordinates, set to 1 to have keyboard entry override running object snaps, set to 2 (the default) to have keyboard entry override running object snaps except in scripts.
PLINETYPE	Controls the conversion and creation of Release 14 lightweight polylines. When set to 0, polylines in previous release drawings are not converted when opened in Release 14, and AutoCAD creates the old-format polylines. When set to 1, polylines in previous release drawings are not converted when opened in Release 14, and AutoCAD creates lightweight polylines. When set to 2 (the default), polylines in previous release drawings are converted when opened in Release 14, and AutoCAD creates lightweight polylines. Affects all commands that create polylines — for example, PLINE, RECTANG, POLYGON, and so on.

System Variable	Description
PROJECTNAME	Creates a project name for a drawing. Projects add a search path, which AutoCAD uses to search for external references. You generally create them using the Files tab of the Preferences dialog box.
PROXYGRAPHICS	Proxy objects are created when a third-party application (ARX) creates a custom object but AutoCAD can't find the application when it opens the drawing (either you don't have it installed on your system or you unloaded it). AutoCAD temporarily replaces the custom object with a proxy object and displays the Proxy Information dialog box, which is where you usually set this system variable. This system variable determines whether proxy object images are saved in the drawing. Set to 0 if you don't want to save the image — AutoCAD uses a bounding box instead. Set to 1 (the default) to save the image with the drawing.
PROXYNOTICE	Determines whether AutoCAD displays a notice when a proxy is created. Set to 0 to eliminate the notice. Set to 1 (the default) to display the notice.
PROXYSHOW	Determines how AutoCAD displays proxy objects. Set to 0 if you don't want to display them. Set to 1 (the default) to display them. Set to 2 to display a bounding box.
RTDISPLAY	Determines how AutoCAD displays raster images during realtime zoom or pan. Set to 0 to display the raster image (this can slow down your panning and zooming). Set to 1 (the default) to display only an outline.
WRITESTAT	This is a read-only variable. If it's set to 1, you can save the drawing (called writing to the drawing). If it's set to 0, the drawing is read-only and you cannot save any changes to it.
XCLIPFRAME	Specifies whether xref clipping boundaries are visible. If it's set to 0 (the default), they are not visible. If it's set to 1, they are visible.
XLOADCTL	Release 14 offers demand loading of external references, which means that only the portion needed for display is loaded. Set to 0 to turn off demand loading. Set to 1 (the default) to turn on demand loading and keep the xref file open (in case more of it is needed). This prevents anyone else on a networked system from using the xref. Set to 2 to turn on demand loading but open only a copy of the xref file (so that others can work on the original).
XLOADPATH	Sets the location of temporary copies of xref files that are demand loaded when XLOADCTL is set to 2.

The following system variables have been discontinued:

- ✦ ACADMAXMEM
- ✦ ACADMAXOBJMEM
- ✦ ACIS15
- ✦ DWGWRITE
- ✦ FFLIMIT
- ✦ LONGFNAME
- ✦ MAXOBJMEM
- ✦ RIASPECT
- ✦ RIBACKG
- ✦ RIEDGE
- ✦ RIGAMUT
- ✦ RIGREY
- ✦ RITHRESH
- ✦ SAVEIMAGES

Table C-5 lists some changed system variables.

Table C-5 Changed System Variables	
System Variable	**Change**
FILLMODE	Affects the display of hatches (as well as wide polylines and SOLID command objects).
OSMODE	When object snaps are switched off using the OSNAP button on the status bar, a value of 16384 is returned in addition to the normal value of OSMODE.
RASTERPREVIEW	The values have been changed. 0=No Preview, 1 = BMP only.
TEXTFILE	Affects only plotting.
TEXTQLTY	Affects only printer or plot output. The variable now refers to the dots per inch resolution.

System variables on the command line

If you write AutoLISP routines, you need to work with all system variables. However, for most drawing tasks, you need to know only the system variables that you usually do not set in a dialog box. These are the system variables that you often type on the command line and so need to know by name. In Tables C-6 through C-13, I list them by function so you can find them even if you don't know their names. I've included a few additional system variables that are commonly used on the command line although they're accessible from a dialog box.

Table C-6
System Variables for 3D Drawing

System Variable	Description
DISPSILH	Turns on and off the display of silhouette curves of 3D objects in wireframe display.
FACETRES	Sets the smoothness of 3D shaded and rendered objects and objects with hidden lines removed.
ISOLINES	Sets the number of lines used to represent 3D objects in wireframe. The default is 4, but values can range from 0 to 2047. A value of 8 is a good balance between display and speed.
SHADEDGE	Controls the way edges are shaded. 0 shades faces but does not highlight edges; 1 shades faces and highlights edges; 2 doesn't shade faces, hides lines, and shows edges; 3 highlights edges only, with no lighting effect. The default is 3 although 1 is probably the most useful setting.
SHADEDIF	Sets the percent of diffuse reflective light to ambient light. The default is 70. Values can range from 0 to 100.
SURFTAB1	The number of tabulations used in the RULESURF and TABSURF commands. Sets the M direction for the REVSURF and EDGESURF commands.
SURFTAB2	Sets the N direction for the REVSURF and EDGESURF commands.
SURFU	The surface density in the M direction for polyface meshes.
SURFV	The surface density in the N direction for polyface meshes.
UCSFOLLOW	Determines whether AutoCAD returns you to plan view when you change the UCS. Choose 1 to return to plan view. The default is 0.

Table C-7
System Variables for Attributes

System Variable	Description
ATTDIA	Determines whether you get a dialog box when you use the INSERT command to insert a block that contains attributes. A setting of 0 turns off the dialog box.
ATTREQ	If you set this to 0, AutoCAD uses default attribute values when you insert a block with attributes. If you set it to 1, the default, AutoCAD prompts you for values.

Table C-8
System Variables for Dimensioning

System Variable	Description
DIMASO	Turns associative dimensioning on and off. The values are ON and OFF.
DIMSHO	When on, the default, AutoCAD continually recomputes associative dimensions as you drag an object.

Table C-9
System Variables for Drawing Aids

System Variable	Description
BLIPMODE	Turns blips on and off.
EXPERT	Controls whether certain prompts are issued, according to the following values:
	0 Issues all prompts normally.
	1 Suppresses "About to regen, proceed?" and "Really want to turn the current layer off?"
	2 Suppresses the prompts for 1 plus "Block already defined. Redefine it?" and "A drawing with this name already exists. Overwrite it?"
	3 Suppresses the prompts for 1 and 2 plus those displayed when you try to load a linetype that's already loaded or create a new linetype in a file that already defines it.

System Variable	Description
	4 Suppresses the prompts for 1, 2, and 3 plus those displayed by UCS Save and VPORTS Save if the name you supply already exists.
	5 Suppresses the prompts for 1, 2, 3, and 4 plus those issued by the DIMSTYLE Save option and DIMOVERRIDE if the dimension style name you supply already exists.
	When EXPERT suppresses a prompt, AutoCAD acts as if you entered y at the prompt.
	Warning: EXPERT's value affects scripts, menu macros, and AutoLISP routines.
MAXACTVP	The maximum number of viewports that can be regenerated at one time. The default is 16.
UNITMODE	Determines how fractional, feet-and-inches, and surveyor's angle units are displayed on the status line. Set it to 1 to display them in input format, as in 3'2-1/2". A value of 0, the default, displays the same number as 3'-2 1/2".
VISRETAIN	A setting of 0 means that xrefs take on the layer settings (on/off, thawed/frozen, and so on) in the current drawing. A setting of 1 means that the layer settings in the xref drawing take precedence, meaning that these settings persist each time you open a drawing with the xref. The default is 1.
WORLDVIEW	Determines whether the UCS changes to the WCD when you use DVIEW or VPOINT. If you set it to 0, the UCS remains unchanged. If you set it to 1, the default, the UCS switches to the WCS during the DVIEW or VPOINT command.

Table C-10
System Variables for Editing

System Variable	Description
EXPLMODE	The default, 1, lets you explode nonuniformly scaled blocks (the X and Y scales are different). Set to 0 to disallow exploding nonuniformly scaled blocks.

(continued)

Table C-10 (*continued*)

System Variable	Description
MIRRTEXT	By default, the MIRROR command mirrors selected text. Set to 0 to keep the text reading from left to right.
PICKSTYLE	Determines the way groups and hatches can be selected: 0 — No group selection. Hatches are selected without their boundaries. 1 — Group selection. Hatches are selected without their boundaries. 2 — No group selection. Hatches are selected along with their boundaries. 3 — Group selection. Hatches are selected along with their boundaries.

Table C-11
System Variables for Information and Customization*

System Variable	Description
ACADPREFIX	The path of the ACAD environment.
ACADVER	The AutoCAD version number, as in 14.
AREA	The last area calculated by AREA, LIST, or DBLIST.
AUDITCTL	Set to 1 to create an audit report file, to 0 if you don't want a report.
CDATE	Stores the date and time.
CMDACTIVE	Stores whether a regular command, transparent command, script, or dialog box is active.
CMDDIA	Turns dialog boxes on. Set to 0 to suppress dialog boxes. Set to 1, the default, to use them.
CMDNAMES	The name of the active regular and transparent commands.
DATE	The date and time in Julian format.
DBMOD	Saves the types of modifications done in the drawing. Its value is the sum of the following: 1 — Objects have been modified. 4 — System variables have been modified. 8 — A window has been modified. 16 — The view has been modified.

System Variable	Description
DCTCUST	The custom spelling dictionary file.
DCTMAIN	The main spelling dictionary file.
DELOBJ	Determines whether objects used to create other objects are maintained in the drawing database — for example when using the EXTRUDE command to create a 3D object from a 2D object. The default, 1, deletes these objects. A value of 0 retains them.
DIASTAT	Stores the exit method from the last used dialog box (usually OK or Cancel).
DISTANCE	The last distance calculated by the DIST command.
DWGNAME	The drawing name.
DWGPREFIX	The path for the drawing.
DWGTITLED	0 if your drawing has not been named; 1 if it has.
EXTMAX	The upper right corner of the drawing extents.
ENTMIN	The lower left corner of the drawing extents.
FILEDIA	Turns on and off the display of dialog boxes that deal with files, such as the Select File dialog box. Set to 0 to turn off file dialog boxes.
INSNAME	Stores a default block name for DDINSERT or INSERT.
LASTANGLE	The end angle of the last arc that you drew.
LASTPOINT	The last point entered.
LASTPROMPT	Stores the last text string that appears on the command line, including user input.
LIMMAX	The upper right corner of the drawing limits.
LIMMIN	The lower left corner of the drawing limits.
LISPINIT	Determines whether AutoLISP functions and variables are retained from drawing to drawing (value of 0) or whether they are valid only in the current drawing (a value of 1, the default).
LOCALE	The ISO language code of the current AutoCAD version.
LOGINNAME	The user's name required to log in on a network system.
MENUECHO	Sets the display (echo) of menu items. By default (0), all items are echoed. Its value is the sum of these values:
	1 Suppresses echo of menu items (^P in a menu item toggles echoing).
	2 Suppresses display of system prompts during menu use.
	4 Disables ^P menu toggle.
	8 Displays input/output strings; used for debugging DIESEL macros.

(continued)

Table C-11 (*continued*)

System Variable	Description
MENUNAME	The current menu name.
OLEHIDE	Determines whether OLE objects are visible on screen and printed/plotted. By default (value = 0), they are visible. 1 makes them visible in paper space only, 2 makes them visible in model space only, and 3 suppresses their visibility.
PERIMETER	The last perimeter calculated by AREA, LIST, or DBLIST.
PFACEVMAX	The maximum number of vertices per face.
PLATFORM	The computer platform you are using, that is, Windows 95, Windows NT 3.51, or Windows NT 4.0.
FILENAME	Stores the filename.
SCREENSIZE	The size, in pixels, of the current viewport.
SHPNAME	The default shape name.
STATUS	Drawing status information, such as the drawing limits, current color, layer, and so on.
TDCREATE	The date and time the drawing was created.
TREEDEPTH	Configures the spatial index, which structures the database of objects.
VIEWCTR	The center of the view of the current viewport.
VSMAX	The upper right corner of the virtual screen.
VSMIN	The lower left corner of the virtual screen.
WORLDUCS	Stores whether the UCS is the same as the World Coordinate System. A value of 0 means that the UCS is different; a value of 1 means that the UCS and the WCS are the same.
XREFCTL	Set to 1 to create an xref log file. Set to 0 if you don't want to create a log file.

*Many of these system variables are *read-only*, which means that they just provide information but can't be changed.

Table C-12
System Variables for Object Creation

System Variable	Description
PELLIPSE	A setting of 0, the default, creates a true ellipse. Set to 1 to create a polyline representation of an ellipse.
PLINEGEN	When set to 0, the default, linetypes start each vertex of a polyline with a dash. When set to 1, the linetype is generated in a continuous pattern regardless of the vertices.
POLYSIDES	The default number of sides for polygon.
SKPOLY	If set to 0, SKETCH creates lines. If set to 1, it creates polylines.
SPLFRAME	Sets spline-fit polyline display. If set to 0, the default, it doesn't display the control polygon for splines and spline fit polylines, displays the fit surface of a polygon mesh but not the defining mesh; doesn't display the invisible edges of 3D faces or polyface meshes. If set to 1, it displays the control polygon for splines and spline fit polylines, displays the defining mesh of a polygon mesh but not the fit surface, and shows invisible edges of 3D faces and polyface meshes.
SPLINESEGS	Sets the number of line segments that each spline generates. A higher number results in a curve that more precisely matches the frame.
SPLINETYPE	Determines the type of spline curve created by the Spline option of the PEDIT command. Use 5 for a quadratic B-spline and 6 (the default) for a cubic B-spline.
SURFTYPE	Sets the type of surface fitting used by the Smooth option of the PEDIT command. Set 5 for a quadratic B-spline, 6 (the default) for a cubic B-spline, and 8 for a Bezier surface.

Table C-13
System Variables for Text

System Variable	Description
FONTALT	Sets an alternative font that AutoCAD will use if the specified font cannot be found.
TEXTSIZE	Stores the default or last height for text styles without a fixed height.
TEXTSTYLE	The current text-style name.

AutoCAD Resources

Ways to Learn AutoCAD

Aside from using this book, you have many other resources
for learning AutoCAD. They range from AutoCAD's tutorial to
online tutorials and everything in-between.

Learning from your AutoCAD dealer

You are supposed to learn AutoCAD from your AutoCAD
dealer. Most dealers include some training when you
purchase AutoCAD. However, the amount of training and
follow-up support varies greatly — and so does the price. If
there is more than one AutoCAD dealer nearby, check not
only the cost of AutoCAD but the cost of training as well.

Dealers also offer upgrade seminars and courses. For Release
14 they may offer one seminar for those upgrading from
Release 12 and another for those upgrading from Release 13.

If you are going to use either third-party applications that
work with AutoCAD or other Autodesk products, check how
much experience the dealer has with these products and
what kind of support is offered.

Autodesk has an Authorized Training Center program,
which certifies trainers. Your dealer may or may not be an
Authorized Training Center. It's good to ask. Some dealers
are also Authorized Systems Centers. They take additional
training in certain disciplines to offer more specialized
solutions to their customers.

Taking a course

You may be able to take a course in AutoCAD at a local university or Authorized Training Center. Many universities and community colleges offers courses in AutoCAD. They may fit your schedule since they are often offered in the evening, over a period of several weeks. Of course, that may not work if you need to get up and running very quickly.

AutoCAD University (an Autodesk event) holds a once-a-year conference that offers training courses by top AutoCAD "gurus." On Autodesk's Web site (http://www.autodesk.com), choose Company, then Events.

Learning from other users

If you work in an office with several AutoCAD users, you will find that they are usually happy to share information and tips with you. This won't generally get you started from scratch, but it's great for rounding out your knowledge.

Reading the magazines

There are two major magazines that are pretty much devoted to AutoCAD: *Cadence* (800-289-0484) and *CADalyst* (800-346-0085 ext 477). These magazines come out monthly. They contain many helpful articles (as well as advertisements, of course). In addition, both magazines have extensive Web sites — more about that later.

If you're interested in the CAD industry in general, try Ralph Grabowski's shareware newsletter upFront.eZine, which you can subscribe to by sending the e-mail message 'subscribe upfront' to ralphg@xyzpress.com.

Using AutoCAD's tutorials

As explained in Chapter 3, AutoCAD comes with its own tutorial. If you don't find it on your system, it may not be installed. Insert the AutoCAD CD-ROM, start Setup as you did when you installed AutoCAD, and choose Add as the type of installation. Choose Next. In the next screen, check Learning Tools and follow the instructions on your screen. You can then add the tutorial to your AutoCAD installation.

Don't forget the Learning Assistance CD-ROM that comes with Release 14. This is a multimedia extravaganza, and it comes with its own instructions.

Autodesk

Autodesk now offers several online training courses in AutoCAD at its virtual campus Web site (http://vcampus.com). No, it's not free. But it's available when you are. One is an AutoCAD Release 14 Update Course. You can take a free preview of one of the fifteen lessons. The full course is $125.

Getting Technical Support

Autodesk has always referred customers to their dealer for technical support. As with training, you should check out the provisions of the technical support. Some dealers charge for each phone call while others provide free support to all the customers for as long as Autodesk supports the product.

However, by popular demand, Autodesk has now instituted the AutoCAD Safety Net program, which offers direct phone access to technical support from Autodesk. You pay a flat fee of $65 per incident. Call 800-225-6531 in the U.S. and Canada. Currently, Safety Net supports only AutoCAD releases 14 and 13. For more information, go to Autodesk's Web site, choose Support, and find the Phone Support link.

Autodesk's Web site (`http://autodesk.com`) contains technical documents that answer many common questions. Click Support on the main page. Many of these deal with upgrade issues.

Autodesk also offers the VIP Subscription Program. It costs $295 per seat (copy) per year for AutoCAD, but you must subscribe for two years. It is not technical support per se but automatically provides you with all upgrades and a quarterly CD Library that includes the upgrades, a searchable database of support documents, computer-based training modules, and utility and application programs that Autodesk thinks you'll find useful.

There are independent services that provide technical support, usually through 900 numbers. One such service is AutoCAD HELPLINE, provided by the people who write the Dr. Debug column for *CADalyst*. You can call 900-820-2223 to have the cost ($3 per minute) charged to your phone bill or 800-537-3338 to charge to your credit card. AutoCAD HELPLINE also has a Web site at `http://www.cadhelp.com`.

AutoCAD User's Groups

AutoCAD User's Groups (AUGs) meet regularly, offer courses and seminars, bring in speakers, and generally offer the type of resources that all AutoCAD users need. You can find the one nearest you on Autodesk's Web site. Click on Support, then User Groups. If you want a User Group in North America, click that link to get to the user group page. Then click on the location you want to get a listing.

Several user groups have their own Web sites. Here are a couple:

The Silicon Valley AutoCAD Power Users is the largest AUG. Its Web site is at `http://www.power.org`, shown in Figure D-1. This is a great Web site from a great AUG that is active in all AutoCAD matters.

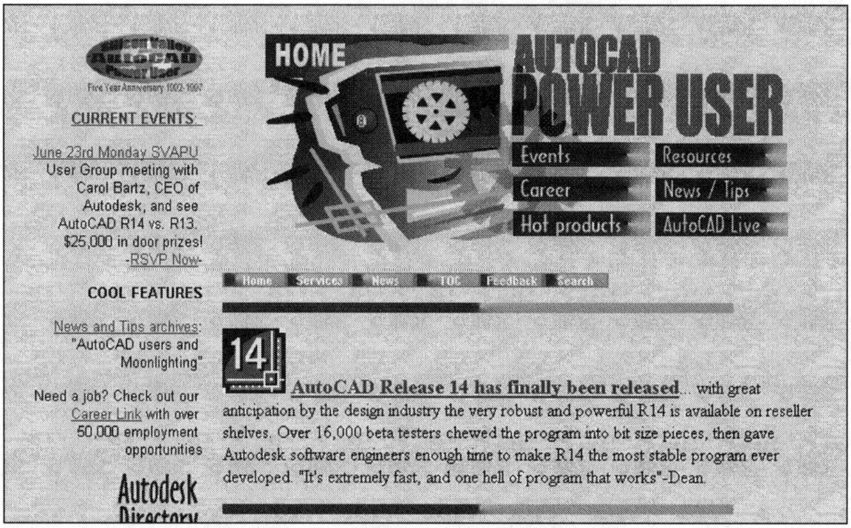

Figure D-1: The Silicon Valley AutoCAD Power User Web site.

The Vancouver AutoCAD Users Society was the first AUG. Its Web site, shown in Figure D-2, is `http://www.vaus.bc.ca/` (It doesn't look flashy but wait until you hear the music!)

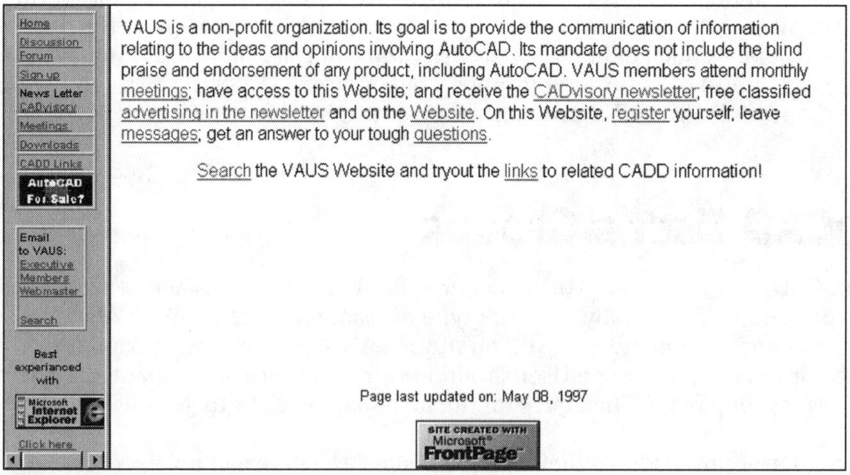

Figure D-2: The Vancouver AutoCAD Users Society Web site.

Internet Resources

The Internet provides a rich source of knowledge about AutoCAD. There are two independent newsgroups, one at `comp.cad.autocad` and the other at `alt.cad.autocad`. You can ask questions and get answers from other users. You can even answer a few questions yourself. Autodesk also administers its own discussion groups at `news://adesknews.autodesk.com` (also accessible from the Autodesk Web site).

In addition, Autodesk maintains an AutoCAD forum on CompuServe. If you have CompuServe (if you don't, you can call 800-848-8199), get to it at GO ACAD. This forum has a huge collection of shareware and AutoLISP routines, Autodesk's technical papers, and drawings you can download. There is also a bulletin board where you can post questions. These may be answered directly by someone at Autodesk or by another user, usually within a day or two.

There are hundreds of AutoCAD-related Web sites. Here are some of the most prominent:

✦ Autodesk's Web site at `www.autodesk.com` is divided into four parts — company, products, industry solutions, and support. At `www.autodesk.com/autocad`, you can find a great deal of information about AutoCAD and Release 14, including training, technical papers, and tips & tricks. There are even discussion groups, organized by topic. You can find the AutoCAD dealer nearest you or search for third-party applications that meet your needs.

✦ *CADalyst*'s Web site at `www.cadonline.com`, shown in Figure D-3, is another huge resource. When you enter this Web site for the first time, click on the Welcome Page link to register. This lets you access the entire site. Here you find the New, Cool & Exciting section, which offers late-breaking news, recent and upcoming conventions, and so on. World of CAD On-line lists the best AutoCAD Web sites. Solutions & Viewpoints offers AutoCAD HelpOnLine, a service for receiving technical support, a beginner's course in AutoLISP, and other goodies. The *CADALYST* Files offers all the AutoLISP code the magazine has published since 1993.

✦ The *Cadence* Web site at `www.cadence-mag.com`, shown in Figure D-4, is also one of those endless resources. Its sections include: News, which details the latest CAD news; Current Issue, an extended table of contents for the current issue of *Cadence*; CAD Sites, which offers a list of valuable Web sites; Code Archive, which contains all the AutoLISP code back to 1986 (when AutoCAD was a baby); and Issue Archive, which contains a listing of articles from back issues, including the entire text of selected articles.

Figure D-3: The *CADalyst* Web site.

Credit: Thanks to Advanstar, publisher of *CADalyst*.

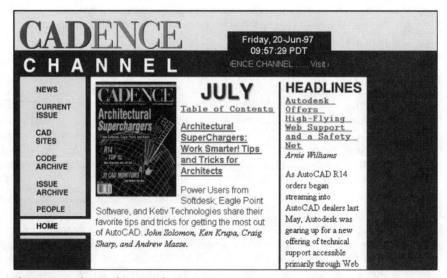

Figure D-4: The *Cadence* Web site.

Credit: Thanks to Miller Freeman, Inc., publisher of *CADENCE*.

✦ The AutoCAD Shareware Clearinghouse at www.cadalog.com, shown in Figure D-5, has one of the largest listings of AutoCAD-related shareware, including drawings, AutoLISP routines, blocks, and so on. This site has a great new search engine that lets you search for shareware by keyword. For example, if you want a routine that works on text, type in text as the keyword to get a listing of all the applicable shareware.

Figure D-5: The AutoCAD Shareware Clearinghouse.

✦ Digital Business Media's Web site from Melbourne, Australia (www.dbm.com.au), also has great AutoLISP software and shareware libraries, as well as lots of other goodies.

✦ *CADsyst*'s Web site at www.buildingWeb.com/cadsyst offers a huge library of AutoLISP routines, blocks, and shareware. It was my first stop when looking for shareware for the CD-ROM of this book.

✦ The CAD Shack, at www.cadshack.com/support.htm, also offers blocks, files, a list of more than 500 AutoCAD books, tips & tricks, fonts, hatch patterns — you name it.

✦ CADII (which stands for CAD Internet Index) is a web site that you can use to start searching for CAD-related resources on the Internet. It's at www.nuwebny.com/cadii.

There are many, many more, but most of them are more specialized. Table D-1 lists some useful sites.

Table D-1
Useful AutoCAD Web Sites

Name	URL	Description
ACAD plus	http://ourworld.compuserve.com/homepages/pshan/	AutoCAD news, code tips & tricks, want ads, utilities, and a list of other sites.
CADIT	http://www.archit.ncl.ac.uk/sess/index.html	A very complete course in AutoCAD based on the DOS version.
ExecNet	http://explorer.execnet.com/filelibs/	This site has many types of down-loadable files. Scroll down to the CAD section.
InstArchives	http://www.renature.com/instarc/cad_net.html	An excellent list of AutoCAD Internet resources.
Learning AutoLISP	http://ucad1.uccb.ns.ca/acad/lisp.htm	Free AutoLISP tutorial and links to other tutorials.
Mark Powell's AutoCAD & Autolisp links	http://web2.airmail.net/markpowl/acad.html	Another good list of links to Internet sites.
Reini Urban's AutoCAD page	http://xarch.tu-graz.ac.at/autocad/	A list of AutoCAD tips and tools, AutoLISP documents, and so on, from Austria.
SimpleCAD	http://www.simplecad.com/	AutoLISP resources and block libraries. Also another list of Internet links.
University of New South Wales	http://www.arch.unsw.edu.au/helpdesk/software/autocad	UNSW has placed some of its AutoCAD courses on its Web site. These are for Release 13, but they're still useful and free.
Army Corps of Engineers	http://cadlib.wes.army.mil	The COE offers a selection of drawings from various disciplines you can download. I used several for the exercises in this book.

What's on the CD-ROM

◆   ◆   ◆   ◆

In This Appendix

Using the CD-ROM

How the CD-ROM is structured

A list of software

◆   ◆   ◆   ◆

Using the CD-ROM

The *AutoCAD 14 Bible* CD-ROM contains all the drawings and files you need to work through and complete the exercises, as well as the results of those exercises. In addition, I've tried out as many useful shareware programs and AutoLISP routines as I could to see if they work with Release 14 and selected those I felt would be most useful. I hope you will find the CD-ROM a useful addition to your AutoCAD arsenal.

How the CD-ROM Is Structured

I have placed all the files you need for the exercises in the root of the CD-ROM so that you don't have to navigate through folders to access them. Almost all these files are named as in the following examples — *ab15-a.dwg*, *ab15-b.dwg*, *ab15-c.dwg*, and so on. In these examples, 15 is the chapter number, and the letters indicate that these are the first, second, and third drawings you need to open.

The files for Chapters 4 through 9 come after the files for Chapter 34 (because 4 through 9 come after 3). Don't forget to scroll down to find them.

A few files have other names, such as *sky.gif* and others. In each case, I give you the name of the file you need to open. You can easily find them with Explorer, since Explorer automatically alphabetizes the files. (If they are not alphabetized, click the Name column of the right window. If Explorer alphabetizes them backwards, click one more time.)

There are three folders in the root of the CD-ROM: *Results, Registered Dvprs & Products,* and *Software*. Figure E-1 shows a partial listing of the CD-ROM in Explorer.

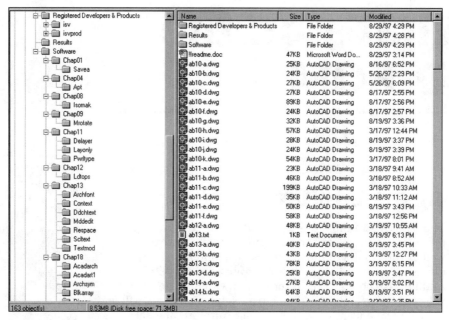

Figure E-1: A partial listing of the CD-ROM contents in Microsoft Explorer.

Using the *Results* folder

In the *Results* folder, you can find the results of all the exercises. You may wish to check your work in the exercise. Also, sometimes I use the result of one exercise as the basis for a second exercise (although I try not to do this very often). If you haven't done the first exercise, you can get the resulting file from the *Results* folder and use it for the second exercise.

Using the Registered Dvprs & Products folder

The information in this folder contains all of Autodesk's registered developers and their products, over 2,000 pages in all. Use this data whenever you are looking for a solution to a problem that might be solved using third-party software that works with AutoCAD. You can look up available software in the following categories:

Computer-Aided Design (CAD)
- ✦ Architectural
- ✦ Document Management
- ✦ Drafting Utilities
- ✦ DTM/Civil/Survey
- ✦ Electrical Design
- ✦ Electronics Design

✦ Facilities Planning & Mgmt

✦ Fashion/Textile Design

✦ Graphics Translators

✦ HVAC

✦ Hydrologic Analysis

✦ Manufacturing Engineering

✦ Mapping/GIS/Utility

✦ MCAE

✦ Mechanical Design

✦ Mining/Geology/Environment

✦ Naval Architecture

✦ Plotting Utilities

✦ Plumbing

✦ Process Plant Design & Piping

✦ Raster to Vector

✦ Scheduling & Estimating

✦ Structural Engineering

✦ User Interface Enhancements

✦ Utilities

✦ Visualization Tools

✦ Other

WorkCenter

✦ AEC/FM

✦ Bulk Loading

✦ Mapping/GIS

✦ Process and Power

Multimedia

✦ Content

✦ 3D Studio Animation

✦ 3D Studio Modeling

✦ 3D Studio Rendering/Particles

✦ Game Development

Changing the Windows read-only attribute

You can use the exercise drawings directly from the CD-ROM, but you may get better results by copying them to your hard drive. In most cases the exercises instruct you to do this. The software should be copied to a folder in AutoCAD's support file search path.

You may not be able to access files on the CD-ROM after you copy them to your computer, or you may get the following error message when you attempt to open a file with its associated application:

```
[Application] is unable to open the [file].
Please make sure the drive and file are writable.
```

Windows sees all files on a CD-ROM drive as "read-only." This makes sense normally since a CD-ROM is a read-only medium — that is, you can't write data back to the CD. However, when you copy a file from a CD to your hard disk or to a Zip drive, Windows doesn't automatically change the file attribute from read-only to writable. Installation software normally takes care of this chore for you, but in this case, since the files are intended to be manually copied to your disk, you have to change the file attribute yourself. Luckily, this is easy:

1. Click the Start menu button.

2. Choose Programs.

3. Choose Windows Explorer.

4. Highlight the file name(s) on the hard disk or Zip drive.

5. Right click the highlighted file name(s) to display a pop-up menu.

6. Select Properties to display the Properties dialog box.

7. Click the Read-only option so that it is no longer checked.

8. Click OK.

You should now be able to use the file(s) with the specific application without getting the annoying error message.

These pages are in HTML format, so you need a Web browser to access them. In most cases, if you double-click on an HTML file in Windows Explorer, Windows automatically opens the file with your browser.

Here's how to access this wealth of information:

1. Open Windows Explorer and select the *Registered Dvprs & Products* folder of the *AutoCAD Bible* CD-ROM.

2. Find and double-click the *index.htm* file, which is the starting point for all the information in this folder. Windows should open the file with your Web browser, as shown in Figure E-2.

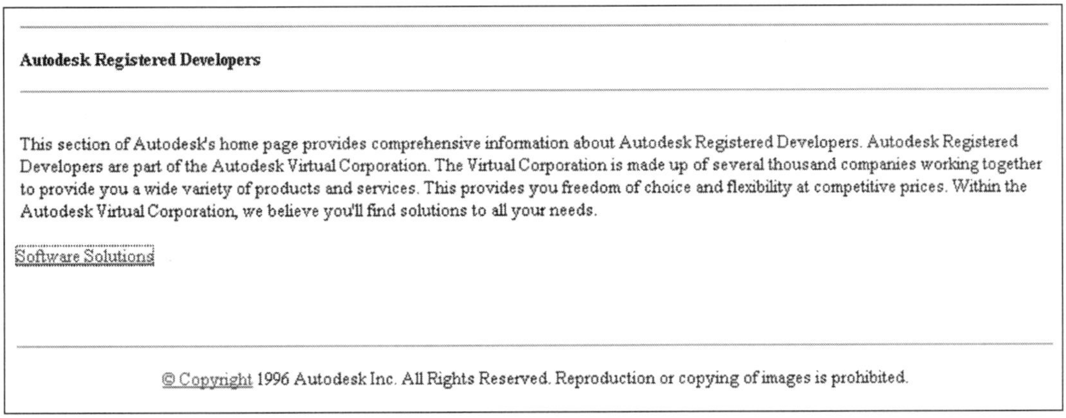

Autodesk Registered Developers

This section of Autodesk's home page provides comprehensive information about Autodesk Registered Developers. Autodesk Registered Developers are part of the Autodesk Virtual Corporation. The Virtual Corporation is made up of several thousand companies working together to provide you a wide variety of products and services. This provides you freedom of choice and flexibility at competitive prices. Within the Autodesk Virtual Corporation, we believe you'll find solutions to all your needs.

Software Solutions

© Copyright 1996 Autodesk Inc. All Rights Reserved. Reproduction or copying of images is prohibited.

Figure E-2: The *index.htm* file is the starting point for all the information on registered developers and their products.

Credit: Thanks to Brian Souder at Autodesk for providing the information in this folder.

3. Click the Software Solutions link. Your browser switches to the Resource Guide for Software Solutions.
4. Choose one of the categories listed previously. For example, if you choose Utilities you see the page shown in Figure E-3. This page lists hundreds of utilities, including a brief description, the price, and the supplier. Note that the supplier is also a link.

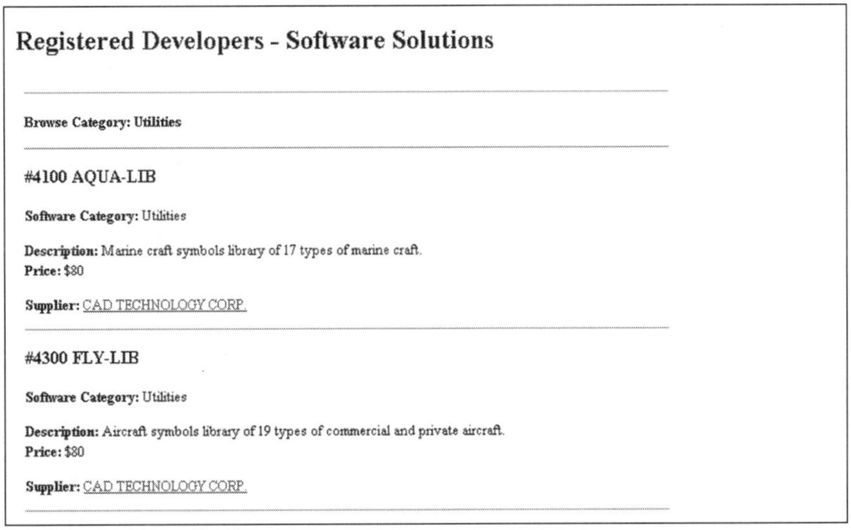

Registered Developers - Software Solutions

Browse Category: Utilities

#4100 AQUA-LIB

Software Category: Utilities

Description: Marine craft symbols library of 17 types of marine craft.
Price: $80

Supplier: CAD TECHNOLOGY CORP.

#4300 FLY-LIB

Software Category: Utilities

Description: Aircraft symbols library of 19 types of commercial and private aircraft.
Price: $80

Supplier: CAD TECHNOLOGY CORP.

Figure E-3: The beginning of the Utilities category, which contains hundreds of entries.

5. If you are interested in a program, click the supplier link to get contact information for the company, as shown in Figure E-4. This company has many products, including the utilities shown in Figure E-3.

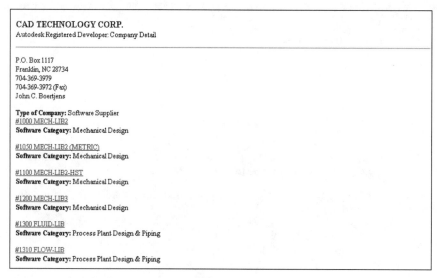

CAD TECHNOLOGY CORP.
Autodesk Registered Developer: Company Detail

P.O. Box 1117
Franklin, NC 28734
704-369-3979
704-369-3972 (Fax)
John C. Boertjens

Type of Company: Software Supplier
#1000 MECH-LIB2
Software Category: Mechanical Design

#1050 MECH-LIB2 (METRIC)
Software Category: Mechanical Design

#1100 MECH-LIB2-HST
Software Category: Mechanical Design

#1200 MECH-LIB3
Software Category: Mechanical Design

#1300 FLUID-LIB
Software Category: Process Plant Design & Piping

#1310 FLOW-LIB
Software Category: Process Plant Design & Piping

Figure E-4: The company detail provides contact information.

Note

If your browser doesn't automatically open when you double-click, Windows might open the Open With window to let you associate the *.htm* file type with an application. Choose your Web browser from this list and click OK. Or, open your browser first and type in the path to *index.htm* where you usually type in Web site addresses (URLs). For example, if your CD-ROM drive is named *d:,* type **d:\Registered Dvprs & Products\index.htm**.

This data comes from Autodesk's Web site, so it contains a few elements that don't apply to the CD-ROM. For example, the CD-ROM has no search engine, so you can't search for data by keyword as you can on the Web site. Of course, you can go to Autodesk's Web site to find this information, but having it on the CD-ROM makes it more accessible.

Using the Software folder

The *Software* folder contains an excellent collection of useful software that works with Release 14, as well as a collection of block and symbol libraries. Most of these libraries are simply collections of useful drawings.

The *Software* folder is divided up into subfolders by chapter. Not all chapters have software so there is a subfolder only for the chapters that have software. This makes it easy for you to find software by function. For example, you can find software for text objects by looking in the *Chap13* subfolder, since Chapter 13 covers text. Table E-1 lists the software alphabetically so you can review it at a glance. Within each chapter subfolder there are other subfolders for each program or AutoLISP routine.

To find out in detail what the software or AutoLISP routine does, read the text (*.txt)* file if there is one. It provides details about what the software does and how to install it. Sometimes details are at the beginning of the *.lsp* file. You can open and read it.

Most of the software on the CD-ROM is freeware — you can use it at no cost. Most of these are AutoLISP routines. However, some of it is shareware. Here's the scoop on shareware — you try it out and if you like it, you buy it. It works on the honor system, so please be honorable and pay for the shareware you use. All shareware comes with a text file that explains how much to pay for it, what you get when you register, and where to send the check. Often, you get additional features when you register.

There are also a couple of demos on the CD-ROM. Demos are not fully functional — usually they either shut down after a short time or they do not work to the fullest extent. Demos are not shareware; they are regular software that you must buy.

AutoLISP routines are easy to install. Follow these steps:

1. Copy the *.lsp* file to AutoCAD's */Support* folder or to a folder that you have placed in AutoCAD's support file search path.

Note

To add a folder to AutoCAD's support file search path, choose Tools⇨Preferences and click the plus sign (+) next to Support File Search Path on the Files tab. Choose Add. Type in a folder path or choose Browse to locate one.

2. In AutoCAD, type **(load "filename")**, where *filename* is the name of the *.lsp* file. You don't need the *.lsp,* but don't forget the parentheses or the quotation marks. AutoCAD responds with the name of the last function defined in the routine.

3. Type the name of the function to use the AutoLISP routine.

You can also choose Tools⇨Load Application to load an AutoLISP or ARX program. If there is a setup or install file, use that to install the software.

Tip

Many of the AutoLISP routines were written before Release 14 came out. Sometimes the installation instructions are out of date and don't include Release 14's new capability to add a folder to the support file search path.

Table E-1
The CD-ROM Software

Software & Subfolder Name	CD-ROM Folder	Description	Type
Acadarch	Chap18	A furniture library of 79 drawings.	Shareware
Acadart1	Chap18	87 drawings of electronic and electrical symbols for schematics. Includes a few isometric connectors.	Freeware
Actrees	Chap24	A library of 3D trees.	Freeware
Album	Chap26	Displays all the drawings in a folder. You can open or insert them.	Freeware
Apt	Chap04	Replaces the Quadrant object snap with an object snap that snaps to any specified angle on a circle or arc.	Freeware
Archfont	Chap13	A set of architectural fonts that look hand drawn.	Shareware
Archsym	Chap18	A collection of architectural symbols — fixtures, appliances, and so on.	Freeware
Blkarray	Chap18	Creates a BLOCKARRAY command to create arrays of blocks	Freeware
Context	Chap13	Continues existing text with the same style and spacing.	Freeware
Ddchtext	Chap13	Changes the properties of text objects.	Shareware
Ddscript	Chap30	Writes a script-file to run on multiple drawings and runs it.	Demo
Delayer	Chap11	Deletes all objects on selected layers.	Freeware
Disney	Chap18	A drawing of Mickey, Minnie, Donald, and Goofy. Just for fun.	Freeware
Elect-001	Chap18	A library of electrical and electronic symbols	Freeware
Elect-002	Chap18	A library of electrical and electronic symbols	Freeware
Elect-003	Chap18	A library of electrical and electronic symbols	Freeware
Epdxf001	Chap18	A dxf library of electrical schematic symbols	Freeware
Flatten	Chap21	Changes the Z coordinate of objects to zero	Freeware
Hidden	Chap27	Five chances to guess the word. Just for fun.	Hidden
Isomak	Chap08	Tools for creating isometric drawings.	Shareware
Layonly	Chap11	Turns off all layers except the one you choose.	Freeware
Lck	Chap34	An AutoLISP checker	Shareware

Software & Subfolder Name	CD-ROM Folder	Description	Type
Ldtops	Chap12	Adds a command, RDA, that works with the DIST command, giving the distance in feet and inches, in decimal format, and in meters, as well as the angle.	Freeware
Libeltr	Chap18	A drawing containing a library of electronic and electrical symbols	Freeware
Lisplink	Chap34	An AutoLISP checker and text editor	Demo
Mddatte	Chap18	Edits any number of block attributes without having to use the DDATTE command for each block.	Freeware
Mddedit	Chap13	Prompts you to select as many text objects as you want and opens the Edit Text dialog box for each, letting you quickly edit all the text objects without having to start DDEDIT for each object individually.	Freeware
MPE-arch	Chap18	A library of mechanical, plumbing, and electrical symbols for architectural drawings, mostly lights and outlets.	Freeware
Mrotate	Chap09	Rotates multiple objects each from their respective insertion points	Freeware
Nuts	Chap18	A symbol library of nuts, screws, bolts, and washers	Shareware
Pipesym1	Chap18	A collection of piping block symbols for creating flow chart diagrams.	Freeware
Pipesym2	Chap18	A collection of piping block symbols for creating flow chart diagrams.	Freeware
Pwrltype	Chap11	A set of complex linetypes.	Freeware
Quicklsp	Chap35	A quick reference chart of AutoLISP functions	Freeware
Respace	Chap13	Respaces lines of text.	Freeware
Savea	Chap01	Saves a drawing to the A: drive and lets you continue to work on the hard drive.	Freeware
Sclblock	Chap18	Rescales multiple selected blocks from their respective insertion points.	Freeware
Scltext	Chap13	Rescales all selected text objects from their respective insertion points.	Freeware
Screwit	Chap18	A library of screws	Freeware

(continued)

Table E-1 (*continued*)

Software & Subfolder Name	CD-ROM Folder	Description	Type
Sharelib	Chap18	Two drawings of architectural symbols.	Freeware
Stairs	Chap23	Creates a 3D stair of 3D faces	Freeware
Textmod	Chap13	Globally or individually modifies text height, text style, rotation angle, obliquing angle, text width, and content. Also mirrors text.	Shareware
VRML	Chap28	Exports drawings to VRML format (a 3D format used on the Web).	Freeware (commercial version available)
XferPro	Chap28	Encodes and decodes files for sending over the Internet	Shareware

Index

C

(continued)

F

(continued)

(continued)

(continued)

T

(continued)

W

WBLOCK command, 509
WCS (World Coordinate System)
    icon indicating, 157
    setting North location, 736
    3D views and, 611
    See also UCS
Web
    AutoCAD Shareware Clearinghouse, 1017
    Autodesk sites, 1012, 1015
    CADalyst Web site, 1015, 1016
    Cadence Web site, 1012, 1015, 1016
    getting drawings from, 812–813
    launching Web browser in AutoCAD, 813–814
    Silicon Valley AutoCAD Power User Web site, 1013, 1014
    useful AutoCAD sites on, 1017, 1018
    Vancouver AutoCAD Users Society Web site, 1013, 1014
    viewing drawings on, 809–812
wedge
    creating 3D, 660
    3D solid, 688–689
Wedge button, 660, 689
welding, 449
WHIP!, 809–812
width of fonts, 311
window blocks, 493
Window option (Select objects: prompt), 181
Window option (ZOOM command), 136
Window Polygon option (Select objects: prompt), 185
Windows 95
    defining environment in Windows registry, 560
    Find feature, 510
    keyboard shortcuts for applications in, 827
    starting AutoCAD from, 4–6
    swap file, 774–775
Windows Clipboard, 508–513
    buttons for, 509
    cutting and copying blocks, 509
    using drag-and-drop feature, 510–511
Windows NT system requirements, 955, 956
wireframe mode, 730
wireframe models, 598, 601
wiring diagram, 237
wizards for setting up drawings, 83
WMF files
    exporting, 782
    importing, 783–785
Wood option (Materials dialog box), 752
worksheets, 799–801
World Coordinate System. *See* WCS
WPolygon option (Select objects: prompt), 185

X

X, Y coordinate system, 51–81
    about the, 51–52
    coordinates on drawing area, 8, 52
    displaying coordinates, 59–61
    drawing units, 52
    picking coordinates on the screen, 61–81
        object snaps, 66–76
        point filters, 79–81
        snap settings, 61–62
        tracking, 76–79
        using the grid, 62–63
    types of measurement notation, 52
    typing coordinates, 53–59
        absolute Cartesian coordinates, 53–54
        direct distance entry, 58–59
        orthogonal mode, 58
        polar coordinates, 56–57
        relative Cartesian coordinates, 55–56
        using relative and polar coordinates, 57–58
X axis, 589
X Axis Rotate option (UCS), 607
XBIND command, 543–544
Xbind dialog box, 544
XCLIP command, 544–546
XLINE button, 111
XLINE command, 111–112
xlines, 111–112
XPLODE command, 502–503
Xref Manager. *See* External References dialog box
xrefs. *See* external references

Y

Y axis, 589
Y Axis Rotate option (UCS), 607

Z

Z axis, 589
Z Axis Rotate option (UCS), 607
Z Axis Vector option (UCS), 607
Z coordinate, 602, 603
ZOOM command, 135–144
    Dynamic option for, 137–138
    options for, 136–137
Zoom flyout/toolbar, 988
Zoom option (DVIEW command), 633
Zoom submenu, for View menu, 978
zooming
    actual size of objects and, 135
    on WHIP!, 811
    xlines and, 111

IDG BOOKS WORLDWIDE
END-USER LICENSE AGREEMENT

READ THIS. You should carefully read these terms and conditions before opening the software packet(s) included with this book ("Book"). This is a license agreement ("Agreement") between you and IDG Books Worldwide, Inc. ("IDGB"). By opening the accompanying software packet(s), you acknowledge that you have read and accept the following terms and conditions. If you do not agree and do not want to be bound by such terms and conditions, promptly return the Book and the unopened software packet(s) to the place you obtained them for a full refund.

1. **License Grant.** IDGB grants to you (either an individual or entity) a nonexclusive license to use one copy of the enclosed software program(s) (collectively, the "Software") solely for your own personal or business purposes on a single computer (whether a standard computer or a workstation component of a multiuser network). The Software is in use on a computer when it is loaded into temporary memory (RAM) or installed into permanent memory (hard disk, CD-ROM, or other storage device). IDGB reserves all rights not expressly granted herein.

2. **Ownership.** IDGB is the owner of all right, title, and interest, including copyright, in and to the compilation of the Software recorded on the disk(s) or CD-ROM ("Software Media"). Copyright to the individual programs recorded on the Software Media is owned by the author or other authorized copyright owner of each program. Ownership of the Software and all proprietary rights relating thereto remain with IDGB and its licensers.

3. **Restrictions on Use and Transfer.**

    (a) You may only (i) make one copy of the Software for backup or archival purposes, or (ii) transfer the Software to a single hard disk, provided that you keep the original for backup or archival purposes. You may not (i) rent or lease the Software, (ii) copy or reproduce the Software through a LAN or other network system or through any computer subscriber system or bulletin-board system, or (iii) modify, adapt, or create derivative works based on the Software.

    (b) You may not reverse engineer, decompile, or disassemble the Software. You may transfer the Software and user documentation on a permanent basis, provided that the transferee agrees to accept the terms and conditions of this Agreement and you retain no copies. If the Software is an update or has been updated, any transfer must include the most recent update and all prior versions.

4. **Restrictions on Use of Individual Programs.** You must follow the individual requirements and restrictions detailed for each individual program in Appendix E, "What's on the CD-ROM," of this Book. These limitations are also contained in the individual license agreements recorded on the Software Media. These limitations may include a requirement that after using the program for a specified period of time, the user must pay a registration fee or discontinue use. By opening the Software packet(s), you will be agreeing to abide by the licenses and restrictions for these individual programs that are detailed in Appendix E and on the Software Media. None of the material on this Software Media or listed in this Book may ever be redistributed, in original or modified form, for commercial purposes.

5. Limited Warranty.

    (a) IDGB warrants that the Software and Software Media are free from defects in materials and workmanship under normal use for a period of sixty (60) days from the date of purchase of this Book. If IDGB receives notification within the warranty period of defects in materials or workmanship, IDGB will replace the defective Software Media.

    (b) IDGB AND THE AUTHOR OF THE BOOK DISCLAIM ALL OTHER WARRANTIES, EXPRESS OR IMPLIED, INCLUDING WITHOUT LIMITATION IMPLIED WARRANTIES OF MERCHANTABILITY AND FITNESS FOR A PARTICULAR PURPOSE, WITH RESPECT TO THE SOFTWARE, THE PROGRAMS, THE SOURCE CODE CONTAINED THEREIN, AND/OR THE TECHNIQUES DESCRIBED IN THIS BOOK. IDGB DOES NOT WARRANT THAT THE FUNCTIONS CONTAINED IN THE SOFTWARE WILL MEET YOUR REQUIREMENTS OR THAT THE OPERATION OF THE SOFTWARE WILL BE ERROR FREE.

    (c) This limited warranty gives you specific legal rights, and you may have other rights that vary from jurisdiction to jurisdiction.

6. Remedies.

    (a) IDGB's entire liability and your exclusive remedy for defects in materials and workmanship shall be limited to replacement of the Software Media, which may be returned to IDGB with a copy of your receipt at the following address: Software Media Fulfillment Department,
Attn.: *AutoCAD 14 Bible*, IDG Books Worldwide, Inc., 7260 Shadeland Station, Ste. 100, Indianapolis, IN 46256, or call 1-800-762-2974. Please allow three to four weeks for delivery. This Limited Warranty is void if failure of the Software Media has resulted from accident, abuse, or misapplication. Any replacement Software Media will be warranted for the remainder of the original warranty period or thirty (30) days, whichever is longer.

    (b) In no event shall IDGB or the author be liable for any damages whatsoever (including without limitation damages for loss of business profits, business interruption, loss of business information, or any other pecuniary loss) arising from the use of or inability to use the Book or the Software, even if IDGB has been advised of the possibility of such damages.

    (c) Because some jurisdictions do not allow the exclusion or limitation of liability for consequential or incidental damages, the above limitation or exclusion may not apply to you.

7. U.S. Government Restricted Rights. Use, duplication, or disclosure of the Software by the U.S. Government is subject to restrictions stated in paragraph (c)(1)(ii) of the Rights in Technical Data and Computer Software clause of DFARS 252.227-7013, and in subparagraphs (a) through (d) of the Commercial Computer — Restricted Rights clause at FAR 52.227-19, and in similar clauses in the NASA FAR supplement, when applicable.

8. General. This Agreement constitutes the entire understanding of the parties and revokes and supersedes all prior agreements, oral or written, between them and may not be modified or amended except in a writing signed by both parties hereto that specifically refers to this Agreement. This Agreement shall take precedence over any other documents that may be in conflict herewith. If any one or more provisions contained in this Agreement are held by any court or tribunal to be invalid, illegal, or otherwise unenforceable, each and every other provision shall remain in full force and effect.

CD-ROM INSTALLATION INSTRUCTIONS

Insert CD-ROM into your disc drive.

Windows sees all files on a CD-ROM drive as "read-only." This makes sense normally since a CD-ROM is a read-only medium — that is, you can't write data back to the CD. However, when you copy a file from a CD to your hard disk or to a Zip drive, Windows doesn't automatically change the file attribute from read-only to writable. Installation software normally takes care of this chore for you, but in this case, since the files are intended to be manually copied to your disk, you have to change the file attribute yourself. Luckily, this is easy:

1. Click the Start menu button.

2. Choose Programs.

3. Choose Windows Explorer.

4. Highlight the file name(s) on the hard disk or Zip drive.

5. Right click the highlighted file name(s) to display a pop-up menu.

6. Select Properties to display the Properties dialog box.

7. Click the Read-only option so that it is no longer checked.

8. Click OK.

You should now be able to use the file(s) with the specific application without getting the annoying error message.

Refer to Appendix E for more detailed instructions and a listing of the software on the CD-ROM.